Working with
Lotus®1-2-3®

Working with Lotus® 1-2-3®

A Comprehensive Manual

Hossein Bidgoli
California State University, Bakersfield

West Publishing Company
St. Paul   New York   Los Angeles   San Francisco   • Release 2.01

Copy Editor: Sheryl Rose
Composition: green apple graphics
Cover Photograph: David Bishop

Library of Congress Cataloging-in-Publication Data

Bidgoli, Hossein.
    Working with Lotus 1-2-3: a comprehensive manual (release 2.0 and 2.01)/Hossein Bidgoli.
    p. cm.
    Includes index.
    1. Lotus 1-2-3 (Computer program) I. Title. II. Title. Working with Lotus One-Two-Three.
HF5548.4.L67B53 1987 005.36'9—dc19   87-25268
ISBN 0-314-65031-8

To my brother Mohsen
For his uncompromising belief in the power of education

About The Author

Dr. Hossein Bidgoli is Professor and Coordinator of Management Information Systems at California State College, Bakersfield. He holds a Ph.D. degree in systems science from Portland State University with a specialization in design and implementation of MIS. His master's degree is in MIS from Colorado State University. Dr. Bidgoli's background includes experience as a systems analyst, EDP consultant, and financial analyst. He was director of the Microcomputer Center at Portland State University and has done computer-related consulting for numerous organizations including Tektronix, Inc. in Oregon.

Dr. Bidgoli has authored two texts and numerous professional papers and articles presented and published throughout the United States on the topics of computers and MIS. For the past eight years, he has been conducting executive seminars on all aspects of computers.

Table of Contents

Chapter 13 – The PrintGraph Program

Chapter 14 – Database Operations/Part One: Lotus as an Electronic File Cabinet

Preface

There are several books about Lotus on the market. Some of the texts are brief and do not cover the entire Lotus package. Some are detailed and teach Lotus commands but do not tell the reader what to do with them. This book, using Release 2.0/2.01, tries to cover the entire Lotus package in an easy-to-understand, step-by-step manner. For Release 1A users, we have provided comprehensive coverage in Appendix E to highlight the differences between Release 2.0/2.01 and Release 1A.

All programs and screens shown throughout the book are available from the publisher on three diskettes. Readers of the book can access all programs, assisting either computer sophisticates or students to understand the material presented. This should also save a lot of time and frustration by not having to type these programs from scratch.

Although the text follows a logical sequence, the chapters have been written independently. This means that a reader with no previous background can understand any part of this text with minimum difficulty.

Lengthy topics, such as functions, data base operations, and macros, have been divided into logical parts. We present the most important parts first and least important last. This should make easy reading and provide not only a text book but also an invaluable reference.

In each chapter we present examples highlighting some real-life situations. This should put Lotus into perspective and emphasize the specific command or series of commands being discussed.

Each chapter ends with 15-35 review questions, divided into two groups. Group 1 reinforces the material covered in the chapter; group 2 questions have a "hands-on" nature. In order to answer these questions, students must get Lotus started and use the actual package. This should encourage a lot of hands-on sessions. We provide the answers to selected questions in Appendix G. Readers can use these questions as a self-test on a particular topic.

Appendix A provides brief microcomputer coverage for first-time users, to enhance their understanding of Lotus material.

Appendix B provides basic DOS information. This should benefit inexperienced as well as experienced users.

We discuss technical matters regarding Lotus operations in Appendix C. This presentation should clear up confusion for the first-time user about Lotus installation and utilization.

In Appendix D we provide guidelines for file transfer to and from Lotus. This should ease some of the frustration for users who are trying to import or export data.

This text teaches use of commands by example. In this fashion, the command is clear to the reader in context rather than in an abstract discussion. Limitations and strengths of these commands are also discussed.

Comprehensive coverage of data base operations, graphics, and Lotus macro commands is extremely important for advanced Lotus users. The text provides excellent coverage of these topics, using many real-life examples.

Every example and worksheet in the text is fully documented. By looking at the worksheet, the reader should be able to understand the concept underlying a particular command or series of commands.

At the end of several chapters, when appropriate, we have added a series of misconceptions and solutions. In some cases they may not be misconceptions but improper operating procedures or outright mistakes in operation. In any case, these should guide readers and provide some tips for avoiding some of the common mistakes and, at the same time, show how to resolve some of these problems.

At the end of the text, we provide a comprehensive command reference list. This should help the reader review the entire Lotus command structure in a few minutes, aiding in a better understanding of Lotus commands. It is also a refresher when the reader isn't sure about the function of a command.

Versions of this material have been tested by groups of students including college students (freshmen to graduates), bankers, financial officers, and chief executive officers for profit and nonprofit organizations. Classroom testing provided us with excellent feedback about the suitability of the material for different levels.

Note to Users:

This book has been written for a variety of audiences with a different computer backgrounds. We suggest the following guidelines:

1. If this is your first exposure to microcomputers, go directly to Appendix A. Material in this appendix describes the world of microcomputers for you in a nontechnical fashion.
2. If you don't know anything about the disk operating system (DOS), study Appendix A and read Appendix B. The first group of DOS commands in Table

B-1 has been organized for the novice. The second group of DOS commands has been selected for advanced DOS users.

3. If you just purchased your Lotus program and are trying to get it started, refer to Appendix C. This material should help you install Lotus on your system.

4. If you are interested in transferring files between Lotus and other programs, such as dBASE and VisiCalc, read Appendix D.

5. To reinforce your understanding of materials presented in the book, we provide answers to selected chapter review questions in Appendix G.

6. First-time Lotus users should read Chapter 1–10 and the beginning of Chapters 11–14, and 19.

7. Advanced Lotus users, after a quick review of Chapters 1–11, should spend more time on Chapters 12 and 14–18. Chapter 19 provides numerous real-life examples of Lotus applications. Advanced Lotus users can develop these applications.

8. Students interested only in Lotus macros should study Chapters 16–19.

9. Students interested in Lotus database capabilities should study Chapters 14–15.

10. For graphics users, Chapter 12 provides a comprehensive coverage of Lotus graphics.

We hope you decided to read the entire book. You will see the real power of Lotus when you put all the pieces together.

Acknowledgments

Several colleagues reviewed different versions of this manuscript and made constructive suggestions. Their help and comments are greatly appreciated.

Al Bird – University of Houston
Donnie Byers – Johnson County Community College
Robert Crews – Pan American University
Diane Drozd – College of DuPage
Pat Green – Temple Junior College
Mike Harris – Del Mar College
Robert McGlinn – Southern Illinois University
Beth Murphy – DePaul University
Beverly Oswalt – University of Central Arkansas
Roy Pipitone – Erie Community College
Jim Stacey – Ithaca College
Robert Taylor – Berkshire Community College
Mark Wayne – Chabot College
Louis Wolff – Moorpark College
Chuck Zebrowski – Texas Southmost College

Many different groups assisted me in completing this project. I am grateful to the students who attended my executive seminars and Lotus and MIS classes. They helped me fine-tune the manuscript during its various stages. My students Linda Worley, Glen Del Tour, Adrienne Cole, and Ihsan Ismail helped me run, edit, and debug some of the screen presented in the text. Their help is greatly appreciated.

I am indebted to my assistant, Ching-Sung Ng, for her thoroughness in checking and double-checking the majority of screens in the text. I also want to thank my friend and colleague, Dr. Reza Azarmsa, for his assistance in preparing the text's instructor's manual. The help of the women in the reprographics center at California State College, Bakersfield, who typed and prepared the manuscript, is very much appreciated. Sylvia O'Brien, a true problem-solver, deserves special recognition; her thoroughness and dedication made it easier to complete this project. Denise Simon, Theresa O'Dell, and Janine Wilson, all of West Educational Publishing, were supportive and constructive in their suggestions concerning this project.

Last but not least, I want to thank my family for their support and encouragement throughout my education. My two sisters, Azam and Akram, deserve my very special thanks.

1

Lotus 1-2-3 at a Glance

1-1 Introduction

This chapter provides you with an overview of Lotus 1-2-3, beginning with a brief history of earlier spreadsheets in order to appreciate this powerful package. We will explain the technical requirements of Lotus and give a brief description of the entire Lotus package. Then we will discuss Lotus as a decision support system tool in detail. This discussion will be reinforced throughout the book. At the end of this chapter, we provide a brief summary of the entire book to give you an idea of what to expect.

1-2 What is a Spreadsheet?

A *spreadsheet* is simply a table or a matrix of rows and columns, very similar to an accounting journal. The intersection of each row and column is called a cell. A *cell* can hold any type of data, including numbers, formulas, texts, and so forth. The major difference between an electronic spreadsheet and an accounting journal is the enhanced flexibility, speed, and accuracy provided by an electronic spreadsheet.

Theoretically, the number of applications that can be handled by an electronic spreadsheet is unlimited. In general terms, any application that can fit into a row and column setting can be handled by a spreadsheet program. This includes such applications as balance sheets, income statements, budgeting analyses, mailing lists, databases, and sales analyses.

The size and sophistication of a spreadsheet depends on the type of program. Some are dedicated spreadsheets such as VisiCalc, while some are integrated packages such as Lotus and Framework that perform many more applications than just spreadsheet analysis. We will discuss these applications in the next section.

1-3 Spreadsheets Prior to Lotus

The spreadsheet era began in 1978 when Robert Frankston, Dan Bricklin, and Dan Fylstra designed and marketed VisiCalc, the most popular microcomputer software prior to Lotus.

VisiCalc was very impressive for its time. The package, designed to perform spreadsheet analysis, included a matrix of 254 rows and 63 columns, many commands, and several built-in functions such as formulas for performing different tasks. However, it had some serious shortcomings. Earlier VisiCalc did not have Boolean operations such as OR, AND, NOT, and IF. It could not communicate directly with other software. Furthermore, it performed very limited graphics and database operations.

Some of these limitations were improved in later versions of VisiCalc. Several Boolean operations were introduced. A DIF (Data Interchange Format) utility program developed by Software Arts translated VisiCalc spreadsheets to other programs for graphics, databases, and word processing applications. VisiTrend/ VisiPlot and VisiFile could communicate with VisiCalc through the DIF utility. Yet there was still a need for a more sophisticated spreadsheet program.

SuperCalc (by Sorcim Corporation), a CP/M-based program introduced in 1980, was an improvement on VisiCalc. This package also included 254 rows and 63 columns.

Later releases of VisiCalc, ProCalc, and SuperCalc tried to eliminate the shortcomings of the earlier VisiCalc. Integrated packages were introduced that could perform spreadsheet analysis, data management, graphics, word processing, and communication operations. These new packages included Multiplan (by Microsoft Corporation), Context MBA (by Context Management Systems), Framework (by Ashton-Tate), and Lotus 1-2-3 (by Lotus Development Corporation). Some experts believe Lotus is not a true integrated package because it does not have word processing and communication capabilities. This is by no means a serious problem because Lotus files can communicate with several popular word processing programs, as well as with some communication packages.

1-4 Lotus: The Ultimate Spreadsheet

Lotus 1-2-3 Release 1 was introduced in 1982. Within six months it was upgraded to Release 1A and in mid-1985, Release 2 appeared on the market. Lotus Development Corporation has been continuously improving this product. After VisiCalc, Lotus has been one of the best sellers of all time.

Lotus includes three functions in one. Besides spreadsheet analysis, it is able to perform graphics and data management operations.

Lotus Release 2 features a spreadsheet of 8,192 rows and 256 columns, which equals 2,097,152 cells. To utilize this capacity, a huge main memory is needed. At the present time there is no microcomputer that can use this spreadsheet without upgrading its memory.

By using a series of commands and built-in functions, Lotus can perform some very impressive operations. Its data management functions are quite effective. Since the database generated by Lotus resides in RAM, the speed of manipulation is impressive (see Chapters 14 and 15).

The Lotus graphics function is also relatively sophisticated. Using spreadsheet data, Lotus can generate bar, pie, stacked bar, line, and XY graphs. Again, since the data for graphics is provided by the spreadsheet component of Lotus, the speed of calculation and redrawing is very high. As you will see in Chapter 12, doing "WHAT-IF" analysis with Lotus graphics is fast and simple.

Release 2 of Lotus increased the size of the worksheet from 2,048 rows to 8,192 rows and added many new functions. By itself, Lotus can serve as a forecasting package (see the discussion of data regression in Chapter 15). Throughout this book you will see these impressive features in action.

1-5 New Upgrade: Release 2.01

There are specific technical improvements in Release 2.01 as compared to Release 2, but they are minor and will not change the way you have been using Release 2. These specific improvements are as follows:

1. File retrieval time is faster than before.
2. Labels (nonnumeric data) are now equal to zero in mixed formulas.
3. Financial functions can have positive as well as negative arguments.
4. COMMAND.COM (see Appendix C) is not required on the utility disk.
5. A fractional number can be defined specifically (in Release 2, financial functions ignored any fractional portion of the term argument).

There are also some minor changes in driver installation and installation for hard disk systems. If you are using Release 2.01, we advise you to spend a few minutes reading its brief manual.

1-6 Lotus Technical Requirements

Lotus is written in assembly language (see Appendix A), the closest language to machine language. This has improved the speed of calculation in Lotus as compared to earlier spreadsheet programs. Lotus is available for PC or PC-compatible machines such as the IBM PC, NEC Advanced PC, Wang Professional, AT&T 6300, Zenith Data System, Texas Instruments Professional Computer, etc.

Two 360K double-sided disk drives are needed or a hard disk. Your computer must also have a minimum of 256K of RAM. Remember, Lotus Release 2 requires almost 192K of RAM to load (if it is loaded directly to the memory without going through the Lotus Access System; see Chapter 2). A color or monochrome display with Hercules graphics or another graphics adapter is also needed if you want to use the graphics capability. The operating system needed by Lotus is either PC or MS DOS, version 2 and above (see Appendix B).

1-7 Lotus: The Entire Package

The Lotus package includes the following:

1. Reference manual
2. Quick Reference
3. Tutorial
4. Getting Started
5. Six disks
6. Customer Assurance Plan
7. Four keyboard guides
8. Three keyboard templates
9. One hardware chart

You will use the System disk most of the time because all Lotus operations except graphics printing are on this disk. The second disk is the backup copy. In case of damage to the original System disk, you have another to use.

The third disk, called A View of 1-2-3, is a simple, quick review of Lotus operations. If you are a first-time user, it would be a good idea to spend a few hours working with this disk.

The fourth disk is the PrintGraph, which allows you to transfer the graphs generated on your monitor to your printer or plotter.

The fifth disk is the Install Library. This will help you to tailor Lotus programs to your particular computer system (see Appendix C for more information).

The last disk is the Utility disk. This includes the Install program for customizing Lotus to your system and a series of programs for file transfer between different software. Appendix C has more detailed information on these six disks.

The first manual is a tutorial that covers Lotus operations step by step. We recommend that you read this manual in conjunction with the A View of 1-2-3 disk. The second manual is a reference manual that gives guidelines for Lotus operation and covers all the items mentioned in the reference manual in detail.

The third document in the Lotus package is a brief manual on getting Lotus started. If you are just getting Lotus out of the box, you may want to spend a few minutes with this manual.

1-8 Lotus Access System

When your entire package is installed (see Appendix C), you can access any part of Lotus 1-2-3 through the Lotus Access System. All Lotus operations are stored on the

System disk except instructions for printing graphics, which is done by the PrintGraph disk. To start Lotus Access System, put the DOS disk in drive A. At the A> prompt, pull DOS out and put the Lotus System disk in drive A. Type LOTUS and hit Return. Your screen will display the material in Figure 1-1.

You can choose any of the options shown in the figure either by moving the cursor to one of the options and pressing the Return key or by typing the first letter of the option name. The last option, Exit, takes you out of the Lotus Access System and puts you back at the DOS A> prompt.

To get into the main section of Lotus, first put the System disk in drive A. Then you can either go through the Lotus Access System or type 123 at the A> prompt. If your computer has 256K of RAM memory, the latter option will give you approximately 15K more memory.

When you are in Lotus, you can always access the on-line Help menu by just pressing the F1 key. The Help menu will appear. You have access to more than 200 screens of the Help menu. Figure 1-2 shows an example of the Help menu.

You can move around the Help menu by using the cursor. If you look at the bottom left corner of this menu, you will see the words Help Index. The Help Index will give you several options. Figure 1-3 shows the Help Index menu. Point the cursor to any of these options and press the Return key. The section on Error Messages, for example, tells you how and when an error might occur and how to resolve the error. To leave the Help menu, just press the Escape (ESC) key.

Figure 1-1 Lotus Access System

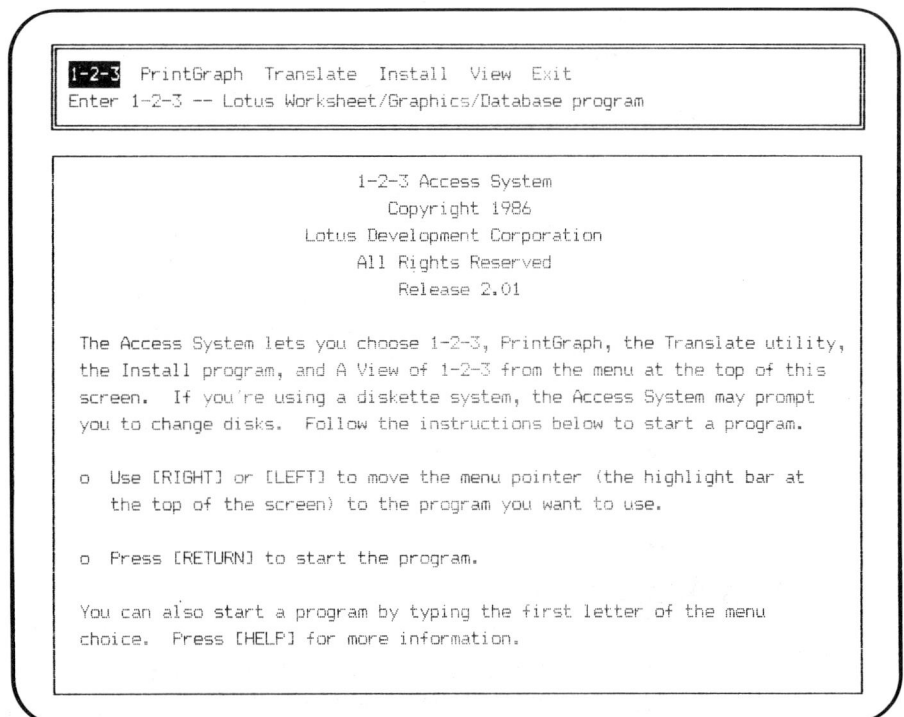

```
1-2-3  PrintGraph  Translate  Install  View  Exit
Enter 1-2-3 -- Lotus Worksheet/Graphics/Database program


                        1-2-3 Access System
                          Copyright 1986
                     Lotus Development Corporation
                          All Rights Reserved
                           Release 2.01


        The Access System lets you choose 1-2-3, PrintGraph, the Translate utility,
        the Install program, and A View of 1-2-3 from the menu at the top of this
        screen.  If you're using a diskette system, the Access System may prompt
        you to change disks.  Follow the instructions below to start a program.

        o  Use [RIGHT] or [LEFT] to move the menu pointer (the highlight bar at
           the top of the screen) to the program you want to use.

        o  Press [RETURN] to start the program.

        You can also start a program by typing the first letter of the menu
        choice.  Press [HELP] for more information.
```

```
A1:                                                                    HELP


_____

READY Mode

The mode indicator, READY, in the upper right corner of the screen means you
can select a command or type a cell entry.  The first key you press
determines your action:

Formula or Number:   Type a digit (0..9) or one of the characters
                     +, -, ., (, @, #, or $.
Label:               Type any character except those that begin a
                     formula or number.  Start with a label-prefix character to
                     create a label of a particular type: ' for left-aligned,
                     " for  right-aligned, ^ for centered, or \ for repeating.
Command:             Type /.
Special Function:    Press a special key.

To learn more about this Help facility, press [END], then [RETURN].
_____

Cell Entries            Mode Indicators
Help Index              How to Use Help

01-Jan-80  03:24 AM
```

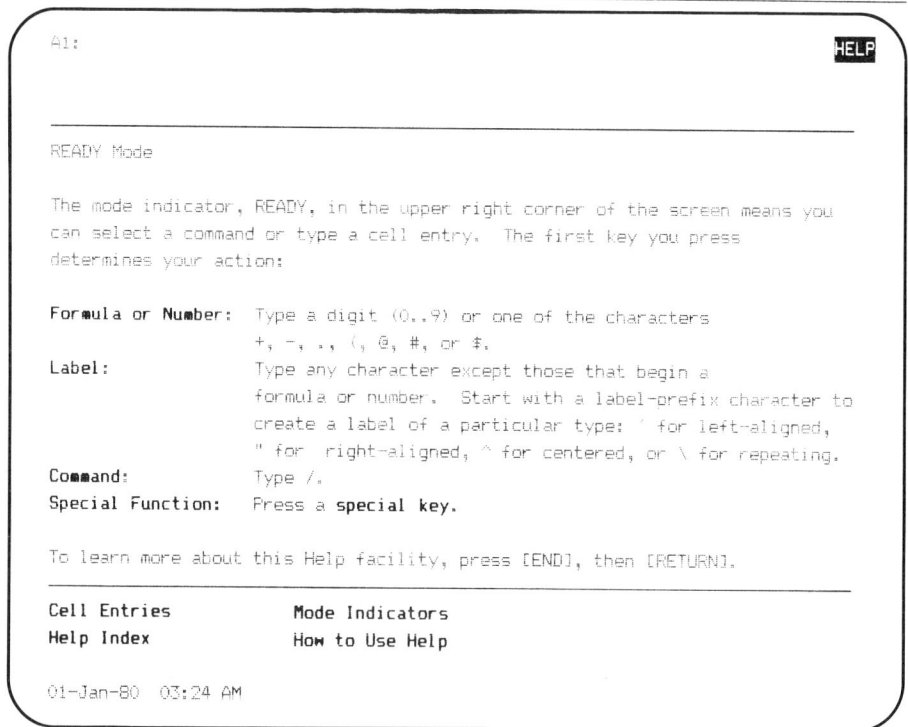

Figure 1-2 A Sample Screen of the Help Menu

To return to the Lotus Access System, invoke the main menu by pressing the question mark key (the slash key on the IBM keyboard or its equivalent on other keyboards) and then choose the Quit option. This option give you two choices, NO and YES. If you choose YES, you will return to the Lotus Access System.

To choose A View of 1-2-3, move the cursor to View and press the Return key. Now the prompt asks for A View of 1-2-3 disk. Put this disk in drive A and press the Return key. You will be given the screen shown in Figure 1-4. As you see, there are three options. Parts A and B are introductory material on Lotus for beginners and Part C is a review of new material on Release 2 for those who are unfamiliar with it. It is a good idea to spend a few minutes on this material, which will also prepare you for the Tutorial manual. This disk also includes a worksheet file called REALITY.WK1, used with the Tutorial.

To leave A View of 1-2-3, press the ESC key. To access any other disk (PrintGraph, Translate, or Install), point the cursor to the name of the program and press the Return key. The prompt will tell you to insert the proper disk and press the Return key.

If you do not want to access 1-2-3 and its companion programs from the Lotus Access System, you can access any of them directly from DOS. To do so, at the A> prompt do the following:

- To access 1-2-3, type 123, assuming the 1-2-3 System disk is in drive A.
- To access A View of 1-2-3, type VIEW, assuming the A View of 1-2-3 disk is in drive A.

```
A1:                                                                          HELP


     ───────────────────────────────────────────────────────────────────
     Help Index              Select one of these topics for additional Help.

     Using The Help Facility          How to Start Over
     Errors and Messages              How to End a 1-2-3 Session
     Error Message Index
                                      Moving the Cell Pointer
     Special Keys                     Cell Entries
     Control Panel                    Erasing Cell Entries
     Modes and Indicators
                                      1-2-3 Commands
                                      Command Menus
     Formulas
     @Functions                       Column Widths
     Cell Formats -- Number vs. Label
                                      Macros
     Operators                        Function Keys

     Ranges                           Menus for File, Range, and Graph Names
     Pointing to Ranges               File Names
     Reenterng Ranges
     01-Jan-80  03:26 AM
```

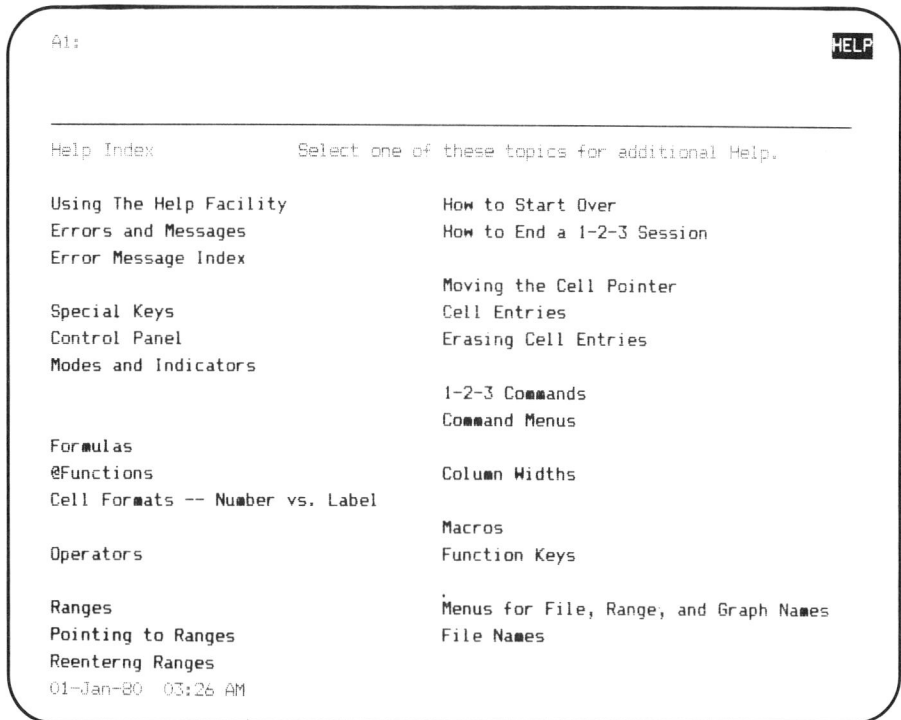

Figure 1-3 Help Index Menu

- To access PrintGraph, type PGRAPH, assuming the PrintGraph disk is in drive A.
- To access Translate, type TRANS, assuming the Utility disk is in drive A.
- To access Install, type INSTALL, assuming the Utility disk is in drive A.
- To access Access, type LOTUS, assuming the 1-2-3 System disk is in drive A.

1-9 What Can Lotus Do for You

The number of applications handled by Lotus is practically unlimited. Lotus can be used in any discipline, although its major applications have been in the areas of finance and accounting. In the next sections we will provide you with an overview of some of the more common Lotus applications. Chapter 19 presents specific applications in the areas of finance, accounting, production, forecasting, and so on.

1-10 Lotus as a Decision Support System (DSS) Tool

In the past couple of years, Lotus has been utilized and evaluated as a *Decision Support System (DSS) tool*. A DSS tool or product is any package that can help a decision maker in making a decision, or making a better decision. It must be able to perform "WHAT-IF" analysis, goal-seeking operations, sensitivity analysis, and

```
                A   V I E W    O F    1 - 2 - 3

A.   INTRODUCTION

     An introduction to the worksheet, graphs, and database

B.   A SAMPLE SESSION

     Using 1-2-3 to evaluate alternative business strategies

C.   NEW FEATURES IN RELEASE 2

     An assortment of new features in this release of 1-2-3


              Press A, B, or C to select a topic,
         or press [ESCAPE] to leave a View of 1-2-3
```

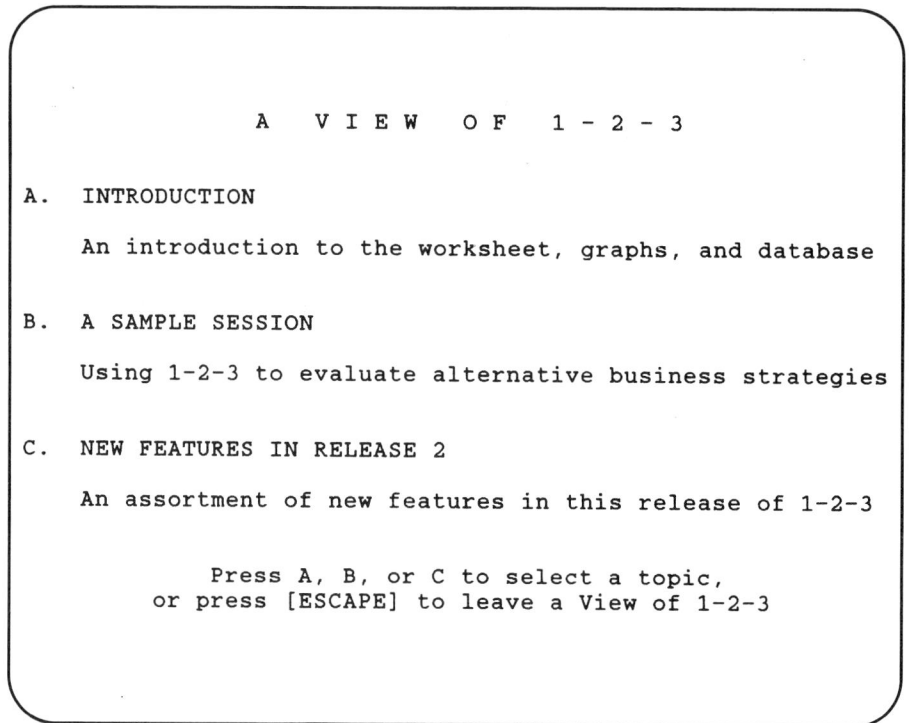

Figure 1-4 A View of 1-2-3

modeling analysis. As you will see throughout this book, Lotus can perform any of these functions. Some of these capabilities are readily available in the Lotus command structure. Others can be done by developing a series of macros (see Chapters 16 – 18). Let us explain these major functions.

1-11 Using Lotus for What - If Analysis

WHAT-IF analysis calculates the effects of a change in one variable over other variables or the entire worksheet. A simple example is a break-even analysis. The break-even point (see Chapter 18) is the number of units generated in which total cost is equal to total revenue. For example, if the fixed cost of an operation is $500, the variable cost of a unit is $10, and the selling price is $15, the break-even point would be 100 units. At this point the company will neither lose nor gain. Above this point, the company will gain; below this point, the company will lose. Lotus can help you discover what will happen to the break-even point if the selling price is increased to $17; or what will happen to the break-even point if the variable costs are decreased by $3.

This feature can be used in a much more complex environment. Think about a budgeting problem. Let us say you have projected the budget of your company for the next five years. Suddenly you notice that the projected income for 1989 will be reduced by 5 percent. What is the impact of this income reduction on the entire budget? Thousands of accurate calculations must be done in order to answer this question. But if the budget is on a Lotus spreadsheet, this amazing program can perform all the recalculations almost instantly with no errors! Just change the old value to the new value and press the Return key.

WHAT-IF analysis can be done with graphics as well. Change any data item and press the F10 (Graph) key in READY mode and your graph will be redrawn instantly (see Chapter 12).

As you will see in Chapter 15, Lotus provides you with table-handling procedures; that in itself is a good application of WHAT -IF analysis. You can monitor the impact of one or two variables on the entire worksheet, or on a specific range.

1-12 Using Lotus for Goal-Seeking Analysis

Goal-seeking analysis is the reverse of WHAT-IF analysis. Here you may ask a question such as, "In order to generate $5,000,000 of total sales, how much should I advertise?" If you build an advertising model (Lotus provides you with the facilities to do this), performing such goal-seeking analysis will be easy.

Goal-seeking can be done by changing one variable or many variables; it depends on the complexity of your model. Remember, using Lotus macros (see Chapters 16 – 18) you can build fairly complex mathematical models. When the model is built, leave the rest of the calculations to the speed and accuracy of Lotus.

1-13 Using Lotus for Sensitivity Analysis

Sensitivity analysis basically means monitoring the range, elasticity, or variation within a model. Let us say that you are paying $15 per hour to the workers on the assembly line. If the workers ask for more money, how much more can you pay and still make a profit? Sensitivity analysis studies the range of variation for a variable and calculates its effect over the entire system. Again, Lotus will provide you with such a facility.

1-14 Building Integrated DSS Using Lotus

By combining a powerful spreadsheet, database management, and graphics, Lotus can be used as an integrated DSS package.

The database component can be used for storing data. Basic database operations (see Chapters 14 – 15) can be performed. Data can be organized in different orders, sorted, or searched. This data can be used for modeling analysis. Lotus Release 2 has provided you with many different models. Many of the built-in functions, especially the financial functions, can be used directly. The data matrix and data regression commands can be used for building sophisticated forecasting models (see Chapter 15). When the analysis and model building is done, the graphics portion of Lotus provides you with five different graphs. Since all operations (database, spreadsheet, and graphics) are performed within one package, the speed and effectiveness is amazingly high.

1-15 Overview of the Entire Book

Following is a quick overview of the entire book to give you an idea of what to expect.

Chapter 2: Getting Started With Lotus

Walking through worksheets. The first worksheet. Correcting mistakes. Types of data. Types of label prefixes. Arithmetic operations using Lotus. A final example.

Chapter 3: Getting In and Getting Out of Lotus

A view of Lotus as a black box. A brief explanation of the Lotus commands menu. Guidelines for entering, processing, and printing data. Saving and retrieving simple worksheets.

Chapter 4: A Complete Overview of the Lotus Worksheet

An overview of mode indicators, cell and address, control panel, column letter, row number, current position, target position, status indicators, date and time indicators, and so forth.

Chapter 5: Lotus Commands/Part One

A complete review of Copy and Move, Global, Insert, Delete, Column, Erase, Titles, Window, Status, and Page Commands.

Chapter 6: Lotus Commands/Part Two

A complete review of range commands such as Label, Erase, Name, Justify, Protect, Unprotect, Input, Value, and Transpose. A detailed explanation of relative, mixed, and absolute addressing.

Chapter 7: Formats: Dressing Up Your Worksheet

A comprehensive review of format commands for both the worksheet and specific ranges. This includes Fixed, Scientific, Currency, ", ", General, Percent, Date, Text, and Hidden formats.

Chapter 8: File Operations: Interaction Between Memory and Disk Files

A comprehensive review of Save, Retrieve, Combine, Xtract, Erase, List, and Directory commands.

Chapter 9: Report Generation

A comprehensive review of report generation, including printers and files. A complete coverage of options (Range, Line, Page, Align, etc.).

Chapter 10: Functions/Part One

A comprehensive review of mathematical functions (@ABS, @INT. etc.), financial functions (@DDB, @FV, etc.), and statistical functions (@STD, @VAR, etc.)

Chapter 11: Functions/Part Two

A comprehensive review of logical functions (@IF, @TRUE, etc.), special functions (@CHOOSE, @CELL, etc.), string functions (@MID, @LOWER, etc.), and date and time functions (@DATE, @TIME, etc.).

Chapter 12: Graphics: Converting Figures into Pictures

A comprehensive review of graphs generated by Lotus (line, bar, XY, stacked bar, and pie), highlighting specific usage of each graph.

Chapter 13: The PrintGraph Program

A comprehensive discussion of the PrintGraph program for graphics printers and plotters, including a detailed discussion of how to print graphs from files created with the /Graph Save command.

Chapter 14: Database Operations/Part One: Lotus as an Electronic File Cabinet

A comprehensive review of database creation, addition, modification, deletion, searching, and sorting. Searching is broken down into single criteria, double criteria, multiple criteria, and searching with wild-cards.

Chapter 15: Database Operations/Part Two: Lotus as a Sophisticated Database

A comprehensive review of advanced database operations, including statistical functions, table handling, frequency distribution, regression analysis, and so on.

Chapter 16: Macros/Part One: Typing Alternatives

A comprehensive review of macro operations. Creation, documentation, and debugging of macros. A table of more than 50 commonly used macros with complete documentation.

Chapter 17: Macros/Part Two: Advanced Commands

A comprehensive review of advanced macro commands. This will include BRANCH, BREAKOFF, GET, BEEP, INDICATE, etc.

Chapter 18: Macros/Part Three: Using Lotus Macros as a Super Programming Language

An overview of the program development life cycle, structured programming, modular programming, etc. More than one dozen simple programs written in macros will be presented.

Chapter 19: Lotus Applications in Specific Disciplines

Several simple worksheets demonstrate specific applications of Lotus in several disciplines, such as accounting, finance, marketing, production/operations, forecasting, economics, budgeting, personnel management, and home use.

Appendix A: You and Your PC: A Friendly Interface

An overview of a complete microcomputer system – keyboard, system unit, monitor, disk drive, floppy disk, hard disk, printer, etc.; a discussion of the types of memories; getting started with PC, etc.

Appendix B: Disk Operating System

A comprehensive discussion of DOS as the starting point for Lotus. An overview of more than 50 important DOS commands; disk file creation; an overview of batch files; and customizing Lotus using DOS.

Appendix C: Installing Lotus

Getting Lotus out of the box! An overview of the Install program, using the Lotus Access System, system configuration, and guidelines for installing the entire system.

Appendix D: File Transfer between Lotus and Other Software

A series of guidelines for file transfer to and from Lotus for a number of popular software packages on the market, including dBASE II, III, and III Plus files, VisiCalc files, and more.

Appendix E: Differences between Release 2/2.01 and Release 1A

Highlights of the differences for 1A users, showing the power of Release 2/2.01.

Appendix F: Lotus International Character Set

This appendix, adopted from the Lotus manual, presents ASCII codes and the extended ASCII codes used by Lotus. This appendix shows the numeric value of different characters used by Lotus.

Appendix G: Answers to the Selected Review Questions

This appendix provides answers to selected questions presented at the end of each chapter to reinforce the reader's understanding of materials presented throughout the text.

Summary

This chapter gave an overview of the functions of a spreadsheet. A quick review shows the power and enhanced features of Lotus compared with other spreadsheets. We also discussed the various applications that Lotus handles. As you will see in the rest of this book, this amazing package is capable of doing many things. Just use your imagination!

Review Questions

1. How do you compare Lotus and a manual accounting spreadsheet?
2.* Name four spreadsheet packages prior to Lotus.
3. How many versions of Lotus have there been?
4.* What are some of the unique features of Release 2?
5. What is Release 2.01?
6.* What was the most popular spreadsheet prior to Lotus?
7. What are the memory requirements for Lotus Release 2?
8. What type of PC can utilize Lotus?
9.* How many disks are included in the Lotus package?
10. What is the most important disk in the entire package? Why?
11. Mention ten specific applications of Lotus.
12. Why is Lotus considered a DSS product?
13. Give an example of WHAT-IF analysis using Lotus.
14. What is goal-seeking analysis and how can Lotus perform such a task?
15.* Mention two examples of using Lotus as an integrated DSS package.
16. Get Lotus started using the Lotus Access System. Now change to A View of 1-2-3. What is available on this disk?
17. Get Lotus started and access the on-line Help command
18. Access the Help Index command. What is available here?
*These questions are answered in Appendix G.

Misconceptions and Solutions

M - Lotus provides a very large spreadsheet, 8,192 rows by 256 columns. At the present time there is no way to use this entire facility with a typical PC because of the memory requirements.

S - To utilize most of this facility, some computers can be upgraded to a bigger memory, up to four megabytes. This can be done with either Intel Above Board or AST Rampage Board.

M - Lotus has been written in 8088 assembler language. This means its processing power is higher than that of other spreadsheets. Even so, this speed will not be high enough to deal with very large spreadsheets.

S - Install an 8087 or 80287 coprocessor chip. This will immensely increase the speed of calculation. It will be very helpful when your worksheet includes a lot of mathematical calculations, sorts, table handling, etc.

2

Getting Started With Lotus

2-1 Introduction

In this chapter you will learn the fundamentals of Lotus 1-2-3. After studying the chapter, you should be able to build some simple worksheets, walk through your worksheet, correct your errors, differentiate types of data (numeric, labels, and formulas). We will also discuss priority rules for arithmetic operations using Lotus 1-2-3.

2-2 What Is A Worksheet?

A *worksheet*, or *spreadsheet*, is simply a matrix or a table consisting of rows and columns. Lotus Release 2 features a worksheet of 8,192 rows and 256 columns. Rows are numbered from 1 to 8,192 and columns are indicated by the letters A to IV. The intersection of a row and a column is called a *cell* and is uniquely identified by a column letter and a row number. A cell is nine characters long by default (see section on label prefixes below). Figure 2-1 illustrates an empty Lotus worksheet with a table of 20 rows and 8 columns.

2-3 Walking Through Your Worksheet

After the Lotus system disk has been installed (see Appendix C for detailed explanations of how to install Lotus 1-2-3), put MS/DOS or PC/DOS in drive A and

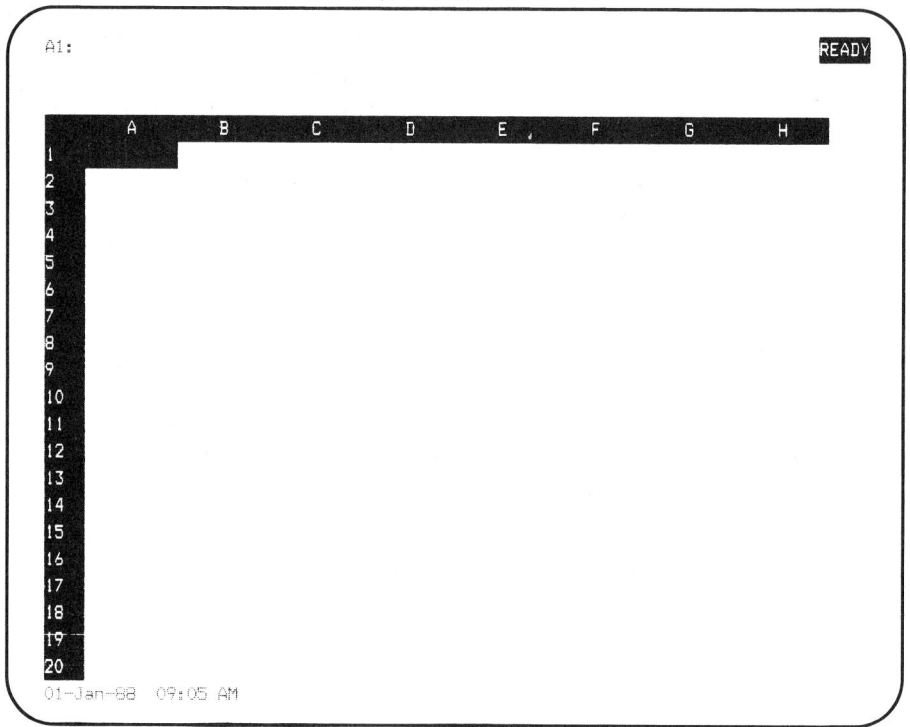

Figure 2-1 A Sample Worksheet

turn on the computer. At the "A" prompt, insert the Lotus system disk in drive A and type Lotus. From the six options presented to you, choose option 1-2-3, the spreadsheet part of Lotus. (For detailed explanations on how to boot your system, see Appendices A and B.)

The cursor is at column A, row 1, or cell A1. You are now able to move around the entire worksheet as follows:

→ (right arrow)	Moves the cursor one cell to the right.
← (left arrow)	Moves the cursor one cell to the left.
↑ (up arrow)	Moves the cursor up one cell.
↓ (down arrow)	Moves the cursor down one cell.
PgUp	Moves the cursor up one screen.
PgDn	Moves the cursor down one screen.
Goto	Will take you to any location in the worksheet. To activate

Goto, hit the F5 function key and the system will request a position. Type the address of the desired cell, hit the **Return** key, and there you go!

Home   Will take you to the cell in the upper left corner of the worksheet (e.g., A1).

End   Used in combination with arrow keys.

End & Home   Moves the cursor to the last occupied cell in any direction (right, left, up or down) or to the intersection of the last two occupied cells.

End & Up arrow   Moves the cursor up to the last cell above the current position (occupied or empty).

End & Down arrow   Moves the cursor down to the last empty cell or last occupied cell below the current position.

End & Right arrow   Moves the cursor to the last right cell of the worksheet to the right of the current position.

End & Left arrow   Moves the cursor to the last left cell of the worksheet to the left of the current position.

2-4 Your First Worksheet

You can enter data items in your worksheet by typing the data item and pressing the **Return** key or one of the arrow keys. Let's create a worksheet. Enter the data shown in Figure 2-2 as follows:

1. Move the cursor to cell A1 and type L.A.
2. Move the cursor to cell B1 and type 1000.
3. Move the cursor to cell A2 and type DENVER.
4. Move the cursor to cell B2 and type 2000.
5. Move the cursor to cell A3 and type PORTLAND.
6. Move the cursor to cell B3 and type 3000.

Figure 2-2 Sample Worksheet with Some Data Items

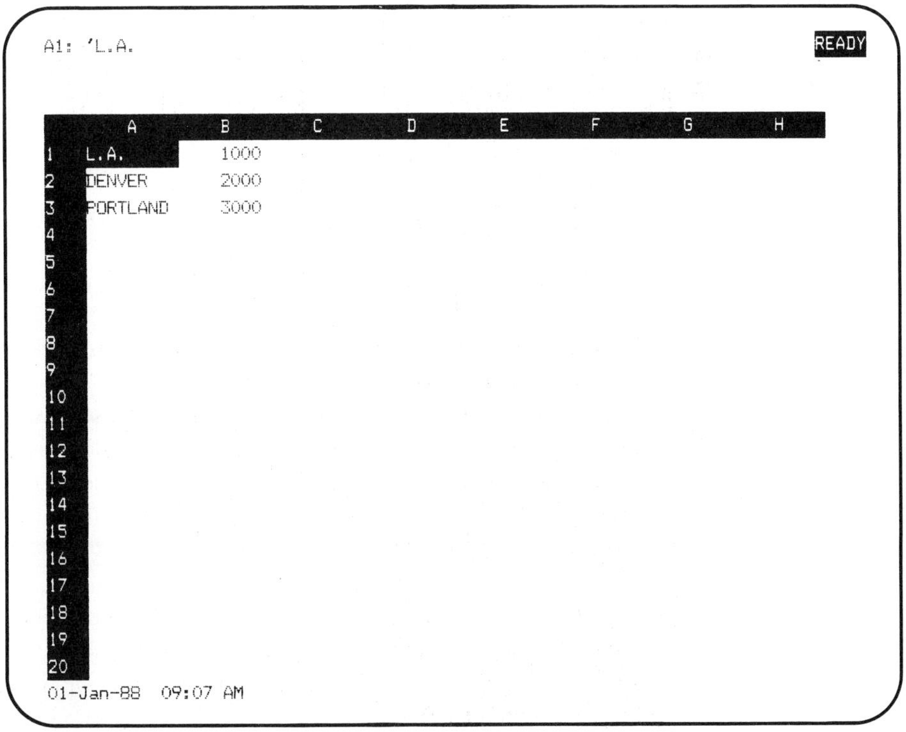

As you see, you can enter the data by typing the data item and moving the cursor or by typing the data, pressing the **Return** key and then moving the cursor to the next cell. The first option is faster but the second will work just as well.

As the worksheet illustrates, L.A. is in row 1, column A. 1000 is in row 1, column B. DENVER is in row 2, column A, and so on.

A new entry will replace an old entry. For example, if you move the cursor to cell A3, type ORLANDO, and hit the **Return** key, the new content of cell A3 will be ORLANDO. Try this on your worksheet.

2-5 How To Correct Your Mistakes

If you make a mistake, do not panic. There are two ways to correct an error. The first method is to replace the content of the cell by reentering the data item. This may not be efficient, especially if the content of a cell is a long series of characters.

The second method, the preferred alternative, is to edit the content of the cell that contains the mistake(s). This is how you do it:

1. Move the cursor to the cell that contains the error.
2. Press the F2 function key (**Edit** key). Now the cursor is at the end of the last character in that cell in the control panel.
3. Using the left or right arrow key, move to where the mistake is and type the correct character(s). The new character will be inserted to the left of the cursor position.
4. Delete the unwanted character(s) by highlighting and pressing the **Del** key.

Let us assume that in Figure 2-2 you have mistakenly typed PORTLAND as PORTLLAND, and you wish to correct the spelling.

1. Move the cursor to cell A3.
2. Press the F2 key.
3. Use the left arrow key to move the cursor to the error.
4. Hit **Del** and then hit the **Return** key.

Other keys are extremely helpful when you are editing data. These are as follows:

Backspace   Erases the character to the left of the cursor.
Insert (**Ins**)   Toggles the **Ins** key on and off. Inserts text by moving existing characters to the right and inserting the new character if the key is off. Replaces the previous character with the new one if the key is on.
Escape (**Esc**)   Cancels the entire line where the cursor resides. The length of the line does not matter.

By using the **Edit** key, arrow keys and special keys you should be able to correct any mistake easily.

2-6 Types of Data

Throughout your Lotus program you will see three types of data:

- numbers
- formulas
- labels

Numbers (values) are any data items starting with the digits 0 through 9, -, $, (, . Numbers can be up to 240 characters long but cannot include spaces or commas. Numbers can have up to 15 decimal places. Very small and very large numbers are presented in scientific notation.

For those of you who have forgotten scientific notation, the following are some examples:

Regular Numbers		Scientific Notation Equivalent	
5000	=	5E+03	$5 * 10^3$
2500000	=	25E+05	$25 * 10^5$
.0000006	=	6E-07	$6 * 10^{-7}$
.00007	=	7E-05	$7 * 10^{-5}$

Formulas must begin with the digits 0 through 9, ., +, -, (, @, #, or $, and can be up to 240 characters long. For example, +A7+AB is a valid Lotus formula. Formulas cannot contain spaces. If the first part of the formula is a cell address, the formula must start with a plus sign (+).

Data items that are neither formulas nor numbers are considered *labels*. Labels can be up to 240 characters long. They either begin with a prefix (see the next section) or start with characters that are not included in the starting position of numbers or formulas. However, labels can be made up of numeric digits, i.e., phone numbers, street addresses, etc., as long as this data will not be used in any arithmetic operations. To enter numeric data as a label, precede it with a label prefix. Long labels occupy the next right cell(s). If the next right cell is already occupied, Lotus will truncate the label on the screen but not in memory.

2-7 Types of Label Prefixes

Labels may begin with four different prefixes indicating whether they are left-justified, right-justified, or centered. By default, Lotus will left-justify a label. Following are the types of prefixes:

' (apostrophe) Left-justified.
" (double quotation)   Right-justified.
^ (caret)   Centered (this character is the uppercase of key 6, i.e., press the **Shift** key and then key 6).
\ (backslash)   Repeat the same character until the length of the cell is filled out.

We have used two words that may not be familiar to you. *Default* means the computer performs a task automatically without input from the user. For example, the length of a cell in Lotus is nine characters by default. You can override this rule any time you wish. *Justified* refers to the order in which the computer fills out a cell.

Right-justified means the characters will occupy the cell from right to left. If you type COBOL in cell A1 as a right-justified data item, Lotus will display three spaces, then COBOL, and leave the rightmost space in the cell empty.

Remember, prefixes are only used for labels. Numbers are always right-justified and don't need a prefix. Figure 2-3 illustrates different prefixes.

2-8 Arithmetic Operations in Lotus

Like any other programming language, Lotus follows a series of rules to perform arithmetic operations. These priority rules are as follows:

1. Expressions inside parentheses have the highest priority.
2. Exponentiation (raising to power) has the next highest priority.
3. Multiplication and division have the third highest priority.
4. Addition and subtraction have the fourth highest priority.
5. When there are two or more operators with the same priority, Lotus proceeds from left to right.

The following examples should make this clear. First, Lotus uses * (asterisk) for multiplication, ^ (caret) for exponentiation, and / (slash) for division. If A=5, B=10, C=2, calculate the following:

1.   A+B/C   =   10
2.   (A+B)/C   =   7.5

Figure 2-3 Examples of Different Types of Prefixes

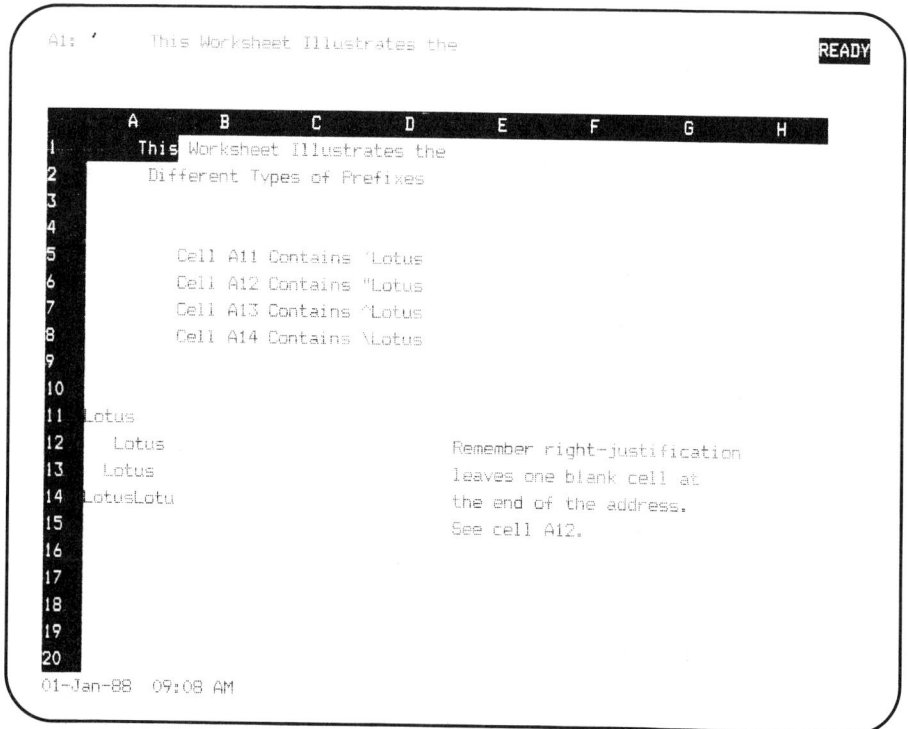

3.	A*B/C	=	25
4.	(A*B)/C	=	25
5.	A^C/2	=	12.50

Figure 2-4 illustrates these examples.

2-9 A More Comprehensive Example

Now that you have learned how to walk through your worksheet and perform simple tasks, let us construct a simple worksheet. Figure 2-5 illustrates three salespersons who have sold four products for Always Smile Merchant. You have been asked to calculate the total sales for each product, for each salesperson and finally for the business.

In cells B10, C10, D10 and E10 we entered PROD 1, PROD 2, PROD 3, and PROD 4. Cells A11, A12, and A13 contain the three salespersons' names. Cells B11 through E13 contain the total sales for each salesperson for different products. As we discussed earlier, you can enter a data item, move the cursor to the next cell and continue until all your data has been entered.

In this particular example, we have added the cells by using the plus sign. Total sales generated by Sue are found by entering +B11+C11+D11+E11 in cell H11. Jack's total sales are in cell H12; we entered +B12+C12+D12+E12. In cell H13, Mary's total sales are stored; we entered +B13+C13+D13+E13. In cell B16 we entered +B11+B12+B13; in cell C16 we entered +C11+C12+C13; in cell D16 we

Figure 2-4 Arithmetic Operations Using Lotus

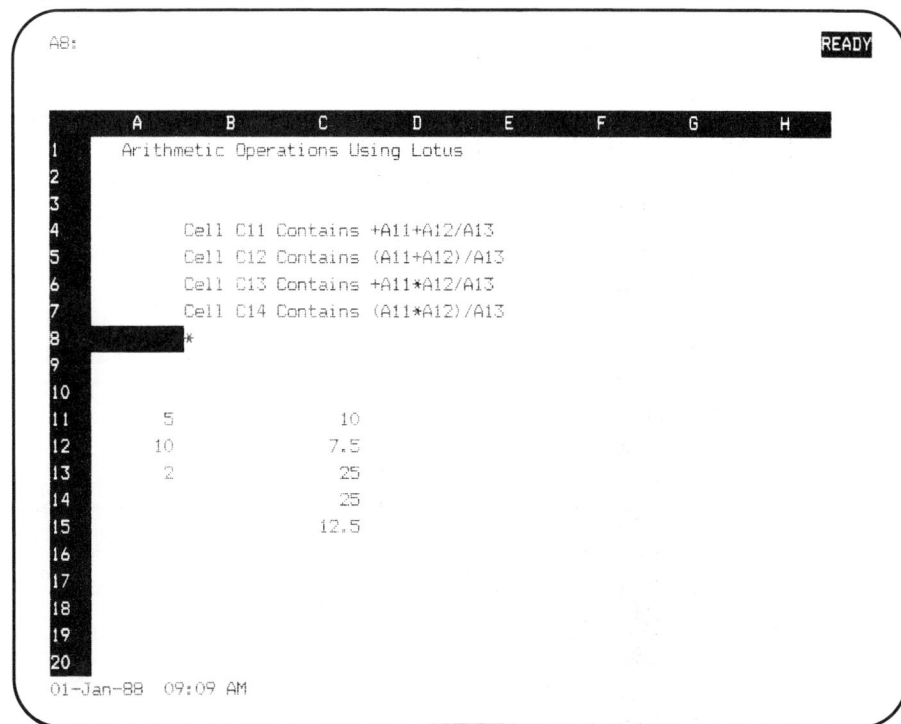

```
A8:                                                          READY

           A       B       C       D       E       F       G       H
    1    Arithmetic Operations Using Lotus
    2
    3
    4         Cell C11 Contains +A11+A12/A13
    5         Cell C12 Contains (A11+A12)/A13
    6         Cell C13 Contains +A11*A12/A13
    7         Cell C14 Contains (A11*A12)/A13
    8    *
    9
   10
   11     5              10
   12    10              7.5
   13     2              25
   14                    25
   15                    12.5
   16
   17
   18
   19
   20
   01-Jan-88  09:09 AM
```

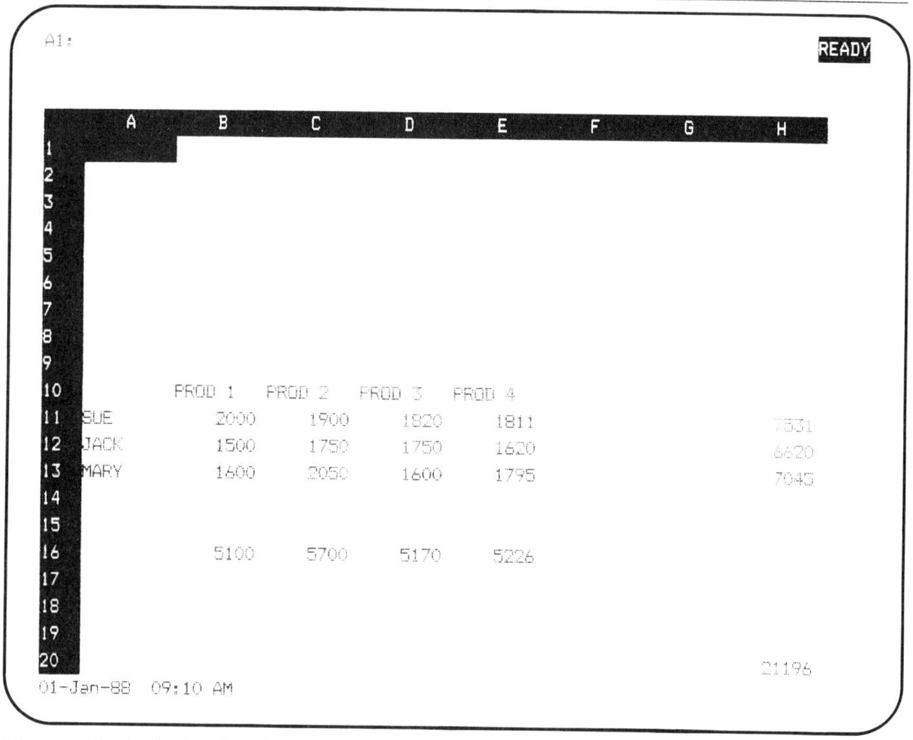

```
A1:                                                                    READY

           A        B        C        D        E       F      G        H
1
2
3
4
5
6
7
8
9
10            PROD 1   PROD 2   PROD 3   PROD 4
11   SUE       2000     1900     1820     1811                       7531
12   JACK      1500     1750     1750     1620                       6620
13   MARY      1600     2050     1600     1795                       7045
14
15
16            5100     5700     5170     5226
17
18
19
20                                                                  21196
01-Jan-88   09:10 AM
```

Figure 2-5 Sales Analysis Using Lotus

entered +D11+D12+D13; and finally, in cell E16 we entered +E11+E12+E13. Cells B16, C16, D16, and E16 contain the total sales for four products. What did we enter in cell H20? As you will see in future chapters, there is a much easier way to do this task.

2-10 Entering Formulas

As you saw in the last example, we entered the formula for addition in different cells by typing. This process is straightforward. However, you must remember to start a formula with a plus sign, +.

There is another way to enter formulas, called *pointing* . Let us say that in the next worksheet (Figure 2-6) we would like to add cells A1, B1, C1, and D1 and store the result in cell G1 by pointing. Do the following:

1. Move the cursor to G1 and enter a + sign.
2. Move the cursor to cell A1 (you will see A1 in the control panel), then add another + sign.
3. Move the cursor to cell B1, then add another + sign.
4. Move the cursor to cell C1, then add another + sign.
5. Move the cursor to cell D1.

Now you are done adding; just press the **Return** key. You will see that the result, 10, is stored in cell G1.

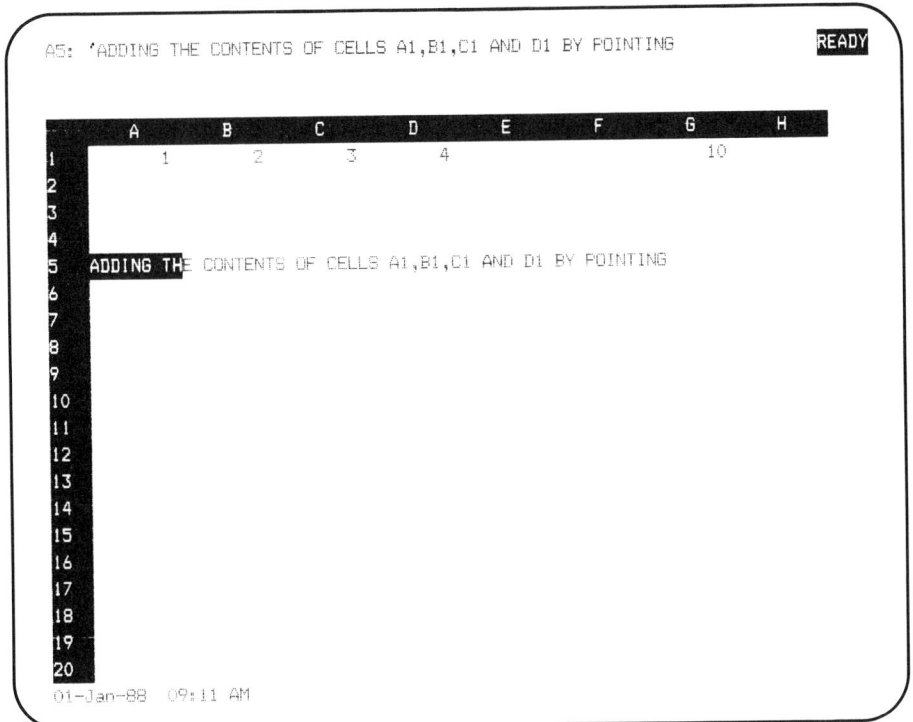

Figure 2-6 Adding the Contents of Four Different Cells by Pointing

When you design a formula, remember to always use the cell address instead of the cell value (A1 vs. 1 or B1 vs. 2 in this example). The reason for this is that you can change the contents of the cells and the result would be automatically recalculated. If you use values instead of cell addresses, you have to change the formula whenever you change the values.

Pointing can be very helpful if you are dealing with long, complicated formulas. You can transfer the content of a cell to another one by just starting with a plus sign in the destination cell, moving the cursor to the target cell and pressing the **Return** key. Pointing is more accurate since we humans are prone to make transpositions and typographical errors.

Summary

In this chapter you learned the basics of Lotus: how to build simple worksheets, enter data items in the worksheet, and edit a cell. We also discussed data types and the arithmetic operations.

Review Questions

1. How do you start your Lotus worksheet?
2.* What is the A prompt? Do we have any other prompts?
3. What is the simplest way to correct errors in your worksheet?

4.* What is the role of the **Home** key?

5. How do you move the cursor to the last row of the worksheet?

6. Which function key performs the editing task?

7.* What is the role of the **Esc** key?

8. How many types of data do we have?

9. How do you make a data item right-justified?

10.* How do you center a data item?

11. In performing arithmetic operations, which expression has the highest priority?

12.* How do you override the priority of operations?

13. Get Lotus started and do the following arithmetic operations in cells A1, A2, A3, and A4:

    2 +2/2
    (2+2)/2
    2*2/2
    2^2/2

    Check your answers manually. See if Lotus is correct!

14. Get Lotus started and calculate the average of the following four test scores:

    100
    95
    85
    80

15. Design a worksheet with ten salespersons in cells A1 through A10. For each salesperson, input a four-digit sales data in column C. In cell H1 calculate the average sales for these ten individuals.

16. Jack's Social Security number is 524-13-1439. Is this numeric data or nonnumeric?

17. Get Lotus started. Enter 555 in cell A10 as nonnumeric data. How does it look? Is it right-or left-justified?

18. The area of a triangle is calculated by B*H/2 where B is the base and H is the height. Enter a value for the base in cell A1 and a value for the height in cell A2. Now enter the formula for the area in cell A3. Enter different values for the base and the height and see how quickly Lotus calculates the area.

19. Get Lotus started and do the following:
    a. Move down one screen.
    b. Move to the right by three screens (*hint*: Use the Tab key).
    c. Move to the last cell of the worksheet.
    d. Move back to cell A1.

20. Mary receives a base salary of $360 a week and three different commissions of 5%, 7%, and 10% on Persian rugs, color TVs and general appliances, respectively. Last week she sold $12,000, $5,000, and $10,000 worth of these three items, respectively. Calculate her total pay.

Misconceptions and Solutions

M - When you perform editing you can move back and forth by using left or right arrows. This may be time-consuming for long labels.

S - Use the Home key to move to the beginning of the label and use the End key to move to the end of the label.

M - Nonnumeric data that starts with numbers, e.g., 29 Avenue, will be considered numeric data. You can always watch the mode indicator at the top right corner of the screen. This will tell you what type of data you are entering. The mode indicator for numbers is VALUE, for labels, LABEL.

S - Enter such data with one of the label prefixes, e.g., ', ", .

M - Cell addresses, e.g., A5, A69, will be considered nonnumeric data by Lotus.

S - These values must be preceded by a plus sign, e.g., +A9, or any other numeric characters, 0-9, +, -, ., (, $, #, @.

M - Entering long formulas may be time-consuming; also, accuracy may be jeopardized.

S - Use the pointing technique to enter long formulas.

M - Sometimes your arrow keys do not move.

S - Hit the **Esc** key to return to Ready mode. If the arrow keys still do not work, check if the **Num Lock** key is on. If this is the case, press the **Num Lock** key again.

M - You are entering a formula and at the end you press the **Return** key. Lotus gives you a beep and you cannot get out of EDIT mode.

S - Check your parentheses to make sure that every left parenthesis is matched with a right one.

3

Getting In and Getting Out of Lotus

3-1 Introduction

In this chapter, we explain the entire cycle of entering and exiting from Lotus, methods of data entry, how to perform mathematical operations, and how to print reports from the worksheet. We will also teach you how to save your worksheet on disk and how to recall data from disk to your computer's memory.

3-2 Lotus as a Black Box

Throughout this book we view Lotus as a black box. This means you will send some information to Lotus, it will perform some calculations, and the result will be given to you either in printed form or on a screen. In order to use this black box you should be able to answer the following three questions:

1. How do I send data or information to Lotus?
2. How does Lotus perform calculations?
3. How do I receive output from Lotus?

Sending data to Lotus, as you have already seen, is very easy. You have two options. You can enter data directly by typing it, moving to the next cell, and continuing this process until all data has been entered. If your data is a formula, you can enter it directly or by pointing.

What happens if you make a mistake? No problem. You can correct your mistake either by reentering the data or by editing the content of a cell. We discussed these options in Chapter 2.

How does Lotus perform calculations? Lotus performs calculations in many ways; we will discuss these methods throughout this text. For now, remember that most basic calculations in Lotus, or any other programming language, are done by performing arithmetic operations. As you saw in Chapter 2, Lotus can do addition, subtraction, multiplication, division, and exponentiation. In Chapters 10 and 11 you will learn Lotus functions (predefined formulas) that can perform mathematical and logical (comparison) operations. You can translate any mathematical formula into Lotus and it will give you the result. We will talk about all this later.

How do you receive output from Lotus? You have seen the output of your Lotus program on the monitor but how do you generate a paper report from the data on the screen? There are two methods for generating reports or hard copies. The simplest way, using an IBM PC or compatible keyboard, is to press the Shift key (the thick arrow key) and the **PrtSc** (print screen) key at the same time. What is displayed on the monitor will be sent to the printer.

Lotus has provided a more convenient method for generating a report. This method uses the Print command. We have not talked about commands yet, but all Lotus operations are done through a series of commands (we will discuss this in the next section). Before we go any further, consider this example of the entire input/process/output cycle, or the black box approach.

Here are some students in our Lotus class. You have been asked to generate a worksheet with their names and grades and the average grade of this group:

Craig Johnson	95
Mary Freeman	98
Debbie Freeman	90
Reid Stuart	92
Debbie Campbell	70
Jack Jones	65

Figure 3-1 is the worksheet generated for this task. Data was entered as usual. Then we entered the formula (C1+C2+C3+C4+C5+C6) /6 in cell E15.

3-3 Lotus Command Menu

To activate the Lotus command menu, press the slash key (the question mark key). You will be given the screen shown in Figure 3-2.

Any of these menu items can be selected. Either type the first letter of each command, or point to the command, moving the right or left arrow to the item and pressing the **Return** key. (For a complete discussion of a Lotus worksheet, see Chapter 4.)

You will see three lines at the top of the worksheet. These three lines are called the *control panel*. The first line shows the present position of the cursor. In this case the cursor is in A1 and cell A1 is empty.

Figure 3-1 Students' Average in Lotus Class

```
A1: 'Craig Johnson                                                    READY


        A        B        C        D        E        F        G        H
1   Craig Johnson         95
2   Mary Freeman          98
3   Debbie Freeman        90
4   Reid Stuart           92
5   Debby Campbell        70
6   Jack Jones            65
7
8
9
10
11
12
13
14
15                                         85
16
17
18
19
20
01-Jan-88  09:38 AM
```

Figure 3-2 Lotus Command Menu

```
A1:                                                                  MENU
Worksheet  Range  Copy  Move  File  Print  Graph  Data  System  Quit
Global, Insert, Delete, Column, Erase, Titles, Window, Status, Page
        A        B        C.       D        E        F        G        H
1
2
3
4
5
6
7
8
9
10
11
12
13
14
15
16
17
18
19
20
01-Jan-88  09:10 AM
```

The second line highlights the Lotus main menu:

Worksheet Range Copy Move File Print Graph Data System Quit

The third line highlights options available under the selected menu item. For example, in Figure 3-2 the options available under Worksheet are:

Global Insert Delete Column Erase Titles Window Status Page

These options will be explained in detail later.

3-4 Lotus as a Black Box: The Second Look

All you need to do to utilize Lotus as a sophisticated programming language is enter data and ask Lotus to perform calculations. No matter how simple or how complicated your application is, it always includes three distinct components: input, process, and output. The diagram shows this process:

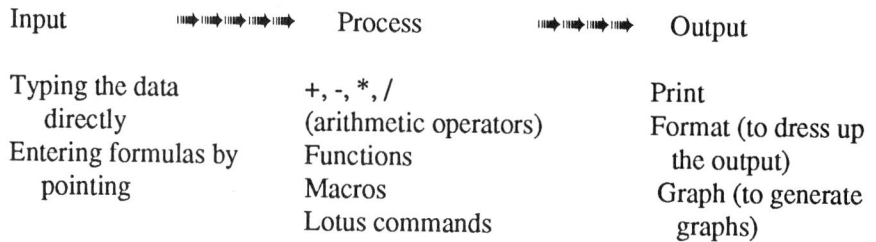

Input	Process	Output
Typing the data directly	$+, -, *, /$ (arithmetic operators)	Print
Entering formulas by pointing	Functions	Format (to dress up the output)
	Macros	Graph (to generate graphs)
	Lotus commands	

After performing the input/process/output cycle, how do you save your work for future reference? And how do you recall your previous work? We will answer these questions in the next section.

3-5 Creating A Worksheet

Let us assume that the following students have taken three tests in our Lotus class:

	Test #1	Test #2	Test #3
Craig	90	78	75
Mary	92	95	80
Debbie	80	85	96
Reid	95	75	94
Debby	70	85	76
Jack	65	75	85

You have been asked to do the following:

1. Create a worksheet for the class.
2. Add an additional column for the average score of each student.

3. Add an additional row for the average of each test.
4. Generate a hard copy of this worksheet.
5. Save your worksheet for future reference.

Figure 3-3 shows this worksheet. Entering data and calculating averages should not pose any problem. For example, Craig's average was calculated by the formula (B3+C3+D3) /3. Mary's average was calculated by (B4+C4+D4) /3. The first test average was calculated by (B3+B4+B5+B6+B7+B8) /6 and so on.

As we mentioned earlier, you have available two options to generate a hard copy. The first option is to press the **Shift** key and the **PrtSc** key at the same time.

The second option is to use the Print command. As you saw in Figure 3-2, one of the selections available in the main Lotus menu is Print. If you choose Print, two choices will be given to you: Printer or File (see Figure 3-4). This means that you can either send the worksheet to the printer directly or send the worksheet to a file for future printing. If you choose either of these options you will be given the screen shown in Figure 3-5.

We will explain these options in detail in Chapter 9. For now, just choose Range, which refers to the part of the worksheet you want to print. Specify the desired area by typing the two opposite corners. For example, A1..B5 means everything from cell A1 to cell B5, inclusive (the entire rectangle). Choose Go and hit the **Return** key. Your worksheet will be printed.

How do you save your worksheet for future reference? First you must have a formatted disk. (To format a disk, see Appendix B.) Put your formatted disk in drive

Figure 3-3 A More Comprehensive Students' Average Problem

	A	B	C	D	E	F	G	H
		Test #1	Test #2	Test #3		Average		
2						Score		
3	Craig	90	78	75		81		
4	Mary	92	95	80		89		
5	Debbie	80	85	96		87		
6	Reid	95	75	94		88		
7	Debby	70	85	76		77		
8	Zeky	65	75	85		75		
11	Average							
12	Score	82	82.16666	84.33333				

AS: 'Debbie READY

01-Jan-88 09:40 AM

Figure 3-4 Options Available under Print Command

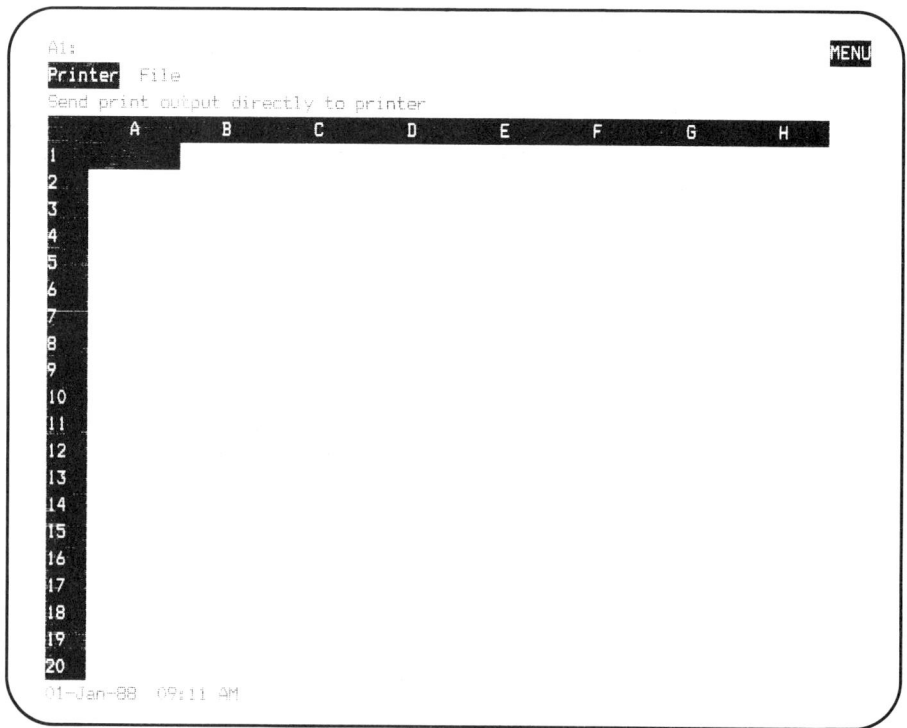

Figure 3-5 Options Available under Either Print Printer or Print File Command

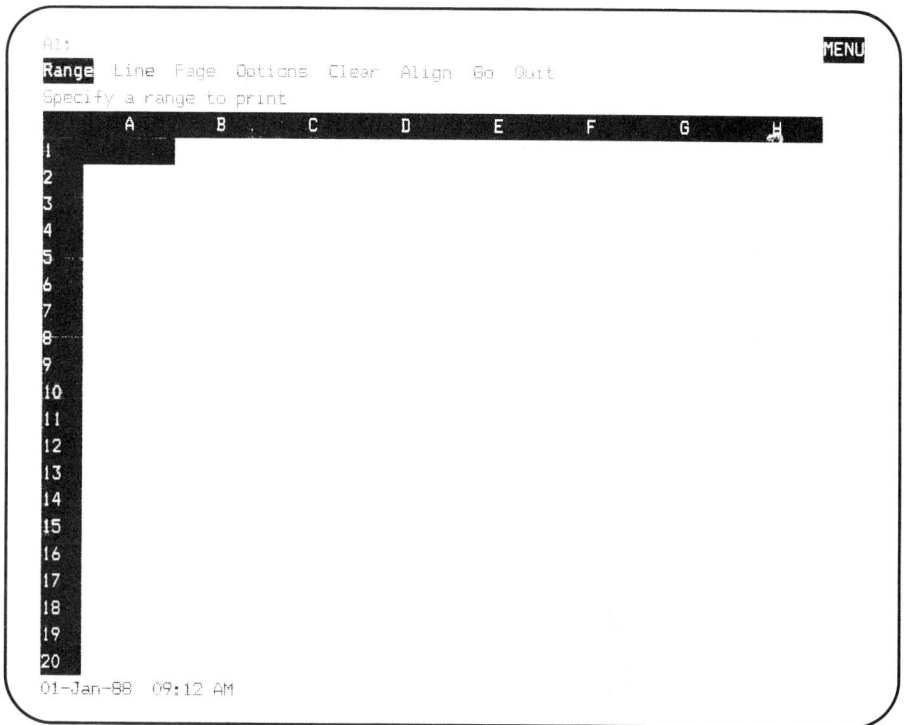

B: and choose the File option from the main menu. You will be given the screen shown in Figure 3-6.

Choose the Save option from this submenu. You will be given the current directory. Save your worksheet using a unique file name of up to eight characters. (For more information on File commands, see Chapter 8.)

You may have access to a hard disk. If this is the case, you can save your worksheet on it. When you save your worksheet on a floppy or a hard disk, you have made a permanent copy of it. This worksheet will remain until it is erased.

How do you recall a previously saved worksheet? Look at the choices given to you under the File command. Retrieve is among them. When you choose the Retrieve option, you will be given the names of all the files in your directory. Either by typing the name of a file or by pointing to it, you will be able to bring a file (a worksheet) back from disk to memory.

Remember, when you bring a file to memory (to the screen), this file will replace the current worksheet in the memory. In other words, the file on the screen will be lost. If you don't want to lose this worksheet, you must save it first and retrieve the other file.

3-6 Exiting From Lotus

When your worksheet has been saved and you are finished working with Lotus, you should exit from the program to maintain control over the contents and provide some security for the system.

Figure 3-6 Options Available under File Command

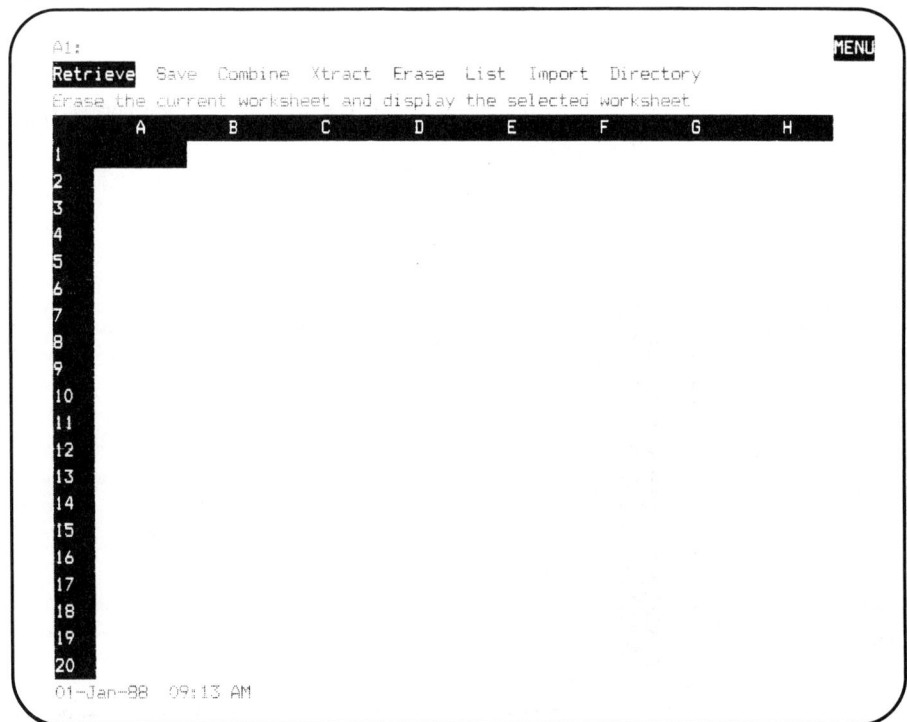

To exit from Lotus, choose the Quit option from the main menu. Lotus will give you the options of No or Yes. If you choose Yes, Quit will put you back to either the DOS A> prompt or the Lotus Access System.

By typing Lotus at the beginning of the session at the A> prompt, you enter the Lotus Access System. By typing 123 at the A> prompt, you go directly to the spreadsheet section of Lotus.

Summary

This chapter explained the cycle of input, process, and output, and methods of data entry. Using arithmetic operators, you can ask Lotus to perform any mathematical operation.

To receive hard copy from Lotus, use the Print command or press both the **Shift** and **PrtSc** keys.

Commands for printing, saving, and retrieving a worksheet were introduced. These commands will be explained in detail in later chapters.

Review Questions

1.* How do you start Lotus?
2. How do you start the Lotus Access System?
3. How do you enter numbers into a worksheet?
4.* Is entering numbers different from entering labels?
5. Generate a worksheet with 10, 20, and 30 in cells A1, A2, and A3. Add them up and store the result in cell H10 by pointing.
6. The hourly pay for employees at Craft-Tie-Corner is $15. Each employee gets 50% extra for each overtime hour (hours above 40). Design a worksheet for the following employees and calculate their weekly total pay.

    Sue   48
    Mary   35
    Bob   41
    John   52

    Your worksheet should include three columns: employee name, total hours, and total pay. Use only a simple formula to do this. Later on you will learn a much easier way by using the @IF function.
7.* How do you activate the Lotus command menu?
8. How many options are available in the Lotus main menu?
9. What is the control panel?
10. What is the third line in the control panel?
11.* How do you generate a hard copy of your worksheet?
12. How do you save your worksheet?
13.* How do you format a blank disk?
14. How do you recall a previous worksheet?

15.* How do you exit from Lotus?

16.   When you recall a file from disk to memory, do you still have the file on disk or is the file destroyed?

17.   Design a worksheet with your first name in cell A1, your last name in cell A2 and your Social Security number in cell A3. Generate a hard copy of this worksheet first by using **Shift** and **PrtSc** keys and then by using the Print command.

18.   Save the worksheet in Question 17 under "First." Exit from the Lotus worksheet. Turn the computer off.

19.   Get Lotus started again and retrieve worksheet "First." In cell A4 enter your age, in cell A5 enter your street address. Save this worksheet under "Second."

20.   When you enter a long label such as the street address, what will happen? Will your data occupy more than one cell or will it be truncated? Try this.

4

A Complete Overview of the Lotus Worksheet

4-1 Introduction

In this chapter we will discuss a Lotus worksheet, areas of a worksheet, the control panel as the starting point of your worksheet, and indicators such as mode, status, time and date. We will explain function keys and special keys. The information provided in this chapter should help you manage your Lotus worksheet more effectively.

4-2 What Is A Worksheet?

As discussed earlier, a Lotus worksheet is a matrix of 8,192 rows and 256 columns. The rows are numbered from 1 to 8,192 and the columns are labeled from A to IV (e.g., A-Z, AA-AZ, etc.).

The intersection of a row and a column is a cell. A cell can hold values, variables, formulas, and so forth. If you look at Figure 4-1, you will see several specific locations on that worksheet. Let us explain these locations.

4-3 Control Panel

The first three lines from the top are called the control panel. The first line usually gives you four types of information.

The first item on the first line is the cell address. This is the present position of the cursor. In our case, cell D16 is the present cell. This position can be changed by using one of the arrows in READY mode.

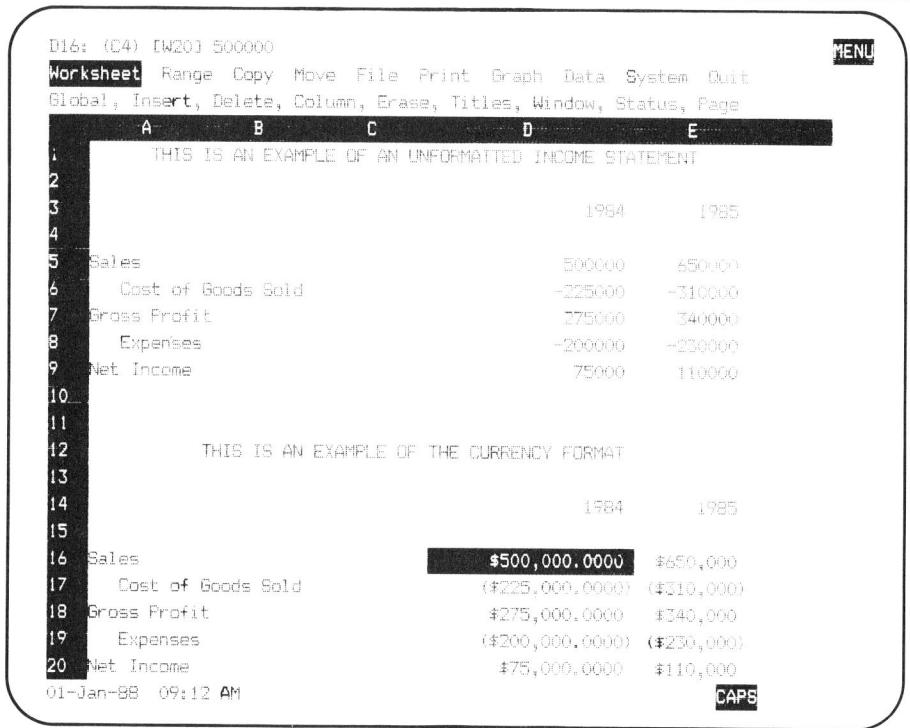

Figure 4-1 A Sample Worksheet

The second item gives the format of the present cell. In our case it is C4, meaning currency with four decimal places (discussed in Chapter 7).

The third item is the column width of the present cell. In this case it is 20 characters (discussed in Chapter 5).

The fourth item is the content of the present cell. This can be labels, numbers, formulas, etc. In our case it is 500000.

The second line of the control panel provides you with the main menu.

The third line of the control panel lists either options available to the menu that can be chosen by the cursor, or the menu selected by the present position of the cursor.

4-4 Indicators

In the upper right corner of Figure 4-1, at the lower right, and at the lower left you will see information called *indicators*. There are three types of indicators.

Mode Indicators

This indicator appears at the upper right corner of the worksheet. There are eleven types of mode indicators, as follows:

WAIT Lotus is executing or processing a command. Wait until this indicator goes off before performing any task. For example, you may have to wait while Lotus recalculates a balance sheet after changing one of the figures.

VALUE The user is entering a number or a formula; for example, +A1+A2 or 655.

READY Lotus is ready to accept the next command or the next action. For example, in this mode you can enter data into the worksheet, call the menu, and so on.

POINT The cell pointer is pointing to a cell or a range. For example, if you copy the contents of cell A1 to B1..B10 and you are at the From or To choices of the copy command, the indicator mode shows POINT (discussed in Chapter 5).

MENU The Lotus menu is being displayed. For example, when you press the / key (the question mark key) in order to invoke the main menu, the indicator shows MENU.

LABEL Indicates that the user is entering a label. This means any nonnumeric data. For example, if you type I AM BUSY, you will see LABEL as the indicator.

HELP Indicates that the user has invoked the HELP facility. To see this, press F1.

FIND This indicator is displayed when the /Data Query Find operation is in progress (see Chapter 14).

FILES This indicator appears whenever a File menu is invoked; for example, /File Save or /File Retrieve, etc. (see Chapter 8).

ERROR This indicator appears whenever an error occurs. For example, if you try to save a file in drive B and it does not have any disk, you will receive the ERROR indicator. To clear the error indicator, press either Return or Escape.

EDIT This indicator appears when you perform any kind of editing. To see this, press F2.

Status Indicators

Status indicators appear at the lower right corner of the worksheet. There are ten of these indicators, as follows:

SST This indicator, which means single step, appears when a macro is being executed one step at a time. As we discuss in Chapter 16, you can execute a Lotus macro one step at a time for debugging purposes.

STEP When this indicator appears, it means the single step mode has been turned on. To turn the step on, press Alt and F2 at the same time. To leave STEP mode, press Alt and F2 again.

SCROLL Shows that the **Scroll Lock** key is on. If you move the cursor down, the worksheet will scroll.

OVR This indicator appears if the **Insert** key is on. This is used when you perform some editing task.

NUM Indicates that the **Num Lock** key is on. When this key is on, the arrow keys serve as a numeric pad (a calculator) and cannot be used for moving the cursor around the worksheet.

END Indicates that the **End** key is on. This is used in combination with any of the arrow keys.

CMD Appears during the execution of a macro. As soon as the macro execution is over, this indicator will disappear.

CIRC This indicator appears if a cell is referring to itself. For example, if you type +A11 in cell A11, you will see CIRC. This will only happen if the recalculation order is natural. (For different types of recalculation, see Chapter 5.)

CAPS Indicates that the **Caps Lock** key is on. To turn it off, press the key again. You will see CAPS in Figure 4-1.

CALC Indicates that the worksheet needs to be recalculated. If you press F9 this indicator will disappear.

Date and Time Indicators

This indicator appears at the lower left corner of the screen. You can change this format by using /Worksheet Global Default Other or delete the indicator with / Worksheet Global Default Other Clock None.

4-5 Function Keys

Lotus utilizes the IBM-type keyboard function keys very effectively. These keys make it much easier for you to perform different tasks. Some of these keys are used individually, such as F1 through F10; some of them are used in conjunction with other keys, such as F2 + **Alt** for STEP. Following are descriptions of these keys.

F1 (Help) Accesses the Lotus on-line help facility.

F2 (Edit) Shifts Lotus into Edit mode. The contents of the current cell will be displayed in the control panel and the cursor will be positioned at the end of the cell's content. Now you can perform any editing. When you are done, hit the **Return** key.

F3 (Name) Displays all the range names in POINT mode. If you press this key a second time, you will receive a full screen listing of all the range names. This is helpful if you would like to know all the range names before issuing another name (discussed in Chapter 6).

F4 (Abs) In POINT mode, changes an address from absolute, to mixed, to relative. The cycle can continue (discussed in Chapter 6).

F5 (Goto) Gives you the opportunity to move to any location in the worksheet.

F6 (Window) Moves the cursor between two split screens (discussed in Chapter 5).

F7 (Query) Performs the most recent /Data Query operation (discussed in Chapter 14).

F8 (Table) Operates the last /Data Table command, e.g., recalculates the present table (discussed in Chapter 15).

F9 (Calc) Recalculates the worksheet. All formulas will be calculated into their most recent values (discussed in Chapters 5 and 17).

F10 (Graph) In READY mode, redraws the most recent graph. This is very handy for what-if analysis performed on a graph by changing different variables.

Alt + F1 (Compose) In conjunction with other keys, used to generate international characters. For example, try Alt + F1 + ((left parenthesis).

Alt + F2 (Step) Switches Lotus into single step mode for debugging a macro.

4-6 Special Keys

Besides function keys, some other very useful keys are:

Backspace Erases a character or a range.

Backtab (←) In READY mode, moves the cursor one screen to the left. In EDIT mode, moves the cursor five positions to the left.

Tab (→) In READY mode, moves the cursor one screen to the right. If the **Shift** and **Tab** keys are pressed together, they move the cursor one screen to the left. In EDIT mode, moves the cursor five positions to the right.

Break Cancels the current operation. (To activate this key, hold down the **Ctrl** key while pressing the **Break** key.)

Delete (Del) In EDIT mode, erases the current character.

Escape Cancels the current operation, e.g., gets you out of Lotus menu, erases a line, etc.

Alt (Macro) In conjunction with a macro name, it will invoke a particular macro.

Period (.) When you try to enter a range, it anchors the cursor if it is unanchored for pointing (discussed in Chapter 5).

Return It finalizes the operation: entering data, issuing a command, and so on.

Summary

This chapter gave an overview of a worksheet, explaining the control panel, indicators, function keys, and special keys. The information in this chapter can help you utilize the Lotus worksheet more effectively.

Review Questions

1. What is a control panel?
2. How many lines are usually included in the control panel?
3. What information is presented in the second line of a control panel?
4. What is a mode indicator?
5. How do you create a POINT mode indicator?
6. How and why might the indicator display ERROR?
7.* What is the most commonly used mode indicator?
8. When the mode indicator shows VALUE, what does it mean?
9. What is a status indicator?
10.* How do you create STEP as your status indicator?
11. When the **Num Lock** key is on, can you use the arrow keys for cursor movements?
12.* When can you see CMD as the status indicator?
13. How is CIRC generated?
14. How many function keys are there?
15. What is the function of F9?
16. What is the function of F10?

17. What does the **Escape** key do?
18. Start your Lotus worksheet and generate as many mode indicators as you can.
19. Generate as many status indicators as you can.
20. Can you erase date and time indicators from the bottom of your worksheet? If yes, how?
21. Try as many function keys as you can. At this point, some of them may not work. Why is this?
22. Get Lotus started. Type you name in cell A1. Now, without putting any disk in drive B, try to save this worksheet under "W1." What will you see in the mode indicator?
23. Enter 55 in cell A5. Check the mode indicator. You must see VALUE. Is this correct? In cell A6, type Lotus. You must see LABEL in the mode indicator. Is this correct?
24. In cell A10, type +A10. Your status indicator must show CIRC. Do you see why?
25. Get Lotus started. Press the **End** key, then press the down arrow. Check your status indicator.
26. Press the **Num Lock** key. Now try to use the arrow keys. They will not show the arrow movement. Why? Now you have a ten-key machine!
27. Press the **F1** key and check the mode indicator. What do you see?
28. Press the **Scroll Lock** key. Check your status indicator. Now, using the **down arrow** key, try to move the cursor down. Do you see what is happening? You always see new cells; the old ones are scrolled out of the screen.

5

Lotus Commands/ Part One

5-1 Introduction

In this chapter we will explain /Copy and /Move commands and the pointing technique; then we will talk about /Worksheet commands. Worksheet commands have been divided into two groups. The first group controls the entire worksheet. These are called /Worksheet Global commands. For example, /Worksheet Global Column-Width is used to set the column width for the entire worksheet. The second group controls only part of a worksheet. For example, /Worksheet Column Set-Width allows you to set the column width for one column of the current worksheet.

5-2 /Copy Command

The /Copy command enables you to copy a portion of a worksheet to another section of the same worksheet. The origin and the destination cells do not need to be symmetrical. This means that you can copy one cell to another cell, one cell to many cells, or many cells to many cells.

To use this command, choose the Copy command from the main menu. Lotus will ask for the range to copy FROM (showing you the present cell). Type the address of the original cell (the cell you want to copy), then hit the **Return** key. If you want to make a copy of the cell in which the cursor is residing, just press the **Return** key. Lotus will ask for the range to copy TO (the destination cell). Type the destination range and then hit the Return key. You can also point to the original and/or destination cells, as discussed in Section 5-4.

Figure 5-1 illustrates an example of the /COPY command. In this example we entered the word LOTUS in cell A4 and chose Copy from the main menu. In response to FROM (original cell) we typed A4; in response to To (destination cell) we typed A8..H20, then pressed the **Return** key.

Since this command is very important, we will summarize the steps involved:

1. From the main menu choose Copy.
2. Type the range that you would like to copy from.
3. Hit the **Return** key.
4. Type the range that you would like to copy to.
5. Hit the **Return** key.

When you are more comfortable with pointing, you will find this process to be much easier. For now this should do it just fine!

5-3 /Move Command

With the /Move command, you can move a portion of a worksheet to another section of the same worksheet. All you need to do is issue the Move command from the main menu. Lotus then prompts you for the FROM range. Type in the cell or range of cells that you want to move and hit the **Return** key. Now Lotus asks for the destination

Figure 5-1 An Example of the Copy Command

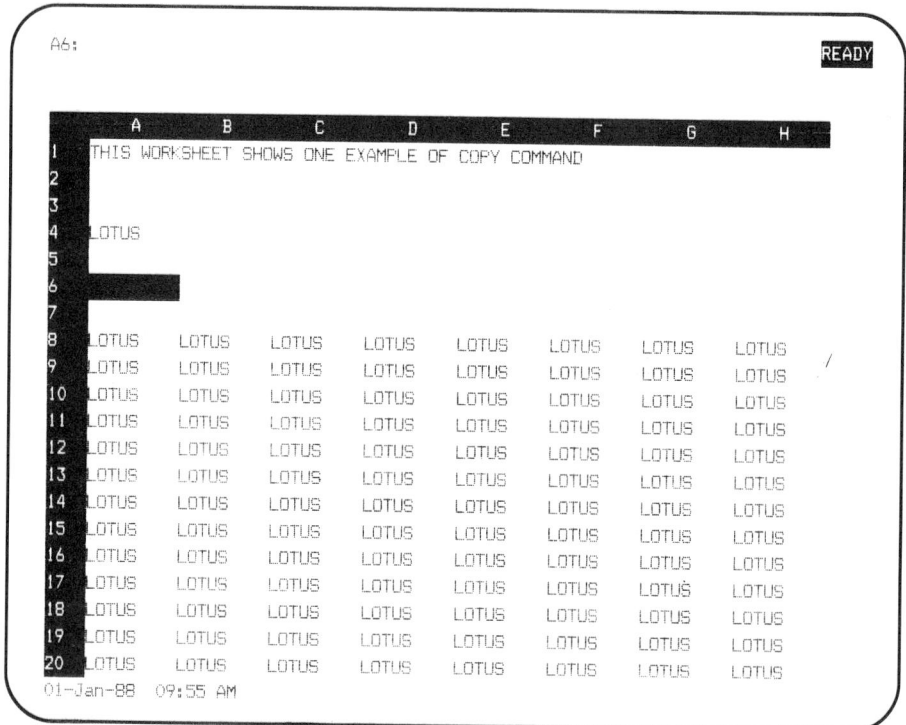

range. Type in the destination range, or point to it, and hit the **Return** key. Figure 5-2 illustrates a sample worksheet before we used /Move. We generated Figure 5-3 by typing /Move A1..G1 (hit Return) A15 (hit Return). This process moved row 1 to row 15.

5-4 Pointing

To define a range in a worksheet, you have two options. The first option is to type the address of a range, for example, a1..a5. The second option is to use *pointing*. To use the pointing technique, the mode indicator must be in POINT. At this time, press the **period** key . (>key). You have now anchored the first corner of the range. You can move the cursor in any direction until you have specified the range. When the desired range is established, press the **Return** key.

The **Esc** key removes the anchor from a range or breaks the pointing process. **Backspace**, **Home** and **End** keys can also be used with pointing.

5-5 Worksheet Global Commands

If you choose the Worksheet Global command from the main menu, you will see the following menu:

Format Label-Prefix Column-Width Recalculation Protection Default Zero

In the next sections we will explain these options.

5-6 /Worksheet Global Label-Prefix

If you choose Worksheet Global Label-Prefix from the main menu, you will be presented with the following three choices:

Left   Right   Center

As we discussed in Chapter 2, either enter a label prefix manually or use these commands for inserting left, right, or center justification. Remember that by default numbers are right-justified and labels are left-justified.

You should always issue the command and then type data into the worksheet. The command has no effect on data already entered in the worksheet.

5-7 /Worksheet Global Column-Width

This command enables you to set the column width for the entire worksheet. By default, the size of the column is nine characters. In many cases this default setting must be changed. For long names or labels you must extend the column width; for

Figure 5-2 A Sample Worksheet before the /Move Command

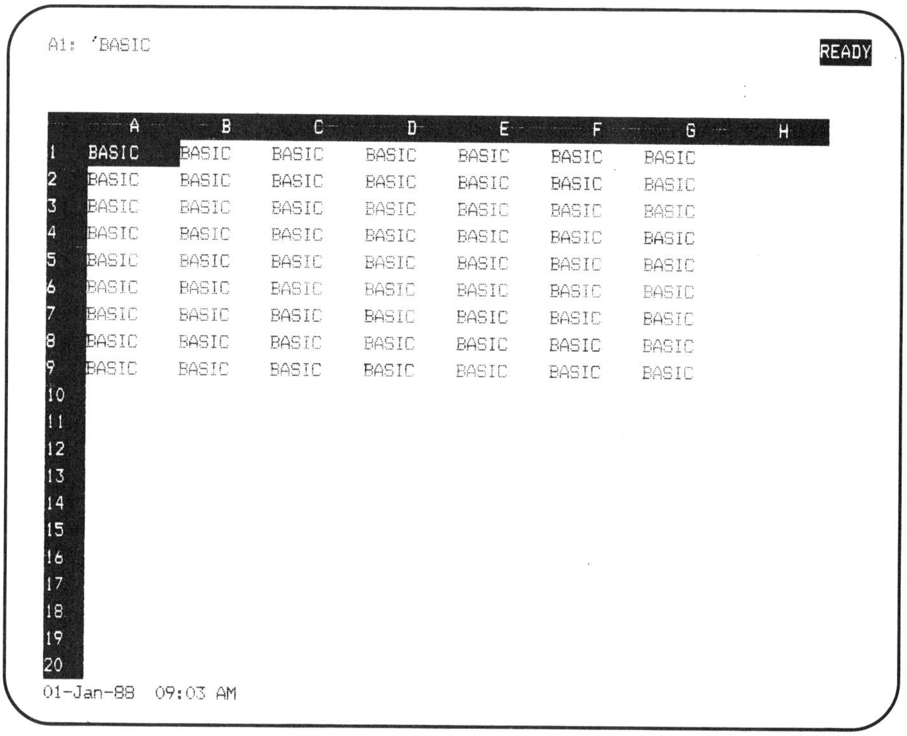

```
A1:  'BASIC                                                          READY

          A        B        C        D        E        F        G       H
1     BASIC    BASIC    BASIC    BASIC    BASIC    BASIC    BASIC
2     BASIC    BASIC    BASIC    BASIC    BASIC    BASIC    BASIC
3     BASIC    BASIC    BASIC    BASIC    BASIC    BASIC    BASIC
4     BASIC    BASIC    BASIC    BASIC    BASIC    BASIC    BASIC
5     BASIC    BASIC    BASIC    BASIC    BASIC    BASIC    BASIC
6     BASIC    BASIC    BASIC    BASIC    BASIC    BASIC    BASIC
7     BASIC    BASIC    BASIC    BASIC    BASIC    BASIC    BASIC
8     BASIC    BASIC    BASIC    BASIC    BASIC    BASIC    BASIC
9     BASIC    BASIC    BASIC    BASIC    BASIC    BASIC    BASIC
10
11
12
13
14
15
16
17
18
19
20
01-Jan-88   09:03 AM
```

Figure 5-3 A Sample Worksheet after the /Move Command

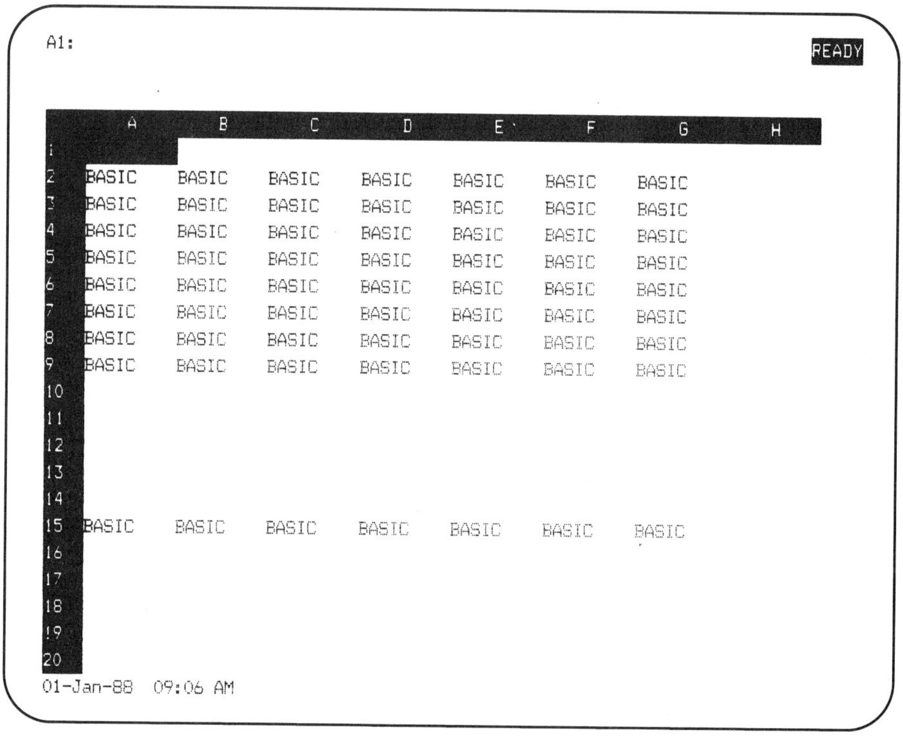

```
A1:                                                                 READY

          A        B        C        D        E        F        G       H
1
2     BASIC    BASIC    BASIC    BASIC    BASIC    BASIC    BASIC
3     BASIC    BASIC    BASIC    BASIC    BASIC    BASIC    BASIC
4     BASIC    BASIC    BASIC    BASIC    BASIC    BASIC    BASIC
5     BASIC    BASIC    BASIC    BASIC    BASIC    BASIC    BASIC
6     BASIC    BASIC    BASIC    BASIC    BASIC    BASIC    BASIC
7     BASIC    BASIC    BASIC    BASIC    BASIC    BASIC    BASIC
8     BASIC    BASIC    BASIC    BASIC    BASIC    BASIC    BASIC
9     BASIC    BASIC    BASIC    BASIC    BASIC    BASIC    BASIC
10
11
12
13
14
15    BASIC    BASIC    BASIC    BASIC    BASIC    BASIC    BASIC
16
17
18
19
20
01-Jan-88   09:06 AM
```

short labels or numbers you may want to reduce this default setting. For example, for a Sex field you need a column width of one character, e.g., M or F. The column width can be changed to any number between 1 and 240, inclusive. Figure 5-4 shows the default setting.

Figure 5-5 shows the column width extended to 12 characters. To select this option, type /Worksheet Global Column-width, then type any number between 1 to 240 inclusive.

5-8 /Worksheet Global Recalculation

If you choose Worksheet Global Recalculation from the main menu, you will be given the following menu:

Natural   Columnwise   Rowwise   Automatic   Manual   Iteration

In the *Natural* option, Lotus will first recalculate all values that have an impact over a particular formula. For example, if a formula in cell A10 depends on cell H35, Lotus first recalculates cell H35 and then goes to cell A10.

In the *Columnwise* option, all columns will be recalculated first, from A to B to C, etc., from top to bottom.

In the *Rowwise* option, all rows will be recalculated first, from 1 to 2, to 3, etc., from left to right.

In *Automatic*, Lotus recalculates the entire worksheet whenever you change any value. This is the default setting.

In the *Manual* option, Lotus recalculates the entire worksheet whenever you hit F9. This is a very useful option if you are dealing with a large worksheet and you do not want to spend a lot of time recalculating the worksheet for a minor change. It is also useful when you are making many changes but you don't need to see intermediate results.

In the *Iteration* option, Lotus uses an iteration number between 1 and 50 for Columnwise, Rowwise, and Natural options or whenever there is a circular reference (a cell referring to itself). When the iteration number is reached, the calculation will stop.

5-9 /Worksheet Global Protection

This command works in conjunction with /Range Protect and /Range Unprotect to protect a worksheet or a portion of a worksheet from unwanted changes. When you issue this command (/WGP) you will be given two choices: Enable or Disable. With the Enable facility on, only unprotected areas can be accessed and modified. Remember, the /Worksheet Erase command can always erase your protected or unprotected worksheet.

To make this discussion more clear, we will walk through an example.

From the main menu choose WGP. You will be given two options: Enable or Disable. Choose the Enable option. As soon as you choose this option you will see the PR sign on the control panel. This means that your worksheet is now protected.

Figure 5-4 Default Column-Width Setting

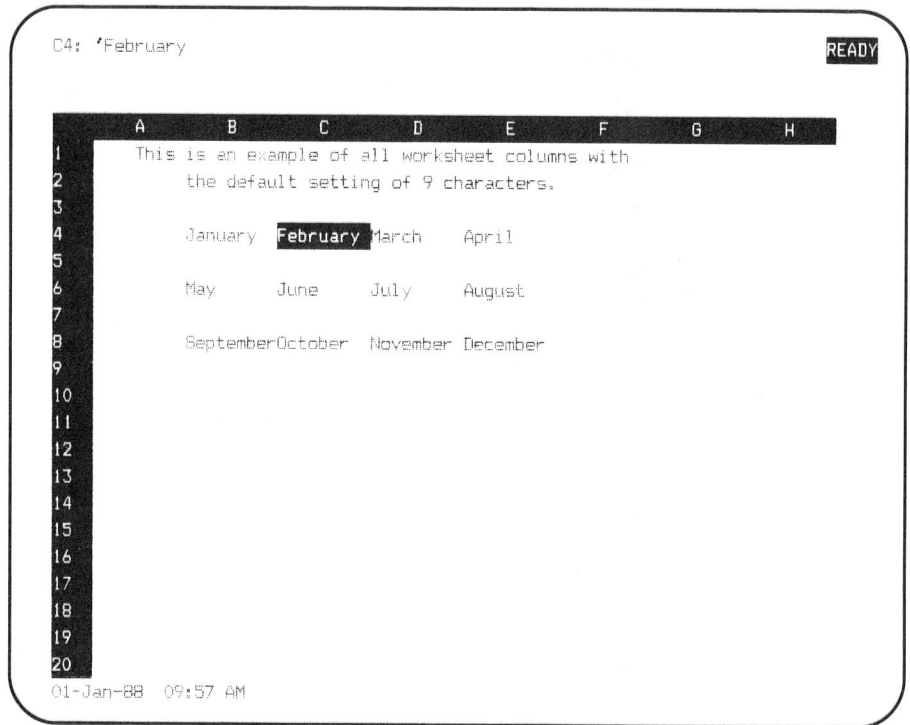

```
C4: 'February                                                          READY


       A      B      C      D      E      F      G      H
 1   This is an example of all worksheet columns with
 2        the default setting of 9 characters.
 3
 4        January  February March    April
 5
 6        May      June     July     August
 7
 8        SeptemberOctober  November December
 9
10
11
12
13
14
15
16
17
18
19
20
01-Jan-88  09:57 AM
```

Figure 5-5 Column Width Extended to 12 Characters

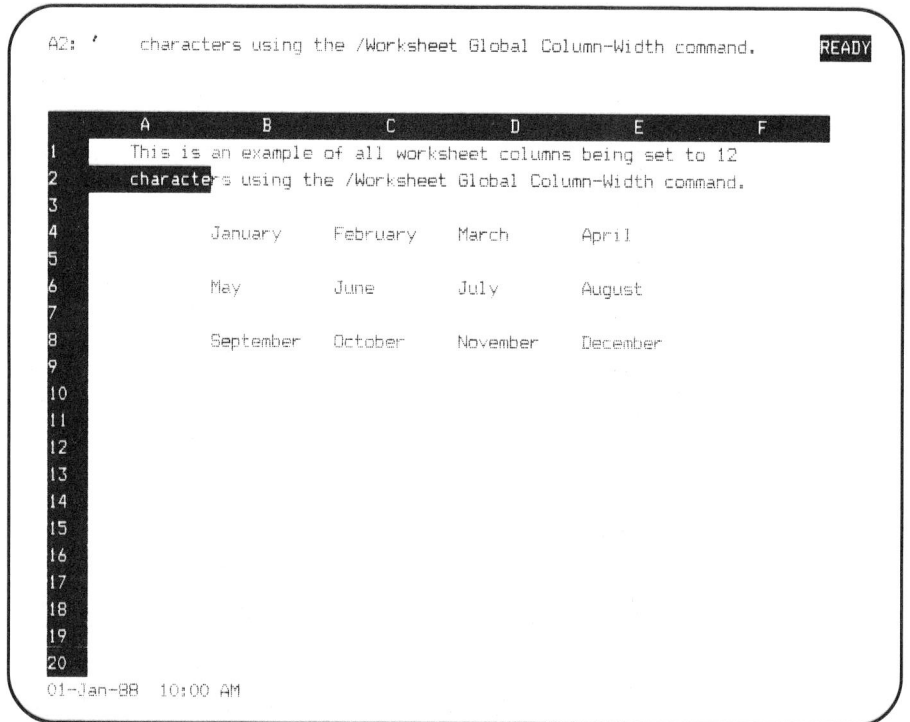

```
A2: '    characters using the /Worksheet Global Column-Width command.   READY


       A         B         C         D         E         F
 1   This is an example of all worksheet columns being set to 12
 2   characters using the /Worksheet Global Column-Width command.
 3
 4        January   February  March     April
 5
 6        May       June      July      August
 7
 8        September October   November  December
 9
10
11
12
13
14
15
16
17
18
19
20
01-Jan-88  10:00 AM
```

To verify this, try to enter a data item anywhere in the worksheet. For example, type check and press the **Return** key. You will hear a beep. This means that you cannot enter anything in this worksheet.

To cancel this facility, again choose WGP from the main menu. This time choose the Disable option. When you do this, the PR sign will disappear.

You may be interested in protecting a portion of the worksheet, but you want a range such as A1..H10 to be unprotected. To do this follow the following steps:

1. Choose WGP from the main menu.
2. Choose the Enable option. Now the entire worksheet is protected.
3. Choose Range Unprotect from the main menu.
4. Type A1..H10 to be unprotected.

Now you can enter data only in range A1..H10. The rest of the worksheet is protected.

Again, to remove the protection from the entire worksheet, choose /WGP and then Disable.

5-10 /Worksheet Global Default

When you choose Worksheet Global Default from the main menu, you will be presented with the following menu:

Printer   Directory   Status   Update   Other   Quit

The Pr*inter* option will give all the settings for the printer, as follows:

• Interface - describes the connection between Lotus and your printer (parallel or serial).

• Auto-LF - tells you whether your printer automatically issues a line-feed after a carriage return.

• Left - sets the left margin; default is 4.

• Right - sets the right margin; default is 76.

• Top - sets the top margin; default is 2.

• Bottom - sets the bottom margin; default is 2.

• Pg-Length - sets page length; default is 66.

• Wait - allows you to pause.

• Setup - specifies a string of control characters; default is a blank (see Chapter 9).

• Name - tells you which printer to use; default is the first printer.

The Directory option tells you the current directory.

The Status option gives you the present default settings of your system, for example, left margin, right margin, and so forth. This is a helpful command to use periodically in order to find out the default settings of your system.

The Update option enables you to save current settings in the configuration file (123.CNF file). If you change the default drive from B: to A: or C:, you must use / Worksheet Global Default Update in order to save these new settings. If you do not do this, the next time you access your worksheet, your current directory will be B:. If you do not want to save this new change, you must use /Worksheet Global Default Quit to leave the menu.

The Other option will give the following choices:

• International – Under this option you get Punctuation, Currency, Date, Time and Quit. Punctuation describes the characters used by Lotus for thousands separators, argument separators, etc. Currency tells you the sign used for currency, e.g., $. Date specifies different date options (discussed in Chapter 7). Time option will give you four different time formats. Quit will put you back into the previous menu.

• Help – This option is used for accessing the Help facility. You have two choices: Instant and Removable. If you choose the Instant option, Lotus provides you with Help when you hit F1. If you choose the Removable option, Lotus closes the Help facility whenever you leave. To make this change permanent, you have to use the Update command.

• Clock – This option gives you the format for the date and time presented in the lower left portion of your screen. There are three options: Standard, International, and None. The Standard option is the default setting. If you choose the International option, you must use the international settings for date (D4) and time (D9), as discussed in Chapter 7. If you choose None, the date and time will not be displayed on the screen. This is nice if you do not want to see these items all the time.

5-11 /Worksheet Global Zero

This command gives you the option of displaying or suppressing zeros in the worksheet. If you invoke /Worksheet Global Zero, you will be given No and Yes options. Choosing Yes will suppress the display of zero. Refer to the worksheet presented in Figure 5-6. As you see in this figure, there is a zero in cell D9. In Figure 5-7 we have used the /WGZY command. As you see, the zero has been suppressed.

5-12 /Worksheet Insert

This command allows you to insert either a row or a column into your worksheet. This command can be very helpful during database operations discussed in Chapter 14. To activate this command, type /Worksheet Insert. Lotus gives you the options of Column or Row. Choose either Row or Column, then hit the **Return** key. Lotus will ask for the cell address of the row or the column. For row or column insertion all you

Figure 5-6 A Sample Worksheet for Zero Suppression

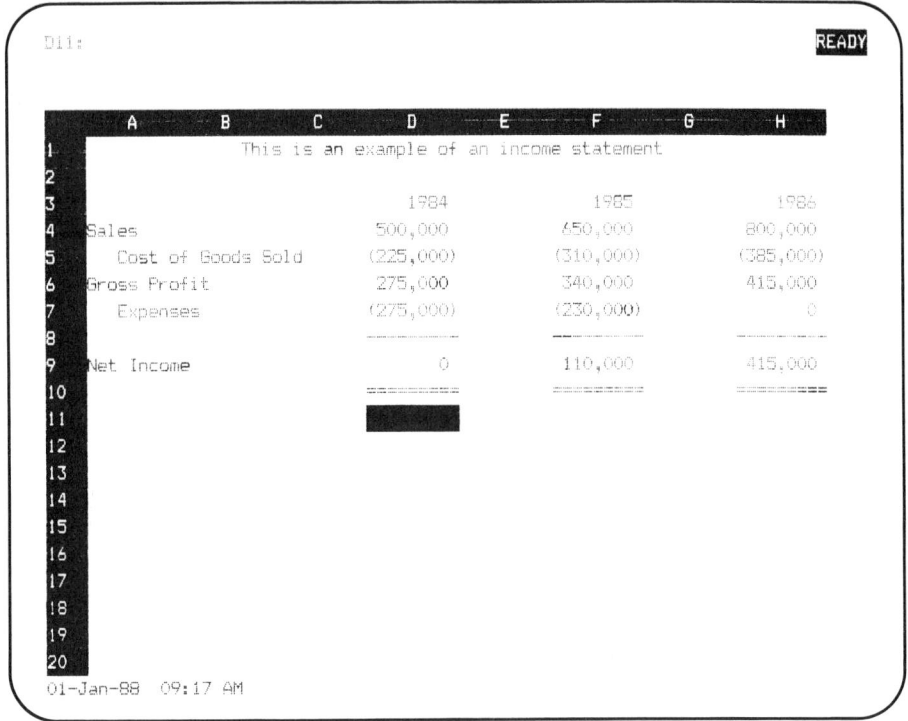

Figure 5-7 Sample Worksheet Using /Worksheet Global Zero

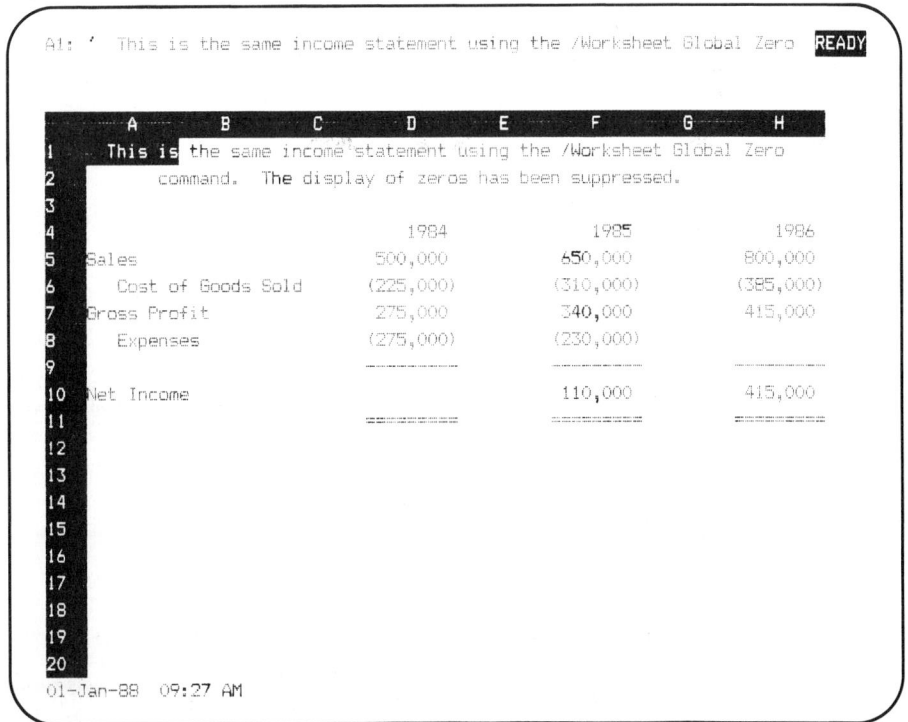

need is the address of one cell. For example, D1..D1 will insert a blank in column D if the option chosen was Column. A1..A1 will insert a blank in Row 1 if the option chosen was Row.

Figure 5-8 is a sample worksheet in which we will insert a row and a column. For row insertion we typed /WIR A5..A5. For column insertion we typed /WIC C1..C1. As you see in Figure 5-9,column C is empty and the other columns have been shifted one column to the right.

5-13 /Worksheet Delete

This command allows you to delete rows or columns. When you invoke /WD you will be given two options: Row and Column. When you delete a row or column with this command, the deleted area will be closed up.

Starting with Figure 5-9, we deleted the empty row and the empty column. The row was deleted with /WDR A5..A5 (Return). The column was deleted with /WDC C1..C1 (Return). The result is presented in Figure 5-10.

5-14 /Worksheet Column

If you type Worksheet Column from the main menu, you will be given the following options:

Set-Width   Reset-Width   Hide   Display

Set-Width allows you to change the width of a column. The default setting is 9 characters. You can extend the size of a column from 1 to 240 characters, inclusive. Reset-Width allows you to return the column width to its default setting.

The Hide option allows you to hide a portion of the worksheet without erasing anything. This command is useful in report generation. You may hide data that you do not want to print and redisplay it after printing.

The Display option redisplays the hidden columns, which will be marked by asterisks next to the column letters.

5-15 /Worksheet Erase

This command allows you to erase the entire worksheet. If you invoke /Worksheet Erase, you will be given two options: Yes and No. The Yes option erases the worksheet. Be careful. Make sure that this is what you want to do. If you haven't saved it, the erased worksheet is gone for good.

5-16 /Worksheet Titles

The /Worksheet Titles command freezes rows or columns along the top or left side of the screen. This enables you to see either the top portion, the side portion, or both

Figure 5-8 A Sample Worksheet for Row and Column Insertion

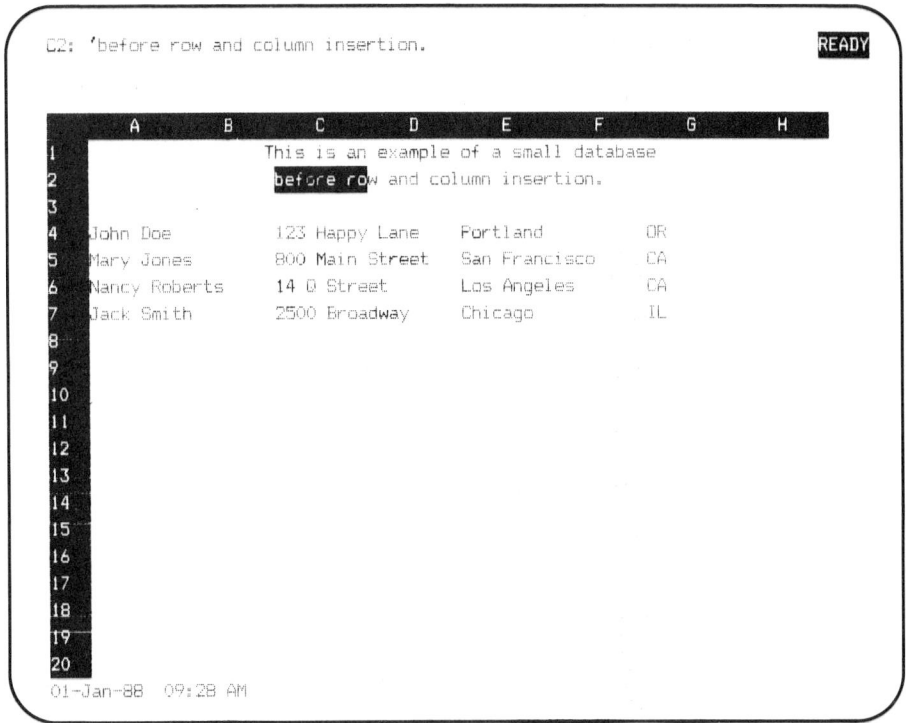

```
C2: 'before row and column insertion.                                        READY

          A          B          C          D          E          F          G          H
1                               This is an example of a small database
2                               before row and column insertion.
3
4    John Doe                   123 Happy Lane    Portland             OR
5    Mary Jones                 800 Main Street   San Francisco        CA
6    Nancy Roberts              14 Q Street       Los Angeles          CA
7    Jack Smith                 2500 Broadway     Chicago              IL
8
9
10
11
12
13
14
15
16
17
18
19
20
01-Jan-88  09:28 AM
```

Figure 5-9 A Worksheet with One Row and One Column Inserted

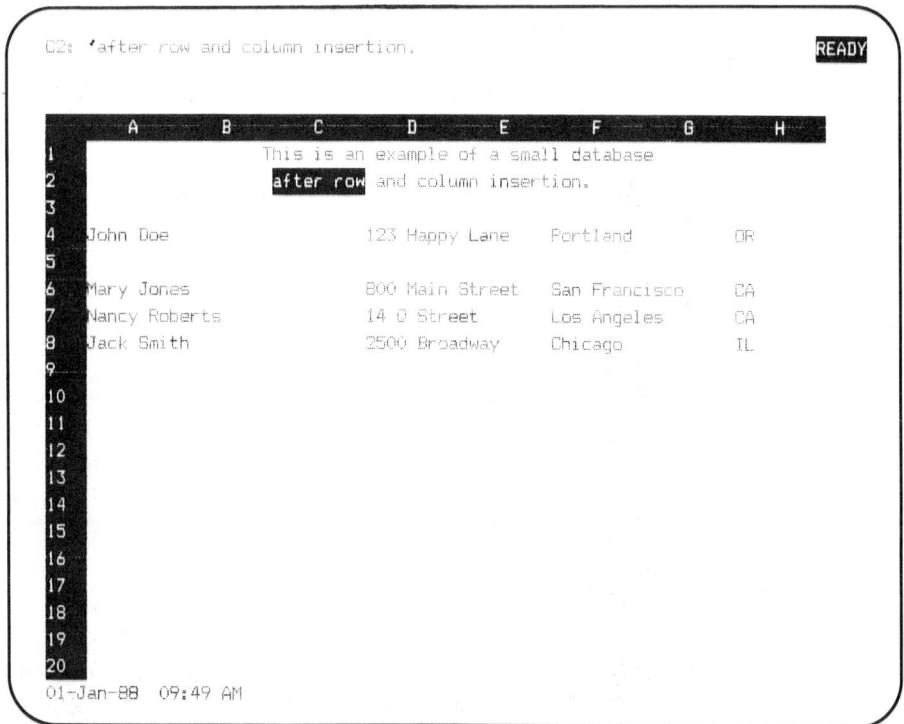

```
C2: 'after row and column insertion.                                         READY

          A          B          C          D          E          F          G          H
1                               This is an example of a small database
2                               after row and column insertion.
3
4    John Doe                              123 Happy Lane    Portland          OR
5
6    Mary Jones                            800 Main Street   San Francisco     CA
7    Nancy Roberts                         14 Q Street       Los Angeles       CA
8    Jack Smith                            2500 Broadway     Chicago           IL
9
10
11
12
13
14
15
16
17
18
19
20
01-Jan-88  09:49 AM
```

Figure 5-10 A Sample Worksheet after an Empty Row and an Empty Column Have Been Deleted

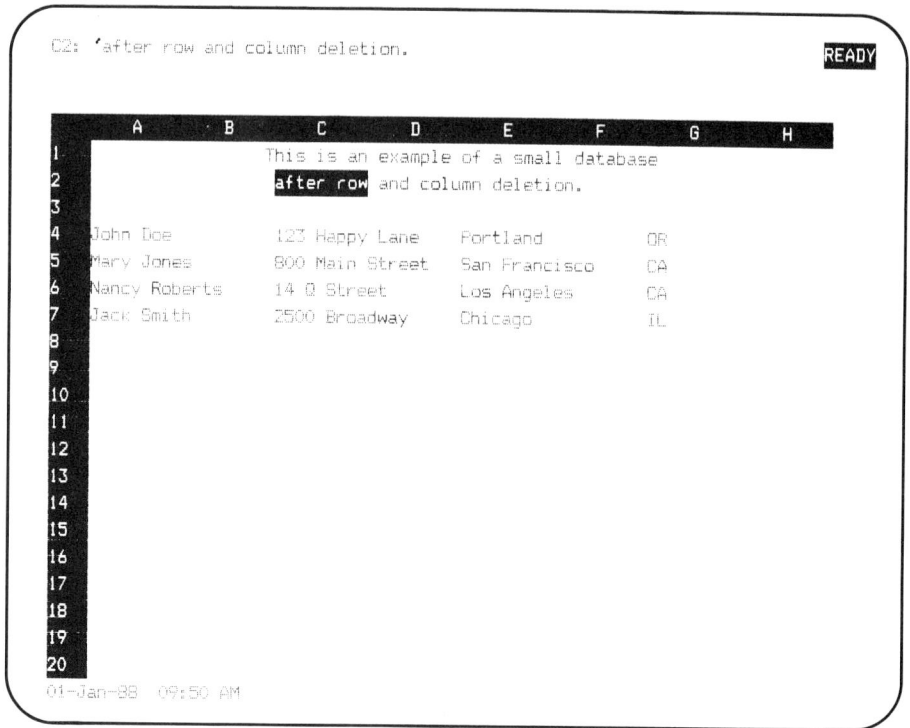

of your worksheet as you move around it. If you use /Worksheet Titles, you will be given the following options:

      Both   Horizontal   Vertical   Clear

• Horizontal – freezes the rows above the cursor. This means you can move around the cursor vertically in the worksheet, but the row or rows above the cursor are fixed.

• Vertical – freezes the columns to the left of the cursor. This means you can move around the cursor horizontally in the worksheet but the column or columns to the left of the cursor are fixed.

• Both – freezes the rows above and the columns to the left of the cursor.

• Clear – unfreezes the worksheet.

To see this command in use, refer to the sample worksheet in Figures 5-11 and 5-12. First we moved the cursor to cell A5, then typed /WTH. Now lines 1 through 4 of this worksheet are frozen, as shown in Figure 5-12. You can move the cursor vertically to any cell and these four lines will be untouched.

In Figure 5-13, we froze column A from Figure 5-11. To do this we moved the cursor to column B, then typed /WTV. You can move the cursor horizontally to any cell and column A will remain untouched.

Figure 5-11 A Sample Worksheet for the /Worksheet Titles Command

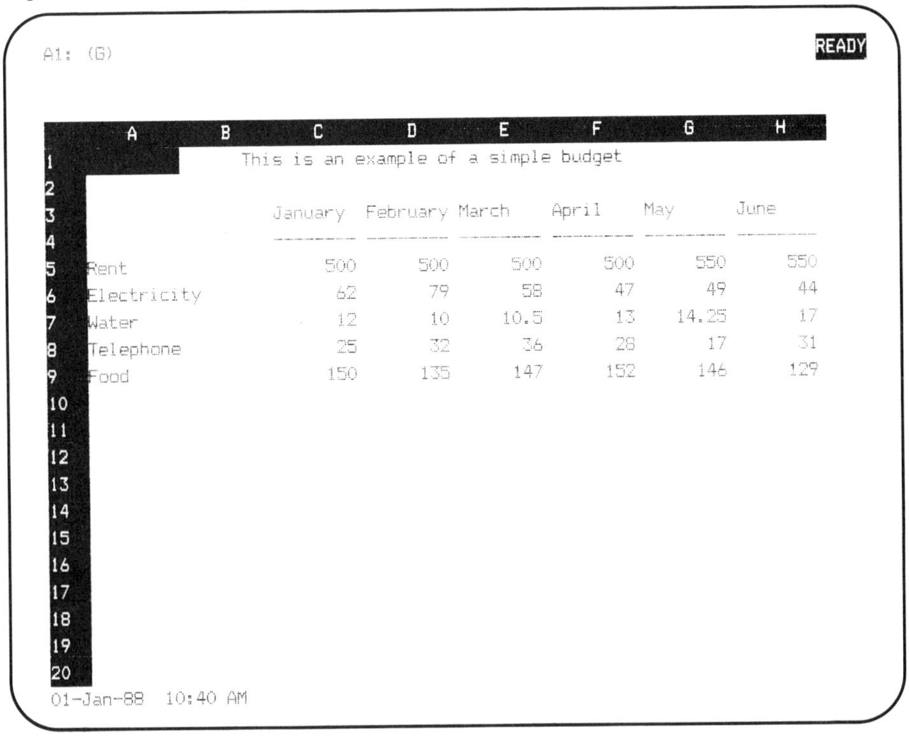

Figure 5-12 An Example of /Worksheet Titles Horizontal

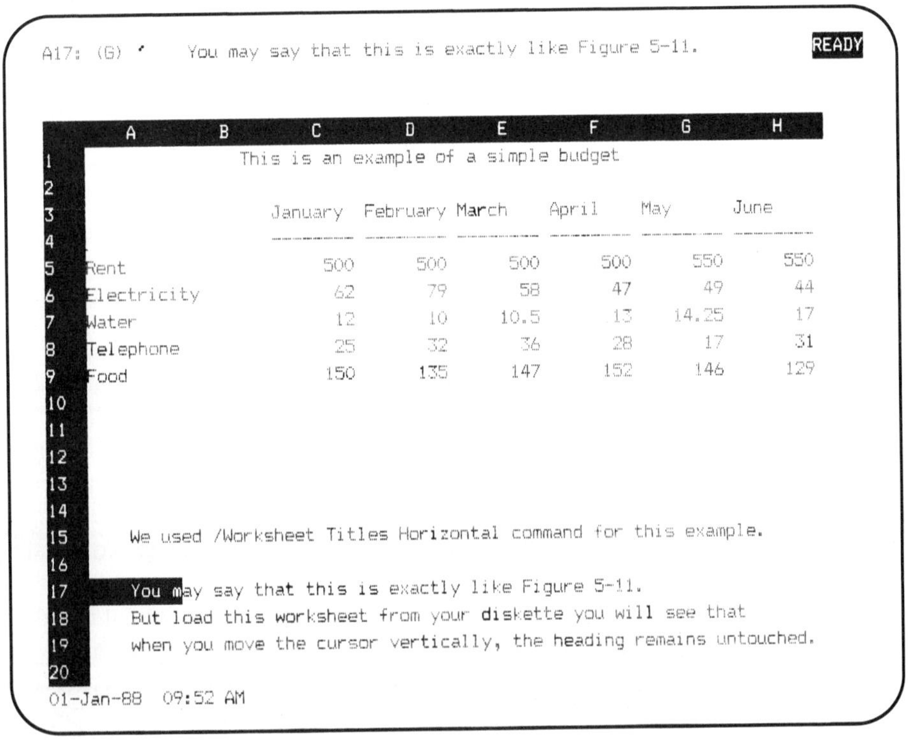

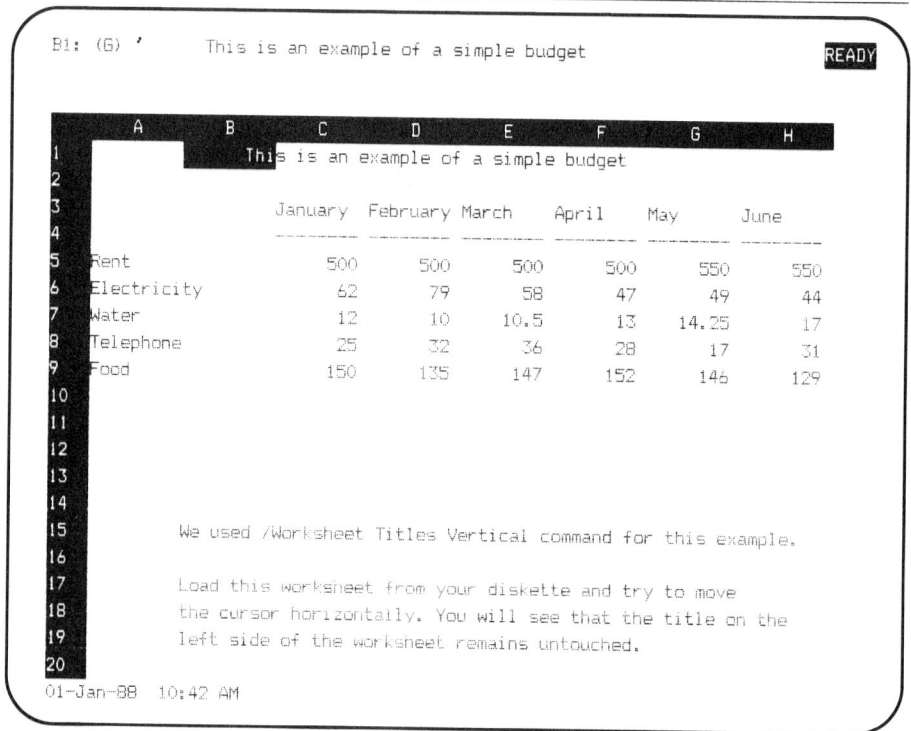

Figure 5-13 An Example of /Worksheet Titles Vertical

5-17 /Worksheet Window

Using /Worksheet Window allows you to split the screen to view two versions of a worksheet, formatted and unformatted, at the same time. When you invoke /Worksheet Window you will be given the following choices:

Horizontal   Vertical   Sync   Unsync   Clear

The Horizontal option creates a split screen with two horizontal windows. To produce such a worksheet, move the cursor to a particular row (row 2 or any row below this), then type /WWH. If you invoke this command in row 1 you will hear a beep. This means you cannot split the screen in row 1.

The Vertical option creates a split screen with two vertical windows. To produce such a worksheet, move the cursor to a particular column (column B or any column to the right of column B), then type /WWV.

The Sync option allows two windows to move harmoniously. This means that data scrolls across the screen in the same direction.

The Unsync option allows independent movement in either window.

The Clear option removes the second window from your worksheet.

To move the cursor between the two windows, press F6. The default for scrolling is Sync. Figures 5-14 and 5-15 show an example of this command.

Figure 5-14 An Example of /Worksheet Window Vertical

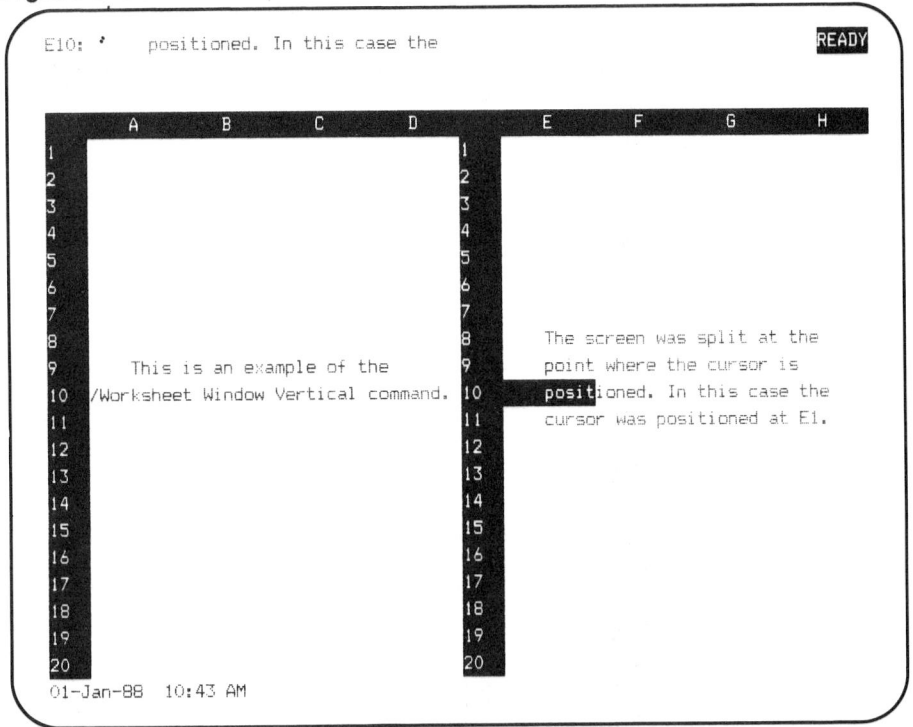

```
E10:  '    positioned. In this case the                                    READY

        A        B        C        D        E       F       G       H
1                                          1
2                                          2
3                                          3
4                                          4
5                                          5
6                                          6
7                                          7
8                                          8    The screen was split at the
9        This is an example of the         9    point where the cursor is
10  /Worksheet Window Vertical command.   10    positioned. In this case the
11                                         11    cursor was positioned at E1.
12                                         12
13                                         13
14                                         14
15                                         15
16                                         16
17                                         17
18                                         18
19                                         19
20                                         20
01-Jan-88   10:43 AM
```

Figure 5-15 An Example of /Worksheet Window Horizontal

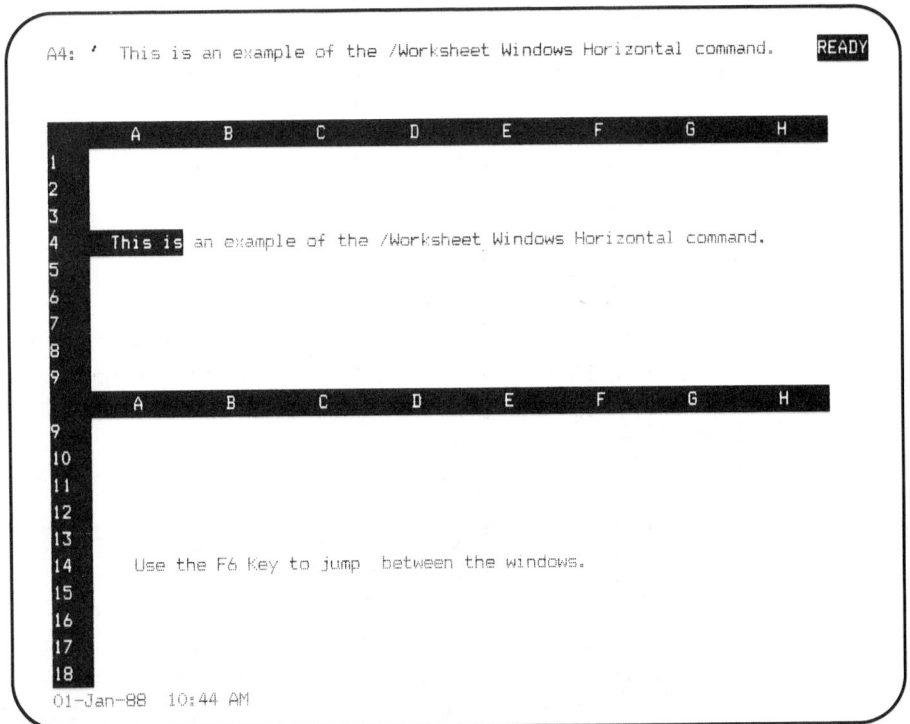

```
A4:  '   This is an example of the /Worksheet Windows Horizontal command.    READY

        A        B        C        D        E       F       G       H
1
2
3
4    This is an example of the /Worksheet Windows Horizontal command.
5
6
7
8
9
        A        B        C        D        E       F       G       H
9
10
11
12
13
14       Use the F6 Key to jump  between the windows.
15
16
17
18
01-Jan-88   10:44 AM
```

5-18 /Worksheet Status

This command provides you with information about available memory, recalculation method, current format, label prefix, column width, zero suppression, and global protection. This can be very helpful when you want to erase some unwanted data, speed up the processing time by changing the recalculation method, get a view of the current settings, and so on.

Figure 5-16 shows the worksheet status of the system used in this text. To generate this figure we first chose /Worksheet, then Status. As you see, this figure reveals a lot of information. It tells us the recalculation method, the format, and so on.

5-19 /Worksheet Page

This command inserts a page break into the worksheet, useful when writing reports. When you print a worksheet, a new page will start at the page break. To use this command, move the cursor to the row below the one where you would like to have a page break, then issue the /Worksheet Page command. The location of the break will be given by ::, which must be positioned in column A. Figure 5-17 shows an example of this command. The page break option can be removed using /Range Erase, / Worksheet Delete Column, etc.

Figure 5-16 The Output of the /Worksheet Status Command

```
                                                                    STAT

        Available Memory:
          Conventional..... 27152 of 27152 Bytes (100%)
          Expanded......... (None)

        Math Co-processor:  (None)

        Recalculation:
          Method........... Automatic
          Order............ Natural
          Iterations....... 1

        Circular Reference: (None)

        Cell Display:
          Format........... (G)
          Label-Prefix..... '
          Column-Width..... 9
          Zero Suppression. Off

        Global Protection:  Off

    01-Jan-88  09:07 AM
```

```
A10:                                                                      READY

          A          B          C          D          E          F          G          H
1                            This is an example of a small database
2
3
4    John Doe              123 Happy Lane              Portland              OR
5    Mary Jones            800 Main Street             San Francisco         CA
6    Nancy Roberts         14 Q Street                 Los Angeles           CA
7    Jack Smith            2500 Broadway               Chicago               IL
8
9
10              This is an example of the /Worksheet Page command.
11                       Page break is in A15
12
13   John Doe              123 Happy Lane              Portland              OR
14   Mary Jones            800 Main Street             San Francisco         CA
15   ::
16   Nancy Roberts         14 Q Street                 Los Angeles           CA
17   Jack Smith            2500 Broadway               Chicago               IL
18
19
20
     01-Jan-88  10:45 AM
```

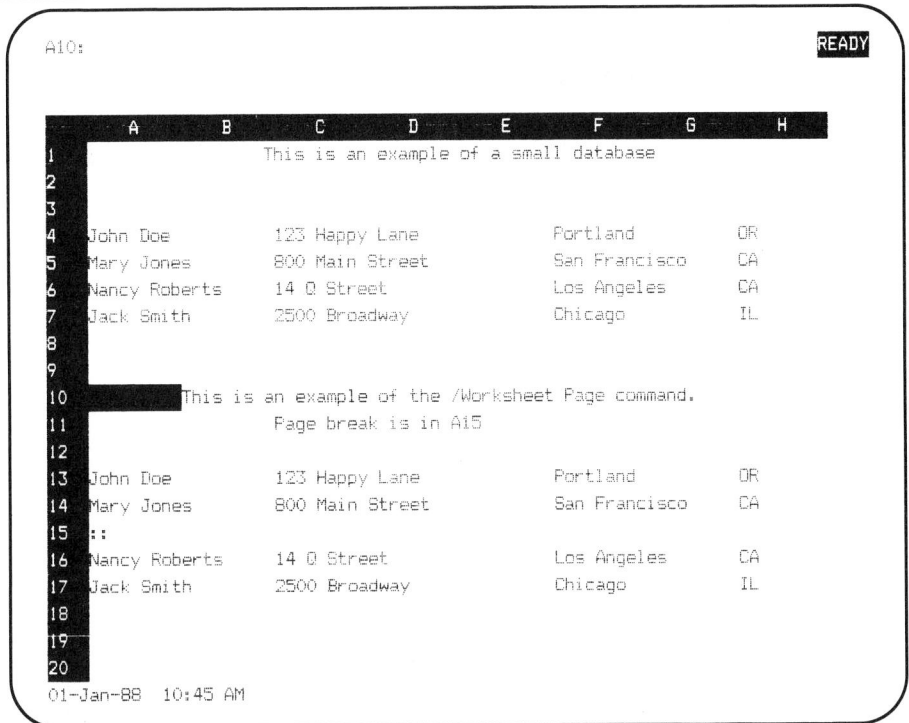

Figure 5-17 An Example of the /Worksheet Page Command

Summary

In this chapter, we discussed /Copy and /Move commands and the pointing technique, useful for working with data. We also discussed the /Worksheet commands. These commands have been divided into two groups. Global commands affect the entire worksheet; for example, setting column widths. The second group controls a portion of the worksheet; for example, inserting a row or a column. These commands and the /Range commands discussed in Chapter 6 will be important as we learn how to work with Lotus. Practice them and learn to understand them.

Review Questions

1. What is the difference between /Worksheet commands and /Worksheet Global commands?
2. What does Global mean?
3.* What is the default value for column-width in your worksheet?
4. How many recalculation methods are available in Lotus?
5.* What are some specific applications of Manual recalculation?
6. What is the default value for the Recalculation method?
7.* When you use /Worksheet Global Label-Prefix, should the data be entered first, before issuing the command?

8.   How do you activate Worksheet Global Protection?

9.   If a worksheet is protected, can you erase it?

10. What is the purpose of /Worksheet Global Zero?

11. What is the difference between /Worksheet Delete and /Range Erase commands?

12. How many options are available under the /Worksheet Column command?

13. What are some applications of the /Worksheet Titles command?

14. How many ways can /Worksheet Window be utilized?

15. How do you move the cursor between two split screens?

16. What are some applications of /Worksheet Window?

17.* What does /Worksheet Page do? Is there any specific column for page break or can it be placed anywhere?

18.* Sometimes the date and time displayed on the lower left corner of the screen is disturbing. What is the command to erase time and date?

19. Create a worksheet with your first name in cell A1 and copy your name into cells A1..H20.

20. In the worksheet created in Question 19, move rows 1 and 2 to row 50.

21. Repeat the process in Question 20 using pointing instead of typing the range coordinates.

22. Extend the column width in the worksheet to 30.

23. Split the worksheet in Question 19 both vertically and horizontally.

24. Using /Worksheet Erase command, erase the above worksheet.

25. Generate a worksheet with row 1 and column A frozen.

26. Enter your last name in cell A1. Then by using the pointing technique copy your name in range A1..H10.

27. Generate a protected worksheet. Then use /Range Unprotect on cell H10. Now enter your last name in cell H10.

28. Invoke /Worksheet Global Default and see the status of your system.

29. Enter the number 10 in cells A1 and A2. In cell A3 enter formula +A1-A2. Naturally you will see zero in this cell. Suppress the zero in the worksheet.

30. In the above worksheet, first hide Column A, then reveal it.

31. Design the following worksheet:

	A	B	C ...
1		Financial Data	
2	Branch A		
3	Branch B		
4	Branch C		
.			
.			

Using worksheet titles, freeze both horizontal and vertical titles. Now, to verity your work, move the cursor to the right, then downward. Both titles must be untouched. Is this correct?

Misconceptions and Solutions

M - If you enter a new data item in very large worksheets, Lotus immediately recalculates the entire worksheet. If you keep entering different values, this may slow down the process.

S - You can use /Worksheet Global Recalculation Manual. This turns the automatic recalculation off. Enter all your numbers, then press F9 (CALC).

M - When you use the /Move or /Copy commands to move or copy a data item or formula to a cell, the content of the cell will be replaced by the new data. Then any formula that refers to this cell will use the new value.

S - Direct /Move or /Copy to an empty cell or an area of the worksheet that does not have any relationship to your earlier formulas.

6

Lotus Commands/
Part Two

6-1 Introduction

In this chapter we will review commands related to range operations. A range can be any rectangular block within your worksheet, varying from a cell to the entire worksheet. We will also discuss relative, absolute, and mixed addressing.

6-2 What Is A Range?

A *range* is a rectangular block within a worksheet. This can be a cell, a row, part of a row, a column, part of a column, or the entire worksheet.

A range in Lotus is presented by two opposite corners, from upper left to lower right. To show a range, we type the first corner, two periods, and then the second corner. For example, A1..B5 means the rectangle of column A to column B and row 1 to row 5. This is a matrix of two columns and five rows. Range A1..H20 is a matrix of eight columns and twenty rows. Following are some more examples of a range:

A1..A1	a cell
A1..A8192	a column
A1..A50	part of a column
A1..IV1	a row
A1..H1	part of a row
A1..H30	a block (8 columns by 30 rows)
A1..IV8192	the entire worksheet

6-3 /Range Protect

You can protect a portion of your worksheet from being deleted by using the /Range Protect command. This means that you will not be able to erase this portion accidentally. To use this command, first you must use /Worksheet Global Protection Enable in order to turn on the protection facility. Now you can remove the protection from any range in the worksheet with the /Range Unprotect command, enter data into the range, and then protect it using the /Range Protect command. If a range is protected and you try to erase its contents, you will get an error message.

6-4 /Range Label

As we discussed in Chapter 2, Lotus enters numbers by default as right-justified and labels by default as left-justified. The arrangement for labels can be changed either by including a label prefix (as in Figure 2-3), or by using /Range Label, Left, Right, or Center. These commands change the label prefix of a cell that contains labels (nonnumeric data). They do not have any effect on numbers. Figure 6-1 illustrates an example. In this example we first entered Lotus in cells A3, A4, and A5. Then we issued /Range Label Left for cell A3, /Range Label Right for cell A4, and /Range Label Center for cell A5.

6-5 /Range Erase

This command can be used for erasing a specified portion of a worksheet. (Remember, it cannot erase a protected area of a worksheet.) To erase a single cell, move the cursor to that particular cell, type /Range Erase and then press the **Return** key. In Figure 6-2 we have generated two identical portions of a worksheet. A portion of the second worksheet was later erased by using /Range Erase B14..C18 (hit Return).

6-6 /Range Name Create

To perform any Lotus operations in a certain range, two options are available. Let us say you are trying to add the contents of cells A1, A2, A3, and A4. You can refer to these four cells as A1..A4 or you can give this range a name; then from this point you may refer to the range by using its name. To name a range you must use the /Range Name Create command. A range name can have up to 14 characters. Try to use meaningful names and avoid names such as A14 or G23. These names are misleading because you do not know if they are cell addresses or range names.

You can use /Range Name Labels to name an adjacent cell. With this option you can use Right, Down, Left, and Up. For example, if cell G1 contains "Commission Rate" as the name for cell H1. Naturally, you can use Up, Left, and Down options, depending upon where the desired cell and cursor are at any specific time.

To delete a range name use /Range Name Delete. This will erase a specific range name. To erase all the range names in your worksheet, you must use /Range Name Reset. What happens if you duplicate a range name? Lotus assigns the most recent range to the specific range name.

Figure 6-1 Example of /Range Label Command

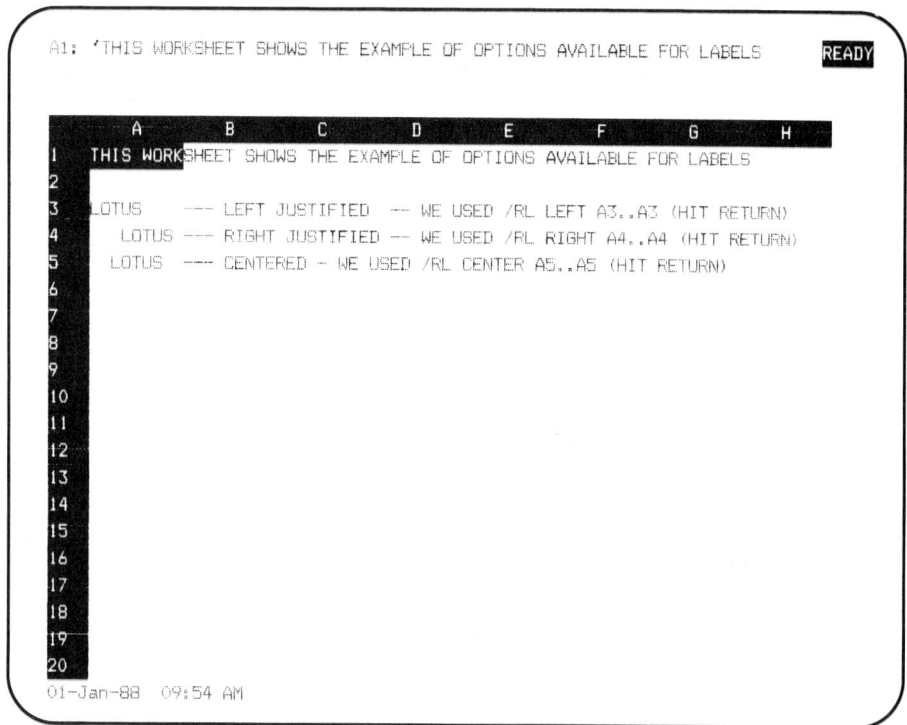

```
A1: 'THIS WORKSHEET SHOWS THE EXAMPLE OF OPTIONS AVAILABLE FOR LABELS        READY


         A       B       C       D       E       F       G       H
1   THIS WORKSHEET SHOWS THE EXAMPLE OF OPTIONS AVAILABLE FOR LABELS
2
3   LOTUS     --- LEFT JUSTIFIED  -- WE USED /RL LEFT A3..A3 (HIT RETURN)
4      LOTUS --- RIGHT JUSTIFIED -- WE USED /RL RIGHT A4..A4 (HIT RETURN)
5     LOTUS  --- CENTERED - WE USED /RL CENTER A5..A5 (HIT RETURN)
6
7
8
9
10
11
12
13
14
15
16
17
18
19
20
01-Jan-88   09:54 AM
```

Figure 6-2 Example of /Range Erase Command

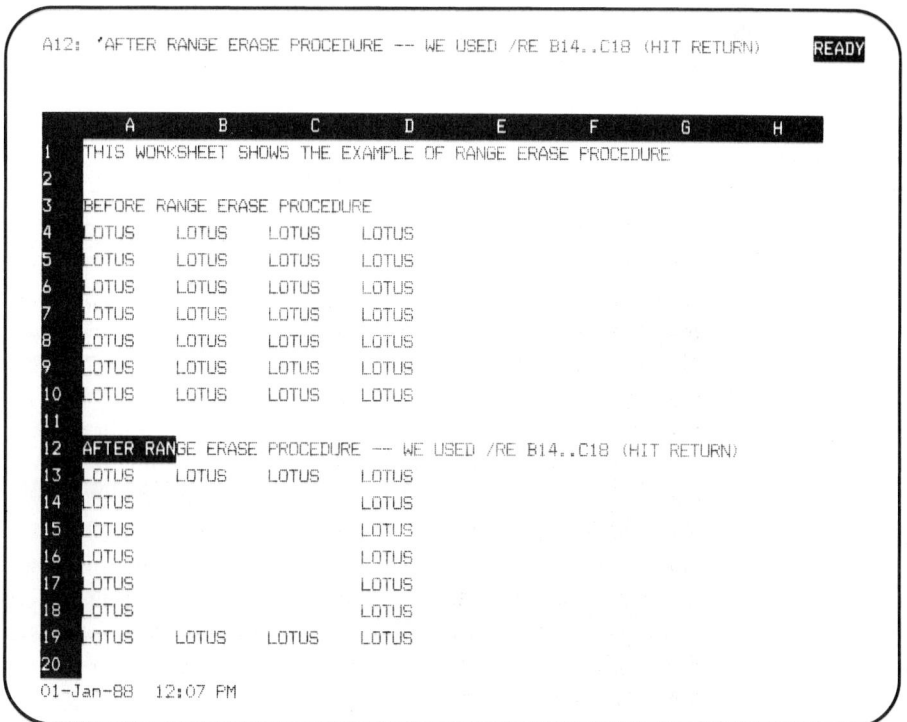

```
A12: 'AFTER RANGE ERASE PROCEDURE -- WE USED /RE B14..C18 (HIT RETURN)      READY


         A       B       C       D       E       F       G       H
1   THIS WORKSHEET SHOWS THE EXAMPLE OF RANGE ERASE PROCEDURE
2
3   BEFORE RANGE ERASE PROCEDURE
4   LOTUS     LOTUS   LOTUS   LOTUS
5   LOTUS     LOTUS   LOTUS   LOTUS
6   LOTUS     LOTUS   LOTUS   LOTUS
7   LOTUS     LOTUS   LOTUS   LOTUS
8   LOTUS     LOTUS   LOTUS   LOTUS
9   LOTUS     LOTUS   LOTUS   LOTUS
10  LOTUS     LOTUS   LOTUS   LOTUS
11
12  AFTER RANGE ERASE PROCEDURE -- WE USED /RE B14..C18 (HIT RETURN)
13  LOTUS     LOTUS   LOTUS   LOTUS
14  LOTUS                     LOTUS
15  LOTUS                     LOTUS
16  LOTUS                     LOTUS
17  LOTUS                     LOTUS
18  LOTUS                     LOTUS
19  LOTUS     LOTUS   LOTUS   LOTUS
20
01-Jan-88   12:07 PM
```

To get a listing of all the range names and their addresses, use /Range Name Table. This command will give you the names of all the ranges in your current worksheet in alphabetical order. Remember to position the cursor in a blank area of the worksheet so the table does not overwrite good data. To issue this command all you need is the upper left corner cell of the table, which will show all range names. From this point on you will get the listing of all the range names.

When you try to use a new range name, if you are not sure which names have been utilized, press F3 in POINT mode. This will give all the range names that are already in your worksheet. Remember, whenever you save a worksheet the range names will also be saved.

Using range names can be much easier than using range addresses. For example, if you are designing a balance sheet your total assets would be the sum of current assets and fixed assets. All you need to use is the @SUM function. Type in the following formula: @SUM (current asset, fixed asset). (All Lotus functions will be discussed in Chapters 10 and 11.)

6-7 /Range Justify

This command treats a continuous column of text as a line. You can use it to break a long title or heading into several shorter ones. The shorter titles will be lined up in one or several columns; it is up to you how many columns will be occupied. In Figure 6-3 we give several examples of this command. All you need to do is type your title and use the /Range Justify command. Remember, if there is data underneath the line that you are justifying, that data will also be justified and moved down. Therefore, your data won't be destroyed. In the first example, Figure 6-3, we have justified the title into one column, Column A. In the second case we have justified the title into two columns.

6-8 /Range Input

This command can be used to limit user input to a particular unprotected portion of the worksheet; thus, it can be very helpful during data-entry routines. If you use the command /Range Input and specify a range, you can move the cursor only to the unprotected cells in the range.

To see how the /Range Input command works, get Lotus started. Use /Worksheet Global Protection Enable in order to protect the entire worksheet. At this point, you cannot enter any data into this worksheet; all of it is protected.

Use the /Range Unprotect command to remove protection from range A1..A10. You can now enter data into this range with no problem. Now use the /Range Input command and define A1..A5 as your input range. At this point you can only move back and forth between A1 and A5, inclusive. There is no way to get out of this area. Using this technique, you can limit beginning users to a specified portion of your worksheet so that they cannot mistakenly erase or damage your worksheet.

Several keys can be used with /Range Input command. These include Backspace, Edit, End, Escape, Help, Home, Return, Down, Left, Right, and Up arrows. End will

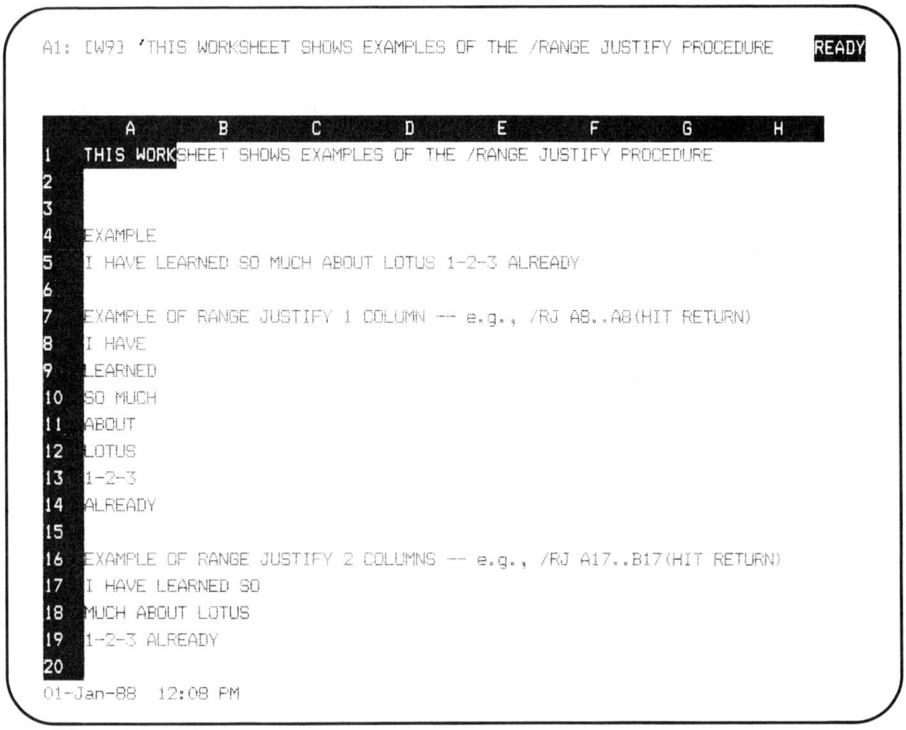

```
A1: [W9] 'THIS WORKSHEET SHOWS EXAMPLES OF THE /RANGE JUSTIFY PROCEDURE    READY

          A       B       C       D       E       F       G       H
1   THIS WORKSHEET SHOWS EXAMPLES OF THE /RANGE JUSTIFY PROCEDURE
2
3
4   EXAMPLE
5   I HAVE LEARNED SO MUCH ABOUT LOTUS 1-2-3 ALREADY
6
7   EXAMPLE OF RANGE JUSTIFY 1 COLUMN -- e.g., /RJ A8..A8(HIT RETURN)
8   I HAVE
9   LEARNED
10  SO MUCH
11  ABOUT
12  LOTUS
13  1-2-3
14  ALREADY
15
16  EXAMPLE OF RANGE JUSTIFY 2 COLUMNS -- e.g., /RJ A17..B17(HIT RETURN)
17  I HAVE LEARNED SO
18  MUCH ABOUT LOTUS
19  1-2-3 ALREADY
20
01-Jan-88  12:08 PM
```

Figure 6-3 Example of /Range Justify Command

move the cursor to the end of the Input range, Home will move the cursor to the beginning of the Input range, and so on. To terminate the /Range Input command, press Escape or Return without typing any data.

6-9 /Range Transpose

This command exchanges the rows and columns of a given range; rows become columns and columns become rows. For example, a two-by-three table (two rows and three columns) becomes a three-by-two table (three rows and two columns). All you need to do is use the /Range Transpose command. Lotus will ask you for the original range. Specify the range and hit the **Return** key. Now Lotus asks you the range for the transposed table. Specify only the upper left corner cell of the range and hit the **Return** key. Be careful. If you direct the transposed table to a part of the worksheet that is already occupied, you will lose that portion of data. Figure 6-4 illustrates an example of this command.

6-10 /Range Value

This command converts formulas in a given range to their numeric values. Let us assume cells A1 and A2 contain values 5 and 10. Cell A3 contains +A1+A2. If you want to copy the exact value of this formula and not the formula itself, you must use

```
A1:  'THIS WORKSHEET SHOWS ONE EXAMPLE OF /RANGE TRANSPOSE PROCEDURE         READY

        A        B        C        D        E        F        G        H
1  THIS WORKSHEET SHOWS ONE EXAMPLE OF /RANGE TRANSPOSE PROCEDURE
2
3  BEFORE RANGE TRANSPOSE
4  LA        SUE       MARY      HARRY
5  DENVER    JACK      JOHN      BOB
6
7  AFTER RANGE TRANSPOSE - WE GENERATED THIS BY USING /RT A4..D5(HIT RETURN
8                                                           A9 (HIT RETURN)
9  LA        DENVER
10 SUE       JACK
11 MARY      JOHN
12 HARRY     BOB
13
14
15
16
17
18
19
20
01-Jan-88  09:58 AM
```

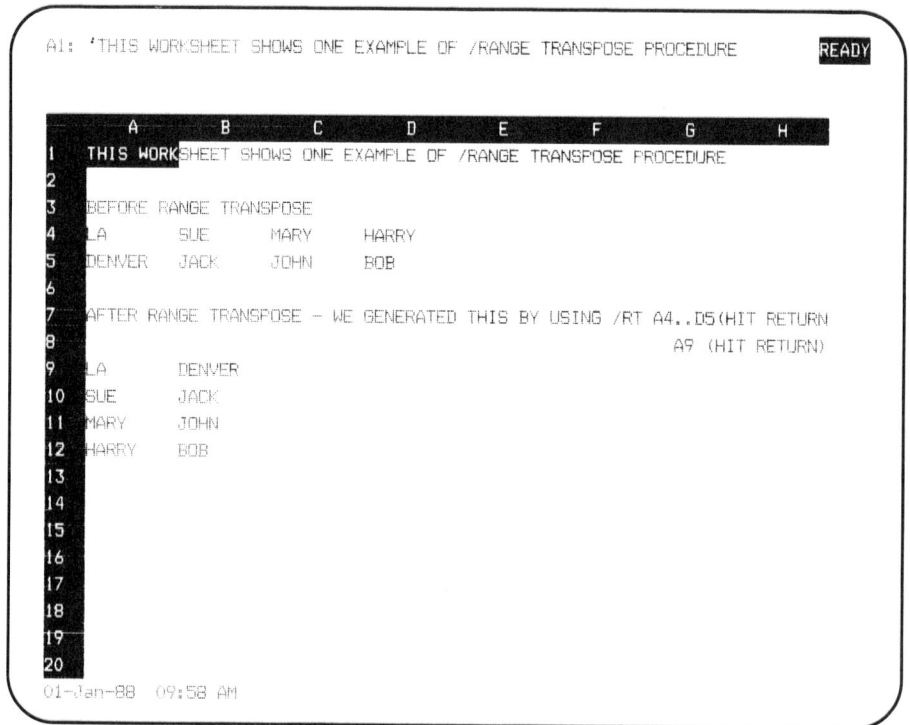

Figure 6-4 An Example of /Range Transpose Command

the /Range Value command first to translate the formula to its numerical value, then do the copying.

To see how this command works, get Lotus started. Type 1 in cell A1 and 2 in cell B1. Move to cell D1 and add the first two cells by typing +A1+B1. You will see 3 in cell D1. With the /Copy command, copy cell D1 to cell D5 and in D5 you will see a zero. Why? As you will learn in the next section, Lotus transfers the relative address of a cell, so in cell D5 you will see +A5+B5, because we are in row 5. Since A5 and B5 are empty, they have the value of zero, therefore the final result is zero.

Go back to cell D1 and use the /Range Value command, then copy to cell D10 (or any other cell). You will now see 3, not 0, in D10.

6-11 Relative Addressing

Lotus maintains the address of a particular cell and compares it to the origin of the worksheet. For example, in relation to a formula in cell E10, cell G4 is two columns to the right and six rows above cell E10. To make this clear, look at Figure 6-5. In cell B11 we have the formula +B9+B8+B7+B6. If we copy this formula to cell C11, Lotus is smart enough to recognize that in this cell you have to add +C9+C8+C7+C6. If you copy the same formula to cells D11 and E11, in cell D11 you will see +D9+D8+D7+D6 and in cell E11 you will see +E9+E8+E7+E6. This is called *relative addressing*, a powerful feature. It will make the task of copying a more efficient operation. Let us say you have sales data related to 100 different businesses in the first 100 columns of a worksheet. To calculate the sum of each column, all you

```
A1:  'THIS WORKSHEET SHOWS ONE EXAMPLE OF THE RELATIVE ADDRESSING PROCEDURE  READY

          A         B         C         D         E         F         G         H
1   THIS WORKSHEET SHOWS ONE EXAMPLE OF THE RELATIVE ADDRESSING PROCEDURE
2
3   EXAMPLE
4                                    DIVISIONS
5   MONTHS        DIV 1     DIV 2     DIV 3     DIV 4
6   JAN             100       343       123       654
7   FEB             234       654       466       453
8   MAR             313       345       245       213
9   APR             321       368       907       790
10              ----------------------------------------
11      TOTAL       968      1710      1741      2110
12              ========================================
13
14  IN CELL B11 WE USED THE FORMULA +B6+B7+B8+B9
15  THEN WE COPIED THIS FORMULA TO C11..E11
16
17
18
19
20
    01-Jan-88   12:12 PM
```

Figure 6-5 An Example of Relative Addressing

need to do is to type a formula for one column and then copy the same formula to the other 99 columns.

6-12 Absolute Addressing

There are many times when you must refer to an exact location or an exact value. Sometimes you may want to use some predefined numbers or ratios. In these cases you have to use *absolute addresses.* For example, in relation to a formula in cell E10, cell G4 is G4, when used as an absolute address.

To make this distinction clear, look at Figure 6-6. Five divisions of XYZ Company sold different amounts of a particular product. Your task is to calculate the percentage of total sales for each division. In cell C5, type the formula +B5/B11. If you copy this formula to range C6..C9, you will get an error. The reason is that in every case the division unit must be divided by the total units currently in cell B11. Relative addressing will not work here. You have to make cell B11 absolute, meaning always fixed.

To make a cell absolute, put a dollar sign ($) in front of the row number and one in front of the column letter. You can either type ($) or use F4, the Abs function key. This key can change and show you four variations of relative, absolute, and mixed addressing. For example, if your cell address is A10 and in Point mode you press F4 four times you will see $A$10, A$10, $A10, and finally A10. Remember, to use this key you must be in POINT mode. The simplest way to enter POINT mode is to press the F5 function key (GoTo key).

Figure 6-6 An Example of Absolute Addressing

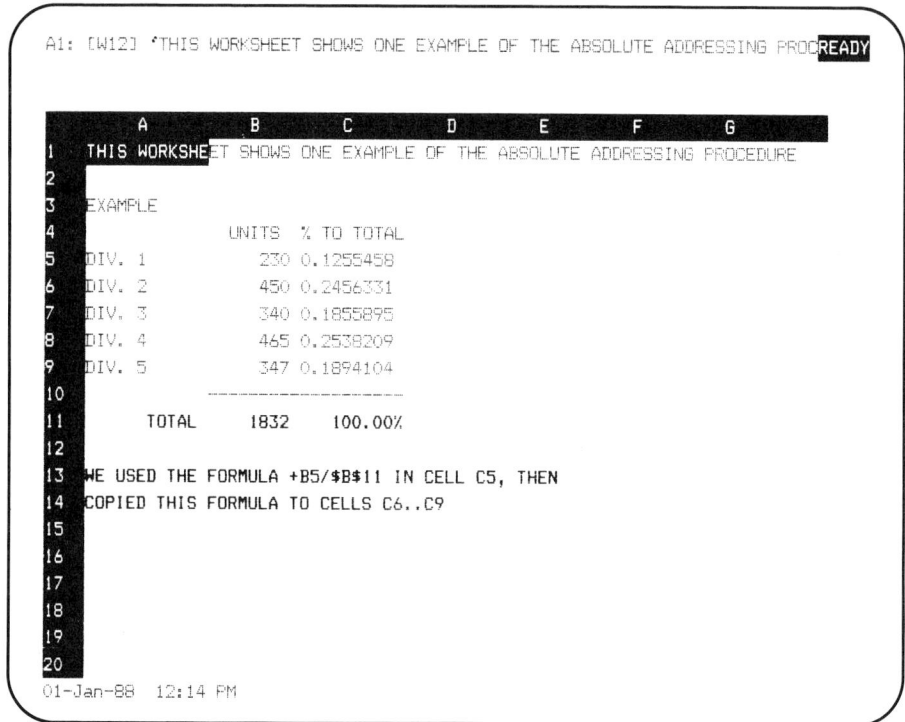

```
A1: [W12] 'THIS WORKSHEET SHOWS ONE EXAMPLE OF THE ABSOLUTE ADDRESSING PROCREADY

         A          B          C          D          E          F          G
 1  THIS WORKSHEET SHOWS ONE EXAMPLE OF THE ABSOLUTE ADDRESSING PROCEDURE
 2
 3  EXAMPLE
 4                  UNITS  % TO TOTAL
 5  DIV. 1            230  0.1255458
 6  DIV. 2            450  0.2456331
 7  DIV. 3            340  0.1855895
 8  DIV. 4            465  0.2538209
 9  DIV. 5            347  0.1894104
10                  ------------------
11         TOTAL    1832    100.00%
12
13  WE USED THE FORMULA +B5/$B$11 IN CELL C5, THEN
14  COPIED THIS FORMULA TO CELLS C6..C9
15
16
17
18
19
20
01-Jan-88  12:14 PM
```

Figure 6-7 An Example of Mixed Addressing

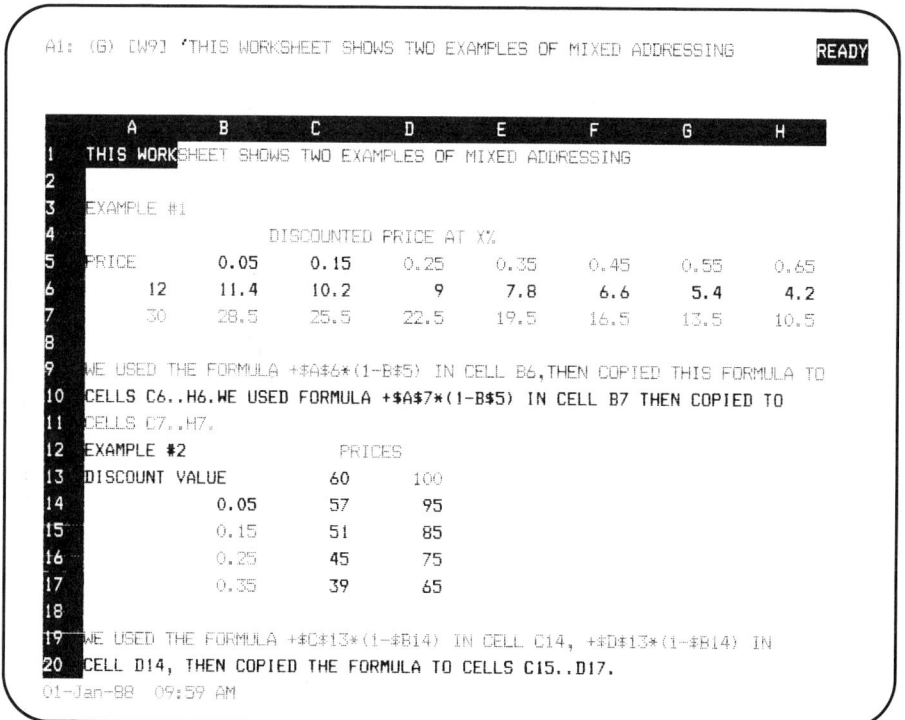

```
A1: (G) [W9] 'THIS WORKSHEET SHOWS TWO EXAMPLES OF MIXED ADDRESSING        READY

         A        B        C        D        E        F        G        H
 1  THIS WORKSHEET SHOWS TWO EXAMPLES OF MIXED ADDRESSING
 2
 3  EXAMPLE #1
 4                  DISCOUNTED PRICE AT X%
 5  PRICE         0.05     0.15     0.25     0.35     0.45     0.55     0.65
 6         12     11.4     10.2        9      7.8      6.6      5.4      4.2
 7         30     28.5     25.5     22.5     19.5     16.5     13.5     10.5
 8
 9  WE USED THE FORMULA +$A$6*(1-B$5) IN CELL B6,THEN COPIED THIS FORMULA TO
10  CELLS C6..H6.WE USED FORMULA +$A$7*(1-B$5) IN CELL B7 THEN COPIED TO
11  CELLS C7..H7.
12  EXAMPLE #2                PRICES
13  DISCOUNT VALUE         60      100
14                0.05     57       95
15                0.15     51       85
16                0.25     45       75
17                0.35     39       65
18
19  WE USED THE FORMULA +$C$13*(1-$B14) IN CELL C14, +$D$13*(1-$B14) IN
20  CELL D14, THEN COPIED THE FORMULA TO CELLS C15..D17.
01-Jan-88  09:59 AM
```

Cell $B$11 is absolute. To make a range name absolute, precede it with a dollar sign, e.g., $ASSET.

In Figure 6-6, first we typed (+B5/$B$11) in Cell C5, then copied this formula to range C6..C9.

6-13 Mixed Addressing

There are cases when you want to have both relative and absolute addressing. You can have either the row or the column fixed and the other absolute. For example, $A10 means that the column remains the same but the row changes; B$10 means that the row is fixed but the column changes. Figure 6-7 illustrates two examples of mixed addressing.

The first example in Figure 6-7 shows the discounted prices under different discount rates for two products whose original prices were $12 and $30.

The second example in this figure shows the same thing with a different format. Can you tell what is different?

Summary

In this chapter we explained a series of commands helpful for manipulating a portion of your worksheet, or a range. You can erase, name, transpose, protect, and remove protection from a range. The /Range Input is useful in advanced Lotus applications. Relative, absolute, and mixed addressing are features that let you manipulate references to cells and ranges.

Review Questions

1. What is a range?
2.* Can a range and a worksheet be the same?
3. What is the function of /Range Label Center?
4. How do you erase a range?
5. How do you name a range?
6.* How do you know a range name has not been used already?
7. How do you erase all range names?
8. How many characters can be used as a range name?
9. What are some applications of the /Range Justify command?
10. What does the /Range Protect command do?
11.* When can you actually see the effect of the /Range Protect command?
12. What is the application of the /Range Value command?
13. What are some uses of the /Range Transpose command?
14. What is relative addressing?
15. Why can relative addressing be dangerous?
16. What is mixed addressing?
17.* How do you make a range name absolute?
18. Can a cell have both absolute and relative addresses at the same time?

19. Type COBOL in cell A1, then center it using /Range Label Center.
20. Type 10, 20, 30, and 40 in cells A1 to A4. Using the appropriate command, give this range a valid name.
21. Using the /Range Input command, generate a data-entry section in range H1..H10. (Remember, you must be able to move around only in this range.)
22. Using /Range Transpose, first generate a five-by-three table, then make it a three-by-five.
23. Enter 10, 20, and 30 in cells A1 to A3. Add them up and store the result in cell G1. Copy this cell to cell H1. Use /Range Value first and do the copying again. What is the difference?

Misconceptions and Solutions

M - If you have a series of range names in a worksheet and delete a portion of that worksheet by using /Worksheet Delete or /Range Erase, your range becomes undefined, even though the names are still intact.

S - First check the addresses and listing of all your range names by using F3 in POINT mode. Then issue the command to erase.

M - The /Move command does not transfer cell addresses in the same way that the /Copy command does. /Copy transfers relative addresses of cells. Absolute cell addresses will be transferred as absolute with /Copy but not with /Move. For example, in cells A1 and B1 type numbers 1 and 2 respectively, then use the formula $A$1+$B$1 in cell C1. Transfer this entire row to row 10 by using /Copy. You will see in cell C10 the same formula as in cell C1. If you move the original row to row 10, you will see $A$10+$B$10 in cell C10.

S - Don't try to transfer absolute addresses with the /Move command.

M - If you try to erase a portion of a row or a column of a worksheet, don't use /Worksheet Delete Row or /Worksheet Delete Column. This command erases the entire row or the entire column.

S - Use /Range Erase to erase a portion of a worksheet.

M - /Range Name Table will give you a listing of all the range names. This command may overwrite a part of your worksheet.

S - Before invoking this command, find an empty location in your worksheet. Then invoke the command.

M - You cannot use /Range Justify if any cells in a particular range are protected.

S - First use /Worksheet Global Protection Disable to turn off the protection facility, then use /Range Justify.

M - Using /Range Transpose, if a particular range contains formulas with relative addresses, Lotus won't adjust relative addresses to refer to the same cells.

S - Use Move instead.

M - In the middle of your spreadsheet you see the error message ILLEGAL CELL OR RANGE ADDRESS.

S - Check your range specification to see if this is what you wanted to do. You may have typed an undefined range.

7

Formats: Dressing Up
Your Worksheet

7-1 Introduction

In this chapter we will discuss the different formatting options available in Lotus. We will present examples to demonstrate a specific application for each option and briefly discuss format limitation. (The /Range Justify command, also used for formatting, was discussed in Chapter 6.)

7-2 Why Formats?

In the business world a good report is one that presented in a format that aids comprehension. Lotus provides a number of formatting options, so a variety of reports can be generated easily.

To access the Format command in Lotus there are two options, /Worksheet Global Format or /Range Format. /Worksheet Global Format is used when the entire worksheet needs to be formatted; /Range Format is used if only a specific portion is to be formatted. Figure 7-1 shows all the options available under the Format command:

Fixed	Scientific	Currency	,	General	+/-
Percent	Date	Text	Hidden	Reset	

The Reset option is used to change the existing setting to the global default setting.

7-3 General Option

The General option is the default format command. You may check the worksheet status to verify this. In this format the insignificant zeros to the right of a decimal place are eliminated. Very large and very small numbers are presented in scientific notation. Labels (nonnumeric data) are left-justified. You can change this setting manually by inserting one of the prefixes, by using /Worksheet Global Label-Prefix, or by using /Range Label. Figure 7-2 illustrates the formatted portion of the worksheet generated by /Worksheet Global Format General.

7-4 Fixed Option

The Fixed option format does not display commas or dollar signs in the formatted worksheet. Numbers can include up to 15 decimal places. If you specify fewer decimal places, the number will be rounded up. For example, if you specify three decimal positions, 6.7786 would be displayed as 6.779. This option is suitable for printing checks or financial statements, such as an income statement or balance sheet. Figure 7-3 compares a formatted and unformatted worksheet.

The formatted portion of Figure 7-3 was generated by /Range Format Fixed 2 (decimal places) Return A17..E20 Return.

7-5 Scientific Option

The Scientific option is used for very large or very small numbers. You may specify up to 15 decimal places. Figure 7-4 illustrates the format generated by /Range Format Scientific 2 (decimal places) Return E15..E18 Return.

7-6 Currency Option

In the Currency option, the dollar sign ($) will appear immediately to the left of the numbers. A comma will separate every third digit. Negative numbers will appear in parentheses. The placement of the decimal is determined as in the other options. If the specified column width does not include enough space, a series of asterisks will be displayed (of course, this is true for all the options). Figure 7-5 illustrates this option. The formatted portion was generated by /Range Format Currency 0 (zero decimal places) Return D16..F20 Return.

7-7 Comma Option

The Comma option is very similar to Currency; the only difference is that the dollar sign is suppressed. This option is suitable for nonfinancial reports. Figure 7-6 illustrates this option. The formatted portion of this figure was generated by /Range Format , (comma) 0 (zero decimal places) Return D16..F20 Return.

Figure 7-1 Different Format Options Available in Lotus

Figure 7-2 Example of General Options

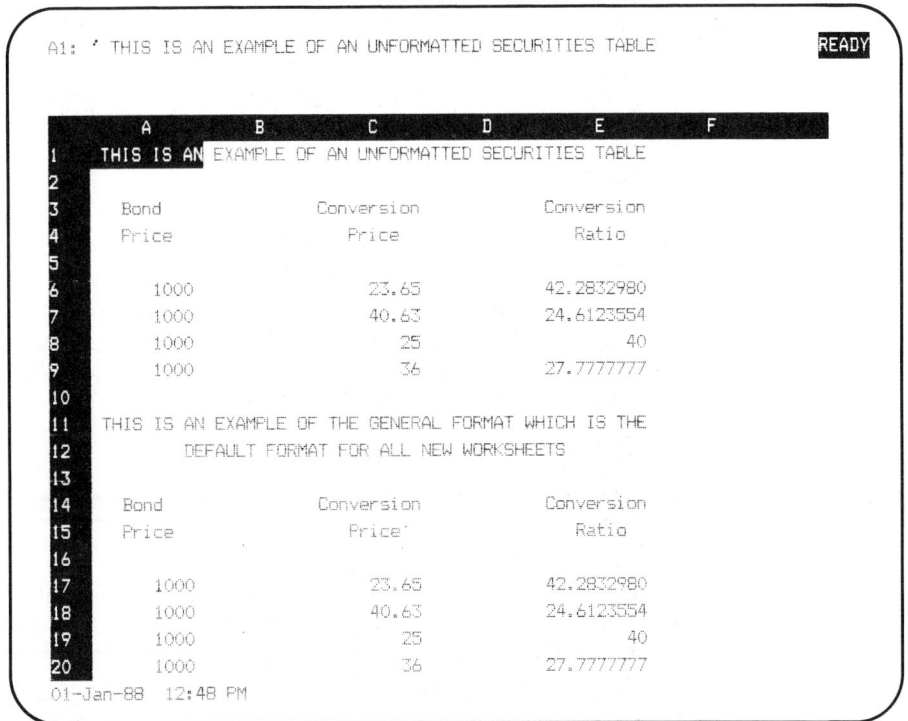

Figure 7-3 Example of Fixed Option

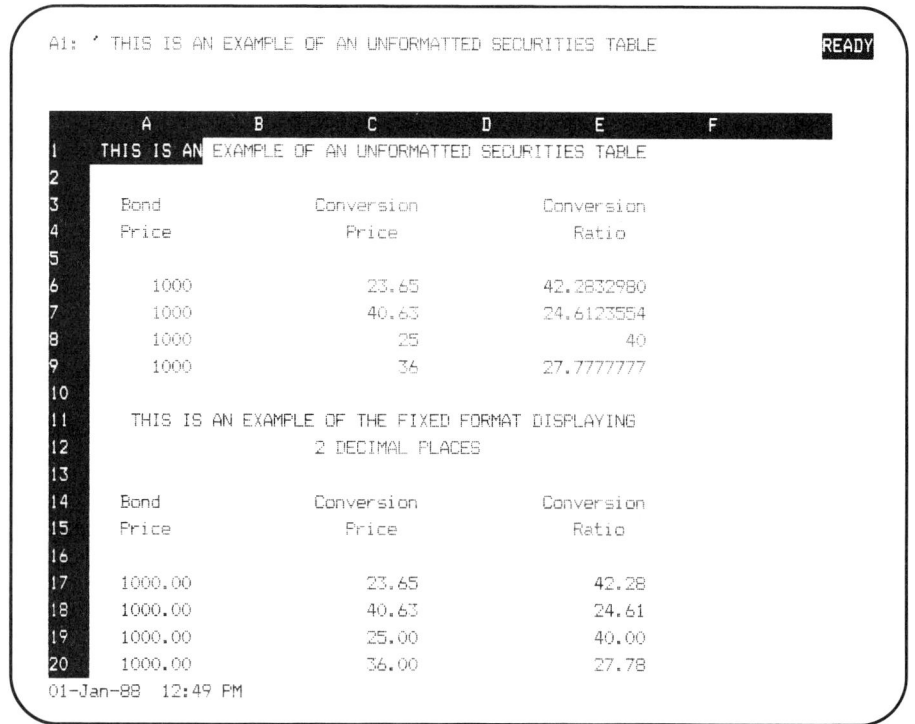

```
A1:  ' THIS IS AN EXAMPLE OF AN UNFORMATTED SECURITIES TABLE                    READY

              A           B           C           D           E           F
   1    THIS IS AN EXAMPLE OF AN UNFORMATTED SECURITIES TABLE
   2
   3     Bond                    Conversion              Conversion
   4     Price                     Price                   Ratio
   5
   6         1000                  23.65                 42.2832980
   7         1000                  40.63                 24.6123554
   8         1000                     25                         40
   9         1000                     36                 27.7777777
  10
  11       THIS IS AN EXAMPLE OF THE FIXED FORMAT DISPLAYING
  12                      2 DECIMAL PLACES
  13
  14     Bond                    Conversion              Conversion
  15     Price                     Price                   Ratio
  16
  17     1000.00                   23.65                      42.28
  18     1000.00                   40.63                      24.61
  19     1000.00                   25.00                      40.00
  20     1000.00                   36.00                      27.78
01-Jan-88  12:49 PM
```

Figure 7-4 Example of Scientific Option

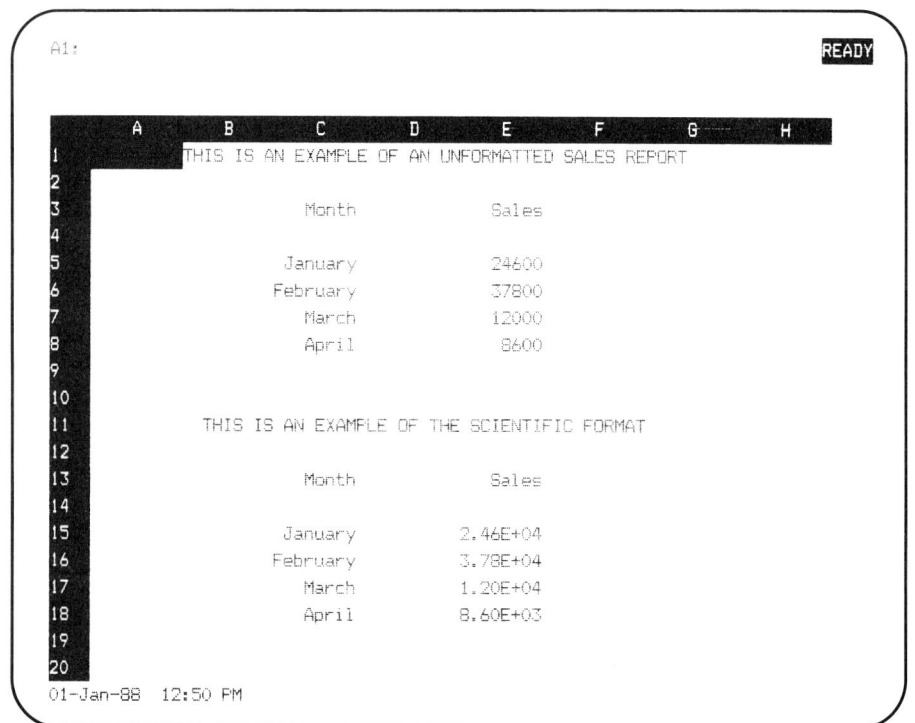

```
A1:                                                                            READY

              A      B      C      D      E      F      G       H
   1       THIS IS AN EXAMPLE OF AN UNFORMATTED SALES REPORT
   2
   3                    Month              Sales
   4
   5                  January              24600
   6                 February              37800
   7                    March              12000
   8                    April               8600
   9
  10
  11       THIS IS AN EXAMPLE OF THE SCIENTIFIC FORMAT
  12
  13                    Month              Sales
  14
  15                  January           2.46E+04
  16                 February           3.78E+04
  17                    March           1.20E+04
  18                    April           8.60E+03
  19
  20
01-Jan-88  12:50 PM
```

Figure 7-5 Example of Currency Option

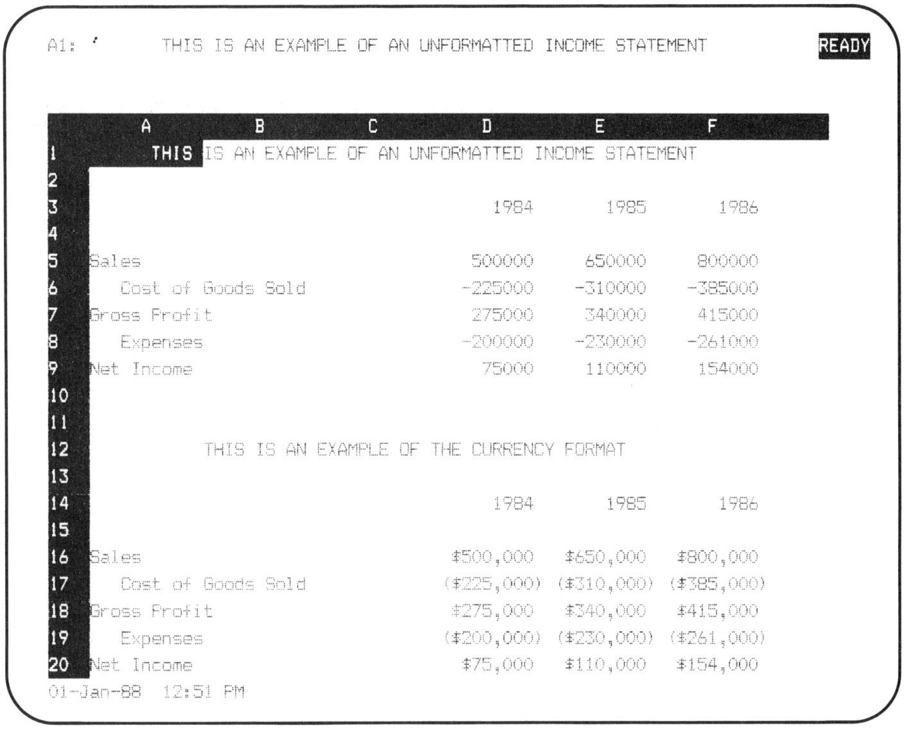

```
A1: '        THIS IS AN EXAMPLE OF AN UNFORMATTED INCOME STATEMENT                    READY


          A          B          C          D          E          F
1       THIS IS AN EXAMPLE OF AN UNFORMATTED INCOME STATEMENT
2
3                                         1984       1985       1986
4
5    Sales                                500000     650000     800000
6       Cost of Goods Sold               -225000    -310000    -385000
7    Gross Profit                         275000     340000     415000
8       Expenses                         -200000    -230000    -261000
9    Net Income                           75000      110000     154000
10
11
12           THIS IS AN EXAMPLE OF THE CURRENCY FORMAT
13
14                                         1984       1985       1986
15
16   Sales                              $500,000   $650,000   $800,000
17      Cost of Goods Sold            ($225,000) ($310,000) ($385,000)
18   Gross Profit                       $275,000   $340,000   $415,000
19      Expenses                       ($200,000) ($230,000) ($261,000)
20   Net Income                          $75,000   $110,000   $154,000
01-Jan-88  12:51 PM
```

Figure 7-6 Example of Comma (,) Option

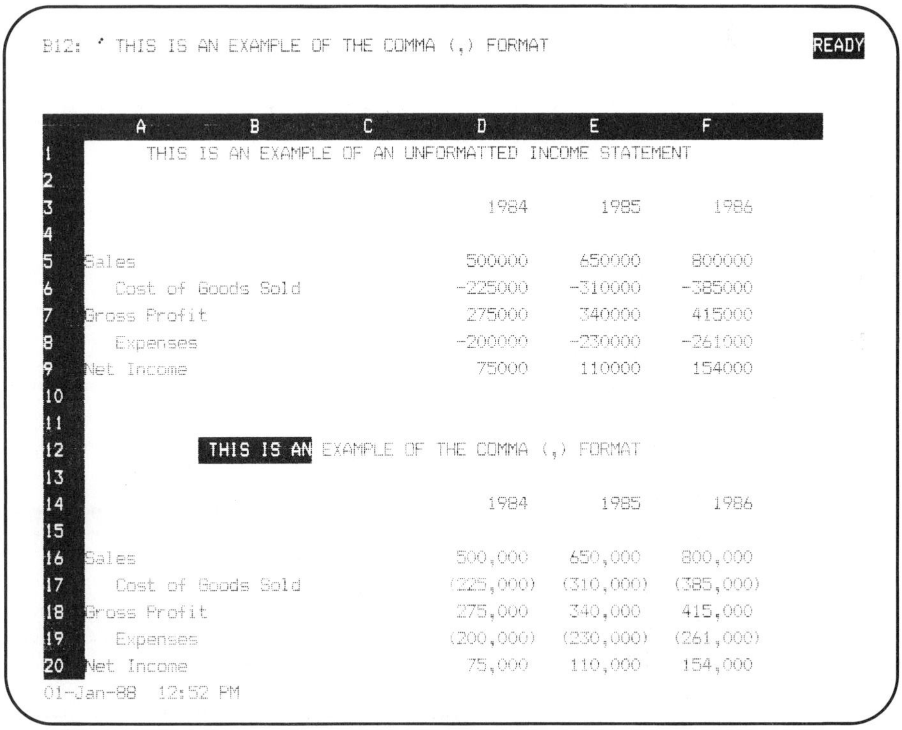

```
B12: ' THIS IS AN EXAMPLE OF THE COMMA (,) FORMAT                                    READY


          A          B          C          D          E          F
1        THIS IS AN EXAMPLE OF AN UNFORMATTED INCOME STATEMENT
2
3                                         1984       1985       1986
4
5    Sales                                500000     650000     800000
6       Cost of Goods Sold               -225000    -310000    -385000
7    Gross Profit                         275000     340000     415000
8       Expenses                         -200000    -230000    -261000
9    Net Income                           75000      110000     154000
10
11
12         THIS IS AN EXAMPLE OF THE COMMA (,) FORMAT
13
14                                         1984       1985       1986
15
16   Sales                               500,000    650,000    800,000
17      Cost of Goods Sold              (225,000)  (310,000)  (385,000)
18   Gross Profit                        275,000    340,000    415,000
19      Expenses                        (200,000)  (230,000)  (261,000)
20   Net Income                           75,000    110,000    154,000
01-Jan-88  12:52 PM
```

7-8 +/- Options

In the +/- format, a positive number will be presented by the plus sign (+), a negative number by the minus sign (-), and zero by a period. This option is considered a limited graphics option, making the job of comparing different numbers an easy task. Figure 7-7 illustrates this option. In this example, we have used the +/- option to present an activity chart known as a Gantt chart. The formatted portion of this worksheet was generated by /Range Format +/- D16..D20 Return.

7-9 Percent Option

The Percent option presents numbers as a percentage of 100, for example, .05 = 5%. This option can be very useful when comparing a portion of data to the total: for example, the portion of total cost of production belonging to raw materials. Figure 7-8 illustrates this option. The formatted portion of this illustration was generated by /Range Format Percent 1 Return F15..F20 Return and /Range Format Percent 1 Return H15..H20 Return.

7-10 Date Options

Lotus allows five different formats for dates. The beginning date in the Lotus calendar is December 31, 1899 and the last date in the calendar is December 31, 2099. December 31, 1899 is defined by Lotus as zero; January 1, 1900 equals 1; and December 31, 2099 equals 73050. Figure 7-9 shows the five different date options. We generated the formatted portion of this worksheet using the following commands:

/Range Format D1 E16..F16 Return

/Range Format D2 E17..F17 Return

/Range Format D3 E18..F18 Return

/Range Format D4 E19..F19 Return

/Range Format D5 E20..F20 Return

7-11 Time options

Lotus has four different time options. In time formats fractional parts of serial numbers represent time (.000 = midnight, .5000 = noon, 20/24 = 8:00 P.M., and so on) as parts of a 24-hour period. You can use the @TIME and @NOW functions to generate these numbers. Figure 7-10 illustrates different time options. The formatted portion of the worksheet was generated using the following commands:

/Range Format Date Time 1 C16..E16 Return

Figure 7-7 Example of +/- Options

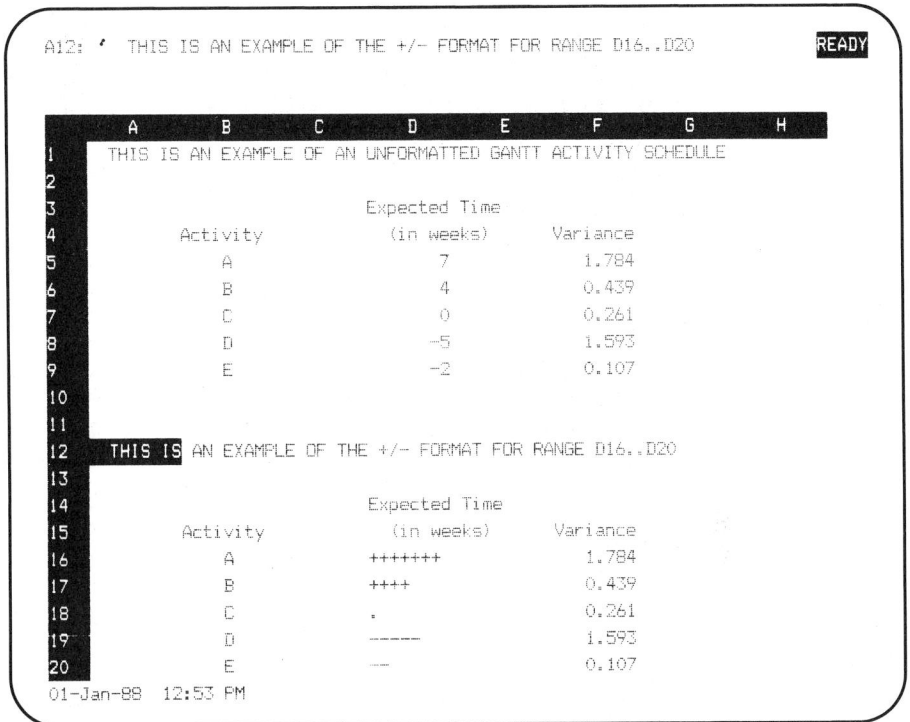

```
A12: '   THIS IS AN EXAMPLE OF THE +/- FORMAT FOR RANGE D16..D20        READY

          A       B       C       D       E       F       G       H
 1     THIS IS AN EXAMPLE OF AN UNFORMATTED GANTT ACTIVITY SCHEDULE
 2
 3                             Expected Time
 4            Activity          (in weeks)       Variance
 5               A                   7             1.784
 6               B                   4             0.439
 7               C                   0             0.261
 8               D                  -5             1.593
 9               E                  -2             0.107
10
11
12     THIS IS AN EXAMPLE OF THE +/- FORMAT FOR RANGE D16..D20
13
14                             Expected Time
15            Activity          (in weeks)       Variance
16               A              +++++++           1.784
17               B              ++++              0.439
18               C                  .             0.261
19               D              -------           1.593
20               E              --                0.107
01-Jan-88   12:53 PM
```

Figure 7-8 Example of Percent Option

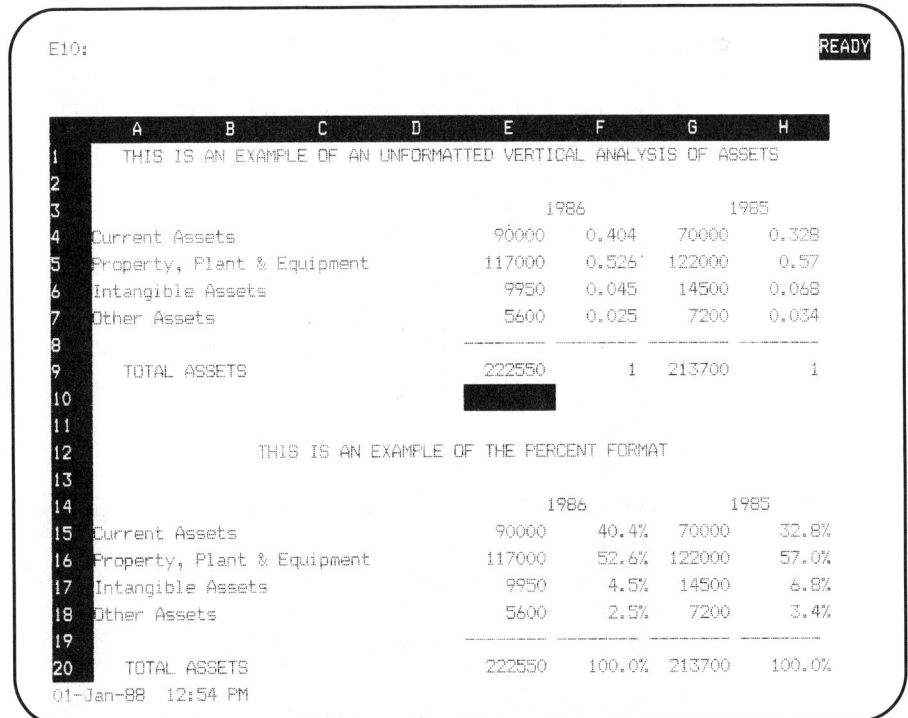

```
E10:                                                                   READY

          A       B       C       D       E       F       G       H
 1        THIS IS AN EXAMPLE OF AN UNFORMATTED VERTICAL ANALYSIS OF ASSETS
 2
 3                                      1986             1985
 4     Current Assets                 90000   0.404    70000   0.328
 5     Property, Plant & Equipment   117000   0.526   122000   0.57
 6     Intangible Assets               9950   0.045    14500   0.068
 7     Other Assets                    5600   0.025     7200   0.034
 8                                   --------  ------  -------  ------
 9        TOTAL ASSETS              222550        1   213700       1
10
11
12              THIS IS AN EXAMPLE OF THE PERCENT FORMAT
13
14                                      1986             1985
15     Current Assets                 90000   40.4%    70000   32.8%
16     Property, Plant & Equipment   117000   52.6%   122000   57.0%
17     Intangible Assets               9950    4.5%    14500    6.8%
18     Other Assets                    5600    2.5%     7200    3.4%
19                                   --------  ------  -------  ------
20        TOTAL ASSETS              222550   100.0%   213700  100.0%
01-Jan-88   12:54 PM
```

Figure 7-9 Example of Date Options

Figure 7-10 Example of Time Options

/Range Format Date Time 2 C17..E17 Return

/Range Format Date Time 3 C18..E18 Return

/Range Format Date Time 4 C19..E19 Return

7-12 Text Option

The content of each cell will be displayed as text using the Text option. For example, if cell A30 contains +H1*P1 (hours multiplied by pay rate), this formula will be displayed using the Text format. The Text option can be helpful in debugging lengthy formulas. Figure 7-11 illustrates this option. We have generated the formatted worksheet by using /Range Format Text H6..H19 Return (on the right window).

7-13 Hidden Option

The Hidden option is useful for hiding a portion of the worksheet or the entire worksheet. This format can generate reports that do not need to display a portion of the worksheet. (Remember that the hidden portion is still a part of your worksheet and is included in any calculations.) This format also provides security by hiding some portions of a worksheet from unauthorized users. To reveal the hidden portion, move the cursor to any other format option and press the **Return** key. Figure 7-12 illustrates this option. We have generated the hidden range by using /Range Format Hidden D14..D20 Return.

7-14 Override Option

As we mentioned earlier, the /Format command can be accessed either by / Worksheet Global Format or /Range Format. /Range Format always has priority over /Worksheet Global Format. This means that the portion of the worksheet formatted by /Range Format is not affected by /Worksheet Global Format.

Figure 7-13 illustrates this case. Column D in the upper worksheet was formatted by /Range Format Currency 0 (zero) Return D5..D9 Return. The lower worksheet was formatted by /Worksheet Global Format, (comma) 0 (zero) Return. As you see, column D is untouched. This is helpful for generating worksheets that use different formats for different tasks.

7-15 A Complete Example

To put the whole thing together we have created a final worksheet that uses the seventeen Format options generated by Lotus to serve as a quick reference. Figure 7-14 demonstrates these options.

Figure 7-11 Example of Text Format

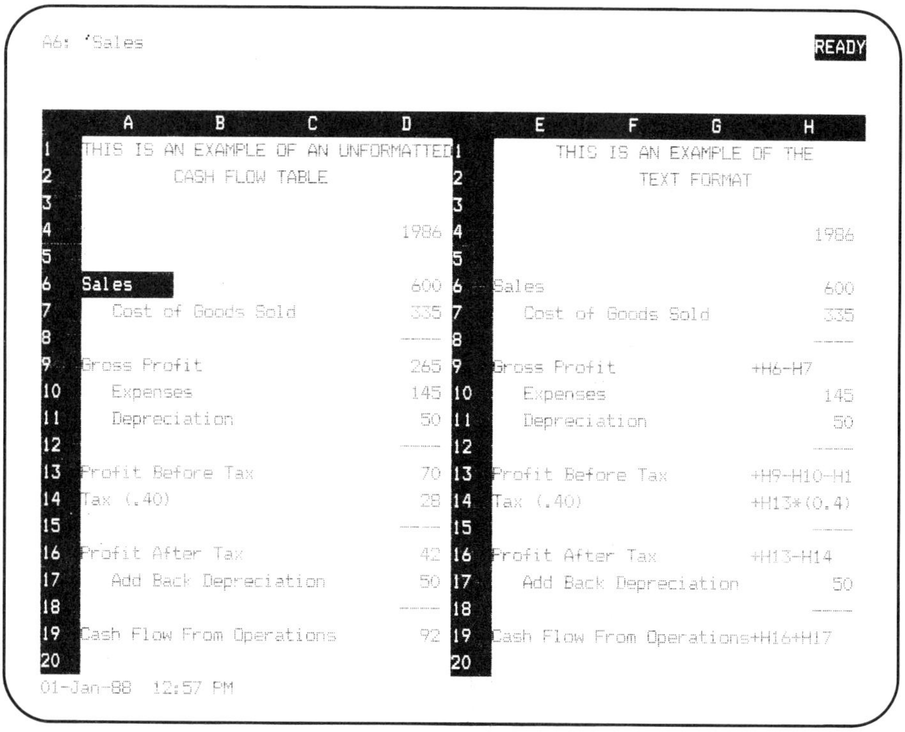

```
A6: 'Sales                                                                    READY

        A       B       C       D           E       F       G       H
1  THIS IS AN EXAMPLE OF AN UNFORMATTED1       THIS IS AN EXAMPLE OF THE
2            CASH FLOW TABLE          2                TEXT FORMAT
3                                     3
4                            1986 4                              1986
5                                     5
6  Sales                      600 6  Sales                        600
7     Cost of Goods Sold      335 7     Cost of Goods Sold        335
8                            ----- 8                             -----
9  Gross Profit              265 9  Gross Profit          +H6-H7
10    Expenses                145 10    Expenses                  145
11    Depreciation             50 11    Depreciation               50
12                                    12
13 Profit Before Tax          70 13 Profit Before Tax     +H9-H10-H1
14 Tax (.40)                   28 14 Tax (.40)             +H13*(0.4)
15                            ----- 15
16 Profit After Tax           42 16 Profit After Tax      +H13-H14
17    Add Back Depreciation    50 17    Add Back Depreciation      50
18                            ----- 18                             -----
19 Cash Flow From Operations   92 19 Cash Flow From Operations+H16+H17
20                                    20
01-Jan-88  12:57 PM
```

Figure 7-12 Example of Hidden Format

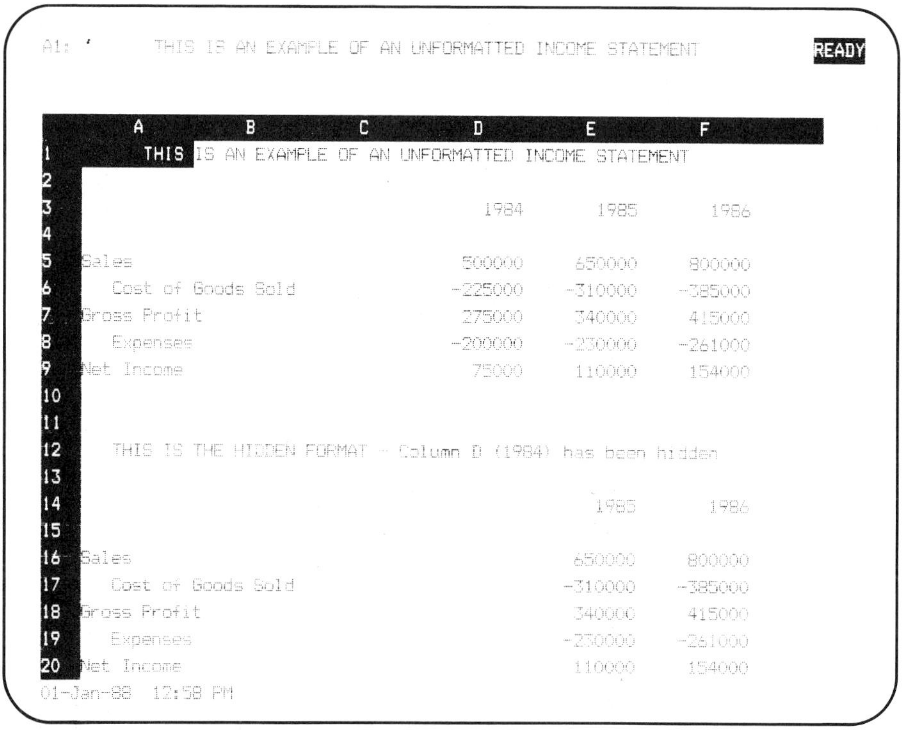

```
A1: '       THIS IS AN EXAMPLE OF AN UNFORMATTED INCOME STATEMENT              READY

        A       B       C       D       E       F
1      THIS IS AN EXAMPLE OF AN UNFORMATTED INCOME STATEMENT
2
3                            1984    1985    1986
4
5  Sales                     500000  650000  800000
6     Cost of Goods Sold    -225000 -310000 -385000
7  Gross Profit              275000  340000  415000
8     Expenses              -200000 -230000 -261000
9  Net Income                 75000  110000  154000
10
11
12    THIS IS THE HIDDEN FORMAT - Column D (1984) has been hidden
13
14                                    1985    1986
15
16 Sales                             650000  800000
17    Cost of Goods Sold            -310000 -385000
18 Gross Profit                      340000  415000
19    Expenses                      -230000 -261000
20 Net Income                        110000  154000
01-Jan-88  12:58 PM
```

Figure 7-13 Example of Override Option

```
A1: ' COLUMN D HAS BEEN FORMATTED WITH THE /RANGE FORMAT CURRENCY  OPTION    READY

            A          B          C          D          E          F
1    COLUMN D HAS BEEN FORMATTED WITH THE /RANGE FORMAT CURRENCY  OPTION
2
3                                          DIV. A     DIV. B     DIV. C
4
5    Sales                                $500,000    650000     800000
6       Cost of Goods Sold               ($225,000)  -310000    -385000
7    Gross Profit                         $275,000    340000     415000
8       Expenses                         ($200,000)  -230000    -261000
9    Net Income                           $75,000     110000     154000
10
11   THIS EXAMPLE SHOWS HOW THE /WORKSHEET GLOBAL FORMAT COMMA  OPTION DOES
12            NOT OVERRIDE THE /RANGE FORMAT CURRENCY  OPTION
13
14                                          DIV. A     DIV. B     DIV. C
15
16   Sales                                $500,000    650,000    800,000
17      Cost of Goods Sold               ($225,000)  (310,000)  (385,000)
18   Gross Profit                         $275,000    340,000    415,000
19      Expenses                         ($200,000)  (230,000)  (261,000)
20   Net Income                           $75,000     110,000    154,000
01-Jan-88  12:59 PM
```

Figure 7-14 A Complete Example of All Format Options

```
E18: (T) [W12] +C7*C8                                                        READY

            A          B          C          D          E          F          G
1    FORMAT OPTION     UNFORMATED          FORMATTED
2
3      GENERAL           25000              25000
4      FIXED             25000              25000.00
5      SCIENTIFIC        25000              2.50E+04
6      CURRENCY          25000              $25,000
7      ,                 25000              25,000
8      +/-               6                  ++++++
9      D1                31621              28-Jul-86
10     D2                31621              28-Jul
11     D3                31621              Jul-86
12     D4                31621              07/28/86
13     D5                31621              07/28
14     T1                0.448263           10:45:30 AM
15     T2                0.448263           10:45 AM
16     T3                0.448263           10:45:30
17     T4                0.448263           10:45
18     TEXT              150000             +C7*C8
19     HIDDEN            25000
20
01-Jan-88  01:00 PM
```

Summary

The Format options should help you generate eye-pleasing and useful reports. As we discussed earlier, Lotus Release 2 is capable of generating 17 format options.

Even with all these options there are still some limitations and we do not see any way around them. Numeric data is always right-justified and nonnumeric data is always left-justified. There is no provision for centering numbers. Large and small numbers are not lined up from the left margin. If a number is larger than the specified column size, a series of asterisks will be displayed until you widen the column. We believe these are minor limitations and the available options are adequate for most operations.

Review Questions

1. Why is formatting necessary?
2.* How many format options are available?
3.* What is the difference between the Currency option and the Comma option?
4. How many Date options are available? What is the application of each?
5. How many Time options are available? What is the application of each?
6.* What is an application of the Text format?
7. What are some applications of the Hidden format?
8. What is the difference between /Worksheet Global Format and /Range Format?
9. What are the beginning and ending dates in the Lotus calendar?
10.* Can you do arithmetic operations with dates and times (e.g., can you subtract two dates or two times from each other)?
11. Design a worksheet with 5, 66, 777, 8888, and 99999 in cells A1 to A5. Now do the following:

   - Format this worksheet using the Comma option.
   - Format this worksheet using the Fixed option with two decimals.
   - Format this worksheet using the Scientific option with two decimals.
   - Format this worksheet using the Currency option with two decimals.

   In some of these cases, you may see a series of asterisks. Why? This means your cell is not wide enough to hold your formatted number. You have to extend the cell width. Do you know how? See Chapters 5 or 6.

12. In cell A1 using D3, enter 32152 (e.g., January, 1988). Now generate the next 11 months by using the /Copy command. *Hint:* In cell A2 enter +A1+30.
13. In cells H1 and H2 enter 500 and 1000. In cell H3 enter +H1+H2. Naturally you will see 1500. Which format option will give you the formula +H1+H2 in cell H3, not its numeric value?
14. Enter 2, 22, 222, 2222 and 22222 in cells A1 to A5. Copy these numbers in cells F1 to F5. Now split the screen vertically in column D. Format the first screen using the Currency option. Format the second screen using the Comma option. Do you see the difference?

Misconceptions and Solutions

M - You invoke a particular /Format command and stroke the **Return** key. The particular cell may give you a solid line of asterisks.

S - The cell is not wide enough. Use the appropriate command in order to widen the cell width.

8

File Operations: Interaction Between Memory and Disk Files

8-1 Introduction

File operations enable you to save a worksheet file on disk, retrieve a file, incorporate parts of a file in your current worksheet, erase a file on disk, and import an ASCII file (discussed in Appendix D) from other programs to your worksheet. We will discuss these features, except file import, in this chapter. Appendix D gives a comprehensive presentation of file transfer between Lotus and other programs.

8-2 An Overview of File Operations

When you choose the File option from the main menu, you will be given the following choices:

Retrieve   Save   Combine   Xtract   Erase   List   Import   Directory

In the following pages we will explain these commands using several examples.

8-3 /File Save and Retrieve

The Save option enables you to save a Lotus file on a disk to make it permanent. A file can be saved under any valid file name (valid names are discussed in the next section). Remember that your disk must be formatted first (see Appendix B on formatting a disk).

To Save a new file, simply choose the /File Save option and enter a name. However, if you are working with an old file that has already been saved at least once and you try to save it again, Lotus will give you two options:

Cancel   Replace

If you choose the Cancel option, nothing will be saved and you return to READY mode. Your old file will stay on the disk, untouched. If you choose the Replace option, the current worksheet will replace the old version on the disk, regardless of any difference in size.

To retrieve a file from a disk, choose the Retrieve option, then hit the **Return** key. Lotus will give you a listing of all your worksheet files. Either type the name of the file or move the cursor to a particular file and hit the **Return** key.

8-4 Lotus File Specifications

Lotus file specifications are very similar to those for disk files (discussed in Appendix B). Lotus accepts any valid file name up to eight characters in length. Digits zero through 9 and the underscore are accepted as part of a file name. Spaces are not allowed. The following are some examples of valid and invalid Lotus file names:

PAYROLL   Valid

PAY-ROLL   Valid

ROLL55   Valid

PARTNUMBER   Lotus cuts it to eight characters, then accepts it

PAY ROLL   Invalid (a space is not accepted)

Lotus generates and manipulates three types of files. These include Worksheet (WK1), Graph (PIC), and Print (PRN). Non-Lotus files are identified under Others (non-Lotus type ASCII files, discussed in Appendix D). For example, when you save a worksheet, Lotus automatically attaches the extension WK1 to it. When you save a file, you can type your own extension. However, this file will not be retrieved automatically by Lotus nor will it appear on your menu. To retrieve such a file, type the name with the extension. Any Lotus file created in version 1A can be retrieved when using version 2.0 but the opposite is not true. Version 2.0 files must be translated prior to retrieval when using version 1A.

Two wild card characters are accepted by Lotus: the question mark (?) and the asterisk (*). The question mark, used for one character only, means any character in a particular position. For example, B:\PAYROLL?.WK1 will give you all the files whose first seven characters are payroll and which are worksheet files. The asterisk, used for one or more characters, means any character at the end of the file name or extension. For example, B:*.WK1 will give you all the worksheet files (all files with the extension WK1).

Lotus always starts its root directory with the drive name and a backslash (B:\). Within the root directory you can establish a subdirectory. (For more information on directories and subdirectories, see Appendix B.)

You can make your Lotus file self-booting. If you save your worksheet under AUTO123, Lotus will automatically load this file as soon as you start the spreadsheet.

To erase a permanent file, use the /File Erase command. But remember that if you erase a file, it is gone for good. You can use wild card characters to erase Lotus files in order to expedite the process, but this maximizes the danger of losing a file.

You can have one current file and many permanent files at any time. The current file is your current worksheet and permanent files are the files saved on your disk. If you retrieve another file, the current worksheet will be erased. If you do not want to lose this worksheet, you must save it before retrieving another file.

Lotus also allows you to save a file with a password. To do this, follow the following steps:

1. Create or load a file.
2. Type /File Save from the main menu.
3. Type your desired file name.
4. Hit the Space bar.
5. Type P (for password).
6. Hit the **Return** key.
7. Type the desired password. Your password can be any of the LICS (Lotus International Character Set) characters, up to 15 characters. Do not use spaces. (See appendix F for Lotus LICS).
8. Hit the **Return** key.
9. Type the password again to verify it and hit the **Return** key.

If you change your mind, you can always change or delete the password. To delete a password but save the file itself, first retrieve the file with the present password. When you are ready to save it again (/File Save), you will be given the following message: B:\Myfile.WK1 [PASSWORD PROTECTED] (Myfile.WK1 is any valid file name). Hit the backspace to erase [PASSWORD PROTECTED], then hit the **Return** key. Now your file will be saved under the desired name, in this case Myfile. To change a password, first delete the password as we just did, hit the space bar, and type P followed by the **Return** key.

If you forget the password, you cannot retrieve the file. The password must be typed exactly as you created it every time you retrieve the file. Uppercase characters are considered to be different from lowercase characters.

8-5 /File Combine

The Combine option gives you three choices:

Copy   Add   Subtract

The Copy option enables you to copy an entire file or a portion of a file to the current worksheet. Be careful to remember the present position of the cursor; Copy can overwrite the current worksheet. This option gives you two choices:

Entire-File   Name/Specified-Range

Either the entire file or a specific range can be copied. Lotus will ask you for the name of the file, the range name, or range coordinates. Copy will not change the current worksheet *if* the cursor is in an empty location of the current worksheet.

The Add option enables you to add a file or a portion of a file to the current worksheet. Again, the position of the cursor is important. When you choose Add you will be given two choices:

Entire-File   Name/Specified-Range

You can choose either of these. The difference between Add and Copy is that Add adds the contents of the incoming file or range to the current worksheet. For example, if the cursor is at cell A1 and cell A1 contains 5 and if cell A1 from the incoming file contains 15, the final value of cell A1 in the current worksheet will be 20.

The Subtract option gives you the opportunity to subtract an entire file or a portion of a file from the current worksheet. Remember the present position of the cursor. In each of these three options the incoming data will be entered in the worksheet from the present position of the cursor to the right and down.

Remember, when you use the Add option, if an incoming file overlays a cell containing a label or a formula, Lotus discards the incoming value and retains the label or formula in the current worksheet. For example, if cell A1 in the current worksheet contains the label "COBOL", the incoming data will not have any effect on it. To see how this powerful command works, study the following examples.

Figure 8-1 is an example of an income statement for Division A of a company. Figure 8-2 shows the income statement for Division B.

Figure 8-3 was generated by using the Copy option. The income statement for Division B was copied at the bottom of Division A's income statement. This was done by using /File, Combine, Copy, Entire-file, Ch8-2 (the file name for Figure 8-2), and Return. Remember, the cursor must be in an empty area of the worksheet. In this example, the cursor was placed at cell A12.

Figure 8-4 is the consolidated income statement of Division A and Division B, using the Add option. Figures from Division B were added to those from Division A. Figure 8-4 was generated by choosing /File, Combine, Add, Name/Specified-Range, D5..D9, Return, Ch8-2, and Return.

The cursor must be positioned at the top left corner of the range for which you want to add the incoming data. In this case, the cursor was placed at cell D5.

Figure 8-5 shows the Subtract option. Figures for Division A were subtracted from the figures of Division B. In this example, the cursor was placed at cell D5. This figure was generated by using /File, Combine, Subtract, Name/Specified-Range, D5..D9, Return, Ch8-1 (the file name for Figure 8-1), and Return.

8-6 /File Xtract

This option extracts and saves a portion of the current worksheet in a file on disk. Unlike Combine, Xtract does not change information in the current worksheet. Two

Figure 8-1 An Example of an Income Statement for Division A

```
A1: ' THIS IS AN EXAMPLE OF AN INCOME STATEMENT FOR DIVISION A          READY

          A          B          C          D          E          F
1    THIS IS AN EXAMPLE OF AN INCOME STATEMENT FOR DIVISION A
2
3                                      1986
4
5   SALES                            $500,000
6      COST OF GOODS SOLD           ($225,000)
7   GROSS PROFIT                     $275,000
8      EXPENSES                     ($200,000)
9   NET INCOME                        $75,000
10
11
12
13
14
15
16
17
18
19
20
01-Jan-88   01:02 PM
```

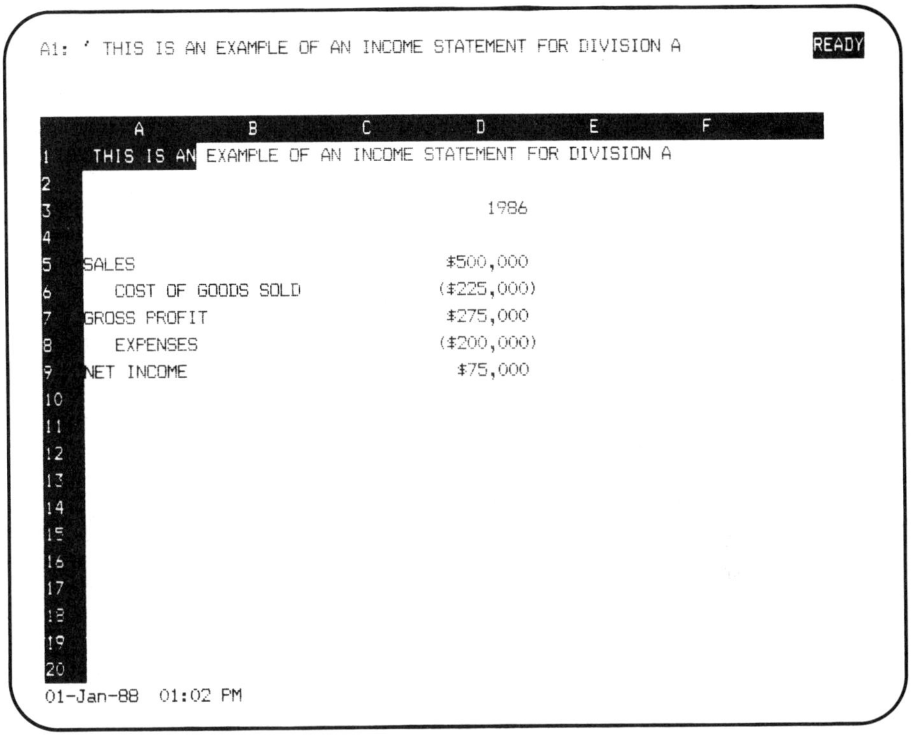

Figure 8-2 An Example of an Income Statement for Division B

```
A1: ' THIS IS AN EXAMPLE OF AN INCOME STATEMENT FOR DIVISION B          READY

          A          B          C          D          E          F
1    THIS IS AN EXAMPLE OF AN INCOME STATEMENT FOR DIVISION B
2
3                                      1986
4
5   SALES                            $650,000
6      COST OF GOODS SOLD           ($310,000)
7   GROSS PROFIT                     $340,000
8      EXPENSES                     ($230,000)
9   NET INCOME                       $110,000
10
11
12
13
14
15
16
17
18
19
20
01-Jan-88   01:02 PM
```

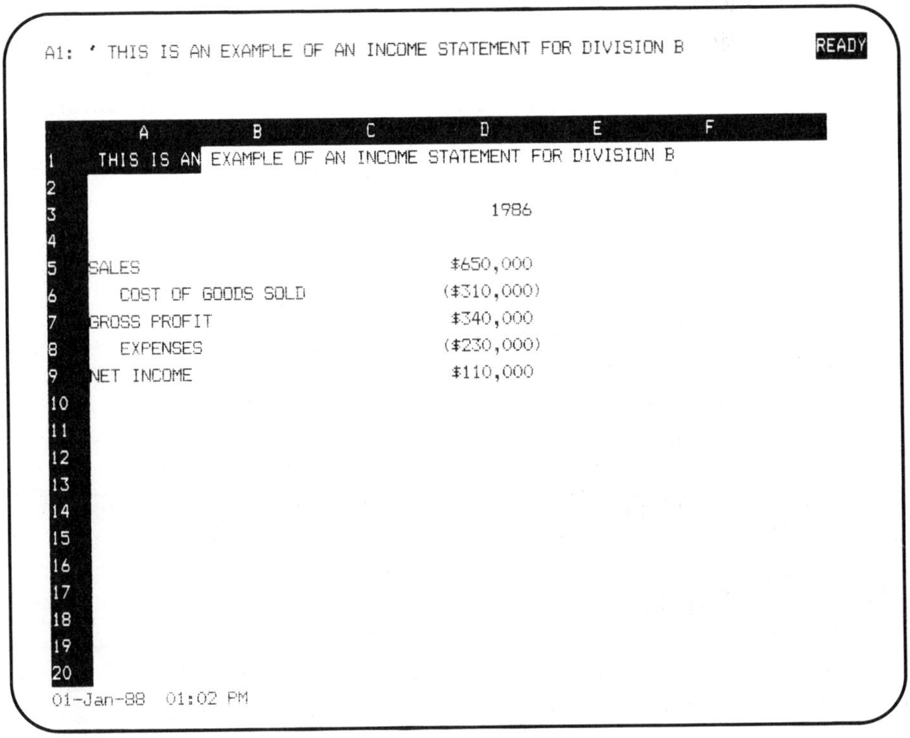

Figure 8-3 An Example of the Copy Option

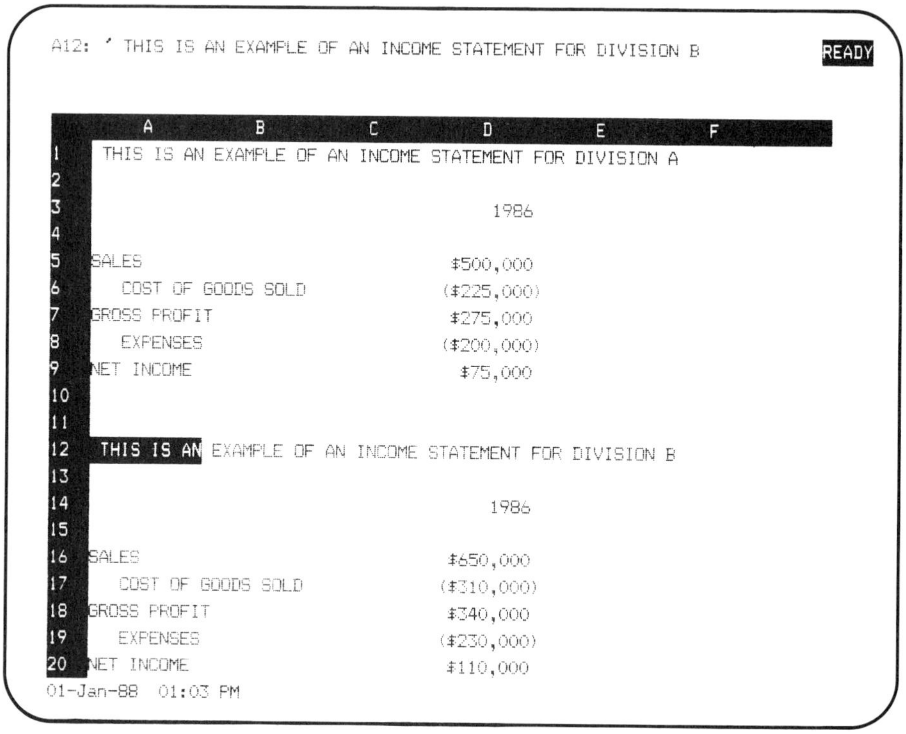

```
A12:  ' THIS IS AN EXAMPLE OF AN INCOME STATEMENT FOR DIVISION B       READY

              A         B         C         D         E         F
   1      THIS IS AN EXAMPLE OF AN INCOME STATEMENT FOR DIVISION A
   2
   3                                      1986
   4
   5    SALES                          $500,000
   6       COST OF GOODS SOLD         ($225,000)
   7    GROSS PROFIT                   $275,000
   8       EXPENSES                   ($200,000)
   9    NET INCOME                      $75,000
  10
  11
  12    THIS IS AN EXAMPLE OF AN INCOME STATEMENT FOR DIVISION B
  13
  14                                      1986
  15
  16    SALES                          $650,000
  17       COST OF GOODS SOLD         ($310,000)
  18    GROSS PROFIT                   $340,000
  19       EXPENSES                   ($230,000)
  20    NET INCOME                     $110,000
   01-Jan-88   01:03 PM
```

Figure 8-4 Example of the Add Option

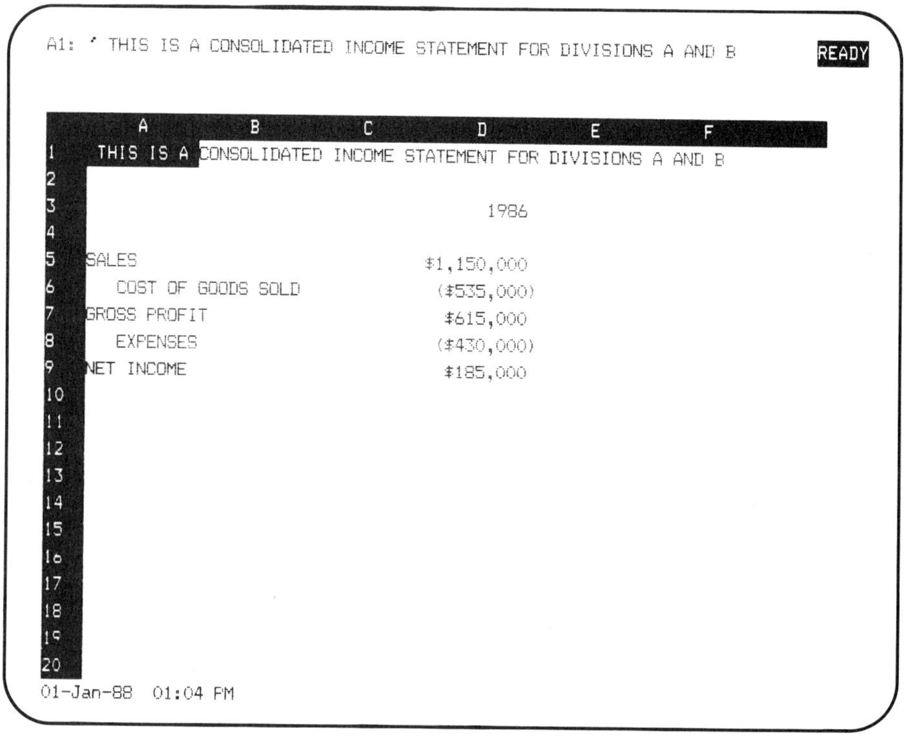

```
A1:  ' THIS IS A CONSOLIDATED INCOME STATEMENT FOR DIVISIONS A AND B     READY

              A         B         C         D         E         F
   1      THIS IS A CONSOLIDATED INCOME STATEMENT FOR DIVISIONS A AND B
   2
   3                                      1986
   4
   5    SALES                        $1,150,000
   6       COST OF GOODS SOLD         ($535,000)
   7    GROSS PROFIT                   $615,000
   8       EXPENSES                   ($430,000)
   9    NET INCOME                     $185,000
  10
  11
  12
  13
  14
  15
  16
  17
  18
  19
  20
   01-Jan-88   01:04 PM
```

A2: ' IS SUBTRACTED FROM DIVISION B   READY

```
            A        B        C        D        E        F
1    THIS IS THE INCOME STATEMENT AFTER DIVISION A
2    IS SUBTRACTED FROM DIVISION B
3                                      1986
4
5    SALES                          $150,000
6       COST OF GOODS SOLD          ($85,000)
7    GROSS PROFIT                    $65,000
8       EXPENSES                    ($30,000)
9    NET INCOME                      $35,000
10
11
12
13
14
15
16
17
18
19
20
01-Jan-88  09:01 AM
```

Figure 8-5 Example of the Subtract Option

options are given under Xtract: Formulas and Values. With the Formulas option, Lotus saves the worksheet with any formulas from the current worksheet to the extracted file. For example, if cells A1 and A2 contain 5 and 10 cell A3 contains their sum, e.g., +A1+A2, then the Formulas option saves this worksheet and the formula.

With the Values option, Lotus saves the worksheet with only calculated values for formulas. In the above example, 15 will be extracted and saved with the worksheet, not +A1+A2. This means that you will not know how the value was obtained.

Figure 8-6 is an income statement for three divisions of a company. In Figure 8-7 we have extracted Division A from Figure 8-6 with the Formulas option. We used /File, Xtract, Formulas, Ch8-7 (the file name for Figure 8-7), Return, A3..D9, and Return.

In Figure 8-8 we have extracted Division A from Figure 8-6 with the Values option. We used /File, Xtract, Values, Ch8-8 (the file name for Figure 8-8), Return, A3..D9, and Return.

As you can see, with the Formulas option, the original formulas are transferred exactly, while with the Values option, only the values are transferred, not the formulas. Remember, to see the formulas in any worksheet you must choose the Text option from the Format command.

Now, if you go to Figure 8-8 and try the Format Text option in cell D5, you will see the value 275000.

If you go to Figure 8-7 and try the Format Text option in cell D5, you will see the formula +D3-D4, because this was transferred by /File Xtract Formulas.

Figure 8-6 Example of an Income Statement for Three Divisions of a Company

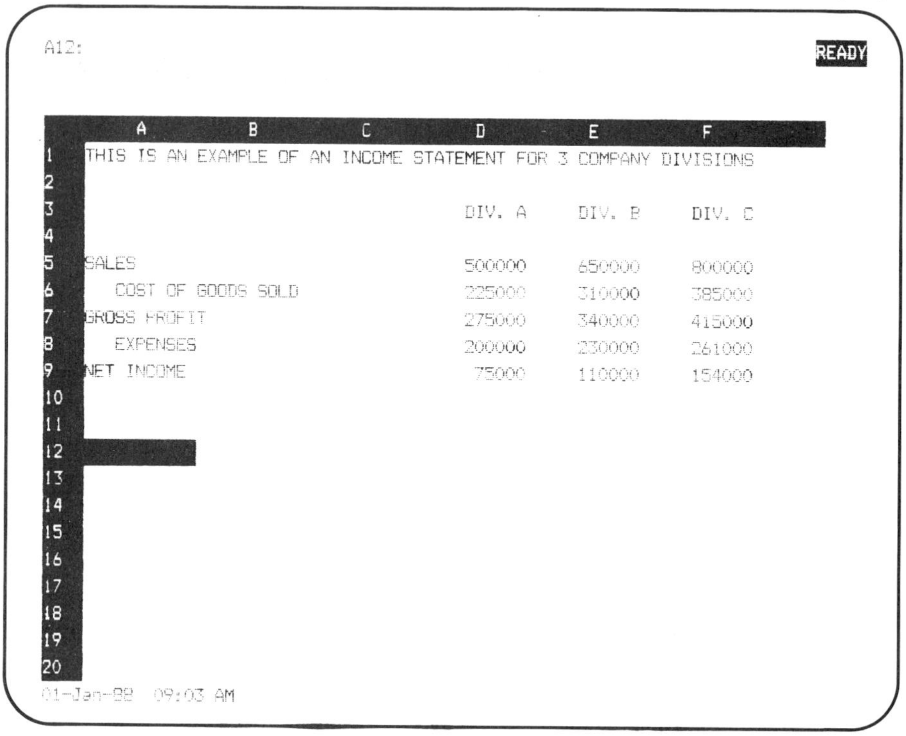

```
A12:                                                                    READY

        A          B          C          D         E         F
1 THIS IS AN EXAMPLE OF AN INCOME STATEMENT FOR 3 COMPANY DIVISIONS
2
3                                       DIV. A    DIV. B    DIV. C
4
5 SALES                                 500000    650000    800000
6    COST OF GOODS SOLD                 225000    310000    385000
7 GROSS PROFIT                          275000    340000    415000
8    EXPENSES                           200000    230000    261000
9 NET INCOME                             75000    110000    154000
10
11
12
13
14
15
16
17
18
19
20
01-Jan-88  09:03 AM
```

Figure 8-7 Example of the Xtract Option with Formulas

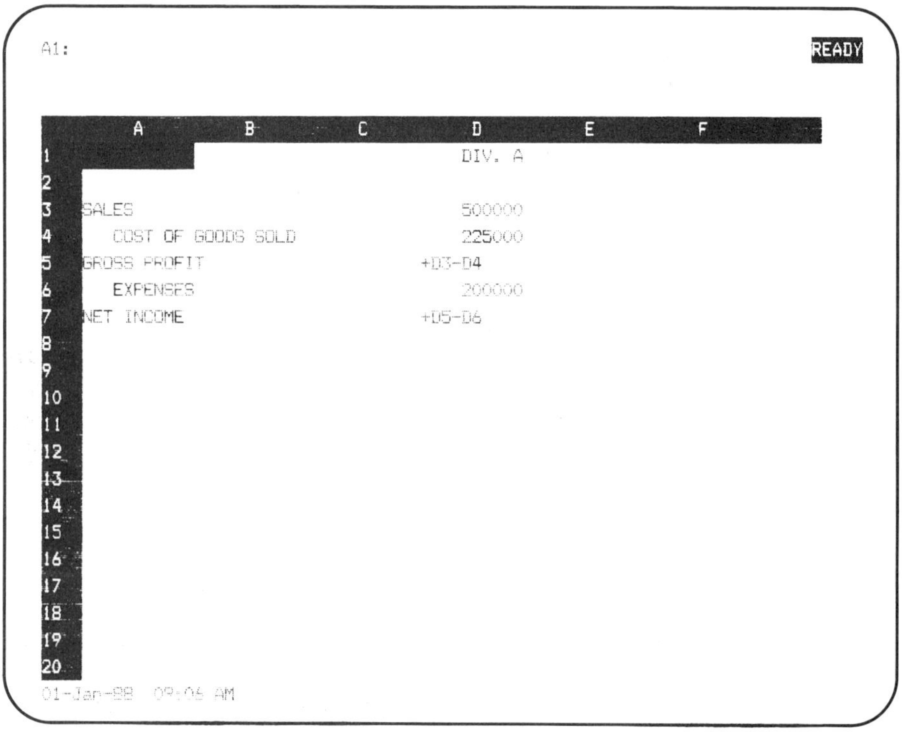

```
A1:                                                                     READY

        A          B          C          D         E         F
1                                       DIV. A
2
3 SALES                                 500000
4    COST OF GOODS SOLD                 225000
5 GROSS PROFIT                          +D3-D4
6    EXPENSES                           200000
7 NET INCOME                            +D5-D6
8
9
10
11
12
13
14
15
16
17
18
19
20
01-Jan-88  09:06 AM
```

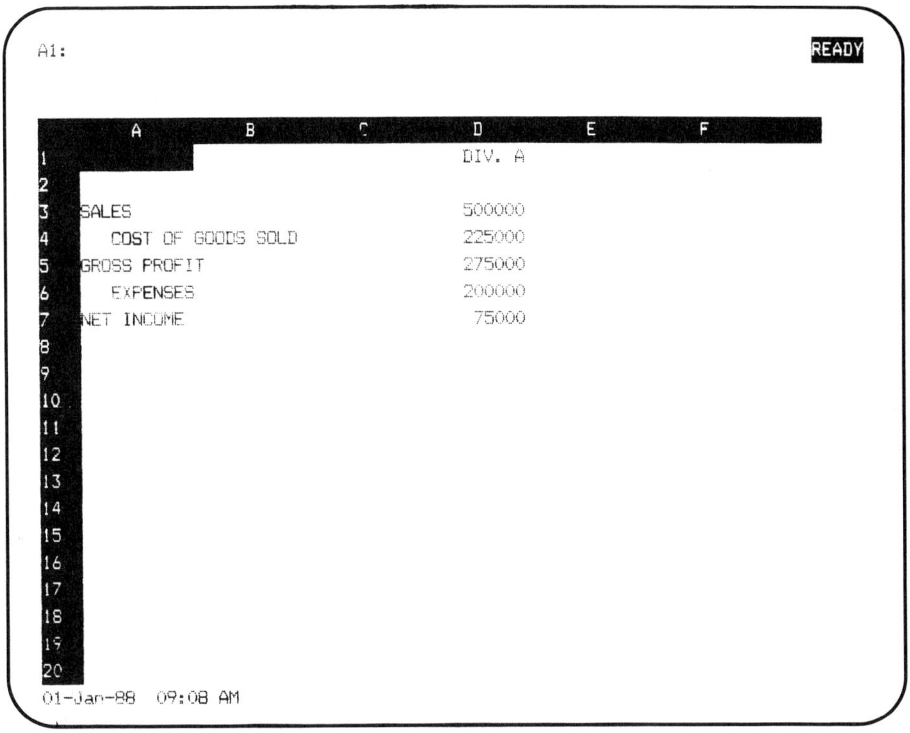

Figure 8-8 Example of the Xtract Option with Values

8-7 /File List, Erase, and Directory

With the /File List command you can get the listing of your entire directory. Your Lotus directory will include four types of files: WK1, PIC, PRN, and Others. You can choose any of these options and Lotus will give you a complete listing of files within any group.

The Erase option allows the deletion of files WK1, PIC, PRN, and Others. (Others includes all the files in your directory, both Lotus and non-Lotus files.)

The Directory option will tell you the current directory of your system. Usually your directory is in drive B, but it can be changed. To find the status of your directory, you can also use the /Worksheet Global Default Status command. This will display the current directory. If you have access to a hard disk, type /File Directory A:\ to access files on a floppy disk and then place the floppy disk in drive A: for example, if you have a hard disk and you are trying to use the disks provided with this book, you have to first issue /File Directory A:\, then put one of the disks in drive A.

Summary

Using the file operations provided by Lotus, you can save a worksheet, combine several worksheets together, erase an unwanted worksheet, and so forth. Lotus provides a series of choices within the /File command. You can add a password to a file for security purposes, extract a portion of a file and send it to another worksheet, and so on. Appendix D discusses file transfer between Lotus and other programs.

Review Questions

1. How many choices are provided by the File options?
2. What is a Lotus file?
3.* How many types of files can be generated by Lotus?
4. How many current and permanent worksheets can you have at one time?
5. How do you generate a password for a disk file?
6.* What are the requirements for a password?
7. How many options do you have under /File Combine?
8.* What is the difference between /File Combine Add and /File Combine Copy?
9. Why is the present position of the cursor so important in the /File Combine command?
10.* Is it possible for you to lose your current worksheet when you use /File Combine options? If yes, how?
11. What is the difference between /File Combine Copy and /File Xtract?
12. What are some of the uses of /File Xtract?
13. What is the purpose of /File Directory?
14.* How can wild card characters be used with the /File Erase option?
15. Can you change your directory? If yes, how?
16. Can the /File Combine Add or /File Combine Copy commands generate the same final result? If yes, under what circumstances?
17. Store 10, 20, 30, and 40 in cells A1, A2, A3, and A4. Save this worksheet under W1. Now retrieve this file using the /File Combine Add, /File Combine Copy, and /File Combine Subtract commands. What command should you use in order to generate a worksheet with zeros in cells A1, A2, A3, and A4?
18. Generate three worksheets with five values in column A for the first one, five values in column B for the second one, and five values in column C for the third one. Now, using the /File Combine command, generate a worksheet that includes three columns with values from worksheet 1, 2, and 3.
19. Using the /File Xtract command, transfer column A of the above worksheet to another file called W5.
20. Store values 5, 10, and 15 in cells A1, A2, and A3, respectively. Store the sum of these values in cell A10 (+A1+A2+A3). Using the /File Xtract command, save this worksheet once with the Values option in a file called Value. Use the Formulas option and save this worksheet in a file called Formula. What is the difference between files Value and Formula?
21. Generate the following worksheet for Branch A of Tasty Pizza:

Column A	Column B
Quarter 1	10,000
Quarter 2	15,000
Quarter 3	12,500
Quarter 4	11,500

Save this file with the password "Secret."

22. Retrieve this file and change the password to "not-secret." Is this a valid name?

23. The following data comes from Branch B of Tasty Pizza:

Column C	Column D
Quarter 1	8,000
Quarter 2	11,200
Quarter 3	10,000
Quarter 4	10,500

   - Add Branches A and B together using /File Combine Add.
   - Subtract Branch A from Branch B using /File Combine Subtract.
   - Save Branch B data under BranchB.

24. Start Lotus and copy Branch A data in range A1..B4. Now copy Branch B data underneath Branch A with one empty line between.

25. Extract Quarter 1 and Quarter 2 data for Branch A and save it in a file called "Half."

26. Retrieve Branch B data, add the four quarters, and store the result in cell D10. Now extract this total once with the option Formulas and once with the option Values. What is the difference?

27. Using /File List, get a listing of all your worksheet files in your drive B: or C:.

Misconceptions and Solutions

M - When you save a file with a password, if you forget the password, you will never be able to retrieve that file.

S - Use a password that has a special meaning for you

.

M - One of the options in the Lotus main menu is Quit. When you choose this option, you will leave Lotus and your work will not be saved.

S - Save your worksheet first; Lotus will not save your worksheet automatically.

M - FILE NOT FOUND is a common unfriendly error message.

S - Either the particular file is not on the disk or you spelled the name wrong. Type the right file name and possibly the drive identifier. If it still doesn't work, there should not be such a file.

M - You try to save or retrieve a file, but the mode indicator says DISK DRIVE NOT READY.

S - Check if there is a disk in your default Drive, or if the door is closed.

9

Report Generation

9-1 Introduction

In this chapter we discuss the /Print command, one that enables you to generate reports. Using this command and its subcommands, you can print directly to a printer or to a file for future printing. You have flexibility in determining the look of your report by specifying such aspects as margins and lengths. This command also assists you in generating reports that can be utilized later by other software such as databases, word processors, other spreadsheets, and so on (for more information see Appendix D).

9-2 Printing to a File or a Printer

As mentioned earlier, a report can be printed directly to a printer or to a file. Since the commands are the same for both printer and file, we will only refer to the printer as the print device.

When you try to print to a file, a file name must be defined, following the rules discussed in Chapter 8. The file generated by the /Print command will use PRN as an extension, as opposed to WK1 (for worksheet) or PIC (for graphic files).

Files generated by /Print File can later be printed in DOS. At the A> prompt type TYPE filename.PRN. This file can be brought to the worksheet by the /File Import command; however, the file will lose its column and row structures. The reason for this transformation is that filename.PRN is an ASCII file (see Appendix D).

Whether printing to a printer or to a file, you have complete control over a file's size and format. This means that you can choose a specific range or ranges.

9-3 Overview of the /Print Command

When you invoke the /Print command, you will be given two options: Printer and File. Both have the following further options:

Range   Line   Page   Options   Clear   Align   Go   Quit

Range allows you to print either a specific portion of the worksheet or the entire worksheet. As usual, you can specify the range address or use pointing.
Line inserts a line or skips a line. If the printer is at the bottom of the report, this command will advance the printer to the next page.
Page skips a page or advances a page. If there is a footer, it will be printed at the bottom of the page.
Options includes several interesting choices:

Header   Footer   Margins   Borders   Setup   Pg-Length   Other   Quit

Header prints a line of text up to 240 characters below the top margin.
Footer prints a line of text up to 240 characters above the bottom margin.
Margins allows you to define Left, Right, Top, and Bottom margins.
Borders prints designated column or row headings on every page.
This can be either above or to the left of the specified range you are printing. With this option you can choose rows or columns. The areas you have identified as borders are not supposed to be included in your print range. If they are, you will get duplicate information.
Setup specifies the style and font size for a printer. The setup string, up to 39 characters, comes from a printer control code (you should consult your printer manual for specifics). It must begin with a backslash (\) and a three- or four-digit code. For Example, \015 on an Epson FX80 prints compressed output.
Pg-Length defines the number of lines of text to be printed. This can be any number between 1 and 100.
Other options include several powerful commands:

As-Displayed   Cell-Formulas   Formatted   Unformatted

As-Displayed prints the report as it appears on the monitor.
Cell-Formulas prints the contents of each occupied cell in the specified print range, one cell per line.
Formatted restores the previous format settings for headers, footers, and page breaks.
Unformatted prints a specified range without headers, footers, and page breaks. This option can be very helpful when printing to a file.
The *Clear* command in the main menu provides you with the following options:

All   Range   Borders   Format

All cancels print range, borders, footers, and headers. Everything is returned to the default settings.

Range cancels the present print range.

Borders clears the present borders.

Format restores page length, margins, and setup settings to their default settings.

Align tells the printer that the user has positioned the paper at the top of a new page. This command should be used before printing a worksheet. If you do not use this command, there may be gaps in the middle of the report.

Go in the main menu executes the Print command.

Quit, as usual, gets you out of the Print menu.

9-4 Default Settings

In most cases, the printer's default settings should satisfy your needs (to see the entire default settings, use /Worksheet Global Default Printer). The default settings include the following:

Page Length	66 lines
Left Margin	4 characters from the left side of the paper
Right Margin	76 characters from the left side of the paper
Top Margin	2 lines from the top of the page
Bottom Margin	2 lines from the bottom of the page

As you have seen in the main menu of the /Print command, any of these settings can be changed, either temporarily or permanently. For temporary changes issue the command /Print Printer Options. Under Options you have:

Header   Footer   Margins   Borders   Setup   Pg-Length   Other   Quit

For permanent changes first issue the command /Worksheet Global Default Printer. Change whatever you want, then choose /Worksheet Global Default Update.

9-5 Controlling Your Printer More Effectively

Several commands that we have already discussed can be used individually or collectively to enhance the effectiveness of your printer by reducing manual intervention and generating more readable output. You will see the enhanced features more clearly when you design a macro (discussed in Chapters 16-18) for printing and /or when you print to a file rather than to the printer.

/Print Printer Line skips a line. If you would like to skip a page, choose /Print Printer Page. After printing a report, select /Print Printer Align. This command will skip the printer to the beginning of a new page.

As we discussed in Chapter 5, /Worksheet Page gives a page break. This command will start a new page no matter how much of the present page is empty. When you use /Worksheet Page, you must check to see how many lines you have specified in /Print Printer Options Pg-Length. /Worksheet Page may not override this command *if* the number of lines specified by /Print Printer Options Pg-Length is less than the number of lines covered by /Worksheet Page.

9-6 Special Characters

Three special characters can be utilized for entering page numbers and the current date and for specifying the position of the header or footer, as follows:

(number sign)   Enter a page number starting at 1.

@ (at sign)   Enter current date in international format (month/day/year).

¦ (split vertical bar)   Separate portions of the header or footer, either left, center, or right-justified. We show examples of this at the end of the chapter. Text by itself will be left-justified. Preceded by one split vertical bar it will be centered; preceded by two split vertical bars (¦¦), it will be right-justified.

9-7 Planning Your Printed Report More Accurately

A standard page is 66 lines; standard means 11 inches, or six lines per inch. By default, Lotus leaves two lines blank between the text and the header or footer. If your printed line is longer than the right margin, Lotus will wrap around to the next line. To avoid this, use compressed type in your setup string. Of the 66 lines, only 56 lines are available for the text.

Lines 1-2	Top margin
Line 3	Header, if any
Lines 4-5	Blank by default
Lines 6-61 (56 lines)	Your text
Line 64	Footer, if any
Lines 65-66	Bottom margin

Different printers have different setup options. With the Epson FX80 printer we used \015 to generate compressed output. To stop a printing session use the **Ctrl** and **Break** keys together. This may not stop the printer immediately, but it will stop as soon as its buffer is empty.

9-8 Printing Reports with Different Options

To show you how the /Print command works, we developed several examples. Figure 9-1 is a balance sheet for four quarters of Ocean City Tourist Attraction.

In Figure 9-2, we printed three worksheets in one report using the default option. This report was generated by using /Print, Printer, Range, A1..E52, Return, Align, Go. As you see, even the default setting will give you a readable report.

Figure 9-1 Ocean City Tourist Attraction Balance Sheet in Worksheet Form

```
A1: [W32] '                        OCEAN CITY TOURIST ATTRACTION              READY


          A                          B          C          D          E
 1                    OCEAN CITY TOURIST ATTRACTION
 2              (1986-87  Figures in thousands of dollars)
 3        ----------------------------------------------------------------
 4                                Spring    Summer     Fall     Winter
 5        ----------------------------------------------------------------
 6   Current Assets
 7      Cash                      $36,249   $42,495   $58,761   $72,300
 8      Accounts Receivable        26,700    23,821    22,545    22,768
 9      Inventory                   8,000     7,625     9,025     8,475
10                                --------  --------  --------  --------
11   Total Current Assets          70,949    73,941    90,331   103,543
12
13   Fixed Assets
14      Property, Plant and Equipment
15         Land                     49,121    48,700    45,600    40,410
16         Building                 82,212    82,212    79,100    78,275
17         Leasehold Improvements   22,400    18,506    17,900    20,145
18         Equipment                 8,364     8,544     9,106     9,364
19      Gross P, P and E           162,097   157,962   151,706   148,194
20      Accumulated Depreciation   (48,814)  (37,600)  (36,945)  (29,725)
01-Jan-88   01:05 PM
```

Figure 9-1 (Continued)

```
A21: [W32]                                                                  READY


          A                          B          C          D          E
21                                --------  --------  --------  --------
22      Net P, P and E            113,283   120,362   114,761   118,469
23
24      Other Assets                 545       489       513       606
25
26   Total Fixed Assets           113,828   120,851   115,274   119,075
27
28   Total Assets               $184,777  $194,792  $205,605  $222,618
29                                ========  ========  ========  ========
30
31   ::
32   Current Liabilities
33      Accounts Payable           34,522    37,819    33,245    31,009
34      Notes Payable              10,000    11,321     7,369     8,655
35      Income Tax Payable          4,500     4,789     5,802     6,134
36                                --------  --------  --------  --------
37   Total Current Liabilities     49,022    53,929    46,416    45,798
38
39   Noncurrent Liabilities
40      Long Term Debt             52,242    48,700    46,345    40,300
01-Jan-88   01:06 PM
```

```
A41: [W32]                                                              READY

                    A          ·        B         C         D         E
 41                                   ---------  --------  --------  --------
 42   Total Liabilities               101,264   102,629    92,761    86,098
 43
 44   Stockholders' Equity
 45      Common Stock                   2,555     2,644     2,750     2,936
 46      Retained Earnings             80,958    89,519   110,094   133,584
 47                                   ---------  --------  --------  --------
 48   Total Stockholders' Equity       83,513    92,163   112,844   136,520
 49
 50   Total Liabilities and Equity   $184,777  $194,792  $205,605  $222,618
 51                                   ========  ========  ========  ========
 52
 53
 54
 55
 56
 57
 58
 59
 60
  01-Jan-88   01:07 PM
```

Figure 9-1 (Continued)

In Figure 9-3, we generated a page of a report with Header and Footer options. This report was generated by /Print, Printer, Range, A1..E52, Return, Options, Header¦¦, @, Return, Footer¦, Page #, Return, Pg-Length 66, Return, Margins Right 78, Return, Margins Top 4, Return, Margins Bottom 4, Return, Quit, Align, Go.

In Figure 9-4, we generated two pages of a report using a page break. We used the Borders Rows command under Options to show headings on both pages. This report was generated by /Print, Printer, Range A6..E52, Return, Options, Borders, Rows, A1..E5, Return, Quit, Align, Go.

In Figure 9-5, we used the Borders Columns command showing winter figures with column headings. In this case, Borders Columns was A6..A52 and Print Range was E3..E52. The report was generated by /Print, Printer, Range E3..E52, Return, Options, Borders, Columns A3..A52, Return, Quit, Align, Go.

In Figure 9-6, we used the Compressed option to print the spring quarter. The setup character on the Epson FX80 is \015. The report was generated by /Print, Printer, Range A3..B52, Return, Options, Setup \015, Return, Quit, Align, Go.

In Figure 9-7 we displayed the spring quarter without enhancements. We used / Print, Printer, Range B3..B52, Return, Options, Other, As-Displayed, Quit, Align, Go.

In Figure 9-8 we displayed the spring quarter using cell formulas. We used /Print, Printer, Range B3..B52, Return, Options, Other, Cell-Formulas, Quit, Align, Go.

```
                    OCEAN CITY TOURIST ATTRACTION
               (1986-87  Figures in thousands of dollars)
----------------------------------------------------------------------
                            Spring   Summer    Fall    Winter
----------------------------------------------------------------------
Current Assets
   Cash                     $36,249  $42,495  $58,761  $72,300
   Accounts Receivable       26,700   23,821   22,545   22,768
   Inventory                  8,000    7,625    9,025    8,475
                            -------  -------  -------  -------
Total Current Assets         70,949   73,941   90,331  103,543

Fixed Assets
   Property, Plant and Equipment
      Land                   49,121   48,700   45,600   40,410
      Building               82,212   82,212   79,100   78,275
      Leasehold Improvements 22,400   18,506   17,900   20,145
      Equipment               8,364    8,544    9,106    9,364
   Gross P, P and E         162,097  157,962  151,706  148,194
   Accumulated Depreciation (48,814) (37,600) (36,945) (29,725)
                            -------  -------  -------  -------
   Net P, P and E           113,283  120,362  114,761  118,469

   Other Assets                 545      489      513      606

Total Fixed Assets          113,828  120,851  115,274  119,075

Total Assets               $184,777 $194,792 $205,605 $222,618
                           ======== ======== ======== ========


Current Liabilities
   Accounts Payable          34,522   37,819   33,245   31,009
   Notes Payable             10,000   11,321    7,369    8,655
   Income Tax Payable         4,500    4,789    5,802    6,134
                            -------  -------  -------  -------
Total Current Liabilities    49,022   53,929   46,416   45,798

Noncurrent Liabilities
   Long Term Debt            52,242   48,700   46,345   40,300
                            -------  -------  -------  -------
Total Liabilities          101,264  102,629   92,761   86,098

Stockholders' Equity
   Common Stock               2,555    2,644    2,750    2,936
   Retained Earnings         80,958   89,519  110,094  133,584
                            -------  -------  -------  -------
Total Stockholders' Equity   83,513   92,163  112,844  136,520

Total Liabilities and Equity $184,777 $194,792 $205,605 $222,618
                            ======== ======== ======== ========
```

Figure 9-2 Ocean City Tourist Attraction Balance Sheet

```
                    OCEAN CITY TOURIST ATTRACTION
              (1986-87  Figures in thousands of dollars)
         ----------------------------------------------------------
                          Spring    Summer     Fall    Winter
         ----------------------------------------------------------
Current Assets
   Cash                  $36,249   $42,495  $58,761   $72,300
   Accounts Receivable    26,700    23,821   22,545    22,768
   Inventory               8,000     7,625    9,025     8,475
                         -------   -------  -------   -------
Total Current Assets      70,949    73,941   90,331   103,543

Fixed Assets
   Property, Plant and Equipment
      Land                49,121    48,700   45,600    40,410
      Building            82,212    82,212   79,100    78,275
      Leasehold Improvements 22,400 18,506   17,900    20,145
      Equipment            8,364     8,544    9,106     9,364
   Gross P, P and E      162,097   157,962  151,706   148,194
   Accumulated Depreciation (48,814)(37,600)(36,945) (29,725)
                         -------   -------  -------   -------
   Net P, P and E        113,283   120,362  114,761   118,469

   Other Assets             545       489      513       606

Total Fixed Assets       113,828   120,851  115,274   119,075

Total Assets            $184,777  $194,792 $205,605  $222,618
                        =======   =======  =======   =======


Current Liabilities
   Accounts Payable       34,522    37,819   33,245    31,009
   Notes Payable          10,000    11,321    7,369     8,655
   Income Tax Payable      4,500     4,789    5,802     6,134
                         -------   -------  -------   -------
Total Current Liabilities 49,022    53,929   46,416    45,798

Noncurrent Liabilities
   Long Term Debt         52,242    48,700   46,345    40,300
                         -------   -------  -------   -------
Total Liabilities        101,264   102,629   92,761    86,098

Stockholders' Equity
   Common Stock            2,555     2,644    2,750     2,936
   Retained Earnings      80,958    89,519  110,094   133,584
                         -------   -------  -------   -------
Total Stockholders' Equity 83,513   92,163  112,844   136,520

Total Liabilities and Equity $184,777 $194,792 $205,605 $222,618
                        =======   =======  =======   =======
```

Figure 9-3 Ocean City Tourist Attraction: A Fancier Report!

Figure 9-4 Ocean City Tourist Attraction: With Borders Rows and Page Break

```
                    OCEAN CITY TOURIST ATTRACTION
              (1986-87  Figures in thousands of dollars)
--------------------------------------------------------------------
                            Spring    Summer    Fall     Winter
--------------------------------------------------------------------
Current Assets
   Cash                    $36,249   $42,495   $58,761   $72,300
   Accounts Receivable      26,700    23,821    22,545    22,768
   Inventory                 8,000     7,625     9,025     8,475
                           -------   -------   -------   -------
Total Current Assets        70,949    73,941    90,331   103,543

Fixed Assets
   Property, Plant and Equipment
      Land                  49,121    48,700    45,600    40,410
      Building              82,212    82,212    79,100    78,275
      Leasehold Improvements 22,400   18,506    17,900    20,145
      Equipment              8,364     8,544     9,106     9,364
   Gross P, P and E        162,097   157,962   151,706   148,194
   Accumulated Depreciation (48,814) (37,600)  (36,945)  (29,725)
                           -------   -------   -------   -------
   Net P, P and E          113,283   120,362   114,761   118,469

   Other Assets               545       489       513       606

Total Fixed Assets         113,828   120,851   115,274   119,075

Total Assets              $184,777  $194,792  $205,605  $222,618
                           =======   =======   =======   =======
```

Figure 9-4 (Continued)

```
                    OCEAN CITY TOURIST ATTRACTION
              (1986-87  Figures in thousands of dollars)
--------------------------------------------------------------------
                            Spring    Summer    Fall     Winter
--------------------------------------------------------------------
Current Liabilities
   Accounts Payable          34,522    37,819    33,245    31,009
   Notes Payable             10,000    11,321     7,369     8,655
   Income Tax Payable         4,500     4,789     5,802     6,134
                            -------   -------   -------   -------
Total Current Liabilities    49,022    53,929    46,416    45,798

Noncurrent Liabilities
   Long Term Debt            52,242    48,700    46,345    40,300
                            -------   -------   -------   -------
Total Liabilities          101,264   102,629    92,761    86,098

Stockholders' Equity
   Common Stock               2,555     2,644     2,750     2,936
   Retained Earnings         80,958    89,519   110,094   133,584
                            -------   -------   -------   -------
Total Stockholders' Equity   83,513    92,163   112,844   136,520

Total Liabilities and Equity $184,777 $194,792 $205,605 $222,618
                            =======   =======   =======   =======
```

```
-------------------------------------------
                               |  Winter
-------------------------------------------
Current Assets
   Cash                           $72,300
   Accounts Receivable            22,768
   Inventory                       8,475
                                 -------
Total Current Assets            103,543

Fixed Assets
   Property, Plant and Equipment
      Land                        40,410
      Building                    78,275
      Leasehold Improvements      20,145
      Equipment                    9,364
   Gross P, P and E             148,194
   Accumulated Depreciation     (29,725)
                                 -------
   Net P, P and E               118,469

   Other Assets                      606

Total Fixed Assets              119,075

Total Assets                   $222,618
                                =======


Current Liabilities
   Accounts Payable               31,009
   Notes Payable                   8,655
   Income Tax Payable              6,134
                                 -------
Total Current Liabilities        45,798

Noncurrent Liabilities
   Long Term Debt                 40,300
                                 -------
Total Liabilities                86,098

Stockholders' Equity
   Common Stock                    2,936
   Retained Earnings             133,584
                                 -------
Total Stockholders' Equity      136,520

Total Liabilities and Equity   $222,618
                                =======
```

Figure 9-5 Ocean City Tourist Attraction: With Borders Columns

```
-------------------------------------------
                                Spring
-------------------------------------------
Current Assets
    Cash                        $36,249
    Accounts Receivable          26,700
    Inventory                     8,000
                                -------
Total Current Assets             70,949

Fixed Assets
    Property, Plant and Equipment
        Land                     49,121
        Building                 82,212
        Leasehold Improvements   22,400
        Equipment                 8,364
    Gross P, P and E            162,097
    Accumulated Depreciation    (48,814)
                                -------
    Net P, P and E              113,283

    Other Assets                    545

Total Fixed Assets              113,828

Total Assets                   $184,777
                                =======


Current Liabilities
    Accounts Payable             34,522
    Notes Payable                10,000
    Income Tax Payable            4,500
                                -------
Total Current Liabilities        49,022

Noncurrent Liabilities
    Long Term Debt               52,242
                                -------
Total Liabilities               101,264

Stockholders' Equity
    Common Stock                  2,555
    Retained Earnings            80,958
                                -------
Total Stockholders' Equity       83,513

Total Liabilities and Equity   $184,777
                                =======
```

Figure 9-6 Spring Quarter of Ocean City Tourist Attraction, Compressed

```
          ---------
           Spring
          ---------

          $36,249
           26,700
            8,000
          -------
           70,949


           49,121
           82,212
           22,400
            8,364
          162,097
          (48,814)
          -------
          113,283

              545

          113,828

         $184,777
          =======


           34,522
           10,000
            4,500
          -------
           49,022

           52,242
          -------.
          101,264

            2,555
           80,958
          -------
           83,513

         $184,777
          =======
```

Figure 9-7 Spring Quarter of Ocean City Tourist Attraction As Is

```
B3:  \-
B4:  ^Spring
B5:  \-
B7:  (C0) 36249
B8:  (,0) 26700
B9:  (,0) 8000
B10: "-------
B11: (,0) @SUM(B7..B10)
B15: (,0) 49121
B16: (,0) 82212
B17: (,0) 22400
B18: (,0) 8364
B19: (,0) @SUM(B15..B18)
B20: (,0) -48814
B21: "-------
B22: (,0) +B19+B20
B24: 545
B26: (,0) +B22+B24
B28: (C0) +B11+B26
B29: "=======
B33: (,0) 34522
B34: (,0) 10000
B35: (,0) 4500
B36: "-------
B37: (,0) @SUM(B33..B35)
B40: (,0) 52242
B41: "-------
B42: (,0) +B37+B40
B45: (,0) 2555
B46: (,0) 80958
B47: "-------
B48: (,0) +B45+B46
B50: (C0) +B42+B48
B51: "=======
```

Figure 9-8 Spring Quarter of Ocean City Tourist Attraction: Cell-Formulas

Summary

Using the /Print command and its subcommands, you can generate reports. You can print to a printer or to a file for future printing. Margins, headers, and footers can be specified. Depending upon the type of printer you use, you can specify strings. This means you can print with different type sets, in compressed types, and so forth. The /Print command also gives you the Cell-Formulas option, which lets you print the "guts" of your worksheet in order to debug it or make further modifications.

Review Questions

1. What is the difference between printing to a file and printing to a printer?
2.* If you print to a file, how do you print the content of this file in DOS?
3. What are some of the advantages of printing to a file over printing to a printer?
4. What are the printer default settings?
5. What is the maximum and the minimum page length?
6.* Which character is used to display the current date?
7. What is the role of the Borders command?
8. How many ways can you split 58 lines of text into two pages?
9.* Does /Worksheet Page always override Pg-Length?
10.* What are some uses of the Cell-Formulas option?

11.   When do you use the Align option?

12.   How do you advance the printer to the top of a new page?

13.   What is the file extension of a file generated by /Print File?

14.* How many of the 66 lines of a page (by default) are available to you for writing text (excluding top and bottom margins)?

15.   How do you change default settings temporarily?

16.* How do you change default settings permanently?

17.   When and why do you use the Clear option?

18.   Generate a ten-row by five-column worksheet. Print this worksheet as follows:

- Using the **Shift** and **PrtSc** keys.

- Using /Print Printer with default settings.

- Using /Print Printer with top and bottom margins of eight.

- Using the Cell-Formulas option.

- Using the Compressed option.

Misconception and Solution

M - You try to use the /Print Printer command and receive an error message, PRINTER-ERROR.

S - Check your printer. It may be loosely connected, not connected at all, out of paper, or turned off!

10

Functions/Part One

10-1 Introduction

In this chapter we will explain the general format of mathematical, financial, and statistical functions. Numerous examples will accompany our discussion. Chapter 11 continues the discussion by covering string, date and time, and special functions. Database statistical functions will be the subject of Chapter 15.

10-2 What Is A Lotus Function?

A Lotus *function* is a built-in formula for the calculation of a specific task. Lotus has eight function groups. Each has been designed to perform a unique task. For example, you have learned how to add the contents of cells A1, A2, A3 and A4 by adding +A1+A2+A3+A4. Instead of doing this, you could simply type @SUM(A1..A4). Now you can see how easy it is to perform the task using a function.

Every function follows this format:

@FUNCTION(argument1,argument2,...)

A function must begin with the at sign (@). Next comes the name of the function and one or a series of arguments in parentheses. The *argument* is the information Lotus needs in order to perform a task. Consider the function @SUM(X1,X2,X3). The function name is SUM and the arguments are X1, X2, and X3. Some functions, however, do not need any arguments.

10-3 Argument Types

Lotus accepts three types of arguments:
1. Numeric values. In the function @ABS(y), y is a value; @ABS(-5) = 5.
2. Range values. In the function @SUM(A1..A9), A1..A9 is the range address. In the function @SUM(Asset), Asset is a range name.
3. String values. In the function @UPPER("rose") = ROSE, rose is the string value. Remember, strings must be enclosed in double quotation marks.

Numeric values can have one of the following forms:

actual value	@ABS(-5)
cell address	@ABS(A11)
cell range name	@SUM(asset)
formula	@ABS((-20/4)/5)
function	@INT(@ABS(A11)+@SQRT(64))
combination	@INT(@SUM(A1..A10)+asset+2500)

Range values can have one of the following forms:

range name	@SUM(DIVISION1)
range address	@SUM(A1..A10)
combination	@SUM(DIVISION1,A1..A9,DIVISION9)

And finally, string values can have one of the following forms:

cell address	@LOWER(A1)
cell name	@LOWER(STREET) (remember street is a cell name)
actual value	@LOWER("I AM A STUDENT")
formula	@LENGTH("TITLE"&"SUB-TITLE")

When you are working with functions you must keep in mind the exact type of argument accepted by each function. For example, @SUM("TITLE") will cause an error because the @SUM function requires a numeric value or a range value, not a string value.

Seven functions do not require any arguments. These include @ERR, @FALSE, @NA, @NOW, @PI, @RAND, and @TRUE. We will talk about these in Chapter 11.

The functions @CELL, @N, and @S require single-cell values as arguments; however, you must enter these values as a range, for example @N(A1..A1), or a cell address preceded by an exclamation mark, as in @N(!A1). We will discuss these in Chapter 11.

10-4 Mathematical Functions

Lotus offers 17 mathematical functions. All except @PI require arguments. The arguments can be values, cell addresses, range names, formulas, or other functions. Arguments for sine, cosine, and tangent must be expressed in radians. (To convert degrees to radians, multiply the number of degrees by @PI/180.)

The trigonometric functions arc sine, arc cosine, and arc tangent return all angles in radians. (To convert radians to degrees, multiply the number of radians by 180/@PI.)

10-4-1 @ABS(A)

This function's argument must be numeric. The function always returns the positive value of the argument. Examples:

```
@ABS(5)     = 5
@ABS(0)     = 0
@ABS(-5)    = 5
@ABS("Happy Birthday") = ERR – invalid argument
```

10-4-2 @ACOS(A)

The function calculates the arc cosine of an angle and returns the angle, in radians, whose cosine is A. Argument A must be between -1 and +1. Examples:

```
@ACOS(.25)          = 1.318116 (radians)
@ACOS(-0.5)         = 2.094395 (radians)
@ACOS(1)*180/@PI    = 0 (degrees)
@ACOS(.75)*180/@PI  = 41.40962 (degrees)
@ACOS(9.5)          = ERR – invalid argument
```

10-4-3 @ASIN(A)

Argument A must be between -1 and +1. The function calculates the arc sine of an angle and returns the angle, in radians, whose sine is A. Examples:

```
@ASIN(0.25)         = 0.252680 (radians)
@ASIN(-0.5)         = -0.52359 (radians)
@ASIN(.5)*180/@PI   = 30 (degrees)
@ASIN(1)*180/@PI    = 90 (degrees)
@ASIN(9.5)          = ERR – invalid argument
```

10-4-4 @ATAN(A)

This function's argument can take any value. It calculates the two-quadrant arc tangent of an angle and returns the angle, in radians, whose tangent is A. Examples:

```
@ATAN(90)           = 1.559685 (radians)
@ATAN(-45)          = -1.54857 (radians)
@ATAN(1)*180/@PI    = 45 (degrees)
```

10-4-5 @ATAN2(A,B)

The arguments can take any numeric value. The function calculates the four-quadrant arc tangent of an angle and returns the angle, in radians, whose tangent is B/A. If both A and B are zero, the result is ERR. Examples:

@ATAN2(4,590)	= 1.564016
@ATAN2(-30, -60)	= -2.03444
@ATAN2(0, 0)	= ERR

10-4-6 @COS(A)

This function calculates the cosine of angle A, which must be measured in radians. The result is always between -1 and 1. Examples:

| @COS(90*PI/180) | = 3.4E-19 |
| @COS(60*@PI/180) | = 0.5 |

10-4-7 @EXP(A)

This function calculates the result of e (2.7182) to the A th power. The upper limit for A is 709; beyond this the result is too large to be stored by Lotus. Examples:

@EXP(0)	= 1
@EXP(1)	= 2.718281
@EXP(-2)	= 0.135335
@EXP(2)	= 7.389056
@EXP(1000)	= ERR – too large

10-4-8 @INT(A)

This function returns the integer portion of the argument, but it does not round the number. If you would like to round a number, either use the @ROUND function or simply add .50 to the argument of the @INT(A) function. Examples:

@INT(5.5645)	= 5
@INT(-6.45698)	= -6
@INT(9.9)	= 9
@INT(9.9+.50)	= 10

10-4-9 @LN(A)

Argument A must be greater than zero. The function calculates the natural logarithm of A. Examples:

@LN(58)	= 4.060443
@LN(1)	= 0
@LN(-5)	= ERR – invalid argument

10-4-10 @LOG(A)

Argument A must be greater than zero. The function calculates the logarithm (base 10) of A. Examples:

@LOG(25)	= 1.397940
@LOG(1)	= 0
@LOG(-5)	= ERR – invalid argument

10-4-11   @MOD(A,B)

Argument A can be any number; argument B can be any number except zero. The function calculates the remainder of A/B. The sign returned by this function will always be the same as the sign of A. Examples:

@MOD(13,7)	= 6
@MOD(11,3)	= 2
@MOD(-14,2)	= 0
@MOD(-15,4)	= -3
@MOD(15,-4)	= 3
@MOD(7,0)	= ERR – invalid argument

10-4-12   @PI

This function returns 3.141592 or PI, the ratio of the circumference of a circle to its diameter $(2*PI*R/(2*R) = PI$, where R is the radius of a circle).

10-4-13   @RAND

This function generates a random number between zero and one. You can use it to generate a random number between any range of numbers as follows:

$$@INT(@RAND*(U-L+1)+L)$$

where U is the upper bound, L is the lower bound. For example, if you are interested in a random number between 1000 and 100, your formula would be @INT(@RAND*(901)+100). This formula will return an integer between 100 and 1000.

10-4-14   @ROUND(A,n)

Argument n must be a value between -15 and +15. The function rounds argument A to n places. This function can round on either side of the decimal point. Examples:

@ROUND(2.435678,3)	= 2.436
@ROUND(5.567564,3)	= 5.568
@ROUND(145.267,-1)	= 150
@ROUND(145.267,-2)	= 100
@ROUND(145.267,-3)	= 0

10-4-15   @SIN(A)

This function returns the sine of angle A. The angle must be measured in radians. Examples:

$$@SIN(45*@PI/180) \quad = 0.707106$$
$$@SIN(60*@PI/180) \quad = 0.866025$$

10-4-16 @SQRT(A)

Argument A must be a positive number. The function returns the positive square root of A. Examples:

@SQRT(16)	= 4
@SQRT(25)	= 5
@SQRT(56)	= 7.483314
@SQRT(-4)	= ERR – invalid argument

10-4-17 @TAN(A)

Argument A must be measured in radians. The function returns the tangent of angle A. Examples:

@TAN(45*@PI/180)	= 1
@TAN(90*@PI/180)	= 2.9E+18
@TAN(180*@PI/180)	= -3.4E-19

10-5 Financial Functions

Lotus has 11 financial functions. They can be utilized for cash flow analysis, investment analysis, loan installment, and three methods of depreciation analysis. Before you use these functions, you should remember that term and interest rate must be expressed for the same time frame (for monthly payment, the yearly interest rate must be divided by 12 and the term must be multiplied by 12). Interest rate can be entered either as a percentage (10%) or as a decimal (.10). Lotus assumes ordinary annuity. This means that a payment is made at the end of each period and the annuity due is made at the beginning of each period.

10-5-1 @FV(payment,interest rate,term)

This function calculates the future value of a series of equal payments with a given interest rate over a period of time. The @FV function uses the following formula:

$$FV = Payment * \frac{(1 + interest)^{n-1}}{interest} \quad \text{where } n = \text{number of periods}$$

Figure 10-1 shows the future value of an IRA plan over 20 years with a $2,000 payment and an interest rate of 9 percent. This function can be very helpful for calculating the future value of an investment.

10-5-2 @PV(payment,interest rate,term)

This function calculates the present value of an investment. The payments must be equal. The function uses the following formula:

$$PV = \text{Payment} * \frac{(1 - (1 + \text{interest})^{-n})}{\text{interest}} \quad \text{where } n = \text{term}$$

This function can be used for discounting a series of future income payments to today's value. Let us say somebody will pay you $5,000 for the next five years. How much can you sell this portfolio for today? Figure 10-2 shows an example of this function.

10-5-3 @IRR(estimate,range)

This function calculates the internal rate of return (IRR) of a series of cash inflows and outflows. Estimate can be any figure between zero and one. Range is the entire cash inflow and outflow of a particular investment. This function can be very helpful for investment analysis. Let us assume you have an investment portfolio that includes a series of cash outflows (initial cost, labor, raw materials, etc.) and a series of cash inflows (the income that may be generated by the investment). Let us assume that you have no money to invest in this project. You go to a bank for a loan. At what interest rate can you afford to implement the project? It depends on the internal rate of return. If the IRR is 12 percent and the bank is willing to lend you money at a rate less than 12 percent, you can proceed. At an interest rate of 12 percent you will neither lose nor gain and at a rate more than 12 percent you will lose. Figure 10-3 illustrates an example of this function.

Figure 10-1 Future Value of an IRA Investment

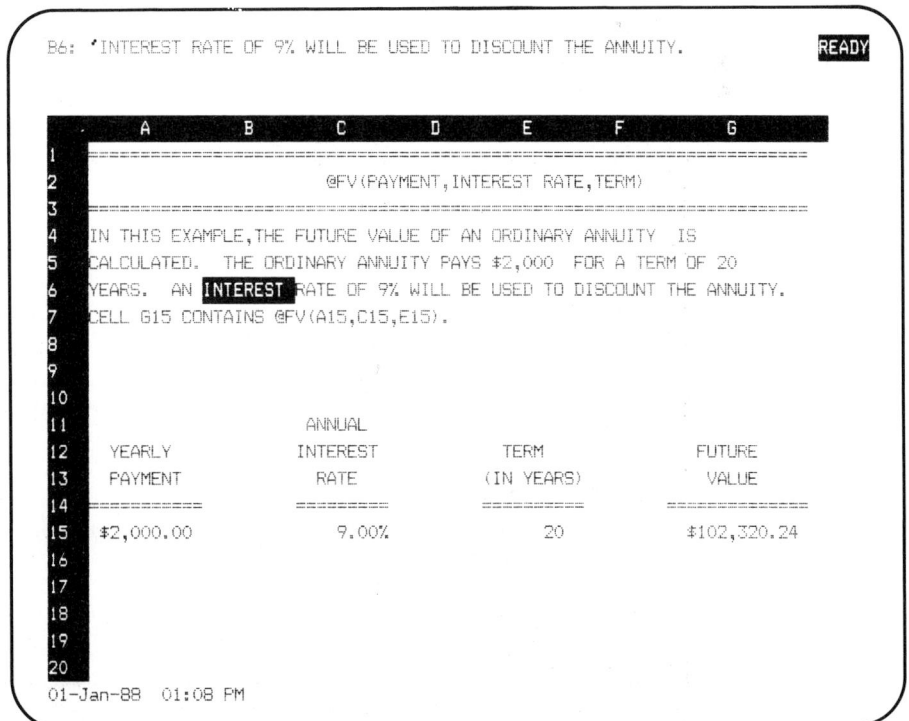

```
 B6:  'INTEREST RATE OF 9% WILL BE USED TO DISCOUNT THE ANNUITY.              READY


        .     A        B         C         D        E         F          G
  1     ================================================================
  2                        @FV(PAYMENT,INTEREST RATE,TERM)
  3     ================================================================
  4     IN THIS EXAMPLE,THE FUTURE VALUE OF AN ORDINARY ANNUITY   IS
  5     CALCULATED.   THE ORDINARY ANNUITY PAYS $2,000  FOR A TERM OF 20
  6     YEARS.   AN  INTEREST RATE OF 9% WILL BE USED TO DISCOUNT THE ANNUITY.
  7     CELL G15 CONTAINS @FV(A15,C15,E15).
  8
  9
 10
 11                        ANNUAL
 12     YEARLY            INTEREST             TERM               FUTURE
 13     PAYMENT             RATE             (IN YEARS)           VALUE
 14     ==========       ==========        ===========        ===============
 15     $2,000.00          9.00%               20               $102,320.24
 16
 17
 18
 19
 20
 01-Jan-88   01:08 PM
```

Figure 10-2 Present Value of an Ordinary Annuity

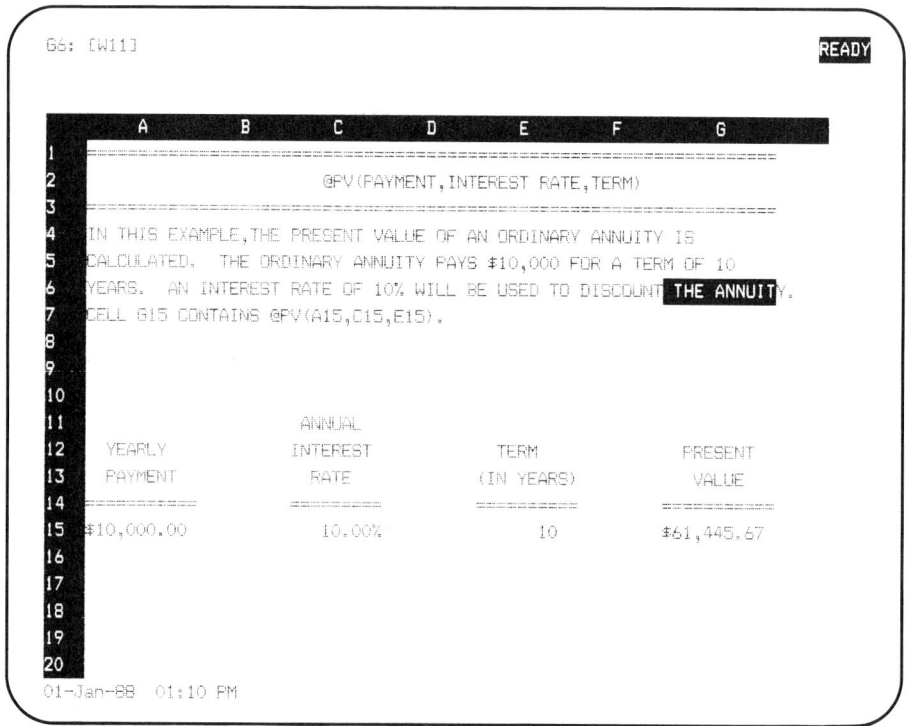

```
G6: [W11]                                                              READY

          A         B         C         D         E         F         G

1
2                        @PV(PAYMENT,INTEREST RATE,TERM)
3
4    IN THIS EXAMPLE,THE PRESENT VALUE OF AN ORDINARY ANNUITY IS
5    CALCULATED.   THE ORDINARY ANNUITY PAYS $10,000 FOR A TERM OF 10
6    YEARS.   AN INTEREST RATE OF 10% WILL BE USED TO DISCOUNT THE ANNUITY.
7    CELL G15 CONTAINS @PV(A15,C15,E15).
8
9
10
11                        ANNUAL
12   YEARLY              INTEREST            TERM                PRESENT
13   PAYMENT               RATE           (IN YEARS)             VALUE
14   ========           ========          ========             ========
15   $10,000.00           10.00%              10               $61,445.67
16
17
18
19
20
01-Jan-88   01:10 PM
```

Figure 10-3 Internal Rate of Return Analysis

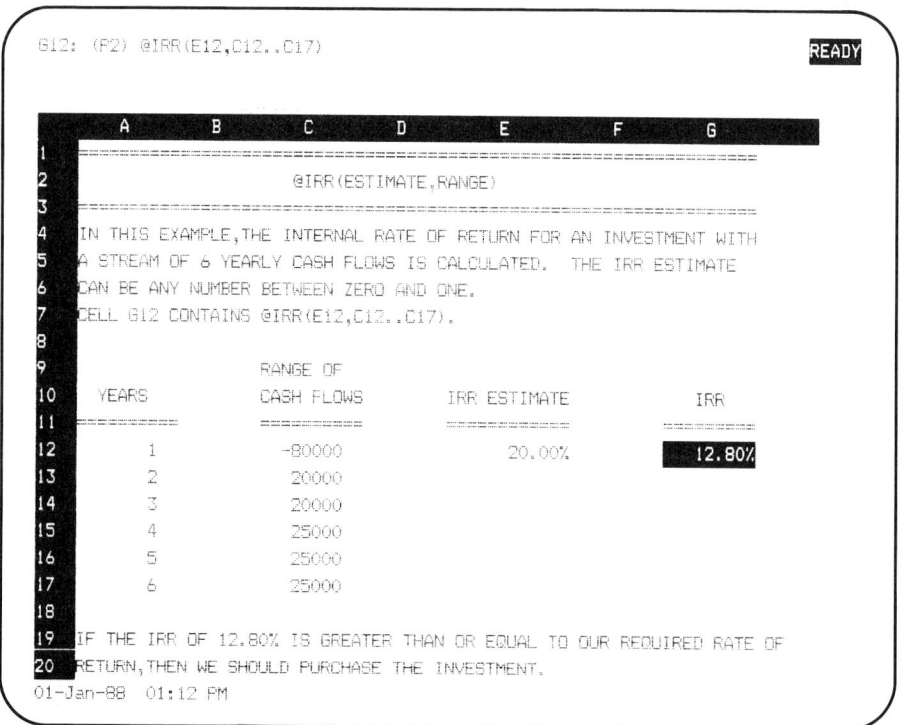

```
G12: (P2) @IRR(E12,C12..C17)                                           READY

          A         B         C         D         E         F         G

1
2                         @IRR(ESTIMATE,RANGE)
3
4    IN THIS EXAMPLE,THE INTERNAL RATE OF RETURN FOR AN INVESTMENT WITH
5    A STREAM OF 6 YEARLY CASH FLOWS IS CALCULATED.   THE IRR ESTIMATE
6    CAN BE ANY NUMBER BETWEEN ZERO AND ONE.
7    CELL G12 CONTAINS @IRR(E12,C12..C17).
8
9                        RANGE OF
10   YEARS             CASH FLOWS        IRR ESTIMATE            IRR
11   ======            ==========        ============          ====
12     1                 -80000             20.00%            12.80%
13     2                  20000
14     3                  20000
15     4                  25000
16     5                  25000
17     6                  25000
18
19   IF THE IRR OF 12.80% IS GREATER THAN OR EQUAL TO OUR REQUIRED RATE OF
20   RETURN,THEN WE SHOULD PURCHASE THE INVESTMENT.
01-Jan-88   01:12 PM
```

10-5-4 @NPV(interest rate,range)

This function calculates the present value of a series of future cash flows discounted at a fixed interest rate, assuming that each cash flow occurs at the end of each period. This function uses the following formula:

$$\sum \frac{Vi}{(1 + interest)^i} \quad \text{where } Vi \dots Vm = \text{series of cash flows}$$

$$m = \text{number of cash flows}$$

$$i = \text{number of iterations (1 to m)}$$

The cash inflows or outflows do not need to be equal. This function is very helpful for calculating today's worth of an investment that may generate different future cash inflows and outflows. Figure 10-4 illustrates an example of this function.

10-5-5 @PMT(principal,interest rate,term)

This function calculates the amount of the periodic payment on a loan, using the following formula:

$$PMT = principal \quad \frac{interest\ rate}{1 - (interest\ rate + 1)^{-n}} \quad \text{where } n = term$$

This function is very helpful for determining the payments for a new car, house, boat, and so forth. Figure 10-5 illustrates an example of this function.

10-5-6 @CTERM(interest rate,future value,present value)

This function calculates the number of compounding periods an investment reaches from a given present value to a given future value with a given fixed interest rate. Lotus utilizes the following formula in this function:

$$\frac{LN\ (future\ value/present\ value)}{Ln\ (1 + interest\ rate)} \quad \text{where } Ln = \text{natural logarithm}$$

This function can be very helpful for future planning, let us say for your children's college expenses. It tells you how many years it will take to accumulate a certain amount of money. Figure 10-6 shows an example of this function.

10-5-7 @TERM(payment,interest rate,future value)

This function calculates the number of payment periods necessary to accumulate a given future value. All payments must be equal. The function uses the following formula:

$$\frac{LN\ (1 + (Future\ value * interest/payment))}{Ln\ (1 + interest)} \quad \text{where } Ln = \text{natural logarithm}$$

To calculate the term of an annuity that is due, the following formula should be used:

@TERM(payment, interest rate, future value/(1+ interest))

Figure 10-7 illustrates an example of this function.

Figure 10-4 Net Present Value Analysis

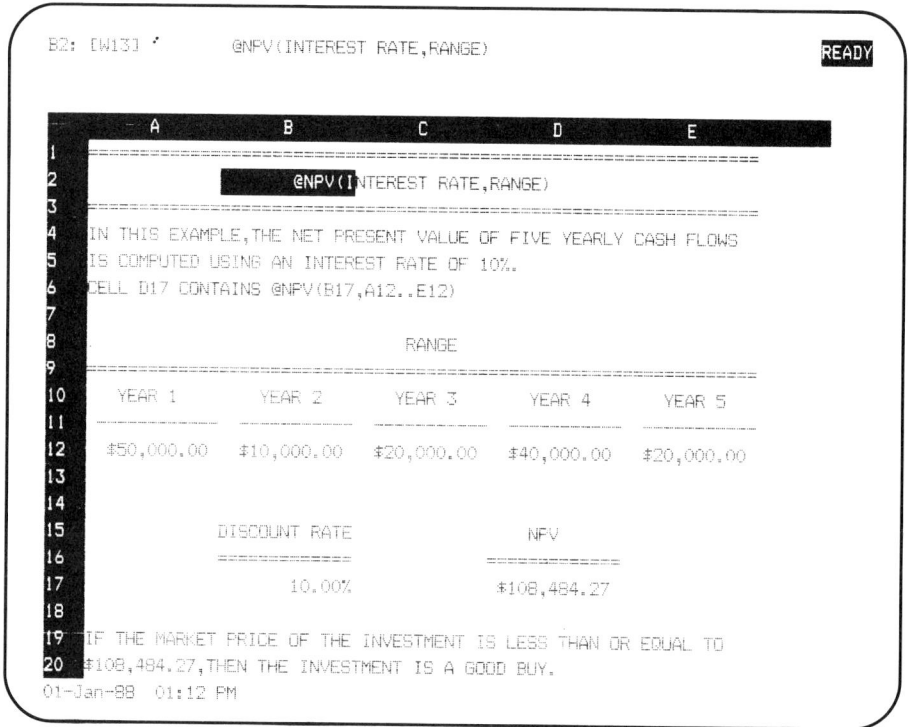

```
B2: [W13] '        @NPV(INTEREST RATE,RANGE)                        READY

         A            B            C            D            E
1  ================================================================
2                     @NPV(INTEREST RATE,RANGE)
3  ================================================================
4  IN THIS EXAMPLE,THE NET PRESENT VALUE OF FIVE YEARLY CASH FLOWS
5  IS COMPUTED USING AN INTEREST RATE OF 10%.
6  CELL D17 CONTAINS @NPV(B17,A12..E12)
7
8                            RANGE
9  ================================================================
10   YEAR 1       YEAR 2       YEAR 3       YEAR 4       YEAR 5
11 --------------------------------------------------------------
12  $50,000.00   $10,000.00   $20,000.00   $40,000.00   $20,000.00
13
14
15              DISCOUNT RATE              NPV
16              =============          =============
17                 10.00%               $108,484.27
18
19 IF THE MARKET PRICE OF THE INVESTMENT IS LESS THAN OR EQUAL TO
20 $108,484.27,THEN THE INVESTMENT IS A GOOD BUY.
   01-Jan-88  01:12 PM
```

Figure 10-5 Payment Analysis of a Particular Loan

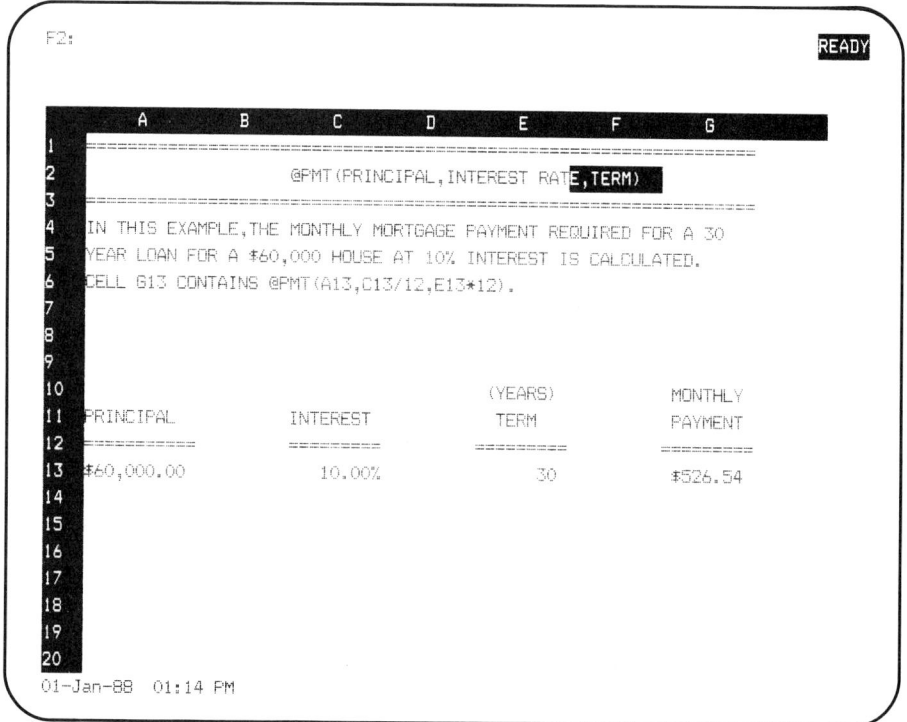

```
F2:                                                             READY

        A       B       C       D       E       F       G
1  ================================================================
2              @PMT(PRINCIPAL,INTEREST RATE,TERM)
3  ================================================================
4  IN THIS EXAMPLE,THE MONTHLY MORTGAGE PAYMENT REQUIRED FOR A 30
5  YEAR LOAN FOR A $60,000 HOUSE AT 10% INTEREST IS CALCULATED.
6  CELL G13 CONTAINS @PMT(A13,C13/12,E13*12).
7
8
9
10                                 (YEARS)           MONTHLY
11 PRINCIPAL       INTEREST         TERM             PAYMENT
12 =========       ========       =========         =========
13 $60,000.00       10.00%           30              $526.54
14
15
16
17
18
19
20
   01-Jan-88  01:14 PM
```

Figure 10-6 Number of Compounding Periods Analysis

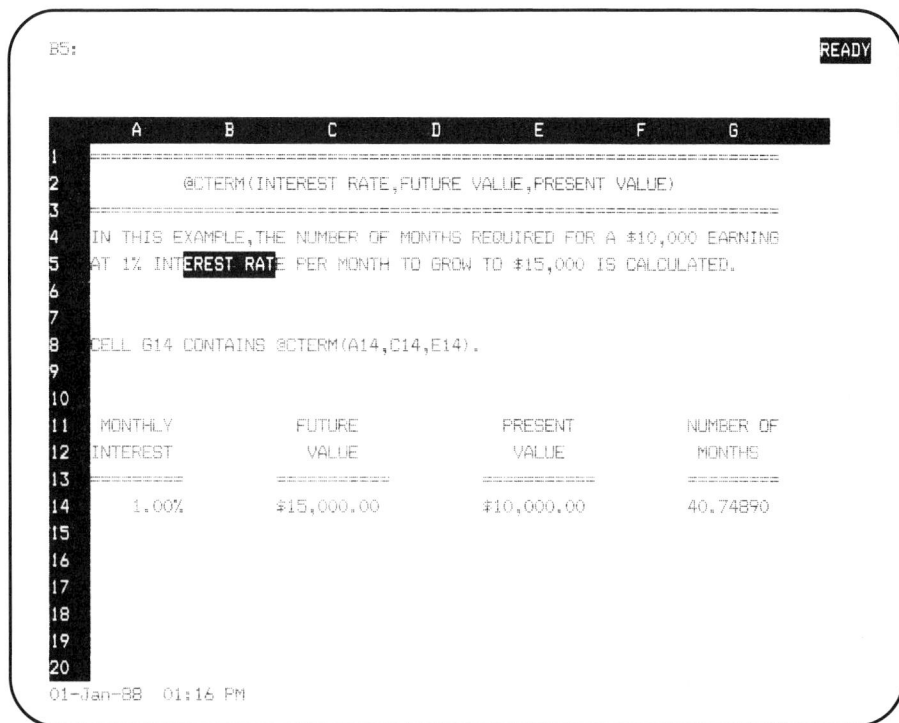

```
B5:                                                                    READY

          A         B         C         D         E         F         G
1     ==========================================================================
2              @CTERM(INTEREST RATE,FUTURE VALUE,PRESENT VALUE)
3     ==========================================================================
4     IN THIS EXAMPLE,THE NUMBER OF MONTHS REQUIRED FOR A $10,000 EARNING
5     AT 1% INTEREST RATE PER MONTH TO GROW TO $15,000 IS CALCULATED.
6
7
8     CELL G14 CONTAINS @CTERM(A14,C14,E14).
9
10
11     MONTHLY            FUTURE             PRESENT            NUMBER OF
12     INTEREST            VALUE              VALUE              MONTHS
13     --------          ----------         ----------         ----------
14       1.00%          $15,000.00         $10,000.00           40.74890
15
16
17
18
19
20
01-Jan-88   01:16 PM
```

Figure 10-7 Number of Payment Periods Analysis

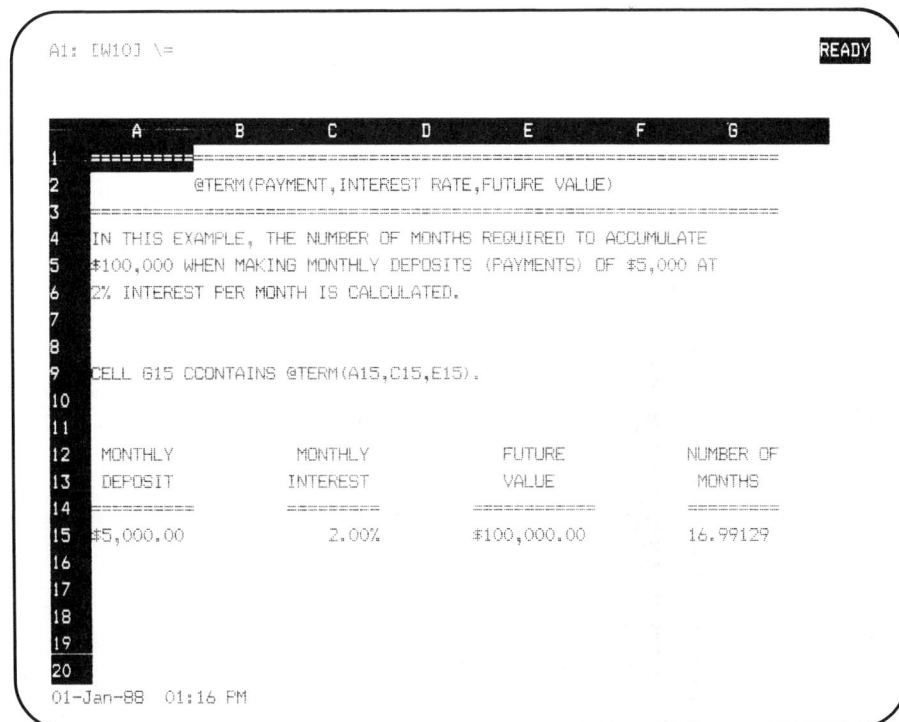

```
A1: [W10] \=                                                           READY

          A         B         C         D         E         F         G
1     ==========================================================================
2               @TERM(PAYMENT,INTEREST RATE,FUTURE VALUE)
3     ==========================================================================
4     IN THIS EXAMPLE, THE NUMBER OF MONTHS REQUIRED TO ACCUMULATE
5     $100,000 WHEN MAKING MONTHLY DEPOSITS (PAYMENTS) OF $5,000 AT
6     2% INTEREST PER MONTH IS CALCULATED.
7
8
9     CELL G15 CCONTAINS @TERM(A15,C15,E15).
10
11
12     MONTHLY            MONTHLY            FUTURE             NUMBER OF
13     DEPOSIT            INTEREST            VALUE              MONTHS
14     --------          ----------         ----------         ----------
15    $5,000.00           2.00%           $100,000.00          16.99129
16
17
18
19
20
01-Jan-88   01:16 PM
```

10-5-8 @RATE(future value,present value,term)

This function calculates the interest rate necessary for a present value to reach a future value over the number of compounding periods, using the following formula:

$$\left(\frac{\text{Future value}}{\text{present value}}\right)^{\frac{1}{n}} -1 \quad \text{where } n = \text{term}$$

Figure 10-8 illustrates an example of this function.

10-5-9 @SLN(cost,salvage value,life)

This function calculates the straight-line depreciation of a piece of equipment for one period, assuming the same amount of depreciation for every period. The function uses the following formula:

$$\frac{(\text{Cost - Salvage Value})}{\text{useful life of the asset}}$$

Figure 10-9 illustrates an example of this function.

10-5-10 @SYD(cost,salvage value,life,period)

This function calculates the sum-of-the-years'-digits depreciation for a selected period using the following formula:

$$\frac{(\text{Cost - Salvage Value}) * (\text{Useful life} - P + 1)}{(n * (n + 1)/2)}$$

where n   = useful life of the equipment

P   = period for which depreciation is being computed

This method accelerates the rate of depreciation; therefore, more depreciation expenses occur in earlier periods than in later ones. Since the maintenance costs are minimal in the first few years, this method will balance out the total cost of a piece of equipment. In later years there are fewer depreciation costs and more maintenance costs. Figure 10-10 illustrates an example of this function.

10-5-11 @DDB(cost,salvage value,life,period)

This function calculates the depreciation for a selected period of time, using the double-declining-balance method. Depreciation stops when the book value of the equipment reaches the salvage value. At any given period, the book value is equal to the total cost minus total depreciation over all prior periods. This function uses the following formula:

$$\frac{(\text{Book value in that period} * 2)}{(\text{life of the equipment})}$$

Figure 10-11 illustrates an example of this function.

Figure 10-8 Interest Rate Analysis

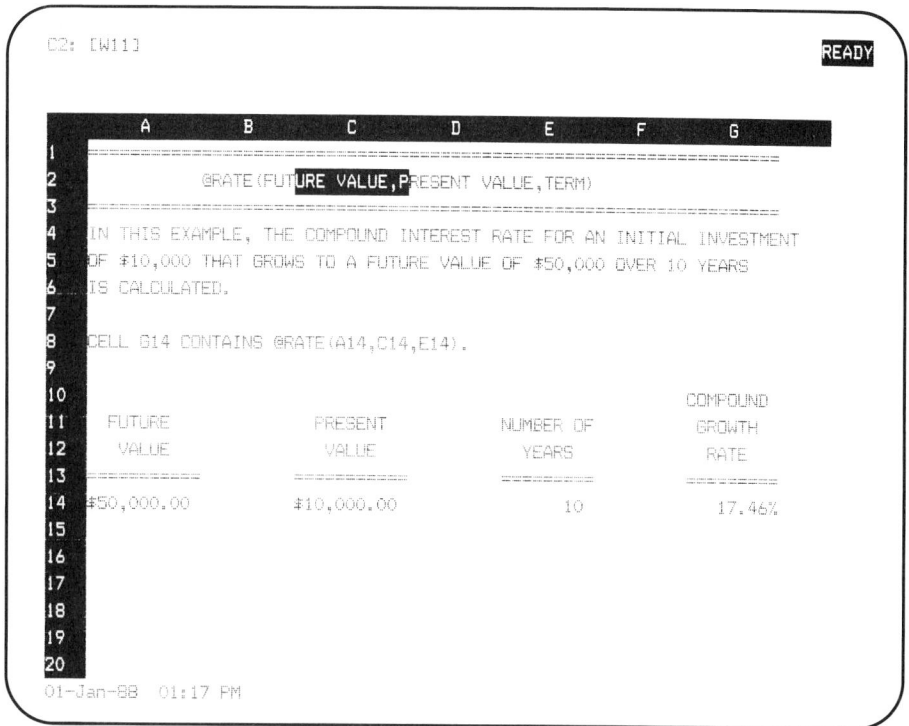

```
C2: [W11]                                                                      READY

            A           B           C           D           E           F           G
1  =========================================================================
2                  @RATE(FUTURE VALUE,PRESENT VALUE,TERM)
3  -------------------------------------------------------------------------
4  IN THIS EXAMPLE, THE COMPOUND INTEREST RATE FOR AN INITIAL INVESTMENT
5  OF $10,000 THAT GROWS TO A FUTURE VALUE OF $50,000 OVER 10 YEARS
6  IS CALCULATED.
7
8  CELL G14 CONTAINS @RATE(A14,C14,E14).
9
10                                                             COMPOUND
11    FUTURE              PRESENT           NUMBER OF          GROWTH
12    VALUE               VALUE              YEARS              RATE
13  ===========        ===========        ===========        ===========
14 $50,000.00          $10,000.00             10               17.46%
15
16
17
18
19
20
01-Jan-88   01:17 PM
```

Figure 10-9 Straight-Line Depreciation

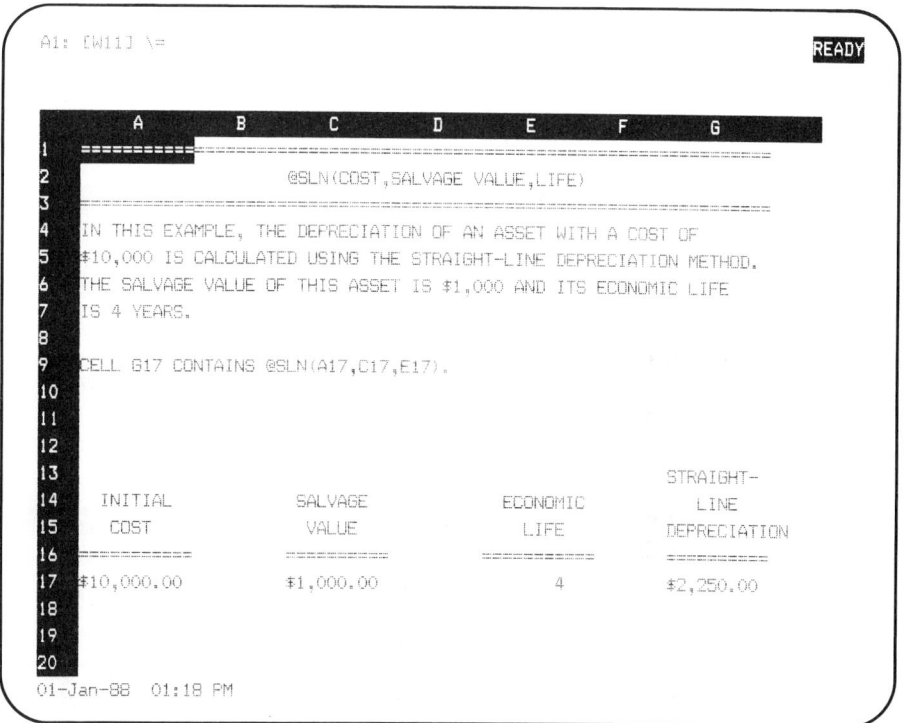

```
A1: [W11] \=                                                                   READY

            A           B           C           D           E           F           G
1  ==========
2                  @SLN(COST,SALVAGE VALUE,LIFE)
3  -------------------------------------------------------------------------
4  IN THIS EXAMPLE, THE DEPRECIATION OF AN ASSET WITH A COST OF
5  $10,000 IS CALCULATED USING THE STRAIGHT-LINE DEPRECIATION METHOD.
6  THE SALVAGE VALUE OF THIS ASSET IS $1,000 AND ITS ECONOMIC LIFE
7  IS 4 YEARS.
8
9  CELL G17 CONTAINS @SLN(A17,C17,E17).
10
11
12
13                                                             STRAIGHT-
14    INITIAL             SALVAGE           ECONOMIC           LINE
15    COST                VALUE              LIFE             DEPRECIATION
16  ===========        ===========        ===========        ===========
17 $10,000.00          $1,000.00              4              $2,250.00
18
19
20
01-Jan-88   01:18 PM
```

Figure 10-10 Sum-of-the-Years'-Digits Depreciation

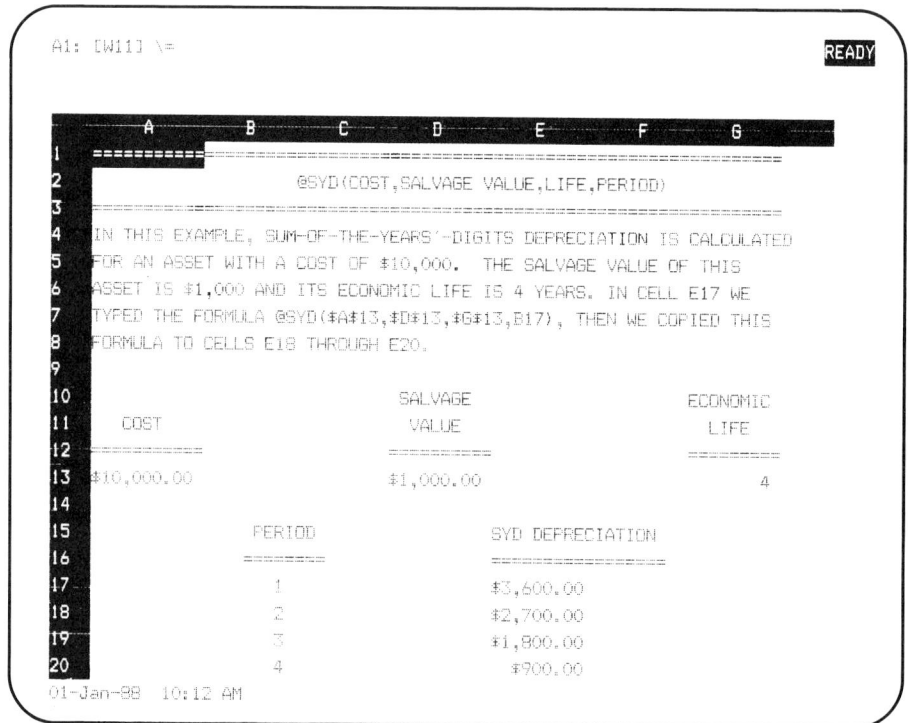

```
A1: [W11] \=                                                              READY


        A         B         C         D         E         F         G
1  ===========
2                          @SYD(COST,SALVAGE VALUE,LIFE,PERIOD)
3
4  IN THIS EXAMPLE, SUM-OF-THE-YEARS'-DIGITS DEPRECIATION IS CALCULATED
5  FOR AN ASSET WITH A COST OF $10,000.  THE SALVAGE VALUE OF THIS
6  ASSET IS $1,000 AND ITS ECONOMIC LIFE IS 4 YEARS. IN CELL E17 WE
7  TYPED THE FORMULA @SYD($A$13,$D$13,$G$13,B17), THEN WE COPIED THIS
8  FORMULA TO CELLS E18 THROUGH E20.
9
10                             SALVAGE                      ECONOMIC
11     COST                     VALUE                         LIFE
12  ===========              ===========                   ==========
13 $10,000.00               $1,000.00                         4
14
15            PERIOD                    SYD DEPRECIATION
16            ========                  ================
17              1                         $3,600.00
18              2                         $2,700.00
19              3                         $1,800.00
20              4                           $900.00
01-Jan-88  10:12 AM
```

Figure 10-11 Double-Declining-Balance Depreciation

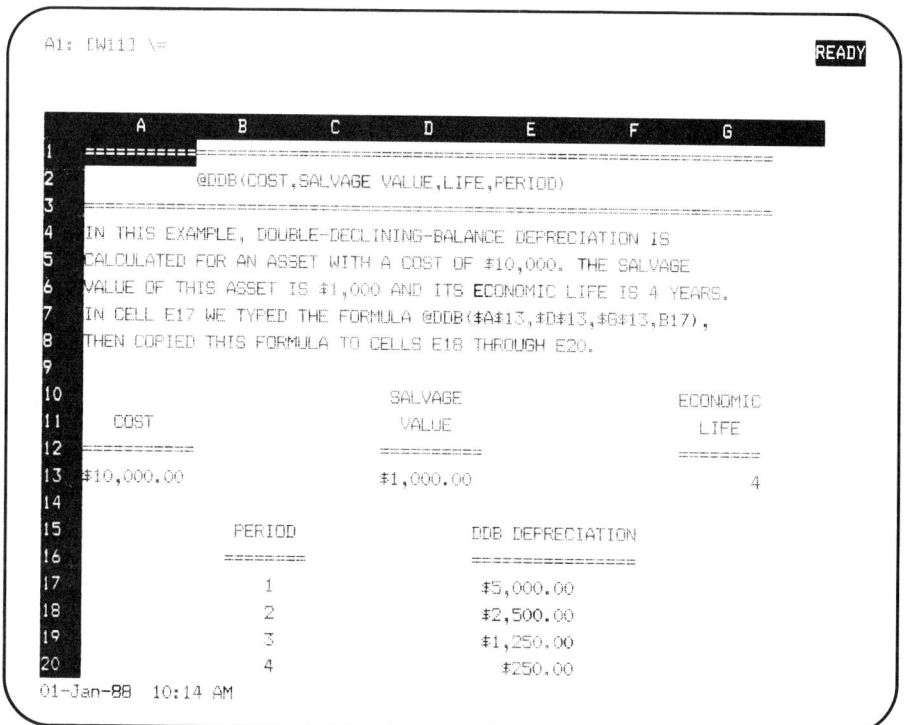

```
A1: [W11] \=                                                              READY


        A         B         C         D         E         F         G
1  ===========
2                          @DDB(COST,SALVAGE VALUE,LIFE,PERIOD)
3
4  IN THIS EXAMPLE, DOUBLE-DECLINING-BALANCE DEPRECIATION IS
5  CALCULATED FOR AN ASSET WITH A COST OF $10,000. THE SALVAGE
6  VALUE OF THIS ASSET IS $1,000 AND ITS ECONOMIC LIFE IS 4 YEARS.
7  IN CELL E17 WE TYPED THE FORMULA @DDB($A$13,$D$13,$G$13,B17),
8  THEN COPIED THIS FORMULA TO CELLS E18 THROUGH E20.
9
10                             SALVAGE                      ECONOMIC
11     COST                     VALUE                         LIFE
12  ===========              ===========                   ==========
13 $10,000.00               $1,000.00                         4
14
15            PERIOD                    DDB DEPRECIATION
16            ========                  ================
17              1                         $5,000.00
18              2                         $2,500.00
19              3                         $1,250.00
20              4                           $250.00
01-Jan-88  10:14 AM
```

10-6 Statistical Functions

Lotus offers seven statistical functions. All except the @COUNT function accept both numeric and range values for arguments. The @COUNT function accepts numeric as well as string values. In all these functions arguments can be a single address or group addresses. For example, @SUM (A1..A9, B5, ASSET) is valid.

Lotus considers a blank cell used as an argument in the list as the value zero.

10-6-1 @AVG(range)

This function calculates the average of all values included in the list or range. Examples: @AVG (A1..A15) or @AVG(Asset).

If you do not want to use the @AVG function you can use its equivalent, which is @SUM(range)/@COUNT(range).

10-6-2 @COUNT(range)

This function counts the number of occupied (nonblank) cells in the range. For example, if cells A1, A2, and A5 are occupied, @COUNT(A1..A5) = 3. If range includes only blank cells, the result is zero; for example, if cells A1 through A5 are all empty, @COUNT(A1..A5) = 0. However, if you use @COUNT(A10), even if A10 is empty, you still receive 1.

10-6-3 @MAX(range)

This function returns the maximum value in the range.

10-6-4 @MIN(range)

This function returns the minimum value in the range.

10-6-5 @STD(range)

This function calculates the standard deviation of the values included in the range. The standard deviation is the square root of the variance, a measure of deviation around the mean. If you deal with two populations, let us say two sales regions, and their mean (average) is equal, the one with smaller standard deviation is considered to be a more harmonic population. Lotus uses the following formula for standard deviation calculations:

$$\sqrt{\frac{(\text{Value i - average})^2}{n}} \quad \text{where} \quad \begin{array}{ll} n & = \text{number of items in the range} \\ \text{value i} & = \text{the } i\text{th item in the range} \end{array}$$

10-6-6 @SUM(range)

This function calculates the sum of all values in the range.

10-6-7 @VAR(range)

This function computes the variance of the values included in the range. Lotus uses the following formula in this function:

```
C7: '@SUM(A7..A19)   =                                                    READY

         A      B      C       D       E       F       G
1   =======================================================================
2   IN THIS EXAMPLE, THE STATISTICAL FUNCTIONS BELOW WILL BE
3   CALCULATED.
4   =======================================================================
5
6
7       -500        @SUM(A7..A19)   =      1300
8       -400
9       -300        @AVG(A7..A19)   =       100
10      -200
11      -100        @MIN(A7..A19)   =      -500
12         0
13       100        @MAX(A7..A19)   =       700
14       200
15       300        @VAR(A7..A19)   =     140000
16       400
17       500        @STD(A7..A19)   =   374.16573
18       600
19       700        @COUNT(A7..A19) =        13
20
01-Jan-88   01:21 PM
```

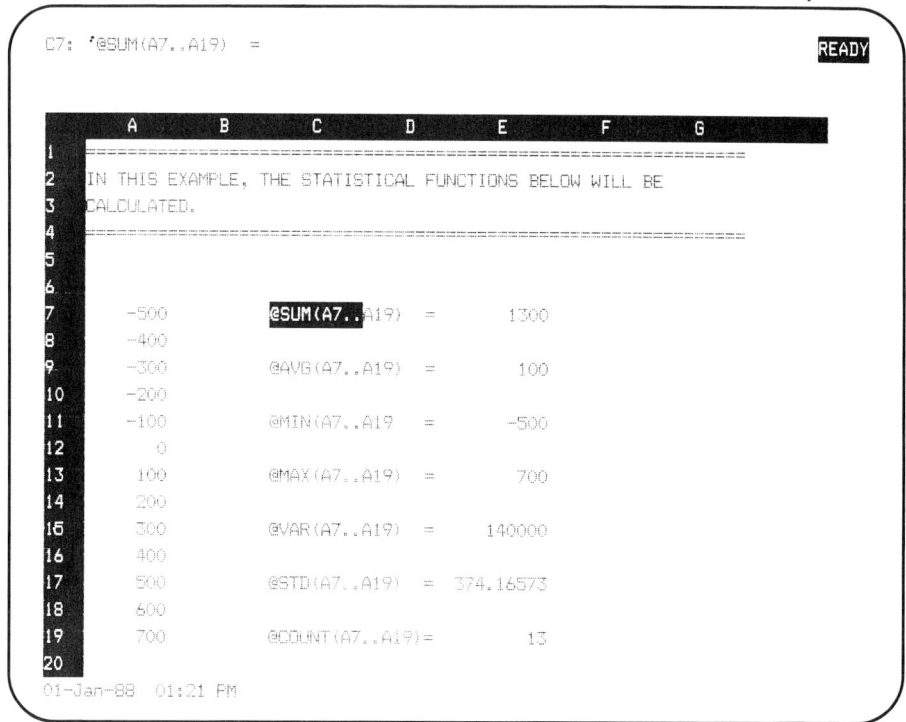

Figure 10-12 Statistical Functions

$$\sum \frac{(\text{Value i - average})^2}{n} \text{ where Value i } \quad = \text{ the } i\text{th item in the range}$$
$$n \quad = \text{ number of items in the range}$$

The formulas for variance and standard deviation are for a population (the entire group). To calculate the variance and standard deviation of the sample (random sample), use the following formulas:

Variance   = @COUNT(range)/(@COUNT(range)-1) * @VAR (range)

Standard Deviation = @SQRT(@COUNT(range)/(@COUNT(range)-1))* @STD(range)

Figure 10-12 illustrates an example of these seven statistical functions.

Summary

In this chapter we reviewed three groups of Lotus functions: mathematical, financial, and statistical. These functions can be very helpful for a variety of applications in different fields. In the next chapter we will talk about more advanced functions offered by Lotus.

Review Questions

1. What is a Lotus function?
2.* What is the major task performed by a Lotus function?
3. How many groups of functions are offered by Lotus?
4. What is a function argument?
5. How many types of arguments are accepted by Lotus?
6.* What is an invalid argument?
7. Do all Lotus functions require arguments?
8.* What is one use of @ABS function?
9. What are some of the uses of the @INT function?
10.* Can you do rounding with the @INT function?
11. What does the @MOD function do?
12. The @RAND function has many business applications. Name three of these applications.
13.* If you do not want to use the @SQRT function, for example, @SQRT(B10), what is its equivalent?
14.* What are some of the applications of the @FV and @PV functions?
15. In general, is a higher or lower @IRR more desirable for any project?
16.* What is the difference between the @PV and @NPV functions?
17. If you are trying to buy a house, which function in this chapter can help you the most? Why?
18. What is the difference between the @CTERM and @TERM function?
19. What depreciation method assumes an accelerated rate in the first few years of its life?
20. How many statistical functions are offered by Lotus?
21. One statistical function allows for a string argument. Which one?
22. What is the difference between variance and standard deviation of a population and a random sample?
23. Using the @RAND function, generate five random numbers between 100 and 200.
24. What is the IRR of a project with the following cash flows:
   -500,000, -300,000, -50,000, 32,000, 200,000, 700,000
25. What is the NPV of the above project with the calculated IRR from Question 24?
26. Let us say the IRR of a project is 15 percent. What is the NPV of this project with a 15 percent interest rate?
27. Perform the seven statistical functions on the following data:
   10, 15, 20, 90, 60, 70, 85, 5, 85
28. What is the future value of a pension plan over 30 years with a $1,500 payment, if the interest rate is 8.25 percent?
29. What is the NPV of a portfolio with the following cash flows (interest rate is 10 percent):
   -25,000, -22,000, 1,000, 20,000, 36,000, 40,000
30. If you buy a car for $30,000, with no down payment and a fixed interest rate of 9.25 percent, how much is your payment in a five-year agreement?
31. Using the straight-line method, how much is the yearly depreciation of a piece

of equipment with an original price of $10,000, a salvage value of $2,000, and six years' economic life?

32. How much is the depreciation for the next six periods using sum-of-the-years'-digits depreciation?

33. Using the double-declining-balance method, how much is the depreciation for the next six periods?

Misconceptions and Solutions

M - Usually the interest rate in a mortgage problem is stated as yearly and the payment is monthly. Using yearly interest rate and monthly payment will cause mistakes in payment calculation.

S - Divide the yearly interest rate by 12 and multiply the number of years by 12. This adjustment will calculate the correct payment.

M - You are entering a function. When you try to enter the function by pressing the **Return** key, Lotus gives you a beep.

S - Check the syntax of any @ functions that you have used to make sure you have typed the name and the syntax of the function correctly.

11

Functions/Part Two

11-1 Introduction

In this chapter we will explain logical, string, date and time, and special functions with numerous examples. Database statistical functions will be discussed in Chapter 15.

11-2 Logical Functions

Lotus offers seven logical functions that generate values based on the results of conditional statements. When you use logical functions, remember that a blank cell has the value of zero. If you use a range name that represents a multiple cell range, Lotus examines the upper left corner cell.

11-2-1 @FALSE

This function returns the logical value zero. For example, if you type @FALSE in cell A1, you will get zero.

11-2-2 @IF(condition,A,B)

The condition must be a numeric value or one that results in a numeric value. The function returns the value A if the condition is true or the value B if the condition is false. Examples:

@IF(3<0,"F","T")   T
@IF(3>0,"T","F")   T
@IF(3<5,10,-50)   10
@IF((10+5)/2<10,"T","F") T

This function has many applications in macro design and use, including designing loops (doing a process for certain number of times) and conditional branching (transfer to a particular cell depending on a condition).

11-2-3 @ISERR(A)

This function examines cell A to see if it contains the value ERR. The function will return one if cell A contains the value ERR; otherwise it returns zero. Examples:

@ISERR(5/0) =   1
@ISERR(2/2) =   0

In the first example the value 1 is returned because 5/0 is invalid.

11-2-4 @ISNA(A)

This function tests A to see if it contains the value NA (not available). The function returns one if A contains the value NA; otherwise, it returns zero. Let us say in cell A15 we have stored function @NA, @ISNA(A15) = 1, and @ISNA(A16) = 0. Cell A16 can contain anything except @NA. This function is used to show a particular number is not available to calculate a formula, therefore it shows NA in the current cell and in all other cells that depend on a particular formula. This is useful for building worksheets when they need values that are not yet defined.

11-2-5 @ISNUMBER(A)

This function tests cell A to see if it contains a numeric value. The function returns one if cell A contains a number or a calculation (formula) resulting in a numeric value; otherwise it returns zero. Examples:

@ISNUMBER(5)   =   1
@ISNUMBER("7")   =   0
@ISNUMBER(68/8+@SQRT(16)) =   1
@ISNUMBER("PORTLAND")   =   0

11-2-6 @ISSTRING(A)

This function is similar to @ISNUMBER(A), but it tests for a string. It returns one if A is a string, otherwise it returns zero. Examples:

@ISSTRING(7)   =   0
@ISSTRING("LOTUS")   =   1

11-2-7 @TRUE

This function returns the logical value one. Let us assume cell A10 contains the string "BASIC". Then @IF(A10="BASIC",@TRUE,@FALSE) = 1, so TRUE or 1 are the same.

11-3 String Functions

Lotus offers 19 string functions that are extremely helpful for nonnumeric manipulations. If a string is used as an argument, it must be enclosed in a pair of quotation marks. The characters of strings enclosed in quotation marks are numbered starting from zero. For example, string "DISK" is numbered from zero to 3.

11-3-1 @CHAR(A)

Argument A can be any numeric value between 0 and 255. The function returns the ASCII/LICS character corresponding to the number A (see Appendix F). For values outside this range, you get ERR. If your argument is a decimal, Lotus will convert it to an integer. Examples:

@CHAR(77)	=	M
@CHAR(100)	=	d
@CHAR(81.5)	=	Q
@CHAR(280)	=	ERR

(ASCII, American Standard Code for Information Interchange, is a data presentation code accepted by a majority of computer manufacturers. LICS, Lotus International Character Set, includes numbers 0 to 255 for all the codes and characters accepted by Lotus.)

11-3-2 @CODE(string)

This function returns the ASCII/LICS code number for the first character in the string (argument). If the argument is not a string, you will get ERR. Examples:

@CODE("TEST")	=	84
@CODE("T")	=	84
@CODE("PASCAL")	=	80
@CODE("JONES")	=	74
@CODE(65)	=	ERR

11-3-3 @CLEAN(string)

Strings imported with the /File Import command, especially if they are imported by modem from a different site, may contain nonprintable characters or noise (ASCII codes below 32). This function eliminates the nonprintable characters from the strings. The argument of this function must be a string value or a cell address that contains a string value. The cell address cannot be a range.

11-3-4 @EXACT(String1,String2)

This function compares two strings to see if they are identical. If they are, the function returns one, otherwise it returns zero. Remember, uppercase and lowercase characters are different. Both arguments must be strings, otherwise you get ERR. Examples:

@EXACT("TRYOUT","TRYOUT") = 1

```
@EXACT("TRYOUT","TRYUT")        = 0
@EXACT("555","555")             = 1
@EXACT("555",555)               = ERR
```

11-3-5 @FIND(Search String,String,Start Number)

This function searches for a string starting from a specified position. It returns the exact position of the first occurrence of the desired string. If the search fails, you get ERR. The starting number must be either zero or positive. If the starting number is not an integer, Lotus considers only the integer part. Examples:

```
@FIND("LOTUS","LOTUS IS POWERFUL",0) = 0
@FIND("LOTUS","ONE OF THE BEST SPREADSHEETS IS LOTUS",10)
= 32
@FIND("HAPPY","WE HAVE LEARNED SO MUCH ALREADY",0) =
ERR
@FIND("M", "I HAD A GOOD MONTH IN MEXICO",15.6) = 22
```

11-3-6 @LEFT(String,m)

This function returns the first m characters in the string. Examples:

```
@LEFT("COBOL",3)                = COB
@LEFT("HAPPINESS IS HERE",5)    = HAPPI
```

11-3-7 @LENGTH(String)

This function returns the number of characters included in the string. Examples:

```
@LENGTH("LESSON")               = 6
@LENGTH("YESTERDAY WAS SUNNY")  = 19
@LENGTH("")                     = 0
@LENGTH(555)                    = ERR
```

11-3-8 @LOWER(String)

This function converts all the letters in the string to lowercase. Examples:

```
@LOWER("Portland")      = portland
@LOWER("PORTLAND")      = portland
```

11-3-9 @MID(String,Start Number,m)

This function extracts m characters from a string after skipping the start number characters. Examples:

```
@MID("JACKSON",2,5)              =      CKSON
@MID("I AM GOING HOME NOW",6,60) =      OING HOME NOW
@MID("LOTUS DOES GRAPHICS",0,5)  =      LOTUS
```

11-3-10 @N(RANGE)

This function returns the value of the upper left corner of a particular range as a number. For example, if values 100, 200, 300, and 400 are stored in cells A1, A2, A3, and A4, then @N(A2..A4) will return 200.

11-3-11 @PROPER(String)

This function puts a string into proper order by converting the first letter of each word to a capital letter and the rest to lowercase letters. Examples:

@PROPER("SUSAN BROWN")   =   Susan Brown
@PROPER("Susan BROWN")   =   Susan Brown

11-3-12 @REPEAT(String,m)

This function repeats a particular string m times. Examples:

@REPEAT("HB",2)   =   HBHB
@REPEAT("BH",1)   =   BH
@REPEAT("I AM HAPPY",2)   =   I AM HAPPY I AM HAPPY

11-3-13 @REPLACE(Original String, Start Number,m, New String)

This function removes m characters in an original string beginning at start number and then inserts new string in the same position in the original string. Examples:

@REPLACE("ATTENTION",1,3,"XXXXX")   =   AXXXXXNTION
@REPLACE("ATTENTION",1,-1,11XXXXX)   =   ERR

In the first example, position zero is at A, position one is at T, so TTE will be removed and five Xs will be inserted. The second example is invalid. Why?

11-3-14 @RIGHT(String,m)

M must be >= 1. The function returns the last m characters in a particular string. Examples:

@RIGHT("FORTRAN",3)   =   RAN
@RIGHT("DATABASE",1)   =   E

11-3-15 @S(Range)

This function returns the value in the upper left corner cell of the range as a string value (if the cell contains a value). For example, if cells A1, A2, A3, and A4 contain strings SUE, JACKSON, BOB, and JACK, the following can be seen:

@S(!A1)   =   SUE
@S(A2..A3)   =   JACKSON
@S(A1..A4)   =   SUE

11-3-16 @STRING(Y,m)

In this function, m specifies the number of decimal places from 0 to 15. M must be >= 0. The function converts a number Y to a string with m places to the right of the decimal point. In order to convert a string to its numeric equivalent, use @VALUE. Examples:

@STRING(125.8735,3)	=	125.874
@STRING(125.87,0)	=	126
@STRING(125.87,-1)	=	ERR

11-3-17 @TRIM(String)

This function eliminates excess space characters from a particular string. Examples:

@TRIM("IT   HAS   BEEN   A   LONG   DAY")   = IT HAS BEEN A LONG DAY
@TRIM("THIS   IS   A   TEST")   = THIS IS A TEST

11-3-18 @UPPER(String)

This function converts all the letters in a string to uppercase. Examples:

@UPPER("First Computer")	=	FIRST COMPUTER
@UPPER("happy")	=	HAPPY

11-3-19 @VALUE(String)

This function converts a string to a numeric value. Examples:

@VALUE("12 4/3")	=	13.3333333333
@VALUE("1.567E+5")	=	156700
@VALUE("15.55")	=	15.55
@VALUE("-10/-2*2")	=	ERR

11-4 Date and Time Functions

Lotus offers 11 date and time functions. These functions generate or use numbers to represent dates and times, so that you can use them in calculations. Before you use these functions, remember the following:

1. Any date between January 1, 1900 and December 31, 2099 inclusive is valid and has an equivalent integer serial number.
2. The first serial number is 1, the last is 73050.
3. January 1, 1900 is equivalent to 1 and December 31, 2099 is equivalent to 73050.
4. Each hour of the day has a serial number as well, e.g., midnight = 0, noon = .50, etc.

5. The following functions generate serial numbers: @DATE, @DATEVALUE, @NOW, @TIME, and @TIMEVALUE

6. The following functions use serial numbers: @DAY, @MONTH, @YEAR, @HOUR, @MINUTE, and @SECOND

11-4-1   @DATE(Year,Month,Day)

This function returns the serial number corresponding to a certain year, month, or day. Remember, since there was no February 29, 1900 (we did not have leap year then), Lotus assigns a date number to this particular day. This does not invalidate any of your calculations, unless you use any dates between January 1 and March, 1, 1900. (Remember, D1 through D5 are five date options provided by Lotus, discussed in Chapter 7.) Examples:

@DATE(87,7,1)	=	31959	Equivalent in D1	=	01-Jul-87
@DATE(86,12,1)	=	31747	" " D2	=	01-DEC
@DATE(87,6,1)	=	31929	" " D3	=	Jun-87
@DATE(87,10,1)	=	32051	" " D4	=	10/01/87
@DATE(87,10,1)	=	32051	" " D5	=	10/01

11-4-2   @DATEVALUE(Date String)

This function, similar to @DATE, returns the serial number of a date written as a string. The difference is that @DATEVALUE uses a single string value as its argument. The date string must be in one of the five date formats discussed in section 7-10. Examples:

@DATEVALUE("01-JUL-87") =	31959
@DATEVALUE("01-DEC") =	29556
@DATEVALUE("JUN-87") =	31929
@DATEVALUE("10/01/87") =	32051
@DATEVALUE("02-JUN-86") =	32565

11-4-3   @DAY(Date Number)

This function returns the day of the month (1 through 31) of the argument. Examples:

@DAY(@DATE(87,9,1)) =	1
@DAY(31700) =	15

11-4-4   @MONTH(Date Number)

This function returns a month (1 through 12) of the year in the string. Examples:

@MONTH(DATE(87,9,1)) =	9
@MONTH(31625) =	8

11-4-5   @YEAR(Date Number)

This function returns any year between 0 to 199 of the argument. Examples:

@YEAR(@DATEVALUE("1-SEP-87")) =	87

@YEAR(31629)   =   86

11-4-6   @NOW

This function returns the current date and time. Example:

We typed @NOW on our Lotus worksheet. The function returned 29221.02, indicating January 1, 1980 at 12:36 A.M. The integer part is the date and the decimal portion is the time.

Other examples:

@INT(@NOW)   = 29221
@YEAR(29221)   = 80
@MONTH(29221)   = 1
@DAY(29221)   = 1

One good application of the @NOW function is to generate the serial number for DATE function. Assume that during the log-on time you have entered the correct date and time to the computer. Now, you can convert this serial number to any of the five Date formats.

To generate the time portion, you should do the following:

@NOW-@INT(@NOW), then use any of the four TIME formats.

11-4-7   @TIME(Hour,Minute,Second)

In this function hour must be between 0 and 23, minute must be between 0 and 59 and second must be between 0 and 59. The function returns a serial number between 0 and 1 for hour, minute, and second. The serial number is a fraction of a day. Examples: (Remember T1 through T4 are hour time options provided by Lotus, discussed in Chapter 7)

@TIME(10,52,40)   =   0.453240 is equal to   10:52:40 A.M..   T1
@TIME(2,10,59)   =   0.90960 "   "   "   02:10 A.M.   T2
@TIME(22,50,50)   =   0.951967 "   "   "   22:50:50   T3
@TIME(23,45,10)   =   0.989699 "   "   "   23:45   T4
@TIME(30,30,30)   =   ERR

11-4-8   @TIMEVALUE(Time String)

This function returns a serial time number for the string. It is similar to @TIME except that the argument here is only one string. The time string must be in one of the four accepted Lotus time formats (discussed in section 7-11) and must be enclosed in double quotes. Examples:

@TIMEVALUE("12:30:45") = 0.5213541667
@TIMEVALUE("12:30")   = 0.5208333333

11-4-9 @HOUR(Time Number)

This function extracts and returns the hour from a time number. The returned value is between 0 and 23; 0 refers to midnight and 23 to 11:00 P.M. Examples:

@HOUR(0.1876736111) =   4
@HOUR(31774.5)   =   12

11-4-10 @MINUTE(Time Number)

This function extracts and returns the minutes from a time number. The returned value is between 0 and 59. Examples:

@MINUTE(0.1567)   =   45
@MINUTE(12)   =   0

11-4-11 @SECOND(Time Number)

This function extracts and returns the seconds from a time number. The returned value is between 0 and 59. Examples:

@SECOND(0.639)   =   10
@SECOND(@TIME(10,10,10))   =   10

11-5 Special Functions

Lotus offers 11 special functions, most of which are used for searching for a value in a table.

11-5-1 @@(Cell Address)

The argument of this function can be a cell address written as a label, a range name, or a string formula whose value is a cell address or cell name. This function returns the content of the cell referenced by the cell address. Let us say cell A10 contains label H20 and cell H20 contains 200. Then @@(A10) returns 200.

11-5-2 @CELL(Attribute,Range)

This function returns the attribute of a cell or range from the attribute table (see Table 11-1). The attribute must be enclosed in double quotation marks; uppercase or lowercase does not matter. If you use a single cell as range, you must express it as a range (A1..A1 or !A1). If the range includes more than one cell, Lotus uses the upper left corner of the given range. To update cell attributes, you must press F9, the **CALC** function key. Figure 11-1 illustrates the following examples of this function:

@CELL("row",A10..A10)   =   10
@CELL("ADDRESS",A3..A3) = $A$3
@CELL("CONTENTS",!A7)   =   HELLO

@CELL("FORMAT",!A10)	=	G
@CELL("PREFIX",!A5)	=	"
@CELL("WIDTH",!A10)	=	9
@CELL("TYPE",!A3)	=	V

11-5-3 @CELLPOINTER(Attribute)

This function returns attribute information about the current cell. It is very useful for testing the content of a cell; for example, finding out if a cell holds a value or is blank. Examples:

@CELLPOINTER("width") = 9 (by default each column width is 9 characters in length)

If the current row is row 30, then

@CELLPOINTER("ROW")   =   30

11-5-4 @CHOOSE(Y,V0,V1,V2...Vn)

This function uses the numeric value of Y to return an item from the list V0 to Vn. The first value in the list is 0; therefore if Y = 2, @CHOOSE will select the third item. You can have up to 240 numeric or string values in the list. Examples:

Figure 11-1 Sample Worksheet for the @CELL Function

```
A1: 'CONTENT                                                    READY

        A       B       C       D       E       F       G       H
1   CONTENT             Description of a column
2                       This cell is blank
3       555             This cell has a numeric value
4   HARRY               This cell has a label
5     LOTUS             This cell is right-justified
6     HI                This cell is centered
7   HELLO               This cell is protected
8     55.00             This cell is fixed-formatted to 2 decimal places
9   5.00E+03            This cell is scientific-formatted to 2 decimal places
10    19078             This cell shows the date format (D1)
11  2+2                 This cell shows the text format
12                      This cell shows the hidden format
13
14
15
16
17
18
19
20
01-Jan-88  10:15 AM
```

Table 11-1 Attribute Table for the @CELL Function

ATTRIBUTE	THE CALCULATED RESULT
"ADDRESS"	Returns the current cell address, e.g., A10
"COL"	Returns the current column number (1 to 256)
"CONTENTS"	Returns the content of the current cell:
	b for blank cell
	v for numeric value or formula
	L for label or string
"FORMAT"	Returns the current numeric formula of a given address:
	F0 to F15 for fixed, 0 to 15 decimal places
	S0 to S15 for scientific, 0 to 15 decimal places
	C0 to C15 for currency, 0 to 15 decimal places
	G for general
	P0 to P15 for percent
	D1 to D5 for date 1 to date 5 and D6 to D9 for Time 1 to Time 4 format (see Chapter 7)
	T for Text
	A blank if the content of the cell is an empty string, e.g., ""
"PREFIX"	Returns the current label prefix:
	' (apostrophe) for left-justified
	" for right-justified
	∧ for centered
"PROTECT"	Returns the protection status:
	1 if it is protected
	0 if it is not protected
"ROW"	Returns the current row number (1 to 8192)
"TYPE"	Returns the data type in a cell:
	b for blank
	v for numeric value or formula
	L for label or string
"WIDTH"	Returns the current column width (1 to 240)

@CHOOSE(3,10,17,25,29,35,38,41)	=	29
@CHOOSE(0,10,17,25,29,35,38,41)	=	10
@CHOOSE(3,"TONY","SAM","JOE","STEVE")	=	STEVE

11-5-5 @COLS(Range)

This function returns the number of columns in a specific range. Examples:

| @COLS(A1..C1) | = | 3 |
| @COLS(A1..H20) | = | 8 |

11-5-6 @ERR

This function returns the numerical value ERR. This cannot be substituted with the label ERR, e.g., "ERR".

11-5-7 @HLOOKUP(Y,Range,Row Number)

This function performs a horizontal table search beginning with row zero and comparing the value of Y to each cell in the top row of a specified range. As soon as it finds a number larger than Y, it stops and backs up one cell. It moves down the specified row number and returns the content of the appropriate cell. If there is an exact match to Y, the search stops at that cell without backtracking. Then it moves down the specified row number and returns the content of the appropriate cell. If Y (the search value) is smaller than the first value, the function returns ERR. If Y is larger than all the values, the search stops at the last cell in the top row of the range without backtracking. Then it moves down the specified row number and returns the content of the appropriate cell. Remember, the top row of the table used by @HLOOKUP must be sorted in ascending order; this is row 0. Figure 11-2 illustrates this function. Examples:

@HLOOKUP(475,B4..H9,2)	=	12
@HLOOKUP(850,B4..H9,3)	=	15
@HLOOKUP(450,B4..H9,5)	=	20
@HLOOKUP(375,B4..H9,1)	=	18
@HLOOKUP(150,B4..H9,3)	=	ERR

11-5-8 @INDEX(Range, Column Number, Row Number)

This function returns the content of the cell located at the intersection of the column and row number in a specified range. The first row and column numbers are 0. If the argument is out of range (the row or column number is larger than the table), you get an ERR. We have used the data in Figure 11-2 for this function for the following examples:

| @INDEX(A4..H9,0,0) | = | 0 |
| @INDEX(A4..H9,1,2) | = | 13 |

$$@INDEX(A4..H9,5,5) \quad = \quad 16$$
$$@INDEX(A4..H9,5,15) \quad = \quad ERR$$

11-5-9 @NA

This function returns the numeric value NA whenever a particular number is not available in order to complete a formula. The function can be helpful for alerting the user. For example, if cell A10 contains 100, then @IF(A10/2>25,@NA,"I AM BUSY")   =   NA

11-5-10 @ROWS(Range)

This function returns the number of rows in a given range. If we use data from Figure 11-2, we will see the following:

$$@ROWS(A3..D9) \quad = \quad 7$$
$$@ROWS(A6..E4) \quad = \quad 3$$
$$@ROWS(A6..H20) \quad = \quad 15$$

11-5-11 @VLOOKUP(Y, Range, Column Number)

This function, similar to @HLOOKUP, performs a vertical search.

Figure 11-2 Horizontal Table Search with the @HLOOKUP Function

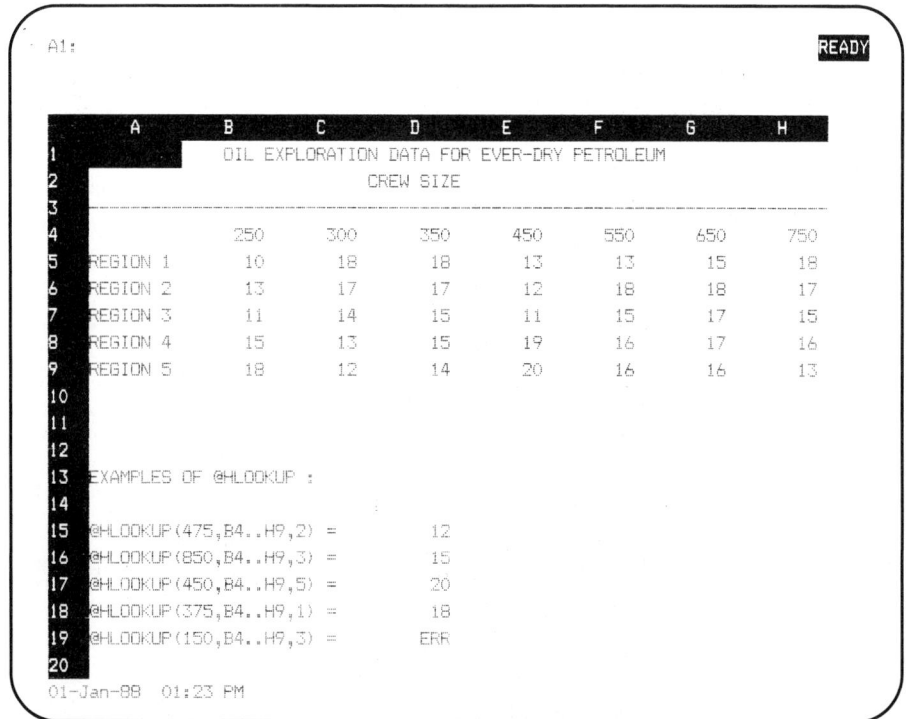

```
A1:                                                                          READY

              A        B        C        D        E        F        G        H
1                     OIL EXPLORATION DATA FOR EVER-DRY PETROLEUM
2                              CREW SIZE
3      ----------------------------------------------------------------------
4                     250      300      350      450      550      650      750
5      REGION 1        10       18       18       13       13       15       18
6      REGION 2        13       17       17       12       18       18       17
7      REGION 3        11       14       15       11       15       17       15
8      REGION 4        15       13       15       19       16       17       16
9      REGION 5        18       12       14       20       16       16       13
10
11
12
13     EXAMPLES OF @HLOOKUP :
14
15     @HLOOKUP(475,B4..H9,2) =         12
16     @HLOOKUP(850,B4..H9,3) =         15
17     @HLOOKUP(450,B4..H9,5) =         20
18     @HLOOKUP(375,B4..H9,1) =         18
19     @HLOOKUP(150,B4..H9,3) =         ERR
20
       01-Jan-88  01:23 PM
```

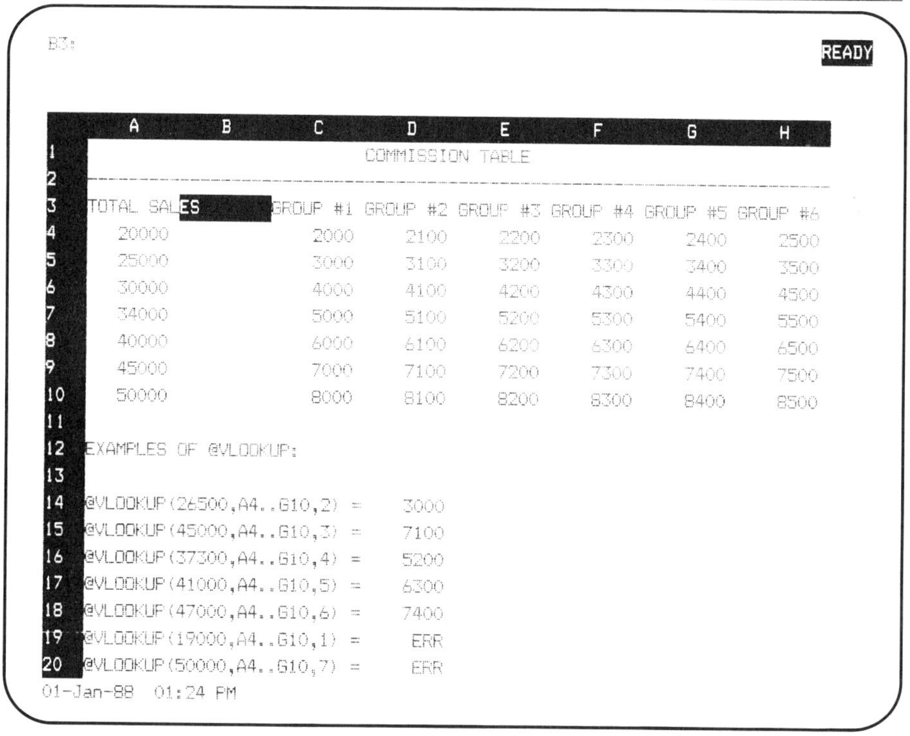

B3: READY

	A	B	C	D	E	F	G	H
1				COMMISSION TABLE				
2								
3	TOTAL SALES		GROUP #1	GROUP #2	GROUP #3	GROUP #4	GROUP #5	GROUP #6
4	20000		2000	2100	2200	2300	2400	2500
5	25000		3000	3100	3200	3300	3400	3500
6	30000		4000	4100	4200	4300	4400	4500
7	34000		5000	5100	5200	5300	5400	5500
8	40000		6000	6100	6200	6300	6400	6500
9	45000		7000	7100	7200	7300	7400	7500
10	50000		8000	8100	8200	8300	8400	8500
11								
12	EXAMPLES OF @VLOOKUP:							
13								
14	@VLOOKUP(26500,A4..G10,2) =			3000				
15	@VLOOKUP(45000,A4..G10,3) =			7100				
16	@VLOOKUP(37300,A4..G10,4) =			5200				
17	@VLOOKUP(41000,A4..G10,5) =			6300				
18	@VLOOKUP(47000,A4..G10,6) =			7400				
19	@VLOOKUP(19000,A4..G10,1) =			ERR				
20	@VLOOKUP(50000,A4..G10,7) =			ERR				

01-Jan-88 01:24 PM

Figure 11-3 Vertical Table Search with the @VLOOKUP Function

The function compares the value of Y to each cell in the first column of a specified range. As soon as it finds a number larger than Y in a cell, it backs up one cell. @VLOOKUP moves across the specified column number and returns the content of the appropriate cell. If there is an exact match to Y, the search stops at the cell (no backup will take place), then moves across the specified column number and returns the content of the appropriate cell. If the search value is smaller than the first value in the search column, the function returns ERR. If Y is larger than all the values, the search stops at the last cell in the first column of the range, then moves across the specified column number and returns the content of the appropriate cell. Remember, the first column in the table is column 0 and the values in the first column (e.g., the index column) must be in ascending order. The following examples are illustrated in Figure 11-3.

@VLOOKUP(26500,A4..G10,2)	=	3000
@VLOOKUP(45000,A4..G10,3)	=	7100
@VLOOKUP(37300,A4..G10,4)	=	5200
@VLOOKUP(41000,A4..G10,5)	=	6300
@VLOOKUP(47000,A4..G10,6)	=	7400
@VLOOKUP(19000,A4..G10,1)	=	ERR
@VLOOKUP(50000,A4..G10,7)	=	ERR

Summary

In this chapter we explained the logical, string, date and time, and special functions. These functions perform numerous operations, mostly for advanced users. As you will see in Chapters 17 and 18, many of these functions can be used effectively with macros.

Review Questions

1. What is the main purpose of logical functions?
2.* What are some of the uses of @ISNUMBER?
3.* What does @CHAR do?
4. What are some of the uses of @EXACT?
5. What are some of the uses of @FIND?
6. What are some of the uses of @LENGTH?
7. What is the main purpose of the @DATE functions?
8.* What is the difference between @DATE and @DATEVALUE?
9. What are some of the uses of @CELL?
10. If the argument of @CELL is "FORMAT", what does this function return?
11. If the argument of @CELL is "PREFIX", what does this function return?
12. What may be returned by @CELLPOINTER?
13.* What is the difference between @HLOOKUP and @VLOOKUP?
14. What is the difference between @INDEX and @HLOOKUP?
15.* What are some of the practical applications of @HLOOKUP and @VLOOKUP?
16. What is the answer to @EXACT("VisiCalc", "Lotus")
17. What is the answer to @LEFT("Database",1)?
18. What is the answer to @LENGTH("Database")?
19. What is the answer to @REPEAT("Lotus",3)?
20. Using Figure 11-2, what are the answers to the following functions:
@HLOOKUP(250,B4..H9,3)   =
@HLOOKUP(275,B4..H9,3)   =
@HLOOKUP(575,B4..H9,5)   =
21. Using Figure 11-3, what are the answers to the following functions:
@VLOOKUP(2000,A4..G10,3)   =
@VLOOKUP(60000,A4..G10,2)   =
@VLOOKUP(47000,A4..G10,5)   =

12

Graphics: Converting Figures into Pictures

12-1 Introduction

In this chapter, we will study the types of graphs generated by Lotus, which include pie charts, bar, line, stacked-bar, and XY graphs. Specific applications of each graph will illustrate its use. In Chapter 13 we will discuss how to print your graph on a graphic printer and/or plotter.

12-2 Why Graphics?

In today's competitive world, business executives and decision makers need to obtain information in the most effective and efficient way. Graphs achieve these goals by condensing massive amounts of data into simple, understandable form.

Lotus generates five different types of graphs:

1. Line graphs show changes in data over time. These graphs are suitable for time series analysis, in which one variable is time and the others could be such items as total sales, total cost, total advertising budget. Using line graphs, you can easily depict budget trends, total sales trends, administrative cost trends, and so forth.

2. Bar graphs emphasize differences between data items. For example, a bar graph can compare the total sales of five products of a particular company, the oil production from five oil wells, or student population of six state universities.

3. XY graphs show relationships between two sets of data. This might be amount of sales and advertising budget, or years of education and yearly income.

4. Pie charts compare parts to the whole. For example, you can compare advertising expenses to total sales expenses.

5. Stacked-bar graphs compare different sets of data by arranging them on top of each other. This helps to visualize the meaning of the data.

There are many graphics packages on the market. Some may offer more variety and more sophistication compared to Lotus graphics. However, since Lotus graphs are based on the data available in the spreadsheet, they can be drawn fast and what-if analysis can be performed quickly. You can change data items, press F10 in Ready mode, and the entire graph will be redrawn immediately.

12-3 Overview of Lotus Graphics

To set up a graph, first invoke Graph from the main menu. The following options will be presented:

Type X A B C D E F   Reset   View   Save   Options   Name   Quit

Type indicates the graphs generated by Lotus: line, bar, XY, stacked-bar, and pie chart.

The X range is used for labeling the X-axis and is also used in the pie chart and the XY graph.

A, B, C, D, E, F indicates six different data ranges, allowing you to plot up to six ranges at the same time in all graphs except the pie chart.

Reset is used if you want to change the graph parameters. This means that all the previous data ranges, settings, and so forth will be erased.

View is used to display the graph on the screen if your computer has graphics capabilities.

Save is used to save a graph to be printed with the PrintGraph program.

Options gives you choices for dressing up your graph.

Name is used to name graph settings. Remember that a single worksheet can generate many different graphs with different names.

Finally, Quit is used to get back to the worksheet.

To create and display a graph, follow this procedure:

1. Select /Graph.
2. Select Type.
3. Select a graph type: line, bar, XY, stacked-bar, or pie chart.
4. Select one or more data ranges (X and/or A through F).
5. Specify the data for each range either by pointing or by typing the address.
6. Select View to display the graph type.
7. Press any key to return to the worksheet and the graph main menu.

12-4 Creating a Simple Pie Chart

Sunset Travel Agency has the following three expenses as part of its operating costs for 1986-1987. Enter the expenses into a worksheet.

Utilities	1850
Rent	1250
Supplies	700

Now plot these expenses using a pie chart.

Figure 12-1 shows this graph. It was generated with the commands /Graph, Type, Pie, X (A4..A6), Return, A (C4..C6), Return, View.

12-5 Saving the Graph Parameters

Once the graph is created, you may give it a name for later reference. In order to save a graph parameter, type /Graph Name Create. You can save a graph parameter under any name having up to 14 characters. After the graph is saved, you can change the parameters and save it under another name if you want. Don't forget to save (/File Save) the worksheet as well, because if you forget to save your worksheet, your graph will be lost. In addition, if you forget to name your graph (/Graph Name Create) and save only your worksheet, your graph will be lost.

To make a graph active (bring it back to memory), use /Graph Name Use. You can have only one graph active at one time. However, a worksheet can generate as many graphs as you want.

Figure 12-1 A Simple Pie Chart

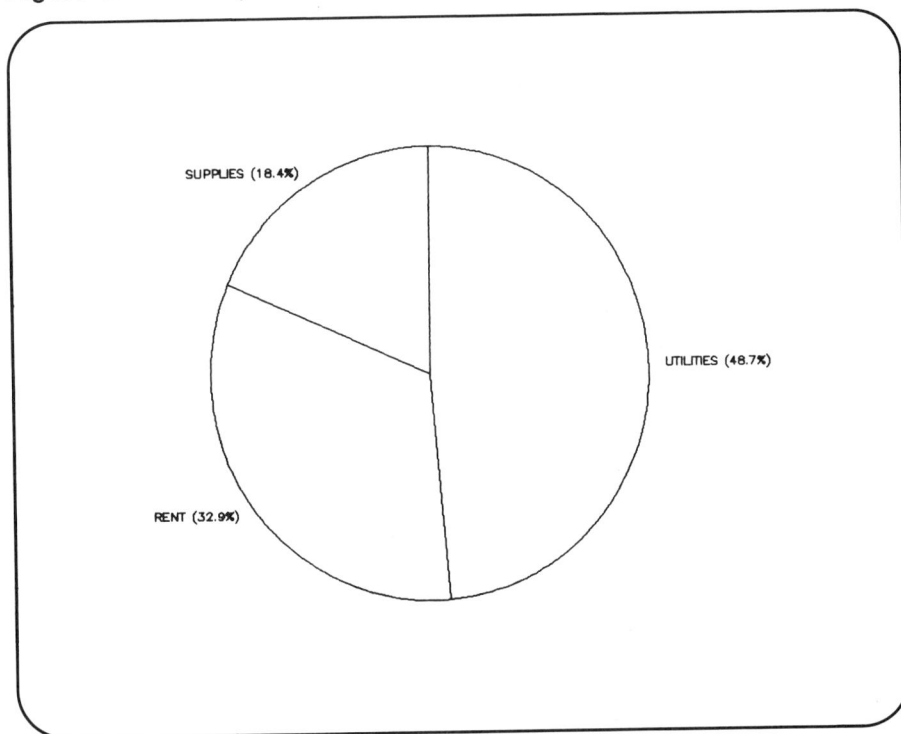

```
B1:  'SUNSET TRAVEL AGENCY                                          READY

          A          B          C          D          E          F          G          H
    1                 SUNSET TRAVEL AGENCY
    2
    3
    4           UTILITIES            1850
    5           RENT                 1250
    6           SUPPLIES              700
    7
    8
    9
   10
   11
   12
   13
   14
   15
   16
   17
   18
   19
   20
   01-Jan-88   12:17 PM
```

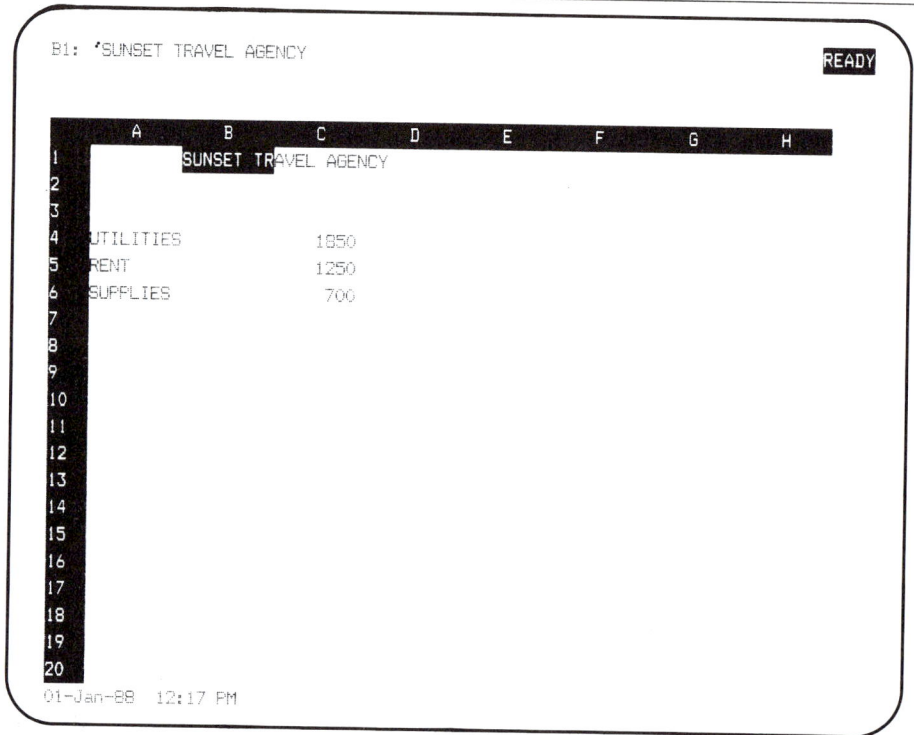

Figure 12-1 (Continued)

12-6 Deleting A Graph

To delete a graph, use /Graph Name Delete. Lotus will display all graph names for the current worksheet. You can either type the name to be deleted or move the cursor to the name and press Return. The graph is deleted. If you want to delete all the graphs under the current worksheet, use /Graph Name Reset. Be careful. When you issue this command all the graphs under the current worksheet will be gone and there is no way to retrieve them.

12-7 Saving a Graph For Printing

The Lotus spreadsheet program is not capable of printing your graph. To print your graph, first you must save it using /Graph Save. Lotus creates a graphic file on your disk with PIC as the extension. Now you can use the PrintGraph disk for printing your graph. When the graph is saved in a graphic file you can access it only from the PrintGraph program.

12-8 Pie Chart – a Second Look

As we mentioned earlier, pie charts are very useful for comparing some data to the whole. To activate the pie chart from the main menu, first select /Graph. Then from the Type menu choose Pie. To draw a pie chart, you need one data range. After you specify your data range, choose View and the graph will appear.

Figure 12-2 shows a pie chart of a simple regional analysis. Sales for each region are compared with total sales. This graph was generated by using /Graph, Type, Pie, X (A11..A13), Return, A (E11..E13), Return, View.

Figure 12-3 uses the same data for a sales performance analysis. This time the performance of each salesperson is compared with total sales. This graph was generated with /Graph, Type, Pie, X (B10..D10), Return, A (B15..D15), Return, View.

Generating a Pie Chart Using Crosshatches

Lotus can generate eight different crosshatches, which make data comparison an easy task. Each crosshatch has its own shape, and with color graphics, each crosshatch has a unique color. (We will discuss color later in this chapter.) Figure 12-4 illustrates these crosshatches. This figure was generated by using the commands /Graph, Type, Pie, X (B2..I2), Return, A (B3..I3), Return, B (B6..I6), Return, View.

To generate a crosshatch, you have to define a separate data range outside your original data range. The location of this new data range is not important. However, you must call this data range the B range. This means you must choose the B range then specify the address of the data in your worksheet. In this data range you can enter any number between 0 to 8 inclusive. Codes 0 or 8 indicate an unshaded wedge.

Regional Analysis Using Crosshatches

In Figure 12-5 we show you another example of the pie chart with crosshatches. This figure performs regional analysis on the data shown in the upper part of the figure. This figure was generated with /Graph, Type, Pie, X (A12..A14), Return, A (E12..E14), Return, B (B18..D18), Return, View.

Exploding A Pie Chart

Sometimes you may be interested in highlighting or "exploding" a portion or portions of a pie chart. Lotus provides you with a facility to perform this task. You can explode one or all portions of your pie chart. To do so, add 100 to the codes of your crosshatches. In Figure 12-6 we added 100 to cell B18. Now this cell contains 101.

This will explode that particular section of the pie with its original crosshatch. This figure was generated with /Graph, Type, Pie, X (A12..A14), Return, A (E12..E14), Return, B (B18..D18), Return, View.

Figure 12-7 illustrates a pie chart with all its components exploded. This figure was generated by using /Graph, Type, Pie, X (A12..A14), Return, A (E12..E14), Return, B (B18..D18), Return, View.

Figure 12-2 Regional Analysis Using a Pie Chart

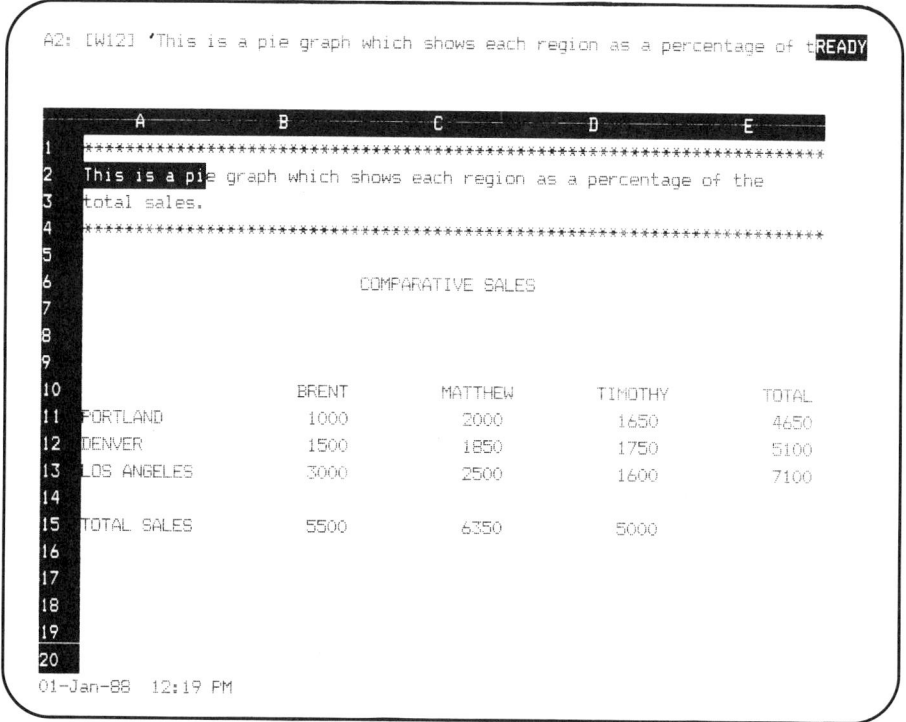

```
A2: [W12] 'This is a pie graph which shows each region as a percentage of t READY

         A            B            C            D            E
1  *****************************************************************************
2  This is a pie graph which shows each region as a percentage of the
3  total sales.
4  *****************************************************************************
5
6                          COMPARATIVE SALES
7
8
9
10                      BRENT        MATTHEW      TIMOTHY        TOTAL
11 PORTLAND             1000         2000         1650          4650
12 DENVER               1500         1850         1750          5100
13 LOS ANGELES          3000         2500         1600          7100
14
15 TOTAL SALES          5500         6350         5000
16
17
18
19
20
01-Jan-88  12:19 PM
```

Figure 12-2 (Continued)

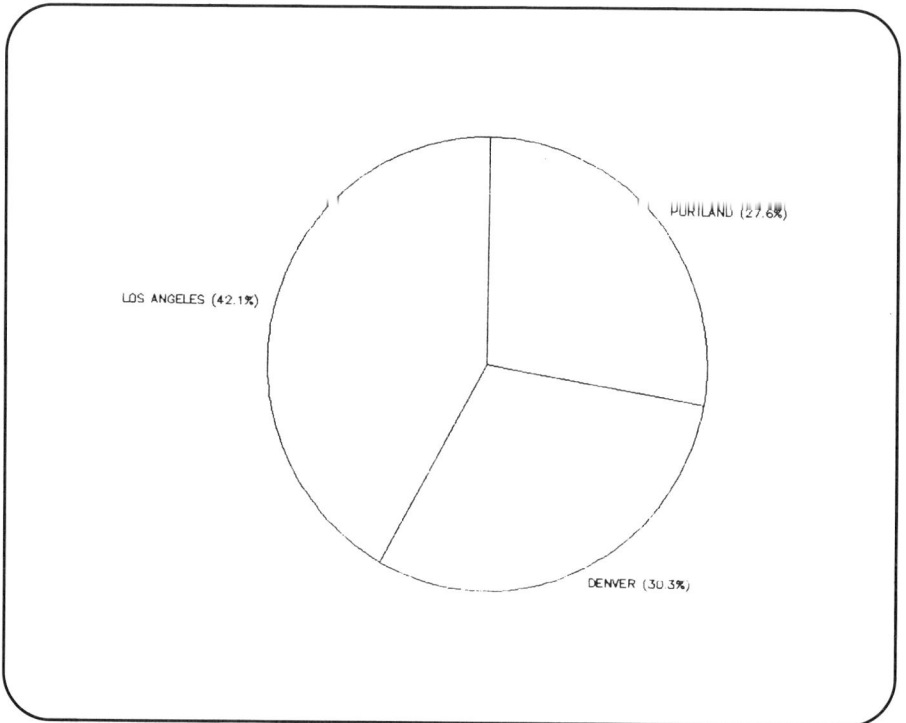

Figure 12-3 Sales Performance Analysis Using a Pie Chart

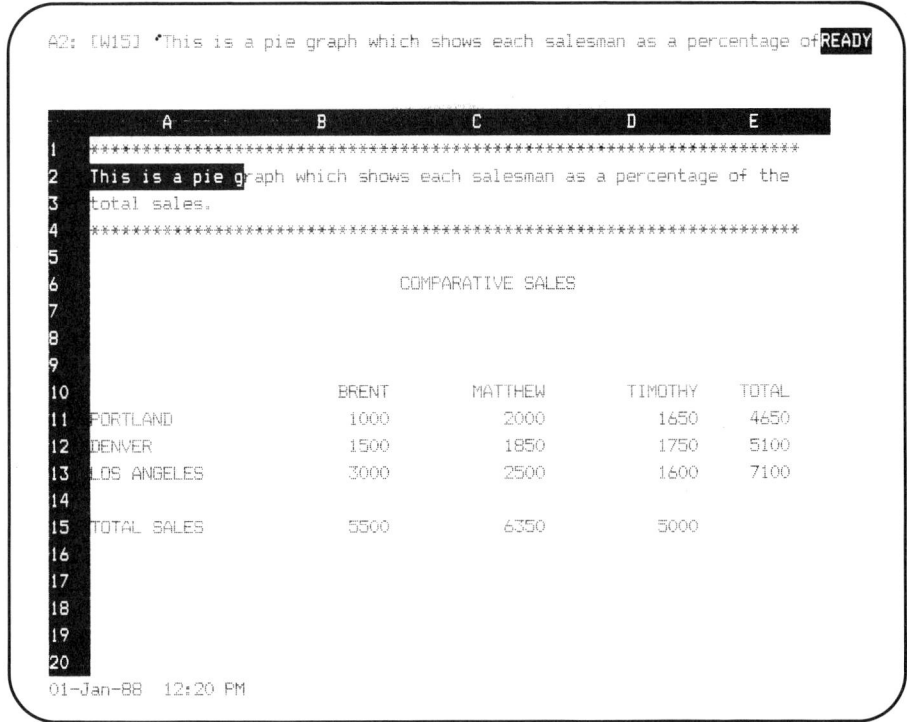

```
A2: [W15] 'This is a pie graph which shows each salesman as a percentage of READY

        A           B           C           D           E
1  ***********************************************************************
2  This is a pie graph which shows each salesman as a percentage of the
3  total sales.
4  ***********************************************************************
5
6                         COMPARATIVE SALES
7
8
9
10                   BRENT       MATTHEW     TIMOTHY     TOTAL
11 PORTLAND          1000        2000        1650        4650
12 DENVER            1500        1850        1750        5100
13 LOS ANGELES       3000        2500        1600        7100
14
15 TOTAL SALES       5500        6350        5000
16
17
18
19
20
01-Jan-88   12:20 PM
```

Figure 12-3 (Continued)

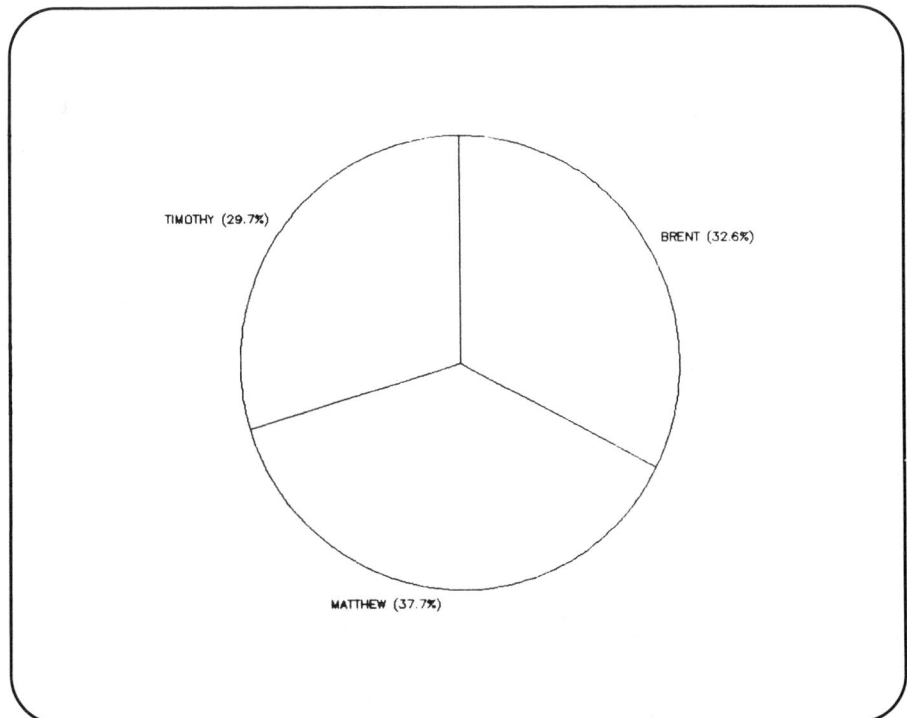

Figure 12-4 Crosshatch Options

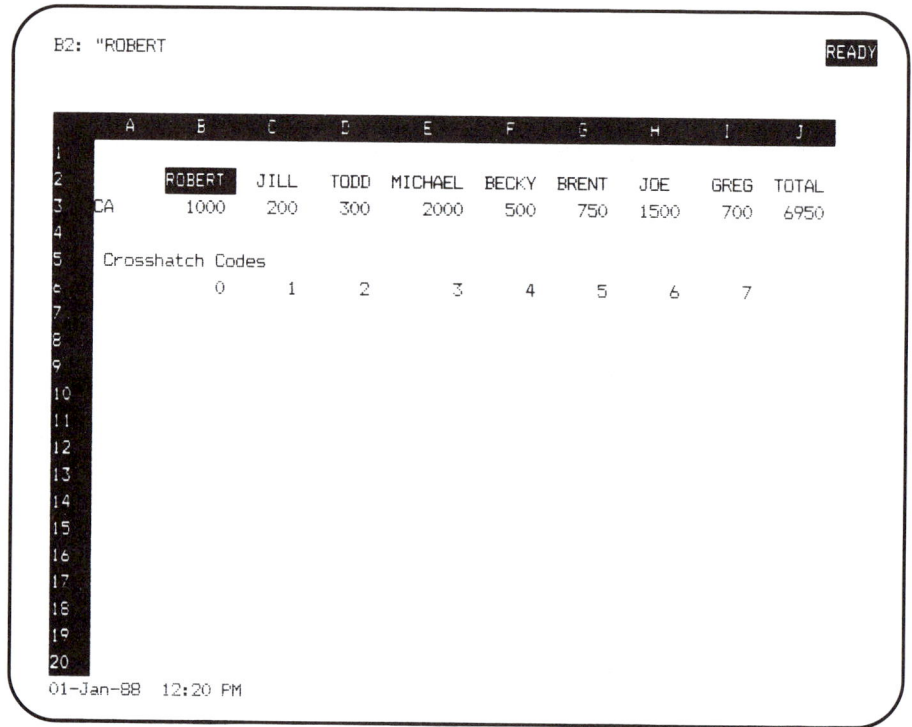

```
B2: "ROBERT                                                              READY

        A      B       C      D        E       F       G       H       I      J
1
2              ROBERT  JILL   TODD    MICHAEL  BECKY   BRENT   JOE     GREG   TOTAL
3    CA        1000    200    300     2000     500     750     1500    700    6950
4
5    Crosshatch Codes
6              0       1      2        3       4       5       6       7
7
8
9
10
11
12
13
14
15
16
17
18
19
20
01-Jan-88   12:20 PM
```

Figure 12-4 (Continued)

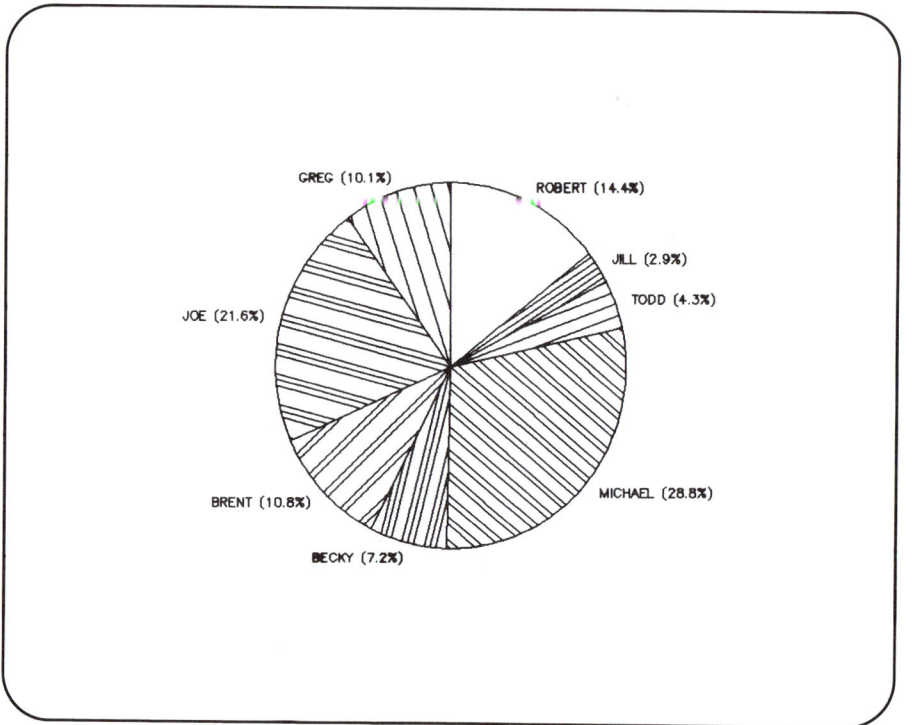

Figure 12-5 Regional Analysis Using Crosshatches

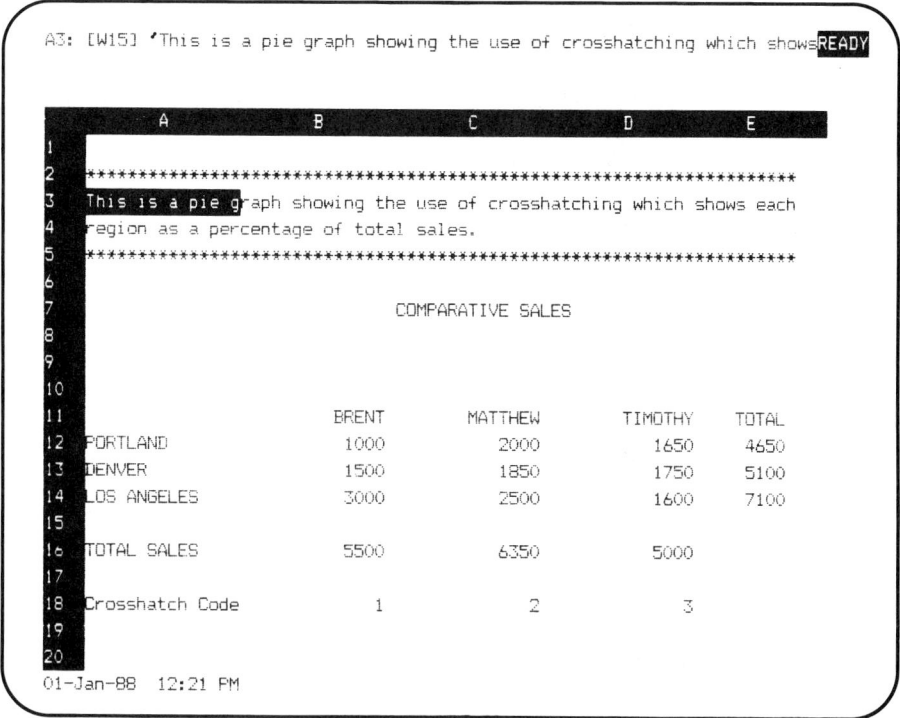

```
A3: [W15] 'This is a pie graph showing the use of crosshatching which shows READY

            A         B           C           D           E
1
2   ****************************************************************
3   This is a pie graph showing the use of crosshatching which shows each
4   region as a percentage of total sales.
5   ****************************************************************
6
7                        COMPARATIVE SALES
8
9
10
11                     BRENT       MATTHEW      TIMOTHY     TOTAL
12  PORTLAND           1000        2000         1650        4650
13  DENVER             1500        1850         1750        5100
14  LOS ANGELES        3000        2500         1600        7100
15
16  TOTAL SALES        5500        6350         5000
17
18  Crosshatch Code      1           2            3
19
20
01-Jan-88   12:21 PM
```

Figure 12-5 (Continued)

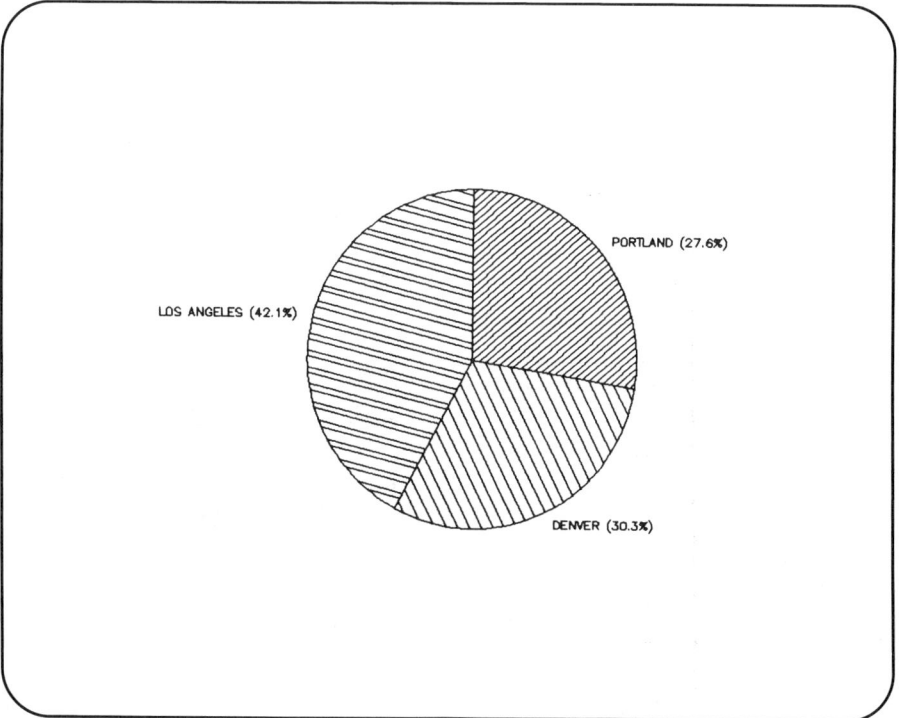

Figure 12-6 Exploding One Section of a Pie Chart

```
A2: [W15] 'This is an exploded pie graph showing region as a percentage of  READY

            A            B            C            D            E
1  ********************************************************************
2  This is an exploded pie graph showing region as a percentage of total
3  sales. To explode a portion, 100 is added to the crosshatch code.
4  ********************************************************************
5
6
7                         COMPARATIVE SALES
8
9
10
11                      BRENT        MATTHEW      TIMOTHY      TOTAL
12 PORTLAND             1000         2000         1650         4650
13 DENVER               1500         1850         1750         5100
14 LOS ANGELES          3000         2500         1600         7100
15
16 TOTAL SALES          5500         6350         5000
17
18 Crosshatch Code      101          2            3
19
20
01-Jan-88  12:22 PM
```

Figure 12-6 (Continued)

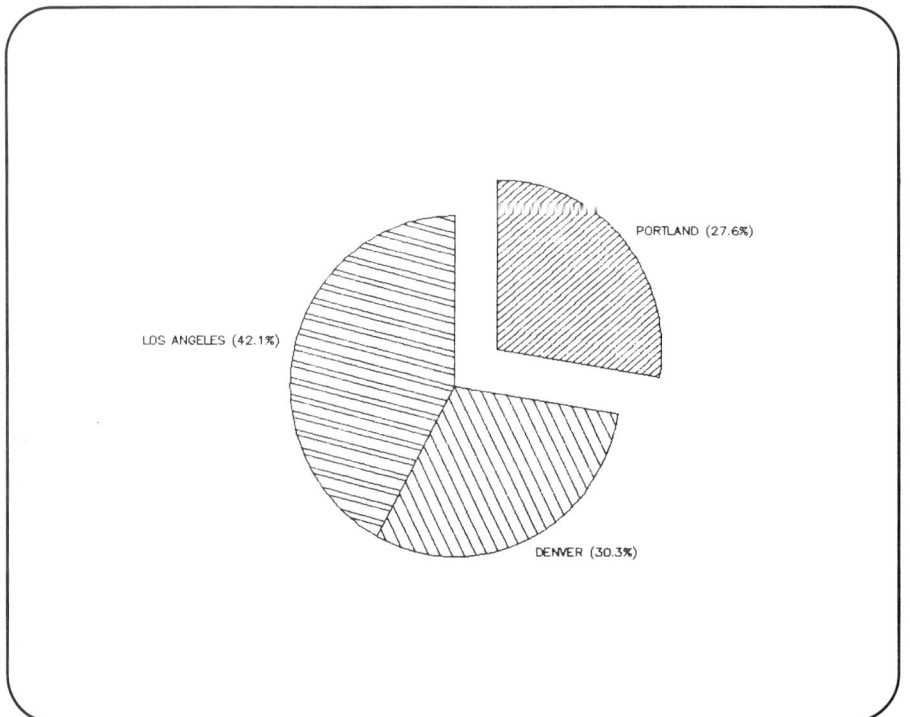

Figure 12-7 Explosion of the Entire Pie Chart

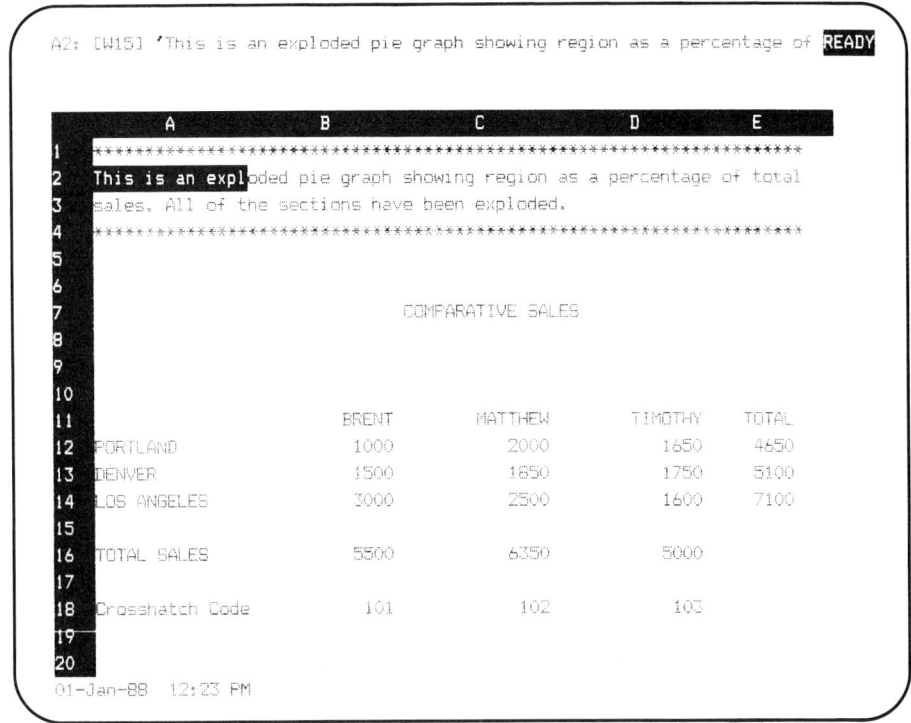

```
A2: [W15] 'This is an exploded pie graph showing region as a percentage of READY

              A            B            C            D            E
1  ***********************************************************************
2  This is an exploded pie graph showing region as a percentage of total
3  sales. All of the sections have been exploded.
4  ***********************************************************************
5
6
7                              COMPARATIVE SALES
8
9
10
11                        BRENT        MATTHEW      TIMOTHY      TOTAL
12 PORTLAND               1000         2000         1650         4650
13 DENVER                 1500         1850         1750         5100
14 LOS ANGELES            3000         2500         1600         7100
15
16 TOTAL SALES            5500         6350         5000
17
18 Crosshatch Code         101          102          103
19
20
01-Jan-88  12:23 PM
```

Figure 12-7 (Continued)

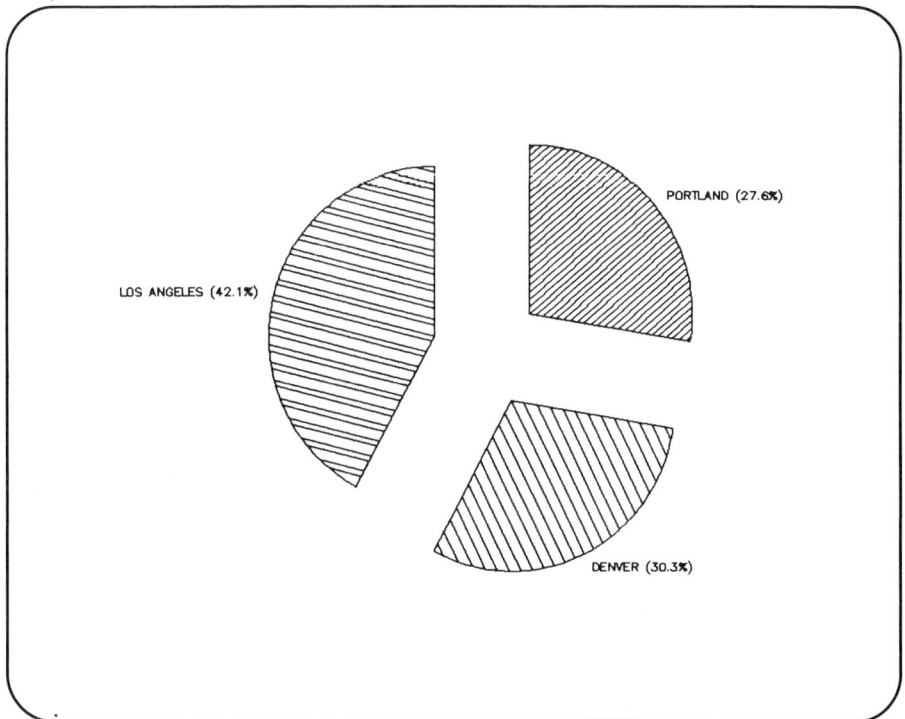

12-9 Bar Graphs

Bar graphs are useful for comparing differences between data items. Lotus allows you to choose up to six data ranges for bar graph presentation. Figure 12-8 is a bar graph showing the performance of three salespersons in three regions. This graph was generated as follows:

/Graph, Type, Bar, X (B10..D10), Return, A (B11..D11), Return, B (B12..D12), Return, C (B13..D13), Return, Options, Titles, First, COMPARATIVE SALES, Return, Titles, Second, FOR THE HAPPY TRAVELER, Return, Titles, X-axis, SALESMEN, Return, Titles, Y-axis, SALES, Return, Legend, A (\A11), Return, Legend, B (\A12), Return, Legend, C (\A13), Return, Quit, View.

As usual, the Graph option was chosen from the main menu. The type chosen was Bar. The X data range can be whatever labels you are interested in showing on the X-axis. In Figure 12-8, we have chosen the names of three salesmen. The A range shows performance of Brent, Matthew, and Timothy in Portland. The B and C ranges show the performances of these three salespersons in Denver and Los Angeles respectively. You can include up to six such labels.

Lotus gives you the option of choosing a title and a subtitle for the graph. Choose Options, then Titles, then First. This is the heading, so we entered COMPARATIVE SALES. To enter this heading, either type it or use a backslash (\) followed by a cell address or a range name containing the heading. In this case, \C6 will do it. The Second option is for the subtitle, which is FOR THE HAPPY TRAVELER.

Now you choose the X-axis. We put SALESMEN on the X-axis and SALES for the Y-axis. To make the presentation clearer, you can choose up to six legends. We chose Legend A for PORTLAND, B for DENVER, and C for LOS ANGELES. These items can be either typed or entered with a backslash followed by the cell reference or range name.

Figure 12-9 is a slightly different version of Figure 12-8. In this figure we display the performance of each region. This figure was generated as follows:

/Graph, Type, Bar, X (A11..A13), Return, A (B11..B13), Return, B (C11..C13), Return, C (D11..D13), Return, Options, Titles, First, COMPARATIVE SALES, Return, Titles, Second, FOR THE HAPPY TRAVELER, Return, Titles, X-axis, REGION, Return, Titles, Y-axis, SALES, Return, Legend, A(\B10), Return, Legend, B(\C10), Return, Legend, C(\D10), Return, Quit, View.

Setting Scale Limits

So far, the graphs we have discussed have been plotted using automatic scaling. This means that Lotus always automatically fits your data in the X and Y axes; for example, your first data item appears first and the last data item appears last. However, there may be cases where you are interested in highlighting a portion of the graph or in changing the automatic scaling. If you issue the command /Graph Options Scale, the following menu will be illustrated:

Y scale   X scale   Skip

Choose Y scale and the following menu will be illustrated:

Automatic   Manual   Lower   Upper   Format   Indicator   Quit

Figure 12-8   Bar Graph for Sales Performance Analysis

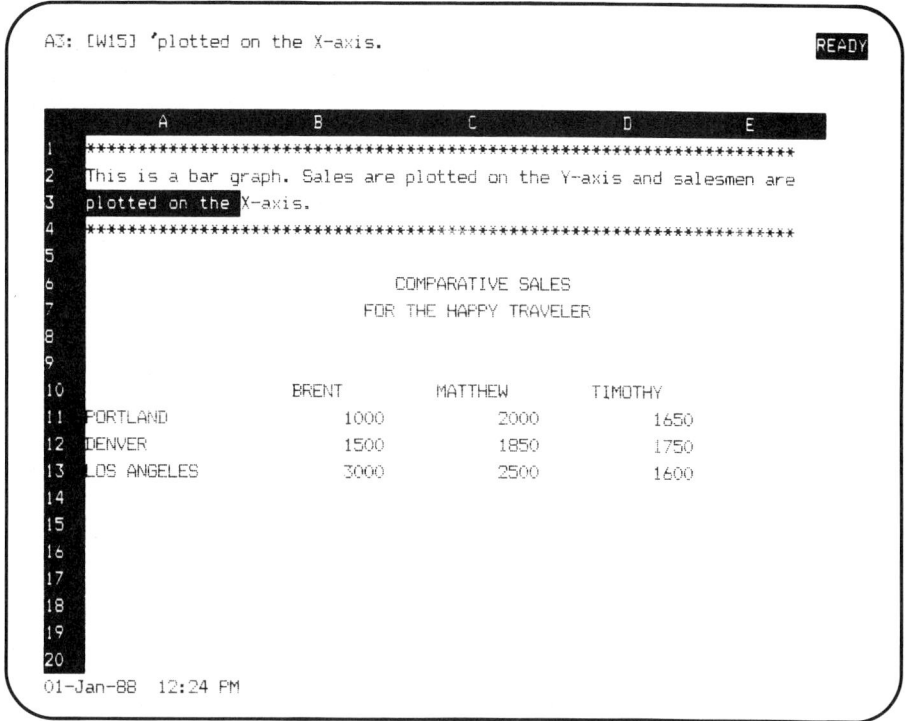

```
A3: [W15] 'plotted on the X-axis.                                    READY

                A           B           C           D           E
1  ****************************************************************
2  This is a bar graph. Sales are plotted on the Y-axis and salesmen are
3  plotted on the X-axis.
4  ****************************************************************
5
6                        COMPARATIVE SALES
7                       FOR THE HAPPY TRAVELER
8
9
10                   BRENT        MATTHEW        TIMOTHY
11 PORTLAND          1000          2000           1650
12 DENVER            1500          1850           1750
13 LOS ANGELES       3000          2500           1600
14
15
16
17
18
19
20
01-Jan-88   12:24 PM
```

Figure 12-8   (Continued)

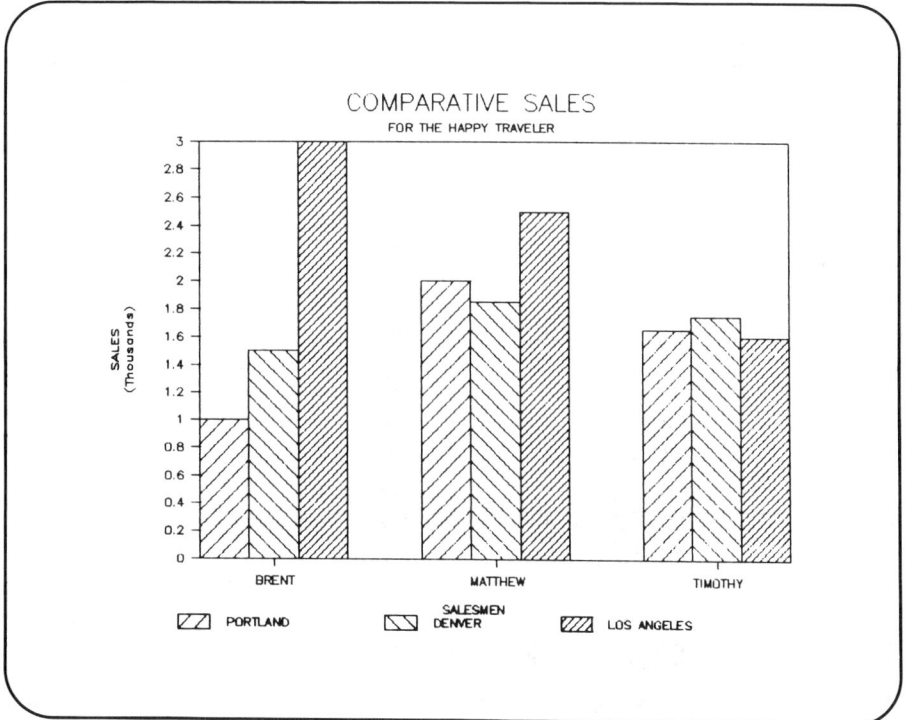

Figure 12-9 Bar Graph for Regional Analysis

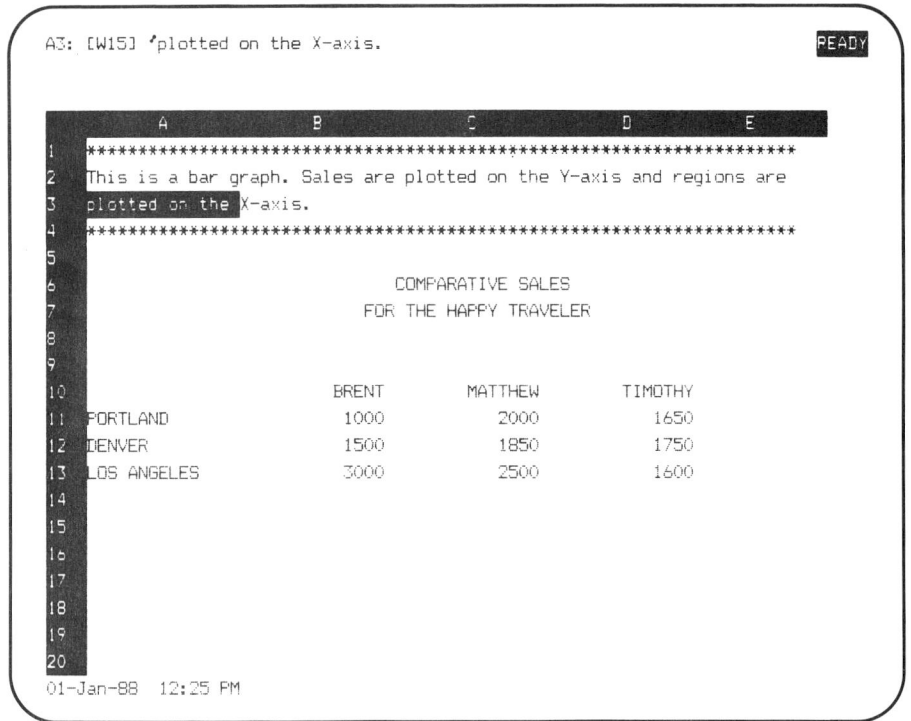

```
A3: [W15] 'plotted on the X-axis.                               READY

              A           B           C           D           E
1  ********************************************************************
2  This is a bar graph. Sales are plotted on the Y-axis and regions are
3  plotted on the X-axis.
4  ********************************************************************
5
6                        COMPARATIVE SALES
7                      FOR THE HAPPY TRAVELER
8
9
10                    BRENT       MATTHEW       TIMOTHY
11 PORTLAND           1000         2000          1650
12 DENVER             1500         1850          1750
13 LOS ANGELES        3000         2500          1600
14
15
16
17
18
19
20
01-Jan-88   12:25 PM
```

Figure 12-9 (Continued)

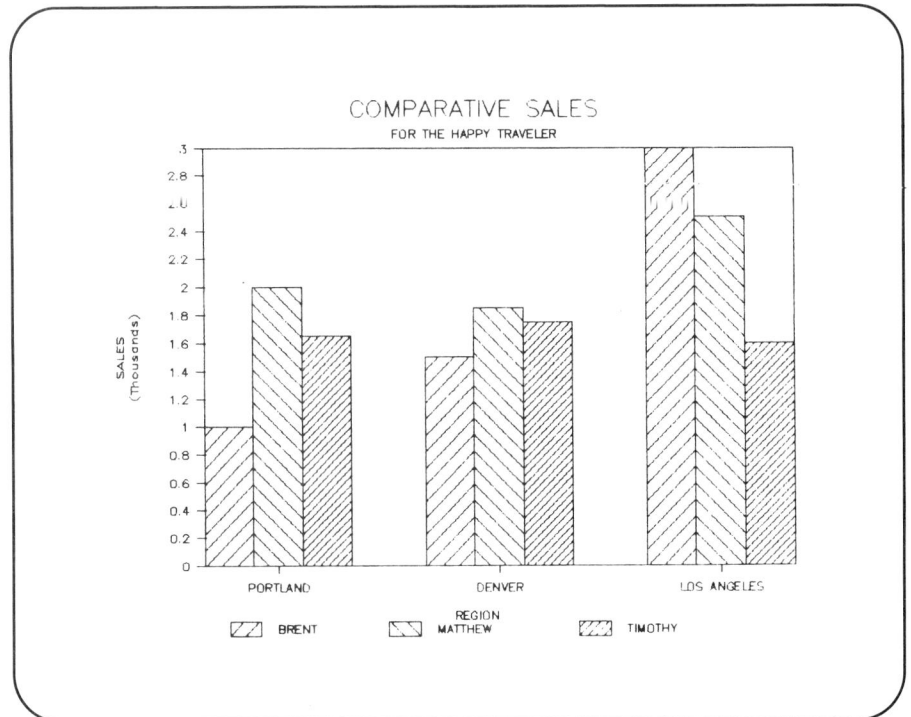

COMPARATIVE SALES
FOR THE HAPPY TRAVELER

If you choose Manual, you will be given all the other choices. The Format option is the same as /Range Format or /Worksheet Global Format. This means you can format your number(s) in the X or Y axis.

Figure 12-10 shows an example of a manual scale. This figure was generated as follows:

/Graph, Type, Bar, X (B11..D11), Return, A (B12..D12), Return, B (B13..D13), Return, C (B14..D14), Return, Options, Legend, A (\A12), Return, Legend, B (\A13), Return, Legend, C (\A14), Return, Titles, First, COMPARATIVE SALES, Return, Titles, Second, FOR THE HAPPY TRAVELER, Return, Titles, X-axis, SALESMEN, Return, Titles, Y-axis, SALES, Return, Scale, Y-scale, Manual, Lower (-1,000), Return, Upper (4,000), Return, Quit, Quit, View.

The Indicator option allows you to suppress the scale indicator, or, more simply put, Lotus rescales the axis in order to fit the data. If your scale is too low and there are large differences between your data ranges you may see only a portion of your data. Figure 12-11 illustrates this case. This graph was generated as follows:

/Graph, Type, Bar, X (B11..D11), Return, A (B12..D12), Return, B (B13..D13), Return, C (B14..D14), Return, Options, Legend, A (\A12), Return, Legend, B (\A13), Return, Legend, C (\A14), Return, Titles, First, COMPARATIVE SALES, Return, Titles, Second, FOR THE HAPPY TRAVELER, Return, Titles, X-axis, SALESMEN, Return, Titles, Y-axis, SALES, Return, Scale, Y scale, Manual, Lower (-1000), Return, Upper (2000),Return, Quit, Quit, View.

12-10 Line Graphs

Line graphs are very useful when you want to observe the performance of one variable over a period of time; for instance, a company's total advertising budget for the years 1976 to 1987. The Format option is used to draw lines or symbols in line or XY graphs. When the Format option is chosen, the following menu will be presented:

Graph   A B C D E F   Quit

The Graph option sets the format for all ranges, while options A-F are used to set the format for a particular range. Lines, Symbols, Both, and Neither are choices under the Graph option. Lines will draw lines between data points; Symbols will draw symbols at data points; Both will draw both lines and symbols; and Neither will display data labels only.

Horizontal and vertical grid lines can be used to make graphs easier to read. These lines can be drawn by using the Grid option. A choice of horizontal grid lines, vertical grid lines, or both are available for the flexible presentation of line graphs.

The Data Labels option is used to specify a label corresponding to the data range. Up to six data ranges can be labeled. These labels can be aligned in five convenient ways relative to data points: center, left, above, right, or below.

Figure 12-12 is an example of a line graph. This figure shows the total sales for Alpha-Talk Company from 1975 to 1986. The graph was generated as follows:

/Graph, Type, Line, X (C11..C15), Return, A (F11..F15), Return, Options, Titles, First, ALPHA-TALK COMPANY, Return, Titles, X-axis, YEAR, Return, Titles, Y-axis, TOTAL SALES, Return, Format, Graph, Lines, Quit, Quit, View.

Figure 12-10 Manual Scaling of Sales Performance Analysis

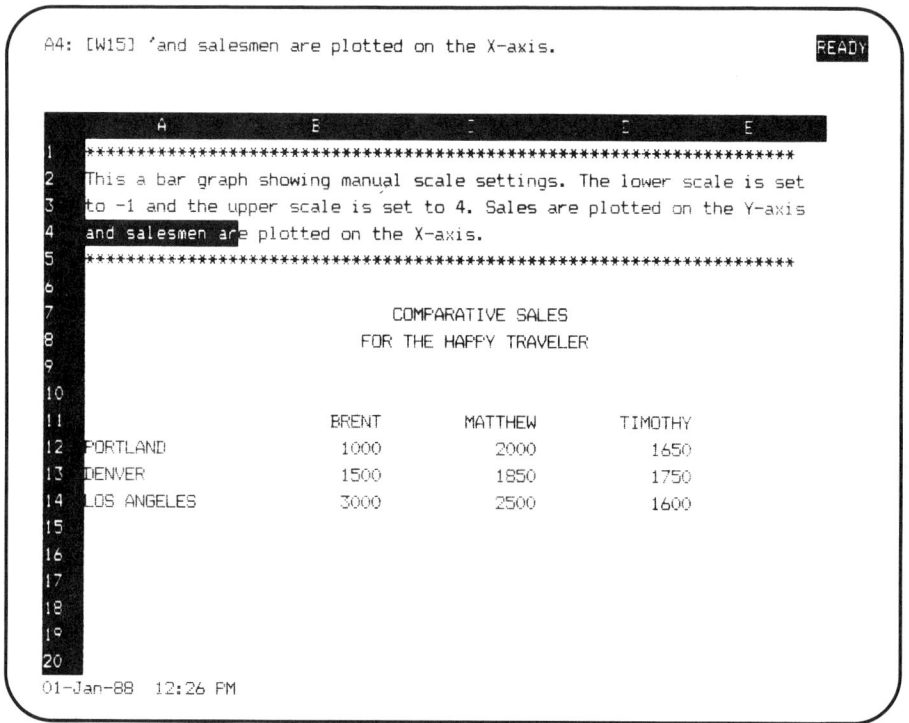

```
A4: [W15] 'and salesmen are plotted on the X-axis.                    READY

          A            B            C            D            E
1  ***********************************************************************
2  This a bar graph showing manual scale settings. The lower scale is set
3  to -1 and the upper scale is set to 4. Sales are plotted on the Y-axis
4  and salesmen are plotted on the X-axis.
5  ***********************************************************************
6
7                              COMPARATIVE SALES
8                            FOR THE HAPPY TRAVELER
9
10
11                    BRENT        MATTHEW        TIMOTHY
12 PORTLAND           1000          2000          1650
13 DENVER             1500          1850          1750
14 LOS ANGELES        3000          2500          1600
15
16
17
18
19
20
01-Jan-88   12:26 PM
```

Figure 12-10 (Continued)

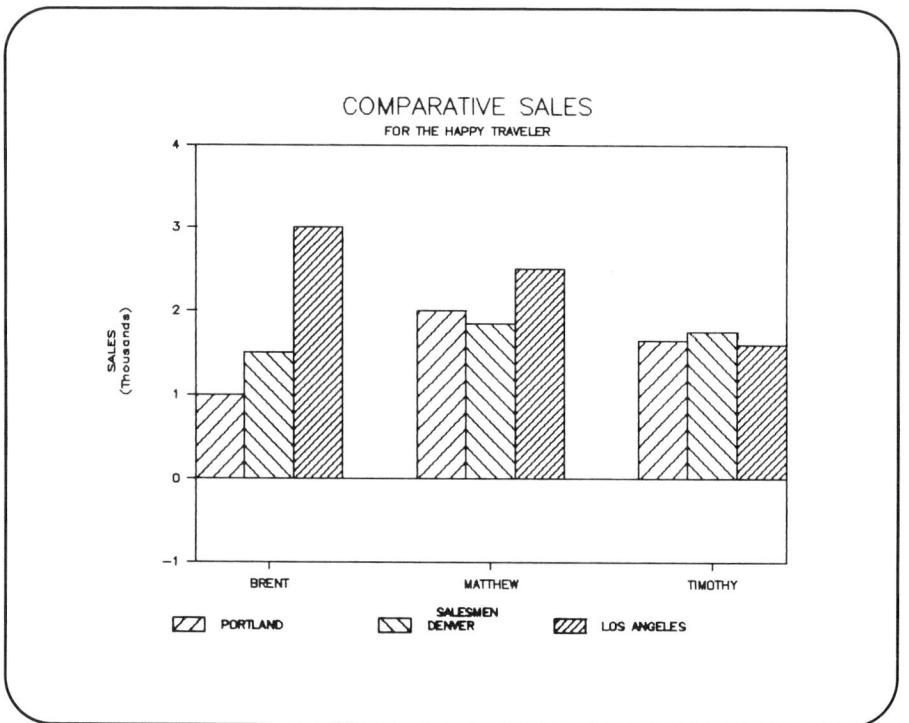

COMPARATIVE SALES
FOR THE HAPPY TRAVELER

Figure 12-11 Manual Scaling of Sales Performance

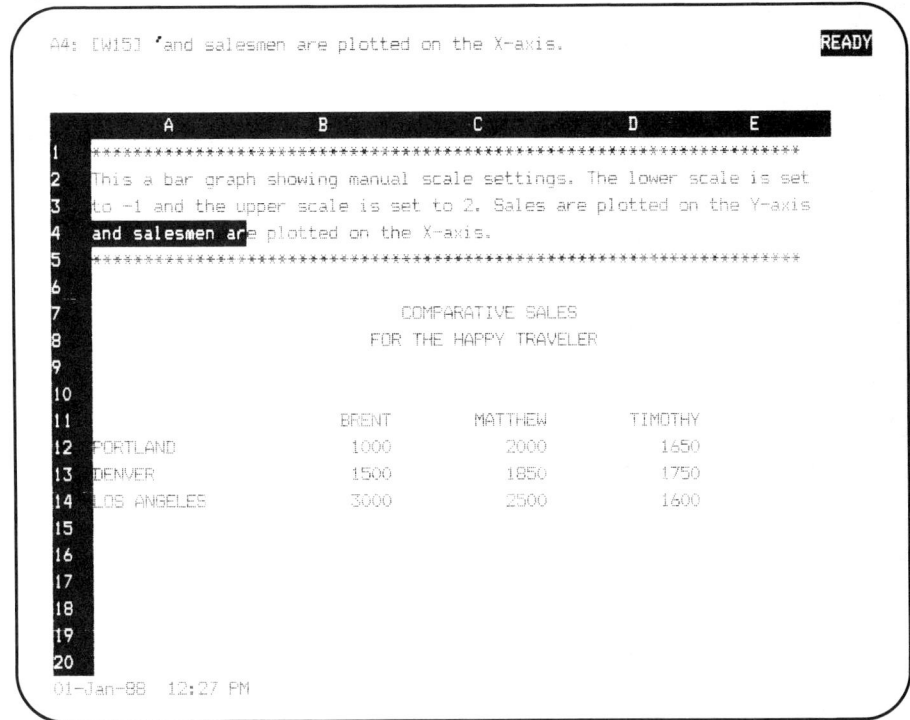

```
A4: [W15] 'and salesmen are plotted on the X-axis.                    READY

          A              B              C              D        E
1  **********************************************************************
2  This a bar graph showing manual scale settings. The lower scale is set
3  to -1 and the upper scale is set to 2. Sales are plotted on the Y-axis
4  and salesmen are plotted on the X-axis.
5  **********************************************************************
6
7                        COMPARATIVE SALES
8                       FOR THE HAPPY TRAVELER
9
10
11                   BRENT        MATTHEW        TIMOTHY
12 PORTLAND          1000          2000           1650
13 DENVER            1500          1850           1750
14 LOS ANGELES       3000          2500           1600
15
16
17
18
19
20
01-Jan-88  12:27 PM
```

Figure 12-11 (Continued)

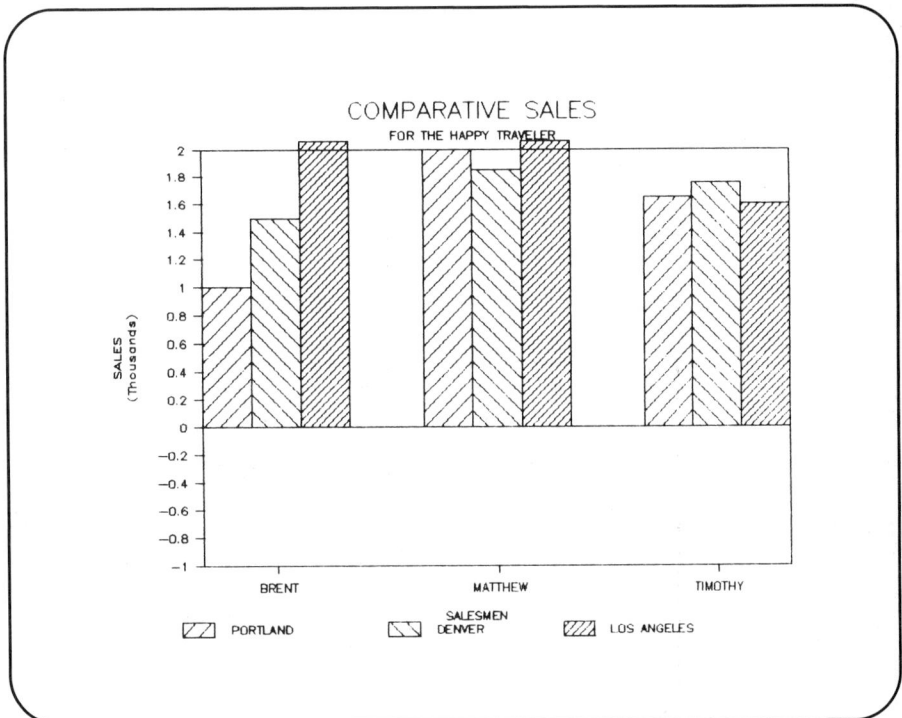

Figure 12-12 Line Graph with Lines Only

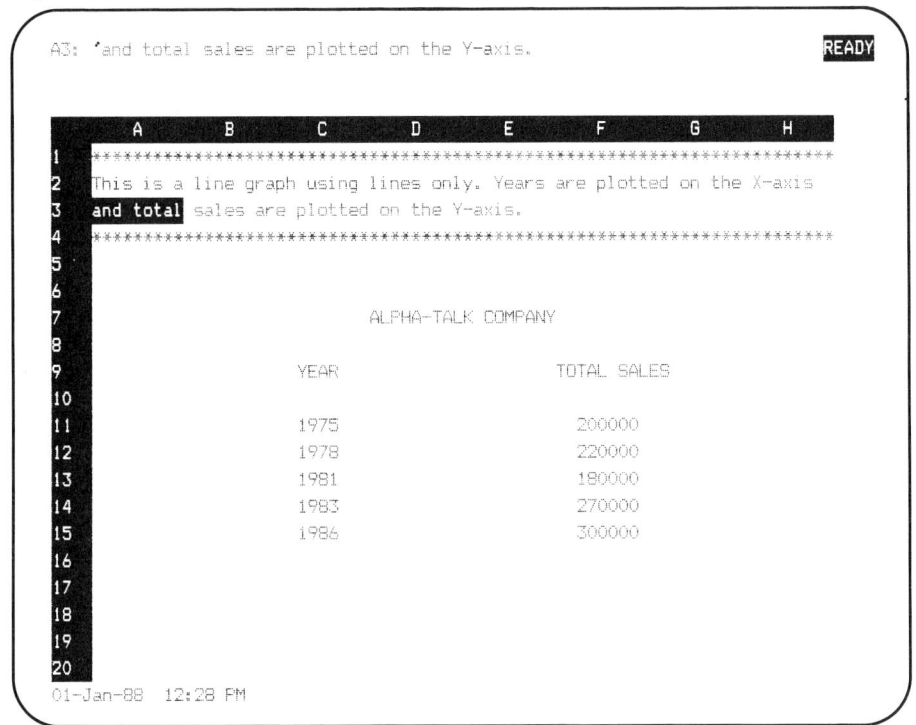

```
A3: 'and total sales are plotted on the Y-axis.                    READY

          A       B       C       D       E       F       G       H
1   **********************************************************************
2   This is a line graph using lines only. Years are plotted on the X-axis
3   and total sales are plotted on the Y-axis.
4   **********************************************************************
5
6
7                              ALPHA-TALK COMPANY
8
9              YEAR                           TOTAL SALES
10
11             1975                             200000
12             1978                             220000
13             1981                             180000
14             1983                             270000
15             1986                             300000
16
17
18
19
20
01-Jan-88  12:28 PM
```

Figure 12-12 (Continued)

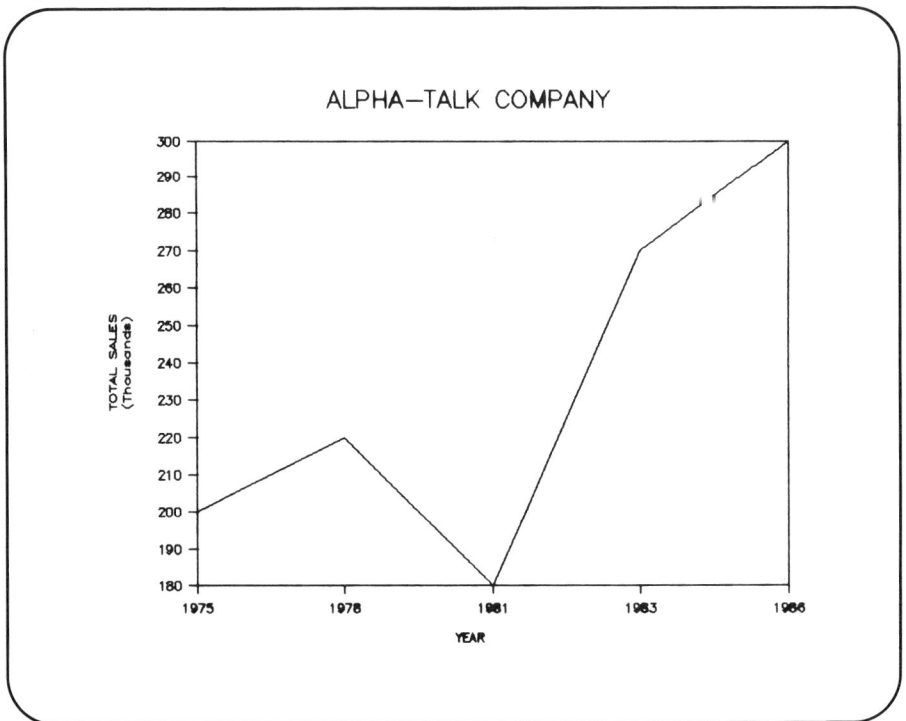

ALPHA-TALK COMPANY

Line Graph with Lines and Symbols

Figure 12-13 displays the same data as Figure 12-12 except that we have chosen both lines and symbols. This graph was generated as follows:

/Graph, Type, Line, X (C11..C15), Return, A (F11..F15), Return, Options, Titles, First, ALPHA-TALK COMPANY, Return, Titles, X-axis, YEAR, Return, Titles, Y-axis, TOTAL SALES, Return, Format, Graph, Both, Quit, Quit, View.

Line Graph with Lines, Symbols, and Grids

Figure 12-14 plots the same data as Figures 12-12 and 12-13 but uses a vertical grid. This figure was generated as follows:

/Graph, Type, Line, X (C12..C16), Return, A (F12..F16), Return, Options, Titles, First, ALPHA-TALK COMPANY, Return, Titles, X-axis, YEAR, Return, Titles, Y-axis, TOTAL SALES, Return, Grid, Vertical, Format, Graph, Both, Quit, Quit, View.

Figure 12-15 shows the same data, this time on a horizontal grid. This figure was generated as follows:

/Graph, Type, Line, X (C12..C16), Return, A (F12..F16), Return, Options, Titles, First, ALPHA-TALK COMPANY, Return, Titles, X-axis, YEAR, Return, Titles, Y-axis, TOTAL SALES, Return, Grid, Horizontal, Format, Graph, Both, Quit, Quit, View.

Figure 12-16 displays the same data once again. This time, we are using both vertical and horizontal grids. This figure was generated as follows:

/Graph, Type, Line, X (C12..C16), Return, A (F12..F16), Return, Options, Titles, First, ALPHA-TALK COMPANY, Return, Titles, X-axis, YEAR, Return, Titles, Y-axis, TOTAL SALES, Return, Grid, Both, Format, Graph, Both, Quit, Quit, View.

Figure 12-17 displays the same graph, this time using only symbols. This graph was generated as follows:

/Graph, Type, Line, X (C12..C16), Return, A (F12..F16), Return, Options, Titles, First, ALPHA-TALK COMPANY, Return, Titles, X-axis, YEAR, Return, Titles, Y-axis, TOTAL SALES, Return, Grid, Both, Format, Graph, Symbols, Quit, Quit, View.

Figure 12-18 displays the same data. This time, however, neither lines nor grids are used, just symbols. This figure was generated as follows:

/Graph, Type, Line, X (C11..C15), Return, A (F11..F15), Return, Options, Titles, First, ALPHA-TALK COMPANY, Return, Titles, X-axis, YEAR, Return, Titles, Y-axis, TOTAL SALES, Return, Format, Graph, Symbols, Quit, Quit, View.

Figure 12-19 displays a line graph that plots an advertising budget for twelve periods, using symbols. This figure was generated as follows:

/Graph, Type, Line, X (A7..A18), Return, A (B7..B18), Return, Options, Format, Graph, Both, Quit, Titles, First, SUNSHINE TRAVEL, Return, Titles, X-axis, YEAR, Return, Titles, Y-axis, PERCENTAGE OF ADVERTISING BUDGET, Return, Quit, View.

Figure 12-20 displays the same data as Figure 12-19, however, this time we have used the Skip option. This option lets you skip every *n*th label on the X axis. The graph was generated as follows:

Figure 12-13 Line Graph with Lines and Symbols

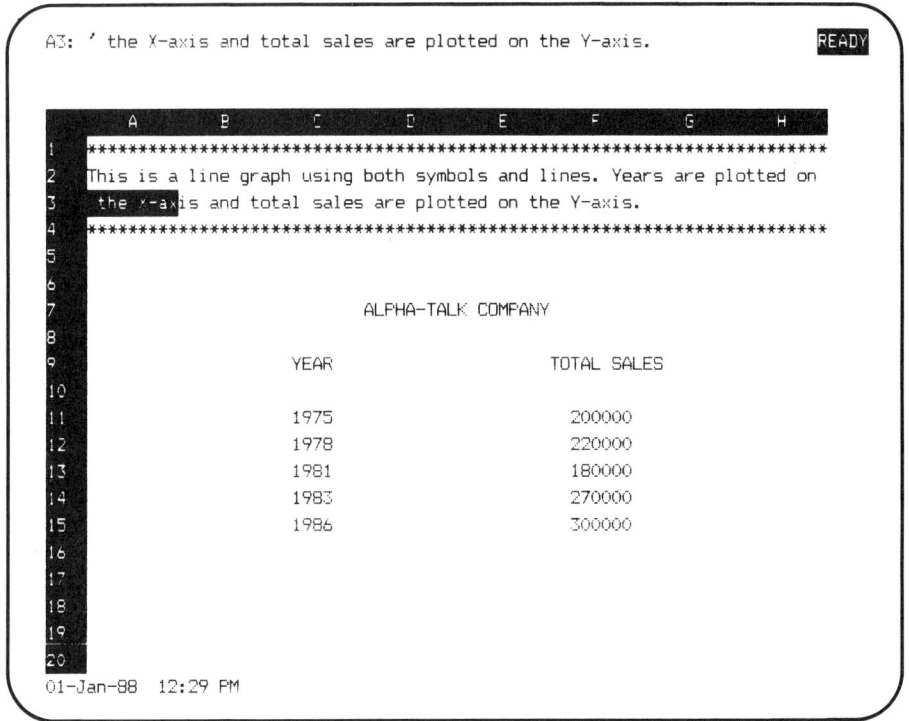

```
A3: ' the X-axis and total sales are plotted on the Y-axis.            READY

         A        B        C        D        E        F        G        H
1 ********************************************************************************
2 This is a line graph using both symbols and lines. Years are plotted on
3  the X-axis and total sales are plotted on the Y-axis.
4 ********************************************************************************
5
6
7                              ALPHA-TALK COMPANY
8
9                    YEAR                    TOTAL SALES
10
11                   1975                       200000
12                   1978                       220000
13                   1981                       180000
14                   1983                       270000
15                   1986                       300000
16
17
18
19
20
01-Jan-88  12:29 PM
```

Figure 12-13 (Continued)

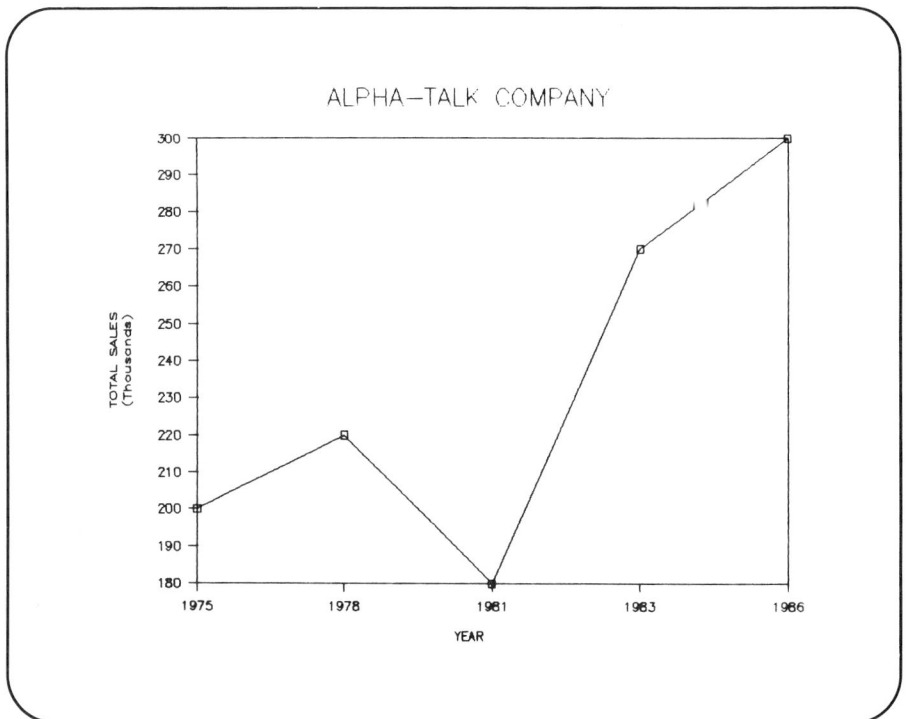

Figure 12-14 Line Graph with Both Lines and Symbols and a Vertical Grid

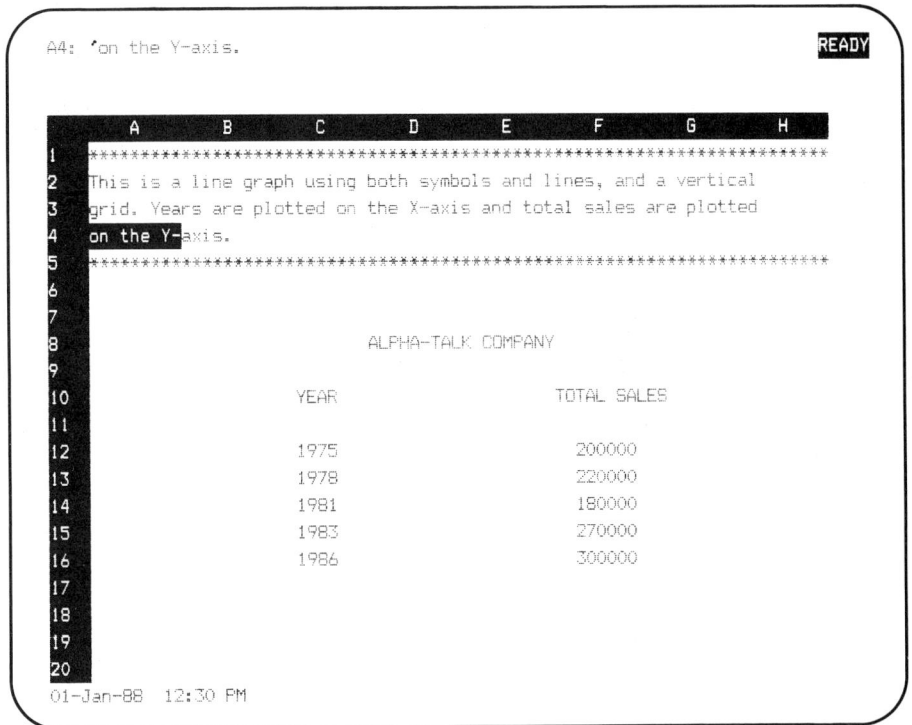

```
A4: 'on the Y-axis.                                                    READY

        A      B      C      D      E      F      G      H
1  *************************************************************************
2  This is a line graph using both symbols and lines, and a vertical
3  grid. Years are plotted on the X-axis and total sales are plotted
4  on the Y-axis.
5  *************************************************************************
6
7
8                             ALPHA-TALK COMPANY
9
10            YEAR                        TOTAL SALES
11
12            1975                          200000
13            1978                          220000
14            1981                          180000
15            1983                          270000
16            1986                          300000
17
18
19
20
01-Jan-88  12:30 PM
```

Figure 12-14 (Continued)

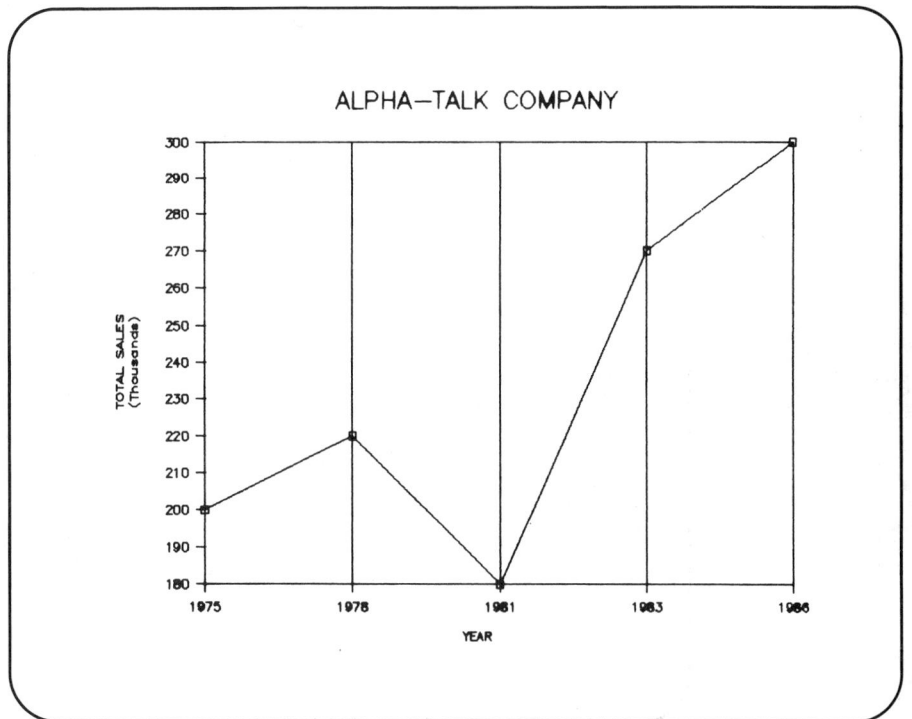

ALPHA—TALK COMPANY

Figure 12-15 Line Graph with Both Lines and Symbols and a Horizontal Grid

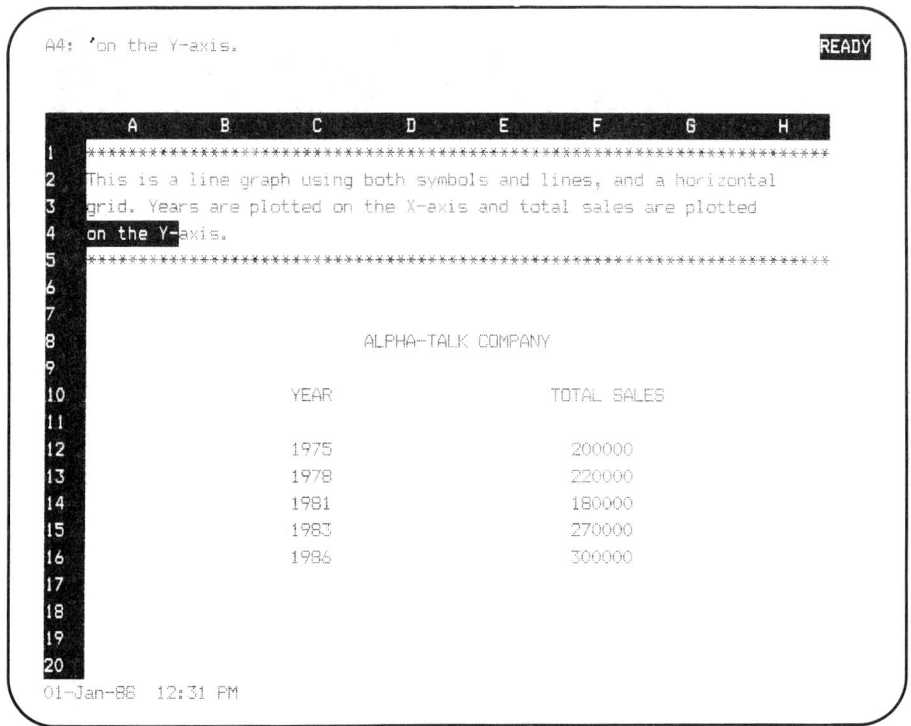

```
A4: 'on the Y-axis.                                                    READY

          A      B      C        D        E        F        G        H
1    *********************************************************************
2    This is a line graph using both symbols and lines, and a horizontal
3    grid. Years are plotted on the X-axis and total sales are plotted
4    on the Y-axis.
5    *********************************************************************
6
7
8                            ALPHA-TALK COMPANY
9
10               YEAR                      TOTAL SALES
11
12               1975                        200000
13               1978                        220000
14               1981                        180000
15               1983                        270000
16               1986                        300000
17
18
19
20
     01-Jan-88  12:31 PM
```

Figure 12-15 (Continued)

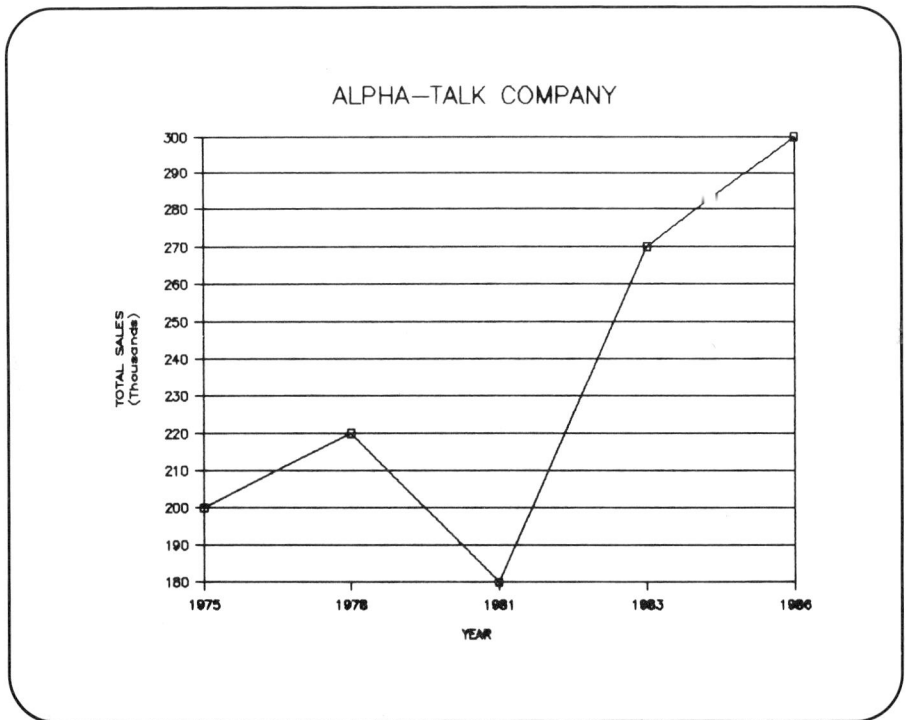

Figure 12-16 Line Graph with Lines, Symbols, Vertical, and Horizontal Grids

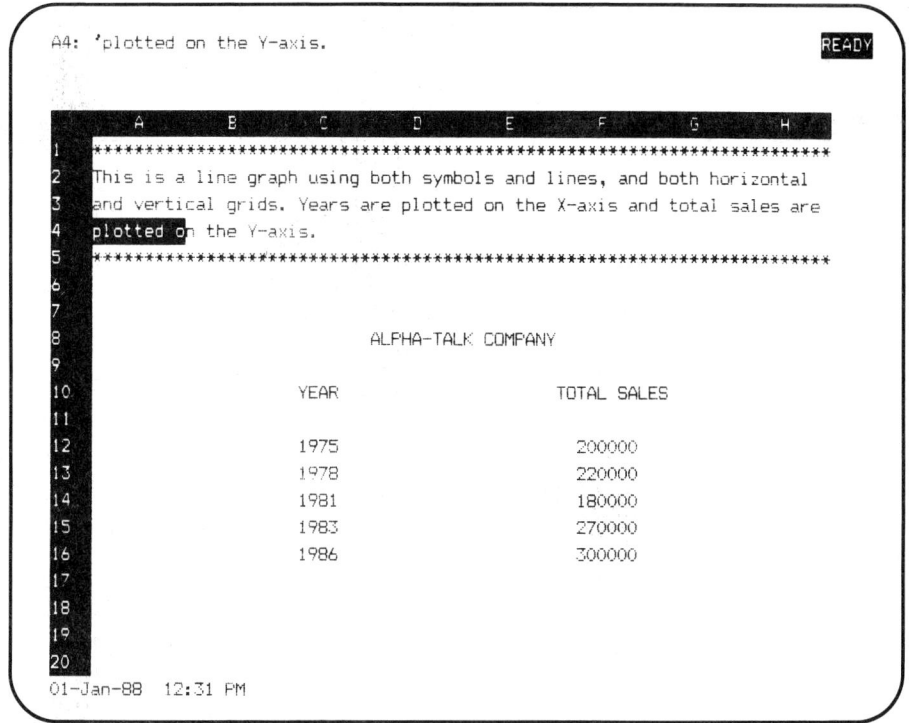

```
A4: 'plotted on the Y-axis.                                              READY

         A        B        C        D        E        F        G        H
1  ****************************************************************************
2  This is a line graph using both symbols and lines, and both horizontal
3  and vertical grids. Years are plotted on the X-axis and total sales are
4  plotted on the Y-axis.
5  ****************************************************************************
6
7
8                              ALPHA-TALK COMPANY
9
10          YEAR                        TOTAL SALES
11
12          1975                          200000
13          1978                          220000
14          1981                          180000
15          1983                          270000
16          1986                          300000
17
18
19
20
01-Jan-88   12:31 PM
```

Figure 12-16 (Continued)

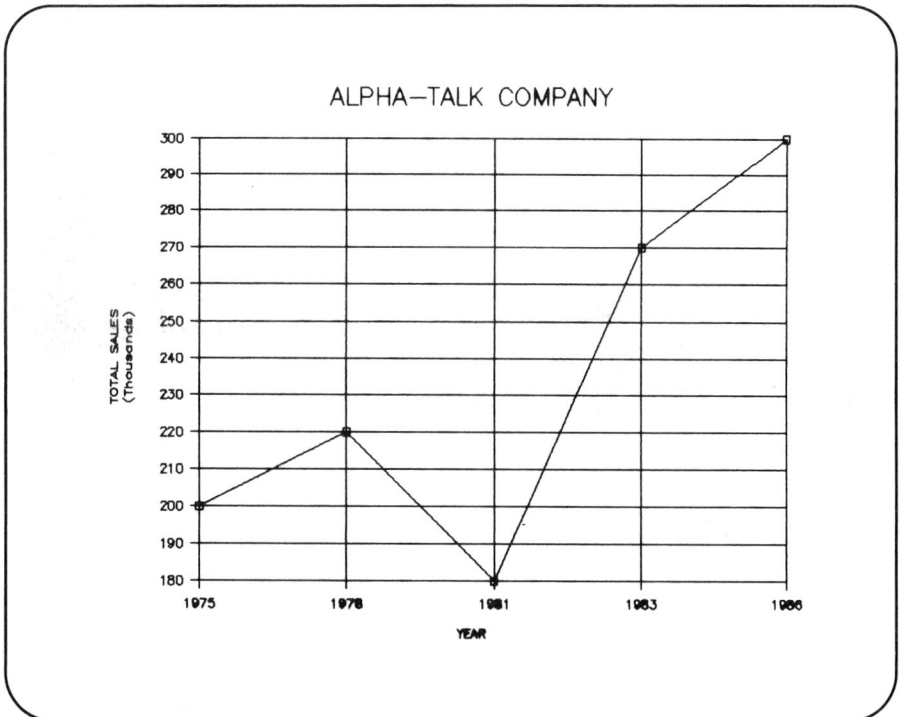

Figure 12-17 Line Graph with Symbols and Vertical and Horizontal Grids

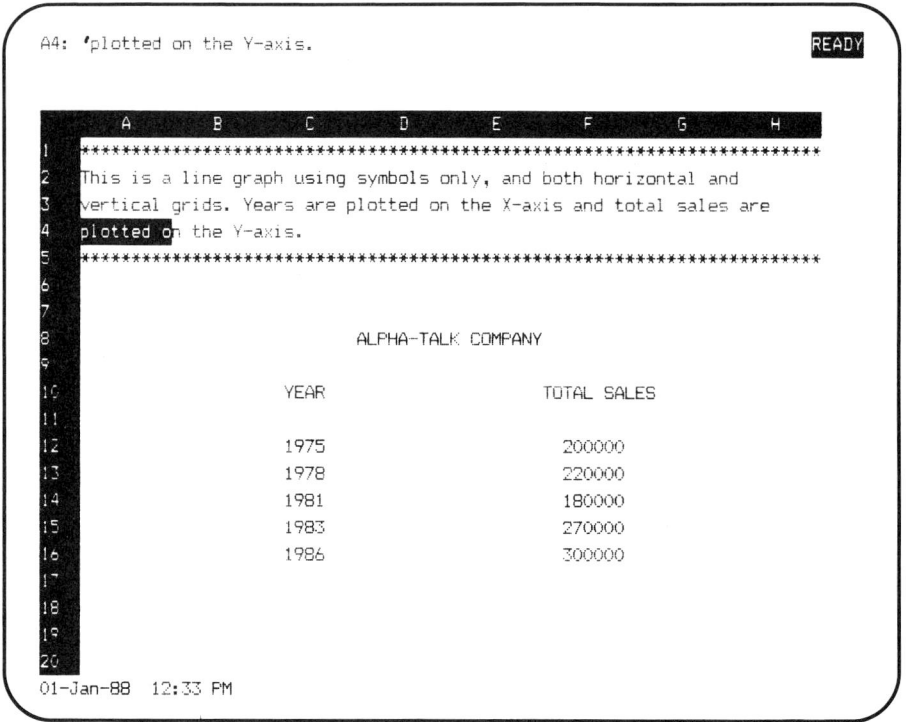

```
A4: 'plotted on the Y-axis.                                            READY

         A        B        C        D        E        F        G        H
1  *************************************************************************
2  This is a line graph using symbols only, and both horizontal and
3  vertical grids. Years are plotted on the X-axis and total sales are
4  plotted on the Y-axis.
5  *************************************************************************
6
7
8                              ALPHA-TALK COMPANY
9
10              YEAR                        TOTAL SALES
11
12              1975                          200000
13              1978                          220000
14              1981                          180000
15              1983                          270000
16              1986                          300000
17
18
19
20
01-Jan-88   12:33 PM
```

Figure 12-17 (Continued)

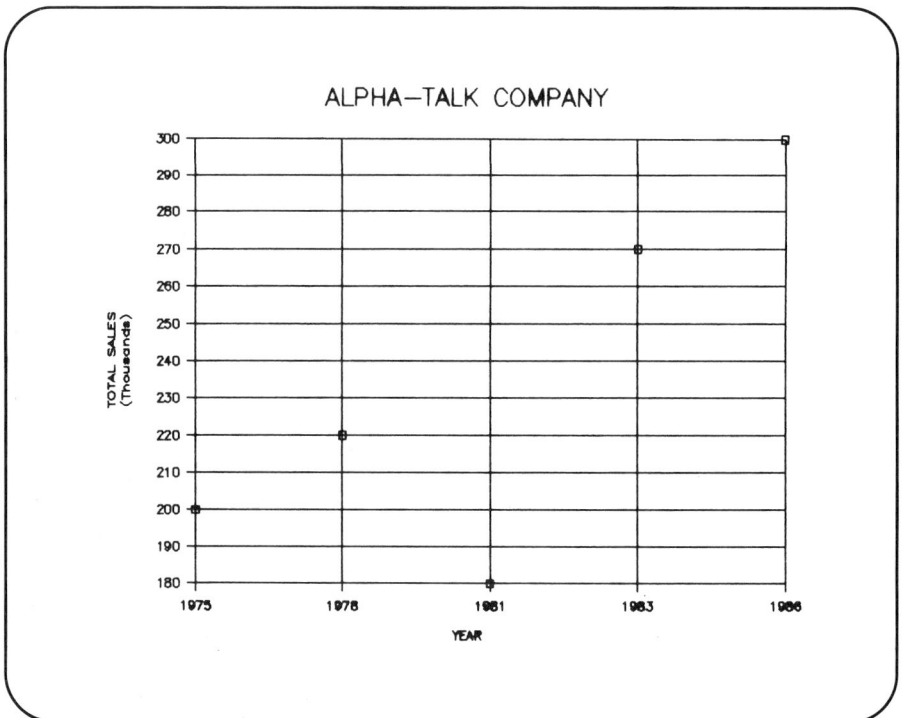

Figure 12-18 Line Graph with Symbols Only

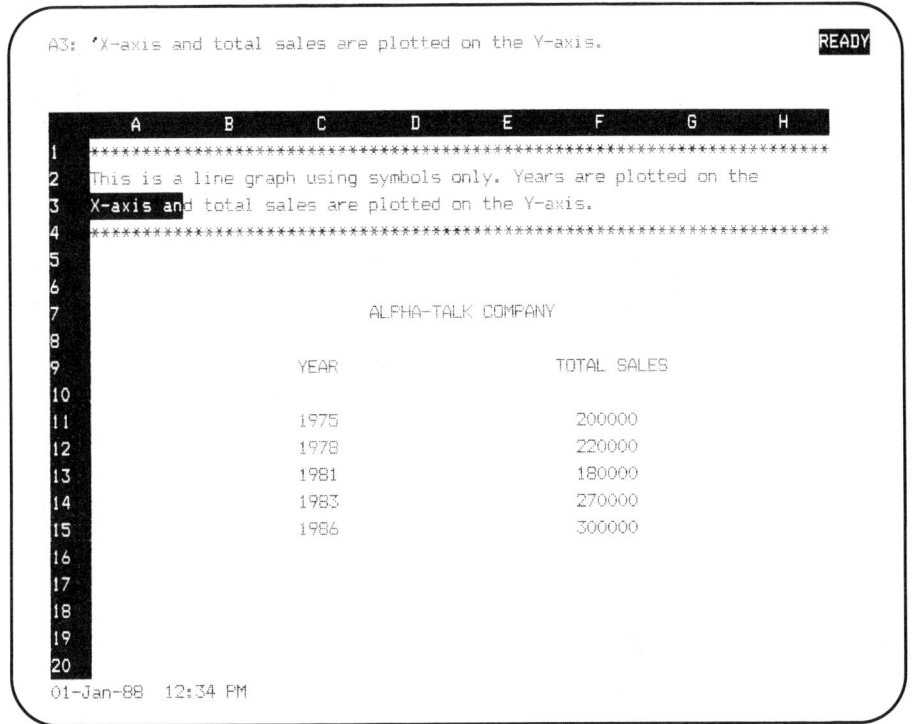

```
A3: 'X-axis and total sales are plotted on the Y-axis.          READY

         A        B        C        D        E        F        G        H
1  ***********************************************************************
2  This is a line graph using symbols only. Years are plotted on the
3  X-axis and total sales are plotted on the Y-axis.
4  ***********************************************************************
5
6
7                          ALPHA-TALK COMPANY
8
9               YEAR                        TOTAL SALES
10
11              1975                          200000
12              1978                          220000
13              1981                          180000
14              1983                          270000
15              1986                          300000
16
17
18
19
20
01-Jan-88  12:34 PM
```

Figure 12-18 (Continued)

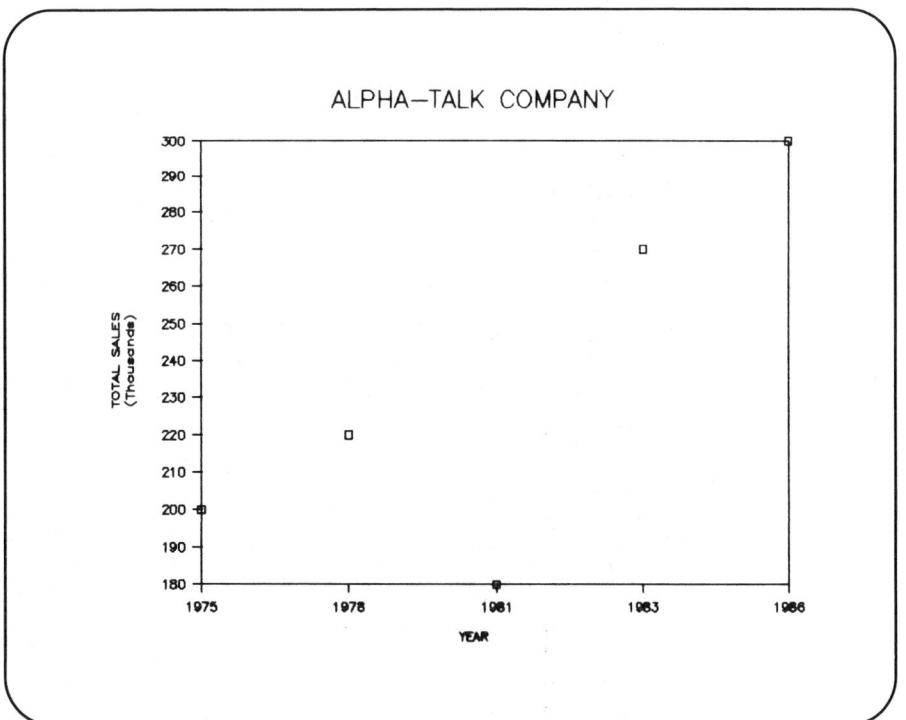

Figure 12-19 Line Graph of Advertising Budget without Skip Options

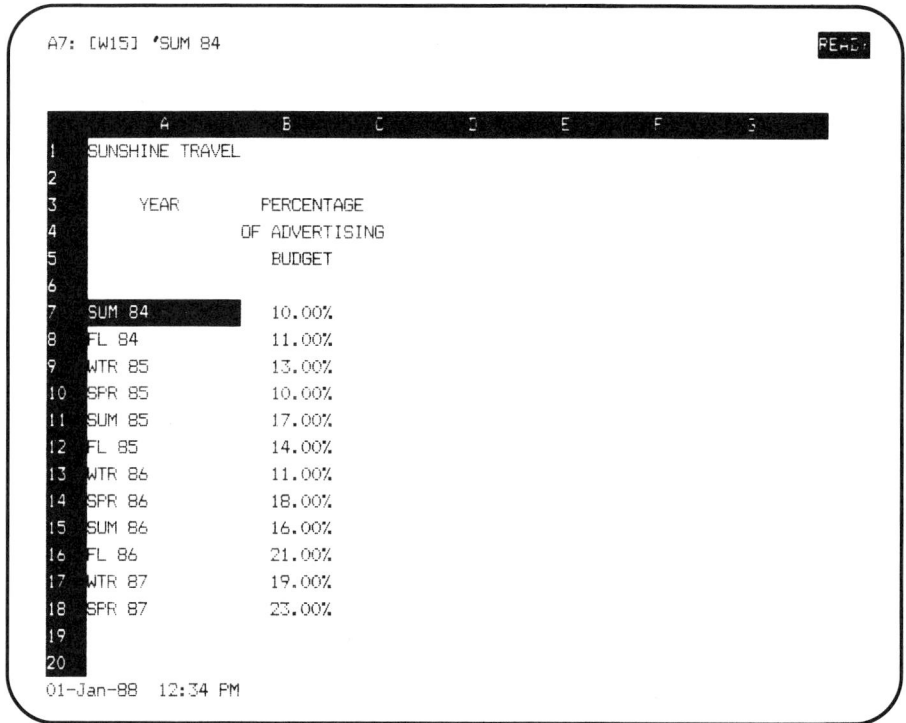

```
A7: [W15] 'SUM 84                                                      READY

            A            B           C          D         E         F         G
1   SUNSHINE TRAVEL
2
3        YEAR          PERCENTAGE
4                      OF ADVERTISING
5                      BUDGET
6
7   SUM 84                10.00%
8   FL 84                 11.00%
9   WTR 85                13.00%
10  SPR 85                10.00%
11  SUM 85                17.00%
12  FL 85                 14.00%
13  WTR 86                11.00%
14  SPR 86                18.00%
15  SUM 86                16.00%
16  FL 86                 21.00%
17  WTR 87                19.00%
18  SPR 87                23.00%
19
20
01-Jan-88   12:34 PM
```

Figure 12-19 (Continued)

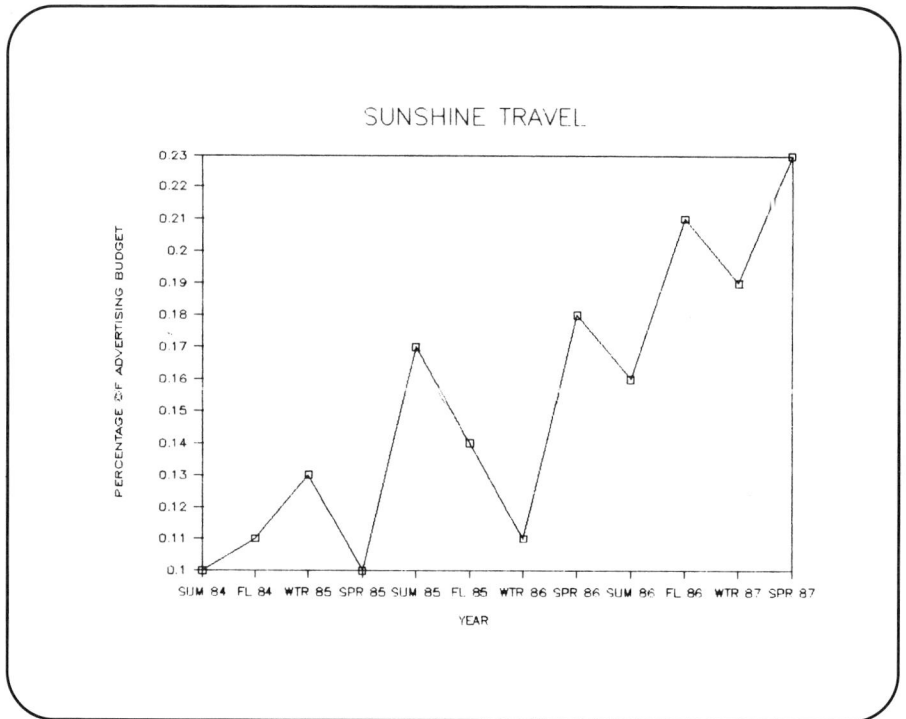

Figure 12-20 Line Graph of Advertising Budget with Skip Options

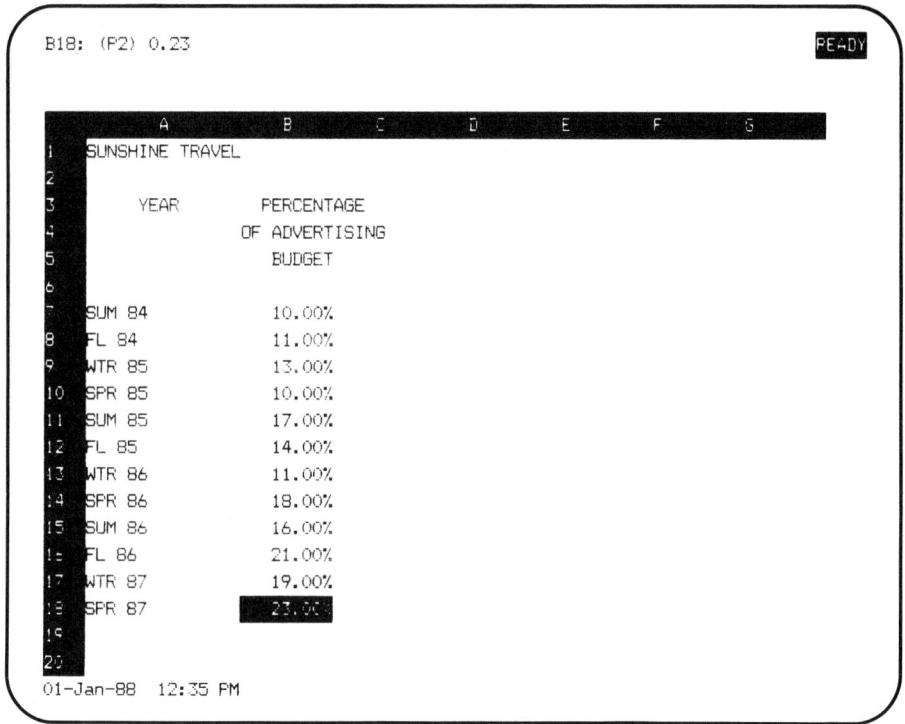

Figure 12-20 (Continued)

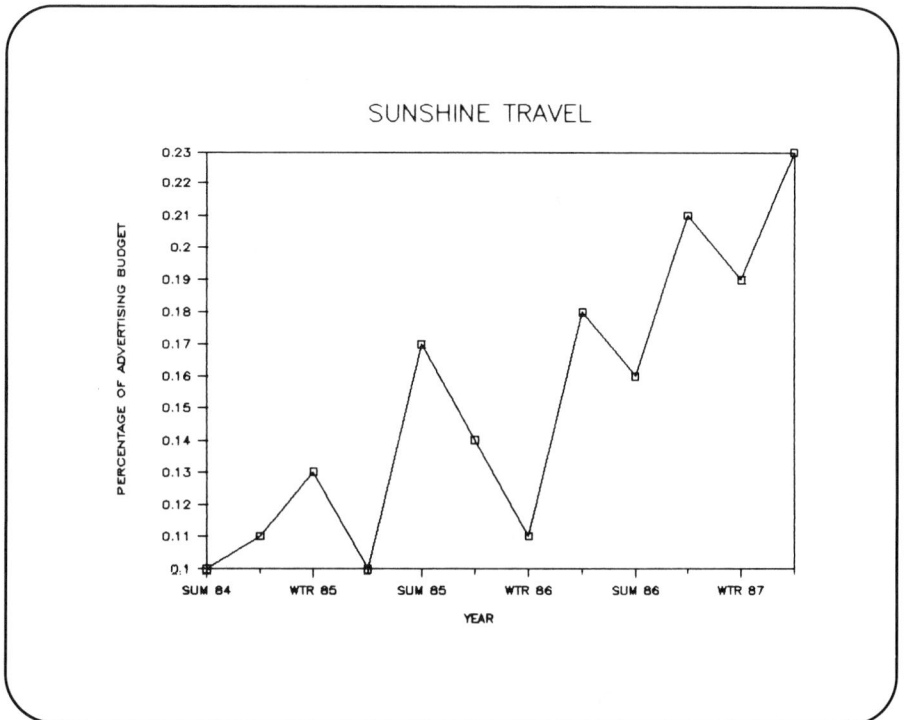

/Graph, Type, Line, X (A7..A18), Return, A (B7..B18), Return, Options, Scale, Skip, 2, Return, Titles, First, SUNSHINE TRAVEL, Return, Titles, X-axis, YEAR, Return, Titles, Y-axis, PERCENTAGE OF ADVERTISING BUDGET, Return, Format, Graph, Both, Quit, Quit, View.

Figure 12-21 compares the total sales of two divisions using a line graph with two lines and different symbols. This figure was generated as follows:

/Graph, Type, Line, X (A4..A13), Return, A (C4..C13), Return, B (E4..E13), Return, Options, Legend, A (DIVISION #1), Return, Legend, B (DIVISION #2), Return, Format, Graph, Both, Quit, Titles, X-axis, YEAR, Return, Titles, Y-axis, TOTAL SALES, Return, Quit, View.

Line Graph with Lines, Symbols, and Data Labels

Figure 12-22 plots the same data as Figure 12-19, but this time data labels are used. This graph was generated as follows:

/Graph, Type, Line, X (A7..A18), Return, A (B7..B18), Return, Options, Format, Graph, Both, Quit, Titles, First, SUNSHINE TRAVEL, Return, Titles, X-axis, YEAR, Return, Titles, Y-axis, PERCENTAGE OF ADVERTISING BUDGET, Return, Data-Labels, A (B7..B18), Return, Above, Quit, Scale, Skip, 2, Return, Quit, View.

12-11 Stacked-Bar Graph

In a stacked-bar graph, Lotus displays the corresponding value from each data range stacked on the top of the preceding data item in each bar. You can build a stacked bar graph with six corresponding data items on the top of each other. Shadings or colors represent each data item. When you define your data ranges, A corresponds to the lowest and F corresponds to the highest. As usual, the X range is used for data labels on the X-axis.

Figure 12-23 illustrates an example of the stacked-bar graph. The performance of each salesperson in the three regions is displayed with the regions stacked on top of each other. The first bar shows Brent's performance in Portland (the bottom portion), Denver (the middle), and Los Angeles (the top). This graph is generated as follows:

/Graph, Type, Stacked-Bar, X (B11..D11), Return, A (B12..D12), Return, B (B13..D13), Return, C (B14..D14), Return, Options, Legend, A (\A12), Return, Legend, B (\A13), Return, Legend, C (\A14), Return, Titles, First, COMPARATIVE SALES, Return, Titles, X-axis, SALESMEN, Return, Titles, Y-axis, SALES, Return, Quit, View.

Figure 12-24 is a different version of Figure 12-23. The performance of each salesperson in the same region is compared with the performances of the other salespeople. The first bar from the left shows Brent's performance (the bottom portion) compared with Matthew and Timothy in Portland. This graph is generated as follows:

/Graph, Type, Stacked-Bar, X (A12..A14), Return, A (B12..B14), Return, B (C12..C14), Return, C (D12..D14), Return, Options, Legend, A (\B11), Return, Legend, B (\C11), Return, Legend, C (\D11), Return, Titles, First, COMPARATIVE

Figure 12-21 Comparative Sales Analysis of Two Divisions

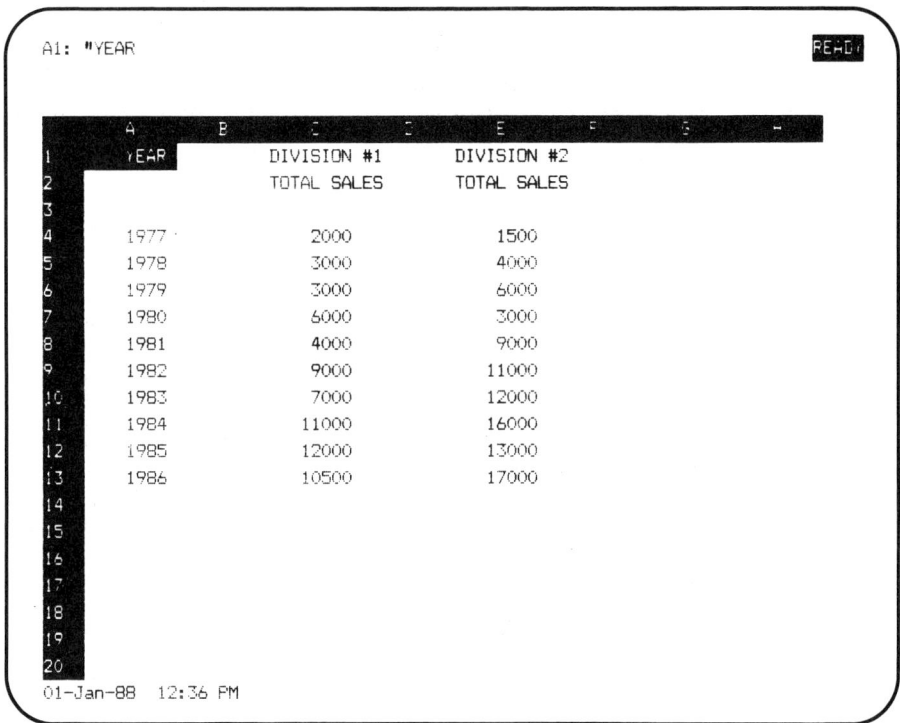

```
A1: "YEAR                                                          READY

        A         B         C         D         E         F         G

1     YEAR                  DIVISION #1         DIVISION #2
2                           TOTAL SALES         TOTAL SALES
3
4     1977                     2000                1500
5     1978                     3000                4000
6     1979                     3000                6000
7     1980                     6000                3000
8     1981                     4000                9000
9     1982                     9000               11000
10    1983                     7000               12000
11    1984                    11000               16000
12    1985                    12000               13000
13    1986                    10500               17000
14
15
16
17
18
19
20
01-Jan-88   12:36 PM
```

Figure 12-21 (Continued)

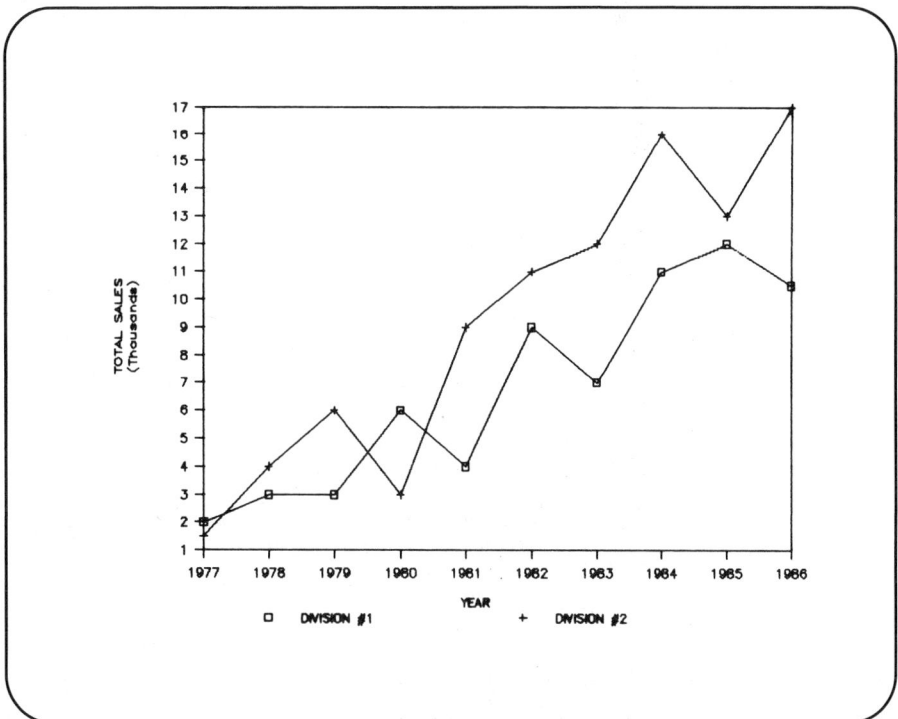

Figure 12-22 Total Budget for Advertising Using Data Labels

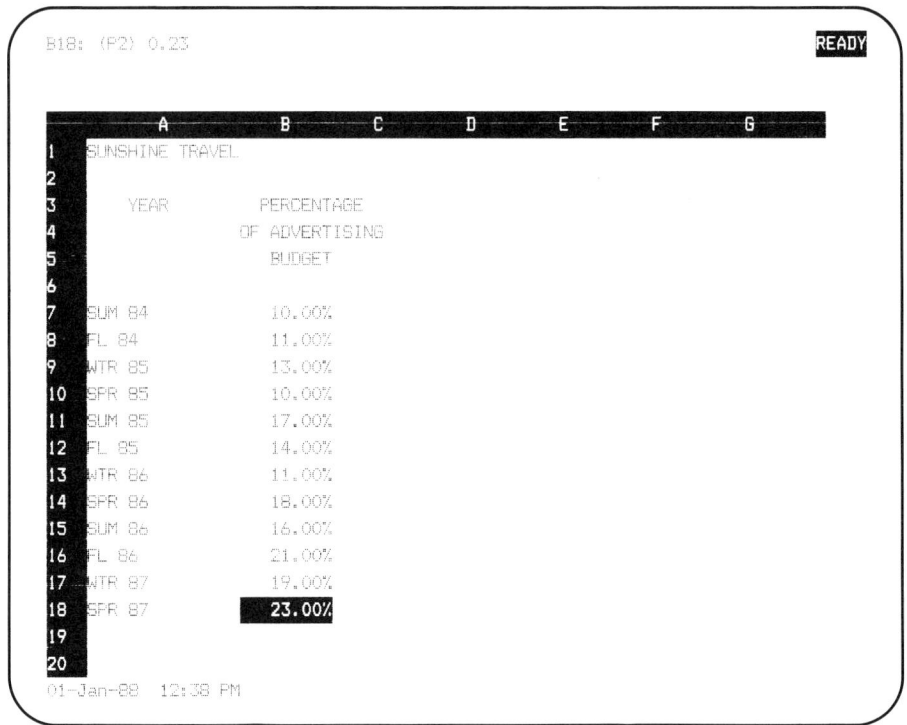

Figure 12-22 (Continued)

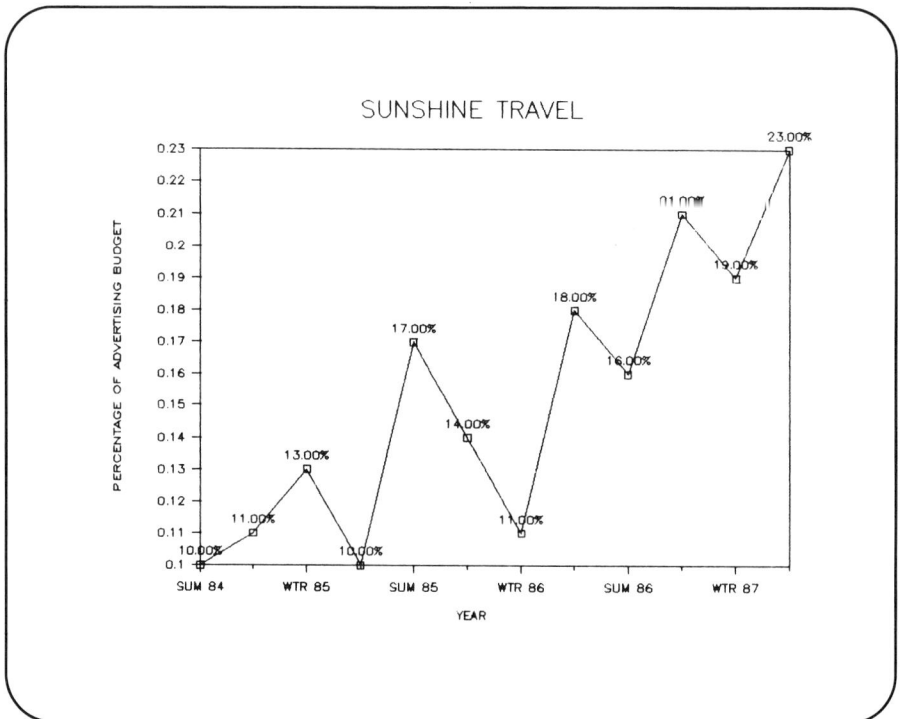

Figure 12-23 Comparative Sales in Three Regions using Stacked-Bar

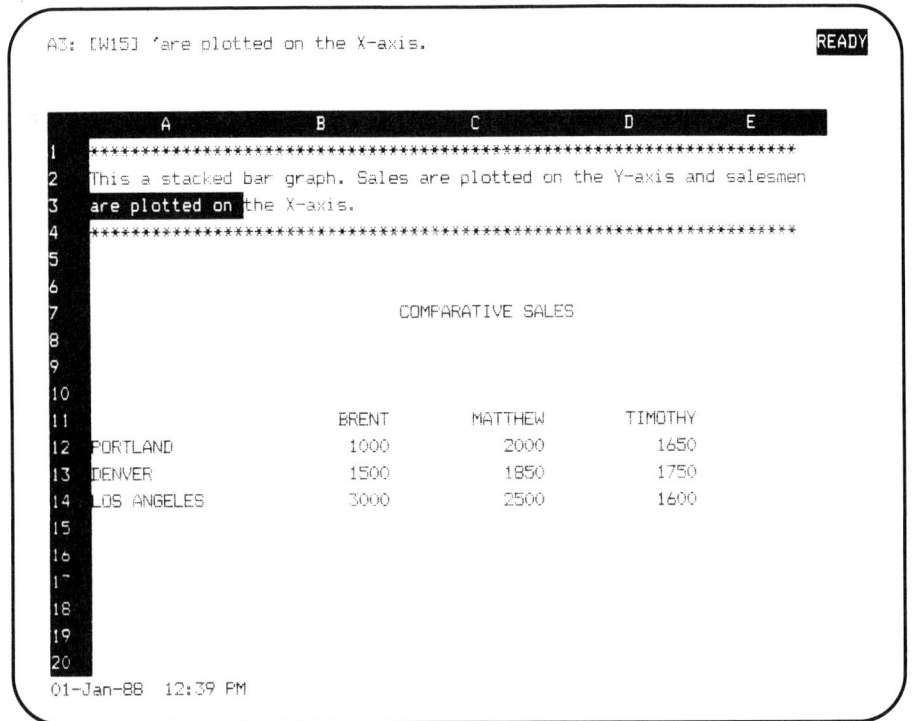

```
A3: [W15] 'are plotted on the X-axis.                              READY

         A           B            C            D            E
1  ****************************************************************
2  This a stacked bar graph. Sales are plotted on the Y-axis and salesmen
3  are plotted on the X-axis.
4  ****************************************************************
5
6
7                           COMPARATIVE SALES
8
9
10
11                   BRENT        MATTHEW        TIMOTHY
12 PORTLAND          1000          2000           1650
13 DENVER            1500          1850           1750
14 LOS ANGELES       3000          2500           1600
15
16
17
18
19
20
01-Jan-88  12:39 PM
```

Figure 12-23 (Continued)

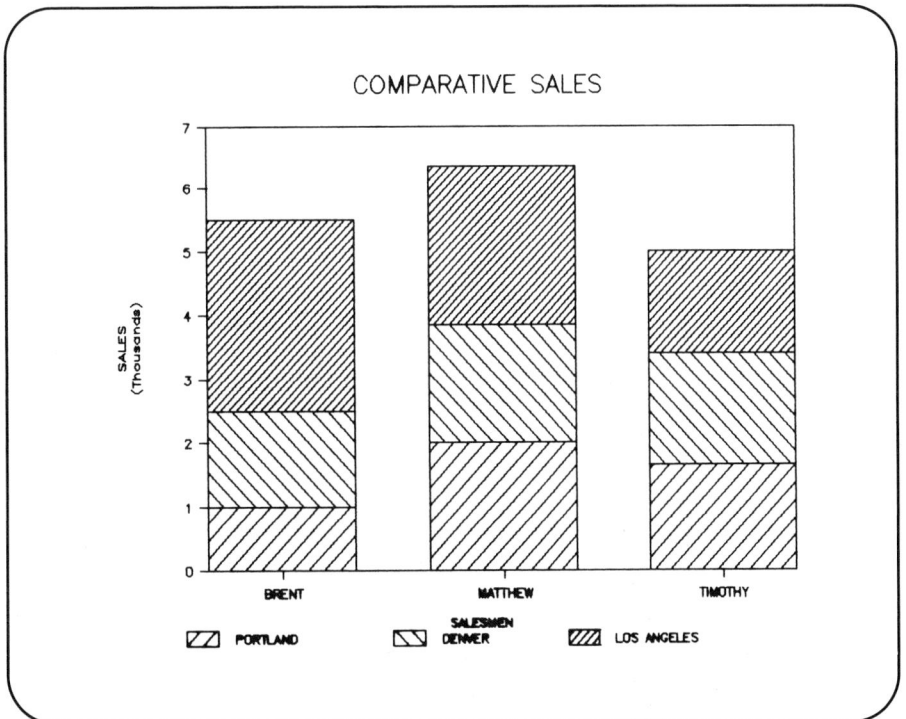

Figure 12-24 Comparative Sales for Three Salesmen in Three Regions using Stacked-Bar

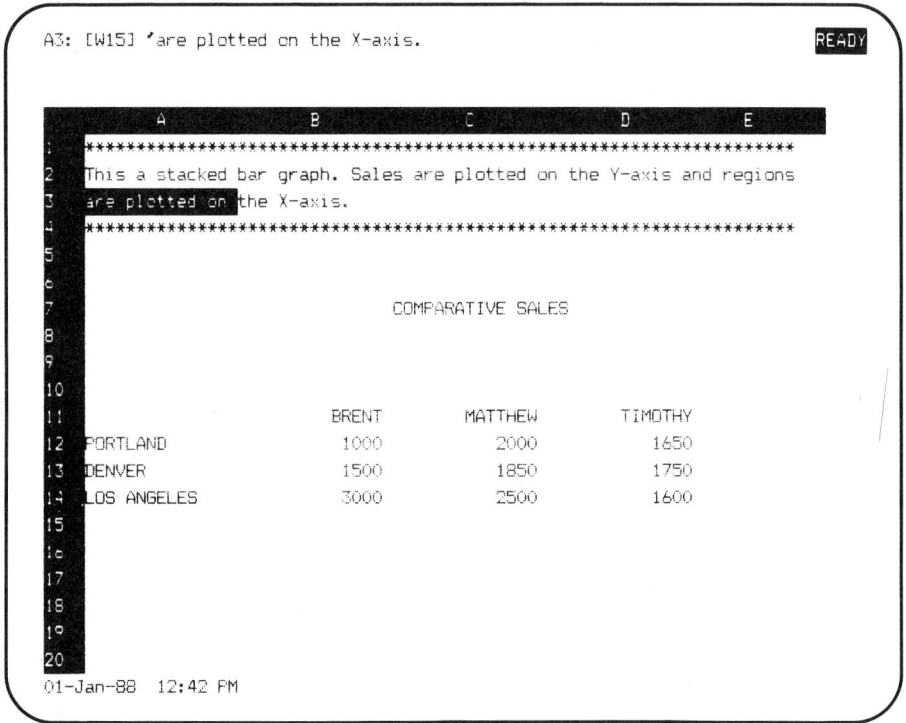

```
A3: [W15] 'are plotted on the X-axis.                              READY

         A            B            C            D            E
1   *******************************************************************
2   This a stacked bar graph. Sales are plotted on the Y-axis and regions
3   are plotted on the X-axis.
4   *******************************************************************
5
6
7                        COMPARATIVE SALES
8
9
10
11                  BRENT        MATTHEW      TIMOTHY
12  PORTLAND        1000         2000         1650
13  DENVER          1500         1850         1750
14  LOS ANGELES     3000         2500         1600
15
16
17
18
19
20
01-Jan-88  12:42 PM
```

Figure 12-24 (Continued)

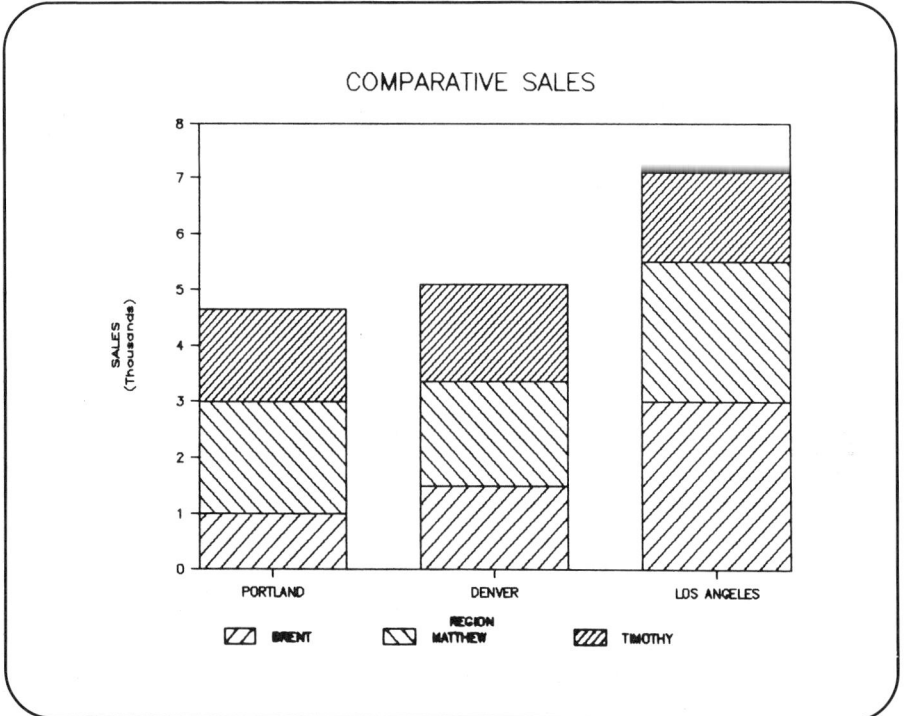

COMPARATIVE SALES

SALES, Return, Titles, X-axis, REGION, Return, Titles, Y-axis, SALES, Return, Quit, View.

Figure 12-25 is another example of a stacked-bar graph. Here we have used manual scaling. Since the scale was not big enough, a portion of the bar lies outside the scale. This figure was generated as follows:

/Graph, Type, Stacked-Bar, X (B11..D11), Return, A (B12..D12), Return, B (B13..D13), Return, C (B14..D14), Return, Options, Legend, A (\A12), Return, Legend, B (\A13), Return, Legend, C (\A14), Return, Titles, First, COMPARATIVE SALES, Return, Titles, X-axis, SALESMEN, Return, Titles, Y-axis, SALES, Return, Scale, Y Scale, Manual, Lower (-1000), Return, Upper (4000), Return, Quit, Quit, View.

12-12 XY Graph

In an XY graph, Lotus pairs each value from the X data range with the corresponding data from each of the A-F ranges to plot the graph. You can generate up to six data ranges in a XY graph. Lotus uses different symbols to show each distinct range. Figure 12-26 is one example of an XY graph. Total sales are shown on the Y-axis and advertising on the X-axis. Remember, in an XY graph, one of your data ranges must be the X range. In a line graph there is no restriction in choosing a data range. This is the major difference between a line graph and an XY graph. We have used both lines and symbols. This was generated as follows:

/Graph, Type, XY, X (C11..C16), Return, A (A11..A16), Return, Options, Titles, First, SALES AND ADVERTISING, Return, Titles, X-axis, ADVERTISING, Return, Titles, Y-axis, TOTAL SALES, Return, Format, Graph, Both, Quit, Quit, View.

12-13 Miscellaneous

We have not talked about the color option yet because many Lotus users do not have access to color graphics. However, the /Graph Options Color command provides this facility. This command displays data range bars, graph lines, and symbols in different colors only if your monitor is capable of displaying color graphics.

/Graph Options B&W displays data ranges in contrasting monochrome crosshatches. You should use /Graph Options B&W *only* if you have previously selected /Graph Options Color and want to return to a monochrome display.

12-14 A Comprehensive Model

To wrap up this chapter we have presented a comprehensive model for Happy Traveler Merchant. A portion of an income statement is presented in Figure 12-27. The following eight graphs (presented in Figures 12-28-1 through 12-28-8) will be illustrated:

1. A pie chart with crosshatches for total expense (in five groups).
2. A stacked-bar graph for six months of five expenses. The X-axis shows months and the Y-axis shows total expense.

Figure 12-25 Sales Analysis Using Stacked-Bar with Manual Scaling

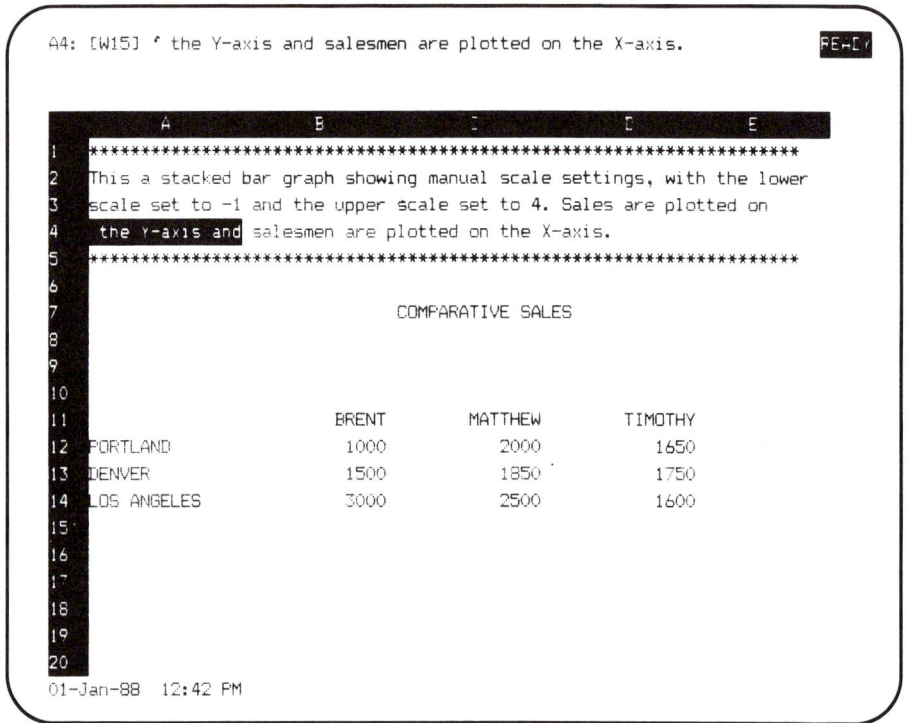

```
A4: [W15] ' the Y-axis and salesmen are plotted on the X-axis.          READY

            A           B           C           D           E
1    *********************************************************************
2    This a stacked bar graph showing manual scale settings, with the lower
3    scale set to -1 and the upper scale set to 4. Sales are plotted on
4    the Y-axis and salesmen are plotted on the X-axis.
5    *********************************************************************
6
7                            COMPARATIVE SALES
8
9
10
11                      BRENT       MATTHEW     TIMOTHY
12   PORTLAND           1000        2000        1650
13   DENVER             1500        1850        1750
14   LOS ANGELES        3000        2500        1600
15
16
17
18
19
20
01-Jan-88  12:42 PM
```

Figure 12-25 (Continued)

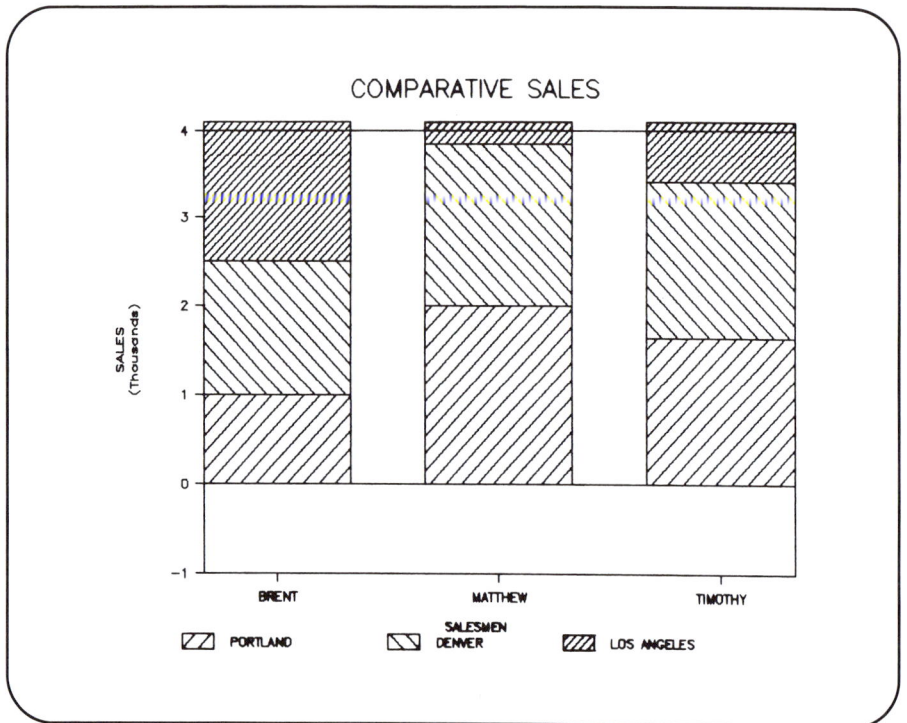

Figure 12-26 XY Graph for Total Sales and Advertising

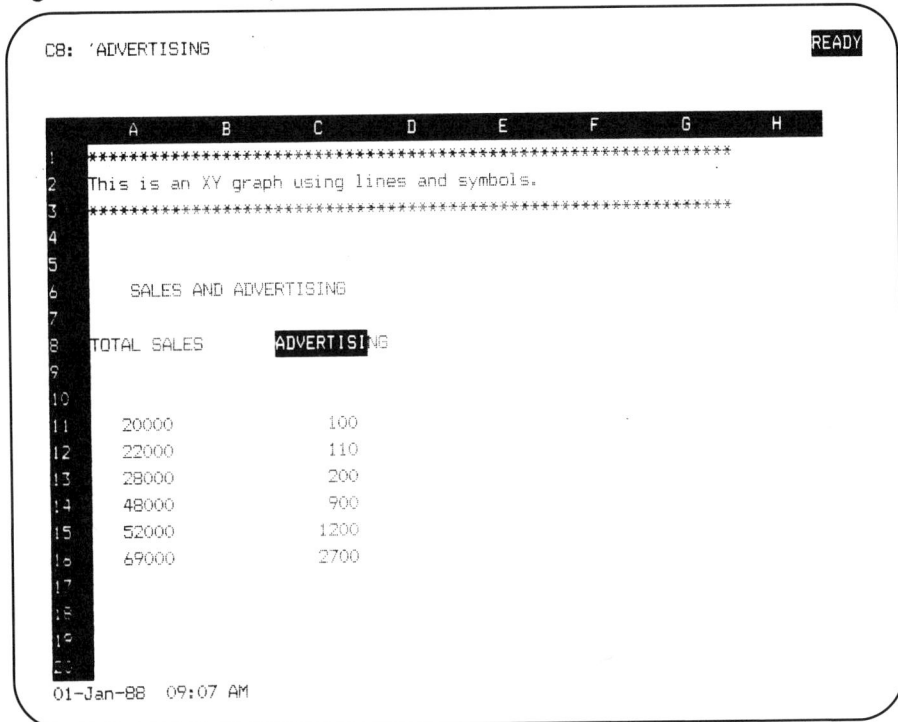

Figure 12-26 (Continued)

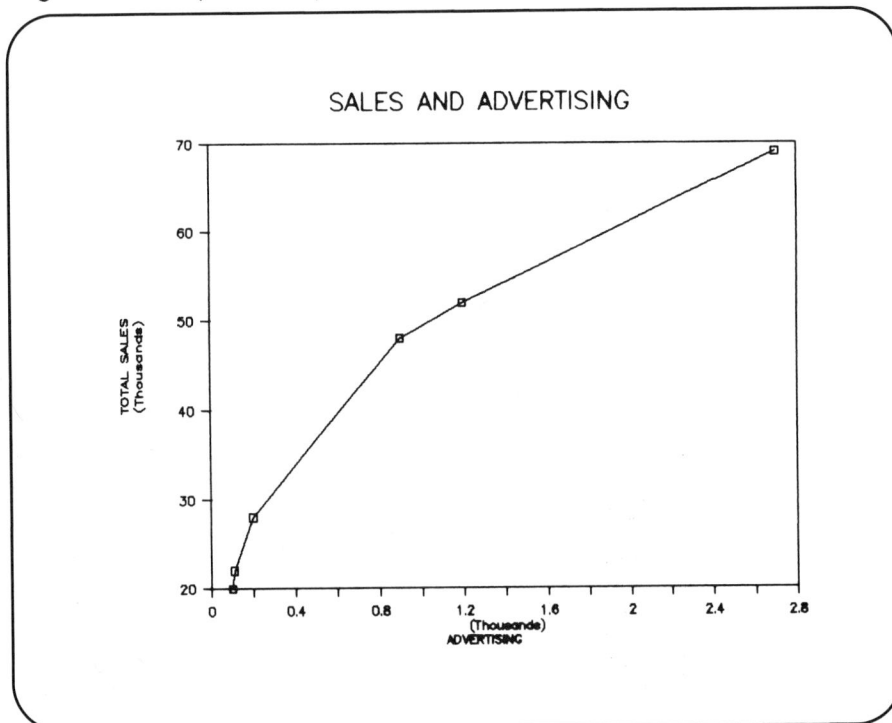

Figure 12-27 A Partial Income Statement for Happy Traveler Merchant

```
I8: [W7] 'crosshatches                                                    READY

              A       B       C       D       E       F       G       H         I
 1
 2                              HAPPY  TRAVELER  MERCHANT
 3
 4                    JAN     FEB     MAR     APR     MAY     JUNE    TOTAL
 5
 6    SALES        $2,000  $2,100  $1,900  $1,750  $2,200  $2,500  $12,450
 7    ===============================================================Code for
 8    EXPENSES                                                         crosshatches
 9    Raw Mat.        600     650     590     550     600     700    3690      1
10    Labor           300     275     310     280     310     375    1850      2
11    Rent            150     175     140     120     150     200     935      3
12    Electric         75     100      95     100     145     165     680      4
13    Advert.          50      65      70      75     100     150     510      5
14    -------------------------------------------------------------------
15    Total Exp.     1175    1265    1205    1125    1305    1590    7665
16    ===============================================================
17    Total Pro.    $825    $835    $695    $625    $895    $910   $4,785
18    ~~~~~~~~~~~~~~~~~~~~~~~~~~~~~~~~~~~~~~~~~~~~~~~~~~~~~~~~~~~~~~~~~~~~~
19    Code for
20    exploded Pie chart         101     102     103     104     105     106
01-Jan-88   12:45 PM
```

Figure 12-28-1 Happy Traveler Merchant in Action

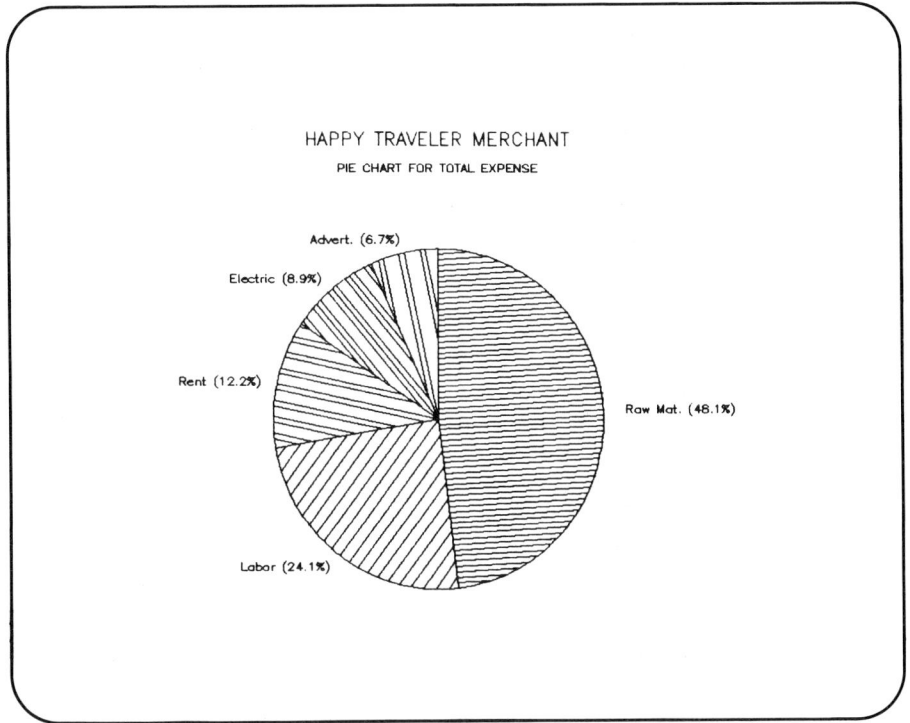

HAPPY TRAVELER MERCHANT

PIE CHART FOR TOTAL EXPENSE

Advert. (6.7%)

Electric (8.9%)

Rent (12.2%)

Raw Mat. (48.1%)

Labor (24.1%)

Figure 12-28-1 (Continued)

```
/Graph Type Pie
    X    A9..A13 Return
    A    H9..H13 Return
    B    I9..I13 Return
    Options Titles First "HAPPY TRAVELER MERCHANT" Return
            Titles Second "PIE CHART FOR TOTAL EXPENSE" Return
            Quit

    View
```

Figure 12-28-2

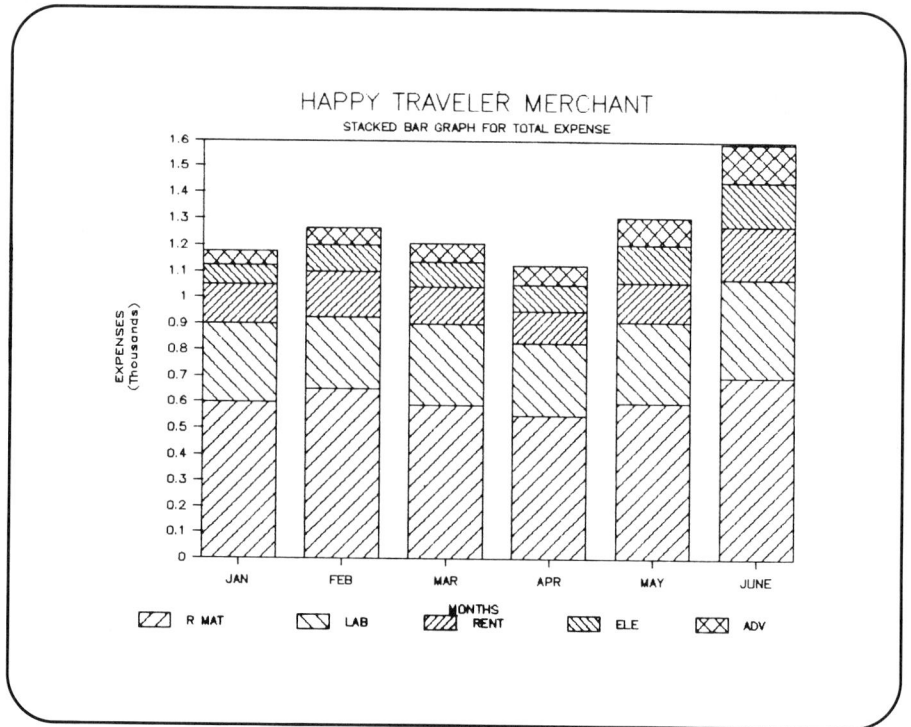

Figure 12-28-2 (Continued)

```
/Graph Type Stacked-Bar
       X    B4..G4 Return
       A    B9..G9 Return
       B    B10..G10 Return
       C    B11..G11 Return
       D    B12..G12 Return
       E    B13..G13 Return

       Options Legend A       "R MAT" Return
               Legend B       "LAB" Return
               Legend C       "RENT" Return
               Legend D       "ELE" Return
               Legend E       "ADV" Return
               Titles First   "HAPPY TRAVELER MERCHANT" Return
               Titles Second  "STACKED BAR GRAPH FOR TOTAL EXPENSE"
                               Return
               Titles X-axis  "MONTHS" Return
               Titles Y-axis  "EXPENSES" Return
               Quit

       View
```

Figure 12-28-3

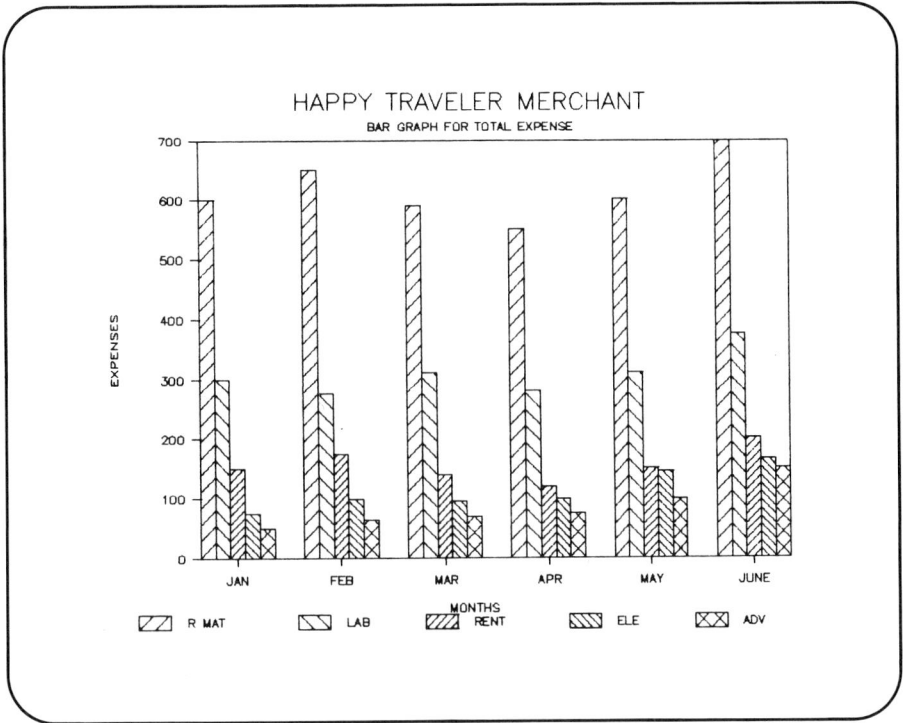

Figure 12-28-3 (Continued)

```
/Graph Type Bar
        X    B4..G4 Return
        A    B9..G9 Return
        B    B10..G10 Return
        C    B11..G11 Return
        D    B12..G12 Return
        E    B13..G13 Return

        Options Legend A      "R MAT" Return
                Legend B      "LAB" Return
                Legend C      "RENT" Return
                Legend D      "ELE" Return
                Legend E      "ADV" Return
                Titles First  "HAPPY TRAVELER MERCHANT" Return
                Titles Second "BAR GRAPH FOR TOTAL EXPENSE" Return
                Titles X-axis "MONTHS" Return
                Titles Y-axis "EXPENSES" Return
                Quit

        View
```

Figure 12-28-4

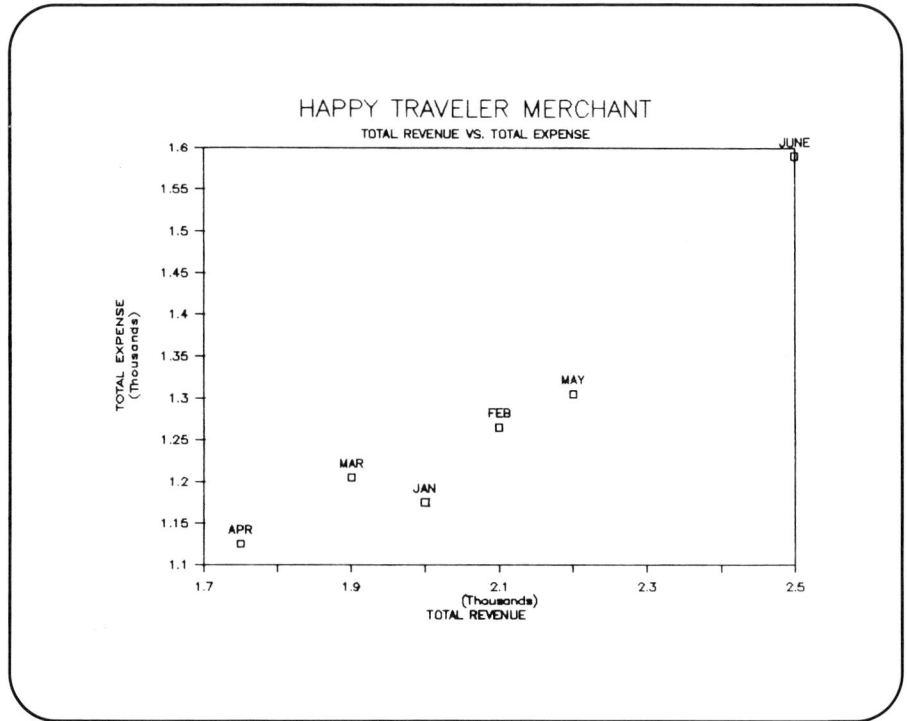

Figure 12-28-4 (Continued)

```
/Graph Type XY

      X    B6..G6 Return
      A    B15..G15 Return

      Options Format  A Symbols
                      Quit
              Titles  First  "HAPPY TRAVELER MERCHANT" Return
              Titles  Second  "TOTAL  REVENUE  VS.  TOTAL  EXPENSE"
                              Return
              Titles  X-axis "TOTAL REVENUE" Return
              Titles  Y-axis "TOTAL EXPENSE" Return
              Data labels A B4..G4  Return Above
                          Quit
              Quit

      View
```

Figure 12-28-5

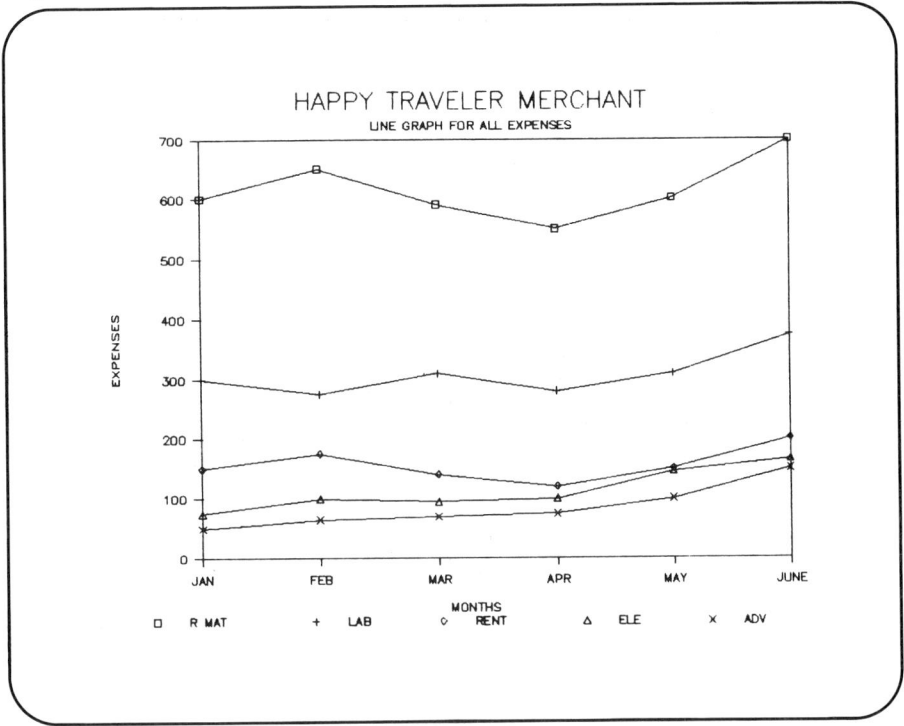

Figure 12-28-5 (Continued)

```
/Graph Type Line
        X    B4..G4 Return
        A    B9..G9 Return
        B    B10..G10 Return
        C    B11..G11 Return
        D    B12..G12 Return
        E    B13..G13 Return

        Options Legend    A      "R MAT" Return
                Legend    B      "LAB" Return
                Legend    C      "RENT" Return
                Legend    D      "ELE" Return
                Legend    E      "ADV" Return
                Titles First     "HAPPY TRAVELER MERCHANT" Return
                Titles Second    "LINE GRAPH FOR ALL EXPENSES" Return
                Titles X-axis    "MONTHS" Return
                Titles Y-axis    "EXPENSES" Return
                Quit

        View
```

Figure 12-28-6

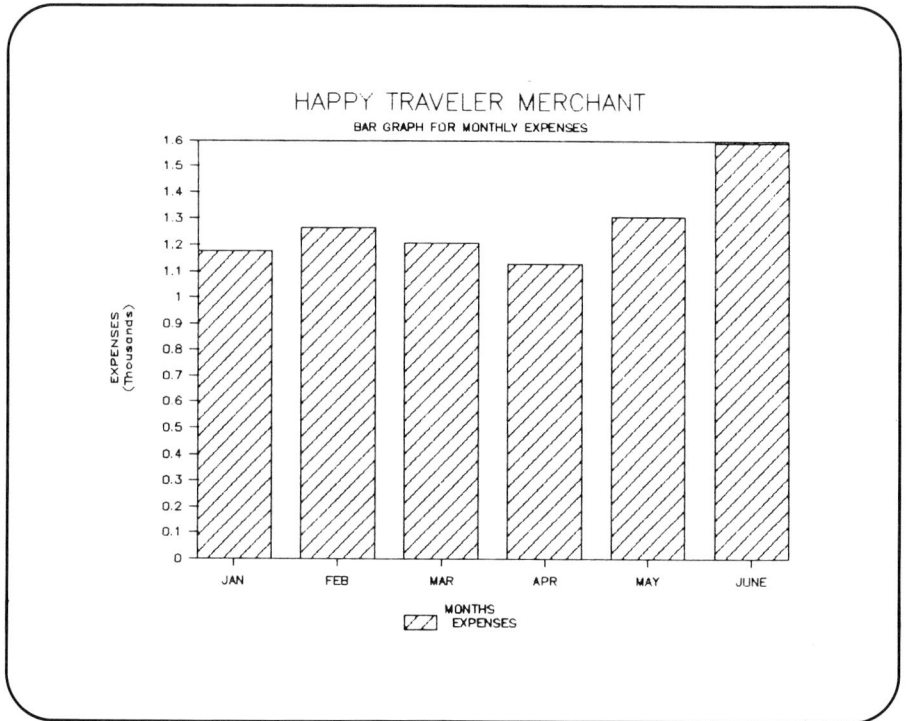

Figure 12-28-6 (Continued)

```
/Graph Type Bar
       X   B4..G4 Return
       A   B15..G15 Return

       Options Legend   A      "EXPENSES" Return
               Titles First    "HAPPY TRAVELER MERCHANT" Return
               Titles Second   "BAR  GRAPH  FOR  MONTHLY  EXPENSES"
                                Return
               Titles X-axis   "MONTHS" Return
               Titles Y-axis   "EXPENSES" Return
               Quit

       View
```

Figure 12-28-7

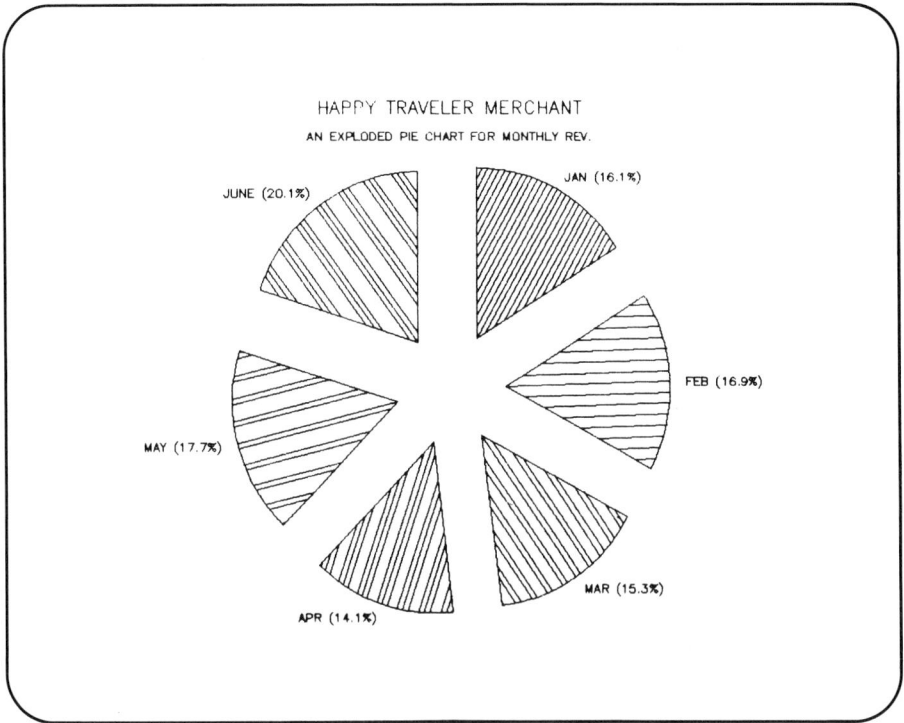

HAPPY TRAVELER MERCHANT

AN EXPLODED PIE CHART FOR MONTHLY REV.

JUNE (20.1%)   JAN (16.1%)

FEB (16.9%)

MAY (17.7%)

MAR (15.3%)

APR (14.1%)

Figure 12-28-7 (Continued)

```
/Graph Type Pie
       X    B4..G4         Return
       A    B6..G6         Return
       B    D20..I20       Return
       Options Titles  First  "HAPPY TRAVELER MERCHANT" Return
               Titles  Second "AN  EXPLODED  PIE  CHART  FOR  MONTHLY
                              REV." Return

              Quit

       View
```

Figure 12-8-8

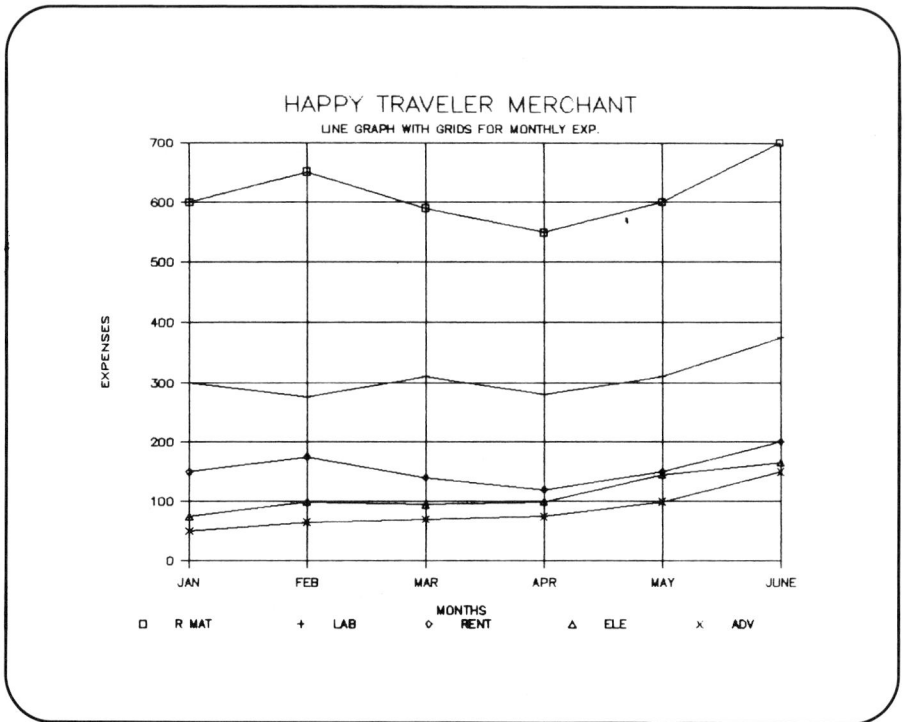

Figure 12-28-8 (Continued)

```
/Graph Type Line
        X    B4..G4      Return
        A    B9..G9      Return
        B    B10..G10    Return
        C    B11..G11    Return
        D    B12..G12    Return
        E    B13..G13    Return

        Options  Legend  A      "R MAT" Return
                 Legend  B      "LAB" Return
                 Legend  C      "RENT" Return
                 Legend  D      "ELE" Return
                 Legend  E      "ADV" Return
                 Titles  First  "HAPPY TRAVELER MERCHANT" Return
                 Titles  Second "LINE  GRAPH  WITH  GRIDS  FOR  MONTHLY
                                      EXP." Return
                 Titles X-axis "MONTHS" Return
                 Titles Y-axis "EXPENSES" Return
                 Grid    Both
                 Quit

        View
```

3. A bar graph with multiple ranges; on the X-axis different months, on the Y-axis the total of different expenses.
4. An XY graph with symbols and data labels. This graph displays total revenue vs. total expense.
5. A line graph of five different expenses over time using different symbols.
6. A simple bar chart for total monthly expenses.
7. An exploded pie chart for total revenue of six different months.
8. A line graph like Figure 12-28-5, but with horizontal and vertical grids.

Summary

Lotus can generate five different graphs: pie charts, bar graphs, stacked-bar graphs, XY graphs, and line graphs. As you can see from the examples, Lotus has a very impressive graphics operation. The last section of this chapter presented a comprehensive model of the variety of information that can be illustrated in Lotus graphics.

Review Questions

1. How many types of graphs can be generated by Lotus?
2. What is the unique application of each type?
3.* What are some of the limitations of Lotus graphics?
4.* What is the difference between XY graphs and line graphs?
5. How many data ranges can be used in Lotus graphics?
6.* What are the specific uses of the X range?
7. How do you save a graph for printing?
8.* Can your graph and your worksheet be saved under the same name?
9.* Can you retrieve a graphic file (e.g., PIC) from a system disk?
10. How do you delete a graph?
11.* How many different graphs can be generated by a worksheet?
12. What are the choices available under Options in the graph menu?
13.* How many types of grids can you have?
14. How many symbols are available for line graphs?
15. What are data labels? What are their applications?
16.* What is the Scale option?
17. Why do you use the Scale option?
18.* What are the uses of legends?
19. How many different legends can you have?
20. What is the function of the reset command in the graph menu?
21. Generate any sets of data comparable to Figure 12-27. Create the eight different graph types as we did in the comprehensive model for Happy Traveler Merchant.

Misconceptions and Solutions

M - When you invoke /Graph Name Delete, Lotus immediately erases the present graph settings and automatically returns you to the graph options menu. There is no confirmation step.

S - Before you use /GND, make sure this is what you want to do.

M - /GNR erases all the named graphs for a particular worksheet. If you issue this command there is no confirmation step.

S - Before issuing this command make sure this is what you want to do.

M - Sometimes no matter what you do, your graph does not show on the screen.

S - Check Graph, Options, Format, Graph, Neither. You may have accidentally formatted your graph to display neither lines nor symbols!

13

The PrintGraph Program

13-1 Introduction

In this chapter, we will explain how graphs generated on the screen can be transferred to graphic printers or plotters and how to generate hard copies of the graphs we studied in Chapter 12. We give an overview of the PrintGraph menu, discussing how to start it and how to exit from it. We explain ways you can control the look of your graph by specifying size, angle, typeface style, and so on. If you have access to a color printer or plotter, you will learn how to generate beautiful color graphics using 1-2-3 and the PrintGraph programs.

13-2 What Is the PrintGraph Program?

As you have seen so far, Lotus operations are stored on the 1-2-3 system disk. The only function not stored on the system disk is the PrintGraph program, which is stored on a separate disk. The reason for storing this program on a separate disk is to keep 1-2-3 at a manageable size. This program enables you to generate hard copies from graphs on your monitor. Using PrintGraph is possible only if you have access to a plotter or if your printer is capable of printing graphics as well as text.

To use the PrintGraph program, first save your graph with the /Graph Save command. Then exit from 1-2-3, and enter PrintGraph.

13-3 Starting PrintGraph

You can get PrintGraph started either from DOS or from the Lotus Access System. To load PrintGraph from DOS, at the A> prompt, put the PrintGraph disk in drive A, type PGRAPH, and press the **Return** key. If you are using a driver other than the default 1-2-3 set, you must type PGRAPH and the driver set, e.g., PGRAPH Name.

To load PrintGraph from the Lotus Access System, move the cursor to PrintGraph, hit the **Return** key, and follow the prompt. To exit from the PrintGraph program, choose the Exit option from the PrintGraph main menu. This will return you either to the Lotus Access System or to the DOS A> prompt.

13-4 Overview of the PrintGraph Main Menu

When you get the PrintGraph program started, you will see the main menu, as shown in Figure 13-1. This menu gives you six options as follows:

Image-Select   Settings   Go   Align   Page   Exit

You can use Left and Right arrows to move around the menu and press the **Return** key to select an option.

The Image-Select option allows you to choose one or more graphs to be printed. When you get the listing of your graph directory, move the cursor to the desired graph and hit the space bar. Your graph will be marked by a # sign. This means the graph is a candidate for printing. To remove the # sign, press the space bar again and the # sign will disappear. Later, if you want to print another graph, first remove the # sign from the present graph and choose your next candidate. If you don't remove the #, you will always print the first graph. Figure 13-2 shows the graph menu and the candidate for printing. This menu also tells you the date when a graph was generated, the time, and the size of the graph in bytes.

At this time, you can display your graph on the monitor (if you have graphics capability) by pressing F10.

The Settings option monitors the settings for the PrintGraph program. This includes size, fonts, color, and so forth.

Go starts the printing.

Align tells PrintGraph if the paper is positioned at the top of the page.

Page advances the paper to the top of the next page.

Exit gets you out of the PrintGraph program. You will return to DOS or to the Lotus Access System.

When you choose a graph from your graph directory for printing, remember that you cannot change any of the graph parameters in the PrintGraph program. If you want to make any changes, you must exit from PrintGraph, get into 1-2-3, retrieve your worksheet file, make the changes on the file, and save it by using /Graph Save. Also remember that a PIC (graphic) file cannot be retrieved in a 1-2-3 worksheet. You have to retrieve the worksheet file that generated the corresponding PIC file in the 1-2-3 worksheet (this file has the WK1 extension).

Figure 13-1 The PrintGraph Main Menu

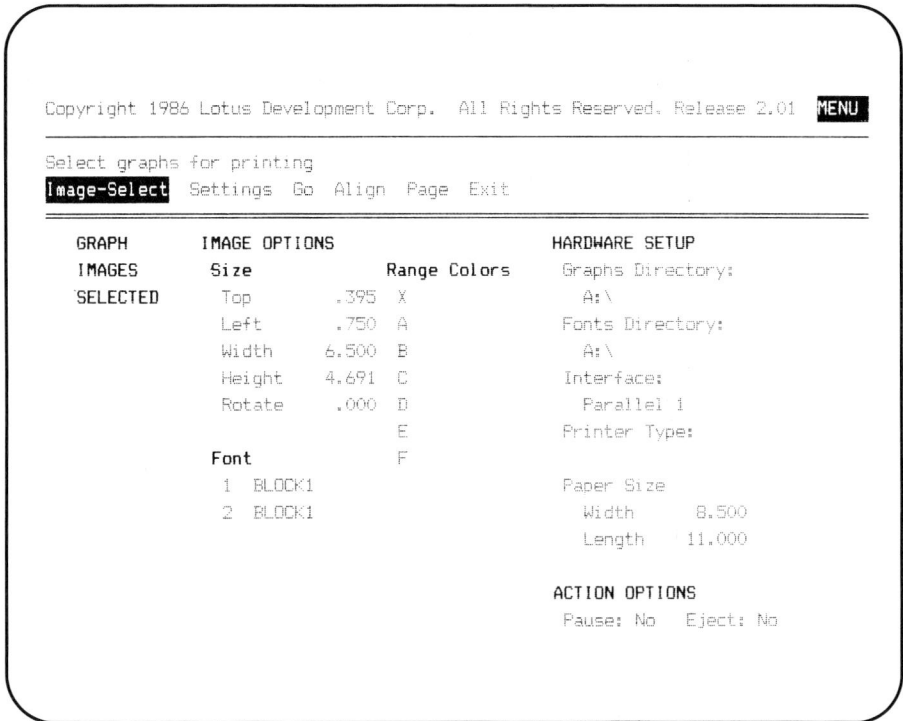

```
Copyright 1986 Lotus Development Corp.  All Rights Reserved. Release 2.01  MENU

Select graphs for printing
Image-Select  Settings  Go  Align  Page  Exit

    GRAPH        IMAGE OPTIONS                        HARDWARE SETUP
    IMAGES       Size              Range Colors       Graphs Directory:
    SELECTED      Top      .395    X                    A:\
                  Left     .750    A                  Fonts Directory:
                  Width   6.500    B                    A:\
                  Height  4.691    C                  Interface:
                  Rotate   .000    D                    Parallel 1
                                   E                  Printer Type:
                 Font              F
                 1  BLOCK1                            Paper Size
                 2  BLOCK1                              Width      8.500
                                                        Length    11.000


                                                    ACTION OPTIONS
                                                      Pause: No   Eject: No
```

Figure 13-2 A Sample of Graphs Directory and a Candidate for Printing

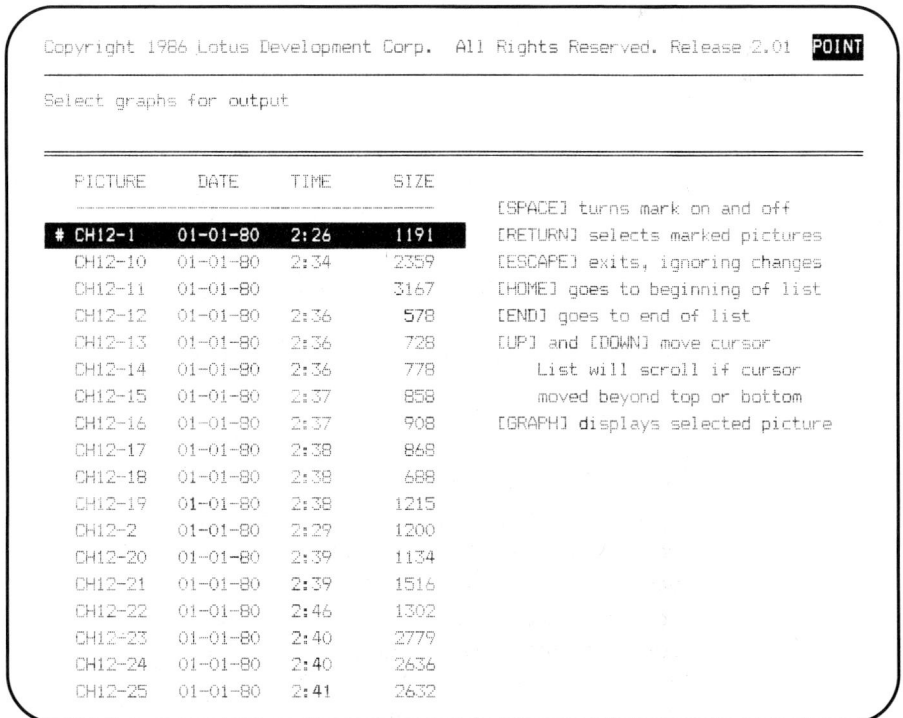

```
Copyright 1986 Lotus Development Corp.  All Rights Reserved. Release 2.01  POINT

Select graphs for output


    PICTURE      DATE      TIME      SIZE
    ─────────────────────────────────────────   [SPACE] turns mark on and off
 #  CH12-1     01-01-80    2:26      1191        [RETURN] selects marked pictures
    CH12-10    01-01-80    2:34      2359        [ESCAPE] exits, ignoring changes
    CH12-11    01-01-80              3167        [HOME] goes to beginning of list
    CH12-12    01-01-80    2:36      578         [END] goes to end of list
    CH12-13    01-01-80    2:36      728         [UP] and [DOWN] move cursor
    CH12-14    01-01-90    2:36      778            List will scroll if cursor
    CH12-15    01-01-80    2:37      858              moved beyond top or bottom
    CH12-16    01-01-80    2:37      908         [GRAPH] displays selected picture
    CH12-17    01-01-90    2:38      868
    CH12-18    01-01-80    2:38      688
    CH12-19    01-01-80    2:38      1215
    CH12-2     01-01-80    2:29      1200
    CH12-20    01-01-80    2:39      1134
    CH12-21    01-01-80    2:39      1516
    CH12-22    01-01-80    2:46      1302
    CH12-23    01-01-80    2:40      2779
    CH12-24    01-01-80    2:40      2636
    CH12-25    01-01-80    2:41      2632
```

13-5 More on the Settings Command

When you choose Settings from the main menu, you will be given the following options:

Image   Hardware   Action   Save   Reset   Quit

Let us briefly explain these options.

13-6 Hardware Considerations

When you choose Settings Hardware, the following menu will be presented to you (see Figure 13-3):

Graphs-Directory   Fonts-Directory   Interface   Printer   Size-Paper Quit

PrintGraph automatically searches drive A for the Graphs and Fonts directories. You can change these directories to drive B by typing B:. With hard disk systems you have to change the default to C drive, or the drive where you have stored your graphs. This procedure is done during the installation of your system (see Appendix C). If you look back at Figure 13-1, you will see the default settings as follows:

Graphs Directory: A:
Fonts Directory: A:
Interface: Parallel 1; etc.

Your interface can be either parallel or serial. If you specify a serial interface for hardware settings (e.g., Settings, Hardware, Interface), you must also specify the baud rate setting of your printer. The baud rate is the speed at which data is transferred. Choose the fastest baud rate available for your printer. The following are baud rates in order of increasing speed:

Setting	Baud Rate
1	110
2	150
3	300
4	600
5	1,200
6	2,400
7	4,800
8	9,600
9	19,200

You must configure the serial printer to the following settings:

Setting	Value
Data bits	8
Stop bits	For baud 110, 2; otherwise,1
Parity	None

Remember, these settings must be changed on your printer, not in the PrintGraph program.

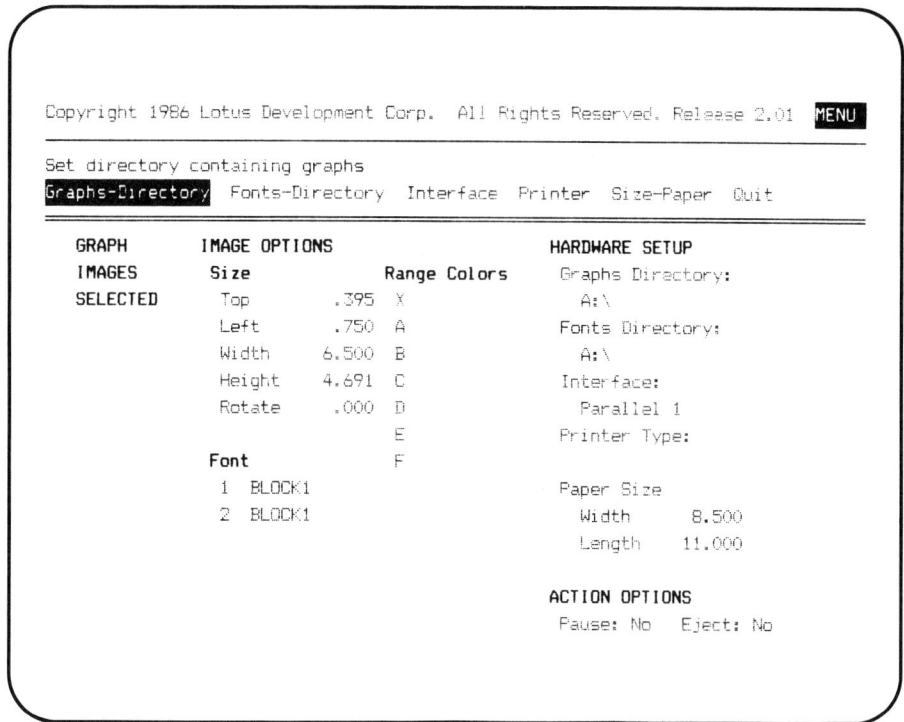

```
Copyright 1986 Lotus Development Corp.  All Rights Reserved. Release 2.01  MENU

Set directory containing graphs
Graphs-Directory  Fonts-Directory  Interface  Printer  Size-Paper  Quit

    GRAPH        IMAGE OPTIONS                   HARDWARE SETUP
    IMAGES         Size              Range Colors  Graphs Directory:
    SELECTED        Top      .395   X               A:\
                    Left     .750   A             Fonts Directory:
                    Width   6.500   B               A:\
                    Height  4.691   C             Interface:
                    Rotate   .000   D               Parallel 1
                                    E             Printer Type:
                  Font              F
                    1  BLOCK1                     Paper Size
                    2  BLOCK1                       Width      8.500
                                                    Length    11.000

                                                ACTION OPTIONS
                                                  Pause: No   Eject: No
```

Figure 13-3 The Menu for Settings Hardware

The Size-Paper option in this menu will give you the following three options:

Length   Width   Quit

These options can change the default settings of PrintGraph.

13-7 The Image Option

The Image option will give the following menu:

Size   Font   Range-Colors   Quit

Choosing the Size option, you can select Full, Half, Manual, or Quit.

With the Full and Half options, PrintGraph will automatically fit your graph onto the entire page or onto half of the page and will set the height and width of the graph accordingly.

The Manual option enables you to change top and left margins manually. It also defines the width, height, and rotation of the graph, from zero to 90 degrees.

The Rotation option sets the number of degrees that the graph is turned counter-clockwise. If PrintGraph sets a graph size automatically, it preserves the aspect ratio or the ratio of graph width to graph height, approximately 1.385 to 1 for X and Y-axes, respectively. Therefore, remember that if you change either X or Y, the other axis must be changed proportionately. For example, if X = 4, then Y = 2.88 (X/Y = 1.385/1, 4/Y = 1.385, Y = 4/1.385 = 2.88).

When you draw a pie chart, you must always maintain the standard aspect ratio of 1.385(X-axis)/1(Y-axis) in order to preserve the circular shape, otherwise you may end up with an ellipse instead of a circle. The default settings for Top, Left, Width, Height, and Rotation are presented in the body of the main menu (see Figure 13-1).

One of the options under Settings Image is the Font option. If this option is chosen you will be given two more choices, 1 or 2. Both graph fonts 1 and 2 have 11 options (see Figure 13-4). In the Font menu, the higher the option, the darker the print; for example, SCRIPT2 is darker than SCRIPT1. You can choose Font 1 for the heading and Font 2 for the rest of the graph. If you don't choose Font 2, PrintGraph will print the entire graph in Font 1.

When you choose Settings, Image, Range-Colors, PrintGraph displays a menu that shows the graph ranges, X and A to F. This setting depends on the type of printer that you are using; you will see different colors only with color printers. Range-Colors can be selected only if you have specified a particular printer or plotter by choosing Hardware, Printer.

Printing a colored pie chart is done in a slightly different way from the other types of graphs. The colors of the wedges are defined by the values in the B range when you save your graph using the /Graph Save command. If you recall from chapter 12, the B range was used for generating crosshatches in B range. Value 1 in the 1-2-3 worksheet corresponds to the X range in PrintGraph, Value 2 to A, value 3 to B and so forth up to Value 7 of the B range in the 1-2-3 worksheet to F in PrintGraph. Besides the color black, there are nine other colors: red, green, blue, orange, lime, gold, turquoise, violet, and brown.

13-8 The Action Option

One of the options under Settings is Action. If you choose Action from this menu, you will be given the following three choices:

Pause   Eject   Quit

The Action option monitors the operations of PrintGraph telling you what PrintGraph does between printing. You can choose Pause or Eject. If you choose the Pause option, you will be given two choices: Yes or No.

The Yes option makes PrintGraph pause. This is useful if you would like to change some of your settings after printing a graph. If you choose the No option, PrintGraph will not pause between printing graphs. This is useful if you are not going to change any of your settings from graph to graph.

The Eject option controls whether PrintGraph automatically advances the paper or not. If you choose this option, you will be given two more choices: Yes or No. Yes will give you one graph per page. No is used if you want more than one graph per page.

```
Copyright 1985 Lotus Development Corp.  All Rights Reserved.  Release 2    POINT

Select font 1

        FONT NAME      SIZE
        ------------------         [SPACE] turns mark on and off
     #  BLOCK1         5737        [RETURN] selects marked font
        BLOCK2         9300        [ESCAPE] exits, ignoring changes
        BOLD           8624        [HOME] goes to beginning of list
        FORUM          9727        [END] goes to end of list
        ITALIC1        8949        [UP] and [DOWN] move cursor
        ITALIC2        11857           List will scroll if cursor
        LOTUS          8679           moved beyond top or bottom
        ROMAN1         6863
        ROMAN2         11847
        SCRIPT1        8132
        SCRIPT2        10367
```

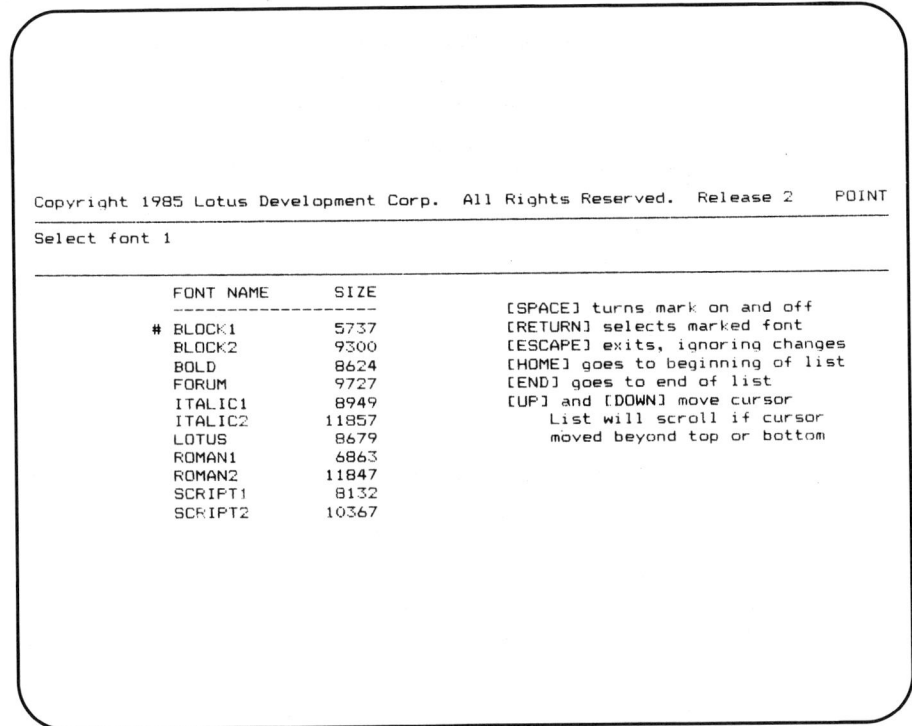

Figure 13-4 The Font Menu

If PrintGraph cannot fit the second graph on the same page, it advances to the next page automatically.

13-9 Save and Reset Options

Under the Settings menu, there are three other options: Save, Reset, and Quit.

The Save option can be used if you wish to save some of the present settings and use them in another session. If you do not choose this option, PrintGraph will not remember the most recent settings, which you may have changed during the last session. Therefore, it reads from the PGRAPH.CNF file (the default settings).

The Reset option is the opposite of Save. It replaces the current settings with those in the PGRAPH.CNF file(the default settings).

The Quit option will let you exit from this menu.

13-10 An Example of the Final Product

To wrap up this chapter, we developed an example using several of the options we have talked about. Look at Figure 13-5. First, by using Settings, Hardware, Printer, we chose the printer, in this case an IBM Graphics printer. Then we chose Image-Select (settings were the default values). Finally, we chose Go.

Figure 13-5 An Example of a Graph Generated by Default Settings

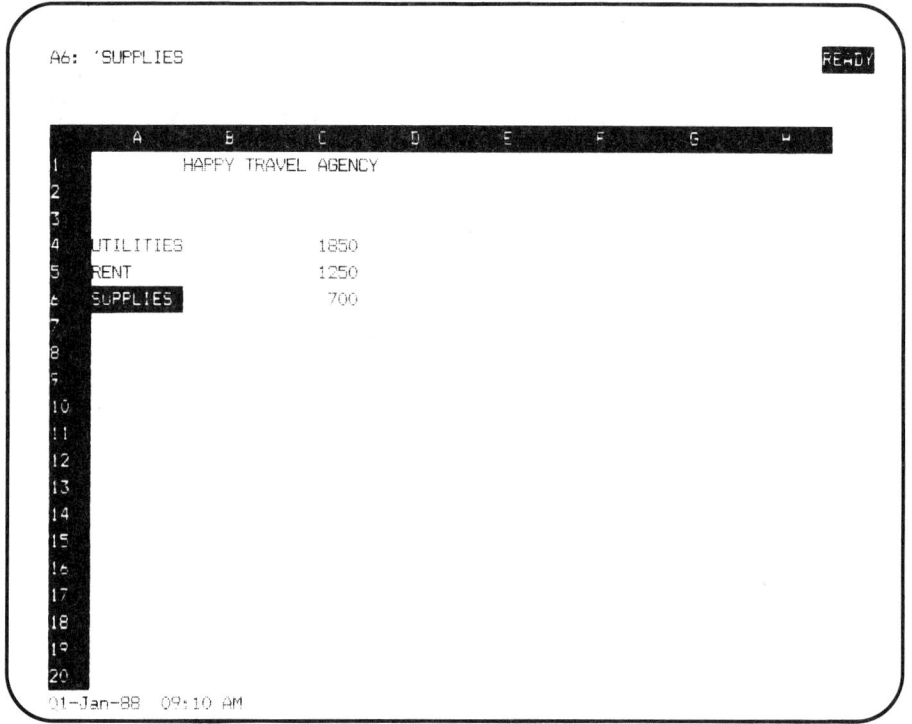

```
A6:  'SUPPLIES                                                    READY


         A        B        C        D       E       F       G       H
1                    HAPPY  TRAVEL  AGENCY
2
3
4   UTILITIES                1850
5   RENT                     1250
6   SUPPLIES                  700
7
8
9
10
11
12
13
14
15
16
17
18
19
20
01-Jan-88   09:10 AM
```

Figure 13-5 (Continued)

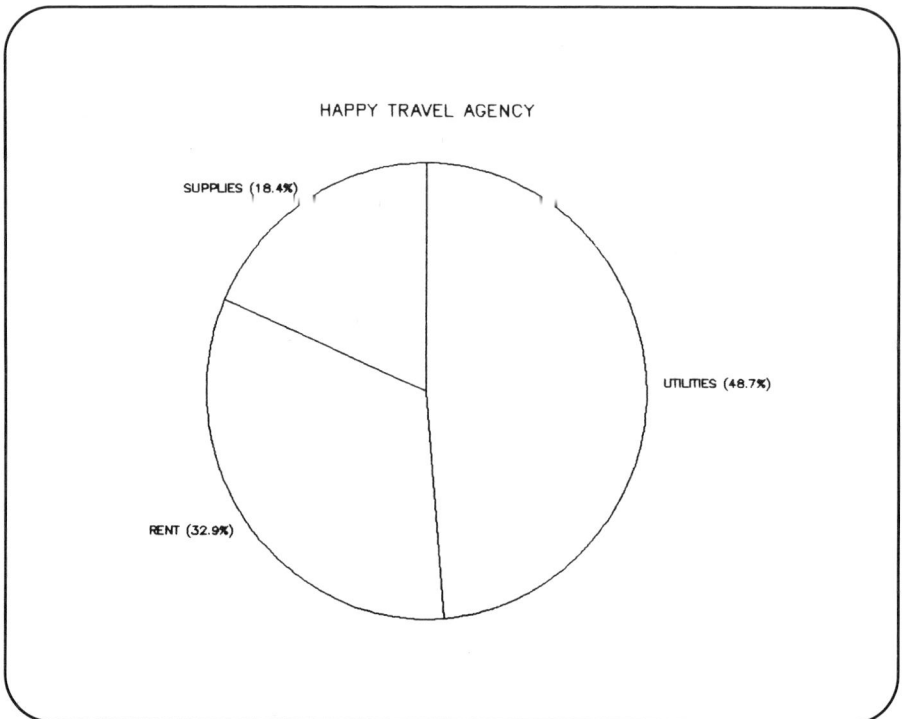

HAPPY TRAVEL AGENCY

SUPPLIES (18.4%)

UTILITIES (48.7%)

RENT (32.9%)

Summary

This chapter reviewed the PrintGraph program. This is the only program not included on the main 1-2-3 systems disk. PrintGraph allows you to generate hard copies of the graphs you have created on your monitor with different settings. You can specify the size of the paper, the angle, the typeface, the size of the graph. The Font option provides you with 11 typefaces for the graph. If you have access to a color printer or plotter, you can generate color graphics.

Remember that at installation time, you must specify the type of printer and /or plotter you are using. As you will see in Appendix C, you can use a wide variety of printers and plotters with Lotus. If yours is not on the list, you may want to contact the Lotus Development Corporation.

Review Questions

1. How do you start PrintGraph?
2. How do you exit from PrintGraph?
3.* When you exit from PrintGraph, do you return to DOS or to the Lotus Access System?
4. What is the purpose of Image-Select in the main menu?
5.* Can you see your graph on the monitor using the PrintGraph program?
6. Can a PIC file (a graphic file) be retrieved in a 1-2-3 worksheet?
7.* How do you modify a graph's parameters in the PrintGraph program?
8. What is the purpose of the Align command in the main menu?
9. How many choices are available under the Font options?
10. How many colors are supported by the PrintGraph program?
11. What is the aspect ratio? What is this ratio in the default setting?
12.* Does the aspect ratio have to be fixed for pie charts? If yes, why?
13. How do you change the Graph directory from A drive to B drive?
14. How many interfaces are available?
15. The baud rate is required for which type of interface?
16.* What are the maximum and minimum baud rates?
17. What choices are available under Action?
18.* What does Pause do?
19. What does Eject do?
20. What is the purpose of Save and Reset in the Settings menu?
21. The following are oil production figures for Exatec Oil Company:

   1981 200,000 barrels
   1982 250,000 barrels
   1983 350,000 barrels
   1984 400,000 barrels
   1985 450,000 barrels
   1986 400,000 barrels
   1987 475,000 barrels

   Design and print a line graph, a bar graph, and a pie chart for this data.

Misconception and Solution

M - In a PrintGraph session, if you change some of the default settings and want to use these settings later, PrintGraph will not save these settings automatically.

S - Use the Settings Save command in order to save the current settings to the PGRAPH.CNF file before you exit from the PrintGraph session.

14

Database Operations/Part One: Lotus as an Electronic File Cabinet

14-1 Introduction

In this chapter we will discuss the principles of database management using Lotus, including file creation, updating, sorting, and searching. We will use examples to illustrate the major database operations. Chapter 15 discusses advanced database operations.

14-2 What Is a Database?

In simple terms, a *database* is an organized collection of data stored in a central location. We all have used many databases, but we may not have called them that. A telephone directory is a good example of a database, one that has been organized alphabetically.

A better example of a database is the Yellow Pages. This database is also organized alphabetically; however, it is organized internally as well. If you are looking for a restaurant, you go to the *R* section, find *Restaurants*, and then search alphabetically for a particular restaurant.

In computer terminology, we call a database a collection of files, or more specifically, a collection of a series of integrated files. A *file* is a collection of records. A *record* is a collection of related fields, and a *field* is a collection of characters.

Your name, age, or occupation is an example of a field. If you put several name, age, and occupation fields together, you have constructed a record. Putting several student records together would establish a student file. At the same time, you can student records together would establish a student file. At the same time, you can have a staff file, a faculty file, and so on. The collection of all these files is a database.

Most small and medium-size businesses use file cabinets to store their data. File cabinets are organized using a series of manila folders. Data in each folder is organized alphabetically, numerically, or by some other organizational scheme. Such a file cabinet and the information it contains can be called a manual database.

There are several differences between a manual and an automated database. An automated database is faster, more accurate, and occupies less space than a manual database.

14-3 Lotus as a Database

Lotus 1-2-3 offers some basic database capabilities. Using Lotus as a database management system, you can store up to 8,192 records. Each record can include up to 256 fields; each field can include up to 240 characters. However, compared to database packages such as dBASE III Plus or R-BASE 5000, Lotus offers limited database capabilities.

The size of a database depends on the size of the memory in your computer (RAM). Each character is equal to one byte of memory. So 1,000 records, each with 200 characters, is equal to 200,000 bytes, or approximately 195K. Lotus Release 2 requires 215K of memory if you load it from the Lotus Access System. If 1-2-3 is loaded directly, the memory requirement is approximately 192K.

Since a database generated by Lotus resides in RAM, processing speed is extremely fast. Using Lotus as a database is also helpful when you import files from other programs to perform database operations (for information on file transfer, see Appendix D).

14-4 Basic Database Operations Using Lotus

The Lotus database is simply an expansion of the spreadsheet. This spreadsheet includes 8,192 rows (records) and 256 columns (fields). Major database operations are:

- Database creation

- Database update

- Database sort

- Database search

Database creation simply means putting labels, formulas, or figures in different cells, something we have been doing all along. If the length of a particular field is larger than nine characters (the default value), it can be modified by using /Worksheet Global Column-Width or /Worksheet Column Set-Width.

Database update includes changing the content of a particular field (simple editing), insertion of a new record or field (/Worksheet Insert Row or /Worksheet Insert Column, respectively), deletion of a record or field (/Worksheet Delete Row or /Worksheet Delete Column, respectively), deletion of an entire database (/Worksheet Erase Yes), or deletion of a portion of a database (/Range Erase).

You can sort your database in either ascending or descending order by using a primary key and a secondary key. A *primary key* is the first field chosen for a sort operation; for example, last name. The *secondary key* is the second field chosen for a sort operation; for example, sex. Finally, you can do any type of search using different criteria.

Other complex database operations, such as the join operation (putting two databases side by side), can be performed with the /File Combine command. A merge operation (adding one database to the bottom of another one) can also be performed by using the /File Combine command. For other database operations, such as label generation or managing multiple databases, macros (discussed in Chapters 16-18) can be developed.

14-5 Your First Database

Figure 14-1 shows an example of a database. This database has fifteen records, each with six fields. Each field starts with a field name. The field name must be a label; however, it can be a numeric label such as "5" or "9", etc. The field name can be more than one line in length but only the last row will be considered the field name. Field names must be unique.

Figure 14-1 has been created in the same fashion as other worksheets. Numbers and figures are right-justified and labels are left-justified.

14-6 Sorting Your Database

The database can be sorted by any field, in ascending or descending order. To access the Sort command, choose Data from the main menu and then select the Sort command. The Sort command has the following options:

Data-Range   Primary-Key   Secondary-Key   Reset   Go   Quit

The data-range usually includes all data items in your database, though in reality you can include only a portion of your database. The field names must not be included in the data-range, otherwise it will be considered as a part of the database itself and will be mixed up with data items.

The primary-key is the first key for the Sort operation. Any field in your database may be selected as the primary-key. The secondary-key is another field that may be used for a Sort operation.

Reset is used when you decide to change the parameter of your database. When you choose the Reset command all current settings will go back to the default setting. For example, if your previous data range was A1..A50, after choosing the Reset

```
A1: [W12]                                                    READY

            A           B          C    D     E            F        G
1                   MY FIRST DATABASE
2
3      FIRST NAME   LAST NAME      AGE  SEX  OCCUPATION     INCOME
4      Randy        Alexander      36   M    Professor      $40,000
5      Fay          Alexander      30   F    Mayor          $30,000
6      Adam         Alexander      31   M    Engineer       $30,000
7      Andrea       Byan           36   F    Teacher        $31,000
8      Moe          Byan           40   M    Officer        $40,000
9      Bob          Adam           32   M    Engineer       $72,000
10     Anna         Adam            4   F    Unemployed     $11,000
11     Vicki        Adam            9   F    Unemployed     $12,000
12     Paula        Bobby          55   F    Housewife      $20,000
13     Jack         Jones          69   M    Artist         $19,000
14     Mary         Fishler        30   F    Interpreter    $19,000
15     Sue          Hayword        22   F    Student        $10,000
16     Tammy        Smith          29   F    Student        $10,000
17     Jacky        Brown          72   F    Engineer       $52,000
18     Lora         Jones          30   F    Nurse          $31,000
19
20
     01-Jan-88  10:34 AM
```

Figure 14-1 An Example of a Database

command your data range will be erased. Now you have to define a new database range.

Go executes the Sort operation. And finally, Quit will let you leave the menu.

Figure 14-2 shows Figure 14-1 after having been sorted by last name. This figure was generated as follows:

/Data, Sort, Data-Range A4..F18, Return, Primary-Key, B4..B18, Return, A, Return, Go

By default, Lotus sorts in descending order. If you do not want this default setting, type A (ascending) and press the **Return** key. Otherwise, hit Return without typing anything; This means you are choosing the default setting. The order in which Lotus performs a sort is determined by a collating sequence. You may choose one of three collating sequences during the install operations (see Appendix C):

- Numbers first

- Numbers last

- ASCII

Uppercase and lowercase letters have the same value. As a general rule, nonlabel, nonnumeric, and composed characters (F1 + Alternate) fall at the end of the listing. (For ASCII codes see Appendix F.) As a general rule do not leave any empty row or column in your database.

```
A1: [W12] 'This database has been sorted by last name.                    READY


          A           B           C    D    E              F         G
 1   This database has been sorted by last name.
 2
 3   FIRST NAME   LAST NAME       AGE  SEX  OCCUPATION     INCOME
 4   Anna         Adam              4   F   Unemployed     $11,000
 5   Bob          Adam             32   M   Engineer       $72,000
 6   Vicki        Adam              9   F   Unemployed     $12,000
 7   Adam         Alexander        31   M   Engineer       $30,000
 8   Fay          Alexander        30   F   Mayor          $30,000
 9   Randy        Alexander        36   M   Professor      $40,000
10   Paula        Bobby            55   F   Housewife      $20,000
11   Jacky        Brown            72   F   Engineer       $52,000
12   Andrea       Byan             36   F   Teacher        $31,000
13   Moe          Byan             40   M   Officer        $40,000
14   Mary         Fishler          30   F   Interpreter    $19,000
15   Sue          Hayword          22   F   Student        $10,000
16   Jack         Jones            69   M   Artist         $19,000
17   Lora         Jones            30   F   Nurse          $31,000
18   Tammy        Smith            29   F   Student        $10,000
19
20
01-Jan-88   10:35 AM
```

Figure 14-2 Figure 14-1 Sorted by Last Name

14-7 Sorting with Two Keys

There are instances when you want to sort a database using two fields. The Yellow Pages, for example, has been sorted by business type and within each type, businesses are sorted alphabetically. In Figure 14-3, we sorted the original database (Figure 14-1) using two keys. The primary-key is sex and the secondary-key is age. Within each group, individuals are sorted by age. Figure 14-3 was generated as follows:

/Data, Sort, Data-Range A4..F18, Return, Primary-Key, D4..D18, Return, A, Return, Secondary-Key, C4..C18, Return, A, Return, Go

14-8 Search Operations

In search operations we are interested in a specific record or series of records that meet certain criteria. For example, in a student grade file we might want to search for all students who have a GPA greater than 3.60, or in an employee file, employees who hold a master's degree. To conduct a search operation, access Data from the main menu and then choose Query. Under Query we have:

Input   Criterion   Output   Find   Extract   Unique   Delete   Reset   Quit

Input includes the entire database, including the field names. For example, in Figure 14-1 the Input range is A3..F18.

```
A1: [W12] 'This database has been sorted by sex and age.          READY
```

	A	B	C	D	E	F	G
1	This database has been sorted by sex and age.						
2							
3	FIRST NAME	LAST NAME	AGE	SEX	OCCUPATION	INCOME	
4	Anna	Adam	4	F	Unemployed	$11,000	
5	Vicki	Adam	9	F	Unemployed	$12,000	
6	Sue	Hayword	22	F	Student	$10,000	
7	Tammy	Smith	29	F	Student	$10,000	
8	Mary	Fishler	30	F	Interpreter	$19,000	
9	Lora	Jones	30	F	Nurse	$31,000	
10	Fay	Alexander	30	F	Mayor	$30,000	
11	Andrea	Byan	36	F	Teacher	$31,000	
12	Paula	Bobby	55	F	Housewife	$20,000	
13	Jacky	Brown	72	F	Engineer	$52,000	
14	Adam	Alexander	31	M	Engineer	$30,000	
15	Bob	Adam	32	M	Engineer	$72,000	
16	Randy	Alexander	36	M	Professor	$40,000	
17	Moe	Byan	40	M	Officer	$40,000	
18	Jack	Jones	69	M	Artist	$19,000	
19							
20							

```
01-Jan-88   10:36 AM
```

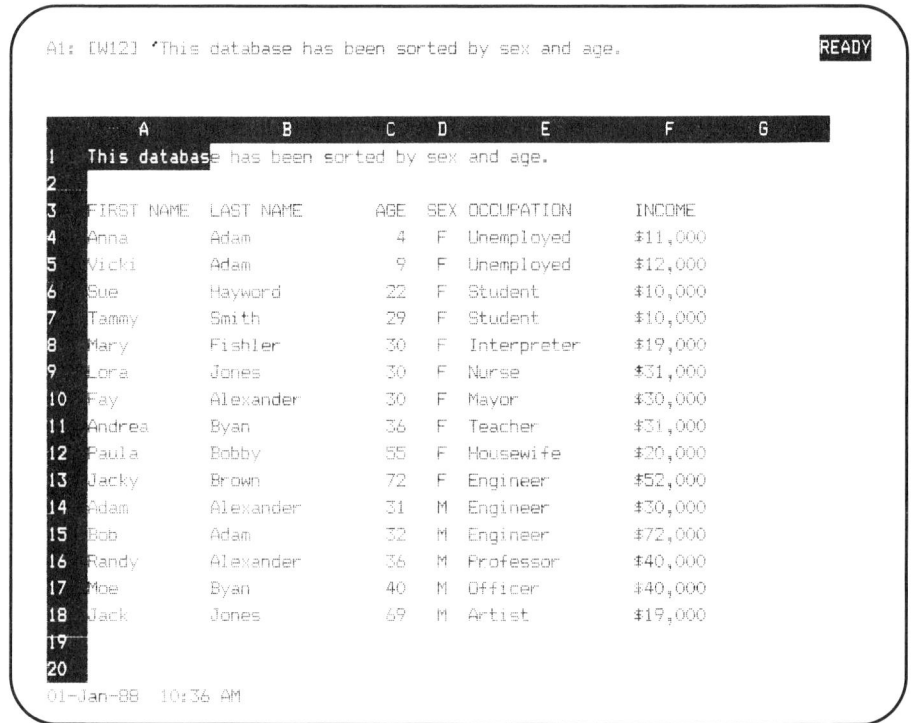

Figure 14-3 Figure 14-1 Sorted by Sex and Age

The criterion range is a part of the worksheet entered separately outside the database range, which includes the name of the field and the criterion we are searching for. The criterion range must have field names identical to those used in the database; therefore, the Copy command is optimal for creation of the criterion range field names. For example, in our database (Figure 14-1), the criterion range for all the engineers would be:

Occupation
Engineer

Occupation is the field name in which we have a field containing Engineer. Up to 32 fields can be considered for the search in the criterion range.

The output range is a selected portion of a worksheet outside the database range used to store records based on the criterion range. It must contain the names of the fields in the database which you want to extract (uppercase or lowercase doesn't matter).

The Find option is used to choose a record or a series of records based on the criterion range (output range is not needed with the Find option). To use the Find option all you need to define is the Input range and the Criterion range, and then choose the Find option. When the option is executed, the selected records will be highlighted.

With the Extract option, a portion of a database can be copied to the output range, based on the criterion range (assuming you have already defined the output range).

The Unique option is used in order to extract only a unique portion of a database. In this case, duplicate records will not be chosen. For example, if you would like to choose one representative of each occupation, only one engineer will be selected, one professor, and so forth.

The Delete option is used to erase a portion of a database, based on the criterion range. The following section illustrates these options.

14-9 Search with Single Criterion

In Figure 14-4 we have searched the database on the left side of the figure for all engineers. This example was generated as follows:

/Data, Query, Input A5..D13, Return, Criterion F6..F7, Return, Find

As you see, when you choose the Find option, the cursor will point to the first record that meets a particular criterion. If you move the cursor down to the records below the first selected one, you will see it point to the next candidate (if there is any). This will continue until all the candidates are highlighted. Now, if you try to move the cursor farther down, you will hear a beep. This means there are no more candidates to be highlighted.

To demonstrate the actual output we have used the Extract option. Figure 14-5 was generated as follows:

Figure 14-4 Example of Search with Single Criteria (All Engineers)

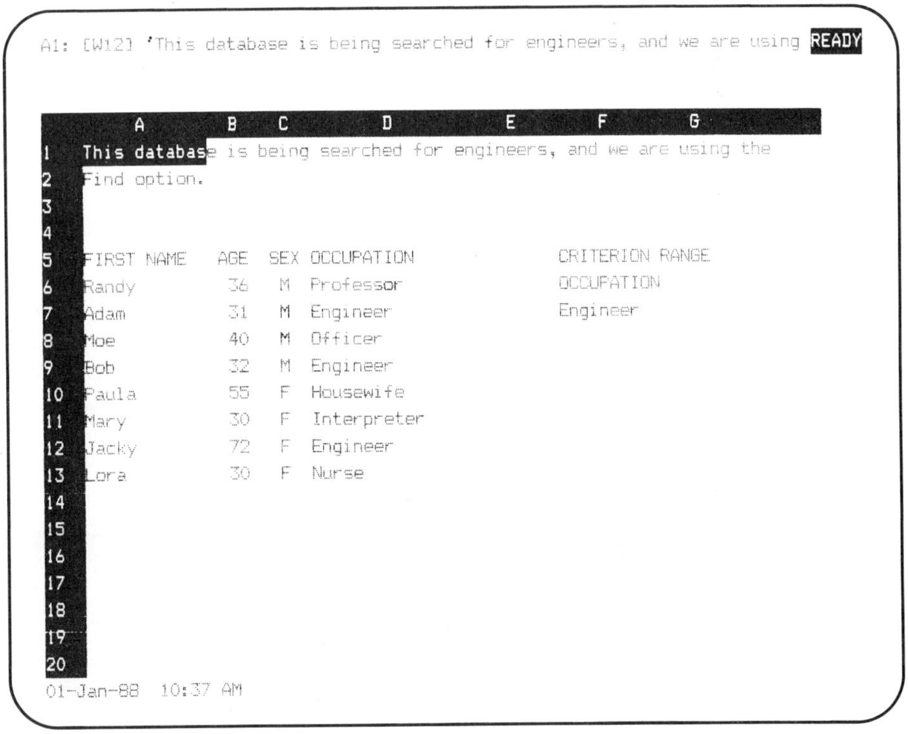

/Data, Query, Input A5..D13, Return, Criterion F6..F7, Return, Output A16..D20, Return, Extract

Remember, the output range does not need to include the entire range for the extracted output (assuming you have enough empty space for the extracted data). If you copy only the names of the fields from the database and specify the first line of the output range, that would be adequate. The first line of the output range is always the row containing the name of the fields for the extracted output.

14-10 Search for Either Criterion

There are numerous occasions when you are interested only in a couple of criteria; either one would be acceptable. For example, you might look for an employee with a bachelor's degree *or* 17 years of experience, or a student who is majoring in MIS *or* computer science. In computer terminology this is called an OR condition (either condition is acceptable). (The opposite is the AND condition, meaning that all the conditions must be met.) The OR criteria must be in a vertical line; that is, in a column. The AND criteria must be in a horizontal line; that is, in a row. In Figure 14-6, we searched the database for individuals who are either engineers or teachers. This figure was generated as follows:

/Data, Query, Input A3..E11, Return, Criterion G4..G6, Return, Output A15..E20, Return, Extract

Figure 14-5 Example of Search with Single Criteria (All Engineers) with Output Range

```
A1: [W12] 'This database is being searched for all engineers, and we are us READY


            A         B     C     D              E        F          G
 1    This database is being searched for all engineers, and we are using the
 2    Extract option.
 3
 4
 5    FIRST NAME    AGE   SEX  OCCUPATION              CRITERION RANGE
 6    Randy          36    M   Professor               OCCUPATION
 7    Adam           31    M   Engineer                Engineer
 8    Moe            40    M   Officer
 9    Bob            32    M   Engineer
10    Paula          55    F   Housewife
11    Mary           30    F   Interpreter
12    Jacky          72    F   Engineer
13    Lora           30    F   Nurse
14
15    OUTPUT RANGE
16    FIRST NAME    AGE   SEX  OCCUPATION
17    Adam           31    M   Engineer
18    Bob            32    M   Engineer
19    Jacky          72    F   Engineer
20
01-Jan-88  10:38 AM
```

```
A1: [W12] 'This database is being used to search for engineers or teachers.  READY


        A        B    C       D            E         F          G
1  This database is being used to search for engineers or teachers.
2
3  FIRST NAME  AGE  SEX  OCCUPATION   INCOME              CRITERION RANGE
4  Adam         31   M   Engineer     $30,000             OCCUPATION
5  Andrea       36   F   Teacher      $31,000             Engineer
6  Moe          40   M   Officer      $40,000             Teacher
7  Bob          32   M   Engineer     $72,000
8  Paula        55   F   Housewife    $20,000
9  Mary         30   F   Interpreter  $19,000
10 Jacky        72   F   Engineer     $52,000
11 Lora         30   F   Nurse        $31,000
12
13
14 OUTPUT RANGE
15 FIRST NAME  AGE  SEX  OCCUPATION   INCOME
16 Adam         31   M   Engineer     $30,000
17 Andrea       36   F   Teacher      $31,000
18 Bob          32   M   Engineer     $72,000
19 Jacky        72   F   Engineer     $52,000
20
01-Jan-88  10:39 AM
```

Figure 14-6 Examples of Search with Either Criteria (Engineer or Teacher)

14-11 Search with Wild Cards

Lotus includes three wild card characters that can be used in the criterion range. Each has its own unique application. The three are the asterisk (*), the question mark (?), and the tilde (~). Placing an asterisk after a character means that you will retrieve that character *plus* any and all characters that follow it. For example, you would use *B* and an asterisk if you are interested in everyone who has a last name starting with B: Byan, Brown, Bandary, and so on.

The question mark will retrieve any character in one position. For example, ?anny will give you Fanny and Danny; ?ortland will give you Portland and sortland.

Finally, the tilde will retrieve all values *except* those that follow it. For example, ~engineer gives you every occupation listed except engineers. Figures 14-7, 14-8, and 14-9 show the effects of using these wild cards.

Figure 14-7 was generated as follows:

/Data, Query, Input A4..D11, Return, Criterion F5..F6, Return, Output A15..D20, Return, Extract

Figure 14-8 was generated as follows:

/Data, Query, Input A4..B11, Return, Criterion D5..D6, Return, Output A16..B20, Return, Extract

Figure 14-9 was generated as follows:

/Data, Query, Input A3..E11, Return, Criterion G4..G5, Return, Output A15..E25, Return, Extract

Figure 14-7 An Example of Wild Card * (Asterisk)

```
A1: [W12] 'This database is being searched for all records with last name    READY


          A              B           C    D    E         F              G
1   This database is being searched for all records with last name
2   starting with B; the rest is not important.
3
4   FIRST NAME  LAST NAME        AGE  SEX        CRITERION RANGE
5   Andrea      Byan             36   F          LAST NAME
6   Moe         Byan             40   M          B*
7   Adam        Alexander        32   M
8   Paula       Bobby            55   F
9   Jack        Jones            69   M
10  Jacky       Brown            72   F
11  Lora        Jones            30   F
12
13
14  OUTPUT RANGE
15  FIRST NAME  LAST NAME        AGE  SEX
16  Andrea      Byan             36   F
17  Moe         Byan             40   M
18  Paula       Bobby            55   F
19  Jacky       Brown            72   F
20
01-Jan-88  10:40 AM
```

Figure 14-8 An Example of Wild Card ? (Question Mark)

```
A1: [W25] 'This database was generated by using the wildcard "?".          READY


              A                B        C        D         E         F
1   This database was generated by using the wildcard "?".
2
3
4   NAME                   AGE              CRITERION RANGE
5   Mary                    30             NAME
6   Sue                     20             ?anny
7   Sunny                   34
8   Danny                   34
9   Fanny                   34
10  Jacky                   39
11  Adrienne                21
12
13
14
15  OUTPUT RANGE
16  NAME                   AGE
17  Danny                   34
18  Fanny                   34
19
20
01-Jan-88  10:41 AM
```

14-12 Search with Multiple Criteria

Sometimes you may be interested in searching for records meeting multiple criteria. This is called an AND condition. For example, you may want to search for all the students who have a GPA of 3.6 or better *and* are MIS majors, or all the employees who have 10 years of experience and have a bachelor's degree and speak Spanish. An employee must meet all the criteria to be selected. The AND criteria must be in a horizontal line; that is, in a row.

Figure 14-11 illustrates an AND condition: all female engineers who make more than $50,000 and are less then 60 years old. We searched the database in Figure 14-10 to find the names that met all these criteria. Figure 14-11 was generated as follows:

/Data, Query, Input A4..F19, Return, Criterion I5..L6, Return, Output G11..L30, Return, Extract

As we mentioned earlier, you can include up to 32 fields in your criterion range. You can also combine AND and OR conditions as long as you are forming a rectangle in your Criterion range.

Figure 14-12 was searched to give the results in Figure 14-13. Figure 14-13 was generated as follows:

/Data, Query, Input, A4..F19, Return, Criterion I5..L8, Return, Output, G11..L30, Return, Extract

In the first row of the criterion range we are looking for whoever meets the following four criteria: Age < 60, Sex = F, Occupation = Engineer, Income > $50,000. As you see, there is only one candidate who meets all criteria, Adam Alexander.

In the second row of the criterion range, we are looking for candidates who meet the following criteria: Age > 90, Sex = Either, Occupation = Teacher, Income = Any. Only one candidate meets all these criteria, Lora Jones.

In the third line of criteria we are looking for any candidate who is a student; sex, age, and income are not important.

As you see, many of these criteria can be combined with the OR and AND conditions. Remember, if you leave a criterion empty in the criterion range, any data item can fill that range (any profession, any sex, etc.).

Another interesting search would be to apply AND/OR choices to one particular field. In Figure 14-14, we searched for individuals who are between the ages of 30 and 40. The figure was generated as follows:

/Data, Query, Input, A3..B18, Return, Criterion, E4..E5, Return Output, E9..F18, Return, Extract

In Figure 14-15, we searched for individuals who are younger than 10 or older than 70. The figure was generated as follows:

/Data, Query, Input, A3..B18, Return, Criterion, E4..E5, Return, Output, E9..F18, Return, Extract

14-13 Extract vs. Unique Options

Sometimes there are duplicate records in the database. Let us say you would like to generate a mailing list for a series of business organizations and you want to send

Figure 14-9 An Example of Wild Card ~ (Tilde)

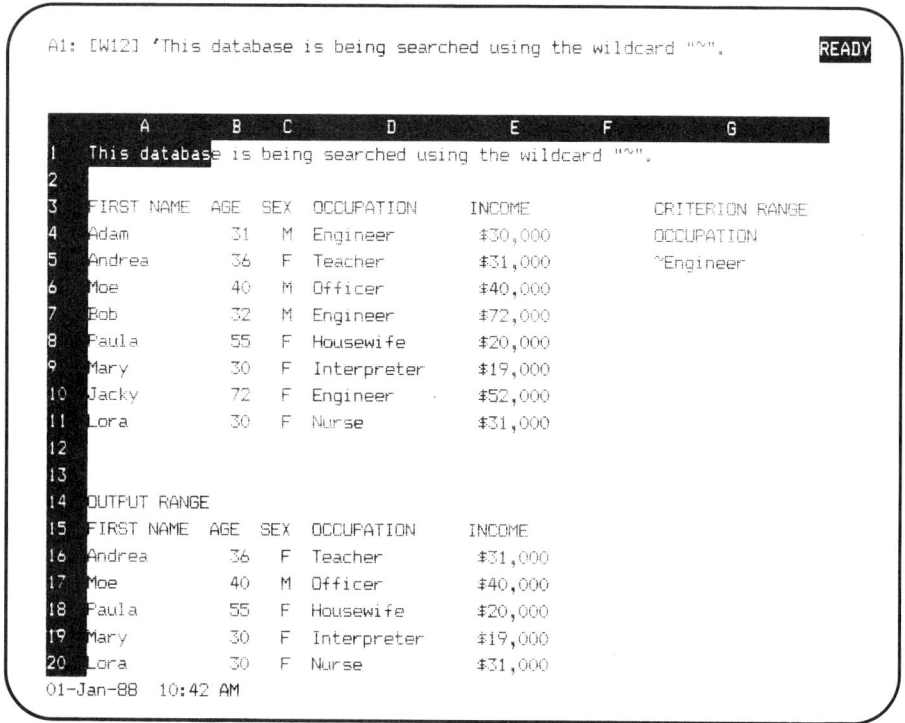

```
A1: [W12] 'This database is being searched using the wildcard "~".            READY

          A         B    C        D              E              F         G
1    This database is being searched using the wildcard "~".
2
3    FIRST NAME AGE  SEX  OCCUPATION     INCOME              CRITERION RANGE
4    Adam       31   M    Engineer       $30,000             OCCUPATION
5    Andrea     36   F    Teacher        $31,000             ~Engineer
6    Moe        40   M    Officer        $40,000
7    Bob        32   M    Engineer       $72,000
8    Paula      55   F    Housewife      $20,000
9    Mary       30   F    Interpreter    $19,000
10   Jacky      72   F    Engineer       $52,000
11   Lora       30   F    Nurse          $31,000
12
13
14   OUTPUT RANGE
15   FIRST NAME AGE  SEX  OCCUPATION     INCOME
16   Andrea     36   F    Teacher        $31,000
17   Moe        40   M    Officer        $40,000
18   Paula      55   F    Housewife      $20,000
19   Mary       30   F    Interpreter    $19,000
20   Lora       30   F    Nurse          $31,000
01-Jan-88   10:42 AM
```

Figure 14-10 Database Used for Multiple Criteria Search

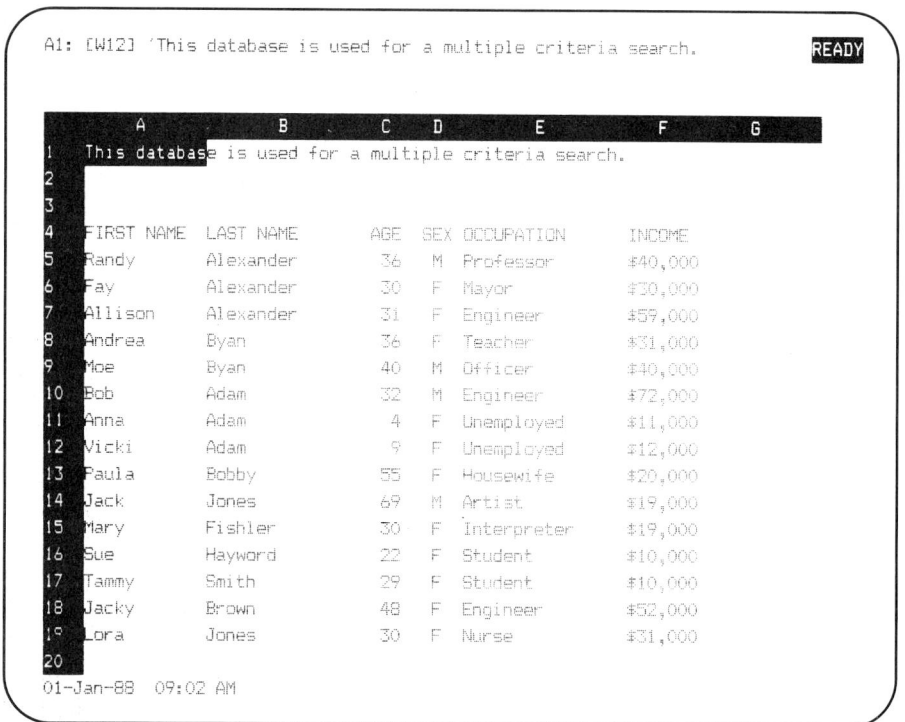

```
A1: [W12] 'This database is used for a multiple criteria search.              READY

          A          B           C    D    E              F         G
1    This database is used for a multiple criteria search.
2
3
4    FIRST NAME LAST NAME    AGE  SEX OCCUPATION     INCOME
5    Randy      Alexander    36   M   Professor      $40,000
6    Fay        Alexander    30   F   Mayor          $30,000
7    Allison    Alexander    31   F   Engineer       $59,000
8    Andrea     Byan         36   F   Teacher        $31,000
9    Moe        Byan         40   M   Officer        $40,000
10   Bob        Adam         32   M   Engineer       $72,000
11   Anna       Adam         4    F   Unemployed     $11,000
12   Vicki      Adam         9    F   Unemployed     $12,000
13   Paula      Bobby        55   F   Housewife      $20,000
14   Jack       Jones        69   M   Artist         $19,000
15   Mary       Fishler      30   F   Interpreter    $19,000
16   Sue        Hayword      22   F   Student        $10,000
17   Tammy      Smith        29   F   Student        $10,000
18   Jacky      Brown        48   F   Engineer       $52,000
19   Lora       Jones        30   F   Nurse          $31,000
20
01-Jan-88   09:02 AM
```

Figure 14-11 An Example of Multiple Criteria (AND Option)

```
G1: [W12] 'This is the result of the multiple search done on Figure 14-10. READY


        G          H          I      J        K          L
1    This is the result of the multiple search done on Figure 14-10.
2
3
4                            CRITERION RANGE
5                            AGE    SEX  OCCUPATION    INCOME
6                            +C5<60 F    Engineer      +F5>50000
7
8
9
10   OUTPUT RANGE
11   FIRST NAME  LAST NAME    AGE    SEX OCCUPATION     INCOME
12   Allison     Alexander     31    F   Engineer       $59,000
13   Jacky       Brown         48    F   Engineer       $52,000
14
15
16
17
18
19
20
01-Jan-88   09:03 AM
```

Figure 14-12 Sample Worksheet for Multiple Search

```
A1: [W12] 'This database is used for a multiple criteria search.          READY


        A          B          C    D      E            F        G
1    This database is used for a multiple criteria search.
2
3
4    FIRST NAME  LAST NAME    AGE  SEX OCCUPATION      INCOME
5    Randy       Alexander     36   M  Professor       $40,000
6    Fay         Alexander     30   F  Mayor           $30,000
7    Allison     Alexander     31   F  Engineer        $59,000
8    Andrea      Byan          36   F  Teacher         $31,000
9    Moe         Byan          40   M  Officer         $40,000
10   Bob         Adam          32   M  Engineer        $72,000
11   Anna        Adam           4   F  Unemployed      $11,000
12   Vicki       Adam           9   F  Unemployed      $12,000
13   Paula       Bobby         55   F  Housewife       $20,000
14   Jack        Jones         69   M  Artist          $19,000
15   Mary        Fishler       30   F  Interpreter     $19,000
16   Sue         Hayword       22   F  Student         $10,000
17   Tammy       Smith         29   F  Student         $10,000
18   Jacky       Brown        100   F  Engineer        $52,000
19   Lora        Jones         99   F  Teacher         $31,000
20
01-Jan-88   09:06 AM
```

Figure 14-13 An Example of a Multiple Search

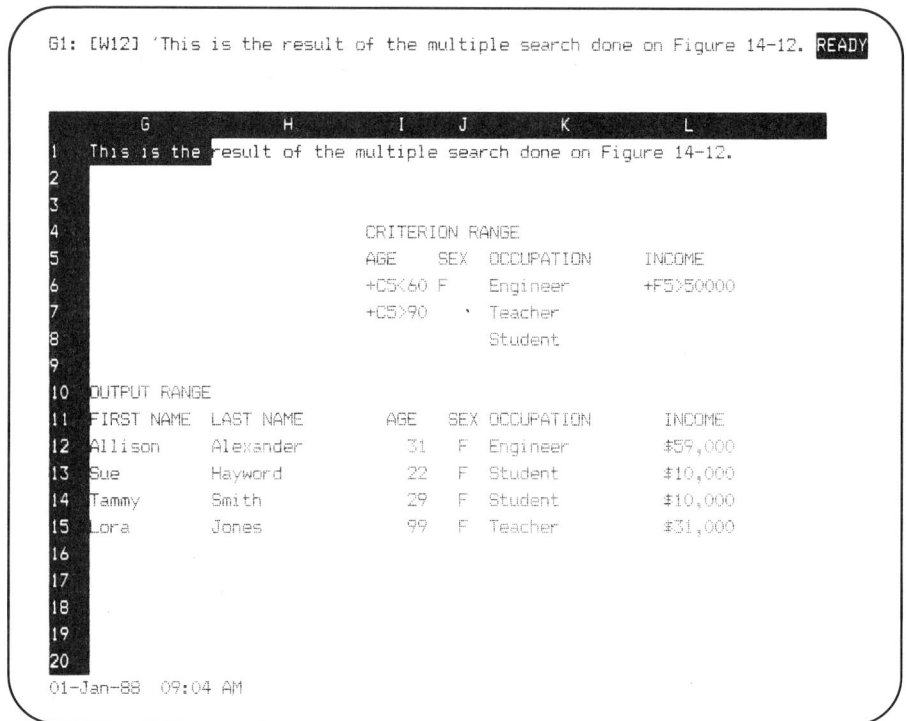

```
G1: [W12] 'This is the result of the multiple search done on Figure 14-12.    READY

            G           H         I    J       K          L
1    This is the result of the multiple search done on Figure 14-12.
2
3
4                                CRITERION RANGE
5                                AGE     SEX  OCCUPATION        INCOME
6                                +C5<60  F    Engineer          +F5>50000
7                                +C5>90   .   Teacher
8                                             Student
9
10   OUTPUT RANGE
11   FIRST NAME  LAST NAME       AGE   SEX OCCUPATION       INCOME
12   Allison     Alexander        31    F  Engineer         $59,000
13   Sue         Hayword          22    F  Student          $10,000
14   Tammy       Smith            29    F  Student          $10,000
15   Lora        Jones            99    F  Teacher          $31,000
16
17
18
19
20
01-Jan-88  09:04 AM
```

Figure 14-14 Search with AND within One Field

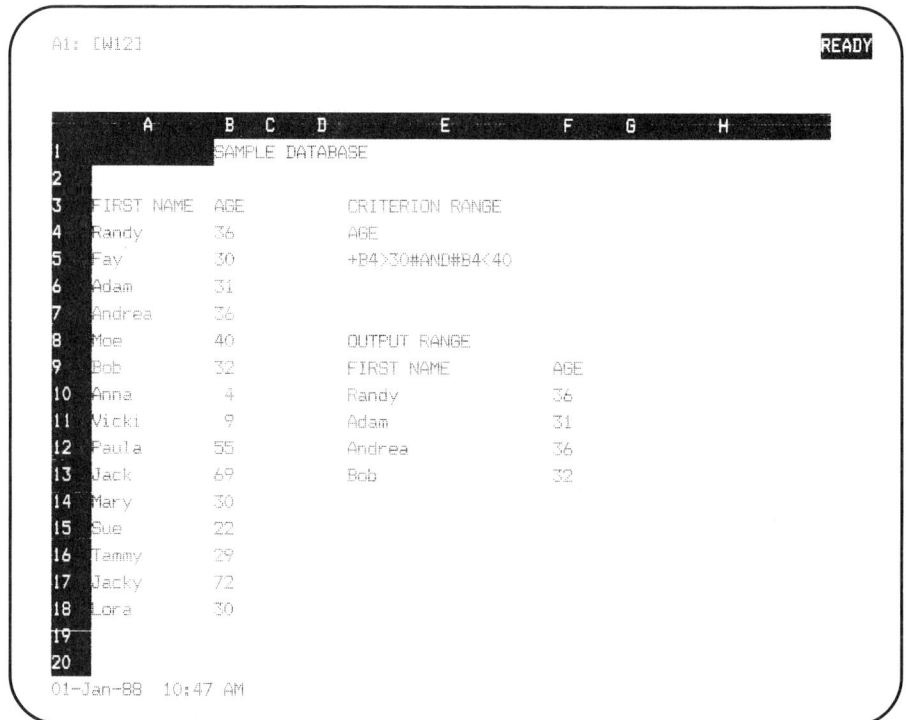

```
A1: [W12]                                                              READY

       A        B   C   D        E            F       G       H
1               SAMPLE DATABASE
2
3    FIRST NAME  AGE          CRITERION RANGE
4    Randy       36           AGE
5    Fay         30           +B4>30#AND#B4<40
6    Adam        31
7    Andrea      36
8    Moe         40           OUTPUT RANGE
9    Bob         32           FIRST NAME        AGE
10   Anna        4            Randy             36
11   Vicki       9            Adam              31
12   Paula       55           Andrea            36
13   Jack        69           Bob               32
14   Mary        30
15   Sue         22
16   Tammy       29
17   Jacky       72
18   Lora        30
19
20
01-Jan-88  10:47 AM
```

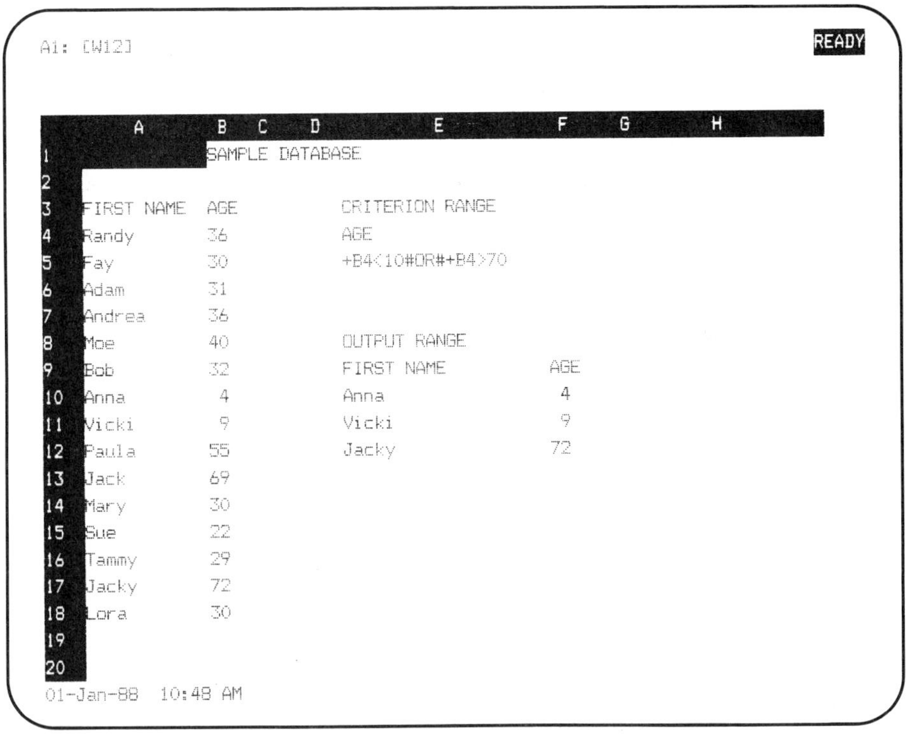

Figure 14-15 Search with OR within One Field

a memo to each organization. As an example, you would like to send a memo to one university in each system; one memo to the Cal State system, one to the UC system, and so forth. In this case, the Extract option may not do the job if the organization is listed more than once in your database. If you use the Unique option, only one occurrence of each record will be selected.

Figure 14-16 shows a database used to compare the Extract and Unique options. Figure 14-17 compares the results of using these two options. This figure was generated as follows:

For the Extract option:

/Data, Query, Input A5..B20, Return, Criterion M18..N19, Return, Output G4..J21, Return, Extract

For the Unique option:

/Data, Query, Input A5..B20, Return, Criterion M18..N19, Return, Output K4..N16, Return, Unique

Remember when the Unique option is used the entire record must be unique, not just one or more fields.

14-14 Delete Option

Besides using the /Worksheet and /Range commands for deleting a portion of your database, you can use the Delete option. Figure 14-19 was generated by using the

Figure 14-16 Database Used for Extract and Unique Options

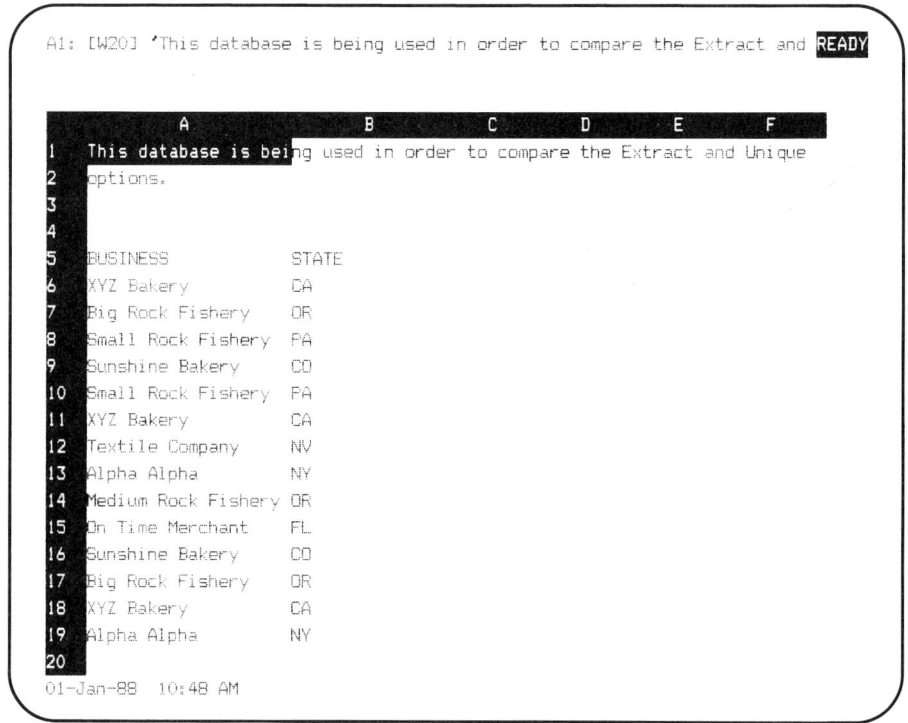

```
A1: [W20] 'This database is being used in order to compare the Extract and  READY


           A                    B        C        D        E        F
1   This database is being used in order to compare the Extract and Unique
2   options.
3
4
5   BUSINESS             STATE
6   XYZ Bakery           CA
7   Big Rock Fishery     OR
8   Small Rock Fishery   PA
9   Sunshine Bakery      CO
10  Small Rock Fishery   PA
11  XYZ Bakery           CA
12  Textile Company      NV
13  Alpha Alpha          NY
14  Medium Rock Fishery  OR
15  On Time Merchant     FL
16  Sunshine Bakery      CO
17  Big Rock Fishery     OR
18  XYZ Bakery           CA
19  Alpha Alpha          NY
20
01-Jan-88  10:48 AM
```

Figure 14-17 Comparison of Extract and Unique Options

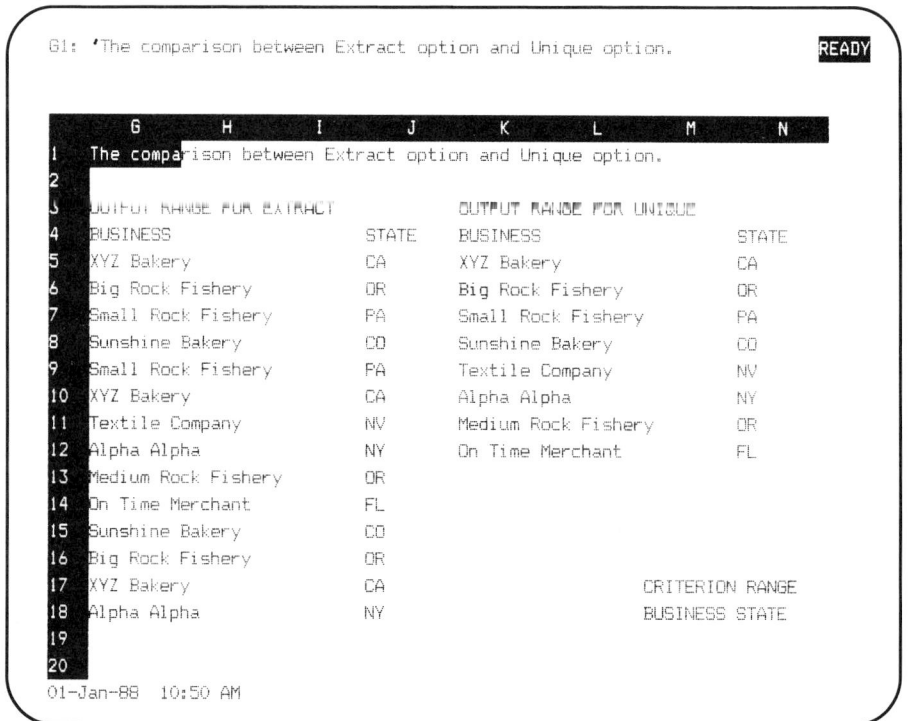

```
G1: 'The comparison between Extract option and Unique option.               READY


           G       H       I        J       K       L       M       N
1   The comparison between Extract option and Unique option.
2
3   OUTPUT RANGE FOR EXTRACT            OUTPUT RANGE FOR UNIQUE
4   BUSINESS             STATE          BUSINESS             STATE
5   XYZ Bakery           CA             XYZ Bakery           CA
6   Big Rock Fishery     OR             Big Rock Fishery     OR
7   Small Rock Fishery   PA             Small Rock Fishery   PA
8   Sunshine Bakery      CO             Sunshine Bakery      CO
9   Small Rock Fishery   PA             Textile Company      NV
10  XYZ Bakery           CA             Alpha Alpha          NY
11  Textile Company      NV             Medium Rock Fishery  OR
12  Alpha Alpha          NY             On Time Merchant     FL
13  Medium Rock Fishery  OR
14  On Time Merchant     FL
15  Sunshine Bakery      CO
16  Big Rock Fishery     OR
17  XYZ Bakery           CA                          CRITERION RANGE
18  Alpha Alpha          NY                          BUSINESS STATE
19
20
01-Jan-88  10:50 AM
```

Figure 14-18 Database Used for the Delete Option

```
A1: [W12]                                                              READY

              A            B          C   D        E            F      G
1                    MY FIRST DATABASE
2
3    FIRST NAME   LAST NAME       AGE  SEX OCCUPATION     INCOME
4    Randy        Alexander        36   M  Professor      $40,000
5    Fay          Alexander        30   F  Mayor          $30,000
6    Adam         Alexander        31   M  Engineer       $30,000
7    Andrea       Byan             36   F  Teacher        $31,000
8    Moe          Byan             40   M  Officer        $40,000
9    Bob          Adam             32   M  Engineer       $72,000
10   Anna         Adam              4   F  Unemployed     $11,000
11   Vicki        Adam              9   F  Unemployed     $12,000
12   Paula        Bobby            55   F  Housewife      $20,000
13   Jack         Jones            69   M  Artist         $19,000
14   Mary         Fishler          30   F  Interpreter    $19,000
15   Sue          Hayword          22   F  Student        $10,000
16   Tammy        Smith            29   F  Student        $10,000
17   Jacky        Brown            72   F  Engineer       $52,000
18   Lora         Jones            30   F  Nurse          $31,000
19                OCCUPATION
20                Engineer
01-Jan-88  10:52 AM
```

Figure 14-19 An Example of the Delete Option

```
A1: [W12]                                                              READY

              A            B          C   D        E            F      G
1                    MY FIRST DATABASE AFTER DELETION OF ALL THE ENGINEERS
2
3    FIRST NAME   LAST NAME       AGE  SEX OCCUPATION     INCOME
4    Randy        Alexander        36   M  Professor      $40,000
5    Fay          Alexander        30   F  Mayor          $30,000
6    Andrea       Byan             36   F  Teacher        $31,000
7    Moe          Byan             40   M  Officer        $40,000
8    Anna         Adam              4   F  Unemployed     $11,000
9    Vicki        Adam              9   F  Unemployed     $12,000
10   Paula        Bobby            55   F  Housewife      $20,000
11   Jack         Jones            69   M  Artist         $19,000
12   Mary         Fishler          30   F  Interpreter    $19,000
13   Sue          Hayword          22   F  Student        $10,000
14   Tammy        Smith            29   F  Student        $10,000
15   Lora         Jones            30   F  Nurse          $31,000
16
17
18
19                OCCUPATION
20                Engineer
01-Jan-88  10:53 AM
```

database in Figure 14-18 and deleting all the engineers. Figure 14-19 was generated as follows:

/Data, Query, Input A3..F18, Return, Criterion B19..B20, Return, Delete, Delete

This command should be used carefully. You may find it useful to make a copy of the database before executing this command.

Summary

This chapter covered the rudiments of database operations and creation, update, sort and search procedures. Having the Lotus database in RAM makes the processing speed extremely fast. For this reason, a Lotus database is an impressive tool for business database applications. Chapter 15 will discuss advanced database operations in detail.

Review Questions

1. What is a database?
2. How do you create a database using Lotus?
3. What is the difference between numeric and nonnumeric data in a database?
4.* How do you erase a record in a database?
5. How do you erase a field in a database?
6. How many fields can you have in your database?
7. How many records can you have in your database?
8. How do you perform editing in your database?
9. How do you sort your database?
10.* What is the difference between the primary-key and secondary-key options?
11. How many ways can you sort your database?
12.* How many ways can you search your database?
13. What is the difference between the AND condition and the OR condition in the criterion range?
14. How many wild cards are available? What is the unique application of each wild card?
15.* What is the difference between the Extract option and the Unique option?
16.* How many fields can be included in your criterion range for AND search?
17. What is the difference between a sort and a search range?
18. Generate the following database:

First Name	Last Name	Major	Age	Sex	GPA
Cora	Barnes	CS	22	F	3.20
Sue	Jones	MIS	29	F	2.80
Bobby	Trana	CS	30	F	3.70
Tamy	Smith	Marketing	22	F	3.85
John	Porsche	Management	36	M	3.60
Brian	Raban	Accounting	19	M	2.20
Adam	Vigen	MIS	21	M	3.70

First Name	Last Name	Major	Age	Sex	GPA
Clark	Standard	CS	28	M	3.00
Stanley	Jones	Personnel	24	M	2.90
Harry	Mohan	Management	26	M	2.75

a. Add two more students to this list.

b. Sort this list by GPA.

c. Sort this list by age.

d. Sort first by sex, then by age.

e. Extract all MIS majors.

f. Extract all MIS majors with GPA > 3.7.

g. Extract either MIS or accounting majors.

h. Extract students with age > 25 and GPA > 3.50 and who are female.

i. Extract students who are between 20 and 30.

j. Extract students who are either younger than 20 or older than 30.

Misconceptions and Solutions

M - If you try to sort a worksheet in order to generate a sorted worksheet, but leave out a portion of the worksheet in your data range, there is no way to return to the original database.

S - Either save the original database in a file or make sure that you have included the entire database in your sort range.

M - You have used the Extract option, but not all the appropriate data has been extracted.

S - Check that your output range is large enough.

15

Database Operations/Part Two: Lotus as a Sophisticated Database

15-1 Introduction

In this chapter we will study some of the sophisticated operations performed by the Lotus database functions, including statistical functions. As you will see, these functions provide a lot of flexibility. We will explain table building using the /Data Fill command, what-if analysis performed by /Data Table 1 and /Data Table 2, and distribution analysis using the /Data Distribution command.

/Data Matrix and /Data Regression will be discussed at the end of this chapter. With these two commands, you can use the tremendous power of Lotus. A matrix of up to 90 rows by 90 columns can be easily inverted. This means that a 90 by 90 system of linear equations can be solved. Using /Data Regression, Lotus can handle a multiple linear regression of up to 16 variables. A dependent variable, such as income, can be predicted based on several independent variables (up to 16), such as education, number of years of experience, or field of study. /Data Matrix and /Data Regression can help you to develop fairly sophisticated forecasting models.

15-2 Database Statistical Functions

The seven statistical functions you saw in Chapter 10 can be used with database data with a minor variation. A database statistical function follows this format:

(@Dfunction name(database range, offset value, criterion range))

The database range or input range is usually the entire database or a selected portion, and the offset value defines which column of the database is under investigation.

This value starts from zero and goes to N-1, where N is the number of columns in a database. So if the offset value is 2, it means you are interested in column 3 of the database or field 3. If it is 10, it means you are interested in column 11. The criterion range must have a field heading. Below it you can define any criteria that you may be interested in.

There are seven database statistical functions: @DAVG, @DCOUNT, @DMAX, @DMIN, @DSTD, @DSUM, and @DVAR. These functions provide more flexibility than their statistical counterparts. By just changing the criterion range, you can perform all sorts of analyses. Figures 15-1 and 15-2 show some examples of database statistical functions.

In Figure 15-1, the database range is A3..C18; the offset value is 1, which means column 2 is under investigation; and the criterion range is H19..H20. In this example we are only interested in individuals who are older than 10 years. (In cell H20, we used the Text format in order to show the actual content of this cell.)

In Figure 15-2 we used the previous worksheet (Figure 15-1), but we changed a couple of the criterion ranges. This demonstrates the flexibility provided by database statistical functions. You can include or exclude any portion of the database just by changing the criterion range.

15-3 Table Building Using the /Data Fill Command

You can use the /Data Fill command to build tables. All you need is to define a range, which becomes the table that you wish to build, then define the start, step, and stop values. These values will be filled in the table from top to bottom and from left to right. If you do not specify any value and press the **Return** key at the prompt, Lotus will use default values for start (0), step (1) and stop (8191).

Table building will continue until either the range is filled or the stop value has been reached. Any of the three values can be a formula if the formula is defined at the time that it is needed by /Data Fill. An excellent application of the /Data Fill command is to return a sorted database to its original unsorted form. To do this, you can either use the /Data Fill Command in order to number all the records in the database into an adjacent column or just number them by entering a sequence number. When the entire database is sorted, this column will be sorted as well. To return the database to its original form, choose this column as the primary key and sort the database again. You will see the original database. Figures 15-3 and 15-4 show some examples of the /Data Fill command.

In the upper portion of Figure 15-3, we defined a high value for stop (5,000), but the table building was stopped as soon as range A1..D1 was filled. In the lower portion of Figure 15-3, table building stopped when the stop value was reached (19,000), and the specified table was not filled.

In Figure 15-4, we created a simple database in cells A3..C8. We made a copy of the database in cells A11..C16 and this database was sorted in ascending order.

The sequence numbers are no longer ordered. To return this database to its original form, we made a copy of it in cells E11..G16 and sorted this database using the sequence number field as the primary key, returning the database back to its original form.

Figure 15-1 Database Statistical Functions

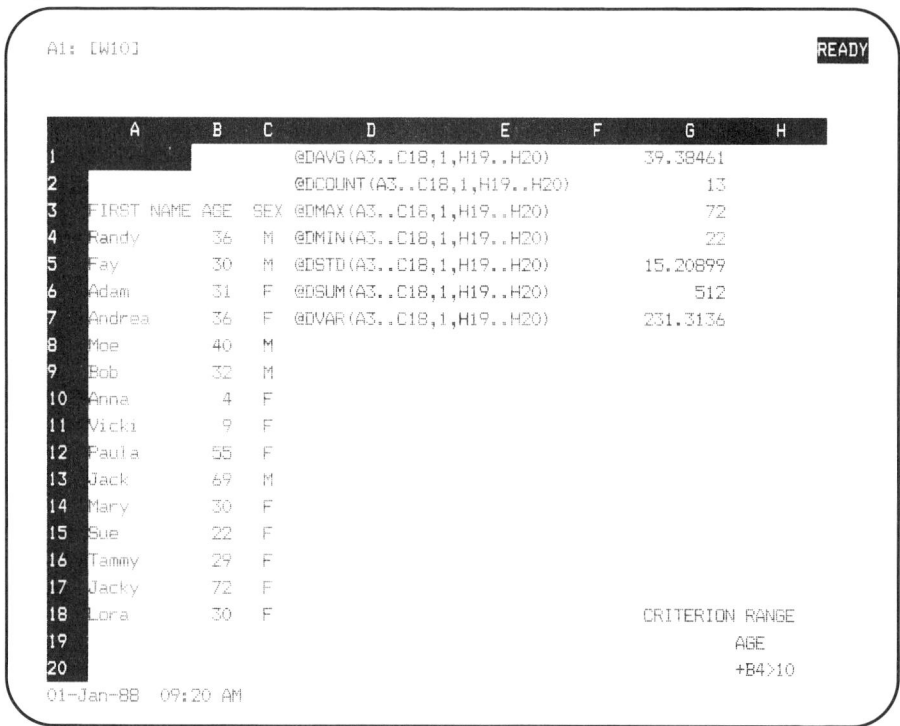

```
A1: [W10]                                                              READY

          A        B    C        D              E        F      G        H
1                           @DAVG(A3..C18,1,H19..H20)          39.38461
2                           @DCOUNT(A3..C18,1,H19..H20)             13
3   FIRST NAME  AGE   SEX  @DMAX(A3..C18,1,H19..H20)              72
4   Randy       36    M    @DMIN(A3..C18,1,H19..H20)              22
5   Fay         30    M    @DSTD(A3..C18,1,H19..H20)          15.20899
6   Adam        31    F    @DSUM(A3..C18,1,H19..H20)             512
7   Andrea      36    F    @DVAR(A3..C18,1,H19..H20)          231.3136
8   Moe         40    M
9   Bob         32    M
10  Anna         4    F
11  Vicki        9    F
12  Paula       55    F
13  Jack        69    M
14  Mary        30    F
15  Sue         22    F
16  Tammy       29    F
17  Jacky       72    F
18  Lora        30    F                                  CRITERION RANGE
19                                                            AGE
20                                                           +B4>10
01-Jan-88   09:20 AM
```

Figure 15-2 Database Statistical Functions with a Different Criterion Range

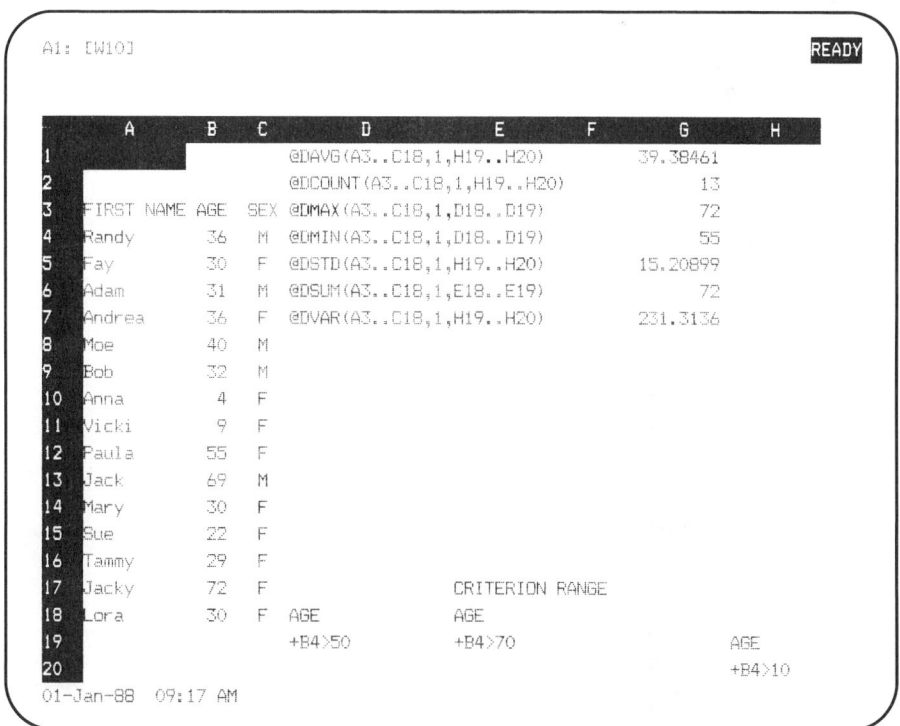

```
A1: [W10]                                                              READY

          A        B    C        D              E        F      G        H
1                           @DAVG(A3..C18,1,H19..H20)          39.38461
2                           @DCOUNT(A3..C18,1,H19..H20)             13
3   FIRST NAME  AGE   SEX  @DMAX(A3..C18,1,D18..D19)              72
4   Randy       36    M    @DMIN(A3..C18,1,D18..D19)              55
5   Fay         30    F    @DSTD(A3..C18,1,H19..H20)          15.20899
6   Adam        31    M    @DSUM(A3..C18,1,E18..E19)              72
7   Andrea      36    F    @DVAR(A3..C18,1,H19..H20)          231.3136
8   Moe         40    M
9   Bob         32    M
10  Anna         4    F
11  Vicki        9    F
12  Paula       55    F
13  Jack        69    M
14  Mary        30    F
15  Sue         22    F
16  Tammy       29    F
17  Jacky       72    F              CRITERION RANGE
18  Lora        30    F  AGE         AGE
19                          +B4>50     +B4>70                 AGE
20                                                           +B4>10
01-Jan-88   09:17 AM
```

Figure 15-3 /Data Fill Command

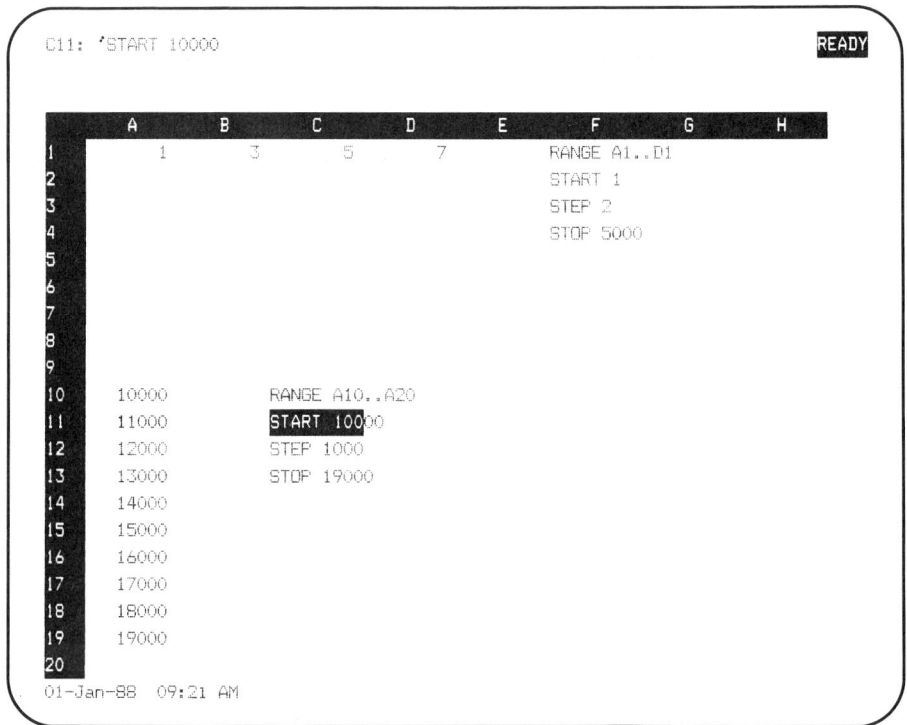

```
C11: 'START 10000                                                    READY


          A        B        C        D        E        F        G        H
1         1        3        5        7        RANGE A1..D1
2                                             START 1
3                                             STEP 2
4                                             STOP 5000
5
6
7
8
9
10     10000                 RANGE A10..A20
11     11000                 START 10000
12     12000                 STEP 1000
13     13000                 STOP 19000
14     14000
15     15000
16     16000
17     17000
18     18000
19     19000
20
01-Jan-88   09:21 AM
```

Figure 15-4 /Data Fill Command for Restoring a Sorted Database

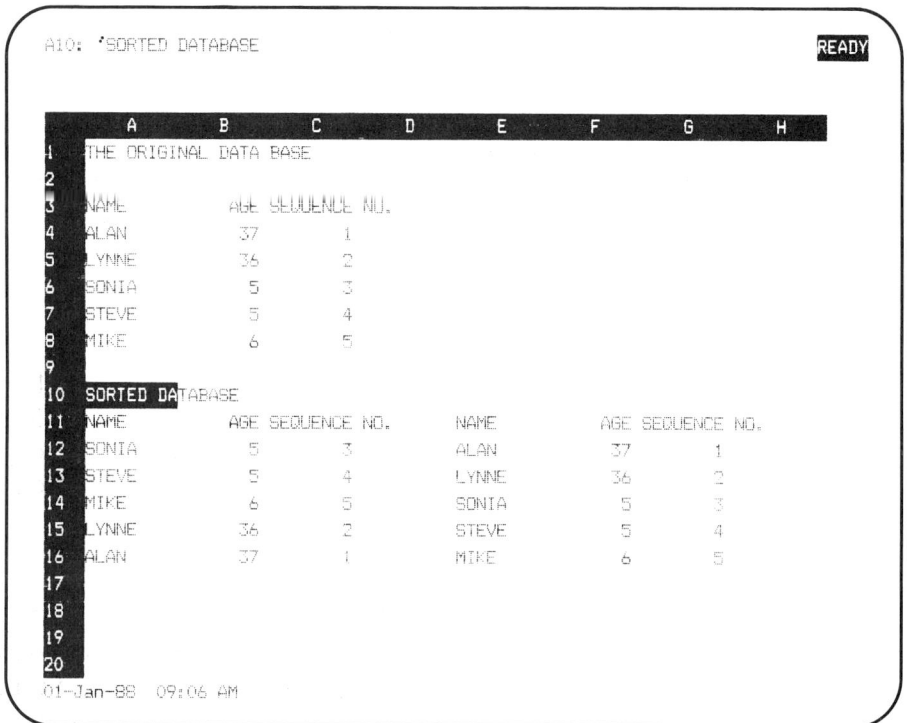

```
A10: 'SORTED DATABASE                                                READY


          A        B        C        D        E        F        G        H
1      THE ORIGINAL DATA BASE
2
3      NAME         AGE  SEQUENCE NO.
4      ALAN         37       1
5      LYNNE        36       2
6      SONIA        5        3
7      STEVE        5        4
8      MIKE         6        5
9
10     SORTED DATABASE
11     NAME         AGE  SEQUENCE NO.      NAME         AGE  SEQUENCE NO.
12     SONIA        5        3             ALAN         37       1
13     STEVE        5        4             LYNNE        36       2
14     MIKE         6        5             SONIA        5        3
15     LYNNE        36       2             STEVE        5        4
16     ALAN         37       1             MIKE         6        5
17
18
19
20
01-Jan-88   09:06 AM
```

15-4 What-If Analysis Using /Data Table 1

The /Data Table 1 command can be used to determine the effect of one variable on a formula or an entire worksheet. There are many areas where this command can be useful; for example, the effect of different interest rates on an IRA plan, the effect of different interest rates on a loan, or the effect of different commission percentages on the total commission generated by a salesperson.

To use /Data Table 1, you must first establish a table range. The table range can be anywhere in the worksheet. In Figure 15-5, C4..E15 is the table range. You must choose an empty cell outside the table range as the input cell. The address of this cell will be used to change values in a formula. In our example, the input cell is A5. Now fill out the changing values in a column; in our case, cells C5..C15. Above and to the right of these values is our formula, here the future value, @FV(2000,A5,20). This is the future value of a $2,000 IRA plan for 20 years with a variable interest rate. This formula is in cell D4. The same formula was also copied to cell E4, but we have changed the number of years to 30. Remember, the intersection of these values (interest rates) and the formula is empty. This empty cell will be used by /Data Table 2.

As soon as the parameters are defined, the entire future value will be calculated for different interest rates and for two different years. Figure 15-5 shows one application of this command. If you change some of the input values, press F8 while in READY mode and the entire table will be recalculated. As you can see, this table can be a lot more complicated. You can do this calculation for several annuity periods. Simply define these periods and leave the rest of it to Lotus' amazing power and accuracy.

15-5 /Data Table 1 Using Database Data

Database statistical functions can be used as formulas with the /Data Table 1 and /Data Table 2 commands. The procedure is straightforward. In Figure 15-6, we used the database to the left of the screen as our input range (A3..B18). The offset value is 1, meaning column 2 (income) is under investigation and the criterion range has been set up in cells C10..C11. As before, this range includes the field title and the specific criteria are below it. Since we have left cell C11 empty, this means any occupation can be entered here. Cell C11 is used also as the input cell for /Data Table 1.

In /Data Table 1, the input range is D3..F6. The entire table range includes three occupations in the column and two formulas in the row. The input cell is C11. Now Lotus matches any of these three occupations with the original database and calculates the average salary and standard deviation of these salaries.

15-6 What-If Analysis Using /Data Table 2

In /Data Table 2 the effects of two variables over the entire worksheet or a specified range can be calculated. Let us walk through an example. Sunrise Electronic Firm has designed a formula for calculating the total salary of its employees, based on the

Figure 15-5 /Data Table 1 Showing the Effects of Different Interest Rates for Two Different IRA Plans

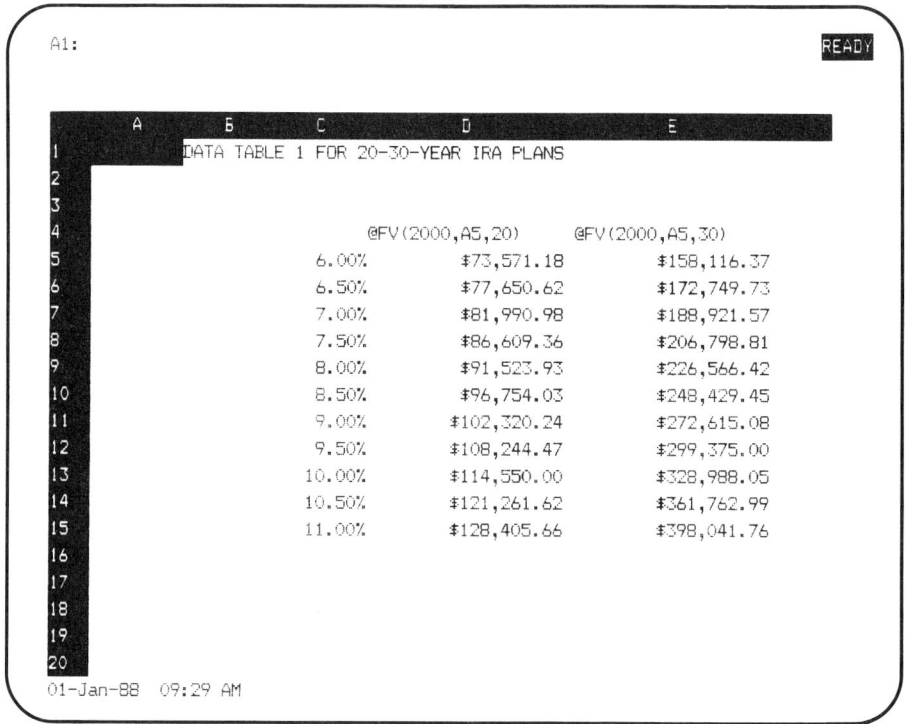

```
A1:                                                                    READY

        A       B       C           D                   E
1              DATA TABLE 1 FOR 20-30-YEAR IRA PLANS
2
3
4                          @FV(2000,A5,20)      @FV(2000,A5,30)
5                   6.00%       $73,571.18          $158,116.37
6                   6.50%       $77,650.62          $172,749.73
7                   7.00%       $81,990.98          $188,921.57
8                   7.50%       $86,609.36          $206,798.81
9                   8.00%       $91,523.93          $226,566.42
10                  8.50%       $96,754.03          $248,429.45
11                  9.00%      $102,320.24          $272,615.08
12                  9.50%      $108,244.47          $299,375.00
13                 10.00%      $114,550.00          $328,988.05
14                 10.50%      $121,261.62          $361,762.99
15                 11.00%      $128,405.66          $398,041.76
16
17
18
19
20
01-Jan-88   09:29 AM
```

Figure 15-6 Using Data Table 1 with Database

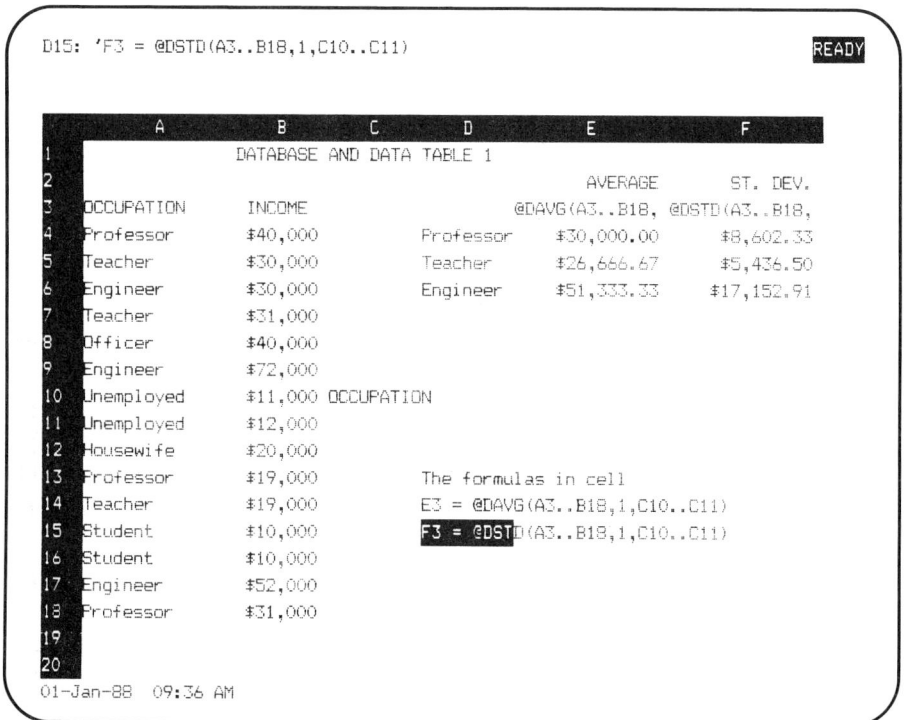

```
D15:  'F3 = @DSTD(A3..B18,1,C10..C11)                                  READY

        A           B           C       D           E           F
1                  DATABASE AND DATA TABLE 1
2                                                AVERAGE       ST. DEV.
3      OCCUPATION   INCOME                     @DAVG(A3..B18, @DSTD(A3..B18,
4      Professor    $40,000          Professor    $30,000.00      $8,602.33
5      Teacher      $30,000          Teacher      $26,666.67      $5,436.50
6      Engineer     $30,000          Engineer     $51,333.33     $17,152.91
7      Teacher      $31,000
8      Officer      $40,000
9      Engineer     $72,000
10     Unemployed   $11,000 OCCUPATION
11     Unemployed   $12,000
12     Housewife    $20,000
13     Professor    $19,000          The formulas in cell
14     Teacher      $19,000          E3 = @DAVG(A3..B18,1,C10..C11)
15     Student      $10,000          F3 = @DSTD(A3..B18,1,C10..C11)
16     Student      $10,000
17     Engineer     $52,000
18     Professor    $31,000
19
20
01-Jan-88   09:36 AM
```

years of education (high school diploma, BS, MS, PhD) and the number of years of experience (1 to 15 years). In any case, $1,000 would be the base salary. The formula is 1000 + A1*50+B1*75, where A1 is the number of years of experience and B1 is the number of years of education. These are the input cells. For example, an employee with 5 years of experience and 12 years of education will make 1000+5*50+12*75 = $2150.

In Figure 15-7, we have used /Data Table 2 to calculate the entire table for the Sunrise Electronics Firm. The table range is D3..H18. Input cell 1 is A5 (years of experience), input cell 2 is B5 (years of education). Remember, the formula 1000+A5*50+B5*75 was copied into cell D3, the intersection of row 3 (years of education) and column D (years of experience).

You can change any of these values and press F8. The entire table will be recalculated immediately.

15-7 /Data Table 2 Using Database Data

/Data Table 2, like /Data Table 1, can be used effectively with database statistical functions. To show this we have collected a summary of a large survey in Figure 15-8. A group of professors in different disciplines were surveyed in different states. We are interested in finding out the average salary of each type of professor in three different states.

The table range is F4..I7, which includes three types of professors (CS, ACC, MIS, the column) in three states (OR, CA, ND, the row). Input cell 1 is D6, which will be either CS (computer science), ACC (accounting), or MIS (management information systems). Input cell 2 is E6, which will be either OR (Oregon), CA (California), or ND (North Dakota). The criterion range is defined in cells D5..E6. Cell F4, the intersection of row and column, contains the formula @DAVG(A3..C18,0,D5..E6).

Lotus searches for a CS professor in the state of Oregon (there are three of them) and calculates the average salary; ($31,000+$41,000+$39,000)/3 = $37,000. In California there is only one with a salary of $40,000; and so forth. We used Text Format in cell F4 to show you the actual formula used for our calculations.

15-8 Distribution Analysis Using the /Data Distribution Command

There are many cases where you may be interested in classifying a series of data into an orderly group, for example, classifying the salary of all the employees of Jack's Manufacturing into ten groups, or classifying your customers in nine sales groups. The /Data Distribution command will perform these types of analysis for you.

To use this command, define the range of values you would like to classify. Then select two empty columns. The first one is used for your bin range in ascending order, for example, salaries of 10,000, 12,000, 15,000, 18,000, etc. The empty column adjacent to the bin range will be used by Lotus to provide the frequency distribution. Figure 15-9 shows an example of the /Data Distribution command.

In this figure, the value range is B4..B17 and the bin range is D4..D8 (we have organized salaries into five groups in ascending order). As you see, the first number under frequency is 6. This means there are six individuals whose income is between

```
A1: [W9] 'DATA TABLE 2 TO CALCULATE SALARY BASED ON EDUCATION AND EXPERIENCE  READY

          A    B  C         D            E        F        G        H
 1   DATA TABLE 2 TO CALCULATE SALARY BASED ON EDUCATION AND EXPERIENCE
 2                                     YEARS OF EDUCATION
 3                     1000+A5*50+B5*75      12       16       18       21
 4   INPUT 1   INPUT 2              1      1950     2250     2400     2625
 5                                  2      2000     2300     2450     2675
 6                                  3      2050     2350     2500     2725
 7                                  4      2100     2400     2550     2775
 8                                  5      2150     2450     2600     2825
 9   YEARS OF EXPERIE               6      2200     2500     2650     2875
10                                  7      2250     2550     2700     2925
11                                  8      2300     2600     2750     2975
12                                  9      2350     2650     2800     3025
13                                 10      2400     2700     2850     3075
14                                 11      2450     2750     2900     3125
15                                 12      2500     2800     2950     3175
16                                 13      2550     2850     3000     3225
17                                 14      2600     2900     3050     3275
18                                 15      2650     2950     3100     3325
19
20
     01-Jan-88  09:07 AM
```

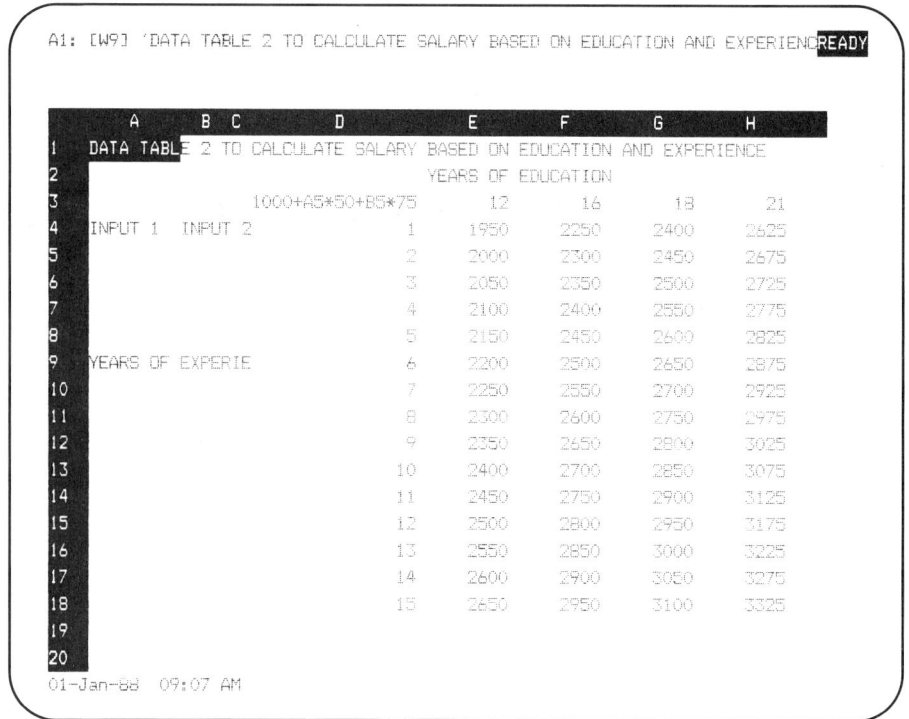

Figure 15-7 /Data Table 2 Showing the Effect of Years of Experience and Education on Salary

$0 and $20,000. There are four individuals whose income is between $20,001 and $40,000; and so on. The last frequency value is 0. This means nobody is making more than $100,000.

15-9 Inverting a Matrix Using the /Data Matrix Invert Command

Inverting a matrix that can be used in solving a system of linear equations is a time-consuming and complex task. Lotus provides an easy solution. The inverse of a matrix is a matrix which, if multiplied by the original matrix, will create an identity matrix. An *identity matrix* is one that has a diagonal of ones and the rest of the matrix filled by zeros. Figure 15-10 shows an original matrix, its inverse, and the result of the multiplication of the original matrix by its inverse. As you see, the result is an identity matrix. All the nonzero numbers are indeed very close to zero. If you format this matrix with two decimals, you will see the zeros.

To generate this result first we enter the original matrix in range B4..D6, then invoke the /Data Matrix Invert command. The range chosen was B4..D6, the output range was B9..D11. To verify this result we multiplied the original matrix by its inverse.

15-10 Matrix Addition, Subtraction, and Multiplication

Matrix addition and subtraction can be done by using /File Combine Add and /File

Figure 15-8 Data Table 2 Using Database Data to Calculate the Average Salary of Three Different Types of Professors in Three Different States

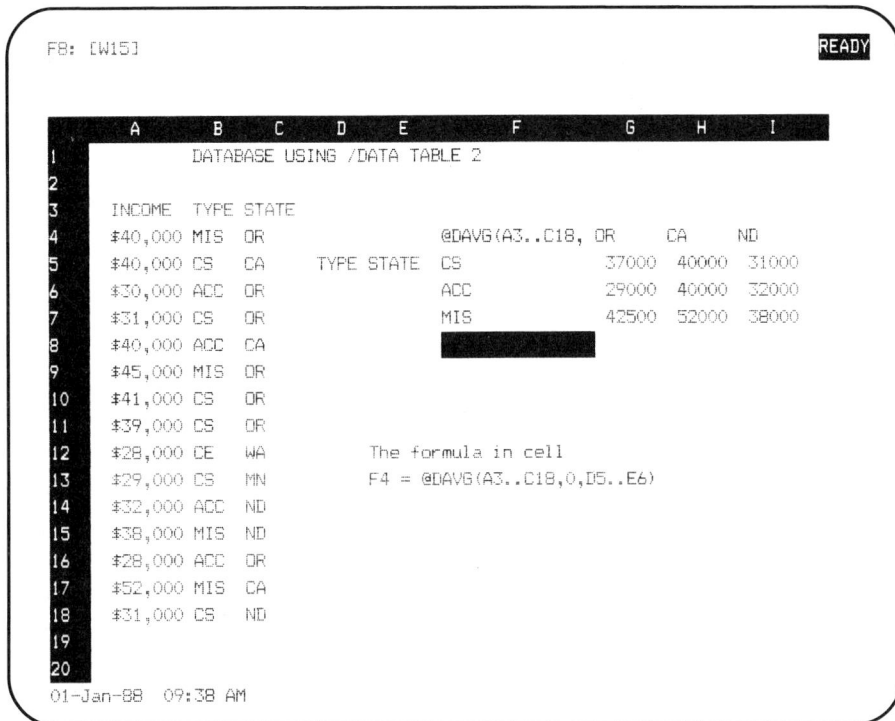

```
F8: [W15]                                                              READY

        A       B    C    D     E       F        G     H     I
1               DATABASE USING /DATA TABLE 2
2
3     INCOME  TYPE STATE
4    $40,000 MIS  OR            @DAVG(A3..C18, OR    CA    ND
5    $40,000 CS   CA   TYPE STATE  CS           37000 40000 31000
6    $30,000 ACC  OR            ACC             29000 40000 32000
7    $31,000 CS   OR            MIS             42500 52000 38000
8    $40,000 ACC  CA
9    $45,000 MIS  OR
10   $41,000 CS   OR
11   $39,000 CS   OR
12   $28,000 CE   WA            The formula in cell
13   $29,000 CS   MN            F4 = @DAVG(A3..C18,0,D5..E6)
14   $32,000 ACC  ND
15   $38,000 MIS  ND
16   $28,000 ACC  OR
17   $52,000 MIS  CA
18   $31,000 CS   ND
19
20
01-Jan-88  09:38 AM
```

Figure 15-9 An Example of /Data Distribution

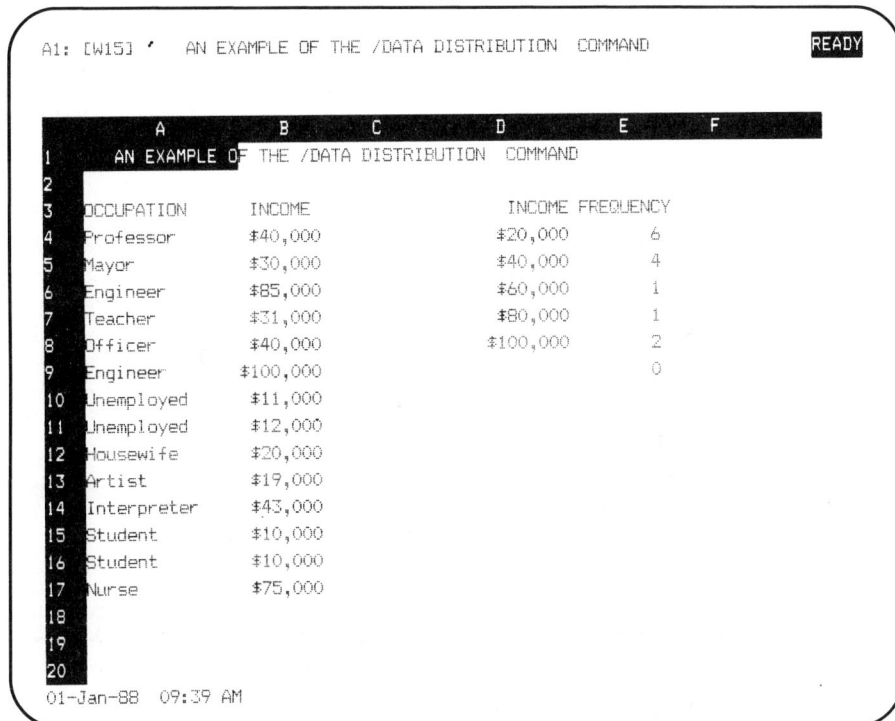

```
A1: [W15] '   AN EXAMPLE OF THE /DATA DISTRIBUTION  COMMAND          READY

        A           B        C        D          E       F
1    AN EXAMPLE OF THE /DATA DISTRIBUTION  COMMAND
2
3    OCCUPATION    INCOME               INCOME FREQUENCY
4    Professor    $40,000              $20,000     6
5    Mayor        $30,000              $40,000     4
6    Engineer     $85,000              $60,000     1
7    Teacher      $31,000              $80,000     1
8    Officer      $40,000             $100,000     2
9    Engineer    $100,000                          0
10   Unemployed   $11,000
11   Unemployed   $12,000
12   Housewife    $20,000
13   Artist       $19,000
14   Interpreter  $43,000
15   Student      $10,000
16   Student      $10,000
17   Nurse        $75,000
18
19
20
01-Jan-88  09:39 AM
```

Combine Subtract. For matrix multiplication, Lotus provides an additional facility under /Data Matrix Multiply.

To multiply two matrices by each other, the number of the columns of the first matrix must be equal to the number of the rows of the second matrix. For example, a 5 by 5 matrix can be multiplied by a 5 by 1 matrix. Invoke /Data Matrix Multiply, then define the data range and the output range for your two matrices. Figure 15-11 shows an example of the operations.

15-11 Solving a System of Linear Equations Using the Lotus /Data Matrix Command

A combination of /Data Matrix Invert and /Data Matrix Multiply can be used to solve a system of linear equations. The solution to a system of linear equations with n variables is as follows:

$$
\begin{bmatrix}
X1 \\
X2 \\
X3 \\
X4 \\
\cdot \\
\cdot \\
\cdot \\
Xn
\end{bmatrix}
=
\begin{bmatrix}
\text{inverse of matrix} \\
\text{of} \\
\text{Coefficients} \\
 \\
 \\
 \\

\end{bmatrix}
*
\begin{bmatrix}
b1 \\
b2 \\
b3 \\
b4 \\
\cdot \\
\cdot \\
\cdot \\
bn
\end{bmatrix}
$$

where $X1, X2, \ldots Xn$ are the number of unknowns and $b1, b2, \ldots bn$ are the righthand side of equations $1, 2, 3, \ldots n$. Therefore to solve a system of linear equations, the inverse of the matrix of coefficients will be multiplied by the array of the righthand side. The result of this multiplication is the solution to the system of the linear equations. Figure 15-12 shows an example using Lotus to solve a system of linear equations. The following equations were used in this example:

$$-10x1+18x2+ \quad 30x3 \quad -40x4 \quad +12x5 \quad = \quad 10$$

$$120x1+30x2+ \quad 100x3 \quad -140x4 \quad -10x5 \quad = \quad 100$$

$$25x1+15x2+ \quad 10x3 \quad -20x4 \quad -5x5 \quad = \quad 25$$

$$38x1+16x2+ \quad 24x3 \quad -30x4 \quad -8x5 \quad = \quad 40$$

$$20x1+10x2+ \quad 40x3 \quad -10x4 \quad +20x5 \quad = \quad 60$$

The answers for x1, x2, x3, x4 and x5 are presented at the bottom of Figure 15-12.

15-12 Regression Analysis Using the /Data Regression Command

Simple linear regression is a tool used for either medium-range (less than two years) or long-range forecasting (two years or more). The formula for a simple linear regression is as follows:

Figure 15-10 Calculation of the Inverse of a Matrix

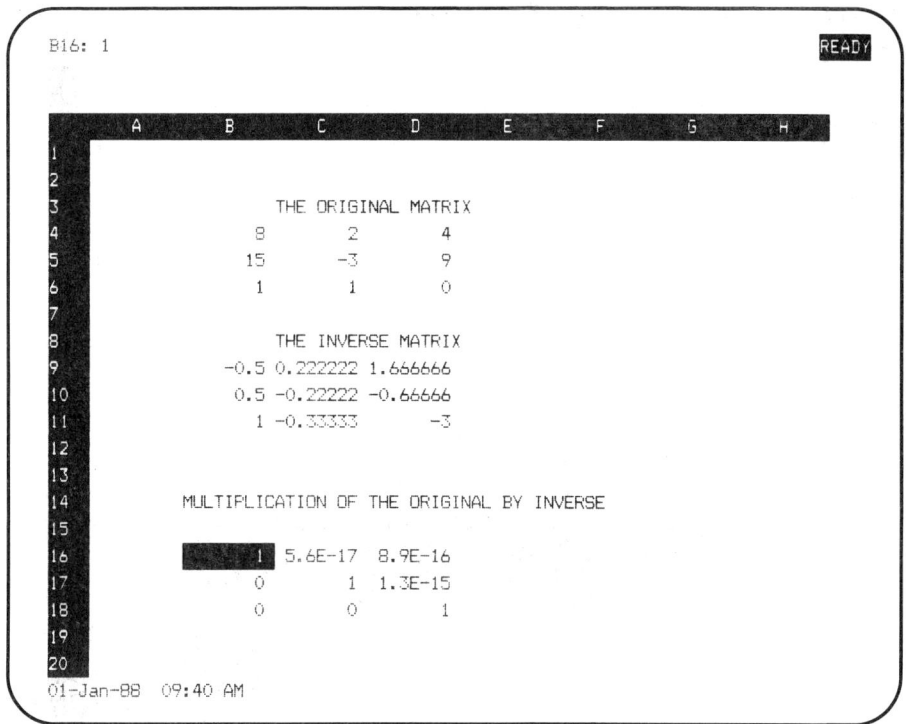

Figure 15-11 Matrix Multiplication

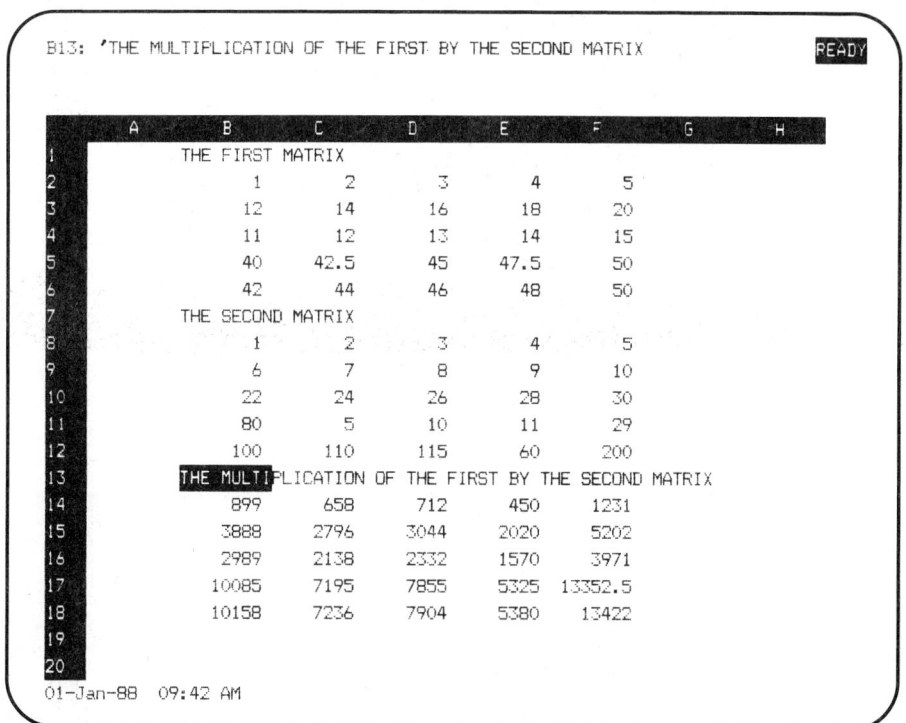

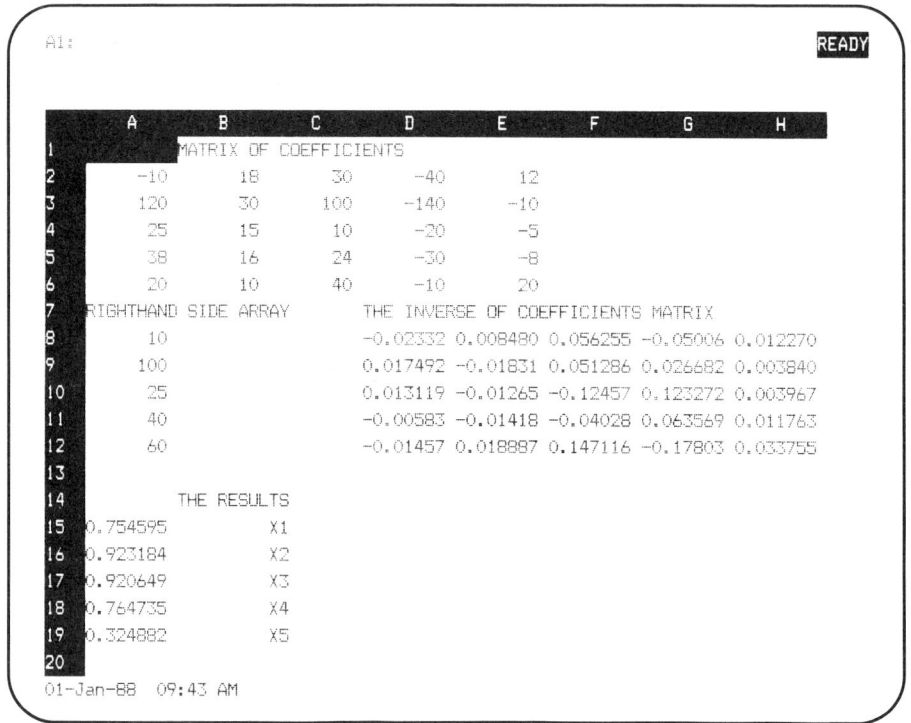

Figure 15-12 Solving a System of Linear Equations

Y = A + BX (equation for a straight line)

where Y is the dependent variable, such as income, total sales, total costs; X is the independent variable, such as education, advertising budget, fixed cost; A is the intercept; and B is the slope of the line.

In order to apply this model to forecasting problems, values for A and B must be estimated. One way of estimating these values is by using the least squares method.

The least squares method estimates the values of A and B in such a way that the mean squared deviation between actual and predicted values is as small as possible. The following two formulas will be used to satisfy the requirements of the least squares method:

$$B = \frac{N\Sigma XY - \Sigma X \Sigma Y}{N\Sigma X^2 - (\Sigma X)^2}$$

$$A = \frac{\Sigma Y}{N} - \frac{B \Sigma X}{N}$$

To measure the strength of the relative association between two variables we use the *correlation coefficient*. The correlation coefficient, r, can vary from -1 to +1; r = 0 indicates no correlation, r = -1 indicates perfect negative correlation, and r = +1 indicates perfect positive correlation.

The formula for the correlation coefficient is as follows:

$$r = \frac{N\Sigma XY - \Sigma X\Sigma Y}{\sqrt{[N\Sigma X^2 - (\Sigma X)^2][N\Sigma Y^2 - (\Sigma Y)^2]}}$$

The square of the correlation coefficient is called the *coefficient of determination.* The coefficient of determination is the ratio of the sum of explained variation over the sum of total variation. The following formula indicates this:

$$r^2 = \frac{[N\Sigma XY - \Sigma X\Sigma Y]^2}{[N\Sigma X^2 - (\Sigma X)^2][N\Sigma Y^2 - (\Sigma Y)^2]}$$

This ratio shows how well a regression line can define the total variation in a series of data points. This ratio varies from 0 to 1; 0 means that the regression line does not explain any variation in the data points and 1 means that total variation is perfectly explained by the regression line.

Let us say you have an equation of $Y = 10,000 + 250X$, where Y is the total sales and X is the amount of advertising. This equation indicates that if you do not advertise at all, your estimated total sales would be $10,000. For every one dollar of advertising, your estimated total sales would increase by $250.

Figure 15-13 shows an example of simple linear regression for total sales and advertising for Pacific Rain Glass Company. This forecast is based on the past 12 years of available data. To generate this forecast, invoke the /Data Regression command. For the X range, independent variable, we have data in cells C5..C16. For the Y dependent variable we have data in cells B5..B16. For the output range we chose E1 (only the left corner). We chose the intercept to be calculated. Then choose Go and you will see the result. As you see the final equation is:

$$Y = -247,600 + 20.04091x$$

Also, as R squared shows, there is a high correlation between the amount of advertising and the total sales (0.840304).

15-13 Multiple Linear Regression Using Lotus

Simple regression finds the relationship between two variables. Lotus has provided you with the ability to include up to 16 independent variables. Naturally a multiple regression can be more comprehensive and more accurate information can be revealed. In Figure 15-14 we have demonstrated an example of a multiple regression.

In this analysis, the independent variables are a salesperson's age, high school GPA, and number of years' selling experience. The dependent variable is the total sales generated by the salespeople.

In this example the /Data Regression command was invoked. For the X range we defined B5..D14, for the Y range, we defined A5..A14, and the output range starts at cell F3. You need only one empty cell. Lotus will provide you with all the calculated results.

Figure 15-13 Simple Regression

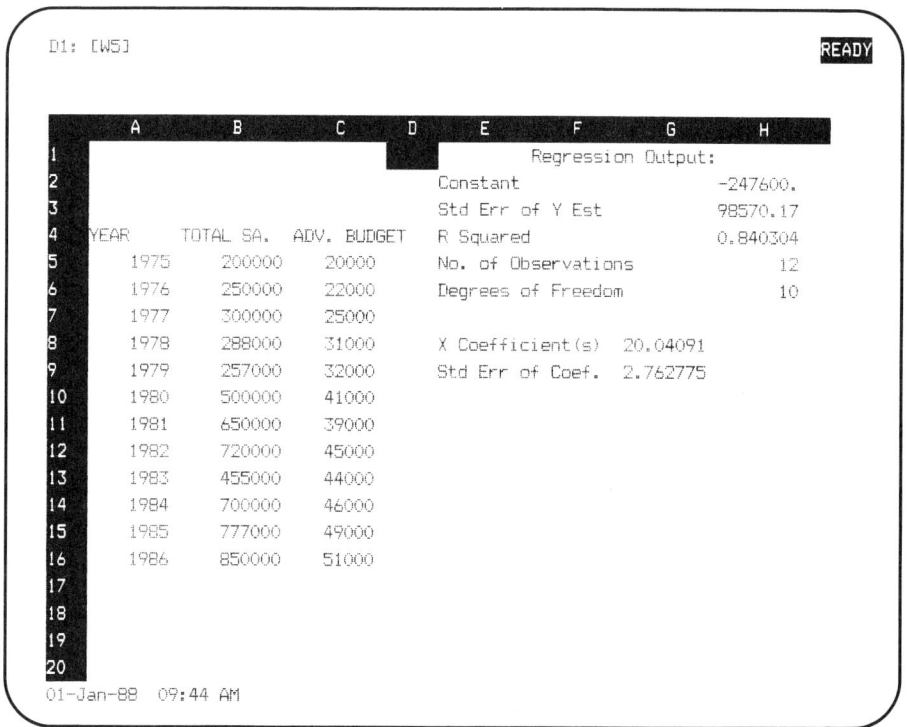

```
D1: [W5]                                                                READY


          A          B          C       D        E          F        G        H
 1                                               Regression Output:
 2                                        Constant                -247600.
 3                                        Std Err of Y Est        98570.17
 4  YEAR       TOTAL SA.  ADV. BUDGET     R Squared               0.840304
 5     1975     200000      20000         No. of Observations           12
 6     1976     250000      22000         Degrees of Freedom            10
 7     1977     300000      25000
 8     1978     288000      31000         X Coefficient(s)   20.04091
 9     1979     257000      32000         Std Err of Coef.   2.762775
10     1980     500000      41000
11     1981     650000      39000
12     1982     720000      45000
13     1983     455000      44000
14     1984     700000      46000
15     1985     777000      49000
16     1986     850000      51000
17
18
19
20
   01-Jan-88   09:44 AM
```

Figure 15-14 Multiple Regression

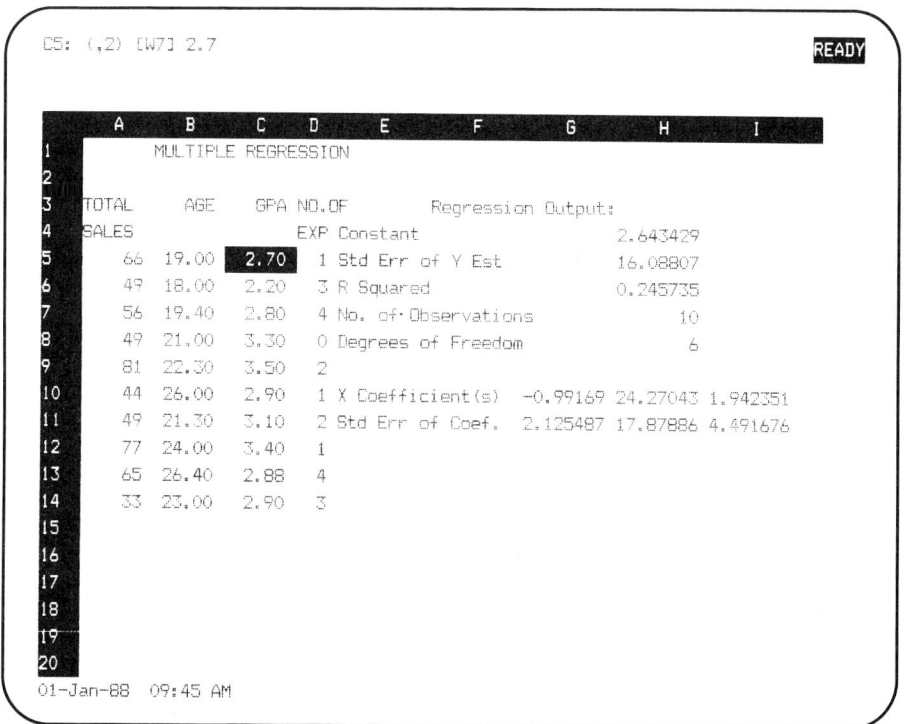

```
C5: (,2) [W7] 2.7                                                       READY


          A     B      C     D      E          F         G        H        I
 1              MULTIPLE REGRESSION
 2
 3  TOTAL      AGE    GPA  NO.OF        Regression Output:
 4  SALES                  EXP  Constant                 2.643429
 5       66  19.00   2.70   1  Std Err of Y Est          16.08807
 6       49  18.00   2.20   3  R Squared                 0.245735
 7       56  19.40   2.80   4  No. of·Observations             10
 8       49  21.00   3.30   0  Degrees of Freedom               6
 9       81  22.30   3.50   2
10       44  26.00   2.90   1  X Coefficient(s)   -0.99169 24.27043 1.942351
11       49  21.30   3.10   2  Std Err of Coef.   2.125487 17.87886 4.491676
12       77  24.00   3.40   1
13       65  26.40   2.88   4
14       33  23.00   2.90   3
15
16
17
18
19
20
   01-Jan-88   09:45 AM
```

Even though Lotus can perform all these calculations, it cannot report some very important statistical measures, such as a t-test, Durbin-Watson test, and so on. We believe these are some of the limitations of this otherwise very powerful command.

Summary

In this chapter we have covered some of the advanced operations performed by a Lotus database: database statistical functions, table building using /Data Fill, sophisticated what-if analysis using /Data Table 1 and /Data Table 2, and /Data Distribution. At the end of this chapter, we spent some time on /Data Matrix and / Data Regression commands. These two sets of commands are extremely powerful since Lotus can solve a system of linear equations with up to 90 variables. Multiple linear regression in Lotus is also capable of handling up to 16 independent variables.

Review Questions

1. How many database statistical functions does Lotus have?
2. What is the major difference between these database functions and their statistical counterparts?
3. What are two applications of the /Data Fill command?
4. What are the default values for the /Data Fill command?
5.* When does table building in the /Data Fill command stop?
6. Why and how can /Data Table 1 and /Data Table 2 be used as a DSS tool?
7. Give two applications of /Data Table 1 and /Data Table 2.
8.* When you use a database with /Data Table 1 or /Data Table 2, are the input cell and criterion range the same?
9. What are some of the applications of the /Data Distribution command?
10. Why must bin range in data distribution be in ascending order?
11.* What will happen in /Data Distribution if one of your data items does not fall within the bin range?
12. How do you invert a matrix?
13. Do all matrices have an inverse?
14. How do you multiply two matrices?
15.* Can you multiply any two matrices?
16. How do you solve a system of linear equations?
17.* What is the righthand side array?
18.* What are some limitations of the /Data Regression command?
19. What statistics are generated by the /Data Regression command?
20. Using the /Data Fill command, build a table with the following values: Start value = 10, step value = 5, and stop value = 200.
21. Generate an example of your own using /Data Table 1.
22. Generate an example of your own using /Data Table 2.
23. Using the /Data Distribution command, classify the following sales data into six groups. The interval between each group is 20,000.

100,000, 150,000, 135,000, 200,000, 164,000, 169,000, 220,000, 300,000, 250,000

24. Using the /Data Matrix Invert command, invert the following matrix:

5   -5   15
10   -7   -3
6   -3   -3

25. Using the /Data Matrix command, solve the following system of linear equations:

5x1	-5x2	+15x3	=	5
10x1	-7x2	-3x3	=	0
6x1	-3x2	-3x3	=	0

26. Following are sales data for the past seven years for Cotton Textile Firm. Using /Data Regression, generate a forecast for total sales for 1988:

1981	100,000
1982	130,000
1983	175,000
1984	155,000
1985	200,000
1986	250,000
1987	300,000

16

Macros/Part One:
Typing Alternatives

16-1 Introduction

In this chapter we will discuss the principles of macro design and use. We will provide guidelines for naming, debugging, and documenting macros, and we will introduce more than 50 of the most commonly used macros. In Chapters 17 and 18 we introduce advanced features of macro operation.

16-2 What Is a Macro?

In simple terms, a *macro* is a collection of a series of keystrokes. As you have learned, everything in Lotus is a series of keystrokes, therefore everything in Lotus can be done by using a macro. Let us assume that you have to type the following statement in many different locations of your worksheet:

THE TOTAL COSTS OF PRODUCTION FOR THIS PERIOD

You have two alternatives. Either type this statement over and over, or create a macro. Whenever you are doing something repeatedly, think of using macros. They increase the speed and accuracy of operations, since they repeat the same sequence over and over.

16-3 Your First Macro

The first question asked by new macro users is, where do we put a macro? You can put a macro in any of the empty cells in your worksheet. It is a good practice to put a macro in a location that is easy to reach but where it will not get in your way. Most users put their macros in column AA. This is one worksheet to the right, close enough for easy access. Let us move the cursor to column AB1 (save AA1 for the macro name) and type the label:

THE TOTAL COSTS OF PRODUCTION FOR THIS PERIOD

The next task is to name the macro. A macro name can be any letter of the alphabet. It does not matter if it is uppercase or lowercase. The name must start with a backslash (\). You must also enter the name as a label. This means you must use one of the label prefixes (, or " or ^). If you do not use a prefix, the letter used for the macro name will be repeated, which you do not want. Next, you should name the location in which the macro is residing. Use /Range Name Create and name your macro \A. To name a macro, you can also use /Range Name Label Right (assuming the cursor is to the left of the macro, at the name cell). Figure 16-1 shows your first macro.

The next question is, how do you execute this macro? It can be executed from any location in the worksheet. Move the cursor to cell A1, hold down the **Alt** key (macro key), and at the same time, type A (the name of your macro). You will see THE TOTAL COSTS OF PRODUCTION FOR THIS PERIOD appear at the top of the screen in the control panel. Just hit the **Return** key in order to enter this label into cell A1.

Can you include *Return* in your macro? The answer is yes. Each key on your keyboard has a representative in macro design. Table 16-1 shows all key representations and certain commands. As you can see in this table, the representative for Return is the tilde (~). Move to cell AB1 and edit the content of this cell by pressing F2. Add a tilde to the end of the label. Now the content of cell AB1 is as follows:

THE TOTAL COSTS OF PRODUCTION FOR THIS PERIOD~

Now move the cursor to cell A2 and invoke your macro. Hold down the **Alt** key and type A. You will see that the label enters directly to cell A2.

Which cell is the address for naming your macro? All you need to do is to use the first cell as the address for the range. In this case cell AB1 is the beginning of the range. However, if you want to provide the entire range address, AB1..AF1, you may.

16-4 Your Second Macro

Your first macro only included a label. You can use a macro to automate a command or a series of commands. In order to do this, you must first record all the steps that you follow for performing a command. Let us assume you are interested in formatting 20000 with the Currency format and two decimal places. Let us record the steps involved:

- / (call the menu)
- R (invoke range)
- F (invoke format)
- C (invoke currency)
- 2 (2 decimal places)
- Return (to enter 2)
- Return (to enter the correct cell as the desired range to be formatted)

Table 16-1 Keyboard Representatives*

DESCRIPTION	MACRO KEY
ABS	{ABS}
BACKSPACE	{BACKSPACE} or {BS}
BIG LEFT (move to left one screen)	{BIGLEFT}
BIG RIGHT (move to right one screen)	{BIGRIGHT}
CALC	{CALC}
DELETE (you must use only in EDIT mode)	{DELETE} or {DEL}
DOWN	{DOWN}
EDIT	{EDIT}
END	{END}
ESCAPE	{ESCAPE} or {ESC}
GOTO	{GOTO}
GRAPH	{GRAPH}
HOME	{HOME}
LEFT	{LEFT}
NAME	{NAME}
PAGE DOWN	{PGDN}
PAGE UP	{PGUP}
QUERY	{QUERY}
RETURN (tilde)	~
RIGHT	{RIGHT}
TABLE	{TABLE}
To have braces appear as {and}	{{}and{}}
To have tilde appear as ~	{~}
UP	{UP}
WINDOW	{WINDOW}

* In order to specify two or more consecutive uses of the same key, you can always include a repetition factor within the braces. For example:

DOWN 6   tells Lotus to move the cursor six cells down
UP 2   tells Lotus to move the cursor two cells up

First, we set the column width to 12, now move the cursor to cell AA3 and enter \B (as label with apostrophe). In cell AB3 enter /RFC2~~ (as label with apostrophe). Using /Range Name Create, name cell AB3 as \B.

Now move the cursor to cell AA10, which contains number 20000, and invoke your B macro. Your number is formatted. Figure 16-2 shows this process.

16-5 An Interactive Macro

In your second macro, the number which was formatted was predefined. It is possible to include a question mark (?) within your macro in order to make it interactive. This means that when you execute your macro the process stops when it encounters the question mark until you enter a number, then the process continues. Let us start with an empty worksheet. Move the cursor to column AB1 and type the following:

YOU TELL ME A NUMBER~
{DOWN}

Figure 16-1 Your First Macro

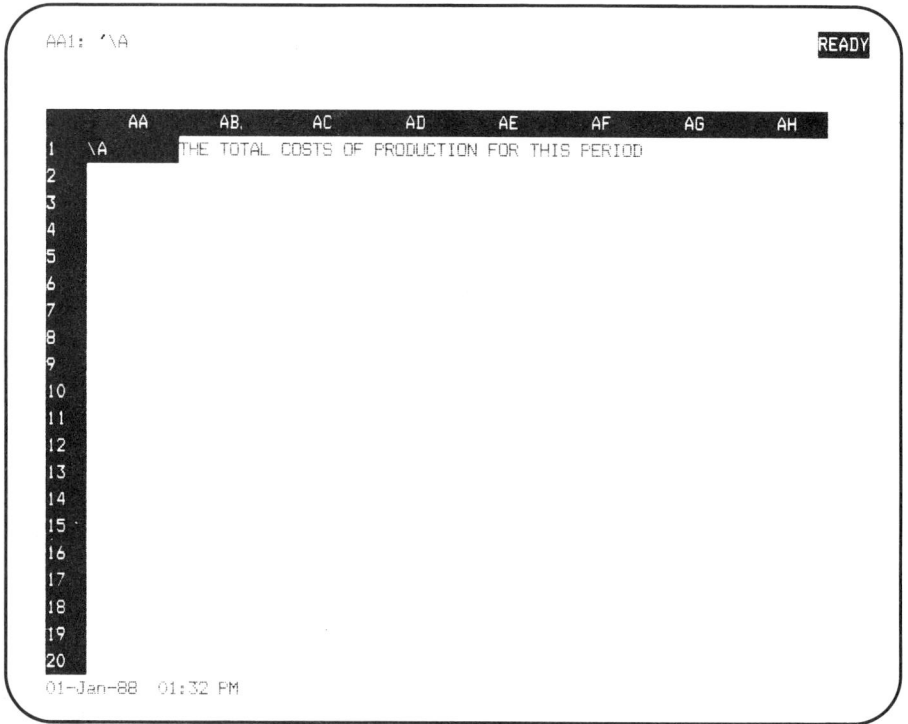

Figure 16-2 Your Second Macro

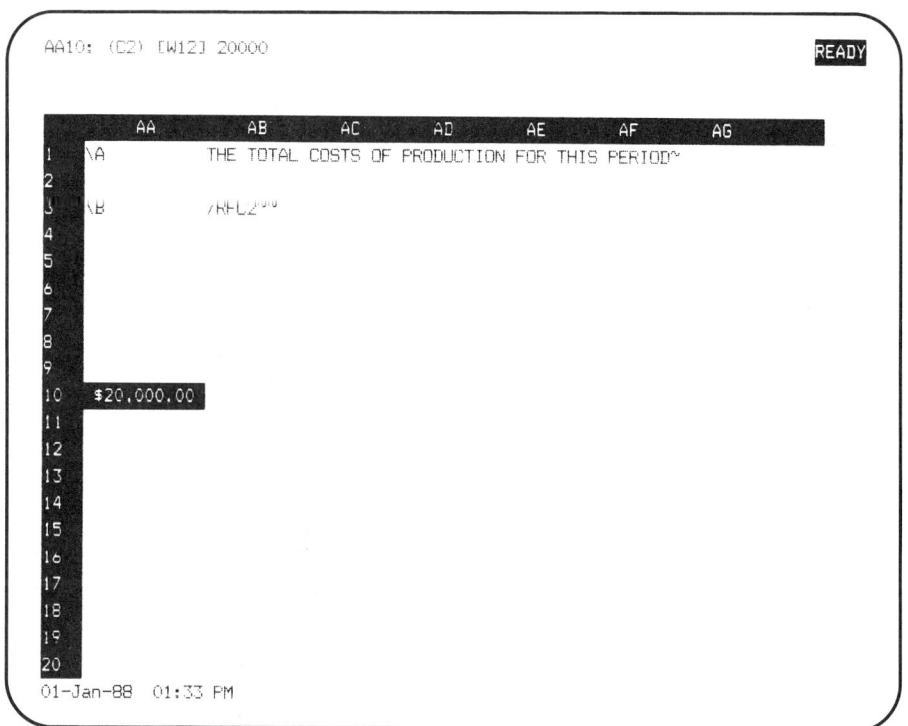

{?}
/RFC2~~

Name this macro \C. Remember, only cell AB1 needs to be indicated as the range since the macro will execute all rows until an empty row is encountered. Now move the cursor to cell AA6 and invoke the macro. As you see, the label YOU TELL ME A NUMBER appears in cell AA6 and CMD is displayed at the bottom of the screen, meaning the macro is in progress. The macro waits for you to enter a number. Type 36000 and hit Return. Your number is formatted. We have set column width to 12. So the question mark within the braces in the macro makes the macro interactive. Figure 16-3 shows this process.

We can enhance the macro by including W(worksheet)C(column)S(set-width) {?} or /WCS{?}~. In this case, the column width is set by the user. We could also include a question mark in place of the number of decimal places. Figure 16-4 shows these variations of our original macro.

To stop a macro, press the **Ctrl** and **Break** keys together.

16-6 How Is a Macro Executed?

As you have seen so far, a macro is a column of keystrokes. The number of keystrokes can be as many as 240. The macro is executed from left to right and top to bottom. As soon as the macro encounters a blank cell, it halts execution. Therefore, if you are putting more than one macro in a worksheet, make sure there is at least one empty line between each macro.

It is also a good idea to document your macro. Since the name of your macro is only one letter there is no way to remember what each macro does. So to the right of the macro, after leaving one empty cell, always indicate briefly what task a particular macro performs. In Figure 16-5 we show an example of a macro. In column AA1, the letter G is the name of the macro. We call this name *documentation*. In column AB1 is the macro itself. And finally, in column AD1 we have mentioned the function of the macro. We call this function *documentation* also.

16-7 Debugging Your Macro

Macros are executed extremely fast. There is always the possibility of making mistakes. Lotus provides a facility for debugging your macro. You can process your macro step by step as follows:

1. Press the **Alt** key and the **F2** key at the same time. Now the status indicator shows STEP.
2. Invoke your macro. Now the status indicator shows SST (single step). 1-2-3 pauses after the execution of each keystroke. To continue, press any key.
3. If you see anything wrong, press **Ctrl** and **Break** keys at the same time to abort the execution of the macro.
4. By editing, correct your mistake(s).

   If you continue hitting a key until the macro is fully executed, SST changes to

Figure 16-3 An Example of an Interactive Macro

```
AA7: (C2) [W12] 36000                                                    READY

          AA          AB          AC          AD          AE          AF
1    \C          YOU TELL ME A NUMBER~
2                {DOWN}
3                {?}~
4                /RFC2~~
5
6    YOU TELL ME A NUMBER
7    $36,000.00
8
9
10
11
12
13
14
15
16
17
18
19
20
01-Jan-88  01:38 PM
```

Figure 16-4 More Complicated Interactive Macro

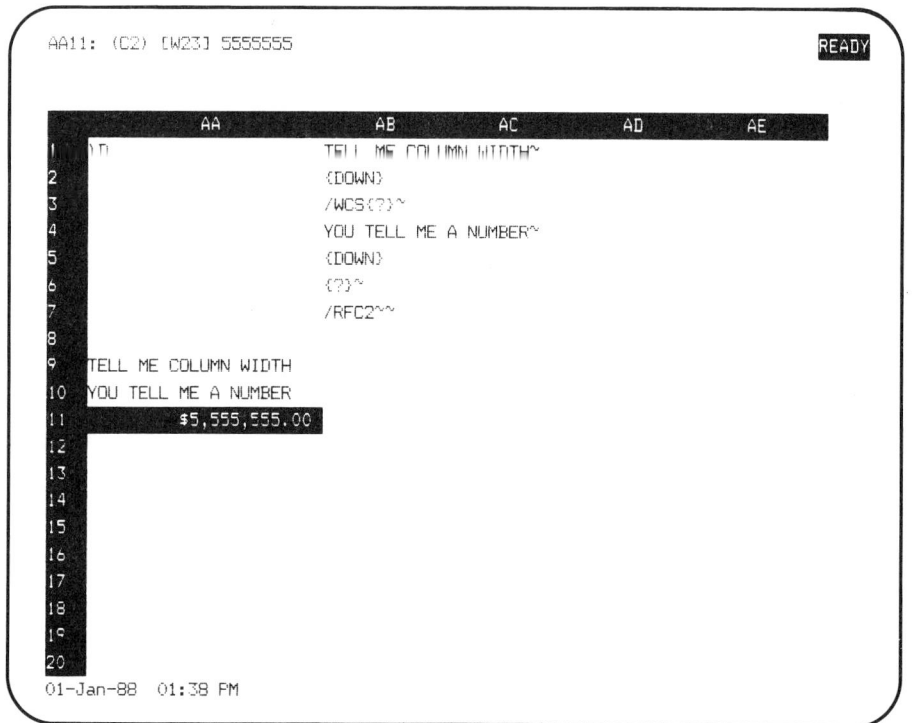

```
AA11: (C2) [W23] 5555555                                                 READY

          AA              AB              AC          AD          AE
1    \D              TELL ME COLUMN WIDTH~
2                    {DOWN}
3                    /WCS{?}~
4                    YOU TELL ME A NUMBER~
5                    {DOWN}
6                    {?}~
7                    /RFC2~~
8
9    TELL ME COLUMN WIDTH
10   YOU TELL ME A NUMBER
11                $5,555,555.00
12
13
14
15
16
17
18
19
20
01-Jan-88  01:38 PM
```

```
AA1: '\G                                                    READY

        AA        AB        AC        AD       AE       AF       AG       AH
1    \G          /FCC                  Copies an entire worksheet or named range to
2                                       the current worksheet depending on the cursor
3                                       position. User must identify the name of the
4                                       incoming file.
5
6
7
8
9
10
11
12
13
14
15
16
17
18
19
20
01-Jan-88   01:39 PM
```

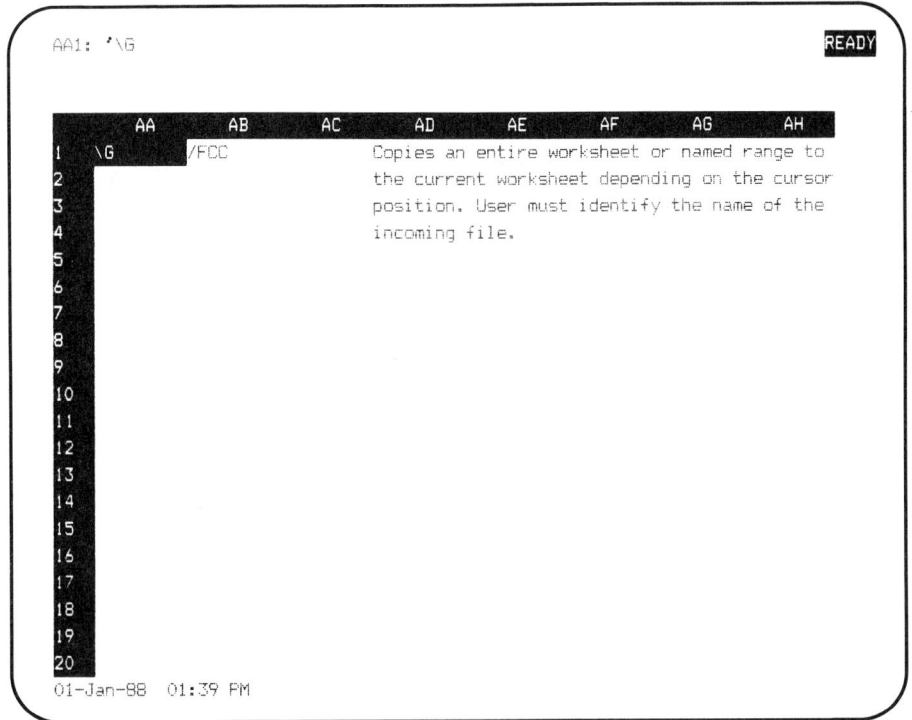

Figure 16-5 An Example of a Documented Macro

STEP, which means the macro is fully executed. To get out of the STEP mode, press Alt and F2 together. The STEP indicator will disappear.

16-8 An Automatic Macro

If you name your macro Zero (\0), it will automatically execute when the worksheet that includes it is loaded. This is very useful for designing menus. If you save the worksheet that includes the \0 macro as AUTO123.WK1, this worksheet will be automatically loaded to RAM as soon as you get the system started. A combination of AUTO123.WK1 and the \0 macro can be used for any application involving first-time computer users giving them easy access to the system. It is also handy for commonly used worksheets. Figure 16-6 shows the \0 macro.

16-9 Creating a Macro Library

When you get used to designing and using macros, you may want to use some of them from worksheet to worksheet. If you put all your macros in a remote location of your worksheet, such as column AA, and if you document them properly, you can use them over and over again. However, if you transfer your macros to a different worksheet, you must rename them. Chapter 17 will show you a macro for naming other macros. Figures 16-7 to 16-9 present some of the most commonly used macros. Figure 16-10 presents key representative macros.

Figure 16-6 Automatic Worksheet and Automatic Macro

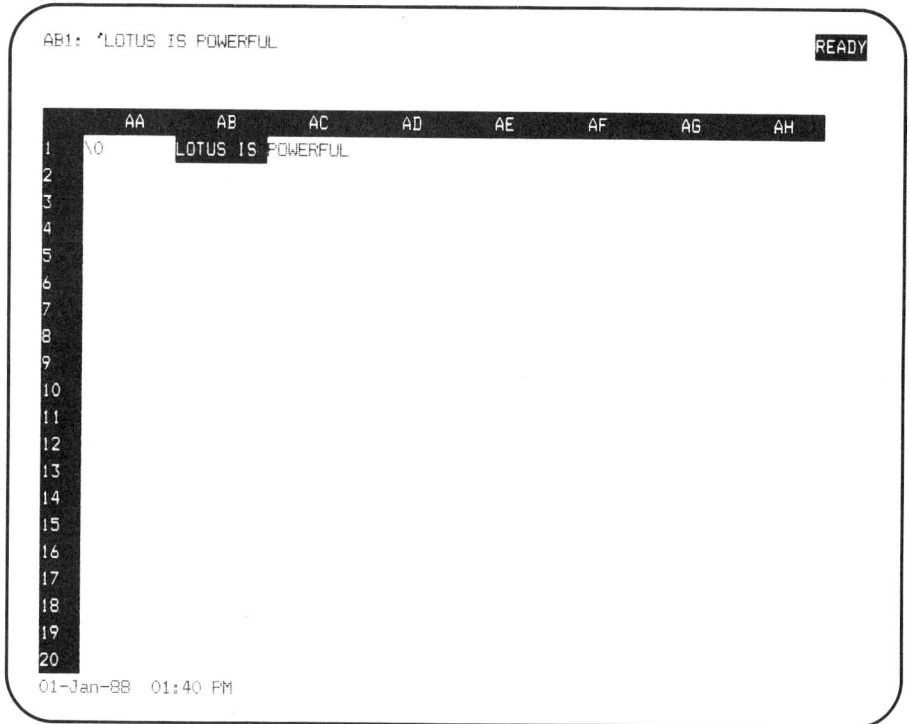

```
AB1: 'LOTUS IS POWERFUL                                         READY

           AA        AB        AC        AD        AE        AF        AG        AH
1    \0         LOTUS IS POWERFUL
2
3
4
5
6
7
8
9
10
11
12
13
14
15
16
17
18
19
20
01-Jan-88  01:40 PM
```

Figure 16-7 Commonly Used Macros Part 1

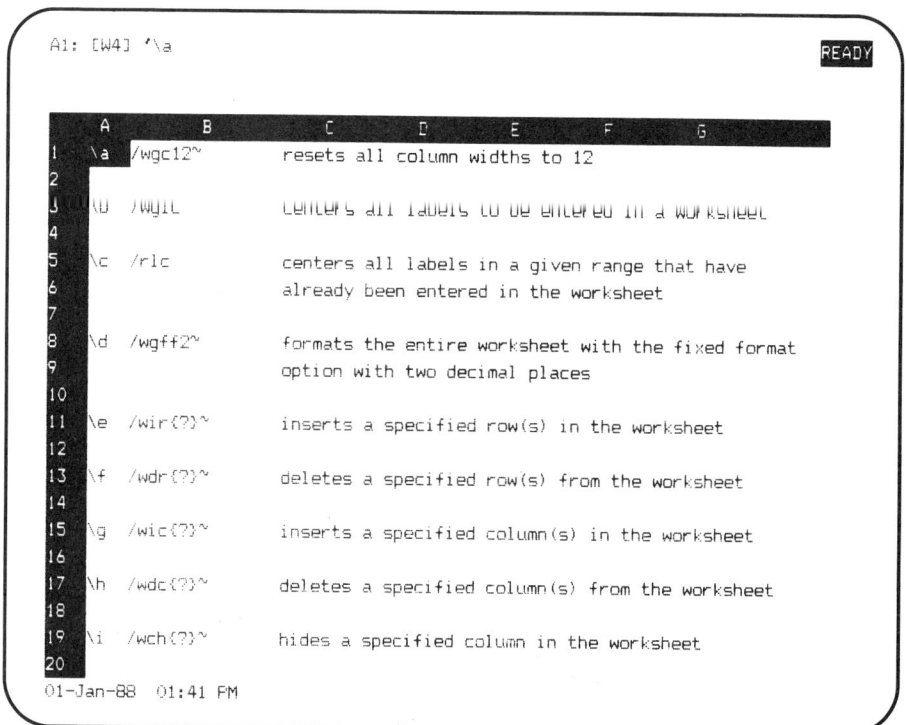

```
A1: [W4] '\a                                                    READY

       A         B           C         D         E         F         G
1    \a    /wgc12~          resets all column widths to 12
2
3    \b    /wgtc           centers all labels to be entered in a worksheet
4
5    \c    /rlc            centers all labels in a given range that have
6                          already been entered in the worksheet
7
8    \d    /wgff2~         formats the entire worksheet with the fixed format
9                          option with two decimal places
10
11   \e    /wir{?}~        inserts a specified row(s) in the worksheet
12
13   \f    /wdr{?}~        deletes a specified row(s) from the worksheet
14
15   \g    /wic{?}~        inserts a specified column(s) in the worksheet
16
17   \h    /wdc{?}~        deletes a specified column(s) from the worksheet
18
19   \i    /wch{?}~        hides a specified column in the worksheet
20
01-Jan-88  01:41 PM
```

Figure 16-7 (Continued)

```
A21: [W4] '\j                                                        READY

       A       B           C        D        E        F        G
21  \j   /wcd{?}~       reveals (displays) a hidden column in the worksheet
22
23  \k   /wey           erases the entire worksheet
24
25  \l   /ru            selectively unprotects a specified range of cells
26
27  \m   /rp            protects a specified range of cells from modification
28
29  \n   /wgzy          suppresses the display of cells that have a numeric
30                      value of zero
31
32  \o   /wwv           splits the screen vertically where the cursor is
33                      positioned
34
35  \p   /wwh           splits the screen horizontally where the cursor is
36                      positioned
37
38  \q   /wtb           freezes all cells to the left and above the cursor
39                      so the cells cannot move off the screen
40
01-Jan-88  01:42 PM
```

Figure 16-7 (Continued)

```
A41: [W4] '\r                                                        READY

       A       B           C        D        E        F        G
41  \r   /wgrm          changes the worksheet from the standard automatic
42                      recalculation to manual recalculation
43
44  \s   /rnc{?}~{?}~   allows the user to specify a name for any range
45
46  \t   /re{?}~        erases a specified range
47
48  \u   /rfc0~{?}~     formats a specified range with the currency format
49                      option and zero decimal places
50
51  \v   @TODAY~        formats today's date with the long international date
52       /rfd4~         format
53
54  \w   /rfdt2{?}~     formats a specified range with the #2 time option
55
56  \x   /rf,2~{?}~     formats a specified range with the comma format
57                      option and two decimal places
58
59  \y   /rfh{?}~       hides a specified range
60
01-Jan-88  01:43 PM
```

Figure 16-7 (Continued)

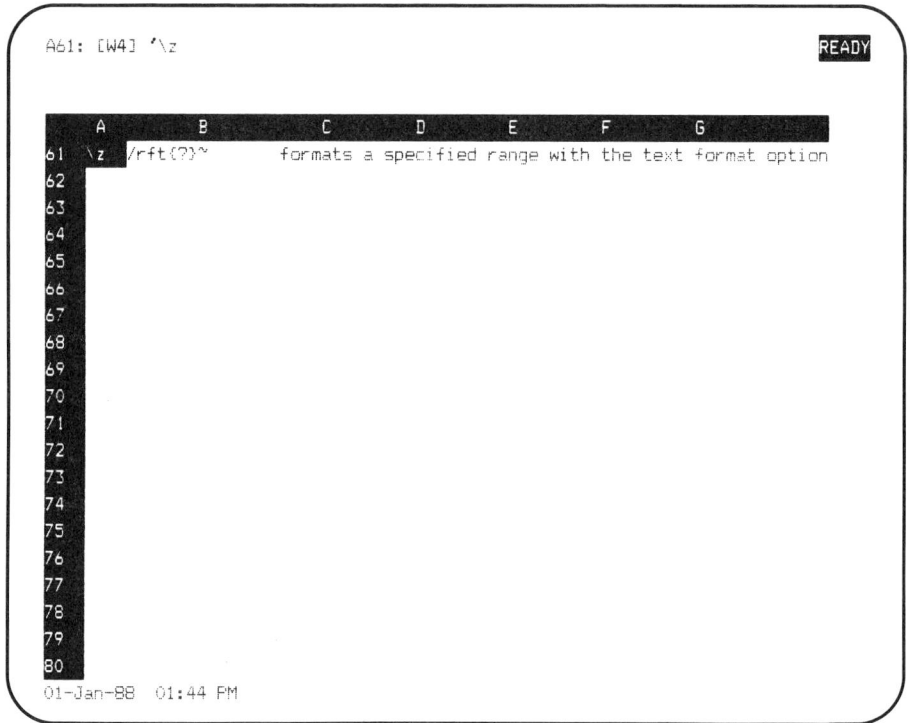

```
A61: [W4] '\z                                                                    READY

        A          B           C          D          E          F          G
61   \z    /rft{?}~           formats a specified range with the text format option
62
63
64
65
66
67
68
69
70
71
72
73
74
75
76
77
78
79
80
01-Jan-88  01:44 PM
```

Figure 16-8 Commonly Used Macros Part 2

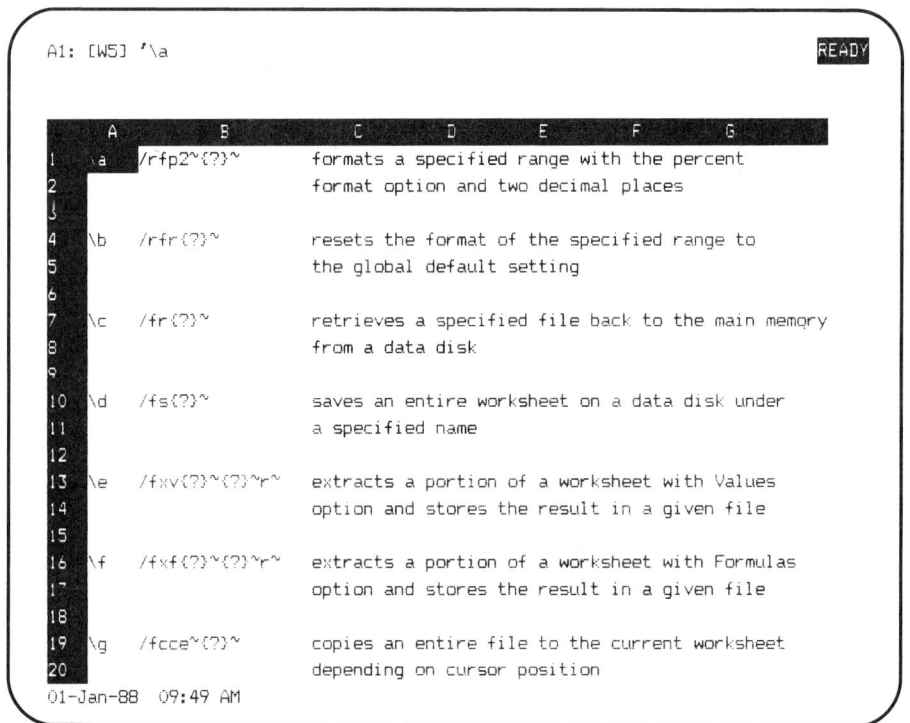

```
A1: [W5] '\a                                                                     READY

        A          B              C          D          E          F          G
1    \a    /rfp2~{?}~        formats a specified range with the percent
2                            format option and two decimal places
3
4    \b    /rfr{?}~          resets the format of the specified range to
5                            the global default setting
6
7    \c    /fr{?}~           retrieves a specified file back to the main memory
8                            from a data disk
9
10   \d    /fs{?}~           saves an entire worksheet on a data disk under
11                           a specified name
12
13   \e    /fxv{?}~{?}~r~    extracts a portion of a worksheet with Values
14                           option and stores the result in a given file
15
16   \f    /fxf{?}~{?}~r~    extracts a portion of a worksheet with Formulas
17                           option and stores the result in a given file
18
19   \g    /fcce~{?}~        copies an entire file to the current worksheet
20                           depending on cursor position
01-Jan-88  09:49 AM
```

Figure 16-8 (Continued)

```
A21: [W5]                                                              READY

       A         B            C         D         E       F       G
21
22  \h    /fcae{?}~         takes the values from an entire file and adds
23                          those values to the corresponding cells in the
24                          current worksheet
25
26  \i    /few{?}~y         deletes a specified worksheet file from a data
27                          disk
28
29  \j    /gtba{?}~v        sets up and views a bar graph with one data
30                          range
31
32  \k    /gtpa{?}~x{?}~otf{?}~qv   sets up and views a pie chart with
33                                  two data ranges and one title
34
35  \l    /gtla{?}~x{?}~otx{?}~ty{?}~qv   sets up and views a line graph
36                                  with two data ranges and a
37                                  title for the x- and y-axis
38
39  \m    /gotx{?}~ty{?}~qv  enters a title for the x-axis and the y-axis
40                           on a specified graph and views the graph
01-Jan-88  09:50 AM
```

Figure 16-8 (Continued)

```
A41: [W5]                                                              READY

       A         B            C         D         E       F       G
41
42  \n    /gosxml{?}~u{?}~qqv   overrides the automatic scale and allows
43                              the user to rescale the x-axis manually
44                              and view the changes
45
46  \o    /gnc{?}~q          names a current graph and saves all the
47                           current parameters defining that graph
48
49  \p    /gnu{?}~q          recalls a graph you have previously named and
50                           saved
51
52  \q    /gnd{?}~q          deletes a single graph name and its parameters
53                           from the worksheet
54
55  \r    /gola{?}~qq        enters a legend below the x-axis
56
57  \s    /gofgsqqv          formats all the graph lines of a graph with
58                           the symbols option and views it
59
60  \t    /dsd{?}~p{?}~g     sorts an entire database or specified data-
01-Jan-88  09:51 AM
```

Figure 16-8 (Continued)

```
A61: [W5]                                                              READY

        A        B          C        D        E        F        G
61                       range according to a primary key field
62
63  \u   /dsd{?}~p{?}~s{?}~g    sorts an entire database or specified
64                         datarange according to primary and
65                         secondary key fields
66
67  \v   /dqi{?}~c{?}~o{?}~e    searches a database and extracts a por-
68                         tion of the database to an output range
69                         based on a specified criterion range
70
71  \w   /dqi{?}~c{?}~o{?}~u    searches a database and extracts a
72                         unique portion of the database to an
73                         output range based on a specified
74                         criterion range. Duplicate records will
75                         not be chosen.
76
77  \x   /pf{?}~r{?}~gq    specifies the range of cells to be printed
78                         into a file
79
80  \y   /ppcrq           clears and resets print range
01-Jan-88  09:52 AM
```

Figure 16-8 (Continued)

```
A81: [W5]                                                              READY

        A        B          C        D        E        F        G
81
82  \z   /ppomr{?}~ml{?}~qq   resets the left and right margins
83
84
85
86
87
88
89
90
91
92
93
94
95
96
97
98
99
100
01-Jan-88  09:53 AM
```

Figure 16-9 Commonly Used Macros Part 3

```
AA1:  '\a                                                              READY

          AA        AB        AC        AD        AE       AF       AG       AH
1   \a            /wgc20~
2                 /rlla1..a7~
3                                          These three macros increase the
4   \b            /wgc20~                  column width (globally) to 20 and
5                 /rlra1..a7~              then left-justifies (\a), right-
6                                          justifies (\b) and center-justifies
7   \c            /wgc20~                  (\c) the label in the range a1..a7.
8                 /rlca1..a7~
9
10  \d            {goto}a15~               This macro changes the date in
11                @NOW~                    cell a15 to today's date.
12                /rfd4~
13
14  \e            {goto}aa1~               This macro loads a macro library.
15                /fcce{?}~
16
17  \f            /ppcrr                   This macro prints any portion of a
18                {?}~g                    worksheet specified by the user.
19
20
01-Jan-88   09:54 AM
```

Figure 16-10 Key Representative Macros

```
AA1:  '\m                                                              READY

          AA        AB        AC        AD        AE       AF       AG       AH
1   \m            {home}
2                 Payment{right}Interest{right}^Term{right}Future Value~
3                 {down}{end}{left}
4                 100{right}.05{right}5{right}@FV(a2,b2,c2)~
5                 /rfc0~a2~
6                 /rfp0~b2~                This macro uses the table
7                 {goto}b4~                building function to deter-
8                 Interest~{down}          mine the future value of
9                 Rate~{right}{up}         a specific payment based on
10                Future~{down}            interest rates from 5% to
11                Value~{down}             14%. The data is then
12                +d2~                     graphed. The payment amount
13                /dfb7..b16~.05~.01~.14~  changes to $200,the
14                /rfp0~b7..b16~           table is rebuilt and the
15                /dt1b6..c16~b2~          graph is redrawn.
16                /wcs12~                  After execution of the
17                /rfc2~c7..c16~           macro, the user can change
18                /gtlab7..b16~xc7..c16~vq any of the values then
19                {goto}a2~                press F9, the entire table
20                200~                     will be recalculated.
01-Jan-88   01:51 PM
```

Figure 16-10 (Continued)

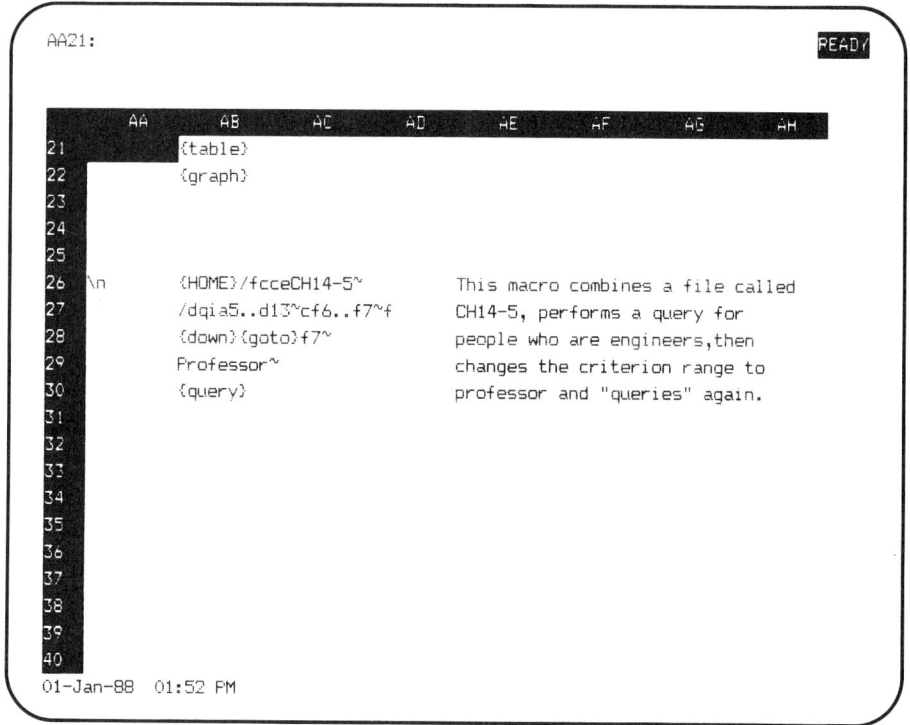

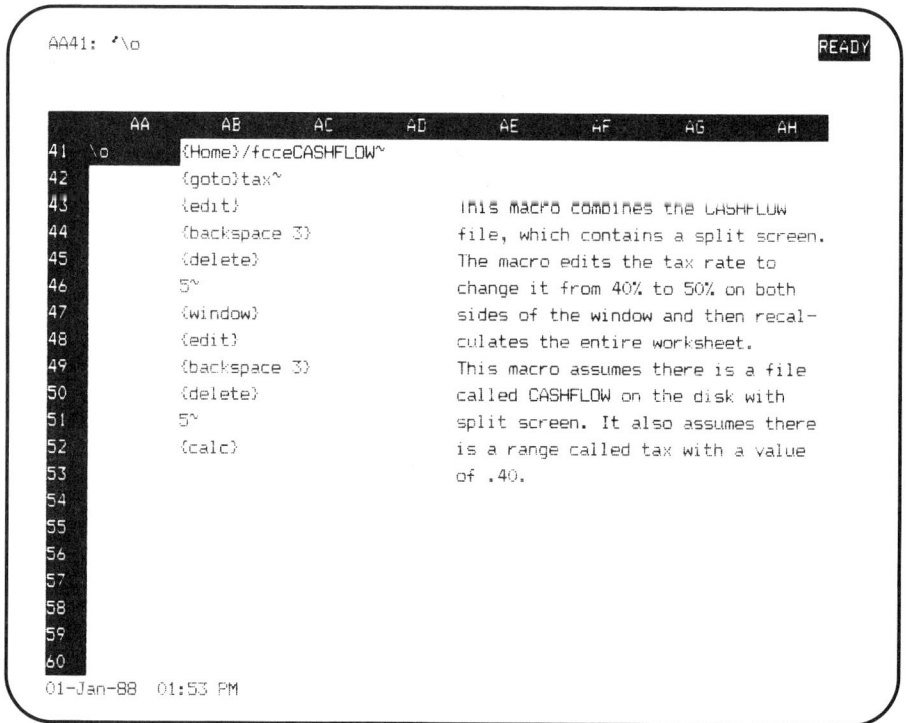

```
AA21:                                                                    READY

         AA        AB        AC        AD        AE        AF        AG        AH
21              {table}
22              {graph}
23
24
25
26    \n        {HOME}/fcceCH14-5~              This macro combines a file called
27              /dqia5..d13~cf6..f7~f          CH14-5, performs a query for
28              {down}{goto}f7~                people who are engineers,then
29              Professor~                     changes the criterion range to
30              {query}                        professor and "queries" again.
31
32
33
34
35
36
37
38
39
40
01-Jan-88  01:52 PM
```

Figure 16-10 (Continued)

```
AA41: '\o                                                               READY

         AA        AB        AC        AD        AE        AF        AG        AH
41    \o        {Home}/fcceCASHFLOW~
42              {goto}tax~
43              {edit}                         This macro combines the CASHFLOW
44              {backspace 3}                  file, which contains a split screen.
45              {delete}                       The macro edits the tax rate to
46              5~                             change it from 40% to 50% on both
47              {window}                       sides of the window and then recal-
48              {edit}                         culates the entire worksheet.
49              {backspace 3}                  This macro assumes there is a file
50              {delete}                       called CASHFLOW on the disk with
51              5~                             split screen. It also assumes there
52              {calc}                         is a range called tax with a value
53                                             of .40.
54
55
56
57
58
59
60
01-Jan-88  01:53 PM
```

Figure 16-10 (Continued)

```
AA61: '\p                                                              READY

         AA      AB      AC      AD      AE      AF      AG      AH
61  \p       {home}
62           This is home~
63           {WAIT @now+@time(0,0,3)}
64           {bigright}
65           You have just moved one screen to the right~
66           {WAIT @now+@time(0,0,3)}
67           {pgdn}
68           You have just moved one screen down~
69           {WAIT @now+@time(0,0,3)}
70           {bigleft}
71           You have just moved one screen to the left~
72           {WAIT @now+@time(0,0,3)}
73           {pgup}
74           You are back home!~
75
76
77           This macro guides the user around the worksheet
78           utilizing BIGLEFT, BIGRIGHT, PGDN, and PGUP.
79
80
01-Jan-88   01:54 PM
```

Figure 16-10 (Continued)

```
AA81:                                                                  READY

         AA      AB      AC      AD      AE      AF      AG      AH
81
82
83
84
85
86
87
88  \q       {HOME}/fcceSALES~          This macro combines a SALES file
89           {name}                     and creates a range named "totals"
90           {esc}                      and a range named "grandtot(als)."
91           {end}{down}                The cells in both ranges are made
92           /rnctotals~a20..h20~       absolute.
93           {abs}a20..h20~             This macro assumes there is a file
94           {end}{right}               called SALES on the disk.
95           /rncgrandtot~i11..i19~
96           {abs}i11..i19~
97
98
99
100
01-Jan-88   01:55 PM
```

Summary

This chapter has covered the principles of macro design and use, creation of a macro, documentation and invoking of a macro. We also discussed debugging a macro, the automatic macro and a self-booting worksheet, and presented a list of more than 50 commonly used macros. This should provide you with a good background for getting started with macros. In the next chapter we will discuss macro commands.

Review Questions

1. What is a macro?
2. What are some of the advantages of using a macro?
3. How do you name a macro?
4.* How do you invoke a macro?
5. How do you document a macro?
6.* What is the function of a \0 macro?
7. How many macros can you have in a worksheet?
8. What is a self-booting worksheet?
9.* What are some of the applications of a self-booting worksheet?
10. How do you debug a macro?
11. What is the STEP indicator?
12. What is the SST indicator?
13.* What is the CMD indicator?
14. How do you get out of STEP mode?
15.* How do you halt the execution of a macro?
16.* How many keystrokes can be included in a macro?
17. How is a macro executed?
18. Design a macro in order to generate a pie chart using the following data:

Sue	2,000
Sam	18,000
Sara	15,000

19. Design a macro to load a file from a disk to a worksheet, then erase the worksheet.
20. Design a macro to print the following message, then exit from the Lotus worksheet:

    IT WAS A PRODUCTIVE SESSION!

21. Design an interactive macro which accepts any three numbers, then calculates their average.
22. Design a macro that accepts any number up to eight digits, then format them using the comma option with three decimal places.
23. Design a macro that prints any portion of a worksheet using default settings.

Misconception and Solution

M - Lotus handles macros and functions differently. Lotus does not adjust cell addresses when you use /Move, /Copy, /Worksheet Delete, or /Worksheet Insert. When your macro is using cell addresses after rearranging, it may no longer work.

S - To avoid this, use range names to refer to cells.

Macros/Part Two: Advanced Commands

17-1 Introduction

As we discussed in the last chapter, macros are extremely handy for automating frequently used Lotus commands, such as repeatedly typing a label in a worksheet, or performing a long task requiring a series of keystrokes. In this chapter, we will teach you how to use advanced features of macro operation. We will explain the structure of an advanced macro command, then divide advanced macro commands into five groups. By using numerous examples we will highlight the real power of Lotus macros. In Chapter 18 we will demonstrate using Lotus macros as a high-level programming language.

17-2 The Structure of Advanced Macro Commands

All advanced macro commands follow a common structure:

{KEYWORD ARGUMENT1, ARGUMENT2, ...}

They must start with a left brace and end with a right brace. KEYWORD includes any valid Lotus advanced command, e.g., LET, BRANCH, INDICATE, and so on. ARGUMENT(S) are one or more of the following four groups:

1. *Address or location.* This includes the address of any of the cells within the entire worksheet. This can also include a range.

2. *Numeric value*. This includes any number, expression, or formula resulting in a specific value. The number can be in standard form (e.g., 5200) or in scientific notation (e.g., 2.002E+3).
3. *Condition*. Any valid logical operation can be used as an argument. The macro command will proceed based on the result of the logical operations.
4. *String*. Any sequence of characters up to 240 can be used as an argument for your advanced macro command.

Argument types can be either numeric or string. Some macro commands such as LET can hold either number or string. For example:

{LET R1, 2 + 3} or
{LET R1, 2 + 3: value} enters number 5 in cell R1
{LET R1, "2 + 3"} or
{LET F1, 2 + 3: String} enters string "2 + 3" in cell R1

Arguments must be separated by a comma (,) or a semicolon (;). There must be a blank space between the KEYWORD and the ARGUMENT. Arguments can be written in either uppercase or lowercase; it does not make a difference.

If you are using a label or a string and if your label contains one of the separators (, or ;), you must include the entire string within a double quotation:

{LET R28, "TYPE YOUR FIRST NAME; THEN YOUR LAST NAME"}

17-3 Valid and Invalid Macro Commands

If you do not follow the rules just mentioned, 1-2-3 will issue an error message. Following are some valid and invalid examples of LET as a macro command.

{LET Q1, 50}	Valid
{let Q2, 55}	Valid
{LET Q3, 2*G1+6*G9}	Valid
{LET Q4, 91	Invalid (second brace is missing)
{LETQ5,65}	Invalid (space is missing)
{LET Q697}	Invalid (separator is missing)
{Q7, 99}	Invalid (keyword is missing)

17-4 An Overview of Advanced Macro Commands

Macro commands have been divided into five groups based on the particular function performed by each group.

Group #1 - Data Manipulation Commands are used for changing the content and/or format of data in a particular location or locations of the worksheet.

Group #2 - Program Flow (branching and looping) Commands are used for controlling the flow of a macro, e.g., performing a loop (printing 200 checks), transferring the control (moving from one part of the macro to another part), and so on.

Group #3 - Testing Keyboard Operations Commands allow you to perform interactive programming with Lotus. For example, a macro pauses during execution, waiting for user input.

Group #4 - Screen Design and Control Commands will help you to change the appearance of the screen, both audibly and visually.

Group #5 - File Operations Commands will help you to perform file operations, such as data transfer between files, writing to a file, reading from a file, and so forth.

Table 17-1 illustrates the commands included in these five groups.

Table 17-1 Summary of Advanced Macro Commands

Command Name	Description
Group #1 - Data Manipulation	
{BLANK address}	Erases the content of a cell or cells
{CONTENTS target-location, source-location}	Places the content of one cell into another cell as label
{LET address, data}	Stores data in an address
{PUT address, column-number, row-number, number}	Stores a number in a specified address within a range
{RECALC address}	Recalculates a formula in a specified address, proceeding row by row
{RECALCCOL address}	Recalculates a formula in a specified address, proceeding column by column
Group #2 - Program Flow (branching and looping)	
{BRANCH address}	Continues macro execution at a specified address
{DEFINE address1: type1, address2: type2 ...}	Specifies address and defines data type
{DISPATCH address}	Branches to a target location which is specified in address
{FOR counter, start, stop, step, starting address}	Executes a macro for a specified number of times
{FORBREAK}	Cancels execution of a FOR loop
{IF condition}	Conditionally executes a macro
{ONERROR branch-address}	Branches to branch-address if an error occurs during macro execution
{QUIT}	Terminates macro execution
{RESTART}	Cancels a subroutine
{RETURN}	Returns from a macro subroutine
Group #3 - Testing Keyboard Operations	
{?}	Halts macro execution temporarily for user input
{BREAKOFF}	Disables the **Break** key during the macro execution
{BREAKON}	Restores the **Break** key
{GET address}	Pauses for the user to input a single character, then stores it in address
{GETLABEL prompt-string, address}	Pauses for the user to input a string, then stores it as a string in address
{GETNUMBER prompt-string, address}	Pauses for the user to input a number, then stores it as a number in address
{LOOK address}	Checks to see if the user has typed a character
{MENUBRANCH address}	Halts macro execution temporarily in order for the user to choose a menu item, then branches accordingly

Table 17-1 (Continued)

Command Name	Description
{MENUCALL address}	Halts the macro execution temporarily in order for the user to choose a menu item, then executes the corresponding macro as a subroutine
{WAIT time}	Waits for a specified amount of time
Group #4 - Screen Design and Control	
{BEEP number}	Causes computer's bell to sound
{INDICATE string}	Changes the mode indicator to string
{PANELOFF}	Suppresses display of the control panel during the execution of the macro
{PANELON}	Restores panel display
{WINDOWSOFF}	Freezes screen display
{WINDOWSON}	Restores normal screen display
Group #5 - File Operations	
{CLOSE}	Closes an open file (the file that was opened by {OPEN} command)
{FILESIZE address}	Determines the size of the file in bytes and puts it in address
{GETPOS address}	Determines correct position of file pointer and displays it in address
{OPEN filename, access-mode}	Opens a specific file for a specific access: reading, writing, or both
{READ bytecount, address}	Reads characters from a file into address
{READLN address}	Copies one line of data from an open file into address
{SETPOS file-position}	Sets a new position for file pointer (of an open file)
{WRITE string}	Copies string into an open file
{WRITELN string}	Copies a complete line into open file (this includes carriage-return, line-feed)

17-5 Data Manipulation Commands

These commands are used for changing the content and format of data in a worksheet. These commands include BLANK, CONTENTS, LET, PUT, RECALC, and RE-CALCCOL.

17-5-1 {BLANK address}

Erases the contents of a cell or cells in a worksheet. This command is equivalent to /Range Erase. For example, {BLANK G1..G5} will erase the contents of cells G1, G2, G3, G4 and G5.

17-5-2 {LET address, number, or string}

Stores a number or string in an address or location. {LET} can be used to generate a label or number entry. For example:

{LET R10, 2 + 3: value}   stores number 5
{LET R11, 2 + 3: string}   stores label 2 + 3

Figure 17-1 illustrates using the LET and BLANK commands.

17-5-3 {CONTENTS target-location, source-location}

This command is similar to LET. The only difference is that {LET} can store either a number or a string, but {CONTENTS} only stores LABEL data. A more elaborate format of this command is as follows:
{CONTENTS target-location, source-location, <width-number>, <format-number>}
The width-number and format-number are optional. If you specify format-number, you must also specify width-number. Table 17-2 contains a complete listing of the numeric format codes for the {CONTENTS} command.

One good use of this command is to use code 117 for text display of formulas for debugging. For example, if the content of H2 is 555.55, {CONTENTS H10,H2,17,36} places the 17-character label $555.550 (currency, three decimal places) in cell H10.

17-5-4 {PUT address, column-number, row-number, number or string}

Stores a number or a string in a specific location within a range. The difference between this command and the {LET} command is that {PUT} stores data in a particular column and row of a specified range. (Remember, column-number and row-number start from zero. {PUT A1..H20,0,5,BASIC} will put BASIC in A6 left-justified.) Figure 17-2 illustrates using the {PUT} and {CONTENTS} commands.

17-5-5 {RECALC address} and {RECALCCOL address}

RECALC recalculates a formula in a specified address, proceeding row by row. This macro command could also include condition and iteration-number as follows:
{RECALC address, <condition>, <iteration-number>}
For example, if your macro changes a value in cell C7 and you are interested in the value in cell B13, which depends on cell C7, macro {RECALC B13..C7} will do the job for you.

{RECALCCOL address, <condition>, <iteration-number>} will recalculate the formulas in a specified address, proceeding column by column. You should always remember to use {RECALC} for a formula that is located below and to the left of the cells that you are referring to. Use {RECALCCOL} if the formula is above and to the right of the cell which it refers. Use {CALC} if the formula is both above and to the left of cells whose values have changed.

If you use a condition and/or iteration number, the process of recalculation will stop regardless of which number is reached first. For example, the macro {RECALC NETPRESENT, (B5>5),12} will cause the NETPRESENT range to be calculated continuously until the value of cell B5 reaches 5 or the number of iterations equals 12. Figure 17-3 illustrates using RECALC and RECALCCOL.

Figure 17-1 Example of BLANK and LET Commands

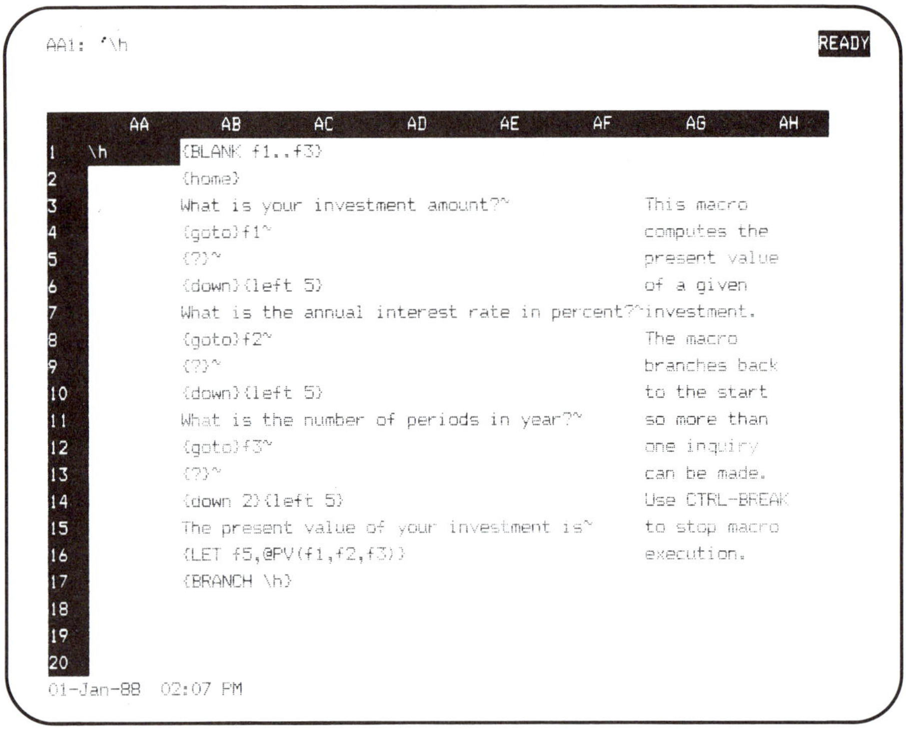

```
AA1: '\h                                                          READY

         AA      AB        AC        AD        AE       AF       AG        AH
1   \h       {BLANK f1..f3}
2            {home}
3            What is your investment amount?~                  This macro
4            {goto}f1~                                         computes the
5            {?}~                                              present value
6            {down}{left 5}                                    of a given
7            What is the annual interest rate in percent?~investment.
8            {goto}f2~                                         The macro
9            {?}~                                              branches back
10           {down}{left 5}                                    to the start
11           What is the number of periods in year?~          so more than
12           {goto}f3~                                         one inquiry
13           {?}~                                              can be made.
14           {down 2}{left 5}                                  Use CTRL-BREAK
15           The present value of your investment is~          to stop macro
16           {LET f5,@PV(f1,f2,f3)}                            execution.
17           {BRANCH \h}
18
19
20
  01-Jan-88   02:07 PM
```

Figure 17-2 Example of CONTENTS and PUT Commands

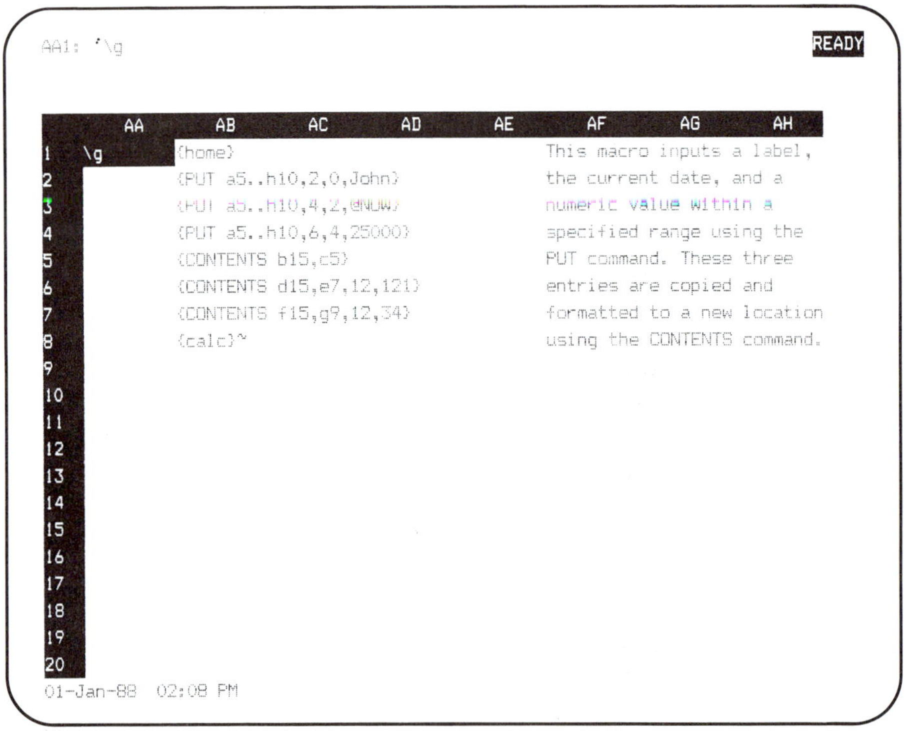

```
AA1: '\g                                                          READY

         AA      AB        AC        AD        AE       AF       AG        AH
1   \g       {home}                                       This macro inputs a label,
2            {PUT a5..h10,2,0,John}                        the current date, and a
3            {PUT a5..h10,4,2,@NOW}                        numeric value within a
4            {PUT a5..h10,6,4,25000}                       specified range using the
5            {CONTENTS b15,c5}                             PUT command. These three
6            {CONTENTS d15,e7,12,121}                      entries are copied and
7            {CONTENTS f15,g9,12,34}                       formatted to a new location
8            {calc}~                                       using the CONTENTS command.
9
10
11
12
13
14
15
16
17
18
19
20
  01-Jan-88   02:08 PM
```

Figure 17-3 Example of RECALC and RECALCCOL Commands

```
AA1: '\d                                                                    READY


        AA      AB       AC      AD      AE      AF      AG      AH
1   \d          /wgrm
2               {goto}b20~
3               Please enter a number in each cell (b4..d6) and press RETURN~
4               /rub4..d6~
5               /rib4..d6~
6               {goto}f4~
7               +b4+c4+d4~{down}
8               +b5+c5+d5~{down}
9               +b6+c6+d6~{down 2}{left 2}        This macro has the user
10              +d4+d5+d6~{left}                  create a matrix and the
11              +c4+c5+c6~{left}                  macro provides the formulas
12              +b4+b5+b6~{down 2}                 to sum the rows and
13              Enter a new number in {down}      columns. The user is then
14              cell b4, c5, and d6~              asked to change three
15              {goto}b4~                         entries, and the sums of
16              {?}~                              the rows and columns are
17              {goto}c5~                         recalculated using the
18              {?}~                              RECALC and RECALCCOL
19              {goto}d6~                         commands.
20              {?}~
01-Jan-88  02:09 PM                                      CALC
```

Figure 17-3 (Continued)

```
AA21:                                                                       READY


        AA      AB       AC      AD      AE      AF      AG      AH
21              {calc}
22              {RECALC b4..d6}
23              {RECALCCOL b4..d6}
24
25
26
27
28
29
30
31
32
33
34
35
36
37
38
39
40
01-Jan-88  02:10 PM                                      CALC
```

Table 17-2 Numeric Format Codes for the CONTENTS Command (the optional part)

CODE	FORMAT EQUIVALENT
0	Fixed, 0 decimal places
1-15	Fixed, 1 to 15 decimal places
16-32	Scientific, 0 to 15 decimal places
33-47	Currency, 0 to 15 decimal places
48-63	% (percent), 0 to 15 decimal places
64-79	, (comma), 0 to 15 decimal places
112	+/- (horizontal bar graph)
113	General
114	D1 (DD-MMM-YY)
115	D2 (DD-MMM)
116	D3 (MMM-YY)
121	D4 (Full international)
122	D5 (Partial international)
119	D6 (HH:MM:SS AM/PM)
123	D8 (Full international)
124	D9 (Partial international)
117	Text format
118	Hidden format
127	Default format display

17-6 Program Flow (Branching and Looping)

Program flow commands are used to perform loops and branches within a macro. They include BRANCH, DEFINE, DISPATCH, FOR, FORBREAK, IF, ONERROR, QUIT, RESTART and RETURN.

17-6-1 {BRANCH address}

Continues macro execution at a specified cell. The specified location or address can be either a single cell or a range. This command is the same as a GOTO command in BASIC. There is a difference between this command and the Lotus GOTO. The Lotus GOTO command moves the cell pointer. The command {BRANCH} transfers the control (or macro execution) to a specified location. Figure 17-4 illustrates an example of this command.

17-6-2 {DEFINE address1: type1, address2: type2, ...}

Specifies the location and arguments to be passed to a subroutine. This must be the first command in the subroutine. The default value for the argument is a string. There must be a match between the number of arguments in the subroutine and the DEFINE command. The following is one example of {DEFINE} and a subroutine:
SUB-GROSS-total H1, N1

DEFINE F1: value, N1: value
Figure 17-5 illustrates an example of this command.

17-6-3 {DISPATCH address}

Transfers macro execution to the location specified in the address. The difference between this command and {BRANCH} is that DISPATCH can execute instructions in several locations specified in the address. Figure 17-6 illustrates one example of this command.

17-6-4 {FOR} and {FORBREAK}

Executes a macro for a certain number of times. This is equivalent to the FOR-NEXT loop in BASIC or the DO loop in FORTRAN. Other programming languages have something similar to this command. The counter keeps track of the number of times the macro has been executed. Start is the starting value stored in the counter location. Stop marks the end of the loop. Step tells the counter how to increment the counter. The starting address is the cell address or range in which the macro starts the execution. Lotus always checks the condition of start, stop, and step before executing the macro. The FORBREAK command cancels the execution of a FOR loop. If the value of step is 0, an endless loop will be generated (a loop that never stops). If the start value exceeds the stop value, the macro will not be executed at all. Figure 17-7 is an example of the FOR command. Figure 17-8 illustrates an example of FOR and FORBREAK.

17-6-5 {IF} {QUIT}, and {ONERROR}

Executes a macro conditionally. This command is similar to the IF-THEN-ELSE command available in many programming languages. The instructions in the cell after the IF are the THEN part and those below the cell are the ELSE part. If the expression does not have a value of zero, 1-2-3 considers it true and the statement in the same cell (the cell that includes IF) will be executed, otherwise the statement in the cell below will be executed.

To protect the accurate execution of IF-THEN-ELSE clauses you may have to use {QUIT} and/or {ONERROR} commands. {ONERROR} branch-address branches to a specified address. You can also include a message in this command. {QUIT} terminates macro execution. Figure 17-9 illustrates the operation of these three commands.

17-6-6 {RESTART}

Cancels a subroutine (a series of instructions that perform a specific task) and clears the subroutine parameters. This is a useful command for canceling a series of commands if a particular condition does not exist. Figure 17-10 illustrates an application of this command.

17-6-7 {RETURN}

Returns control from a subroutine. This command is used either by a routine name or with a MENUCALL. {RETURN} instructs the macro to return to the command

17-4　An Example of the BRANCH Command

```
AA1: '\p                                                              READY

         AA       AB       AC       AD       AE       AF       AG       AH
1   \p         {home}
2              What is your sex? Choose (M)ale or (F)emale {right 6}~
3              {GET sex}
4              {IF sex="F"}{BRANCH no_go}
5              {IF sex="M"}{BRANCH age_rtn}
6
7   age_rtn    {down 2}{LEFT 6}
8              How old are you? {right 2}~
9              {?}~
10             {IF c3<18}{BRANCH no_go}
11             {IF c3>35}{BRANCH no_go}
12             {BRANCH status}
13
14  status     {down 2}{left 2}
15             What is your marital status? Choose (M)arried or (S)ingle {righ
16             {GET marital}
17             {IF marital="M"}{BRANCH no_go}
18             {IF marital="S"}{goto}a15~
19             You qualify for overseas employment. HaHa!~
20
01-Jan-88  02:10 PM
```

Figure 17-4　(Continued)

```
AA21: 'no_go                                                          READY

         AA       AB       AC       AD       AE       AF       AG       AH
21  no_go      {goto}a15~
22             Sorry, you do not qualify for overseas employment.~
23
24
25
26
27             This macro checks to see if an employee meets the
28             requirements for an overseas position by using the
29             BRANCH command to move to various subroutines.
30             The requirements for overseas employment are:
31                         1. male
32                         2. between 18 and 35 years of age
33                         3. single
34
35
36
37
38
39
40
01-Jan-88  02:11 PM
```

Figure 17-5 An Example of the DEFINE Command

```
AB5:  'The amount of your paycheck this week is~                          READY

          AA        AB        AC        AD        AE        AF        AG        AH
1    \o         {GETNUMBER "how many hours did you work this week?:",aa12}
2               {GETNUMBER "what is your hourly wage?:",aa13}
3               {PAYROLL aa12,aa13}
4               {goto}aa15~
5               The amount of your paycheck this week is~
6               {LET af15,ah13}
7               /rfc2~af15~
8
9    PAYROLL    {DEFINE ah11:value,ah12:value}
10              {LET ah13,ah11*ah12}
11
12
13
14
15
16
17              This macro determines the amount of an employee's weekly
18              paycheck utilizing the DEFINE command and a PAYROLL
19              routine-name command.
20
01-Jan-88   02:13 PM
```

Figure 17-6 An Example of the DISPATCH Command

```
AA1:  [W10]  '\n                                                          READY

          AA        AB        AC        AD        AE        AF        AG
1    \n         {GETLABEL "Enter undergraduate or graduate (U or G):",code}
2               {IF code="U"}{LET choice,"undergrad"}
3               {IF code="G"}{LET choice,"grad"}
4               {DISPATCH choice}
5
6    code       g
7
8    choice     grad
9
10   undergrad  {goto}a10~
11              You will need 120 units to graduate with a bachelor's degree~
12
13   grad       {goto}a10~
14              You will need 45 graduate units to obtain your master,s degree
15
16
17              This macro uses the DISPATCH command to branch indirectly
18              to a message based on the user's choice of a code.
19
20
01-Jan-88   10:02 AM
```

Figure 17-7 An Example of the FOR Command

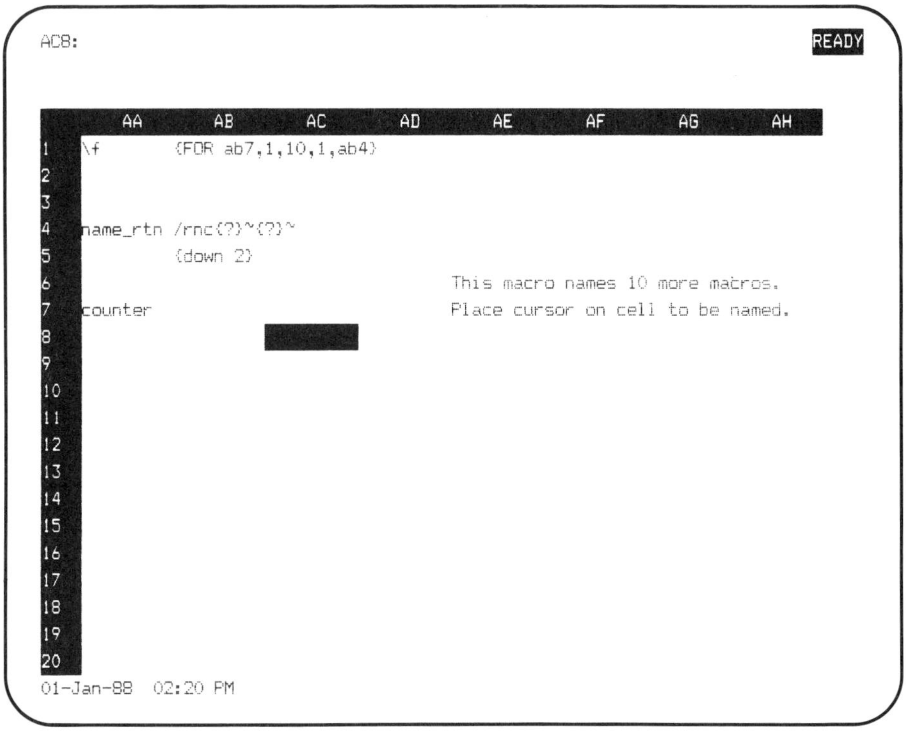

```
AC8:                                                                    READY

            AA        AB        AC        AD        AE        AF        AG        AH
1   \f        {FOR ab7,1,10,1,ab4}
2
3
4   name_rtn /rnc{?}~{?}~
5             {down 2}
6                                                 This macro names 10 more macros.
7   counter                                       Place cursor on cell to be named.
8
9
10
11
12
13
14
15
16
17
18
19
20
    01-Jan-88   02:20 PM
```

Figure 17-8 An Example of the FOR and FORBREAK Commands

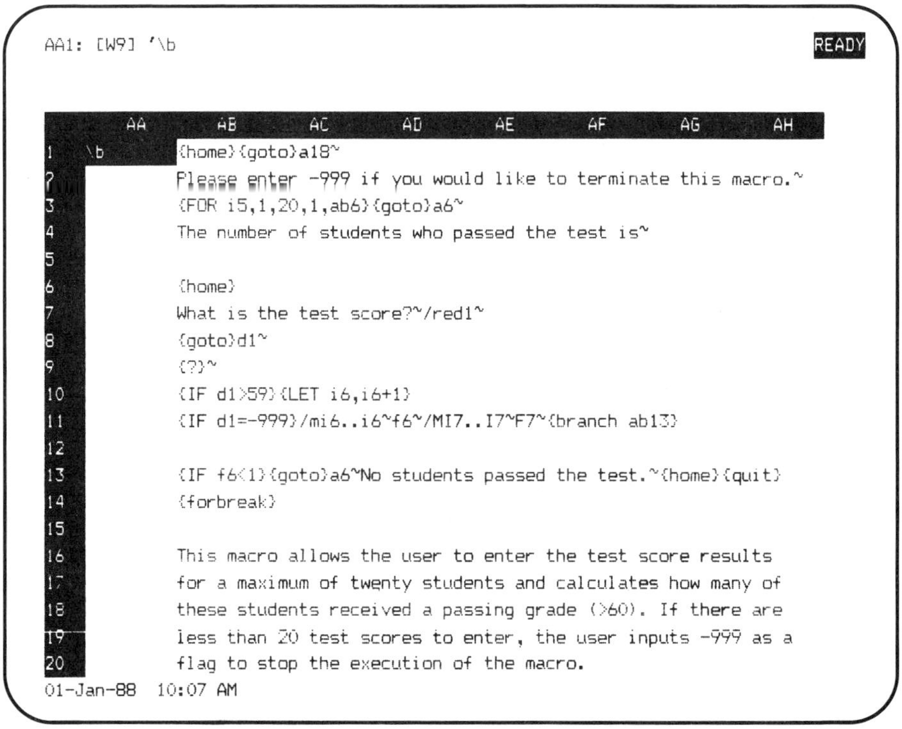

```
AA1: [W9] '\b                                                           READY

            AA        AB        AC        AD        AE        AF        AG        AH
1   \b        {home}{goto}a18~
2             Please enter -999 if you would like to terminate this macro.~
3             {FOR i5,1,20,1,ab6}{goto}a6~
4             The number of students who passed the test is~
5
6             {home}
7             What is the test score?~/red1~
8             {goto}d1~
9             {?}~
10            {IF d1>59}{LET i6,i6+1}
11            {IF d1=-999}/mi6..i6~f6~/MI7..I7~F7~{branch ab13}
12
13            {IF f6<1}{goto}a6~No students passed the test.~{home}{quit}
14            {forbreak}
15
16            This macro allows the user to enter the test score results
17            for a maximum of twenty students and calculates how many of
18            these students received a passing grade (>60). If there are
19            less than 20 test scores to enter, the user inputs -999 as a
20            flag to stop the execution of the macro.
    01-Jan-88   10:07 AM
```

Figure 17-9 An Example of the IF, ONERROR and QUIT Commands

```
AA1: '\a                                                          READY


        AA        AB        AC        AD        AE        AF        AG        AH
1    \a         {home}
2              John{down}
3              Mary{down}
4              Jack{down}
5              Sue{down}~
6              Do you want to save this file? Choose (Y)es or (N)o~
7              {GET answer}
8              {IF answer="N"}{QUIT}
9              {IF answer="Y"}{BRANCH subr_save}
10                                               This macro enters a name
11   answer    y                                 file and then asks the
12                                               user if the file is to be
13   subr_save{ONERROR full_msg}                 saved. If "no" the macro
14             /fsNAMES~                          quits. If "yes" the macro
15                                               goes to the save subroutine
16   full_msg  {goto}a15~                        and tries to save the file.
17             Disk is full~{down}               If the disk is full, or not
18             Replace data disk~{down}          ready  an error message is
19             Press RETURN to continue~{?}~     displayed and the user must
20             {BRANCH subr_save}                replace the data disk
01-Jan-88  10:08 AM
```

Figure 17-10 An Example of the RESTART Command

```
AA1: '\t                                                          READY


        AA        AB        AC        AD        AE        AF        AG        AH
1    \t         {goto}ae2~
2              {SUBR_1}
3              {goto}ae3~
4              {SUBR_1}
5              {goto}ae4~
6              {SUBR_1}
7              {SUBR_2}
8              {goto}ae15~
9              If your macro works,
10             {down}
11             it should never print this line!~
12
13   SUBR_1    1000+ah1~
14             {LET ah1,1000+ah1}                This macro uses the RESTART
15             /rv~~                             command to prevent the
16             {RETURN}                          macro from returning by the
17                                               path it came. In this case,
18   SUBR_2    {goto}ae6~                        when ae6>=10000, the macro
19             +ae2+ae3+ae4~                     stops execution in SUBR_2
20             {IF ae6<10000}{BRANCH \t}         and the RETURN is ignored.
01-Jan-88  02:23 PM
```

```
AA21:                                                          READY

        AA      AB      AC      AD      AE      AF      AG      AH
21              {IF ae6>=10000}{RESTART}
22              {down 2}
23              You are finished!~
24              /reah1~
25              {RETURN}
26
27
28
29
30
31
32
33
34
35
36
37
38
39
40
01-Jan-88  02:24 PM
```

Figure 17-10 (Continued)

cell immediately after the call location. By using several routines you will be able to break down a large problem into several smaller units or modules (see Figure 17-11).

Macro subroutines must be started with SUBR-. The routine name is a range. The routine name cannot be one of the Lotus reserved words such as NAME (see Table 16-1 in Chapter 16 for the listing of reserved words). If duplication occurs Lotus performs the subroutine, not the keystroke (or reserved word).

17-7 Testing Keyboard Operations

These commands are used for interactive programming. During the execution of these commands, 1-2-3 will pause and ask for user input. Commands include ?, BREAKOFF, BREAKON, GET, GETLABEL, GETNUMBER, LOOK, MENUBRANCH, MENUCALL, and WAIT.

17-7-1 {?}

Halts the execution of the macro temporarily and waits for user input. The {?} command is an alternative to GET, GETLABEL, GETNUMBER, LOOK, MENUBRANCH, and MENUCALL.

Figure 17-11 An Example of the RETURN Command

```
AA1:  '\u                                                            READY

          AA       AB       AC       AD       AE       AF       AG       AH
1    \u       {home}
2             What is the retail price?~
3             {goto}f1~
4             {?}~
5             /rfc2~~
6             {LET f12,f1}
7             {down 2}{left 5}
8             Is the item on sale? Choose (Y)es or (N)o~
9             {GET answer}
10            {IF answer="Y"}{subr_sale}
11            {goto}a12~
12            The final purchase price is~
13            {LET f12,f12+(f12*.06)}~
14            /rfc2~f12~
15
16   subr_sale{goto}a5~
17            Sale items are 20 percent off~
18            {LET f12,f1-(f1*.20)}
19            {down 2}
20            Does the price tag have a red star? Choose (Y)es or (N)o~
01-Jan-88  02:25 PM
```

Figure 17-11 (Continued)

```
AA21:                                                                READY

          AA       AB       AC       AD       AE       AF       AG       AH
21            {GET response}
22            {IF response="Y"}{subr_star}
23            {LET f12,f12-g9}
24            {RETURN}
25
26   subr_star{goto}a9~
27            Red star tags get an additional 10 percent off~
28            {LET g9,f1*.10}~
29            {RETURN}
30
31   answer
32
33   response
34
35
36
37            This macro is an example of a nested loop which determines
38            the final purchase price of a retail item that may have
39            one, two or no discounts and has a 6% sales tax.
40
01-Jan-88  02:26 PM
```

17-7-2 {BREAKOFF}

Disables the BREAK key during macro execution. {BREAKON} restores the BREAK key. You must always remember that if your macro enters an endless loop and {BREAKOFF} is active you cannot stop the endless loop. The only solution is to stop the computer. The combination of these two commands is used for applications in which you want to show the execution of the entire macro without user interruption.

17-7-3 {WAIT time-serial-number}

Waits until the time-serial-number is up. You can halt a {WAIT} command by pressing the **Break** key, unless you have executed a {BREAKOFF} command. Figure 17-12 illustrates an application of BREAKOFF, BREAKON and WAIT.

17-7-4 {GET address}

Pauses for the user to input a single character, then stores it in an address. The single character can be either a standard typewriter key or a Lotus standard key (TABLE, QUERY, etc.). Figure 17-13 illustrates an example of this command.

17-7-5 {GETLABEL prompt, address} and {GETNUMBER}

Pauses for the user to type a character string, then stores it as a label in the address. {GETNUMBER} does the same thing, but stores the data as a number. Your prompt (your message or statement) must be short enough to fit into the control panel. Also, if your prompt includes separators (commas or semicolons), you must enclose the prompt in quotation marks. Figure 17-14 illustrates an application of these two commands.

17-7-6 {LOOK address}

Checks to see if the user has typed a character. LOOK is similar to GET except that LOOK does not halt the macro execution. LOOK leaves the character in the type-ahead buffer for future use by GET, GETLABEL or GETNUMBER. Figure 17-15 illustrates an example of this command.

17-7-7 {MENUBRANCH address} and {MENUCALL}

Suspends the execution of the macro temporarily in order to allow the user to choose from a menu and then continues to the macro branch. The MENUCALL address does the same thing, but it executes the corresponding macro as a subroutine. Using MENUCALL you can design your own menu consisting of any of several commands. To establish a menu, remember the following:

1. You can have up to eight commands in your menu.
2. There are three lines available to you. Line one is the name of the command (menu item). Line two is a brief description of the menu item. Line three is the command summary (macro instruction), e.g., /WIC (/Worksheet Insert Column).
3. In your menu the starting character of each menu item must be unique,

Figure 17-12 An Example of BREAKOFF, BREAKON, and WAIT

```
AB19: 'halting macro execution during the eight-second pause.          READY


        AA        AB        AC        AD        AE        AF        AG
1  \c            {goto}instructions~
2               {BREAKOFF}
3               {WAIT @now+@time(0,0,8)}
4               {BREAKON}
5               {goto}aa15~
6               {?}~
7               {right 2}
8               thank you!~
9
10 instructions  Please enter your Social Security number in the
11               following format - XXXXXXXXX
12
13
14
15
16               This macro gives the user eight seconds to read a set
17               of instructions that requests a social security number be
18               entered.  The BREAKOFF/ON commands prevent the user from
19               halting macro execution during the eight-second pause.
20
01-Jan-88  02:27 PM
```

Figure 17-13 An Example of the GET Command

```
AA1: '\i                                                             READY


        AA        AB        AC        AD        AE        AF        AG        AH
1  \i            {home}~
2               /ree1..e3~
3               Please enter the catalogue number~
4               {goto}e1~
5               {?}~                                    This macro simulates
6               {down}{left 4}                          a catalogue order
7               Quantity?~                              process that has the
8               {goto}e2~                               user inputting infor-
9               {?}~                                    mation about that
10              {down}{left 4}                          order, and then asks
11              Item price?~                            if additional orders
12              {goto}e3~                               are to be placed.
13              {?}~
14              /rfc2~{down}~
15              {down}{left 4}
16              Total Price~{goto}e4~
17              (e3*e2)~
18              {down 3}{left 4}
19              Do you have another order? Choose (Y)es or (N)o~
20              {GET answer}
01-Jan-88  10:12 AM
```

Figure 17-13 (Continued)

```
AA21:                                                                    READY

          AA        AB        AC        AD        AE        AF        AG        AH
21            {IF answer="Y"}{BRANCH \i}
22            {IF answer="N"}{down 2}'Thank you for your order!~
23
24
25  answer    y
26
27
28
29
30
31
32
33
34
35  '
36
37
38
39
40
01-Jan-88   10:13 AM
```

Figure 17-14 An Example of GETLABEL and GETNUMBER

```
AA1:  '\k                                                                READY

          AA        AB        AC        AD        AE        AF        AG        AH
1   \k        {goto}a1~
2             {GETLABEL "What is the employee's name?:",a3}~
3             {GETNUMBER "How many hours did employee work?:",d3}'
4             {IF d3<=40}{BRANCH Regular}
5             {IF d3>40}{BRANCH Overtime}
6                                              This macro asks for the
7   Regular   {IF d3<=0}{BRANCH Error}         employee's name and the
8             {LET c5,+d3*10}~                 number of hours worked and,
9             {goto}a5~                        calculates that employee's
10            Your pay is~                     pay based on Regular or
11            /rfc2~c5~                        Overtime hours.  Regular
12                                             pay is $10 per hour and
13  Overtime  {LET c5,40*10+(d3-40)*15}~       Overtime is $15 per hour.
14            {goto}a5~                        If the employee inputs
15            Your pay is~                     zero or negative hours, an
16            /rfc2~c5~                        error message is displayed.
17
18  Error     {goto}a15~
19            Your entry will not compute, please try again!~
20            {BRANCH \k}
01-Jan-88   02:31 PM
```

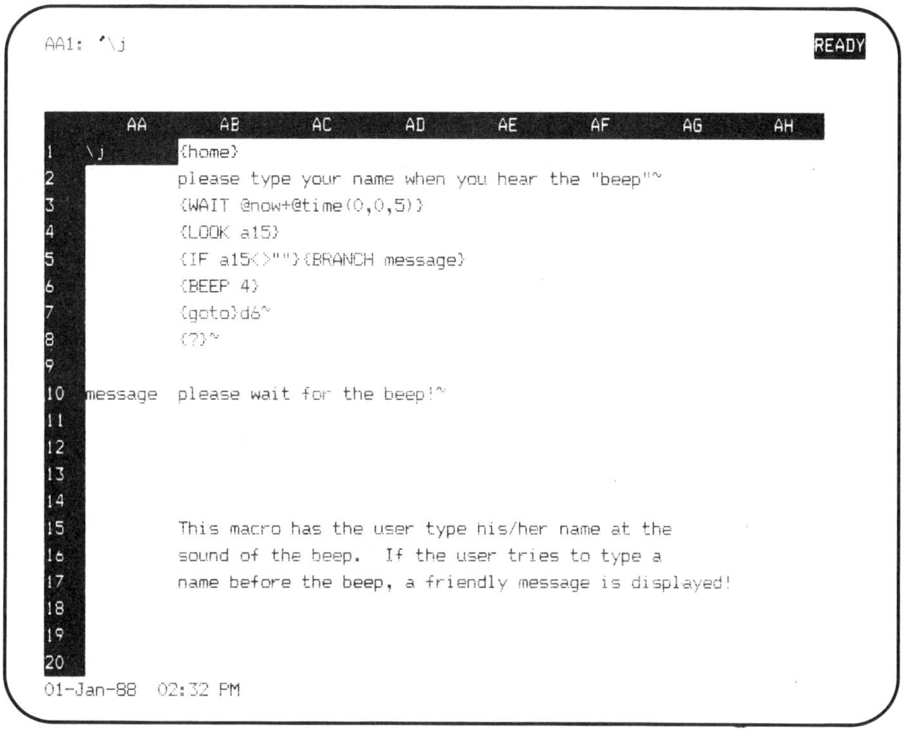

```
AA1: '\j                                                                  READY

            AA        AB        AC        AD        AE        AF        AG        AH
 1   \j        {home}
 2             please type your name when you hear the "beep"~
 3             {WAIT @now+@time(0,0,5)}
 4             {LOOK a15}
 5             {IF a15<>""}{BRANCH message}
 6             {BEEP 4}
 7             {goto}d6~
 8             {?}~
 9
10   message   please wait for the beep!~
11
12
13
14
15             This macro has the user type his/her name at the
16             sound of the beep.  If the user tries to type a
17             name before the beep, a friendly message is displayed!
18
19
20
01-Jan-88  02:32 PM
```

Figure 17-15 An Example of the LOOK Command

otherwise 1-2-3 always chooses the first one. For example, do not use worksheet and window in the same menu.

4. You can extend the column width to any number between 1 and 240, inclusive.
5. Blank cells are not allowed between menu items.
6. The cell to the right of the final menu item must be empty.
7. Uppercase and lowercase are the same.
8. A menu item can be chosen by moving the cursor and pressing the **Return** key, or typing the first character of each command.
9. Pressing the **Escape** key will cancel a menu item.

Figure 17-16 illustrates an example of MENUCALL. Figure 17-17 illustrates an example of MENUBRANCH.

17-8 Screen Design and Control

These commands help you to design the look of the screen and the sound. They include BEEP, INDICATE, PANELOFF, PANELON, WINDOWSOFF, and WINDOWSON.

17-8-1 {BEEP <number>}

Activates the computer bell. The number argument is optional. This command is used to convey a signal to the user. The number can be either 1, 2, 3, or 4, to choose

Figure 17-16 An Example of MENUCALL

```
AA1: '\h                                                              READY

        AA      AB      AC      AD      AE      AF      AG      AH
1    \h       {MENUCALL edit}
2             {BRANCH MENU}
3
4    edit     WIDTH    LABEL    ERASE    FILE     GRAPH    FORMAT
5             reset a ccenters terases thsaves a fsets up aformat a range wit
6             /wgc{?}~ /rlc~    /re~     /fs{?}~  /gtb{?}~v/rfc2~
7
8
9
10
11
12
13            This macro menu contains six different macros that can be
14            used for editing an income statement or balance sheet.
15            The menu is invoked using the MENUCALL command.
16
17
18
19
20
01-Jan-88  10:14 AM
```

Figure 17-17 An Example of MENUBRANCH

```
AA1: [W10] '\q                                                        READY

        AA      AB      AC      AD      AE      AF      AG
1    \q       /rij1..k6~
2             {MENUBRANCH edit_menu}
3
4
5    edit_menu Change   Move     Erase    Quit
6             Make chanMove new Erase newReturn to Ready
7             {BRANCH c{BRANCH m{BRANCH e{home}{quit}
8
9    change   {BRANCH \q}
10
11                                            This macro inputs a set
12   move     {home}/rtk1..k6~                of data (records) to a
13            {home}                          database. Using the
14            {end}{down}                     MENUBRANCH command, the
15            {down}~                         macro allows the user to
16            /rek1..k6~                      edit the entry using the
17            {MENUBRANCH edit_menu}          change, move or erase
18                                            menu choices.
19   erase    /rek1..k6~
20            {BRANCH \q}
01-Jan-88  10:16 AM
```

four different tones. The default value is one. Figure 17-18 illustrates an application of this command.

17-8-2 {INDICATE <string>}

Changes the mode indicator in the upper right corner of the screen. When INDI-CATE is activated the only way to deactivate it is to use another INDICATE command. The default value of string is the READY mode. To remove the mode indicator from the control panel you can use {INDICATE " "}. Figure 17-19 illustrates an example of this command.

17-8-3 {PANELOFF} and {PANELON}

Suppresses redrawing (display) of the control panel during the execution of the macro. {PANELON} restores the setting. {PANELOFF} is very useful when the macro is executing Lotus menu commands. Figure 17-20 illustrates an example of these commands.

17-8-4 {WINDOWSOFF} and {WINDOWSON}

Freezes the screen display (except for the control panel). {WINDOWSON} restores the normal setting. Using WINDOWSOFF will speed up the execution time of a macro since it does not do any redrawing; this is especially useful for long macros. These two commands are similar to PANELOFF and PANELON. Figure 17-21 illustrates an example of these two commands.

17-9 File Operations

The commands in this group enable you to perform file operations. These commands include CLOSE, FILESIZE, GETPOS, OPEN, READ, READLN, SETPOS, WRITE and WRITELN. These are designed only for ASCII files. (For more information on ASCII files, see Appendix D.)

17-9-1 {CLOSE}

Closes a file that was opened with the {OPEN} command.

17-9-2 {FILESIZE address}

Counts the number of bytes (characters) in an open file and then stores the result in address. The address is a cell or a range name.

17-9-3 {GETPOS address}

Determines the present position of the file pointer and displays the result in the address. Naturally the file must be opened first. Remember, the first position in a file is 0 (zero), not 1 (one).

Figure 17-18 An Example of the BEEP Command

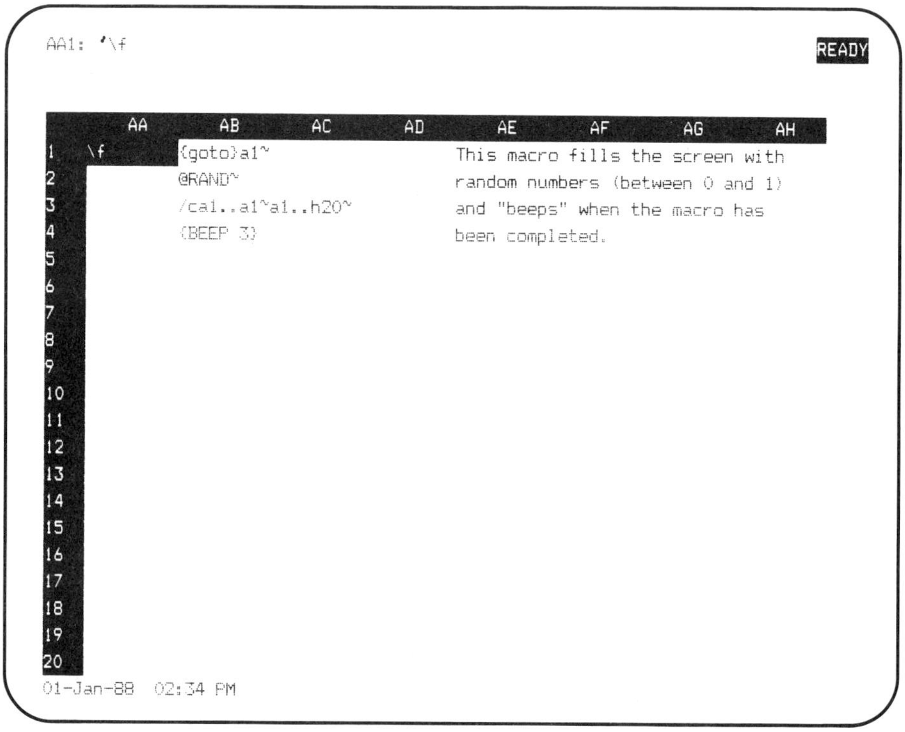

```
AA1: '\f                                                              READY

        AA      AB        AC        AD        AE        AF        AG        AH
1   \f      {goto}a1~                            This macro fills the screen with
2           @RAND~                               random numbers (between 0 and 1)
3           /cal..a1~a1..h20~                    and "beeps" when the macro has
4           {BEEP 3}                             been completed.
5
6
7
8
9
10
11
12
13
14
15
16
17
18
19
20
01-Jan-88  02:34 PM
```

Figure 17-19 An Example of the INDICATE Command

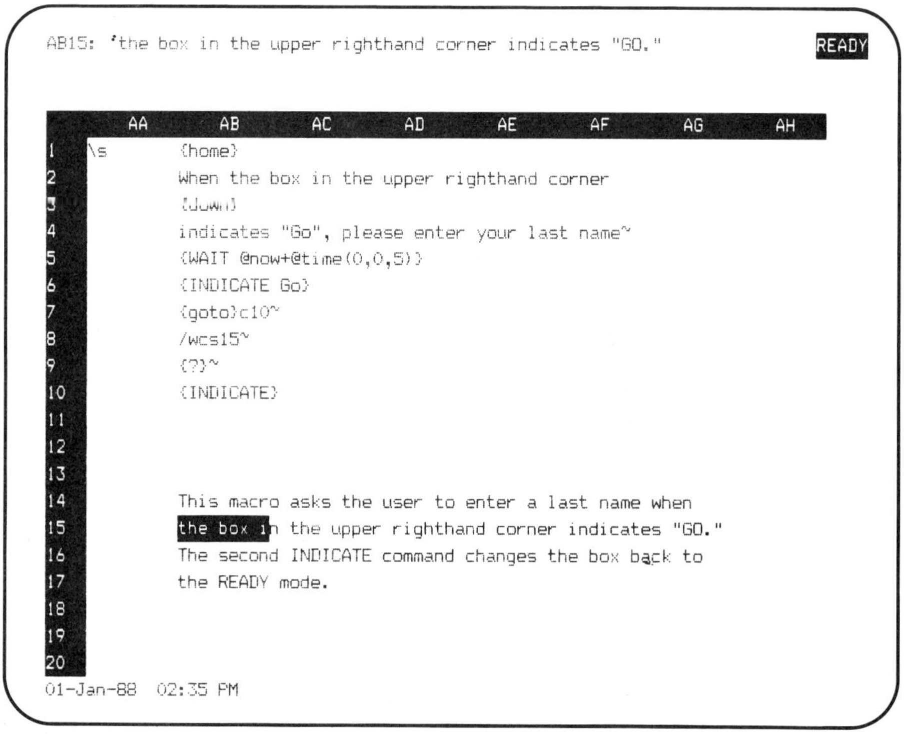

```
AB15: 'the box in the upper righthand corner indicates "GO."              READY

        AA      AB        AC        AD        AE        AF        AG        AH
1   \s      {home}
2           When the box in the upper righthand corner
3           {down}
4           indicates "Go", please enter your last name~
5           {WAIT @now+@time(0,0,5)}
6           {INDICATE Go}
7           {goto}c10~
8           /wcs15~
9           {?}~
10          {INDICATE}
11
12
13
14          This macro asks the user to enter a last name when
15          the box in the upper righthand corner indicates "GO."
16          The second INDICATE command changes the box back to
17          the READY mode.
18
19
20
01-Jan-88  02:35 PM
```

Figure 17-20 An Example of PANELOFF and PANELON

```
AA1: '\e                                                                      READY


           AA             AB              AC            AD          AE         AF
1    \e             /wgc12~
2                   {home}
3                   Enter 5000 in cell a5~
4                   {goto}a5~
5                   {?}~
6                   {PANELOFF}
7                   /ca5~b5..f5~
8                   /rfc2~a5..f5~
9                   {PANELON}
10
11
12                  This macro sets the width of all columns to 12
13                  and prompts the user to input 5000 in cell a5.
14                  The redrawing of the control panel is then frozen
15                  by the PANELOFF command while the macro copies
16                  the contents of cell a5 to cells b5, c5, d5, e5 and
17                  f5 and formats all six cells with the currency format
18                  option to two decimal places.
19
20
01-Jan-88   10:19 AM
```

Figure 17-21 An Example of WINDOWSOFF and WINDOWSON

```
AA1: '\r                                                                      READY


           AA             AB             AC          AD         AE         AF          AG
1    \r             {WINDOWSOFF}
2                   {PANELOFF}
3                   /wgc10~
4                   {goto}d1~                              This macro sets up
5                   January{right}                        a   portion  of  an
6                   June{right}                           income   statement
7                   September{right}                      for four quarters.
8                   December~                             While the commands
9                   /rlcd1..i1~                           are being executed,
10                  {goto}a5~                             the  WINDOWSOFF and
11                  Sales{down}                           PANELOFF command
12                  Cost of Goods Sold{down}              freezes the lower
13                  Gross Profit{down}                    part of the screen.
14                  Expenses{down}NetIncome~
15                  /rfc2~d5..i9~
16                  {home}
17                  {WINDOWSON}
18                  {PANELON}
19
20
01-Jan-88   10:22 AM
```

17-9-4 {OPEN filename, access-mode}

Opens a selected file for reading, writing, or both. The file must be in the current directory. The file name should specify a drive location and subdirectory path if needed. There are three types of access modes:

1. R (Read) allows only the read option for READ and READLN commands.
2. W (Write) allows WRITE and WRITELN commands. This option also allows READ and READLN commands. This access is for a new file.
3. M (Modify) allows READ, READLN, WRITE, and WRITELN commands. This access is for an existing file.

17-9-5 {READ bytecount, address}

Reads characters from an open file into an address. If the bytecount is larger than the number of characters left in the file, Lotus reads the remaining characters. The bytecount must be between 0 and 240. A negative bytecount is equivalent to the maximum positive bytecount of 240.

17-9-6 {READLN address}

Copies an entire line of characters from an open file into an address. This command starts reading from the present position of the file pointer and ends with a carriage return, line feed.

17-9-7 {SETPOS file-position}

Sets a new position for the file pointer in a specified open file. File-position is a number. The first character in the file is always at position 0, the second character at position 1, and so forth. If you specify a large number, you may pass the end of the filo.

17-9-8 {WRITE string}

Copies a series of characters into an open file. This macro command copies from the worksheet to the current position of the file pointer in a file that has been opened with either Write or Modify.

17-9-9 {WRITELN}

This command does the same thing as WRITE, except that it adds a carriage-return line feed to the end of the string in the file.

Figures 17-22 through 17-25 show some simple macros to illustrate file operations.

Figure 17-22 Example of OPEN, WRITELN, WRITE, and CLOSE

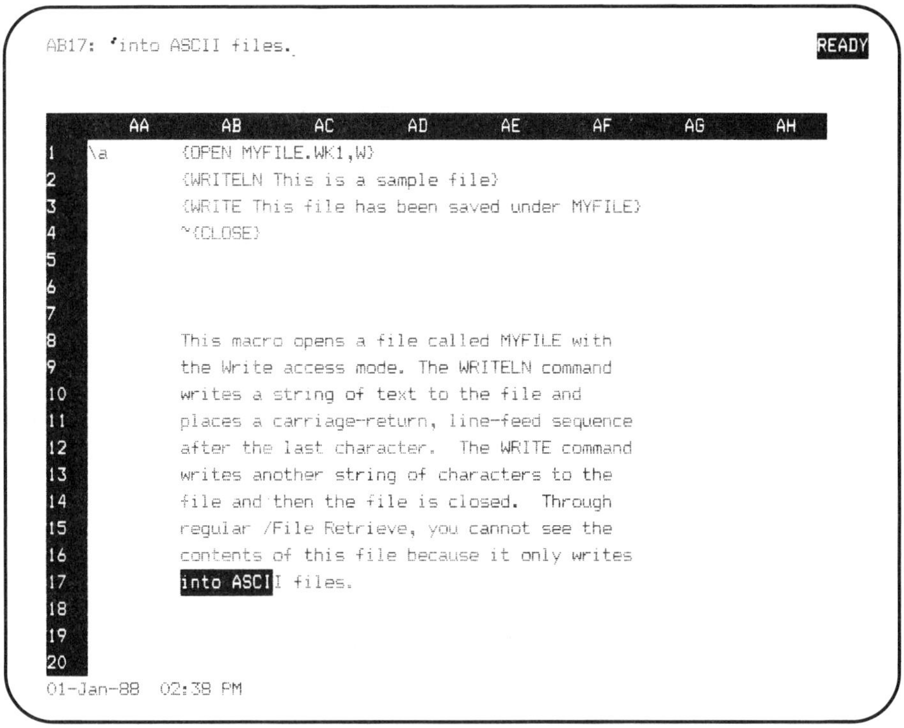

```
AB17:  'into ASCII files.                                                    READY

            AA        AB        AC        AD        AE        AF        AG        AH
1    \a          {OPEN MYFILE.WK1,W}
2                {WRITELN This is a sample file}
3                {WRITE This file has been saved under MYFILE}
4                ~{CLOSE}
5
6
7
8                This macro opens a file called MYFILE with
9                the Write access mode. The WRITELN command
10               writes a string of text to the file and
11               places a carriage-return, line-feed sequence
12               after the last character.  The WRITE command
13               writes another string of characters to the
14               file and then the file is closed.  Through
15               regular /File Retrieve, you cannot see the
16               contents of this file because it only writes
17               into ASCII files.
18
19
20
01-Jan-88   02:38 PM
```

Figure 17-23 Example of FILESIZE

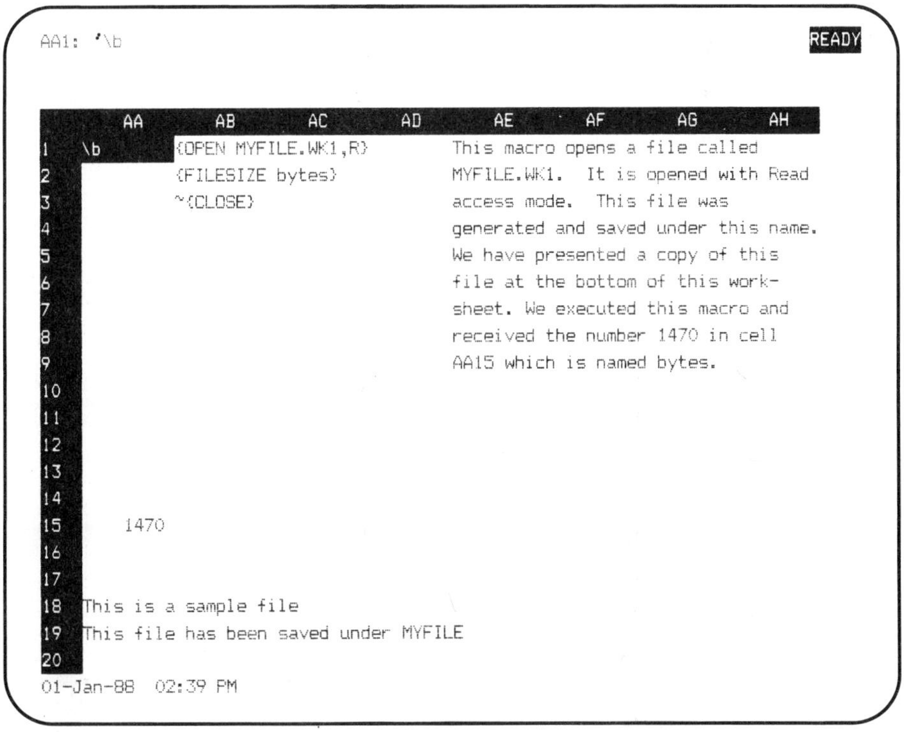

```
AA1:  '\b                                                                    READY

            AA        AB        AC        AD        AE        AF        AG        AH
1    \b          {OPEN MYFILE.WK1,R}         This macro opens a file called
2                {FILESIZE bytes}            MYFILE.WK1.  It is opened with Read
3                ~{CLOSE}                    access mode.  This file was
4                                            generated and saved under this name.
5                                            We have presented a copy of this
6                                            file at the bottom of this work-
7                                            sheet. We executed this macro and
8                                            received the number 1470 in cell
9                                            AA15 which is named bytes.
10
11
12
13
14
15       1470
16
17
18   This is a sample file
19   This file has been saved under MYFILE
20
01-Jan-88   02:39 PM
```

Figure 17-24 Example of READ and SETPOS

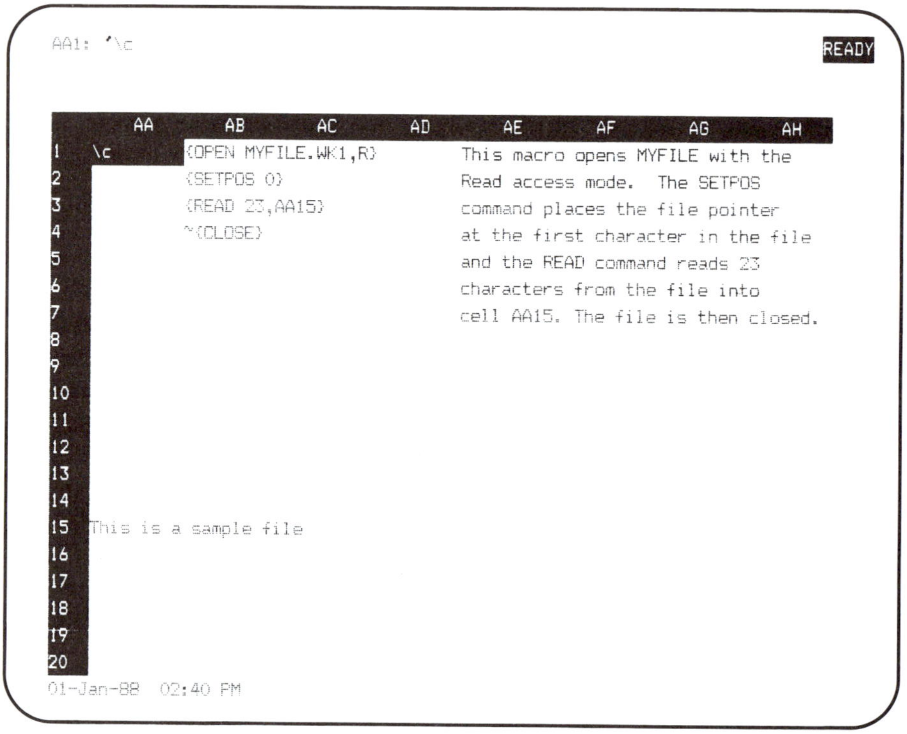

```
AA1: '\c                                                          READY

         AA        AB       AC       AD      AE      AF      AG      AH
1    \c          {OPEN MYFILE.WK1,R}           This macro opens MYFILE with the
2                {SETPOS 0}                    Read access mode.  The SETPOS
3                {READ 23,AA15}                command places the file pointer
4                ~{CLOSE}                       at the first character in the file
5                                              and the READ command reads 23
6                                              characters from the file into
7                                              cell AA15. The file is then closed.
8
9
10
11
12
13
14
15   This is a sample file
16
17
18
19
20
01-Jan-88  02:40 PM
```

Figure 17-25 Example of GETPOS and READLN

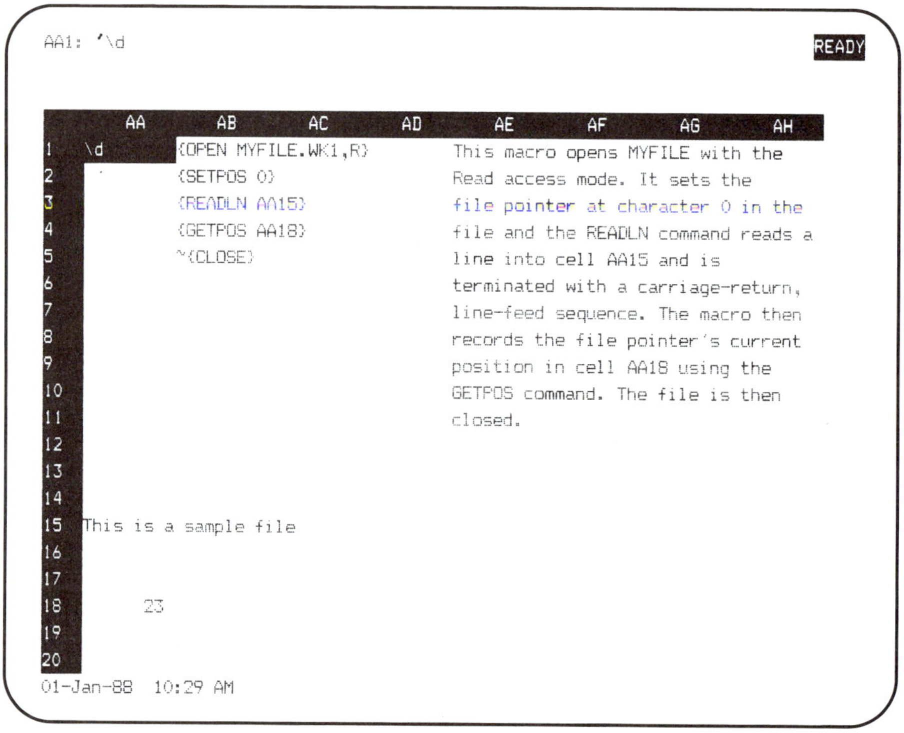

```
AA1: '\d                                                          READY

         AA        AB       AC       AD      AE      AF      AG      AH
1    \d          {OPEN MYFILE.WK1,R}           This macro opens MYFILE with the
2                {SETPOS 0}                    Read access mode. It sets the
3                {READLN AA15}                 file pointer at character 0 in the
4                {GETPOS AA18}                 file and the READLN command reads a
5                ~{CLOSE}                       line into cell AA15 and is
6                                              terminated with a carriage-return,
7                                              line-feed sequence. The macro then
8                                              records the file pointer's current
9                                              position in cell AA18 using the
10                                             GETPOS command. The file is then
11                                             closed.
12
13
14
15   This is a sample file
16
17
18        23
19
20
01-Jan-88  10:29 AM
```

Summary

The Lotus advanced macro commands have been divided into five groups. Each group has been designed to perform a unique task: data manipulation, program flow, testing keyboard operations, screen design and control, and file operations. Lotus advanced commands also serve as a high-level programming language, closely paralleling other high-level programming languages. In Chapter 18 we will utilize these advanced commands in some simple programming assignments.

Review Questions

1. What is a Lotus advanced command?
2. What is the structure of an advanced command?
3.* Is an argument needed for all the advanced commands?
4.* How many different types of arguments do we have in an advanced command?
5. How many different groups of macro commands do we have?
6. Give one command as an example of each group.
7.* What is the equivalent of BLANK in a nonmacro setting (in worksheet or range commands)?
8. What is the difference between CONTENTS and LET?
9. Does LET hold numeric values, nonnumeric values, or both?
10. What is the difference between DISPATCH and BRANCH?
11.* If Start in the FOR command is larger than Stop, what will happen?
12.* Does Return need an argument?
13. What is the application of the LOOK command?
14. How do you design your own menu?
15. How many lines can you have in a menu?
16.* Why must all the commands in your menu be unique (the starting point must be unique)?
17. How many commands are included in the file operations group?
18. What is the difference between the READLN and READ commands?
19. Why must a file be opened before you invoke a command?
20.* How many different access modes do we have?
21. Using the FOR advanced command, design an macro that prints "LOTUS IS EASY TO LEARN" 20 times.
22. Using the MENUCALL advanced command, design a menu with four options:

   a. Extend a column length to any number between 1 and 240 characters.
   b. Center any label typed from the keyboard.
   c. Erase any range specified by the user.
   d. Format any number in Currency with two decimal places.

23. Using the INDICATE advanced command, design a macro to turn the mode indicator to "Bye."
24. Using BRANCH and other advanced commands, design a macro to select

students for a dean's scholarship if they meet the following criteria:

MIS major
GPA > 3.70
Age < 21
Single

25.   Using Figure 17-16, add two more options to this menu.

Misconceptions and Solutions

M - A subroutine name can be any name except reserved Lotus words. If there is a duplicate, Lotus performs the subroutine, not the reserved word.

S - All Lotus reserved words are in Table 16-1. Try not to use any of these as subroutine names.

M - If macro command BREAKOFF is in effect and the macro goes into an endless loop, there is no way to get back to the 1-2-3 command mode.

S - To stop this you have to reset your computer (turn the computer off).

M - In sequential file processing, when you use the OPEN command accompanied with the access mode to open a file you may get an error message.

S - You must use the file extension with the file name.

M - In sequential file processing, Lotus does not prevent you from putting the file pointer past the end of the file.

S - You must use the FILESIZE command to determine the number of the last character in the file.

M - The BRANCH macro command and GOTO both cause branching to different locations not followed in the normal program sequence.

S - Use GOTO only if you want to move the cell pointer. Use BRANCH if you want to transfer the macro execution to a different location which is not the normal program sequence.

18

Macros/Part Three:
Using Lotus Macros as a
Super Programming Language

18-1 Introduction

In this chapter we are wrapping up our discussion of macros. We will present a quick review of the program development life cycle. Modular programming and structured programming also will be briefly discussed. We put a heavy emphasis on program documentation and the types of documentation. We will also compare Lotus macros with a typical high-level programming language.

After this brief presentation we will introduce you to several short programs using Lotus as a programming language. This chapter should provide you with a good background for further investigations into Lotus as a super programming language.

18-2 Steps in the Program Development Life Cycle

The purpose of this chapter is not to teach you how to program. There are several excellent texts available which teach the subject of programming thoroughly. In this chapter, we are trying to provide you with a quick overview of programming and the program development life cycle.

In order to use Lotus as a programming language you should follow these steps:

Step 1 Problem Definition. You should carefully define the nature and scope of the problem which you intend to use Lotus to solve. On a broader scale, you may have to perform an output analysis first. This means that you clearly define all the outputs or answers to the questions you intend to receive from your macro program.

A clear definition of the problem and the output specifications may help you to achieve a solution faster.

A typical problem would be a payroll problem. Your program should be able to print accurate monthly, biweekly, and weekly paychecks for a group of employees. The paycheck is the output of the program. Naturally, some input data is needed in order to print a paycheck. In the simplest case, you need the number of hours a particular employee works, his/her pay rate, overtime rate, deductions, and so forth.

Step 2 Logic Design. In programming terminology, before you attempt to write a program, you must first define how you will reach your solution. For example, if an employee has worked more than 40 hours, what do you do? If the employee has worked less than 40 hours, what do you do? There are many tools to use in clarifying the logic of your program. The flowchart (the most commonly used tool), structure chart, pseudocode, or Nassi-Shneiderman chart are some of the techniques available. If you use these tools, you are safeguarding against logical errors, those that create erroneous results in your program – your program runs but the results are not correct. Other errors you may see are called syntax errors. These include using the wrong keyword or the wrong grammar. The correction of syntactical errors is usually easier than the correction of logical errors.

Using logic design tools such as a flowchart or pseudocode should assist you in minimizing or eliminating errors, especially logical errors. After you design your logic and walk through it to make sure it is working, you move to the next step.

Step 3 Coding. After designing your logic and checking it manually, you are ready to code it. Chapters 16 and 17 taught you how to use Lotus as a programming language.

The best approach for coding your program is a modular approach. This means entering the program as a series of smaller independent blocks. Test these blocks and document them; if one works, begin the next block. We will talk more about modular programming later in this chapter.

Step 4 Execution and Debugging. Usually your program will not run the first time, or it runs partially, or it may run completely but generate the wrong answers. In each case there is a bug (error) in your program. As we discussed in Chapter 16, you can debug each individual macro. To make sure that the entire program is working, you should use some simple data and run it through your program. You can then be pretty sure that your program is working correctly.

Step 5 Documentation. In order to make your program self-explanatory for other people and for your own future reference, you should document it. Documentation can be internal or external. Internal documentation may include a series of statements within your macro to explain its function.

Internal documentation can be three types. Type one is called program documentation. This may include a few lines of explanation at the beginning of the program to describe its function. Type two is called module documentation. This type describes the function of a particular module. Type three is called line documentation or segment documentation. This type of documentation explains lines or segments of a module.

External documentation may include a flowchart, pseudocode, structure chart, or program listing. Comprehensive external documentation may serve as a user's guide or user's manual for future reference. Both internal and external documentation are important and you should get in the habit of using them.

18-3 Modular Programming

Problems you may encounter in real-life situations are usually large and complex. To solve the entire problem in one shot may not be a feasible option. Modular programming methodology advocates the breakdown of a large project into several smaller ones. Solve each small module, then put them together in order to generate the answer to the entire problem. Modular programming has several unique advantages:

1. It is easier to understand.
2. It is easier to code.
3. It is easier to debug.
4. It is easier to document.
5. It is easier to modify.

In order to implement each module in Lotus, use a subroutine. In programming terminology, a subroutine is a series of instructions that performs a particular task. Any large problem can be broken down into a series of subroutines.

18-4 Structured Programming

Since the early 1970s a new methodology has become very common in a programming environment. This new methodology advocates GOTO-less programming. The intention is to eliminate the use of GOTO statements in your program. Proponents of this methodology believe GOTO statements make the program complex and difficult to debug or modify.

In structured programming, four structures are used for performing any tasks. These include sequence, selection, iteration, and CASE structures.

The sequence structure means going from step 1 to step 2 to step 3. There is no looping or branching involved here.

The selection structure is used whenever you have to choose between two options, e.g., regular routine or overtime routine, high commission or low commission.

The iteration structure indicates a loop for a specific task; for example, 100 times printing 100 different checks or 200 times calculating the commissions for a group of salespeople.

The CASE structure is used when you choose from more than two options; for example, selection of a commission formula from 15 different routines. Table 18-1 illustrates the equivalent of these structures in Lotus. The remaining part of this chapter presents some simple macro programs.

Table 18-1 Structured Programming and Lotus

NAME OF THE STRUCTURE	PROGRAMMING EQUIVALENT	LOTUS MACRO EQUIVALENT
Sequence	LET A+10	LET, PUT, BLANK, CONTENTS, etc.
	B=25	
Selection	IF-THEN	IF, BRANCH, etc.
	IF-THEN-ELSE	DISPATCH, etc.
Iteration	FOR-NEXT	FOR, etc.
	DO-WHILE	
	DO-UNTIL	
	DO-CONTINUE	
	REPEAT-UNTIL	
CASE	CASE expression OF	BRANCH, DISPATCH, etc.

18-5 Program 1 - Area and Circumference of a Circle

Our first example calculates the area and circumference of a circle. The program is in interactive mode. The user inputs the radius and the program calculates the area and the circumference of a particular circle. This is illustrated in Figure 18-1.

18-6 Program 2 - Arithmetic Operations with Two Numbers

Example two illustrates a simple program; shown in Figure 18-2. The user inputs two numbers and then the program calculates their sum, their difference, their product, and their quotient.

18-7 Program 3 - Average Score of Five Numbers

In Figure 18-3, if we input five different scores, the program calculates their average.

18-8 Program 4 - Checking the Sign of a Number

Example four, in Figure 18-4, inputs a number with any sign. Then the program examines the number to see if it is positive, negative, or zero. The appropriate message is printed and the program waits for six seconds, erases the previous message, and asks for a new number. To stop this program, type N (for No).

18-9 Program 5 - Random Numbers Generation between Zero and One

Program 5, shown in Figure 18-5, generates as many random numbers as the user specifies. These random numbers are between zero and one.

Figure 18-1 Area and Circumference of a Circle

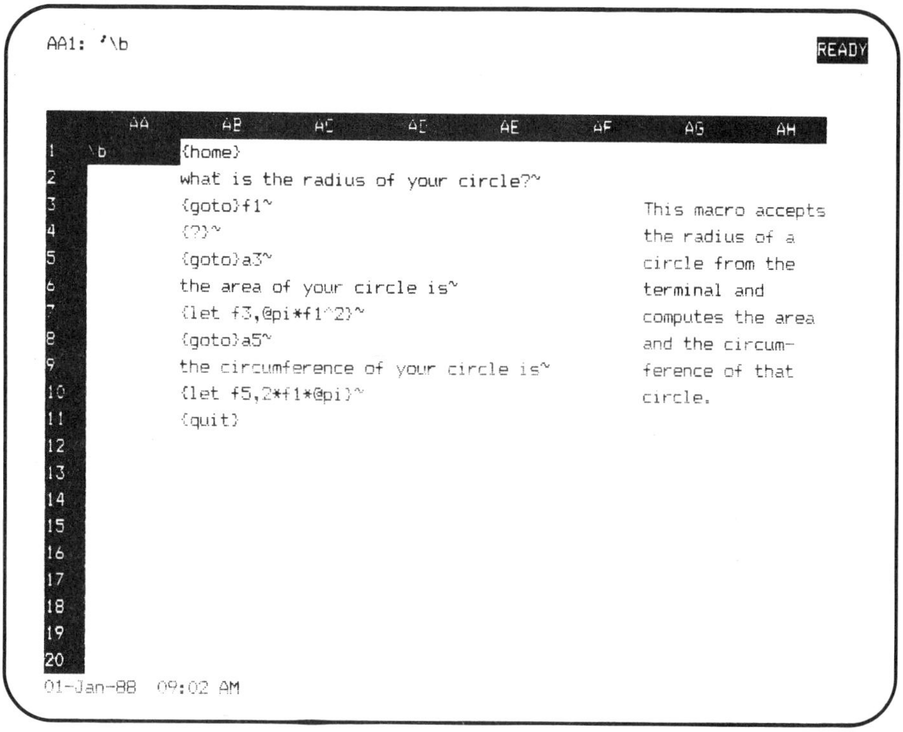

```
AA1: '\b                                                          READY

        AA      AB      AC      AD      AE      AF      AG      AH
1    \b         {home}
2            what is the radius of your circle?~
3            {goto}f1~
4            {?}~                                      This macro accepts
5            {goto}a3~                                 the radius of a
6            the area of your circle is~              circle from the
7            {let f3,@pi*f1^2}~                        terminal and
8            {goto}a5~                                 computes the area
9            the circumference of your circle is~      and the circum-
10           {let f5,2*f1*@pi}~                        ference of that
11           {quit}                                    circle.
12
13
14
15
16
17
18
19
20
01-Jan-88  09:02 AM
```

Figure 18-2 Arithmetic Operations with Two Numbers

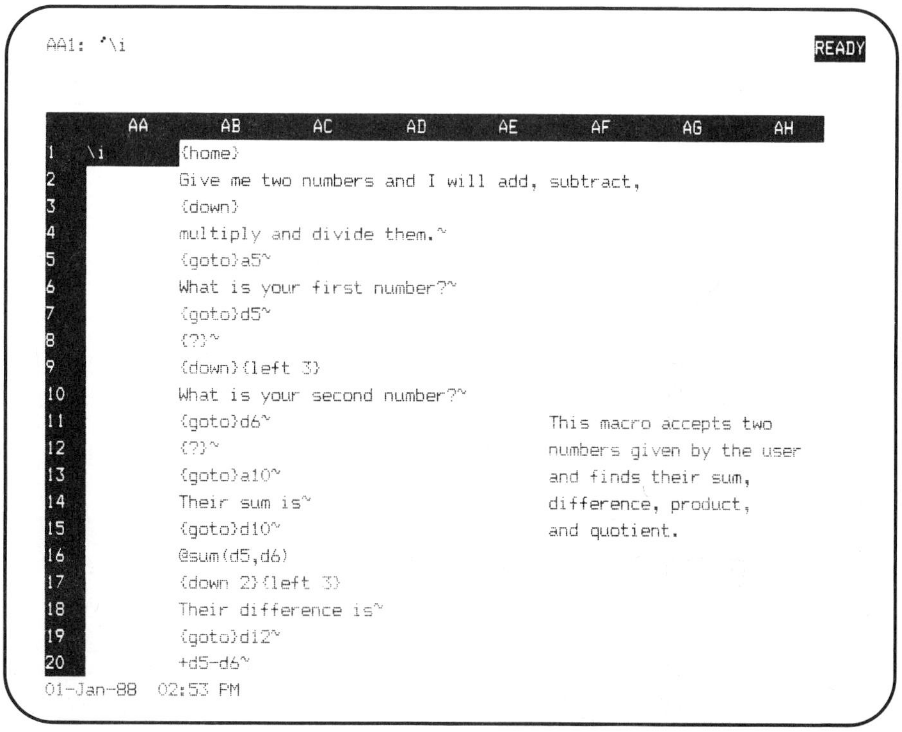

```
AA1: '\i                                                          READY

        AA      AB      AC      AD      AE      AF      AG      AH
1    \i         {home}
2            Give me two numbers and I will add, subtract,
3            {down}
4            multiply and divide them.~
5            {goto}a5~
6            What is your first number?~
7            {goto}d5~
8            {?}~
9            {down}{left 3}
10           What is your second number?~
11           {goto}d6~                                  This macro accepts two
12           {?}~                                       numbers given by the user
13           {goto}a10~                                 and finds their sum,
14           Their sum is~                              difference, product,
15           {goto}d10~                                 and quotient.
16           @sum(d5,d6)
17           {down 2}{left 3}
18           Their difference is~
19           {goto}d12~
20           +d5-d6~
01-Jan-88  02:53 PM
```

Figure 18-2 (Continued)

```
AA21:                                                                    READY

          AA      AB        AC        AD        AE       AF       AG       AH
21              {down 2}{left 3}
22              Their product is~
23              {goto}d14~
24              +d5*d6~
25              {down 2}{left 3}
26              Their quotient is~
27              {goto}d16~
28              +d5/d6~
29
30
31
32
33
34
35
36
37
38
39
40
01-Jan-88  02:54 PM
```

Figure 18-3 Average Scores of Five Numbers

```
AA1:  '\c                                                               READY

          AA      AB        AC        AD        AE       AF       AG       AH
1    \c        {home}
2              What is your first test score?~
3              {goto}e1~
4              {?}~
5              {down}{left 4}
6              What is your second test score?~
7              {goto}e2~
8              {?}~
9              {down}{left 4}
10             What is your third test score?~            This macro calculates
11             {goto}e3~                                  the average score
12             {?}~                                       from five test scores
13             {down}{left 4}
14             What is your fourth test score?~
15             {goto}e4~
16             {?}~
17             {down}{left 4}
18             What is your fifth test score?~
19             {goto}e5~
20             {?}~
01-Jan-88  03:00 PM
```

Figure 18-3 (Continued)

```
AA21:                                                              READY

          AA      AB      AC      AD      AE      AF      AG      AH
21            {down 2}{left 4}
22            Your average score is~
23            {goto}e7~
24            (+E1+E2+E3+E4+E5)/5~
25
26
27
28
29
30
31
32
33
34
35
36
37
38
39
40
01-Jan-88  03:02 PM
```

Figure 18-4 Checking the Sign of a Number

```
AA1:  '\a                                                         READY

          AA      AB      AC      AD      AE      AF      AG      AH
1    \a       {home}
2             What is your number?~
3             {goto}d1~
4             {?}~                              This macro inputs
5             {goto}a3~                         any number from
6             {IF d1>0} Your number is positive~    the keyboard and
7             {IF d1<0} Your number is negative~    will tell you
8             {IF d1=0} Your number is zero~        whether the number
9             {goto}a10~                        is positive,
10            Do you want to try again? Choose (Y)es or (N)negative or zero.
11            {GET answer}
12            {IF answer="Y"}{branch \a}
13
14
15
16
17
18
19
20
01-Jan-88  03:02 PM
```

```
AA1: '\k                                                        READY

        AA       AB       AC       AD       AE       AF       AG       AH
 1   \k          {home}
 2               this macro will generate as many random numbers as you specify~
 3               {down 3}
 4               how many random numbers do you want?~
 5               {goto}e4~
 6               {?}~
 7               {goto}a6~                                   This macro will
 8               {FOR ab15,1,e4,1,ab10}                      generate as many
 9                                                           random numbers as
10   rand_num @RAND                                          the user specifies.
11               {down}                                      The random numbers
12                                                           are between zero
13                                                           and one.
14
15   counter
16
17
18
19
20
01-Jan-88  03:12 PM
```

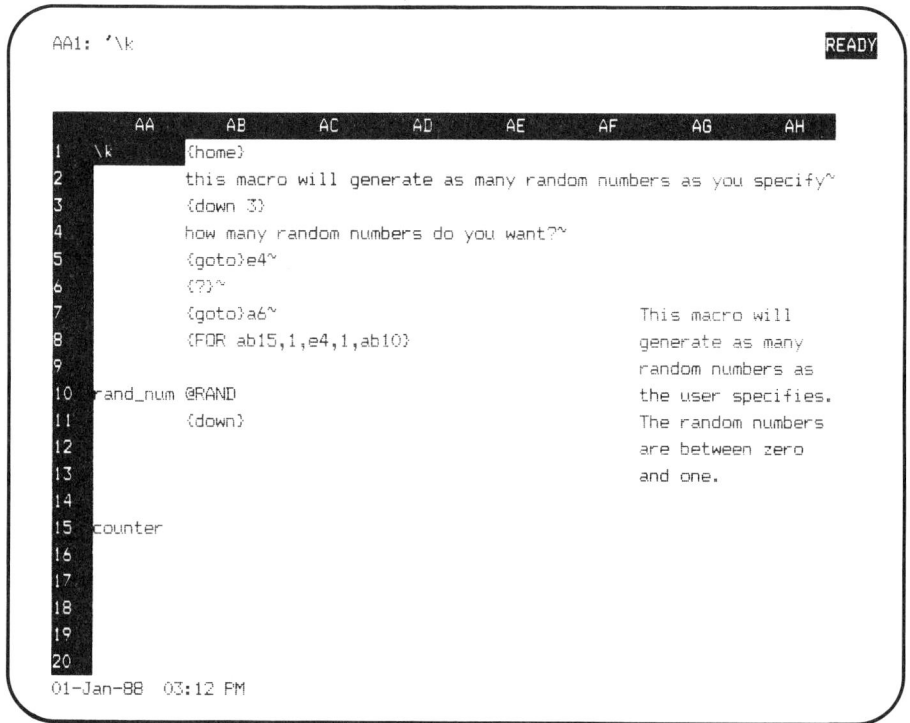

Figure 18-5 Random Number Generation between Zero and One

18-10 Program 6 - Random Numbers between Specific Limits

In the business world random numbers have many different applications, in the production process, in acceptance or rejection of a shipment, in process control, and so forth. In many cases the user may be interested in a random number which is within a certain limit. For example, you are interested in choosing a random number between 1 and 1,000. If this is the case, you have to do some modification of the @RAND function in order to generate a specific random number. The process is very simple.

1. Define your upper limit (in the above example, 1,000), U.
2. Define your lower limit (in the above example, 1), L.
3. Define the difference between the upper and lower limits (in the above example, 999), U-L.

The formula is (upper limit - lower limit + 1). Multiply by the @RAND function, then add the lower limit. In order to generate only an integer portion of the number, you must use the @INT function. The whole formula is @INT((U-L+1)*@RAND+L). Figure 18-6 illustrates this process.

18-11 Program 7 - Many Random Numbers in Any Range

Program 7, shown in Figure 18-7, is an extension of program 6. This program follows the same pattern, but the user can define as many random numbers as he/she is interested in, and in any range.

18-12 Program 8 - Break-Even Analysis

There are many times when a businessperson is interested in calculating the break-even point of the operation. The break-even point is a production point at which there is no loss and no gain, i.e., the total revenue is equal to the total costs. To calculate the break-even point, the following items are needed:

1. FC - Total fixed costs or overhead such as rent and electricity.
2. VC - Variable costs per unit such as raw material and labor.
3. SP - Unit selling price.

The break-even point will be calculated by dividing (FC) by (SP-VC). The difference between SP and VC is called the contribution margin. For example, if FC = 500, VC = 10, SP = 15, the break-even point = 100 units. This means if you sell

Figure 18-6 Random Numbers between Specific Limits

```
AB14: 'Your random number is~                                        READY

        AA       AB        AC        AD        AE        AF       AG       AH
1    \j        {home}
2              This macro will generate one random number~
3              {down}
4              between a specified upper and lower bound~
5              {down 2}
6              What is your upper bound number?~
7              {goto}e4~
8              {?}~                                          This macro
9              {down}{left 4}                               generates one
10             What is your lower bound number?~            random number
11             {goto}e5~                                    between a
12             {?}~                                         specified upper
13             {down 2}{left 4}                             and lower bound.
14             Your random number is~
15             {goto}e7~
16             @INT((+e4-e5+1)*@RAND+e5)~
17
18
19
20
01-Jan-88   03:13 PM
```

Figure 18-7 Many Random Numbers in Any Range

```
AB4: 'between a given upper and lower bound~                              READY

        AA      AB      AC      AD      AE      AF      AG      AH
1   \m          {home}
2               This macro will generate as many random numbers as you want~
3               {down}
4               between a given upper and lower bound~
5               {down 3}
6               How many random numbers do you want?~
7               {goto}e5~
8               {?}~
9               {down}{left 4}
10              What is your upper bound?~          This macro will generate
11              {goto}e6~                           as many random numbers
12              {?}~                                as the user specifies
13              {down}{left 4}                      between a specified upper
14              What is your lower bound?~          and lower bound.
15              {goto}e7~
16              {?}~
17              {goto}a10~
18              {FOR ab23,1,e5,1,ab20}
19
20  rand_num    @INT((+e6-e7+1)*@RAND+e7)~
01-Jan-88   03:27 PM
```

Figure 18-7 (Continued)

```
AB24:                                                                    READY

        AA      AB      AC      AD      AE      AF      AG      AH
21              {down}
22
23  counter         11
24
25
26
27
28
29
30
31
32
33
34
35
36
37
38
39
40
01-Jan-88   03:33 PM
```

less than 100 units, you are losing money; if you sell 100 units, no loss, no gain; if you sell more than 100 units, you are making a profit.

This simple formula can be very helpful when performing what-if analysis. You may ask yourself if the variable cost increases by one dollar, what would be the effect on the break-even point? Or if you reduce the selling price by one dollar, what would be the effect? Figure 18-8 illustrates this calculation in an interactive mode.

18-13 Program 9 - Economic Order Quantity

How much to order and when to order is a major concern for many businesses. Ordering large quantities may increase the cost of capital (tying up money, warehouse space, etc.). At the same time, ordering very small quantities may increase the ordering cost, cost of losing customers, and so on. A model known as the Economic Order Quantity (EOQ) has been utilized by many businesses for minimizing inventory cost. The outcome of this model is the optimum order quantity or the number of units to be ordered that will minimize the business's total inventory costs. This model utilizes the following formula and variables:

$$EOQ = \sqrt{\frac{2*A*B}{C*P}}$$

where A =   annual inventory requirements (annual sales)

B =   cost of placing an order (ordering cost)

C =   single unit cost (sales price)

P =   percentage of inventory value allotted for carrying costs

EOQ =   number of units to order that will minimize the business's total inventory cost.

This formula makes it possible for the user to compute the EOQ for many products with different selling prices and annual sales. Figure 18-9 illustrates this process in an interactive mode.

18-14 Program 10 - Tabulation Analysis

Program 10 is a simple example that keeps track of entries with different code numbers. The user can enter codes 1, 2, 3 and the program keeps track of how many units of each code has been entered. If the user responds with a code that is not 1, 2, or 3, Lotus will beep. The program will also provide a percentage tabulation result. Figure 18-10 shows this example.

Figure 18-8 Break-Even Analysis

```
AA1: '\g                                                            READY

        AA        AB        AC        AD        AE        AF        AG        AH
1   \g          {home}
2               What is the total fixed cost?~
3               {goto}f1~
4               {?}~
5               {down}{left 5}
6               What are the variable costs per unit?~
7               {goto}f2~                              This macro
8               {?}~                                   determines the
9               {down}{left 5}                         break-even point
10              What is the unit selling price?~       in units for a
11              {goto}f3~                              product based on
12              {?}~                                   the unit selling
13              {down 2}{left 5}                       price and the
14              The unit contribution to overhead is~  known production
15              {goto}f5~                              costs.
16              +f3-f2~
17              {down}{left 5}
18              The break-even point in units is~
19              {goto}f6~
20              +f1/f5~
01-Jan-88   03:34 PM
```

Figure 18-9 Economic Order Quantity

```
AA1: '\h                                                            READY

        AA        AB        AC        AD        AE        AF        AG        AH
1   \h          {home}
2               What is the single unit cost?~
3               {goto}g1~
4               {?}~
5               {down 2}{left 6}
6               What are the number of units sold annually?~
7               {goto}g3~
8               {?}~
9               {down 2}{left 6}
10              What is the cost of placing and handling an order?~
11              {goto}g5~
12              {?}~
13              {down 2}{left 6}
14              What is the percentage of inventory value allotted~
15              {down}
16              to carrying costs? (please answer using decimal)~
17              {goto}g8~
18              {?}~
19              {down 2}{left 6}
20              The economic order quanitity (EOQ) is~
01-Jan-88   10:33 AM
```

Figure 18-9 (Continued)

```
AA21:                                                                    READY

        ┌── AA ──── AB ──── AC ──── AD ──── AE ──── AF ──── AG ──── AH ──
     21 │ {LET g10,@ROUND(@SQRT(2*g3*g5/(g8*g1)),0)}~
     22 │
     23 │
     24 │
     25 │
     26 │
     27 │     This macro determines the economic order quantity
     28 │     that will minimize total inventory costs.
     29 │
     30 │
     31 │
     32 │
     33 │
     34 │
     35 │
     36 │
     37 │
     38 │
     39 │
     40 │
    01-Jan-88  10:34 AM
```

Figure 18-10 Tabulation Analysis

```
AA1: '\j                                                                 READY

        ┌── AA ──── AB ──── AC ──── AD ──── AE ──── AF ──── AG ──── AH ──
      1 │ \j    {home}
      2 │       /rea6..e8~
      3 │       This macro keeps totals for Republicans, Democrats and Others~
      4 │       {down}
      5 │       Republicans = 1~
      6 │       {down}
      7 │       Democrats = 2~
      8 │       {down}
      9 │       Others = 3~
     10 │ \P    {goto}a6~
     11 │       Please enter the code number~
     12 │       {goto}e6~/RE~
     13 │       {?}~
     14 │       {IF e6=1}{BRANCH Rep_tot}
     15 │       {IF e6=2}{BRANCH Dem_tot}
     16 │       {IF e6=3}{BRANCH Other}
     17 │       {down}{left 4}
     18 │       You have not entered a proper code number, please try again~
     19 │       {BEEP 2}
     20 │       {WAIT @now+@time(0,0,10)}/RE~
    01-Jan-88  03:37 PM
```

Figure 18-10 (Continued)

```
AA21:                                                                    READY

            AA       AB       AC       AD       AE       AF       AG       AH
21                 {BRANCH \P}                                 This macro uses branching
22                                                             routines to keep track of
23      Rep_tot    {LET i10,i10+1}                             the total number of
24                 {BRANCH Gr_tot}                             Republicans, Democrats,
25                                                             and Others.  It then
26      Dem_tot    {LET i11,i11+1}                             converts the total for
27                 {BRANCH Gr_tot}                             each category to a
28                                                             percentage of the grand
29      Other      {LET i12,i12+1}                             total.
30                 {BRANCH Gr_tot}
31
32      Gr_tot     {goto}a8~
33                 Do you have another entry? Choose (Y)es or  (N)o~
34                 {GET answer}/RE~
35                 {IF answer="Y"}{BRANCH \P}
36                 {goto}a10~
37                 The total number of Republicans is~/mi10..i10~e10~
38                 {down}
39                 The total number of Democrats is~/mi11..i11~e11~
40                 {down}
01-Jan-88   03:38 PM
```

Figure 18-10 (Continued)

```
AA41:                                                                    READY

            AA       AB       AC       AD       AE       AF       AG       AH
41                 The total number of Others is~/mi12..i12~e12~
42                 {down 2}
43                 The percentage of Republicans is~
44                 {goto}e14~
45                 +e10/(+e10+e11+e12)~
46                 /rfp2~e14~
47                 {down}{left 4}
48                 The percentage of Democrats is~
49                 {goto}e15~
50                 +e11/(+e10+e11+e12)~
51                 /rfp2~e15~
52                 {down}{left 4}
53                 The percentage of Others is~
54                 {goto}e16~
55                 +e12/(+e10+e11+e12)~
56                 /rfp2~e16~
57
58      answer     N
59
60
01-Jan-88   03:39 PM
```

18-15 Programs 11, 12, and 13 – Depreciation Assessment

As you saw in Chapter 10, Lotus Release 2 provides functions for three depreciation calculations: straight line, sum-of-the-years depreciation, and double-declining balance. Figures 18-11, 18-12, and 18-13 illustrate the macro version of these functions.

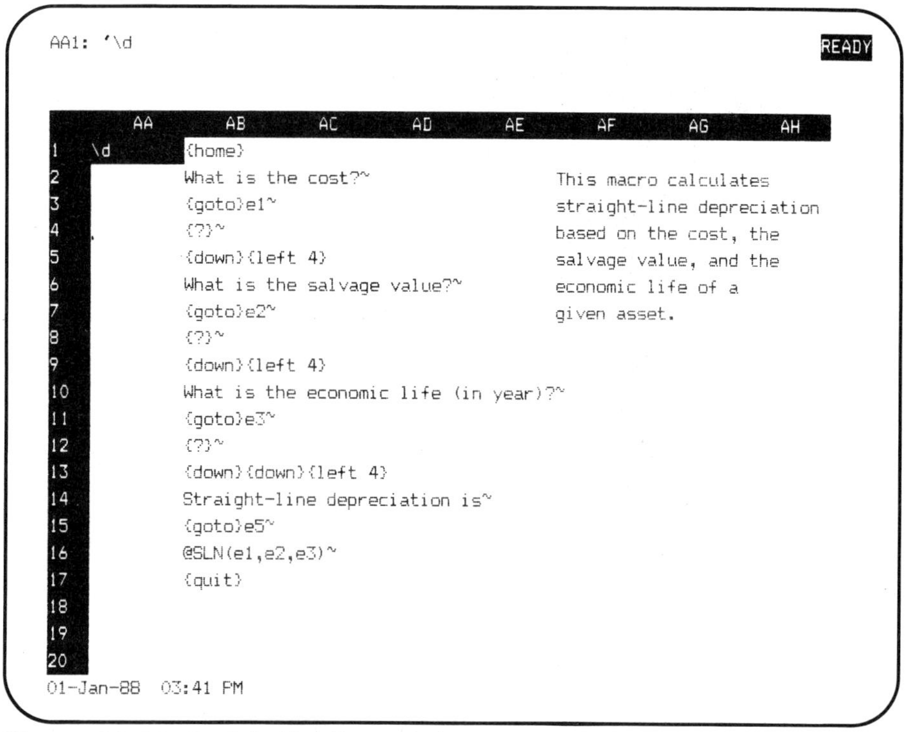

```
AA1: '\d                                                                    READY

          AA        AB        AC        AD        AE        AF        AG        AH
1    \d        {home}
2              What is the cost?~                              This macro calculates
3              {goto}e1~                                       straight-line depreciation
4              {?}~                                            based on the cost, the
5              {down}{left 4}                                  salvage value, and the
6              What is the salvage value?~                     economic life of a
7              {goto}e2~                                       given asset.
8              {?}~
9              {down}{left 4}
10             What is the economic life (in year)?~
11             {goto}e3~
12             {?}~
13             {down}{down}{left 4}
14             Straight-line depreciation is~
15             {goto}e5~
16             @SLN(e1,e2,e3)~
17             {quit}
18
19
20
01-Jan-88   03:41 PM
```

Figure 18-11 Straight-Line Depreciation

Figure 18-12 Sum-of-the-Years Depreciation

```
AB10: 'What is the economic life (in year)?~                          READY

          AA        AB        AC        AD        AE        AF        AG        AH
1    \f         {home}
2               What is the cost?~
3               {goto}f1~
4               {?}~
5               {down}{left 5}
6               What is the salvage value?~
7               {goto}f2~
8               {?}~
9               {down}{left 5}                        This macro calculates
10              What is the economic life (in year)?sum-of-the-years'digits
11              {goto}f3~                             depreciation based on the
12              {?}~                                  cost, the salvage value,
13              {down 3}{left 5}                      and the economic life
14              {LET a7,Period}                       of a given asset.
15              {LET c7,SYD depreciation}
16              {goto}a9~
17              {FOR h1,1,f3,1,ab19}
18
19   calc_rtn   +h1~
20              /rv~~
01-Jan-88  03:42 PM
```

Figure 18-12 (Continued)

```
AB30:                                                                 READY

          AA        AB        AC        AD        AE        AF        AG        AH
21              {right 2}
22              @SYD(f1,f2,f3,h1)~
23              /rv~~
24              {down}{left 2}
25
26
27
28
29
30
31
32
33
34
35
36
37
38
39
40
01-Jan-88  03:43 PM
```

Figure 18-13 Double-Declining-Balance Depreciation

```
AA1:  '\e                                                                    READY


          AA       AB        AC        AD      AE       AF       AG       AH
1    \e           {home}
2                 What is the cost?~
3                 {goto}e1~
4                 {?}~
5                 {down}{left 4}
6                 What is the salvage value?~
7                 {goto}e2~
8                 {?}~                           This macro calculates
9                 {down}{left 4}                 double-declining-balance
10                What is the economic life?~    depreciation based on the
11                {goto}e3~                      cost, the salvage value,
12                {?}~                           and the economic life
13                {down}{left 4}                 of a given asset.
14                {LET a7,Period}
15                {LET c7,DDB depreciation}
16                {goto}a9~
17                {FOR h1,1,e3,1,ab19}
18
19   calc_rtn +h1~
20                /rv~~
01-Jan-88   03:44 PM
```

Figure 18-13 (Continued)

```
AA21:                                                                        READY


          AA       AB        AC        AD      AE       AF       AG       AH
21                {right 2}
22                @DDB(e1,e2,e3,h1)~
23                /rv~~
24                {down}{left 2}
25
26
27
28
29
30
31
32
33
34
35
36
37
38
39
40
01-Jan-88   03:45 PM
```

Summary

In this chapter we have seen that Lotus macros can be used as a super programming language. Basic structures such as sequence, selection, iteration, and CASE can be performed by macros. We reviewed the principles of programming and the program development life cycle. Several simple examples highlighted the application of Lotus macros as a programming language.

Review Questions

1. What is a program development life cycle?
2. Why is problem definition so important?
3. Why is program documentation important?
4.* How many types of documentation do we have?
5. What is the difference between external and internal documentation?
6. What are some of the tools for external documentation?
7.* Logic design methodology is useful for eliminating and reducing one type of error. What kind of error?
8. What is modular programming?
9. What are some of the advantages of modular programming?
10. What is structured programming?
11.* Why has structured programming become so popular?
12. Can Lotus be used as a full-fledged structured programming language? If yes, why? If no, why not?
13.* Why do we use random numbers?
14. What are some of the business applications of random numbers?
15. What is the break-even point? How is it calculated?
16. What is EOQ? How is it calculated?
17.* What is nested subroutine? What are some uses of this type of subroutine?
18.* What are some of the advantages of using macros to calculate depreciation methods?
19. Extend the macro presented in Figure 18-10 in order to generate a bar graph from 10 sets of data; for example, three of code 1, five of code 2, and two of code 3.
20. Design a macro which accepts grades A-F, then calculates a G.P.A. Also, your program should print the following message:

Excellent	for G.P.A. >= 3.8
Good	for G.P.A. >= 3.5
Average	for G.P.A. >= 2.5
In trouble	for G.P.A. <= 2.0

21. Design a macro to generate a mailing list. The output should include three lines as follows:

    First Name   Last Name
    Street Address
    City, State, Zip

    Your macro must accept any number of data items, then generate a mailing label.

19

Lotus Applications in Specific Disciplines

19-1 Introduction

You have seen throughout this book that Lotus can handle an unlimited number of applications. Any application that can utilize row and column settings, any mathematical formula, if it is translated properly, can be solved by Lotus. The amazing speed and user-friendliness of Lotus add to the beauty of the process.

Whenever you want to use Lotus for any application, you have two options. The first option is to use the Lotus worksheet in a straightforward manner. This means putting your figures and numbers in cells and conducting manipulations. The second option is to develop a series of macros and let them do the job. The advantage of the second approach is that the user does not need to know anything about Lotus and/ or the application itself. He/she only needs to answer a series of questions and the rest is done by Lotus.

Applications in this chapter are divided into two groups. First, we introduce you to a series of specific applications and provide you with some guidelines and hints for finishing and expanding them. Later on you may develop macros to perform these tasks with more flexibility. The second group consists of five macro-based applications, to give you the necessary background for developing your own macros. To execute the macros, you need a minimum knowledge of Lotus and the particular application.

The materials presented in this chapter should illustrate the tremendous power and versatility of this amazing software. Try to be creative and invent your own application!

Remember, these applications are by no means a comprehensive coverage of Lotus capabilities. These are only some of the more common applications.

19-2 Lotus for Home Use

Lotus has many applications for home use. Probably the most common is for an automated telephone directory. You can use the Lotus worksheet to keep track of your friends' addresses, telephone numbers, birthdates, and so on.

Forgetting a friend's birthday can be embarrassing. You can keep track of your friends' birthdays in an address database. Then you can ask Lotus to tell you all the birthdays in the next two weeks or so. The design is very easy. Enter the following information:

Column A	First name
Column B	Last name
Column C	Street address
Column D	City
Column E	State
Column F	Zip code
Column G	Telephone number
Column H	Birthdate

Adding to or deleting from this database is no problem. There are 8,192 rows (records) and 256 columns (fields) available to you. Modification would also be an easy job. A sort can be done and any specific values can be searched. The default settings, however, may not be adequate for this application. For example, some of the columns must be extended beyond nine characters (/WCS).

When this database is designed, you could generate mailing labels for Christmas cards or for inviting all your friends to a party.

Another home use could be a database for recipes. The rows would be for recipes, number 1 to number 8,192, and the columns could be for ingredients. Many inquiries can be answered by this database. You could list all the 1987 recipes, all the Chinese recipes, and so on.

Lotus financial functions can be used for home financial planning, mortgage payments, planning for your children's college education, retirement planning, and so forth.

19-3 Accounting Applications

Any task in the accounting environment can be done by Lotus. (However, dedicated accounting packages may be more suitable for specific accounting and bookkeeping applications.) We have developed a series of macros that prepare a balance sheet and an income statement at the end of this chapter. Here, we will show you one very common accounting application: issuing a list of aged accounts receivable.

Let us say column A includes the purchase date, column B is the amount of purchase, column C is the payment, column D is the balance, and column E is today's date. You can perform a variety of analyses using this database. Let us say that if the balance is positive AND the difference between today's date and the purchase date is >= 45 days, issue a message or charge interest. Or you could say if the difference between purchase date and today's date is 30 days OR the balance is >= 5,000, issue a message.

As you remember from Chapter 14, AND (horizontal search), OR (vertical search), and NOT (search with tilde) analysis can be done in a Lotus database. Also, dates in Lotus can be expressed in numbers, so that mathematical calculations can be done with them.

19-4 Tax Analysis

Lotus can be used effectively for calculating taxes. The design process is very easy. Let us say:

Column A	includes the taxpayer's wages
Column B	includes interest income
Column C	includes dividends
Column D	includes other income
Column E	includes adjustments such as moving expenses, medical bills, professional training, etc.
Column F	includes all other itemized deductions
Column G	includes number of exemptions
Column H	includes allowance per exemption

You can make this as complicated as you want. Naturally, the values included in these cells are different for different taxpayers. For example, a single person differs from a family with 18 children or a taxpayer who has a lot of business expenses.

In the above example, the taxable income for a fictitious taxpayer, assuming everything is in row 1, would be:

+A1+B1+C1+D1-E1-F1-G1*H1

The next step would be to build a tax table somewhere in the worksheet. And the final step would be to use a lookup table (horizontal or vertical). The lookup search will tell you how much the tax is, based on a particular taxable income.

You can put as much taxpayer data as you have room for in the worksheet. In theory, you can have up to 8,192 taxpayers in your worksheet.

19-5 Cross-Tabulation Analysis

Cross-tabulation analysis simply means analyzing a row by column data. One common application of this type of analysis is used for questionnaire analysis.

Let us say you have designed a questionnaire with 52 questions regarding customers' reactions to a new product. Each question has a rating scale of one to seven: one means the least satisfaction, four means average satisfaction, and seven means the most satisfaction. When you collect and store this data in your Lotus worksheet, a variety of analyses can be done to answer the following questions:

How many people answered 7?
How many people answered 1?
What is the standard deviation of each question?
What is the mean of each question?

You can use /Data Distribution in order to find out the distribution of each answer; how many ones, how many twos, etc. You can also graph the data in any fashion. When you are more comfortable with macros you may want to develop a macro-based program to analyze a questionnaire and provide important statistics.

Another kind of cross-tabulation application can be used, for example, by a police department. A portion of data collected recently is as follows:

	1985	1986	1987
Homicides	15	17	25
Robberies	22	29	32
Thefts	91	107	99
Rapes	17	13	18
Forgeries	22	25	21
Assaults	62	69	62
Burglaries	73	85	81
Other	19	28	37

You can put this data in the worksheet and answer several interesting questions:

What is the total number of crimes committed in each year?
Which crime had the greatest growth rate for the past three years?
Which crime was the smallest and which crime was the biggest in each year?
Generate a line graph for any of these crimes.
Generate the percentage of each crime to the total number using a pie chart for each year.
Generate a forecast for the year 2000 based on this data using /Data Regression.

19-6 Examination Analysis

Examination analysis is another application of cross-tabulation. Imagine a teacher preparing final grades in the final week of classes. The teacher has given five exams, seven homework assignments, two presentations, and a grade for class participation. Grading can be a time-consuming and complicated task. In this case you are dealing with a matrix of 15 columns and, let us say, 50 rows (50 students).

If this data is stored in a worksheet of 50 by 15, a variety of analyses can be done in a short period as follows:

- Total score of each student, e.g., @SUM.
- Sorted list of students by their total score in descending order.
- Distribution of grade, e.g., how many >= 90, >= 80, >= 70, >= 60.
- Maximum of total score.

- Minimum of total score.
- Mean, variance, and standard deviation of each exam.
- A line graph of total scores of all students.
- Best and worst performance in each of 15 cases of grading.
- Comparing this year's average with the last three years.

19-7 Banking Applications

Lotus has been utilized in the banking industry from the first day of its existence. Accounting and financial analyses, portfolio analysis, and future investment analysis are very common applications of Lotus in the banking industry. What-if, goal-seeking, and sensitivity analyses using different interest rates can be done easily. We would like to show you one common application: a checking account report stating how much the customer should be charged for the number of checks written.

Each bank has a different policy regarding checking accounts. Let us say Plaza Bank of Ocean City has established the following formula for its checking accounts:

Balance >= $500 No charge for writing checks
Balance >= $300 and < $500 15 cents charge per check
Balance < $300 $5 base charge plus 12 cents per check

Your task is to calculate the charge for each customer. If you design a worksheet like the one below, you can do this calculation:

Column A   includes the beginning balance
Column B   includes all the deposits
Column C   includes monthly total checks written
Column D   includes final balance (A + B - C)
Column E   includes number of checks

A simple comparison of Column D against the above formula will tell you to which group a particular customer belongs. Then the charge can be calculated. Of course this analysis and database can be expanded to include more sophisticated analyses, such as:

- The largest check written by a particular customer.
- His/her average amount per check.
- His/her smallest check.
- Average balance of the customer per day.
- Highest and lowest balance of a customer in a particular month.

19-8 Lotus Applications in Personnel Administration

Personnel departments of medium to large organizations often have two application areas that Lotus can handle. One is compiling affirmative action statistics and the other is examination analysis. For the affirmative action case you are usually dealing with a typical data table, as follows:

Column A	Employee name
Column B	Sex
Column C	Age
Column D	Marital status
Column E	Education
Column F	Number of years of experience
Column G	Race
Column H	Handicap status
Column I	Veteran status
Column J	Annual salary

This data matrix can be of any size. Let us say you have 2,000 employees. Your matrix would then be 2,000 by 10. Numerous vital statistics can be generated to answer the following questions:

- Is the average salary of female employees and male employees the same?
- For the same age group, which employees make more money, male or female?
- Which ethnic group makes the highest salary?
- Which ethnic group makes the lowest salary?
- What is the mean salary for male employees?
- What is the mean salary for female employees?
- Plot a line graph of male employees' salary.
- Plot a line graph of female employees' salary.
- Data distribution of different ethnic groups.
- Pie chart of different ethnic groups.
- Pie chart for years of education of all the employees.

You can go on and on, generating more statistics and expanding this database by including other data items.

The second common application for a personnel department is entrance examination score analysis. Let us say you have a data matrix as follows:

Column A	includes prospective employee age
Column B	includes prospective employee high school GPA
Column C	includes prospective employee SAT test score
Column D	includes prospective employee aptitude test score
Column E	includes prospective employee years of experience

Using this database some very useful statistics can be generated:

- The highest and lowest of each test score.
- The youngest and oldest prospective employee.
- Is there any correlation between age and aptitude test?
- Is there any correlation between the aptitude test and the SAT test?
- Is there any correlation between the high school GPA and the aptitude test?

To do the last three analyses you can use /Data Regression and look at the correlation coefficient (also study the discussion in Chapter 15 on simple linear regression).

19-9 Microeconomic Analysis

Lotus can be used to perform cost analysis, revenue analysis, production analysis, and so forth. There is a simple example. Let us say the cost equation of Productive Manufacturing Firm is estimated as $R^3 - 18R^2 + 385$, where R is the number of units produced. Let us further assume that this firm can sell any unit produced at $800 per unit. The revenue equation would be 800R and the profit would be $800R - (R^3 - 18R^2 + 385)$. Lotus can help you to generate a scenario regarding total cost, total revenue and total profit as follows:

Column A	includes +800 *R1 (row10)
Column B	includes +R1^3 - 18 *R1^2 + 385 (row 10)
Column C	includes + A10 - B10 (row 10)

Now you can input any value for R (number of units produced) and Lotus will calculate total cost, total revenue, and total profit.

Also, you can conduct some interesting what-if, goal-seeking, and sensitivity analyses. The production and revenue equation can be a lot more complicated than the one here. Just do the translation and leave the rest to Lotus.

19-10 Computerized Matching System

You can establish a fairly large database of all possible candidates for any selection purposes (up to 8,192). You can also include up to 256 attributes for each candidate (e.g., age, height, education, income). When the database is built, you can perform any database and/or statistical analyses. You can do complicated searches with up to 32 fields with AND, OR, and NOT combinations. You can develop your own dating service or any other search system (see Chapters 14-15).

19-11 World Population Analysis

It is a fact that the birth rate is higher than the death rate. This means that if nothing unexpected happens to reduce the world population, it will eventually explode. The following formula is used for predicting world population growth:

$$P = C * [1 + (X - Y)]^N$$

where:

P	=	Predicted level of future world population
C	=	Current level of world population

X	=	Birth rate
Y	=	Death rate
N	=	Number of years in the future

Put these values in a worksheet as follows:

Column A includes C   (row 1)
Column B includes X   (row 1)
Column C includes Y   (row 1)
Column D includes N   (row 1)
Column E includes A1*(1+(B1-C1))^D

Putting different values in cells A1, B1, C1, D1, you will see some horrifying numbers for the year 2500 and beyond. In 1976 the world population was approximately 4 billion, the birthrate was 2.5 percent and the death rate was .9 percent. Use these numbers and put 13 for N. See what happens?

19-12 Calculation of Quadratic Roots

Quadratic equations have the general formula:

$$Y = AX^2 + BX + C$$

$$X = \frac{-B \pm (B^2 - 4AC)^{1/2}}{2A} = \frac{-B \pm (B \wedge 2 - 4*A*C)^{1/2}}{2*A}$$

Let us use Lotus to calculate different values for X, giving different values for A, B, and C. Build the following worksheet:

	A	B	C	D
(row 1)	10	12	2.70	$\dfrac{-B1+(B1\wedge2-4*A1*C1)^{1/2}}{2*A1}$

We only translated the positive root, not the negative or imaginary root. If you put in any valid values for A, B, and C, Lotus will tell you how much X is.

19-13 Production Analysis*

Suppliers of perishable products and those in service businesses face a serious question: How much to supply in order to satisfy demand but not to oversupply? Spoilage or extra service is a problem. One method for minimizing the cost of oversupply and/or undersupply is known as expected opportunity loss. The following example explains the way this method works.

The manager of Always-Open Rental Car Company is faced with the question of how many rental cars to make available for customers. Oversupply and undersupply is a problem. Past experience shows that the number of rental cars demanded ranges from 15 to 21 with the following probabilities:

15	.12
16	.12
17	.10
18	.08
19	.20
20	.25
21	.13

How many cars should the Always-Open Rental Car Company make available in order to minimize the supply cost? The cost of renting a car for this company is $20 and customers pay $28 for renting a car.

The following table is known as the opportunity loss table. Whenever the supply is equal to demand there is no opportunity loss. Each unit of oversupply will cost the company $20. Each unit of undersupply will have an $8 opportunity cost (the company could have been able to make this much profit).

Opportunity Loss Table for Always-Open Rental Car Company

NUMBER OF RENTAL CARS DEMANDED	PROBABILITY OF PAST DEMAND	NUMBER OF RENTAL CARS SUPPLIED						
		15	16	17	18	19	20	21
15	.12	0	20	40	60	80	100	120
16	.12	8	0	20	40	60	80	100
17	.10	16	8	0	20	40	60	80
18	.08	24	16	8	0	20	40	60
19	.20	32	24	16	8	0	20	40
20	.25	40	32	24	16	8	0	20
21	.13	48	40	32	24	16	8	0

The expected opportunity loss of supplying 15 cars is $27.12, as follows: 0(12) + 8(.12) + 16(.10) + 24(.08) + 32(.20) + 40(.25) + 48(.13) = 27.12 The expected opportunity loss for the other units of supply is as follows:

15	27.12
16	22.48
17	21.20
18	22.72
19	26.48

20   35.84
21   52.20

As we see, supplying 17 cars has the minimum opportunity cost.

We have developed a macro-based program to calculate the opportunity loss for various levels of demand. The macro can plot a graph if your computer has graphics capability. Figure 19-1 shows the documentation, the macro-based program, and the execution of the program.

19-14 Financial Analysis

To measure the financial strength of a company many analysts use financial statement analysis. In order to perform this task a series of ratios are computed and are compared with those of other companies in the same industry or with the past years of the company itself. However, ratio analysis for determining a company's financial strength can be misleading. These ratios can be manipulated in order not to reflect a company's actual financial situation. But if these ratios are calculated periodically in a straightforward manner, they can be a good basis for further financial investigation. Some of the most commonly used ratios are as follows:

Return on investment:

R   =   I/E, where:
R   =   return on investment
I   =   net income
E   =   owners' equity

Figure 19-1 Documentation for Opportunity Loss Table

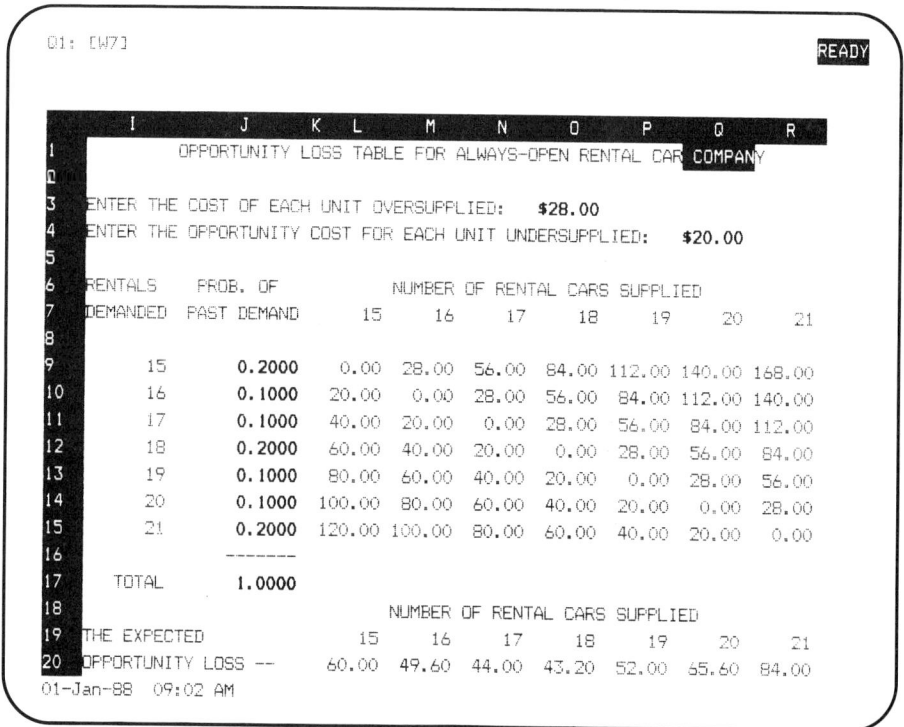

```
        \C      {PANELOFF}{GOTO}INAREA~{GOTO}OVER~  *--- To enter the data ---*
                {GETNUMBER "Enter the cost of oversupplied: ",OVER}
                {GOTO}UNDER~
                {GETNUMBER "Enter the Opp. cost of undersupplied: ",UNDER}
                {GOTO}LOWER~
                {GETNUMBER "Enter the minimum car demanded: ",LOWER}
                {GOTO}PROB15~/re.{down 6}~
        PROBAB/RETEMP~         *--- Entering the probability for each event ---*
                {MENUCALL WARN}
                {GETNUMBER "Enter the probability of the cars demanded: ",PROB15}
                {DOWN}{LET TEMP,TEMP+PROB15}~
                {GETNUMBER "Enter the probability of the cars demanded: ",PROB16}
                {DOWN}{LET TEMP,TEMP+PROB16}~
                {GETNUMBER "Enter the probability of the cars demanded: ",PROB17}
                {DOWN}{LET TEMP,TEMP+PROB17}~
                {GETNUMBER "Enter the probability of the cars demanded: ",PROB18}
                {DOWN}{LET TEMP,TEMP+PROB18}~
                {GETNUMBER "Enter the probability of the cars demanded: ",PROB19}
                {DOWN}{LET TEMP,TEMP+PROB19}~
                {GETNUMBER "Enter the probability of the cars demanded: ",PROB20}
                {DOWN}{LET TEMP,TEMP+PROB20}~
                {GETNUMBER "Enter the probability of the cars demanded: ",PROB21}
                {LET TEMP,TEMP+PROB21}~{GOTO}PROB15~{PANELON}
                {IF TEMP=1}{BRANCH RESULT}
                {GETLABEL "The total prob.<>1, please hit <RET> and reenter.",JUNK}
                {GOTO}PROB15~{BRANCH PROBAB}~

        JUNK2            *--- Temporary storage ---*

        JUNK  Y          *--- Temporary storage ---*

        RESULT{GOTO}OUTPUT~       *--- Arrange the result and draw the graph ---*
                /DSDDATA~PPRIMARY~A~G~{GOTO}BEST~
                {GETLABEL "Enter `Y' or `y' to see the graph: ",JUNK}
                {IF JUNK<>"Y"}{QUIT}~
                {IF JUNK<>"y"}{QUIT}~
                /GRGTLXXAXIS~AVALUE~
                OSYFCO~QTFTHE OPPORTUNITY LOSS GRAPH~
                TXCARS SUPPLIED~TYTHE EXPECTED OPPORTUNITY LOSS~QQ
                {GETLABEL "Hit <RET> & F10 keys to see the graph. ",JUNK2}

        WARN  Now enter the probability of each event and watch out for the total.
              Make sure it is not more than 1. Hit <Return>
                        *--- Warning label for entering the probability ---*
```

Figure 19-1 (Continued) Macro-Based Program for Opportunity Loss Analysis

Earnings per share:

G	=	I/S, where:
G	=	earnings per share
I	=	net income
S	=	number of shares outstanding

Price to earnings ratio:

C	=	P/G, where
C	=	price to earnings ratio
P	=	market price per share
G	=	earnings per share

Quick ratio:

Q	=	A/L1, where
Q	=	quick ratio
A	=	quick assets
L1	=	current liabilities

Figure 19-1 Execution of Macro-Based Program for Opportunity Loss Analysis

```
*************************************************************************
                              DOCUMENTATION
*************************************************************************
THE PURPOSE OF THIS PROGRAM:
     To calculate the opportunity cost of over- and undersupplying
     rental cars for a fictitious car rental company.  It will calculate
     the opportunity cost and give the result according to the lowest
     opportunity cost.  It will also draw the opportunity cost graph.

INSTRUCTIONS:
  1. The macro for this program can be activated by pressing <ALT> and C
     keys simultaneously.

  2. You will be asked to enter several inputs while running the
     program.

  3. The first input is the cost of oversupplying per car, followed by
     the opportunity cost of undersupplying per car. Then you will be
     asked to enter the minimum number of rental cars demanded, then the
     probability for each demand. For example, if the probability of a
     certain number of cars is 12%, enter the probability as 0.12.

  4. If you made any mistakes, hit <CTRL> and <BREAK> keys
     simultaneously.  Hit <ESC> keys and follow step 1 to start again.

LIMITATIONS:
  1. The range of the cars calculated is limited to the [(minimum
     demanded) + additional 6 cars].

  2. You are not allowed to make any changes to the table.
```

Figure 19-1 (Continued)

```
Q22: (F2) [W7]                                                    READY

         I        J      K   L     M      N      O      P      Q      R
21
22 BELOW IS THE TABLE FOR THE OPPORTUNITY LOSS TABLE FOR THE CARS SUPPLIED
23 ARRANGED ACCORDING TO THE LOWEST OPPORTUNITY LOSS
24
25      CARS        OPPOR.
26   SUPPLIED         COST
27        18        $43.20  <------ The optimal solution
28        17        $44.00
29        16        $49.60
30        19        $52.00
31        15        $60.00
32        20        $65.60
33        21        $84.00
34
35
36
37
38
39
40
01-Jan-88  11:40 AM
```

Debt to equity ratio:

D = L2/E, where:
D = debt to equity ratio
L2 = total liabilities
E = owner's equity

We have developed a macro-based program to calculate seven of these ratios. The program is fully interactive. Figure 19-2 shows the documentation, the macro-based program, and the actual execution of the macro-based program.

Figure 19-2 Documentation for Macro-Based Financial Analysis Program

```
***********************************************************************
                            DOCUMENTATION
***********************************************************************
THE PURPOSE OF THE PROGRAM:
     This program will produce a balance sheet and an income statement
     and calculate the financial ratios for a fictitious company after
     the user has entered the values for the different variables upon
     request.

INSTRUCTIONS:
   1. The macro for this program can be activated by pressing <ALT> and
      A keys simultaneously.

   2. The user will be asked to input the values while the program is
      executing.

   3. The first section will ask the inputs for the company's assets. The
      inputs are: CASH, ACCOUNTS RECEIVABLE, INVENTORY, LONG-TERM
      INVESTMENTS, PLANT & EQUIPMENT, and ACCUMULATED DEPRECIATION.

   4. The second section will ask the inputs for the company's
      liabilities and owners' equity. The inputs are: ACCOUNTS
      PAYABLE, TAXES PAYABLE, BONDS PAYABLE, COMMON STOCK, and RETAINED
      EARNINGS.

   5. The program will check the balance of the balance sheet.  It will
      alert the user if the balance sheet is not balanced.

   6. The third section will ask the inputs for the company's income
      statement. It will calculate the company's income. The inputs
      are: SALES, COST OF GOODS SOLD, SELLING EXPENSES, ADMINISTRATIVE
      EXPENSES, INTEREST EXPENSES, and CORPORATE TAX LEVEL.

   7. The fourth section is where all the financial ratios are. They are:
      A. EARNINGS PER SHARE    = Net Income / (Common Stock / Par Value).
      B. PRICE-EARNINGS RATIO  = Stock Price / Earnings Per Share.
      C. RETURN ON ASSETS      = (Net Inc.+(Int.Exp.*(1-Income Tax)))/
                                 Total Assets.
      D. QUICK RATIO           = (Current Asset - Inventory)/Current
                                 Liabilities.
      E. CURRENT RATIO         = Current Assets/Current Liabilities.
      F. DEBT TO EQUITY RATIO  = (Current Liabilities + Bonds)/Total
                                 Stockholders' Equity.
      G. RETURN ON INVESTMENT  = Net Income / Stockholders' Equity.

   8. When you are done entering all the inputs, a menu will appear. Use
      the cursor keys to make the selection and hit <RETURN>.

   9. If you made any mistakes while entering the inputs, hit <CTRL>
      and <BREAK> keys simultaneously followed by <ESC>.  Repeat
      step 1 to start again.

LIMITATIONS:
   1. The user may not change the format of the balance sheet and income
      statement because it is predefined.
```

```
\A   {GOTO}BALANCE~{GOTO}CASH~          *--- To enter the input to Balance Sheet ---*
     {GETNUMBER "Enter the cash amount: ",CASH}{DOWN}
     {GETNUMBER "Enter the amount acc. receivable: ",ACC.REC}{DOWN}
     {GETNUMBER "Enter the amount on Inventory: ",INV}{GOTO}LT.INV~
     {GETNUMBER "Enter the amount of Long Term Investment: ",LT.INV}
     {GOTO}PLANT~
     {GETNUMBER "Enter the amount of Plant & Equipment: ",PLANT}
     {GOTO}DEPRE~
     {GETNUMBER "Enter the amount of Depreciation: ",DEPRE}{GOTO}TOT.AS.~
     /reOFF~{LET OFF,OFF+TOT.AS.}~
     {GETLABEL "Hit <RETURN> key to go to the LIABILITIES section",JUNK}
     {PGDN}{GOTO}ACC.PAY~             *--- Liabilities & Owners' Equities Section ---*
     {GETNUMBER "Enter the amount of Account Payable: ",ACC.PAY}
     {LET OFF,OFF-ACC.PAY}~
     {GOTO}TAX.PAY~
     {GETNUMBER "Enter the amount of Taxes Payable: ",TAX.PAY}
     {LET OFF,OFF-TAX.PAY}~
     {GOTO}BONDS~
     {GETNUMBER "Enter the amount of Bonds Payables: ",BONDS}
     {LET OFF,OFF-BONDS}~
     {GOTO}STOCK~
     {GETNUMBER "Enter the amount of Common Stock: ",STOCK}
     {LET OFF,OFF-STOCK}~
     {GOTO}RET.EARN~
     {GETNUMBER "Enter the amount of Retained Earnings: ",RET.EARN}
     {LET OFF,OFF-RET.EARN}~
     {GOTO}TOT.EQ~{IF (TOT.AS.-TOT.EQ)>0}{BRANCH NO}~
     {IF (TOT.EQ-TOT.AS.)>0}{BRANCH NOT}
     {GETLABEL "Hit <RET> to go to the INCOME STATEMENT. ",JUNK}
     {GOTO}R1~{GOTO}SALES~            *--- Income Statement Section ---*
     {GETNUMBER "Enter the amount Sales: ",SALES}{GOTO}COGS~
     {GETNUMBER "Enter the amount of Cost Of Goods Sold: ",COGS}
     {GOTO}SELL.EXP~
     {GETNUMBER "Enter the amount of Selling Expenses: ",SELL.EXP}
     {GOTO}AD.EXP.~
     {GETNUMBER "Enter the amount of Advertising Expenses: ",AD.EXP.}
     {GOTO}INT.EXP~
     {GETNUMBER "Enter the amount of Interest Expenses: ",INT.EXP}
     {GOTO}TAX~
     {GETNUMBER "Enter the corporate tax level (in percent): ",TAX}{GOTO}NI~
     {GETLABEL "Hit <RET> to go to the calculated RATIOS. ",JUNK}
     {GOTO}Z1~{GOTO}ST.PRICE~         *--- Financial Ratios ---*
     {GETNUMBER "Enter the price of the stock:",ST.PRICE}~
     {GETLABEL "Hit <RETURN> key to get the menu.",JUNK}
     {GETLABEL "Use the cursor keys to make your choice and hit <RETURN>.",JUNK}
O    {MENUBRANCH MENU}

MENUAssets          Liabilities          Income Statement     Financial Ratios     Quit
     View Total AsseView Total LiabilitiView Income StatemenView Financial RatioTo QUIT the program.
     {GOTO}INPUT~     {GOTO}SECOND~       {GOTO}INC~           {GOTO}z1~            {QUIT}
     {BRANCH O}       {BRANCH O}          {BRANCH O}           {BRANCH O}

                 *--- Menu for the result ---*
junk

NO   {BEEP 3}~
     {██████ ██████ ██████ ████ █████ ████ ████████ █ ██████ ████████ " JUNK}
     {BRANCH \A}~


NOT  {BEEP 3}~
     {GETLABEL "TOTAL LIABILITIES & OWNERS' EQUITIES is more than TOTAL ASSETS.",JUNK}
     {BRANCH \A}~
```

Figure 19-2 (Continued) Macro-Based Program Performing Financial Analysis

Figure 19-2 (Continued) Execution of Macro-Based Financial Analysis Program

```
Q1: [W3]                                                          READY

      I  J    K      L       M       N         O        P      Q
1
2                      BALANCE SHEET
3    ==========================================================
4                        ASSETS                        19XX
5    CURRENT ASSETS:
6        CASH ..............................................  $4,309,000
7        ACCOUNTS RECEIVABLE ..............................   2,070,000
8        INVENTORY ........................................     580,000
9                                                            -----------
10          TOTAL CURRENT ASSETS ...........................   6,959,000
11
12   LONG-TERM INVESTMENT ..................................     500,400
13   PLANT & EQUIPMENT ..........................   400,500
14   LESS: ACCUMULATED DEPRECIATION ........    58,000
15                                                -----------
16   NET PLANT & EQUIPMENT ..................................   342,500
17                                                            -----------
18   TOTAL ASSETS ...........................................  $7,859,900
19                                                            ===========
20
01-Jan-88   09:39 AM
```

Figure 19-2 (Continued)

```
Q21: [W3]                                                         READY

      I  J    K      L       M       N         O        P      Q
21
22            CURRENT LIABILITIES AND OWNERS' EQUITY
23   ==========================================================
24   CURRENT LIABILITIES
25        ACCOUNTS PAYABLE ..................................  $4,000,500
26        TAXES PAYABLE ....................................   2,000,500
27                                                            -----------
28          TOTAL CURRENT LIABILITIES ......................   6,001,000
29   BONDS PAYABLE .........................................     550,000
30
31   STOCKHOLDERS' EQUITY
32        COMMON STOCK, $15.00 par value ..........   150,000
33        RETAINED EARNINGS .......................  1,158,900
34                                                -----------
35          TOTAL STOCKHOLDERS' EQUITY .....................   1,308,900
36                                                            -----------
37   TOTAL LIABILITIES & STOCKHOLDERS' EQUITY ...............  $7,859,900
38                                                            ===========
39        This balance sheet is off by           $0
40
01-Jan-88   09:40 AM
```

Figure 19-2 (Continued)

```
R1: [W4]                                                                    READY

        R    S      T       U        V              W           X         Y
1                          INCOME STATEMENT
2        ==========================================================
3                                    19XX
4        SALES ..........................................  $7,800,000
5        COST OF GOODS SOLD ............................   1,500,000
6                                                          --------
7        GROSS MARGIN ..................................   6,300,000
8        OPERATING EXPENSES
9             SELLING EXPENSES ...............    900,500
10            ADMINISTRATIVE EXPENSES ........  1,250,000
11                                              ------------
12            TOTAL OPERATING EXPENSES ...................   2,150,500
13                                                           --------
14       NET OPERATING INCOME  .........................   4,149,500
15       INTEREST EXPENSES .............................      15,000
16                                                          --------
17       NET INCOME BEFORE TAXES .......................   4,134,500
18       INCOME TAXES AT    46% .........................   2,232,630
19                                                          ========
20       NET INCOME ....................................  $1,901,870
01-Jan-88  09:42 AM
```

Figure 19-2 (Continued)

```
AH1: \=                                                                     READY

        Z     AA      AB     AC     AD     AE     AF     AG       AH
1       ==============================================================  ========
2                            FINANCIAL RATIOS
3       --------------------------------------------------------------
4
5          1. EARNINGS PER SHARE ..........................  $190.19
6
7          2. PRICE-EARNINGS RATIO
8             ASSUMING STOCK MARKET PRICE AT $29 .........   0.1525
9
10         3. RETURN ON ASSETS ............................   0.2430
11
12         4. QUICK RATIO .................................   1.0630
13
14         5. CURRENT RATIO ...............................   1.1596
15
16         6. DEBT TO EQUITY RATIO ........................   5.0050
17
18         7. RETURN ON INVESTMENT ........................   1.4530
19
20
01-Jan-88  09:43 AM
```

19-15 Capital Budgeting Analysis

Many financial analyses are classified under the capital budgeting domain. Present value, future value, internal rate of return, and return on investment are some of the most important techniques used in capital budgeting analysis. To show a simple example, we have developed a macro-based program designed to calculate net present value (NPV), internal rate of return (IRR), and the profitability index (PI). Figure 19-3 shows the documentation, the macro-based program, and the execution of this macro-based program.

Figure 19-3 Documentation for Capital Budgeting Problems

```
***********************************************************************
                             DOCUMENTATION
***********************************************************************
THE PURPOSE OF THE PROGRAM:
    To calculate the NPV, IRR, and PI of a proposed project of
    replacing an old machine with a new automated machine.  The old
    machine is currently operated by a worker. The new machine
    requires no worker to operate it.

INSTRUCTIONS:
    1. To activate the macro for this program, press <ALT> and Q keys
       simultaneously.

    2. You will be asked to enter the inputs while running the program.

    3. The first part of the program will ask the information on the old
       equipment: all the costs associated with the old equipment, the
       original price, the expected salvage value, the expected life
       (from beginning), and the current age of the equipment. The
       corporate tax level and the required rate of return are asked in
       this module.

    4. The second part will ask for the information on the new proposed
       equipment. It will ask for the costs of the machine, delivered
       and installed. It will also ask for the expected economic life
       of the machine and expected salvage value after 10 years of
       service.

    5. The third part will show the initial cash outlay for the project.

    6. The fourth part will show the calculation of the cash flow for the
       project. It will calculate all the savings deducted by the costs
       and taxes giving the annual cash flow after taxes.

    7. The last part will show the yearly cash flow, the calculated net
       present value, profitability index, and internal rate of return.
       The conclusion will be given depending on the NPV, IRR and PI.
       The formula used:
       NPV = @NPV(Com. Req. Rate of Return, CashFlow) - Initial
             Cash outflow
       PI  = NPV / ABS(Initial Cash outflow)
       IRR = @IRR (Com. Req. Rate of Return, Cash inflow +
             Initial Cash outflow)

    8. If you make a mistake, hit <CTRL> & <BREAK> keys simultaneously
       to stop the program. To start all over again, hit <ESC> and
       follow step 1.

LIMITATIONS:
    1. The tables are predefined, so you have to follow the instructions
       while running the program.

    2. The cash flow will be calculated for only 10 years.

    3. Depreciation is calculated using the straight-line method.

    4. You are not allowed to make any changes to the table.
```

```
\Q  {GOTO}INPUT~{PANELOFF}               *--- The Current Situation Data ---*
    {GETLABEL "Hit <RETURN> key and enter the current situation data.",JUNK}{GOTO}CSSALARY~
    {GETNUMBER "Enter the salary of the worker (per annum): ",CSSALARY}
    {DOWN}
    {GETNUMBER "Enter the overtime pay (per annum): ",CSO/TIME}
    {DOWN}
    {GETNUMBER "Enter the fringe benefits (insur.,paid vacation, etc. per annum): ",CSBENEFIT}
    {DOWN}
    {GETNUMBER "Enter the cost of defects (per annum) caused by the machine: ",CSDEFECT}
    {DOWN}
    {GETNUMBER "Enter the original price of the machine: ",CSPRICE}
    {DOWN}
    {GETNUMBER "What's the expected life (from beginning) of the old machine: ",CSLIFE}
    {DOWN}
    {GETNUMBER "Enter the expected salvage value of the machine: ",CSSALVAGE}
    {DOWN}
    {GETNUMBER "How old is the machine: ",CSAGE}
    {DOWN 2}
    {GETNUMBER "What's the current book value of old machine: ",CSCURSALVAGE}
    {DOWN}
    {GETNUMBER "Enter the annual maintenance: ",CSMAINTAIN}
    {DOWN}
    {GETNUMBER "Enter the marginal tax rate (in percent): ",CSTAX}
    {DOWN}
    {GETNUMBER "Enter the company required rate of return (in percent): ",CSRROR}{DOWN}
    {GETLABEL "Hit <RETURN> key to go to the proposed situation section",JUNK}
    {GOTO}I21~        *--- The Proposed Situation Data ---*
    {GETLABEL "Hit <RETURN> key and enter the data for the new machine",JUNK}
    {GOTO}PSCOST~
    {GETNUMBER "Enter the cost of new machine: ",PSCOST}
    {DOWN}
    {GETNUMBER "Enter the shipping fee: ",PSFEE}
    {DOWN}
    {GETNUMBER "Enter the installation cost: ",PSINSTALL}
    {DOWN}
    {GETNUMBER "Enter the expected life of new machine: ",PSLIFE}
    {GOTO}PSSALVAGE~
    {GETNUMBER "Enter the expected salvage value of new machine: ",PSSALVAGE}
    {DOWN}
    {GETNUMBER "Enter the expected annual maintenance cost: ",PSMAINTAIN}
    {DOWN}
    {GETNUMBER "What's the exp. cost of defects caused by the new machine (per annum):",PSDEFECT}
    {GETLABEL "Hit the <RETURN> key to get the menu. ",JUNK}
O   {menubranch AX}

TEMP                    *--- Temporary Storage ---*

JUNK                    *--- Temporary Storage ---*

AX  Initial Cash Outlay CashFlow Section The Conclusion    QUIT
    The calculation of IThe calculation oThe Results (NPV,Quit the program.
    {GOTO}I41~          {GOTO}I61~        {GOTO}I81~          {PANELON}
    {BRANCH O}          {BRANCH O}        {BRANCH O}          {QUIT}

    *--- The Menu to see the RESULT ---*
```

Figure 19-3 Macro-Based Program Performing Capital Budgeting Analysis

Figure 19-3 (Cont.) Execution of the Macro-Based Capital Budgeting Program

```
P1: \x                                                              READY

          I    J      K        L         M        N       O        P
1    xxxxxxxxxxxxxxxxxxxxxxxxxxxxxxxxxxxxxxxxxxxxxxxxxxxxxxxxxxxxxxxxxxxxxx
2               INPUT SECTION
3    xxxxxxxxxxxxxxxxxxxxxxxxxxxxxxxxxxxxxxxxxxxxxxxxxxxxxxxxxxxxxxxxxxxxxx
4                      PART ONE:
5
6    Current Situation:
7        Salary one full-time worker ......................  $12,000 /per year
8        Overtime pay .....................................   $1,000 /per year
9        Fringe Benefits ..................................   $2,000 /per year
10       Cost of defect ...................................   $1,000 /per year
11       Original price of hand-operated machine ..........  $20,000
12       Expected life ....................................       20 years
13       Salvage value ....................................       $0
14       Age of the machine ...............................        5 years
15       Depreciation method .............................. Straight line
16       Current salvage value ............................   $5,000
17       Annual maintenance ...............................   $1,500
18       Tax rate .........................................    46.0%
19       Required rate of return ..........................    16.7%
20
01-Jan-88   09:39 AM
```

Figure 19-3 (Continued)

```
P21:                                                                READY

          I    J      K        L         M        N       O        P
21
22
23                     PART TWO:
24
25   Proposed Situation: Automated operation
26       Cost of machine ..................................  $50,000
27       Shipping fee .....................................     $500
28       Installation cost ................................     $450
29       Expected economic life ...........................       20 years
30       Depreciation method .............................. Straight line
31       Salvage value after 10 years .....................       $0
32       Annual maintenance ...............................     $350
33       Cost of defect ...................................     $250 /per year
34
35
36
37
38
39
40
01-Jan-88   09:40 AM
```

Figure 19-3 (Continued)

```
P41: \x                                                                RE-DY


       I     J        K          L            M        N        O          P
41 xxxxxxxxxxxxxxxxxxxxxxxxxxxxxxxxxxxxxxxxxxxxxxxxxxxxxxxxxxxxxxxxxxx.........
42            OUTPUT SECTION
43 xxxxxxxxxxxxxxxxxxxxxxxxxxxxxxxxxxxxxxxxxxxxxxxxxxxxxxxxxxxxxxxxxxxxxxxxxxxx
44
45
46                          Initial Outlay
47 Outflows
48     Cost of new machine ............................. $50,000
49     Shipping fee ...................................     500
50     Installation cost .............................     450
51     Increased taxes ...............................  (4,600)
52 Inflows
53     Salvage value-old machine ...................  -   5,000
54                                                       -------
55     Net Initial Outlay ............................ $41,350
56
57
58
59
60
01-Jan-88  09:41 AM
```

Figure 19-3 (Continued)

```
P61:                                                                   READY


       I     J        K          L            M        N        O          P
61
62                                                          Non-cash
63 Calculation of Differential Cash Flows               flow profit  Cash Flow
64 Savings:
65     Reduced salary ...................................  $12,000   $12,000
66     Reduced overtime .................................    1,000     1,000
67     Reduced fringe benefits .........................     2,000     2,000
68     Reduced defects .................................       750       750
69 Costs:
70     Increased maintenance expenses ..................     (350)     (350)
71     Increased depreciation expenses .................   (1,548)
72                                                         -------   -------
73 Net savings before taxes ............................  $13,853   $15,400
74 Taxes ...............................................    6,372     6,372
75                                                         -------   -------
76 Net Cash Flow after taxes ...........................            $9,028
77
78
79
80
01-Jan-88  09:43 AM
```

```
P81:                                                              READY

     I     J       K       L          M          N        O        P
81
82
83        Year  Cash Flow
84         0   ($41,350)        The Net Present Value (NPV) at
85         1    $9,028               $1,170
86         2    $9,028          The Profitability Index (PI)
87         3    $9,028               1.028
88         4    $9,028          The Internal Rate of Return (IRR)
89         5    $9,028               17.47%
90         6    $9,028          The company's Required Rate of Return
91         7    $9,028               16.70%
92         8    $9,028
93         9    $9,028          * CONCLUSION
94        10    $9,028          Accept the project
95
96
97    *  This conclusion is based on the  NPV, PI, and IRR. The conditions
98       are NPV > 0, PI > 1.00, and IRR > Company Required Rate of Return
99       for the project to be accepted.
100
     01-Jan-88  09:44 AM
```

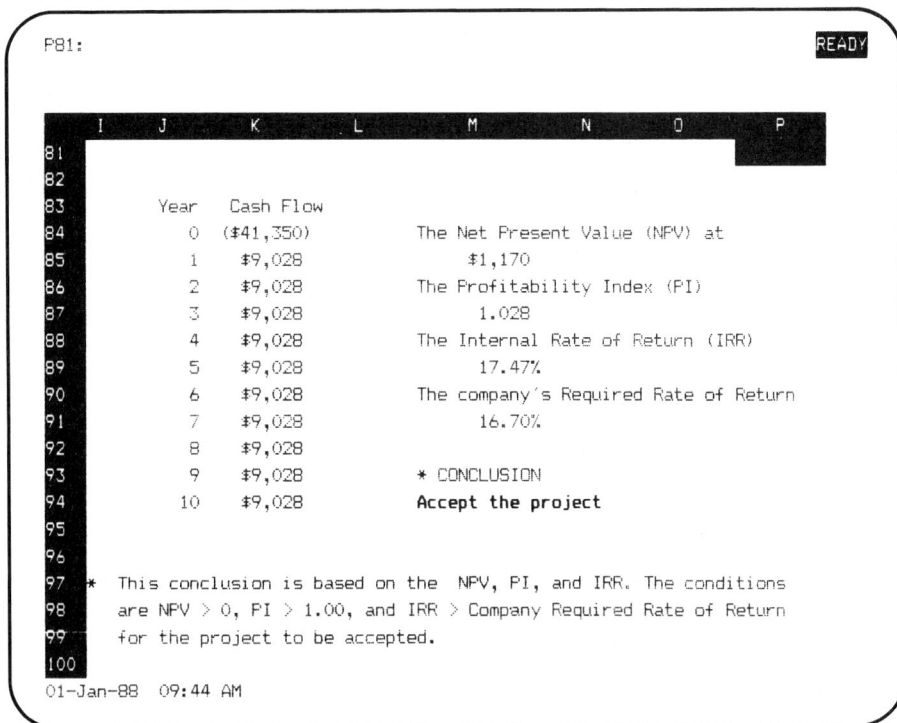

Figure 19-3   (Continued)

19-16 Accounting Applications: A Second Look

Preparing a balance sheet and an income statement are two of the most common tasks performed by any organization. Regardless of the size of the company, a balance sheet and an income statement are needed to determine its financial status. Balance sheets and income statements can be very long and complicated. However, they all follow the same format. We have developed a macro-based program to prepare these two important financial statements for you. This simple model should give you ideas for developing any balance sheet and income statements. Figure 19-4 shows the documentation, the macro-based program, and the execution of this macro-based program.

19-17 S-Curve

Forecasting, or projecting the future of total sales, total expenses, manpower planning, etc., is a common practice in the business world. In order to predict the future of a particular variable, some previous data is needed. Depending on the nature of the data (seasonal, trend, cyclical) and the time horizon for the forecast (short range, medium range, long range), different forecasting models can be chosen. As we discussed in Chapter 15, /Data Regression provides you with a tool for long-range forecasting. There are many forecasting tools, such as moving average, exponential smoothing, and multivariate forecast. Any of these models can

```
**********************************************************************
                            DOCUMENTATION
**********************************************************************
THE PURPOSE OF THIS PROGRAM:
     This program will produce a balance sheet and an income statement
     after the user has entered the values for the different variables
     upon request.

INSTRUCTIONS:
  1. The macro for this program can be activated by pressing <ALT> & A
     keys simultaneously.

  2. The user will be asked to input the values while the program is
     executing.

  3. The first section will ask the inputs for the company's assets. The
     inputs are: CASH, ACCOUNTS RECEIVABLE, INVENTORY, LONG-TERM
     INVESTMENTS, PLANT & EQUIPMENT, and ACCUMULATED DEPRECIATION.

  4. The second section will ask for the company's liabilities and
     owners' equity. The inputs are: ACCOUNTS PAYABLE, TAXES PAYABLE,
     BONDS PAYABLE, COMMON STOCK, and RETAINED EARNINGS.

  5. The program will check the balance of the balance sheet. It
     will make sure that the TOTAL ASSETS will be equal to the TOTAL
     LIABILITIES and OWNERS' EQUITY.

  6. If the balance sheet is balanced, then it will go to the income
     statement. It will calculate the company's income. The inputs are:
     SALES, COST OF GOODS SOLD, SELLING EXPENSES, ADMINISTRATIVE
     EXPENSES, INTEREST EXPENSES, and CORPORATE TAX LEVEL.

  7. When you are done with the income statement, a menu will appear.
     Use the cursor keys to make your selection and hit <RETURN>.

  8. If you made any mistakes while entering the inputs, hit <CTRL>
     & <BREAK> simultaneously followed by <ESC>.  Repeat step
     1 to restart.

LIMITATIONS:
  1. The user may not change the format of the balance sheet and income
     statement because it is predefined.
```

Figure 19-4 Documentation for Macro-Based Balance Sheet and Income Statement

be translated into Lotus in order to generate a forecast. As an example we have chosen the S-curve for such a translation.

The S-curve model is a long-range forecasting model (two years or more). An S-curve model has a slow start, a rather steep growth, and a saturation point that comes after some period of time. The introduction of a new product, an information system life cycle, or the usefulness of a new machine all follow an S-curve model. There are several mathematical presentations of the S-curve model. The following formula is one way of showing this model:

$$Yt = e^{A+B/t}$$

Where Yt is the S-curve estimate, e is the constant equal to 2.718, A is the equivalent of the intercept in the linear regression model, B is the equivalent of the slope in the linear regression model, and t is time.

Since the relationship between the independent variable (t) and the dependent variable (Y) is not linear, the classical least-squares method does not apply to this model. However, by taking the logarithm of both sides, we can convert this form to a linear one, as follows:

$$\text{Log}Yt = (\frac{A + B}{t}) \text{Log } e^e \quad (\text{Log } e^e = 1)$$

```
\A  {GOTO}INPUT~{GOTO}CASH~              *--- The balance sheet input section ---*
    {GETNUMBER "Enter the cash amount: ",CASH}{DOWN}
    {GETNUMBER "Enter the amount acc. receivable:",ACC.REC}{DOWN}
    {GETNUMBER "Enter the amount on Inventory:",INV}{GOTO}LT.INV~
    {GETNUMBER "Enter the amount of Long Term Investment:",LT.INV}
    {GOTO}PLANT~
    {GETNUMBER "Enter the amount of Plant & Equipment:",PLANT}
    {GOTO}DEPRE~
    {GETNUMBER "Enter the amount of Depreciation:",DEPRE}{GOTO}TOT.AS.~
    /reOFF~
    {LET OFF,OFF+TOT.AS.}~
    {GETLABEL "Hit <RETURN> key to go to the LIABILITIES section",JUNK}{PGDN}
    {GOTO}ACC.PAY~                       *--- Liabilities & Owners' Equities Section ---*
    {GETNUMBER "Enter the amount of Account Payable:",ACC.PAY}
    {LET OFF,OFF-ACC.PAY}~
    {GOTO}TAX.PAY~
    {GETNUMBER "Enter the amount of Taxes Payable:",TAX.PAY}
    {LET OFF,OFF-TAX.PAY}~
    {GOTO}BONDS~
    {GETNUMBER "Enter the amount of Bonds Payables:",BONDS}
    {LET OFF,OFF-BONDS}~
    {GOTO}STOCK~
    {GETNUMBER "Enter the amount of Common Stock:",STOCK}
    {LET OFF,OFF-STOCK}~
    {GOTO}RET.EARN~
    {GETNUMBER "Enter the amount of Retained Earnings:",RET.EARN}
    {LET OFF,OFF-RET.EARN}~
    {IF (TOT.AS.-TOT.EQ)>0}{BRANCH NO}
    {IF (TOT.EQ-TOT.AS.)>0}{BRANCH NOT}
    {GETLABEL "Hit <RETURN> key to go to the income statement section",JUNK}
    {GOTO}INC~{GOTO}SALES~               *--- Income Statement Section ---*
    {GETNUMBER "Enter the amount Sales:",SALES}{GOTO}COGS~
    {GETNUMBER "Enter the amount of Cost Of Goods Sold:",COGS}
    {GOTO}SELL.EXP~
    {GETNUMBER "Enter the amount of Selling Expenses:",SELL.EXP}
    {GOTO}AD.EXP.~
    {GETNUMBER "Enter the amount of Advertising Expenses:",AD.EXP.}
    {GOTO}INT.EXP~
    {GETNUMBER "Enter the amount of Interest Expenses:",INT.EXP}
    {GOTO}TAXLEVEL~
    {GETNUMBER "Enter the corporate tax level (in percent): ",TAXLEVEL}
    {GOTO}NI~
    {GETLABEL "Hit <RETURN> key to get the menu.",JUNK}
    {GETLABEL "Use the cursor keys to make your choice and hit <RETURN>.",JUNK}
O   {MENUBRANCH MENU}

MENUAssets           Liabilities         Income Statement    Quit
    View Total AsseView Liabilities & OView Income StatemenQuit the program
    {GOTO}INPUT~      {GOTO}SECOND~       {GOTO}INC~          {QUIT}
    {BRANCH O}        {BRANCH O}          {BRANCH O}

junk                 *--- Temporary storage ---*

NO  {BEEP 5}
    {GETLABEL "TOTAL ASSETS is more than TOTAL LIABILITIES & OWNERS' EQUITIES. ",JUNK}
    {BRANCH \A}

NOT {BEEP 5}
    {GETLABEL "TOTAL LIABILITIES & OWNERS' EQUITIES is more than TOTAL ASSETS. ",JUNK}
    {BRANCH \A}
```

Figure 19-4 (Continued) Macro-Based Program for Preparing a Balance Sheet and an Income Statement

and if we replace $\frac{1}{t}$ by T, Log Yt by t we will have

$$Xt = A + BT$$

As we see, this has a linear form and we can apply the classical least-squares method in order to estimate the values for A and B (see the discussion of simple linear regression in Chapter 15).

We have developed a macro-based program which fits an S-curve to a series of data. Figure 19-5 shows the documentation, the macro-based program, and the execution of the program.

Figure 19-4 (Continued) Execution of Macro-Based Accounting Program

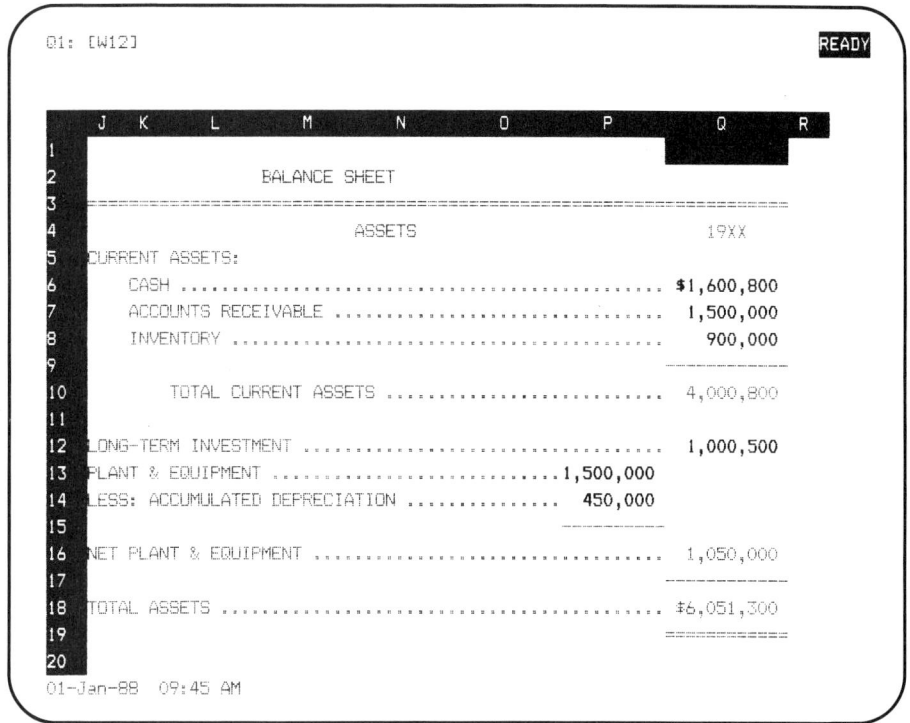

```
01: [W12]                                                              READY

     J   K    L      M       N        O        P         Q        R
1
2                         BALANCE SHEET
3    ==================================================================
4                            ASSETS                        19XX
5    CURRENT ASSETS:
6        CASH ...............................................  $1,600,800
7        ACCOUNTS RECEIVABLE ...............................    1,500,000
8        INVENTORY .........................................      900,000
9                                                             -----------
10          TOTAL CURRENT ASSETS ...........................    4,000,800
11
12   LONG-TERM INVESTMENT ..................................    1,000,500
13   PLANT & EQUIPMENT ......................1,500,000
14   LESS: ACCUMULATED DEPRECIATION ...............  450,000
15                                                   -----------
16   NET PLANT & EQUIPMENT .................................    1,050,000
17                                                             -----------
18   TOTAL ASSETS .........................................   $6,051,300
19                                                             ===========
20
01-Jan-88  09:45 AM
```

Figure 19-4 (Continued)

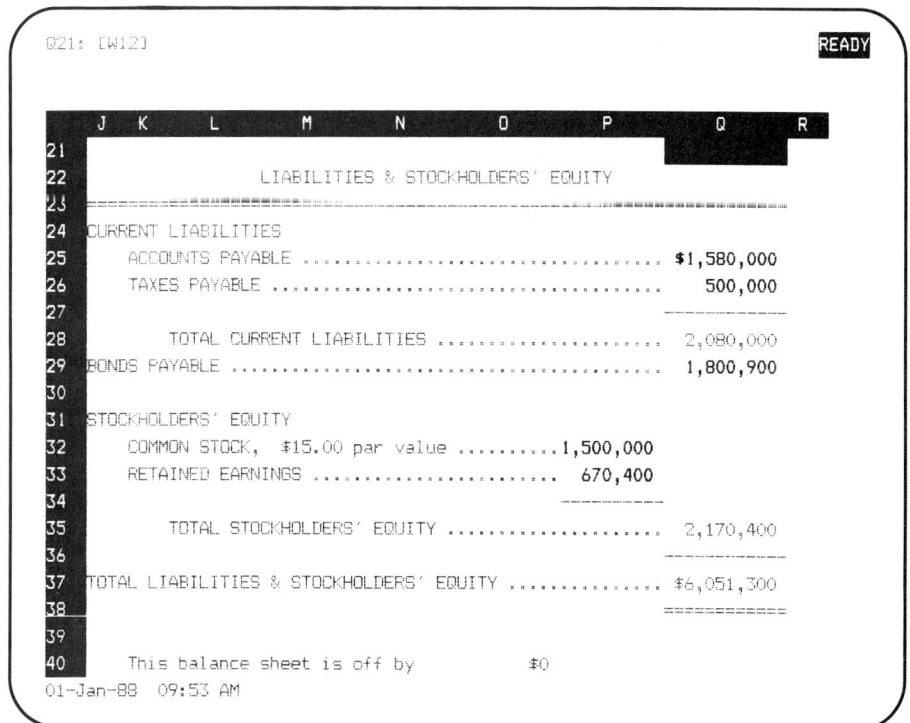

```
021: [W12]                                                             READY

     J   K    L      M       N        O        P         Q        R
21
22               LIABILITIES & STOCKHOLDERS' EQUITY
23   ==================================================================
24   CURRENT LIABILITIES
25       ACCOUNTS PAYABLE ..................................  $1,580,000
26       TAXES PAYABLE .....................................      500,000
27                                                             -----------
28          TOTAL CURRENT LIABILITIES ......................    2,080,000
29   BONDS PAYABLE .........................................    1,800,900
30
31   STOCKHOLDERS' EQUITY
32       COMMON STOCK,  $15.00 par value ..........1,500,000
33       RETAINED EARNINGS ........................  670,400
34                                                   -----------
35          TOTAL STOCKHOLDERS' EQUITY .....................    2,170,400
36                                                             -----------
37   TOTAL LIABILITIES & STOCKHOLDERS' EQUITY ..............   $6,051,300
38                                                             ===========
39
40       This balance sheet is off by           $0
01-Jan-88  09:53 AM
```

Figure 19-4 (Continued)

```
Z1: [W13]                                                              READY

        S   T      U        V       W         X       Y          Z
1                         INCOME STATEMENT
2       ============================================================
3                            19XX
4       SALES .................................................. $2,800,500
5       COST OF GOODS SOLD .....................................  1,200,000
6                                                                ----------
7       GROSS MARGIN ..........................................  1,600,500
8       OPERATING EXPENSES
9            SELLING EXPENSES .......................  580,000
10           ADMINISTRATIVE EXPENSES ................  600,000
11                                                              ----------
12           TOTAL OPERATING EXPENSES ..........................  1,180,000
13                                                                ----------
14      NET OPERATING INCOME  .................................    420,500
15      INTEREST EXPENSES .....................................     12,000
16                                                                ----------
17      NET INCOME BEFORE TAXES ...............................    408,500
18      INCOME TAXES AT .. 46% ................................    220,590
19                                                                ==========
20      NET INCOME ............................................  $187,910
01-Jan-88  09:04 AM
```

Figure 19-5 Documentation for the Macro-Based S-Curve Model

```
****************************************************************
                        DOCUMENTATION
****************************************************************
THE PURPOSE OF THIS PROGRAM:
     To calculate the S-curve model (2 years or more) for the long-range
     forecasting model.  It will calculate the slope and intercept point
     for the S-curve and draw the S-curve graph.

INSTRUCTIONS:
  1. The macro for this program can be activated by pressing <ALT> and Z
     keys simultaneously.

  2. You will be asked to input several variables and some other inputs
     while running the macro.

  3. The first input is how many sets of data the user wants to
     consider. Then it will ask the user to input the first independent
     variable followed by the first dependent variable. This will
     continue until the user has entered all the data.

  4. The next input will be the prediction data. The user will be asked
     if he/she wants to do any predicting; then the user has to input
     the value of independent variables.

  5. Finally, this program will draw the S-curve graph based on the
     calculated values.  The user will be asked if he/she wants the
     program to draw the S-curve graph.

  6. If you made any mistakes while entering the input, hit <CTRL>
     and <BREAK> simultaneously to stop the program.  Hit <ESC>
     and repeat step 1 to start all over again.

LIMITATIONS:
  1. To draw the graph, avoid overflowing, and make it easier to use,
     you should maximize the inputs to 17 sets of data.
```

```
\Z        {GOTO}INAREA~{PANELOFF}
          {GOTO}START~
          {GETNUMBER "How many sets of data to consider? ",DATA}~
          {FOR K,1,DATA,1,INPUT}{BRANCH LOOP}

INPUT     /XNEnter the independent var (X): ~~
          {RIGHT}            *--- To enter the data  ---*
          /XNEnter the dependent var (Y): ~~
          {DOWN}{LEFT}

DATA        10

K           11

LOOP      /RE{RIGHT}{PGDN}~{GOTO}HEAD~/REWORKAREA~      *---  get ready for new calculation  ---*
          {GOTO}TOTAL~/MTOTAL~{END}{UP}{LEFT}{DOWN}{END}{DOWN 3}{RIGHT}~{GOTO}HEAD~{DOWN}
          /C{RIGHT 3}~{DOWN}.{LEFT 2}{END}{DOWN}{RIGHT 5}~
          {GOTO}SUM(X2)~/RE~{GOTO}HEAD~{DOWN}
ONE       /RNCTEMP~~        *--- The accumulator macro for SUM(X2) ---*
          {GOTO}SUM(X2)~
          {IF TEMP>0}{LET SUM(X2),SUM(X2)+TEMP}~
          {IF TEMP>0}{ACCU}
          {IF TEMP>0}{BRANCH ONE}
          /RNDTEMP~
          {GOTO}SUM(Y2)~/RE~{GOTO}HEAD2~
          {DOWN}
DUA       /RNCTEMP~~        *--- The accumulator macro for SUM(Y2) ---*
          {GOTO}SUM(Y2)~
          {IF TEMP>0}{LET SUM(Y2),SUM(Y2)+TEMP}~
          {IF TEMP>0}{ACCU}
          {IF TEMP>0}{BRANCH DUA}
          /RNDTEMP~
          {GOTO}SUM(X2Y2)~/RE~{GOTO}HEAD3~
          {DOWN}
THREE     /RNCTEMP~~        *--- The accumulator macro for SUM(X2Y2) ---*
          {GOTO}SUM(X2Y2)~
          {IF TEMP>0}{LET SUM(X2Y2),SUM(X2Y2)+TEMP}~
          {IF TEMP>0}{ACCU}
          {IF TEMP>0}{BRANCH THREE}
          /RNDTEMP~
          {GOTO}SUM(X2^2)~/RE~{GOTO}HEAD4~
          {DOWN}
FOUR      /RNCTEMP~~        *--- The accumulator macro for SUM(X2^2) ---*
          {GOTO}SUM(X2^2)~
          {IF TEMP>0}{LET SUM(X2^2),SUM(X2^2)+TEMP}~
          {IF TEMP>0}{ACCU}
          {IF TEMP>0}{BRANCH FOUR}          *--- The Prediction Macro ---*
          /RNDTEMP~{GOTO}RESULT~{GOTO}NUM~{RECALC OUTPUT}~{PANELON}
          {GETLABEL "Do you want to do any prediction? (Y)es or (N)o: ",ANSWER}{RECALC OUTPUT}~
          {IF ANSWER<>"y"}{BRANCH DRAW}
          {IF ANSWER<>"Y"}{BRANCH DRAW}
AGAIN     {GETNUMBER "The value of Independent Var: ",NUM}{RECALC ANS}~
          {GETLABEL "Do you want to try another one (Y)es or (N)o ? ",ANSWER}
          {IF ANSWER="y"}{BRANCH AGAIN}
          {IF ANSWER="Y"}{BRANCH AGAIN}
DRAW      {GETLABEL "Do you want to draw the graph? (Yes) or (N)o: ",answer}
          {IF ANSWER<>"y"}{quit}
          {IF ANSWER<>"Y"}{quit}      *---  To draw the S-Curve graph  ---*
          {GOTO}AVAR~/GRGTLXX~A{DOWN}.{END}{DOWN}~
          BTWO~OLAGIVEN VARS~
          LBTHE S-CURVE~
          FASQTXDEPENDENT VARS~
          TYINDEPENDENT VARS~QQ
          {GOTO}RESULT~
          {GETLABEL "Hit the <RET> & F10 key to see the graph ",ANSWER}{PANELON}

ACCU      {GOTO}TEMP~        *--- The accumulator subroutine ---*
          /RNDTEMP~
          {DOWN}/RNCTEMP~~
          {RETURN}


ANSWER          *---  Temporary storage range  ---*
```

Figure 19-5 (Continued) Macro-Based Program for S-Curve Model

Figure 19-5 (Continued) Execution of the Macro-Based S-Curve Model

```
Z1: [W13]                                                                READY

        S  T      U        V        W          X        Y          Z
1                          INCOME STATEMENT
2  ====================================================================
3                               19XX
4       SALES ..................................................  $2,800,500
5       COST OF GOODS SOLD .....................................   1,200,000
6                                                                 ----------
7       GROSS MARGIN ...........................................   1,600,500
8       OPERATING EXPENSES
9            SELLING EXPENSES ........................    580,000
10           ADMINISTRATIVE EXPENSES .................    600,000
11                                                        ----------
12           TOTAL OPERATING EXPENSES ...........................   1,180,000
13                                                                 ----------
14      NET OPERATING INCOME  ..................................     420,500
15      INTEREST EXPENSES ......................................      12,000
16                                                                 ----------
17      NET INCOME BEFORE TAXES ................................     408,500
18      INCOME TAXES AT .. 46% .................................     220,590
19                                                                 ==========
20      NET INCOME .............................................    $187,910
01-Jan-88  09:54 AM
```

Figure 19-5 (Continued)

```
P1: [W12]                                                                READY

      I     J     K        L          M         N          O        P
1              THE INPUT SECTION:
2     X     Y          X2=1/X     Y2=LN(Y)    X2*Y2      X2^2
3     1     35         1.0000      2.3026     2.3026     1.0000
4     2     49         0.5000      3.8918     1.9459     0.2500
5     3     55         0.3333      4.0073     1.3358     0.1111
6     4     69         0.2500      4.2341     1.0585     0.0625
7     5     80         0.2000      4.3820     0.8764     0.0400
8     6    105         0.1667      4.6540     0.7757     0.0278
9     7    140         0.1429      4.9416     0.7059     0.0204
10    8    165         0.1250      5.1059     0.6382     0.0156
11    9    180         0.1111      5.1930     0.5770     0.0123
12   10    173         0.1000      5.1533     0.5153     0.0100
13
14              TOTAL   2.9290     43.8657   10.7314     1.5498
15
16
17
18
19
20
01-Jan-88  09:56 AM                                            CALC
```

```
Q1: [W5] "X'                                                   READY

        Q       R     S      T           U        V      W        X
1       X'          Y '    THE OUTPUT SECTION:
2       1      9.28
3       2     42.87
4       3     71.38    THE INTERCEPT FOR THE S-CURVE MODEL =      5.2827
5       4     91.63    THE SLOPE FOR THE S-CURVE MODEL =         -3.0594
6       5    106.78
7       6    118.24    VALUE OF THE INDEPENDENT VARS (X) =           13
8       7    127.18    ESTIMATED VALUE OF DEPENDENT VARS (Y) =   155.60
9       8    134.32
10      9    140.15
11     10    145.00
12     11    149.09
13     12    152.58
14     13    155.60
15     14    158.24
16     15    160.56
17     16    162.62
18     17    164.46
19     18    166.12
20     19    167.61
01-Jan-88   09:57 AM                            CALC
```

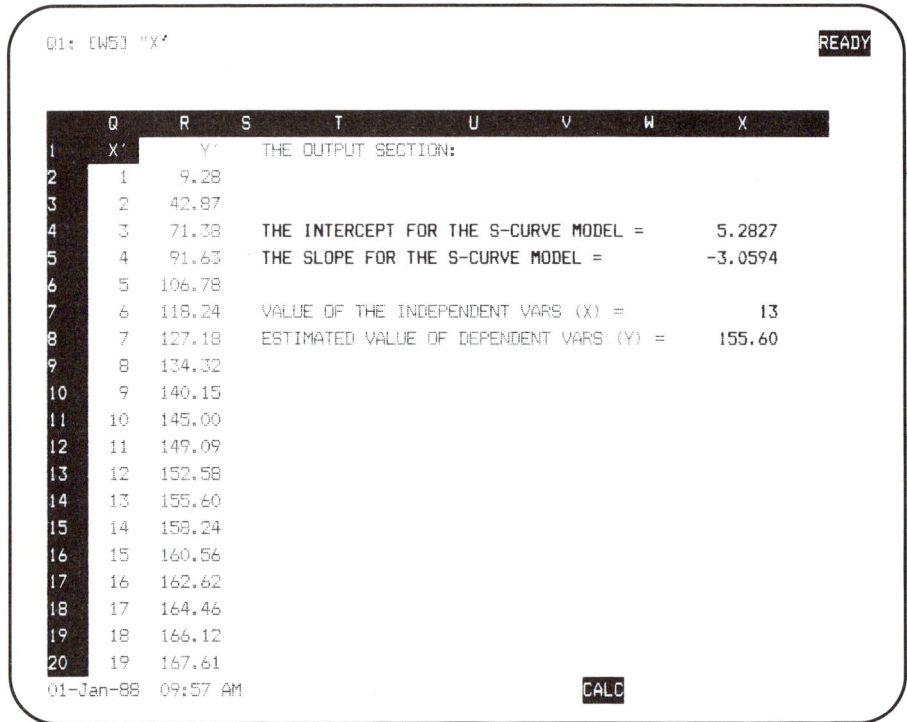

Figure 19-5 (Continued)

Summary

In this chapter we have discussed some of the common applications performed by Lotus. As you have seen Lotus can theoretically handle an unlimited number of applications. These applications can be solved directly using the Lotus worksheet or by developing a series of macros. The advantage of using macros is the user-friendliness of the process. The user of such a program does not need to have any previous knowledge about Lotus and/or the application area. Materials presented in this chapter should prepare you with enough background to develop much more sophisticated applications. Put your creativity into action!

Review Questions

1.* If A, B, and C are 1, 10, and 1, respectively, what is the positive root in quadratic equation?

2. If X, Y, and Z are 5, 10, and 12, respectively, what is the value of R in the following formula:

$$R = X^3 - XYZ + (X/Z)^Y$$

3.* If the world population is 4 billion now, the birth rate 2.6 percent and the death rate .9 percent, what is the world population predicted to be in the year 2010?

4. The following are grades of students in a Lotus class. Using /Data Distribution, organize this data into five groups in ascending order.

Jack	91	Susan	75
Joe	62	Mark	81
Mary	79	Valerie	83
Harry	79	Tina	72
Sherry	81	Steve	91
Bob	98	David	69
Barbara	46	Brad	85
Luke	98	Ellen	91

5. Design a home phone directory for 50 people. Sort it by two keys. The fields include first name, last name, street address, city, state, zip, age, sex, and telephone number.
6. Choose a balance sheet and calculate 7 ratios discussed in this chapter.
7. Using the S-curve model, create a forecast for the following data items:

X	Y
1	120
2	144
3	95
4	218
5	312

If $X = 14$, what is Y, based on your model?

8. Let us say that in the year 2000 you will need $58,000 for your children's college education. How much should you deposit in a bank now in order to have this amount in 2000 (assuming the interest rate is fixed at 10 percent)?
9.* What are some Lotus applications for running a small business?
10. In what capacity can Lotus be used in the marketing department of a travel agency?
11. What are some Lotus limitations in general?
12. The production of Generous Oil Well in Cactus City for the past six years is as follows:

1982	240,000 barrels
1983	290,000 barrels
1984	310,000 barrels
1985	285,000 barrels
1986	360,000 barrels
1987	395,000 barrels

Using simple regression, provide a forecast for the year 1997. Also generate a bar graph for the past six years.

---

* For more information on this technique and other business applications, see Hossein Bidgoli and Grover Rodich, <u>All Purpose BASIC,</u> Burgess, 1982, pp. 193-230.

Appendix A

You and Your PC:
A Friendly Interface

A-1 Introduction

In this appendix we will explain the different components of a microcomputer, discuss types of software, including system software and application software, and introduce some of the popular application software on the market. This should provide you with a better understanding of the operation of a microcomputer.

A-2 What Is a Microcomputer?

The terms personal computer, PC, or microcomputer refer to the smallest type of computer when measured by such attributes as memory size, speed, and sophistication. Although small, these computers are so powerful that sometimes the difference between a PC and minicomputer is blurred. The reason for such confusion is the ever-increasing power and capability of personal computers.

Since the beginning of the microcomputer era in roughly 1975, the capability of these computers has improved beyond imagination. Still, some experts believe this is only the beginning and there is a lot more to be done by these computers.

A typical microcomputer consists of input, output, and memory devices. Figure A-1 illustrates a typical microcomputer system. The input device is usually a keyboard. A keyboard is very similar to a typewriter, with some additional keys. Figure A-2 illustrates an IBM PC keyboard. In the future, there may be voice input devices on the market. Other input devices include mouse, touch technology, light

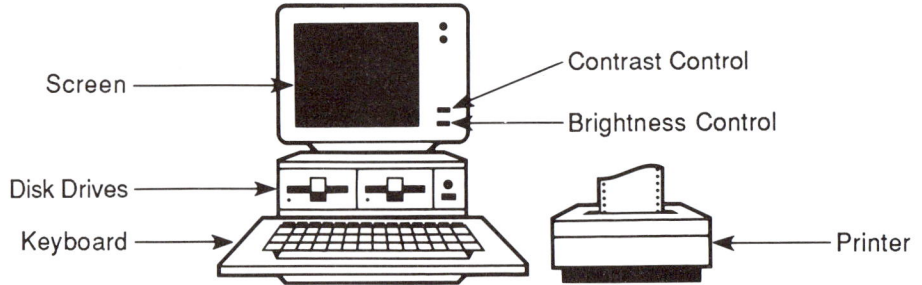

Figure A-1 The Components of a Typical Microcomputer

pens, graphics tablets, optical character readers (OCR), magnetic ink character recognition (MICR), cameras, sensors, and bar codes.

The output device for a microcomputer is either a CRT (cathode-ray tube), VDT (video display terminal), or printer (impact or nonimpact). The output generated on the monitor is called soft copy and the printed output is referred to as hard copy. Other output devices include cameras and plotters.

There are two types of monitors. The majority of microcomputers utilize a monochrome-type screen. As the name indicates, this type of screen generates one color, such as green, although some are amber. Either monochrome or amber can generate graphic output, if you have a graphics card or graphics adapter.

The other type of monitor is called a color monitor. It shows data in a color format.

The processing part of a microcomputer, or its CPU (central processing unit), includes three components:

Main memory stores data, information and instructions.

ALU (arithmetic logic unit) performs arithmetic and logical operations. Arithmetic operations include addition, subtraction, division, and multiplication. Logical operations include any types of comparisons, such as sorting (putting data into a particular order) or searching (choosing a particular data item).

Control unit serves as the commander of the system. It tells the microcomputer what to do and how to do it.

A-3 More on the Keyboard

As you can see in Figure A-2, the typical keyboard has been divided into three sections. In the left section, there are 10 function keys. In most application software these keys perform special functions. They can be programmed to perform a particular task. As we discussed in Chapter 4, Lotus effectively uses all 10 keys for performing different tasks.

The middle part of the keyboard is very similar to a typical typewriter. However, there are some special keys that a typewriter does not use, e.g., the **Alt** key.

The right section can serve both as a 10-key machine (when Num Lock is on) or for arrow movement.

1. Function Keys
2. Escape Key
3. Control (Ctrl) Key

4. Shift Key
5. Alt Key
6. Shift Key

7. Print Screen (PrtSc) Key
8. Number Lock (Num Lock) Key
9. Scroll Lock (Break) Key

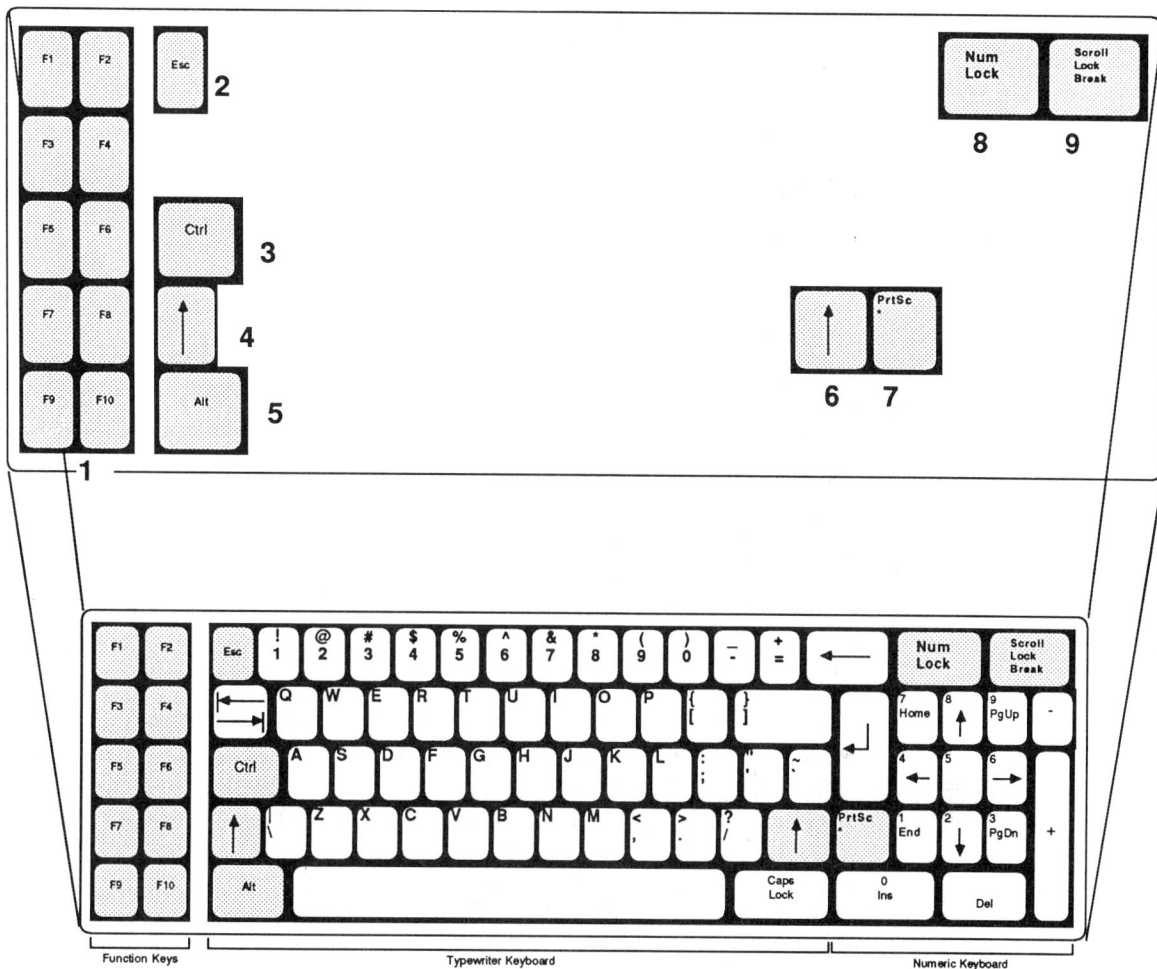

Figure A-2 IBM PC Keyboard

Function keys have been designed for more convenient utilization of a software package or a program. For example, in BASIC, to get a listing of your program, you can either type LIST or just press F1.

The Escape (Esc) key is used either to erase a line or exit from an operation (in Lotus). The **Control** key (Ctrl) is always used with another key. For example, Ctrl and Break together will halt the current operation.

Shift keys are used for generating uppercase characters or characters listed on the upper part of the keys.

Print Screen (PrtSc), if used with the **Shift** key, will print a hard copy of material on the screen. Number Lock (Num Lock) will convert the right side of your keyboard into a 10-key machine for faster numeric data entry.

The purpose of function keys and some of the special keys may vary in different application programs. For example, F1 in BASIC gives you the listing of your program while in Lotus it will access an on-line help command.

A-4 Types of Memories

There are two kinds of memories: main memory and auxiliary memory. Main memory is the heart of the microcomputer, usually referred to as RAM (random-access memory). This is a volatile memory. If you have any data in this memory and there is a power failure, all your work will be lost. To avoid this, you should always save your work on a permanent memory, such as a diskette.

Three other types of memories can be referred to as main memory, but the user cannot have direct access to them. These include:

ROM read-only memory, a prefabricated chip supplied by vendors. This memory stores some general-purpose instructions or programs. For example, some DOS commands and the BASIC language are stored on ROM chips.

PROM programmable read-only memory. By using a special device the user can program this memory. However, when it is programmed, the user cannot erase it.

EPROM erasable programmable read-only memory. This type of memory can be programmed and changed later on.

The second type of memory is called auxiliary or secondary memory. This includes diskette, mini floppy, hard disk, Bernoulli Box, etc. Since the main memory of a microcomputer is limited, expensive, and volatile (in case of a power shutdown, the information will be lost), we have to use secondary memory for storing permanent data. The capacity of a diskette or a hard disk depends on its technical features. There are three types of standard floppies: 3 1/2 inches, 5 1/4 inches and 8 inches. They can be single-density, double density, or high-density. They can also be single-sided or double-sided. A 5 1/4 inch, single-sided, single-density floppy can hold roughly 125K; a 5 1/4 single-sided, double-density floppy can hold roughly 250K; a 5 1/4 double-sided, double-density floppy can hold roughly 500K; and a high-density can hold more than 500K.

A hard disk or Winchester disk can be either 14, 8, 5 1/4 or less than 4 inches in diameter. The capacity of these devices varies from 5 megabytes to 1 gigabyte.

A-5 Memory Capacity and Speed

The capacity of a storage device, either main or auxiliary, is measured in terms of bits of information stored on that device, as follows:

0 or 1 is equal to one bit

8 bits is equal to one byte

1,024 bytes is equal to one K

1,048,576 bytes is equal to one megabyte

1,073,741,824 bytes is equal to one gigabyte

10,995,627,776 bytes is equal to one tribyte

A byte is simply a character. For example, the word Bobby is 5 characters, or 5 bytes. Microcomputers usually start from 256K and go up. Most vendors now offer 512K or 640K PCs. However, this may change in the near future. Some vendors have already started offering 1 and 2 megabyte PCs.

For present and future planning you have to be able to do some calculations to get the memory requirements for your company's computing requirements. For example, if you have a PC with 256K of RAM, all of it may not be accessible to you. A large portion of this memory may be used up by the application software. As an example, Lotus Release 2 (without the access system) takes up almost 192K of RAM. So in a 256K PC, you are only left with 64K of user memory (256 - 192 = 64).

Another consideration regarding memory is speed. The speed of the processor is measured in megahertz (MHz) and usually varies from 4 to 12.50. Naturally, the higher the speed, the faster the computer. Another factor which has direct impact on speed is the word size of the processor. It varies from 8 to 32 bits for microcomputers. The bigger the word size the faster the computer would be. The speed of your microcomputer may have a direct impact on your business operation. With a faster computer you can process more information in a shorter period of time.

A-6 Hardware/Software Concepts

Any computer, regardless of its size, must include two sets of components in order to process data and information. The first component is hardware and the second component is software.

The hardware includes all the physical components of the microcomputer. Keyboard, printer, monitor, and disk drive are some examples of the hardware components of a microcomputer.

Software includes all the programs that run your microcomputer.

Before we go further, let us give a brief definition of a program. A program is simply a series of instructions for performing a particular task. For example, the following is a program in BASIC:

```
10    A    =    5
20    B    =    10
30    C    =    A+B
40    PRINT C
50    END
```

This program is telling a computer to add A and B, store the result in a place called C, then print the result.

Sometimes large programs are broken down into a series of smaller programs or modules. A subprogram or a module is usually called a subroutine. A subroutine is a series of instructions intended to perform a particular task needed in several places in a single program.

Software is divided into two groups: system software and application software. There are two types of system software: programming languages and operating systems.

Programming languages include BASIC, COBOL, FORTRAN, and so on. In order to code in any of these languages, you have to have a compiler (translator) for that language.

There are five classes of programming languages. The first class is called machine language. This language is closest to the machine and the most remote to human beings. It is simply a series of 1s and 0s. Coding in machine language is difficult and slow. Also, machine language coding is hardware dependent; this means a code written for IBM computers may not work for Honeywell computers.

The second class of programming languages is assembly languages. Coding in assembly language is simpler than in machine language. The codes are a series of mnemonics, short codes designed to perform specific tasks. They still must be translated in order to be understood by a computer. The translator for an assembly language program is called an assembler. Assembly languages are also machine dependent.

The third class is called high-level programming languages. There are more than 700 of these languages, which are more like English. Different types have been designed for different applications. For example, FORTRAN is designed for scientific applications and COBOL for business applications. Most of these languages are machine independent.

The fourth class of programming languages is called 4-GL (fourth-generation languages). These languages are very similar to English. There are many of these languages, too. IFPS (by Execucom), EXPRESS (by MDS), and AUTOFAB (by Capex) are some examples of these languages.

The fifth class, and probably the most exciting group from the user's point of view, is called natural languages. These are in the process of being developed further. Their aim is to make the user/computer interface *very* user-friendly.

As we discuss in Appendix B, the operating system, or more specifically, the disk operating system, is a program which runs the entire operation of your microcomputer.

Application software is designed to perform different applications. Some of these programs have a special purpose, for example a general ledger program. The others are general-purpose programs. In this group we can include spreadsheets, databases, word processing, communication, graphics, and so on.

A-7 More on Application Software

There are many different application software programs on the market for microcomputers. This software covers a broad range of applications.

Spreadsheet programs are of two types. The first is a dedicated spreadsheet, which only performs spreadsheet analysis. VisiCalc (by VisiCorp) is a good example of this type.

The other type of spreadsheet, such as Lotus, is integrated software, which can perform more than one task. Lotus can perform spreadsheet analysis as well as creating databases and graphics. In any case, the number of tasks performed by a spreadsheet program is unlimited. Throughout this book, you have seen many applications of Lotus as an integrated package. Other popular spreadsheets include Unicalc (by Lattice, Inc.) and Multiplan (by Microsoft Corp.).

Database programs are designed to perform database operations. This includes file creation, deletion, modification, search, sort, combine, and so on. As we discussed in Chapters 14-15, Lotus is capable of performing some basic database operations. Other popular database programs include dBASE III and III Plus (by Ashton-Tate), Business Filevision (by Telos Software Products), and PC-File III (by Buttonware, Inc.).

A *word processing program* or a dedicated word processor or a microcomputer used as a word processor is very similar to a typewriter with a memory. With such a facility, you can generate documents, delete, insert, cut and paste, and so forth. There are numerous word processing programs on the market. Some of the popular ones include Volkswriter (by Lifetree Software, Inc.), Officewriter (by Office Solutions), and Wordperfect (by Wordperfect Corp.).

Graphics software has been designed to convert data into graphics. As we explained in Chapter 12, Lotus provides some impressive graphics capabilities. However, there are some limitations. For example, you can only plot up to six data ranges. There are some popular dedicated graphic packages on the market. These include Freelance (by Graphic Communications) and Energraphics (by Enertronics Research, Inc.).

Communications software, using a modem, enables your microcomputer to connect you to a wealth of information available in public and private databases. Some packages such as Symphony (by Lotus Development Corp.) include a communication program within the package itself. However, there are many other communications software programs on the market. Among them are On-Line (by Micro-Systems Software), Pfs:Access (by Software Publishing Corp.), Smartcom II (by Hayes Microcomputer Products, Inc.), and Crosstalk (by Microstuf, Inc.).

There are many other application software packages, which cover such areas as education, desktop publishing, finance, general utility, and more. You can do a lot with your microcomputer. Be creative!

A-8 Guidelines for Successful Selection of a Microcomputer

There are many microcomputers on the market, which makes the selection task a difficult one. We will provide you with some general guidelines regarding the purchase and maintenance of a microcomputer. These guidelines may help you to choose a suitable computer and have an easier time maintaining it.

Before you start, you must define your requirements. Sometimes this is called the wish list approach. You should have a clear idea of buying a microcomputer and the specific applications you want it to handle.

After the needs are defined, you have to think about software. Remember, if there is software, there must be hardware to run it but not vice versa.

After defining the software and hardware, you must look at technical support and vendor reputation. We have summarized the important factors regarding selection and maintenance of a microcomputer:

Software Selection
Good software must:

- have a reasonable cost
- be easy to use
- be able to handle your business volume
- have good documentation
- have training available
- have updates available (free of charge or for a minimum charge)
- have local support
- come from a reputable vendor

Hardware Selection (processor and keyboard)
Good hardware must:

- have a reasonable cost
- have a comfortable keyboard
- have function keys
- have a general operating system, e.g., MS-DOS, PC-DOS, CP/M, etc.
- have 16-bit or bigger processor size
- be expandable (memory and peripheral)
- have enough channel capacity or expansion slots (for peripherals to be attached to)

Hardware Selection (CRT)
A good monitor must:

- have a separate CRT (not a built-in one)
- be easy to read
- hold a standard number of characters per row and column

Hardware Selection (disk drive and hard disk)
A good disk drive must:

- have a built-in, not separate, disk drive
- have reasonable storage capacity
- have a hard disk option

Hardware Selection (printer)
A good printer must:

- have a reasonable cost
- have a standard printer interface (without additional devices)
- produce quality output
- have reasonable speed
- have a reasonable amount of noise suppression
- let you change tape and ribbons easily

Vendor Selection
A good vendor must:

- have a good reputation
- have knowledgeable staff
- have training available for hardware and software
- have a hot line available
- support newsletter and user groups
- provide a "loaner" in case of breakdown
- provide updates, e.g., trade-in options

Contract Selection
A good contract must:

- have a reasonable warranty period
- state a flexible time for repair
- have reasonable terms for contract renewal
- allow relocation and/or reassignment of the present contract
- observe confidentiality issues

Taking Care of Your Microcomputer
To maintain the health of your microcomputer you must consider the following factors:

- Protect your microcomputer against dirt, dust, and smoke.
- Make back-ups for security reasons.
- Avoid any kind of liquid spills.
- Maintain steady power. Use surge protectors for power fluctuations and use lightning arresters in mountainous areas.
- Protect the machine from static by using humidifiers or antistatic devices.

A-9 You and Your Microcomputer

If you turn on a typical microcomputer, such as an IBM PC, without having the disk operating system diskette in one of the drives or having a hard disk, the computer will load BASIC (the most commonly used programming language for personal computers). This version of BASIC, minimal BASIC, is stored in ROM. More advanced BASIC, BASICA, is stored on a disk operating system diskette and you can load it into RAM by typing BASICA at the A> prompt.

If the disk operating system is in one of the drives when you turn the computer on, your microcomputer will go through the steps discussed in Appendix B. First it asks you the date, then the time, then it reverts back to the A> prompt. From this mode, or disk operating system mode, you can go to any application software. For example, pull the DOS diskette out, put the Lotus system diskette in, and then type 123. This will load Lotus into RAM. As we mention in Appendix B, from DOS you can access any other application software.

Summary

In this appendix, we explained microcomputer components including hardware and software. We explained main and auxiliary memories. We briefly introduced the memory and speed capabilities of a typical microcomputer. Different types of software were introduced. The information provided in this appendix should help you to better understand the operation of your microcomputer.

Review Questions

1. What is a PC?
2.* Are a PC and a microcomputer the same?
3. What are some of the components of a typical PC?
4. What are the components of the CPU?
5.* What is the purpose of the function keys on the keyboard?
6. Can these function keys be programmed? If yes, how?
7. How many types of memories are there?
8.* What factors determine the speed of a PC?
9. How much is a tribyte?
10. How many different types of software do we have?
11. What is the difference between system software and application software?
12. What are some examples of application software?
13. Where does Lotus fit in software categories?
14.* When you turn on a PC, which mode are you going to be in, DOS or BASIC?
15. Is the A> prompt a DOS prompt or a BASIC prompt?
16.* Is DOS in ROM or RAM or neither?
17. Mention 10 factors that should be considered before choosing a microcomputer.
18. How can your microcomputer communicate with another PC?
19. What is the promised computer language of the future?

Appendix B

Disk Operating System

B-1 Introduction

In this appendix we provide you with a quick review of disk operating system for the IBM PC and PC compatibles. We'll cover disk file creation and use, customizing your system, and manipulation of your directory. We also list more than 50 of the most commonly used DOS commands.

B-2 What Is DOS?

In simple terms, DOS (disk operating system) is a collection of programs which enable you to interact with your computer. There are several uses for DOS:

- getting the system started
- housekeeping (e.g., creating back-up disks)
- house cleaning (e.g., deleting redundant files)
- customizing your PC (changing the prompt, self-booting your system, etc.)
- helping individuals with minimum computer background with easier system access

There are several versions of DOS available. Some of them are general purpose, such as CP/M, MS-DOS, PC-DOS, and UNIX. Many software programs can be run by these operating systems. Each special-purpose DOS has been designed for a particular microprocessor chip and brand of computer, for example, Apple DOS or TRS DOS. Naturally, these operating systems only run the products for which they were designed.

Many advanced features, such as directory designing and program linkage, can be done by DOS. However, these topics are beyond the scope of this appendix. For more information consult your DOS manual.

In this appendix we only discuss MS-DOS or PC-DOS. You can always assume that between you and your application program (Lotus) there is a gate called DOS. To get to your Lotus program you have to go through DOS.

B-3 Types of DOS Commands

When you get your system started have the DOS disk in drive A and turn the computer on. Usually the system will ask you for the date and time. If you respond with the date and time in the proper format, the A> prompt will appear. You can bypass the date and time by hitting the **Return** key twice, but it is a good practice to enter them. If you save a program, the date and time will be saved in your program. You will know which version of your program is the most recent. Figure B-1 shows this process.

The A> prompt means the disk operating system is activated in disk drive A. You can change A to B or C by typing B: or C:. The default drive is always A unless a hard disk is used to boot the DOS (the computer assumes your selected drive is A). It is possible to change the system prompt by using the DOS command PROMPT. For example, if at A> you type PROMPT Good Morning America, your prompt will be changed to Good Morning America.

At this point you can access two types of DOS commands: external and internal. To execute any external command, you must have the DOS disk in your disk drive. An example of an external command is DISKCOPY. All the commands and files with the extensions BAT, COM, or EXE are external. To execute an internal command the DOS disk does not need to be in any of the drives. At the A> prompt, for example, you can type CLS to clear the screen.

B-4 File Specifications

Any disk file will have three distinct parts:

- drive name
- file name
- file extension

A drive name can be A:, B:, C:, etc. If you do not specify a drive name, the computer assumes the default drive is selected.

A file name can be up to eight characters long. It can include digits 0 to 9. Don't use reserved words as file names, such as DISKCOPY or CON (console).

The file extension is optional. If used, it can be up to three characters in length. Digits can be used as well.

You should always remember which drive is the source drive and which is the target drive. The source drive is the one with the original program and the target drive is the one to which you transfer a copy. Mistaking these two drives can be dangerous.

```
Current date is Tue  1-01-1980
Enter new date (mm-dd-yy): 1-1-1988
Current time is  0:00:25.04
Enter new time: 8.45


The IBM Personal Computer DOS
Version 3.00 (C)Copyright IBM Corp 1981, 1982, 1983, 1984

A>
```

Figure B-1 Getting the System Started

It is a good practice to select names that have some meaning. For example, Payroll, Credit, or Commission are some good names for business applications. Don't include any spaces in your file names or extensions. Uppercase and lowercase are treated the same.

B-5 Wild Card Characters

Two characters have specific meaning to DOS. One is the question mark (?) and the other is the asterisk (*). When you use the question mark it means any character in that particular position. For example, A>DIR AB?JACK will give you the following files:

ABAJACK
ABXJACK
ABBJACK
ABZJACK
ABCJACK, etc.

When you use the asterisk, it means that from that position on you can have any characters. For example, A>DIR AB* will list all files starting with the letters AB. The rest of the name is not considered. A>DIR *.* will give you all the files with any name and any extension. A>DIR *.WK1 will give you all the files with extension WK1.

These two wild cards can be very helpful for accessing specific files. For example, COPY B: *.WK1 will copy all the worksheet files from the disk in drive B to the disk in drive A, assuming your current drive is A.

B-6 Redirection and Piping

It is possible to direct the output of a command to a different device other than the standard one, such as a monitor. For example, A>DIR>PRN will transfer the listing of your directory to the printer. A>DIR>Myfile will transfer the listing of your directory to a file called "Myfile."

Piping takes place when you combine two commands. For example, A>DIR ISORT will sort your directory. A>DIR ISORT>Myfile will sort your directory and write the output into a file called "Myfile." Then, at the A> prompt you can type TYPE Myfile and the computer will give you the sorted listing of your files.

B-7 Batch and Autoexec Files

Batch files are disk files designed for a specific use. A batch file can have any standard name but the extension must be always BAT. In theory, batch files can have any length. You can include any valid command or statement in your batch file. To enter a command, you must always hit the **Return** key after the specific command. To generate a batch file you can use EDLIN, the line editor available on DOS, or any word processing program. For simple files you can use a version of the copy command as follows:

```
A> COPY CON Myfile.BAT      (hit Return)
   Command or statement     ( "      " )
        "            "       ( "      " )
        "            "       ( "      " )
```

To save a batch file press Ctrl and Z together (F6 function key). To execute a batch file all you need to do is to type the name of the file at the A> prompt.

We have designed a simple batch file as follows:

```
A> COPY CON HELLO.BAT      (hit Return)
DIR                        ( "      " )
CLS                        ( "      " )
BASICA                     ( "      " )
                           (hit Ctrl +Z) (press Ctrl and Z keys together)
```

If you type HELLO at the A> prompt, you will see your directory, the screen will clear, and BASICA will be loaded to RAM.

The only limitation with COPY CON is that you cannot edit a file that has been created. For editing you have to redo the entire file, use EDLIN, or use some other word processing or editor-type systems.

To stop the execution of a batch file, press Ctrl and Break at the same time.

If you call your file AUTOEXEC.BAT, it will be executed automatically as soon as you get the system started. As a matter of fact, DOS always looks for this file first. If you have such a file all its commands will be executed. This facility can be very helpful. You can design a menu or customize your system and also help other people unfamiliar with computers. Batch files in general are very helpful if you have to do a series of repetitive operations.

B-8 Directory and Subdirectory in DOS

In order to effectively manage all the files in your secondary storage device (diskette and/or hard disk), it is advisable to establish a tree-structured directory. In this fashion, you will be able to organize groups of related files in separate directories. To access a particular file you have to define a path leading to it. Let us assume that Ocean City Manufacturing has stored all its files on a hard disk using a PC as follows:

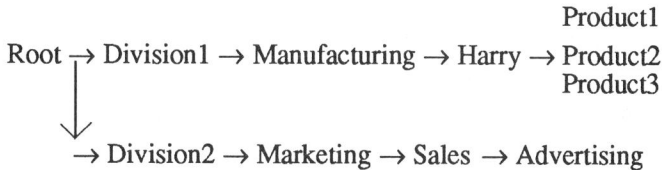

$$\text{Root} \rightarrow \text{Division1} \rightarrow \text{Manufacturing} \rightarrow \text{Harry} \begin{array}{l} \rightarrow \text{Product1} \\ \rightarrow \text{Product2} \\ \rightarrow \text{Product3} \end{array}$$

$$\rightarrow \text{Division2} \rightarrow \text{Marketing} \rightarrow \text{Sales} \rightarrow \text{Advertising}$$

This tree-structured directory can help you access any of these files more effectively than a simple directory. For example, to list all the files under Product1 from the root directory, you have to type:

Division1\Manufacturing\Harry\Product1

The root directory always starts with a backslash (\). This directory is automatically generated when you format a diskette. The distance to reach to a particular file is called the path of that file. The above path for Product1 is one example. A root directory in a single-sided diskette can hold up to 64 files, a double-sided up to 112, and a high-density diskette can hold up to 224 files.

There is another type of directory called the subdirectory. Subdirectory names follow the same format as file names. The extension is optional.

The default directory is called the current directory. You can always change the current directory by using the CHDIR (CD) command. There is no limitation on the number of subdirectories. As we discussed earlier, the subdirectories are separated by a series of backslashes (\). Remember, the length of a directory path cannot exceed 63 characters. To create a directory you use the MKDIR (MD) command. To display the directory structure, you must use the TREE command.

B-9 Important DOS Commands

In Table B-1 we have summarized most of the commonly used commands in DOS. To become more familiar with these commands you have to practice them. All you need is a DOS disk and an empty diskette. Remember that FORMAT and DISKCOPY commands can be very dangerous!

We have divided these commands into two groups. Group 1 is used quite often. Group 2 is for advanced users and advanced applications. Following are brief descriptions of some of these commands.

The COPY command is used for copying one or a series of individual files. The source and target drives can be any drive.

The CHDSK command is used in order to find out about any free space on a particular diskette.

CLS is used to clear the screen. This is an example of a DOS internal command. This command can be used in BASIC as well as in DOS.

DEL or ERASE is used for the deletion of a disk file. Remember, to delete a disk file, you must always use the file name and extension.

DIR is used for displaying the directory of your system. The drive identifier can be A:, B:, C:, etc.

DISKCOPY is used for the duplication of a diskette. When you use this command, the target diskette does not need to be formatted. DISKCOPY formats the target diskette while it is doing the copying.

DISKCOMP and COMP are used for comparing two diskettes and comparing two files, respectively. If two diskettes and/or two files are not identical you receive an error message.

FORMAT is used to format, or prepare, a diskette. If for any reason the diskette is damaged, you will receive an error message.

FORMAT/V command is used for labeling a diskette. Labeling simply means putting a name on your diskette. The label name can be any combination of characters up to 11, including a space. This is a nice feature to have for internal identification of diskettes. For example, one diskette could be for total sales, one for total cost, and so on.

The RENAME command is used for changing a file name to a different one.

The TYPE command will give you a listing of the contents of a file in DOS.

To implement the majority of DOS commands, type the command, then follow the system prompt.

Table B-1 Important DOS Commands

(To execute all these commands we assume the "A" prompt is apparent.)
A stands for A drive
B stands for B drive
ext stands for file extension (any three valid characters)
Filename can be any valid file name

GROUP 1

COPY Filename.ext B:	Copy Filename.ext to B
COPY B:Filename.ext	Copy Filename.ext to A
COPY *.ext B:	Copy all files with the same ext from A to B
COPY B:*.ext	Copy all files with the same ext from B to A
COPY *.*B:	Copy all files from A to B
COPY B:*.*	Copy all files from B to A
COPY Filename1.ext Filename2.ext	Copy a file from A to A with a different name

GROUP 1

COPY B:Filename1.ext B:Filename2.ext	Copy a file from B to B with a different name
COPY Filename1.ext B:Filename2.ext	Copy a file from A to B with a different name
COPY B:Filename1.ext Filename2.ext	Copy a file from B to A with a different name
CHKDSK	Displays free space on diskette
CHKDSK B:	Displays free space on diskette in drive B
COMP	Compares two disk files to determine if they are the same or if they are different
CLS	Clears the screen
CTRL + ALT + DEL	System reset
DATE	To reset system date
DEL Filename.ext	To erase Filename.ext from drive A
DEL B:Filename.ext	To erase Filename.ext from drive B
DEL B:Filename.*	To erase all Filename with any extension from drive B
DEL B:*.ext	To erase all files with the same extension from drive B
DIR	Directory of A
DIR B:	Directory of B
DIR/P	To display a complete directory of drive A with a pause before scrolling of the screen
DIR B:/P	Does the same as above, for drive B
DIR/W	To display a wide directory of drive A
DIR B:/W	To display a wide directory of drive B
DIR |SORT	To display a sorted directory of drive A
DISKCOPY A: B:	Copy a diskette in drive A to a diskette in drive B
DISKCOMP	Compares two diskettes track by track, sector for sector to determine if their contents are identical
ERASE Filename.ext	Erase Filename.ext on A
ERASE B:Filename.ext	Erase Filename.ext on B
ERASE *.ext	Erase all files with same ext on A
ERASE B:*.ext	Erase all files with same .ext on B
FORMAT	Erases and formats a blank diskette
FORMAT B:	Erases and formats a blank diskette in drive B
FORMAT/V	To format a new diskette with a volume label
FORMAT B:/V	To format a new diskette with a volume label in drive B
LABEL	Creates, changes, or deletes a volume label for a disk
RENAME Filename1.ext Filename2.ext	Rename a file on A
RENAME B:Filename1.ext B:Filename2.ext	Rename a file on B
SHIFT + PrtSc key	To print a copy of the screen
TYPE Filename.ext	Display content of Filename.ext on A
TYPE B:Filename.ext	Display content of Filename.ext on B
TIME	To reset system time

GROUP 2

ASSIGN	Tells DOS to use a different disk drive from the one specified by a program or command
BACKUP	Backs up files from a fixed disk or diskette onto a diskette or another fixed disk
CHDIR (CD)	Changes the current directory or displays the current directory path. Changes the current directory of drive A to its root directory

GROUP 2	
MKDIR (MD)	Creates a subdirectory on a disk
PATH	Instructs DOS to search a specified directory for a program that cannot be found in the current directory
PROMPT	Customized the DOS system prompt
RECOVER	Recovers a disk or a file with defective sectors
RMDIR (RD)	Removes a subdirectory from a disk
SYS	Puts a copy of operating system files IBMDOS.COM and IBMBIO.COM on the specified diskette or fixed disk
TREE	Displays the structure of the current directory
VER	Displays the DOS version number on the screen
VERIFY	Checks the data just written to a disk to be sure the data has been correctly recorded and then displays whether the data has been checked
	VERIFY ON → sets verify status on
	VERIFY OFF→sets verify status off
	VERIFY→ shows verify status
VOL	Displays the volume label of a disk, if the label exists

Summary

In this appendix we have provided a brief discussion of disk operating system, DOS, as the starting point for using any application program and Batch and AUTOEXEC files for more convenient system operations. We have also provided you with two sets of DOS commands. Group 1 consists of some of the most commonly used while group 2 commands are used for advanced applications. Knowledge of these commands should be very helpful for more effective use of your PC.

Review Questions

1. What is DOS?
2. How many different types of DOS do we have?
3.* Which DOS is used for the IBM PC? For its clone/compatibles?
4.* What is the difference between external and internal DOS commands?
5. How many different DOS prompts do we have?
6.* What is the purpose of the date and time prompts?
7. How do you bypass these prompts?
8. Can you customize your DOS prompt? If yes, how?
9.* What is the difference between DISKCOPY and COPY *.*?
10. When you use DISKCOPY, do you need to format your diskette first or not?
11. What is a batch file?
12. What are some of the uses of a batch file?
13. How do you design a batch file?
14. What is an AUTOEXEC file?
15. What are some of the uses of an AUTOEXEC file?

16.   How many different ways can you use the DIR command?
17.   How do you rescue a file from a damaged disk?
18.   How do you stop the execution of a batch file?
19.   Get your system started. Format a blank disk, then copy three files from DOS to this empty disk.
20.   Copy your DOS disk to any empty disk.
21.   Using wild card *, get a listing of all files with the BAS extension.
22.   Sort your directory and direct the result to a file called Sfile. Now, using your printer, generate a printed copy of this file.
23.* Generate a batch file that, when it is used, will do the following:

Change directory to B:
Change directory back to A:
Generate a wide directory
Erase the screen

24.   Generate a directory that includes three subdirectories as follows:

Worksheet
Graph
Print
Include three files in each subdirectory.

Misconceptions and Solutions

M - If you want to transfer the content of one diskette to another, you can either use DISKCOPY or COPY*.*. However, DISKCOPY will first erase the content of the second diskette, then copy the first diskette to the second one.

S - Use COPY*.* if you want to keep the content of the second diskette.

M - You turn the computer on, and you may see a message which is not familiar to you, e.g., OK Prompt instead of A> prompt. Your computer has booted the cassette BASIC from ROM.

S - You either forgot to put the DOS disk in drive A or you inserted your disk from the wrong direction. Insert the DOS disk into drive A and reboot the system.

M - You issue a DOS command and the error message says BAD COMMAND.

S - You have probably issued a DOS external command without having the DOS disk in one of the drives. Insert DOS into the right drive and issue the appropriate command again.

Appendix C

Installing Lotus

C-1 Introduction

In this appendix, we will explain how you can tailor Lotus to your particular system. This procedure is needed if you just purchased Lotus or if you made some changes in your existing equipment. You do the installation only once. Installation simply means tailoring Lotus to different hardware. If you do not install Lotus your program will still run, but you won't be able to use your printer or generate any graphs. This appendix should answer questions regarding tailoring the Lotus program to different systems.

C-2 Why Is Installation Needed?

Since Lotus has been designed to work on many different systems, you must tailor this program to your specific hardware. Installation is needed for three different components:

Monitor Which monitor are you planning to use (color, black and white, monochrome with Hercules graphics card, etc.)?

Printer Is it a standard dot matrix printer, letter quality, or a printer with 132 characters?

Secondary Storage (data disk) Which drive will be used for storing data and programs generated by Lotus, drive B or drive C (hard disk)?

C-3 Getting Ready for Installation: Two-Disk Systems

As we mentioned in Chapter 1, Lotus Release 2 comes with six disks:

System Disk
Backup System Disk
A View of 1-2-3 Disk
PrintGraph Disk
Utility Disk
Install Library Disk

The System disk includes everything you need except instructions for printing graphs. This information is stored on the PrintGraph disk. Before you do the installation, it is advisable to make a backup copy of all disks and do the installation with the copies. In case of damage to any of the master disks, you will have a copy of it. Remember, you cannot copy the system disk since it is copy protected. Lotus has provided you with a backup copy of this disk. To make backup copies of the other four disks, follow these steps:

1. Prepare four empty disks. To do so, put the DOS disk in drive A, put an empty disk in drive B, type FORMAT B:, and press the **Return** key. Do this for all four disks. (For more information on formatting, see Appendix B.)
2. Now you have to make a copy of the Install Library, Utility, PrintGraph, and A View of 1-2-3 disks. To do this, put the DOS disk in drive A. At the A> prompt pull DOS out and put one of the four disks in drive A. Put one of the formatted disks in drive B, type COPY *.* B:, and press the **Return** key. Follow these steps for the other three disks. You now have a backup copy of all five disks. You could use the DISKCOPY command for making a backup copy as well; however, Lotus recommends that you use COPY instead of DISKCOPY.
3. The next step is to copy COMMAND.COM to these six disks. If you do not do this, you will get the following error message:
Insert Disk with COMMAND.COM in Drive A and strike any key when ready. Copying this command to your disks helps you get back to DOS when you are exiting 1-2-3 or the Lotus Access System. To copy COMMAND.COM to the six disks, put DOS in drive A, put any of the six disks in drive B, type Copy COMMAND.COM B:, and press the **Return** key. Follow these steps for the other five disks.

C-4 Getting Ready for Installation: Hard Disk Systems

The steps just discussed are used for a two-disk system. If you have a system with hard disks (drive C) and one floppy drive (drive A), follow these steps:

You have to copy all five Lotus disks onto your hard disk. To get Lotus started, you need either your system disk or its backup. This is only for getting started; you can pull it out later and continue working with Lotus.

1. If drive C is not the default drive, make it the default drive by typing C: and pressing the **Return** key.

2. Create a subdirectory to hold 1-2-3 programs. Type MD 123 (see Appendix B for more information on subdirectories).
3. Make this subdirectory the current directory by typing CD 123.
4. Now copy all five Lotus disks onto drive C by putting one of the five disks in drive A and typing COPY *.* C:. Do this for the other four disks.

Now, you are ready to go to the Install program.

C-5 Installing the Drivers

To tailor Lotus to your particular system, you have to transfer a series of drivers to Lotus disks. Drivers are simply a series of programs that monitor and run the hardware. To run the Install program, you must know the specifications of your hardware. To get the procedure started, put the DOS disk in drive A and boot the system. At the A> prompt, pull the DOS disk out, put the Utility disk into drive A, and type INSTALL. This procedure is for a two-disk drive system. For hard disk systems you first have to change the current directory to the subdirectory containing the Lotus programs (CD C:\123) and at the C prompt type INSTALL. In any event, you will be given a screen describing the procedure. Press the **Return** key and the program will ask you to remove the Utility disk and put the Install Library disk in drive A. Do this and press the **Return** key. Now it asks you to put the System disk in drive A and press the **Return** key. The Install menu will appear. You will be given four options:

    First-Time Installation
    Change Selected Equipment
    Advanced Options
    Exit Install Program

If you just purchased Lotus, choose First-Time Installation. Change Selected Equipment is used if you must change one of your components. Advanced Options allows you to do certain things that you can't do elsewhere in the Install program; for example, adding new drivers to the library, modifying the current drivers set, or changing the collating sequence (for sorting, the number to come first or the number to be last). The last option is used to exit the menu. The rest of the procedure basically means following a series of menus. If you follow these menus carefully, you should not have any problem installing the Lotus program for any system that Lotus supports.

Driver programs must be installed on the System disk, A View of Lotus, and PrintGraph. You can do these one by one, replacing the System disk with the next disk.

C-6 Defining Default Settings for Secondary Storage and Printer

You can change and/or maintain the default settings of your secondary storage (drive B or C) and the printer. The /Worksheet Global Default Printer command will tell you the default settings of your printer. This includes:

Interface Auto-LF   Left   Right   Top   Bottom   Pg-Length   Wait
Setup   Name

Any of these settings can be changed and restored in the future by issuing /Worksheet Global Default Update.

/Worksheet Global Default Directory will tell you the current directory or the current secondary storage. These settings can be changed, by issuing /Worksheet Global Default Update.

If you encounter any problems, consult *123 Getting Started*. This brief manual explains these steps in detail.

Summary

In this appendix, we have provided you with some guidelines regarding tailoring Lotus to your system. Since Lotus has been designed to work on several systems, customization is needed. If you don't install Lotus, your 1-2-3 program will still run but you won't be able to generate graphs or use your printer. We gave a quick review of the Utility and Install Library programs. These two programs provide you with the information needed for the installation of 1-2-3 and its companion programs.

Review Questions

1. Why must Lotus be installed?
2. If you do not install Lotus, which part of the program may not work?
3.* Which disk among the six disks cannot be copied and why?
4.* How do you make a backup copy of the PrintGraph disk?
5. Why must COMMAND.COM be copied to all the Lotus disks?
6. How do you copy PrintGraph to a hard disk?
7. What is a directory? A subdirectory?
8. How do you make a directory the current directory?
9. On which disk is the Install program?
10.* How do you get the installation procedure started?
11. What are drivers?
12. How many driver sets can you have?
13.* What is the default driver name for 1-2-3?

Appendix D

File Transfer Between Lotus and Other Software

D-1 Introduction

In this appendix we provide some guidelines for importing and exporting files to and from Lotus. This facility enables you to utilize some of the best features of software packages. Also, by importing other files, you should be able to save time and frustration by not duplicating the same data file.

Lotus provides you with several facilities for data transfer. The Translate utility provided by Release 2 is an excellent program that makes the task of file transfer a very easy job. We will discuss this utility and also the /File Import and /Data Parse commands.

D-2 Why File Transfer?

File transfer simply means the transfer of a file generated by one application software program to another one. There are several reasons for using the file transfer facilities. Three reasons are:

1. To utilize a facility of one software package which is not available in another one; for example, transferring a Lotus spreadsheet to a report generated by a word processing program. you can see why such a task may need to be done. Your report will be more factual and comprehensive.

2. To utilize the enhanced power available for the same basic tasks performed by two application software programs. For example, since the database operations

performed by Lotus are much faster than those of dBASE III Plus, you may want to bring a dBASE file into a Lotus worksheet for processing.

3. To convert data files from earlier application software to more recent ones. This is a very common case; let us say converting VisiCalc files into Lotus files. Without this facility, you must enter all the data again, a time-consuming and boring task.

D-3 What Is an ASCII File?

ASCII (American Standard Code for Information Interchange) is a data format generated and accepted by many applications software.

An ASCII file, or simply a "print image" file, is a file in standard keyboard characters. To verify whether a file is ASCII or not is very simple. At the A> prompt in DOS, type TYPE filename.extension. If a file is listed in standard keyboard characters, it is an ASCII file; otherwise it is not. For example, Lotus files generated by the /Print File command (files with the PRN extension) are ASCII files. VisiCalc generates all its files in ASCII, as do Wordstar, dBASE II and III, and BASICA.

D-4 Lotus Facilities for File Transfer

Lotus Release 2 provides several facilities which make the task of file transfer relatively easy. These include the Translate utility program, /File Import, /Data Parse, /Print File Options Other Unformatted, and Lotus macros related to sequential ASCII files.

In the next few pages we will explain these facilities and provide several examples, to help you understand these powerful features provided by Lotus.

D-5 Lotus Translate Utility Program

When you access the Lotus Access System, one of the options provided is Translate. When you choose this option, Lotus asks you to insert the utility disk. The disk can be loaded here or in DOS at the A> prompt. Type TRANS and press the **Return** key.

This utility gives you nine options that you can translate from:

1-2-3, Release 1A
1-2-3, Release 2
dBASE II
dBASE III
DIF (Data Interchange Format), a well known ASCII file
Jazz
SYMPHONY, Release 1.0
SYMPHONY, Release 1.1
VisiCalc

You can choose any of these options and press the **Return** key. To exit from the Translate utility, press the **Escape** key. You can use F1 to receive on-line help. As an example, we chose 1-2-3, Release 2. When you press the **Return** key, the Translate utility gives you the following options:

1-2-3, Release 1A
dBase II
dBase III
DIF
SYMPHONY, Release 1.0
SYMPHONY, Release 1.1

You can translate from any of the nine options to any of the six options. We chose dBASE III. You will be given a series of instructions. Continue to press Escape. Insert the diskette that includes the desired file. Move the cursor to the file you would like to translate. We chose the file in Figure D-1. The menu will indicate that the source file with the WK1 extension will be changed to a file with the DBF (database file) extension. If you follow the right sequence, the final message will be Translation Successful. Now, if you look at the directory of the diskette, you will see that the file you just translated has DBF as an extension.

Remember, if you do not follow the right sequence, you will receive an error message. You have to follow exactly the instructions provided by the Translate utility.

After translation this is a dBASE III file and you can perform any operation with it using all the dBASE III commands.

D-6 Using File Import and Data Parse Commands

To show how /File Import and /Data Parse work, we will walk through an example. We used /Print File to write the worksheet in Figure D-2 to a new file (Figure D-3). This file is now an ASCII file with the PRN extension. (The /Print File command is discussed in Chapter 9.)

Now we want to bring this file back to the worksheet. When you issue /File Import, Lotus gives you two options: text or numbers. We chose the text option (if you choose the number options, only numeric values will be transferred).

If you play with the cursor, you will see that each line of this file has been entered into one cell. For example, cell A2 contains FIRST NAME AGE SEX OCCUPATION INCOME. Naturally, this file cannot be manipulated by Lotus spreadsheet commands. We have to use the /Data Parse command in order to parse the data (split up the long labels into a series of data items or labels). The procedure with this very powerful command is straightforward. Move the cursor to the left corner of the first row, which contains the first data item. Now invoke the /Data Parse command. You will be given the following options:

Format-Line   Input-Column   Output-Range   Reset   Go   Quit

Format-Line will provide you with a pattern or patterns for splitting up the numbers or labels. You can change it or take it as is. There are two options: Create or Edit. We chose the Create option. You will see a format line starting with four asterisks (four empty cells), L (for labels), 10 asterisks, and V (for value), etc.

Figure D-1 An Example of Lotus Worksheet File Translated into dBASE III File

```
A1: [W12] 'FIRST NAME                                              READY

        A            B           C    D    E             F          G
1   FIRST NAME   LAST NAME     AGE  SEX  OCCUPATION    INCOME
2   Randy        Alexander      36   M   Professor     $40,000
3   Fay          Alexander      30   F   Mayor         $30,000
4   Adam         Alexander      31   M   Engineer      $30,000
5   Andrea       Byan           36   F   Teacher       $31,000
6   Moe          Byan           40   M   Officer       $40,000
7   Bob          Adam           32   M   Engineer      $72,000
8   Anna         Adam            4   F   Unemployed    $11,000
9   Vicki        Adam            9   F   Unemployed    $12,000
10  Paula        Bobby          55   F   Housewife     $20,000
11  Jack         Jones          69   M   Artist        $19,000
12  Mary         Fishler        30   F   Interpreter   $19,000
13  Sue          Hayword        22   F   Student       $10,000
14  Tammy        Smith          29   F   Student       $10,000
15  Jacky        Brown          72   F   Engineer      $52,000
16  Lora         Jones          30   F   Nurse         $31,000
17
18
19
20
01-Jan-88  10:41 AM
```

Figure D-2 A Sample Worksheet

```
A1: [W12]                                                          READY

        A          B    C       D          E          F      G
1              MY FIRST DATABASE
2   FIRST NAME   AGE  SEX  OCCUPATION     INCOME
3   Randy         30   M   Professor     $40,000
4   Fay           30   F   Mayor         $30,000
5   Adam          31   M   Engineer      $30,000
6   Andrea        36   F   Teacher       $31,000
7   Moe           40   M   Officer       $40,000
8   Bob           32   M   Engineer      $72,000
9
10
11
12
13
14
15
16
17
18
19
20
01-Jan-88  10:42 AM
```

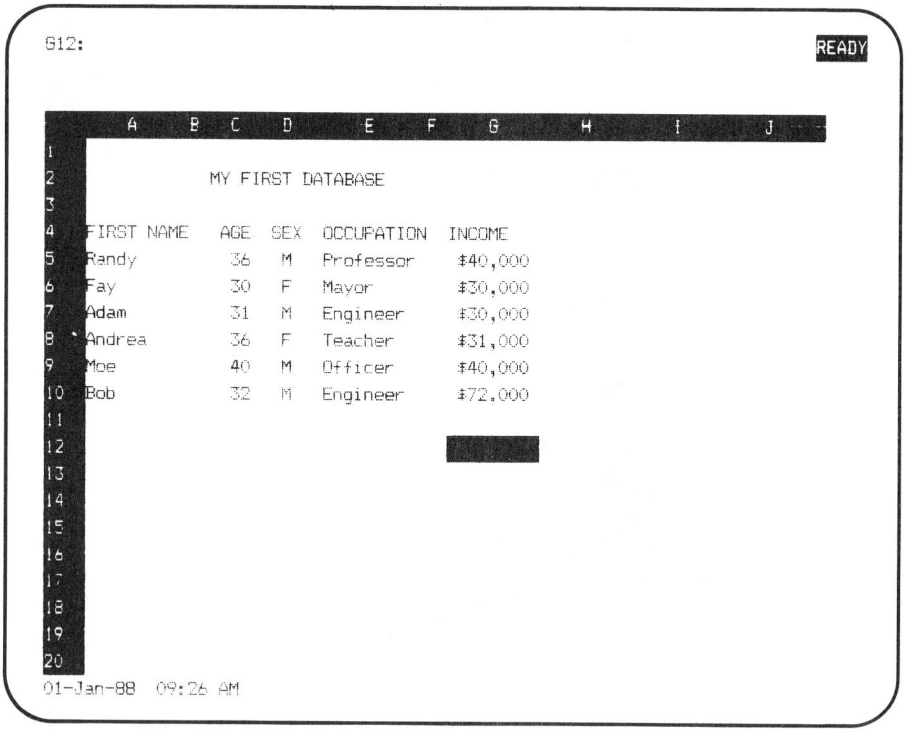

Figure D-3 Sample File was Retrieved by File Import

Input-Column specifies the range to be parsed. In our example, the range is A2..A10.

Output-Range is the left corner of the block for the parsed data. We specified A11.

Reset will cancel the previous settings, and finally, Go will execute the /Data Parse command.

Remember, in this example we have used two format lines; one for database fields FIRST NAME, AGE, SEX, OCCUPATION, and INCOME, and the other for database records. The result of this /Data Parse operation is in cells A12..E18. As you see, the currency format is lost but the data has been split. You will be able to use this database for any Lotus operation. Figure D-4 shows the result.

Other commands provided by Lotus are able to split a long label. The String function can extract a substring from a whole string (@LEFT, @MID, @RIGHT), and the /Range Justify command can split a long label into several shorter ones. The /Data Parse command, however is a lot more flexible and easier to use than the others.

Lotus macros for sequential file processing provide you with some extra features for file handling between Lotus and other standard ASCII files (see Chapter 17).

```
A1: '                    MY FIRST DATABASE                           READY

        A        B        C        D        E        F        G        H
1                     MY FIRST DATABASE
2  ****L>>>>*L>>>***L>>**L>>*L>>>>>>>>>******L>>>>>
3     FIRST NAME    AGE  SEX OCCUPATION      INCOME
4  ****L>>>***********V>***L**L>>>>>>>>*******V>>>>>
5     Randy        36   M  Professor      $40,000
6     Fay          30   F  Mayor          $30,000
7     Adam         31   M  Engineer       $30,000
8     Andrea       36   F  Teacher        $31,000
9     Moe          40   M  Officer        $40,000
10    Bob          32   M  Engineer       $72,000
11
12 FIRST    NAME     AGE      SEX      OCCUPATIOINCOME
13 Randy       36 M          Professor   40000
14 Fay         30 F          Mayor       30000
15 Adam        31 M          Engineer    30000
16 Andrea      36 F          Teacher     31000
17 Moe         40 M          Officer     40000
18 Bob         32 M          Engineer    72000
19
20
01-Jan-88   10:43 AM
```

Figure D-4 An Original Database and Its Parsed Version

Summary

In this appendix, we have provided you with a review of facilities provided by Lotus regarding file transfer between programs. The Translate utility can assist you in transferring files between versions of Lotus, dBASE, DIF, Jazz, VisiCalc, and Symphony. By using the /File Import command, you should be able to import any ASCII file to your worksheet. The /Data Parse command will enable you to parse (split up) long labels into a series of labels and values. Other commands and facilities are available in Lotus for file handling. This includes Lotus macros for sequential files, string functions, and /Print File for generating ASCII files.

Review Questions

1. Why is the file transfer process needed?
2.* What are the requirements for any file transfer?
3. How do you get the Translate utility started?
4.* What application software can directly benefit from the Translate utility?
5.* How do you ask for help in the Translate utility?
6. How do you exit from the Translate utility?
7. When a file is translated from Lotus to dBASE, what is actually changed?
8.* How do you generate an ASCII file using Lotus?
9. How do you know if a file is an ASCII file?

10.   Does all software generate ASCII files?

11.   How do you load an ASCII file into the Lotus worksheet?

12.   What is the major function of /Data Parse?

13.* Why is parsing needed?

14.   Are there other ways to parse data besides using the /Data Parse command?

15.   What are the options available under the /Data Parse command?

16.* What is the function of Reset in the /Data Parse menu?

17.   How many format lines are needed for a typical database?

18.   Choose one of the worksheets in any of the chapters of this book and convert this worksheet into a dBASE III file. How do you know if your translation is successful?

19.   Using the /Print File command, generate an ASCII file.

20.   Using /Data Parse, split a long label into four shorter labels.

Appendix E

Differences Between Release 2.0/2.01 and Release lA

Lotus Release 2.0/2.01 includes a series of enhanced features not available in the earlier releases of this package. These enhancements include new security features, memory management, additional worksheet and range commands, new functions and a number of new macro commands that complement the macro commands available in Release 1A and make Lotus a full-featured programming language.

Memory management gives you complete freedom to utilize a worksheet in any style. For example, a data item in cell A1 or cell A2000 will occupy the same amount of memory. However, in Release 1A, the active area is important. In the above example the active area would be the entire rectangle of A1..A2000. This means you will run out of memory very fast.

Release 2.0/2.01 implements security features by allowing you to have a password for a file. You can also use the /Range Protect or /Worksheet Global Protection commands.

In Release 2.0/2.01 you can access DOS from the 1-2-3 spreadsheet by using the /System command from the main menu. This release also enables you to export or import files between 1-2-3 Release 1A or 2, dBASE II, dBASE III, DIF, Jazz, SYMPHONY Release 1.0 and 1.10, and VisiCalc. We discussed this facility in Appendix D.

For those who are still using Release 1A or who are interested in knowing some of the differences between Release 2.0/2.01 and Release 1A, we have provided Table E-1. This table should assist you in quickly discovering all the features available in Release 2.0/2.01 but not in Release 1A.

In some cases the commands are different but perform the same task; this table also highlights such cases. For easy reference to these new features, we refer you to the section of this book where a particular feature was first presented. This should save you a lot of time in discovering the new enhancements in Lotus.

Table E-1 Release 2.0/2.01 and Release 1A Comparison

FEATURE	RELEASE 2.0/2.01	SECTION NUMBER	RELEASE 1A
	GENERAL INFORMATION		
Worksheet size	256 columns by 8,192 rows	1-4	256 by 2,048
The entire package	System disk	1-7	System disk
	Backup system disk		Backup system disk
	Utility		Utility disk
	PrintGraph		PrintGraph
	A View of Lotus		Tutorial disk
	Install library		
Alt & F1	available	4-5	not available
	WORKSHEET COMMANDS		
/Worksheet Global Protection	available	5-9	not available
/Worksheet Global Default Other International	Currency available	5-10	not available
	Date available		not available
	Time available		not available
/Worksheet Global Zero	available	5-11	not available
/Worksheet Column Hide	available	5-14	not available
/Worksheet Column Display	available	5-14	not available
/Worksheet Status	available	5-18	not available
/Worksheet Page	available	5-19	not available
	RANGE COMMANDS		
/Range Unprotect or Protect	available	6-3	not available
/Range Name Table	available	6-6	not available
/Range Transpose	available	6-9	not available
/Range Value	available	6-10	not available
/Range Format Hidden	available	7-13	not available
File Extension	WK1 (worksheet)	8-4	WKS (worksheet)
	FUNCTIONS		
@ATAN2 (A,B)	available	10-4-5	not available
@CTERM	available	10-5-6	not available
@TERM	available	10-5-7	not available
@SLN	available	10-5-9	not available
@SYD	available	10-5-10	not available

FEATURE	RELEASE 2.0/2.01	SECTION NUMBER	RELEASE 1A
@DDB	available	10-5-11	not available
@ISNUMBER	available	11-2-5	not available
@ISSTRING	available	11-2-6	not available
@CHAR	available	11-3-1	not available
@CODE	available	11-3-2	not available
@CLEAN	available	11-3-3	not available
@EXACT	available	11-3-4	not available
@FIND	available	11-3-5	not available
@LEFT	available	11-3-6	not available
@LENGTH	available	11-3-7	not available
@LOWER	available	11-3-8	not available
@MID	available	11-3-9	not available
@N	available	11-3-10	not available
@PROPER	available	11-3-11	not available
@REPEAT	available	11-3-12	not available
@REPLACE	available	11-3-13	not available
@RIGHT	available	11-3-14	not available
@S	available	11-3-15	not available
@STRING	available	11-3-16	not available
@TRIM	available	11-3-17	not available
@UPPER	available	11-3-18	not available
@VALUE	available	11-3-19	not available
@DATE	available	11-4-1	not available
@DATEVALUE	available	11-4-2	not available
@NOW	available	11-4-6	not available
@TIME	available	11-4-7	not available
@TIMEVALUE	available	11-4-8	not available
@HOUR	available	11-4-9	not available
@MINUTE	available	11-4-10	not available
@SECOND	available	11-4-11	not available
@@	available	11-5-1	not available
@CELL	available	11-5-2	not available
@HLOOKUP	available for both numeric and nonnumeric search	11-5-7	available for numeric search only
@INDEX	available	11-5-8	not available
@VLOOKUP	available for both numeric and nonnumeric search	11-5-11	numeric search only
@CELLPOINTER	available	11-5-3	not available
@COLS	available	11-5-5	not available
@ROWS	available	11-5-10	not available

GRAPHICS

Exploding a pie chart	available	12-8	not available

PRINTGRAPH

Availability of several interfaces for DOS Device

FEATURE	RELEASE 2.0/2.01	SECTION NUMBER	RELEASE 1A
LPT1	available	13-6	not available
LPT2	available	13-6	not available
LPT3	available	13-6	not available
LPT4	available	13-6	not available
Choosing font option	available	13-7	not available

DATABASE

/Data Matrix			not available
Invert	available	15-9	not available
Multiply	available	15-10	not available
/Data Regression	available	15-12	not available

MACRO COMMANDS

BIGLEFT	available	16-3	not available
BIGRIGHT	available	16-3	not available
Multiple action (e.g., DOWN 6 or UP 2)	available	16-3	not available
BLANK	available	17-5-1	not available
LET	available	17-5-2	not available
CONTENTS	available	17-5-3	not available
PUT	available	17-5-4	not available
RECALC	available	17-5-5	not available
RECALCCOL	available	17-5-5	not available
BRANCH	available	17-6-1	/XG
DEFINE	available	17-6-2	not available
DISPATCH	available	17-6-3	not available
FOR and FORBREAK	available	17-6-4	not available
IF	available	17-6-5	/XI
QUIT	available	17-6-5	/XQ
ONERROR	available	17-6-5	not available
RESTART	available	17-6-6	not available
RETURN	available	17-6-7	/XR
SUBR-Name	available	17-6-7	/XC Name
BREAKOFF	available	17-7-2	not available
WAIT	available	17-7-3	not available
GET	available	17-7-4	not available
GETLABEL	available	17-7-5	/XL
GETNUMBER	available	17-7-5	/XN
LOOK	available	17-7-6	not available
MENUBRANCH	available	17-7-7	/XM
BEEP	available	17-8-1	not available
INDICATE	available	17-8-2	not available
PANELOFF	available	17-8-3	not available
PANELON	available	17-8-3	not available
WINDOWSOFF	available	17-8-4	not available
WINDOWSON	available	17-8-4	not available
CLOSE	available	17-9-1	not available
FILESIZE	available	17-9-2	not available

FEATURE	RELEASE 2.0/2.01	SECTION NUMBER	RELEASE 1A
GETPOS	available	17-9-3	not available
READ	available	17-9-5	not available
READLN	available	17-9-6	not available
SETPOS	available	17-9-7	not available
WRITE	available	17-9-8	not available
WRITELN	available	17-9-9	not available

Appendix F

Lotus International Character Set

Lotus uses the Lotus International Character Set (LICS) for displaying, transmitting, printing, and storing characters. These 256 characters are represented by numbers 0 through 255. Numbers 0 through 32 represent control characters (Ctrl + a letter); 32 through 127 represent ASCII codes; and 128 through 255 represent international characters.

The *compose sequence* is a series of keystrokes used to enter a character that is not on the keyboard. To do this, press Alt, then the desired compose sequence.

For printers and monitors which cannot directly represent all LICS characters, there are fallback presentations. These are listed in Table F-1. Table F-1 has been adopted from Lotus Development Corporation, 1987, used with permission.

©Lotus Development Corporation 1987. Used with permission.

LICS Code	Character	Description	Compose Sequence	Fallback Monitor Presentation	Fallback Printer Presentation
0	Control @				
1	Control A				
2	Control B				
3	Control C				
4	Control D		*(Note: Character codes 0 through 31 are not LICS codes.)*		
5	Control E				
6	Control F				
7	Control G				
8	Control H				
9	Control I				
10	Control J	Line feed			

LICS Code	Character	Description	Compose Sequence	Fallback Monitor Presentation	Fallback Printer Presentation
11	Control K				
12	Control L	Form feed			
13	Control M	Return			
14	Control N				
15	Control O				
16	Control P				
17	Control Q				
18	Control R				
19	Control S				
20	Control T				
21	Control U				
22	Control V				
23	Control W				
24	Control X				
25	Control Y				
26	Control Z				
27	[Escape]				
28	FS				
29	GS				
30	RS				
31	US				
32	(Space)				
33	!				
34	"				
35	#		+ +		
36	$				
37	%				
38	&				
39	'	Apostrophe			
40	(				
41	)				
42	*				
43	+				
44	,				
45	-				
46	.				
47	/				
48	0				
49	1				
50	2				
51	3				
52	4				
53	5				
54	6				
55	7				
56	8				
57	9				
58	:				
59	;				
60	⟨				
61	=				
62	⟩				
63	?				
64	@		a a A A		
65	A				
66	B				
67	C				

LICS Code	Character	Description	Compose Sequence	Fallback Monitor Presentation	Fallback Printer Presentation
68	D				
69	E				
70	F				
71	G				
72	H				
73	I				
74	J				
75	K				
76	L				
77	M				
78	N				
79	O				
80	P				
81	Q				
82	R				
83	S				
84	T				
85	U				
86	V				
87	W				
88	X				
89	Y				
90	Z				
91	[		(	(	
92	\		/	/	
93	]		)	)	
94	^		v	v	
95	_				
96	`				
97	a				
98	b				
99	c				
100	d				
101	e				
102	f				
103	g				
104	h				
105	i				
106	j				
107	k				
108	l				
109	m				
110	n				
111	o				
112	p				
113	q				
114	r				
115	s				
116	t				
117	u				
118	v				
119	w				
120	x				
121	y				
122	z				
123	{		(-		
124	¦		^/		

LICS Code	Character	Description	Compose Sequence	Fallback Monitor Presentation	Fallback Printer Presentation
125	}		)-		
126	˜	Tilde	--		
127	DEL				
128	`	Uppercase grave	* ` space		
129	´	Uppercase acute	* ´ space		
130	^	Uppercase circumflex	* ^ space		
131	¨	Uppercase umlaut	* ″ space	″	″
132	˜	Uppercase tilde	* ˜ space		
133					
134					
135			*Do not type* *. *It indicates that*		
136			*compose sequence is order-sensitive.*		
137					
138					
139					
140					
141					
142					
143					
144	`	Lowercase grave	* space `		
145	´	Lowercase acute	* space ´		
146	^	Lowercase circumflex	* space ^		
147	¨	Lowercase umlaut	* space "	"	"
148	˜	Lowercase tilde	space ˜		
149	ı	Lowercase i without dot	i space		
150	_	Ordinal indicator	_ space		
151	▲	Begin attribute (display only)	b a		
152	▼	End attribute (display only)	e a		
153	■	Unknown character (display only)			
154	•	Hard space (display only)	space space		
155	←	Merge character (display only)	m g		
156					
157	►	Tab character			
158					
159					
160	ƒ	Dutch Guilder	f f		f
161	¡	Inverted exclamation mark	! !		¡
162	¢	Cent sign	c¡ C¡ c/ C/		c⟨BS⟩¡
163	£	Pound sign	L= l= L- l-		L⟨BS⟩=
164	"	Low opening double quotes	" ^	"	"
165	¥	Yen sign	Y= y= Y- y-		Y⟨BS⟩=
166	Pts	Pesetas sign	* PT pt Pt		Pt
167	§	Section sign	S0 so S0 s0		Sc
168	¤	General currency sign	X0 xo X0 x0		0⟨BS⟩=
169	©	Copyright sign	C0 co C0 c0	c	(c)
170	ª	Feminine Ordinal	a_ A_		a⟨BS⟩_
171	«	Angle quotation mark left	< <		<<
172	Δ	Delta	d d D D		D
173	π	Pi	* PI pi Pi		pi
174	≥	Greater-than-or-equals	* > =		> =
175	÷	Divide sign	: –		/
176	°	Degree sign	^ 0		o(superscripted, if possible)
177	±	Plus/minus sign	+ –		+⟨BS⟩_
178	²	Superscript 2	^ 2		2 (superscripted, if possible)
179	³	Superscript 3	^ 3	3	3 (superscripted, if possible)
180	„	Low closing double quotes	″ v	″	″
181	μ	Micro sign	* / u		u

LICS Code	Character	Description	Compose Sequence	Fallback Monitor Presentation	Fallback Printer Presentation
182	¶	Paragraph sign	! p ! P		Pr
183	·	Middle dot	^ ·		·(superscripted, if possible)
184	™	Trademark sign	* TM Tm tm	T	TM
185	¹	Superscript 1	^ 1	1	1 (superscripted, if possible)
186	º	Masculine ordinal	o _ 0 _		o⟨BS⟩ _
187	»	Angle Quotation mark right	> >		> >
188	¼	Fraction one quarter	* 1 4		1/4
189	½	Fraction one half	* 1 2		1/2
190	≤	Less-than-or-equals	* = <		= <
191	¿	Inverted question mark	? ?		?
192	À	Uppercase A with grave	A `	A	A
193	Á	Uppercase A with acute	A ´	A	A
194	Â	Uppercase A with circumflex	A ^	A	A
195	Ã	Uppercase A with tilde	A ~	A	A
196	Ä	Uppercase A with umlaut	A "		A
197	Å	Uppercase A with ring	A *		A
198	Æ	Uppercase A with ligature	* A E		AE
199	Ç	Uppercase C with cedilla	C ,		C ⟨BS⟩ 、
200	È	Uppercase E with grave	E `	E	E
201	É	Uppercase E with acute	E ´		E
202	Ê	Uppercase E with circumflex	E ^	E	E
203	Ë	Uppercase E with umlaut	E "	E	E
204	Ì	Uppercase I with grave	I `	I	I
205	Í	Uppercase I with acute	I ´	I	I
206	Î	Uppercase I with circumflex	I ^	I	I
207	Ï	Uppercase I with umlaut	I "	I	I
208	Ð	Uppercase eth (Icelandic)	D –	D	D ⟨BS⟩ –
209	Ñ	Uppercase N with tilde	N ~		N
210	Ò	Uppercase O with grave	O `	0	0
211	Ó	Uppercase O with acute	O ´	0	0
212	Ô	Uppercase O with circumflex	O ^	0	0
213	Õ	Uppercase O with tilde	O ~	0	0
214	Ö	Uppercase O with umlaut	O "		0
215	Œ	Uppercase OE diphthong	* O E	0	OE
216	Ø	Uppercase O with slash	O /		0 ⟨BS⟩ /
217	Ù	Uppercase U with grave	U `	U	U
218	Ú	Uppercase U with acute	U ´	U	U
219	Û	Uppercase U with circumflex	U ^	U	U
220	Ü	Uppercase u with umlaut	U "		U
221	Ÿ	Uppercase Y with umlaut	Y "	Y	Y
222	Þ	Uppercase thorn (Icelandic)	P –	P	P ⟨BS⟩ _
223	ß	Lowercase German sharp s	s s		ss
224	à	Lowercase a with grave	a `		a ⟨BS⟩ `
225	á	Lowercase a with acute	a ´		a ⟨BS⟩ ´
226	â	Lowercase a with circumflex	a ^		a ⟨BS⟩ ^
227	ã	Lowercase a with tilde	a ~	a	a ⟨BS⟩ ~
228	ä	Lowercase u with umlaut	a "		a ⟨BS⟩ "
229	å	Lowercase a with ring	a *		a
230	æ	Lowercase ae with ligature	a e		ae
231	ç	Lowercase c with cedilla	c ,		c ⟨BS⟩
232	è	Lowercase e with grave	e `		e ⟨BS⟩ `
233	é	Lowercase e with acute	e ´		e ⟨BS⟩ ´
234	ê	Lowercase e with circumflex	e ^		e ⟨BS⟩ ^
235	ë	Lowercase e with umlaut	e "		e ⟨BS⟩ `
236	ì	Lowercase i with grave	i `		i ⟨BS⟩ `
237	í	Lowercase i with acute	i ´		i ⟨BS⟩ ´
238	î	Lowercase i with circumflex	i ^		i ⟨BS⟩ ^

LICS Code	Character	Description	Compose Sequence	Fallback Monitor Presentation	Fallback Printer Presentation
239	ï	Lowercase i with umlaut	i "		i ⟨BS⟩
240	ð	Lowercase eth (Icelandic)	d –	d	d ⟨BS⟩ -
241	ñ	Lowercase n with tilde	n ¯		n ⟨BS⟩ ˜
242	ò	Lowercase o with grave	o `		o ⟨BS⟩ `
243	ó	Lowercase o with acute	o ´		o ⟨BS⟩ ´
244	ô	Lowercase o with circumflex	o ^		o ⟨BS⟩ ^
245	õ	Lowercase o with tilde	o ˜	o	o ⟨BS⟩ ˜
246	ö	Lowercase o with umlaut	o "		o ⟨BS⟩ ¨
247	œ	Lowercase oe with diphthong	o e	o	oe
248	ø	Lowercase o with slash	o /	o	o ⟨BS⟩ /
249	ù	Lowercase u with grave	u `		u ⟨BS⟩ `
250	ú	Lowercase u with acute	u ´		u ⟨BS⟩ ´
251	û	Lowercase u with circumflex	u ^		u ⟨BS⟩ ^
252	ü	Lowercase u with umlaut	u "		u ⟨BS⟩ ¨
253	ÿ	Lowercase y with umlaut	y "		y ⟨BS⟩ ¨
254	þ	Lowercase thorn (Icelandic)	p –	p	p ⟨BS⟩ _
255					

Appendix G

Answers to the Selected Review Questions

Chapter 1

2. VisiCalc, SuperCalc, ProCalc, and Context MBA. (Context MBA was introduced approximately at the same time as Lotus.)
4. Release 2 has a larger worksheet, more functions, and utilizes the memory more effectively.
6. VisiCalc.
9. Six.
15. Forecasting to integrate database, spreadsheet, and graphic capabilities; financial analysis to again utilize these three components.

Chapter 2

2. A> prompt means that the disk operating system is in drive A or the default drive is A. Yes, we have other prompts, like B and C for drive B and drive C and OK for the BASIC language.
4. Home will put you back to cell A1.
7. Escape either erases a line in Edit mode, or gets you out of the present operation.
10. Type a caret first (^), then type the data.
12. By putting them inside parentheses.

Chapter 3

1. Type either 123 or Lotus at the A> prompt, assuming your system disk is in Drive A.

4. It is not. However, numbers are right-justified and labels are left-justified.
7. Press the **Slash** key (e.g., /).
11. Use either **PrtSc** and the **Shift** key or use the Print command.
13. At the A> prompt type Format, hit the **Return** key and then follow the prompt.
15. Choose Quit from the main menu.

Chapter 4

7. The READY mode.
10. Press Alt and F2 together.
12. When a macro is being executed.

Chapter 5

3. Nine.
5. For a large worksheet, you choose manual in order to bypass the intermediate results. This can immensely improve the speed of calculations.
7. The command /Worksheet Global Label-Prefix must be issued first. Then enter data.
17. /Worksheet Page generates a page break. It must be in Column A.
18. /Worksheet Global Default Other Clock None will erase both time and date from the bottom of your worksheet.

Chapter 6

2. Yes. Range A1..IV8192 is equal to the entire worksheet.
6. Use the /Range Name Table command; this will give you an alphabetical list of names with their addresses.
11. When you use /Worksheet Global Protection Enable first, then /Range Protect.
17. Precede the range name with a dollar sign, e.g., $Income.

Chapter 7

2. There are 10 options: Fixed, Scientific, Currency, Comma, General, +/-, Percent, Date, Text, and Hidden.
3. The Currency operation separates every three digits by a comma and also includes a dollar sign to the left of a number. The Comma option does the same thing but does not include the dollar sign.
6. To save the actual formulas in a cell for debugging purposes.
10. Yes.

Chapter 8

3. Three types of files: PIC, WK1, and PRN.
6. Any combination of digits and letters of the alphabet, up to 15 characters.
8. /File Combine Add adds the incoming data to the worksheet. /File Combine Copy copies the incoming data to the current worksheet. You must always remember the present position of the cursor.
10. If your worksheet contains numeric data and if the cursor is in the occupied portion of the worksheet, the incoming data will overwrite the current worksheet.

14. Type /File Erase. When Lotus asks for a file name type the name of the file or point to it. For example, type PAY*.*. Lotus will give you a listing of all the files that start with PAY. You can erase them one by one. If you want to erase them all at once, you must use DOS wild card Del or Erase.

Chapter 9

2. At the A> prompt type TYPE Filename.PRN. This will give you a listing of your file on the monitor. Transfer this to the printer.
6. The at sign (@).
9. No. /Worksheet Page may not override this command if the number of lines specified by /Print, Printer, options, Pg-Length is less than the number of lines covered by /Worksheet Page.
10. To print the exact characters, formulas, date, and so forth in a worksheet or a range.
14. Out of 66 lines per page, only 56 lines are available to you.
16. First use /Worksheet Global Default Printer. Change whatever you would like to change, then use /Worksheet Global Default Update.

Chapter 10

2. A Lotus function simplifies operations performed by users. For example, to add 100 different cells, you can either add them up cell by cell or just use the @SUM function.
6. An invalid argument is one that does not follow the convention regarding a function's argument. For example, @SQRT(-25) is invalid because in this function the argument must be positive.
8. The @ABS function treats any numeric value as a positive value. It always returns a positive answer. This can be used when you calculate the root of an equation and you are only interested in the positive root.
10. Yes. Add 0.50 to the argument, then use the @INT function.
13. You may raise the argument of a function to the power of one-half.
14. @FV function can be used to tell you about the future value of an annuity. For example, your IRA Plan. @PV function can tell you what is the present value of a series of equal payments in the future.
16. In the @PV function the cash flows must be equal. In the @NPV function the cash flows need not be equal.

Chapter 11

2. @ISNUMBER is useful for testing the content of a cell. It tells you if the cell holds a numeric value. After this test you may want to conduct some arithmetic operation. If the cell content is not numeric, you cannot perform any arithmetic operations.
3. @CHAR returns the ASCII/LICS equivalent of the argument.
8. The @DATEVALUE function uses a single string value as its argument, while @DATE accepts any Lotus date format.
13. @HLOOKUP conducts a horizontal search, @VLOOKUP conducts a vertical search.

15. They can be used in any table search, for example, searching tax tables, commission tables, production tables, and so on.

Chapter 12

3. One limitation is that you can only use six data ranges. Another limitation is the variety (only five types); a third limitation is that the graphs are only two-dimensional.

4. In an XY graph there must be two sets of data, one for the X-axis and the other for the Y-axis; one of these two data ranges must be X. There is no such limitation in a line graph.

6. The X range is used for labeling the X-axis. It is also used as one of the data ranges in an XY graph and for labeling the pieces of a pie chart.

8. Yes. Your worksheet will have extension WK1; your graph will have extension PIC.

9. No.

11. There is no limit.

13. Two types: horizontal and vertical.

16. The Scale option gives you the opportunity to override the automatic scaling done by Lotus. This means you can tell Lotus how to fit your data on the X and Y axes.

18. Legends are used to make your graph more understandable., They will tell you, for example, which symbol belongs to which data.

Chapter 13

3. It depends on how you got to the PrintGraph program in the first place. If you get to it from DOS, naturally you will return to DOS. If you got to the program from Lotus Access System, you will return to the Lotus Access System when you exit.

5. Yes. Press F10.

7. You cannot. You have to go to the worksheet and retrieve the worksheet file, do all your changes there, save it by using /Graph Save, then go to PrintGraph and print the new graph.

12. Yes. Otherwise you will create an ellipse instead of a circle.

16. Minimum is 110 and maximum is 19,200.

18. Action, Pause, Yes makes PrintGraph pause between printing.

Chapter 14

4. Use /Worksheet Delete Row, then specify the row address.

10. The primary key is the first field chosen to sort and the secondary key is the second field chosen to sort. There are no other differences between these two keys.

12. You can search with single criteria, double criteria, multiple criteria, or with wild cards.

15. The Xtract option extracts all the records that meet a particular criteria. The Unique option will extract only the records that have at least one field different from the others.
16. Up to 32 fields.

Chapter 15

5. It stops either when the range is filled or the stop value has been reached.
8. No.
11. This will show up at the end of Frequency. For example, 1 means there was one data item that was not included in the bin range.
15. Yes, if the number of columns of the first matrix is equal to the number of rows of the second matrix; otherwise, no.
17. The righthand side array is the right side of all the equations. For example, in
$$X1 + X2 \quad\quad = \quad\quad 10$$
$$X1 - X2 \quad\quad = \quad\quad 15$$
10 and 15 are the righthand side array.
18. This command does not provide important statistical measures such as a T-test, Durbin-Watson Test, and so on.

Chapter 16

4. Press the **Alt** key and the name of the macro at the same time.
6. The zero macro will be executed automatically as soon as the worksheet including this macro is loaded.
9. It can be very useful for designing menus and helping non computer experts with easy system access.
13. The CMD indicator means a macro is being executed.
15. Press **Ctrl** and **Break** together.
16. Up to 240.

Chapter 17

3. No. Some advanced commands do not need arguments. For example, QUIT, RETURN, RESTART, etc.
4. There are four types of arguments. These include address or location, numeric value, condition and string.
7. /Range Erase.
11. The macro will not be executed at all.
12. No.
16. Otherwise Lotus will always choose the first item in the menu.
20. Three. Read, Write, and Modify.

Chapter 18

4. Two types: external and internal.
7. Logical errors.

11.   Because this methodology advocates programming techniques which are easier to develop and maintain. Also, this methodology increases a programmer's productivity.

13.   Random numbers are used for investigation of a random process. For example, in an inspection of a shipment, we must decide whether to accept it or reject it. We may take a random sample and based upon this sample we make a decision.

17.   When there is a subroutine within another subroutine, we call this a nested subroutine. There are many uses of such a subroutine. For example, a subroutine calculating the net pay may call another subroutine for tax calculation.

18.   If a macro is designed for depreciation calculation, the user does not need to know detailed operations about Lotus in order to use this function.

Chapter 19

1. $X = \dfrac{(-B+(B2 - 4AC)^{1/2})}{2A} = \dfrac{(-10+(100-4X1X1)^{1/2})}{2X1} = \dfrac{(-10+(96)^{1/2})}{2} = -0.10$

3. $P = C*[1+(X-Y)]^{N} = 4*[1+(.026-.009)]^{13} = 4.98$

9.   Lotus can perform many different tasks for a small business. They may include: balance sheet, income statement, budget analysis, fixed asset, mailing list, database.

Appendix A

2.   Yes.

5.   To make the user's job easier. For example, in BASIC, to run your program you can either type RUN or press the F2 function key.

8.   Word size, type of operating system, type of chip.

14.   In the majority of IBM-type PCs, when you turn the computer on, if you do not have any diskettes in any of the drives, you will go directly to BASIC mode.

16.   DOS is usually in a diskette, so it is in neither ROM nor RAM. You can always transfer DOS from a diskette to RAM.

Appendix B

3.   PC DOS for the IBM PC and MS DOS for its clones.

4.   To execute DOS external commands you have to have the DOS disk in one of the drives. For internal commands, as long as the A> prompt is apparent, you can execute the command.

6.   Date and Time are used to document your file. This means if you save a file it will also save the time and date.

9.   DISKCOPY erases and then copies the source disk to the target disk. Copy will not erase the target disk.

23.   At A> type the following:

```
COPY CON Mybatch.BAT        (Return)
B:                          (Return)
A:                          (Return)
DIR/W                       (Return)
CLS                         (Return)
```
(**Ctrl** and Z to save it)

To execute this batch file, at A> type Mybatch.

Appendix C

3. The System disk cannot be copied because it is copy protected.
4. Put DOS in drive A, type DISKCOPY A: B: and press Return. Then follow the prompt.
10. At the A> prompt put the Utility disk into drive A and type INSTALL. Then follow the prompt.
13. It is 123.

Appendix D

2. The file to be transferred must be compatible to the file structure of the destination system. For example, if a system only accepts an ASCII file, your file must be in ASCII before the transfer can take place.
4. dBASE II and III, VisiCalc, Symphony, DIF, and Jazz.
5. Press the F1 key.
8. You have to use /Print File.
13. It is used to split long labels into a series of shorter ones.
16. Reset will cancel the previous setting. This means, for example, that all your data ranges will be erased.

Index

Lotus Command Menu

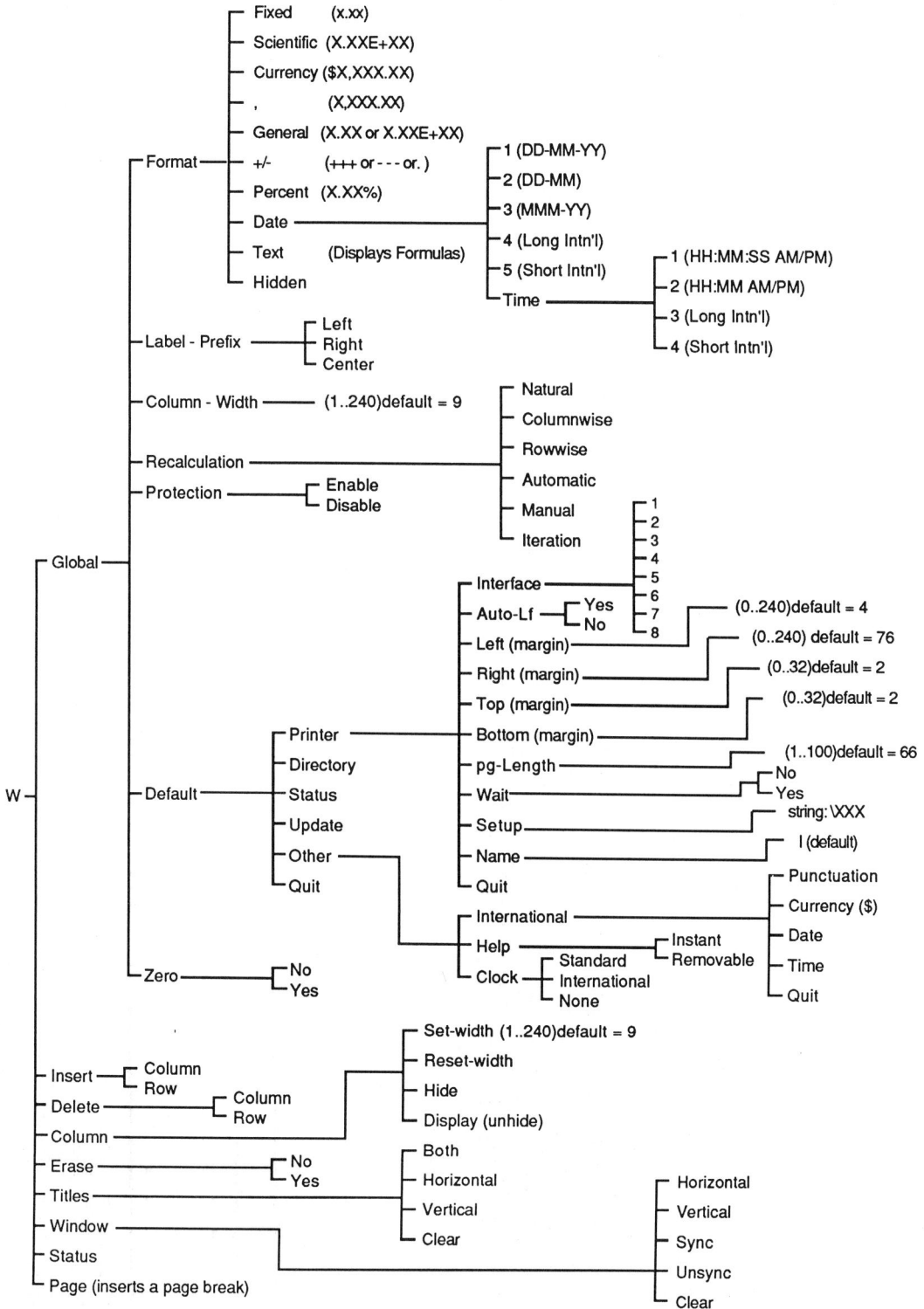

```
W ┬─ Global ─┬─ Format ─┬─ Fixed        (x.xx)
  │          │          ├─ Scientific  (X.XXE+XX)
  │          │          ├─ Currency ($X,XXX.XX)
  │          │          ├─ ,             (X,XXX.XX)
  │          │          ├─ General     (X.XX or X.XXE+XX)
  │          │          ├─ +/-          (+++ or - - - or. )
  │          │          ├─ Percent   (X.XX%)
  │          │          ├─ Date ─┬─ 1 (DD-MM-YY)
  │          │          │        ├─ 2 (DD-MM)
  │          │          │        ├─ 3 (MMM-YY)
  │          │          │        ├─ 4 (Long Intn'l)
  │          │          │        ├─ 5 (Short Intn'l)
  │          │          │        └─ Time ─┬─ 1 (HH:MM:SS AM/PM)
  │          │          │                 ├─ 2 (HH:MM AM/PM)
  │          │          │                 ├─ 3 (Long Intn'l)
  │          │          │                 └─ 4 (Short Intn'l)
  │          │          ├─ Text        (Displays Formulas)
  │          │          └─ Hidden
  │          │
  │          ├─ Label - Prefix ─┬─ Left
  │          │                  ├─ Right
  │          │                  └─ Center
  │          │
  │          ├─ Column - Width ── (1..240)default = 9
  │          │
  │          ├─ Recalculation ─┬─ Natural
  │          │                 ├─ Columnwise
  │          │                 ├─ Rowwise
  │          ├─ Protection ─┬─ Enable    ├─ Automatic
  │          │              └─ Disable   ├─ Manual
  │          │                           └─ Iteration ─┬─ 1
  │          │                                         ├─ 2
  │          │                                         ├─ 3
  │          │                                         ├─ 4
  │          │                                         ├─ 5
  │          │                                         ├─ 6
  │          │                           Interface ─── ├─ 7
  │          │                           Auto-Lf ─┬─ Yes   8
  │          │                                    └─ No
  │          │                           Left (margin) ──── (0..240)default = 4
  │          │                           Right (margin) ─── (0..240) default = 76
  │          │                           Top (margin) ───── (0..32)default = 2
  │          ├─ Default ─┬─ Printer ──── Bottom (margin) ── (0..32)default = 2
  │          │           ├─ Directory    pg-Length ─────── (1..100)default = 66
  │          │           ├─ Status       Wait ─┬─ No
  │          │           ├─ Update             └─ Yes
  │          │           ├─ Other ─┐     Setup ───── string:\XXX
  │          │           └─ Quit   │     Name ────── I (default)
  │          │                     │     Quit
  │          │                     ├─ International ─┬─ Punctuation
  │          │                     │                 ├─ Currency ($)
  │          │                     ├─ Help ─┬─ Instant   ├─ Date
  │          │                     │        └─ Removable ├─ Time
  │          │                     └─ Clock ─┬─ Standard └─ Quit
  │          │                               ├─ International
  │          ├─ Zero ─┬─ No                  └─ None
  │          │        └─ Yes
  │
  ├─ Insert ─┬─ Column
  │          └─ Row         Set-width (1..240)default = 9
  ├─ Delete ─┬─ Column      Reset-width
  │          └─ Row         Hide
  ├─ Column ───────────     Display (unhide)
  ├─ Erase ─┬─ No           Both         ┬─ Horizontal
  │         └─ Yes          Horizontal   ├─ Vertical
  ├─ Titles ────────────    Vertical     ├─ Sync
  ├─ Window ────────────    Clear        ├─ Unsync
  ├─ Status                              └─ Clear
  └─ Page (inserts a page break)
```

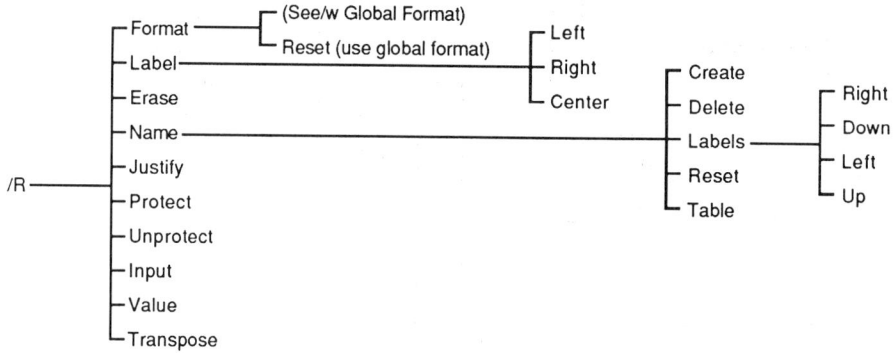

```
/R ──┬─ Format ──┬─ (See/w Global Format)
     │           └─ Reset (use global format)
     ├─ Label ──┬─ Left
     │          ├─ Right
     │          └─ Center
     ├─ Erase
     ├─ Name ─────────────────────────┬─ Create
     │                                ├─ Delete
     │                                ├─ Labels ──┬─ Right
     │                                ├─ Reset    ├─ Down
     │                                └─ Table    ├─ Left
     │                                            └─ Up
     ├─ Justify
     ├─ Protect
     ├─ Unprotect
     ├─ Input
     ├─ Value
     └─ Transpose

/C ───── Enter range to copy FROM , Enter range to copy TO
/M ───── Enter range to move FROM , Enter range to move TO

/F ──┬─ Retrieve
     ├─ Save
     ├─ Combine ──┬─ Copy ────┬─ Entire file
     │            ├─ Add      └─ Named/Specific-Range
     │            └─ Subtract
     ├─ Extract ──┬─ Formulas
     │            └─ Values
     ├─ Erase ──┬────────────┬─ Worksheet
     ├─ List ───┘            ├─ Print
     │                       ├─ Graph
     ├─ Import ──┬─ Text     └─ Other
     │           └─ Numbers
     └─ Directory

/P ──┬─ Printer ──┬─ Range
     └─ File ─────┼─ Line
                  ├─ Page
                  ├─ Options ──┬─ Header
                  ├─ Clear     ├─ Footer
                  ├─ Align     ├─ Margins ──┬─ Left (0..240)default = 4
                  ├─ Go        ├─ Border    ├─ Right (0..240)default = 76
                  └─ Quit      ├─ Setup     ├─ Top (0..32)default = 2
                               ├─ Pg-Length └─ Bottom (0..32)default = 2
                               ├─ Other ──┬─ Columns
                               └─ Quit (Return to Print Menu)  Rows

                                          Pg-Length ── (1..100)default = 66

                                          Other ──┬─ As-Displayed
                                                   ├─ Cell-Formula
                                                   ├─ Formatted
                                                   └─ Unformatted

                               Clear ──┬─ All
                                       ├─ Range
                                       ├─ Borders
                                       └─ Format
```

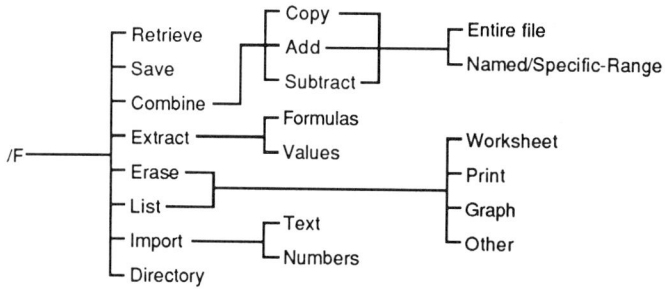

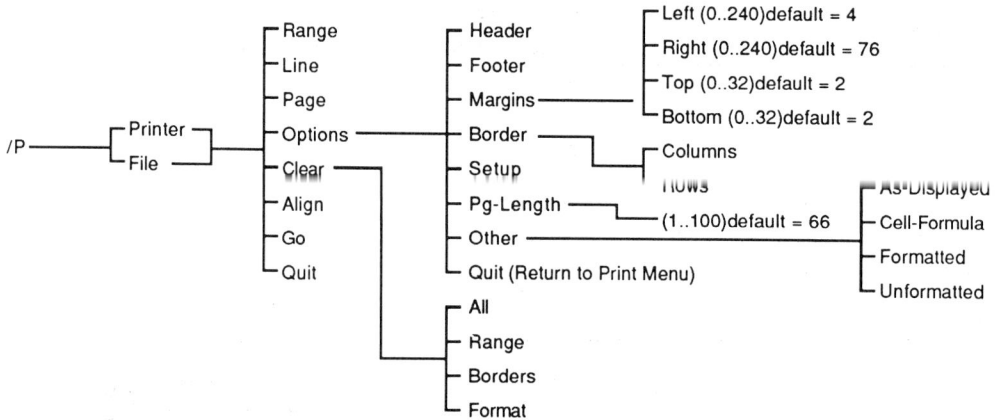

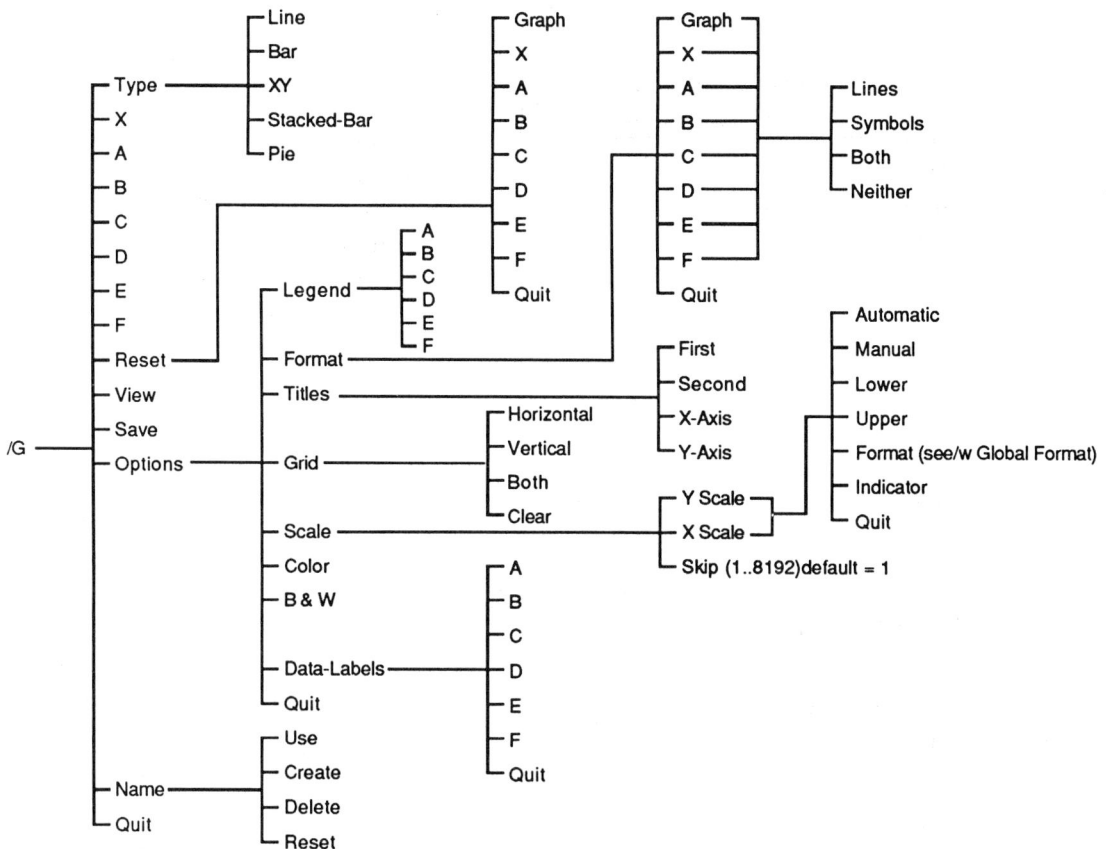

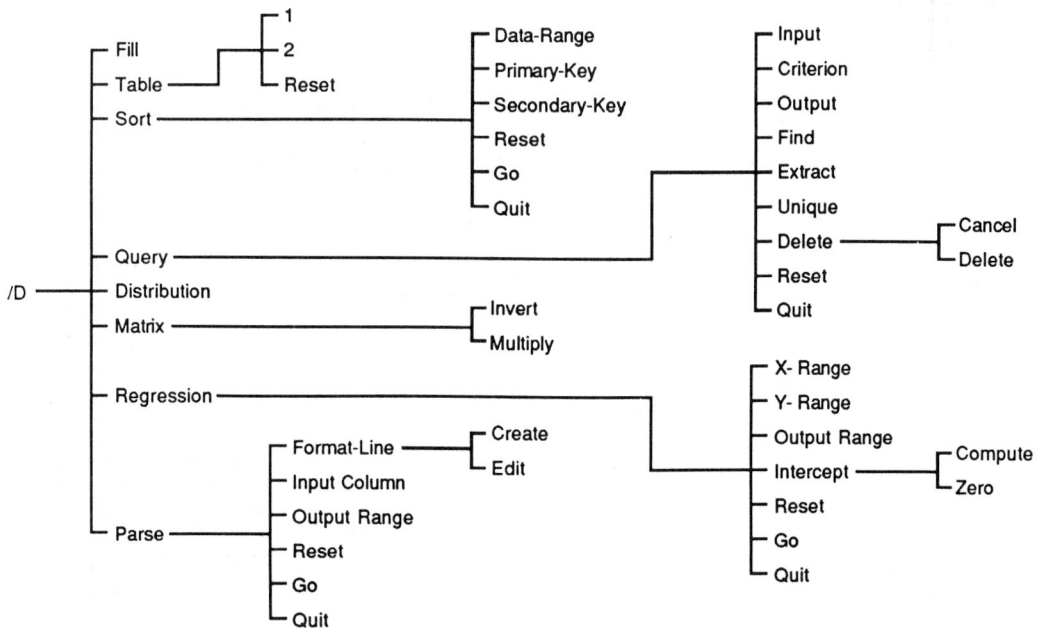

```
/G ─┬─ Type ──────┬─ Line
     │             ├─ Bar
     │             ├─ XY
     │             ├─ Stacked-Bar
     │             └─ Pie
     ├─ X
     ├─ A
     ├─ B
     ├─ C
     ├─ D
     ├─ E
     ├─ F
     ├─ Reset
     ├─ View
     ├─ Save
     ├─ Options ──┬─ Legend ──┬─ A
     │            │            ├─ B
     │            │            ├─ C
     │            │            ├─ D
     │            │            ├─ E
     │            │            └─ F
     │            ├─ Format ──┬─ Graph        Graph ──┬─ Lines
     │            │           ├─ X            X        ├─ Symbols
     │            │           ├─ A            A        ├─ Both
     │            │           ├─ B            B        └─ Neither
     │            │           ├─ C            C
     │            │           ├─ D            D
     │            │           ├─ E            E
     │            │           ├─ F            F
     │            │           └─ Quit         Quit
     │            ├─ Titles ──┬─ First        Automatic
     │            │           ├─ Second       Manual
     │            │           ├─ X-Axis       Lower
     │            │           └─ Y-Axis       Upper
     │            ├─ Grid ────┬─ Horizontal   Format (see/w Global Format)
     │            │           ├─ Vertical     Indicator
     │            │           ├─ Both         Quit
     │            │           └─ Clear
     │            ├─ Scale ───┬─ Y Scale
     │            │           ├─ X Scale
     │            │           └─ Skip (1..8192)default = 1
     │            ├─ Color
     │            ├─ B & W
     │            ├─ Data-Labels ──┬─ A
     │            │                ├─ B
     │            │                ├─ C
     │            │                ├─ D
     │            │                ├─ E
     │            │                ├─ F
     │            │                └─ Quit
     │            └─ Quit
     ├─ Name ──┬─ Use
     │         ├─ Create
     │         ├─ Delete
     │         └─ Reset
     └─ Quit

/D ─┬─ Fill
     ├─ Table ──┬─ 1
     │          ├─ 2
     │          └─ Reset
     ├─ Sort ──┬─ Data-Range
     │         ├─ Primary-Key
     │         ├─ Secondary-Key
     │         ├─ Reset
     │         ├─ Go
     │         └─ Quit
     ├─ Query ──┬─ Input
     │          ├─ Criterion
     │          ├─ Output
     │          ├─ Find
     │          ├─ Extract
     │          ├─ Unique
     │          ├─ Delete ──┬─ Cancel
     │          │           └─ Delete
     │          ├─ Reset
     │          └─ Quit
     ├─ Distribution
     ├─ Matrix ──┬─ Invert
     │           └─ Multiply
     ├─ Regression ──┬─ X- Range
     │               ├─ Y- Range
     │               ├─ Output Range
     │               ├─ Intercept ──┬─ Compute
     │               │              └─ Zero
     │               ├─ Reset
     │               ├─ Go
     │               └─ Quit
     └─ Parse ──┬─ Format-Line ──┬─ Create
                │                └─ Edit
                ├─ Input Column
                ├─ Output Range
                ├─ Reset
                ├─ Go
                └─ Quit

/S        Invoke the DOS Command Interpreter

/Q ──┬─ No   Do not end 1-2-3 session
      └─ Yes  End 1-2-3 session
```